213

PAYMENTS AND CREDITS

SIXTH EDITION

by

WILLIAM D. WARREN
Connell Professor of Law Emeritus
University of California, Los Angeles

STEVEN D. WALT
Professor of Law
University of Virginia School of Law

FOUNDATION PRESS
NEW YORK, NEW YORK
2004

Reprinted in part from Warren and Walt's Commercial Law, Sixth Edition
© 2004 By Foundation Press

Foundation Press, a Thomson business, has created this publication to provide you with accurate and authoritative information concerning the subject matter covered. However, this publication was not necessarily prepared by persons licensed to practice law in a particular jurisdiction. Foundation Press is not engaged in rendering legal or other professional advice, and this publication is not a substitute for the advice of an attorney. If you require legal or other expert advice, you should seek the services of a competent attorney or other professional.

© 1992, 1997, 2000 FOUNDATION PRESS
© 2004 By FOUNDATION PRESS
   395 Hudson Street
   New York, NY 10014
   Phone Toll Free 1–877–888–1330
   Fax (212) 367–6799
   fdpress.com
Printed in the United States of America

ISBN 1–58778–740–7

TEXT IS PRINTED ON 10% POST CONSUMER RECYCLED PAPER

PREFACE

The Sixth Edition substantially revises the Fifth Edition. Now that Revised Articles 3 (Negotiable Instruments) and 4 (Bank Deposits and Collections), new Article 4A (Funds Transfers), and Revised Article 5 (Letters of Credit) have substantially become the law of the land, many cases interpreting these statutes are coming down. The Sixth Edition features a selection of these recent decisions that promise to become leading cases. The 2002 amendments to Articles 3 and 4 are considered, as is the 2003 Federal "Check 21" Act. Materials on technological advances in payment systems have been updated, and emerging consumer issues have been highlighted throughout. The growing importance of federal law in payments law is examined.

We use more problems in the Sixth Edition than we have in previous editions. Problems enable us to raise issues not yet before the courts. These problems force close consideration of relevant statutory provisions and allow for tightly structured class sessions. We gather from the reaction of teachers to our books over the years that most teachers prefer to teach from a mix of cases and problems, and the Sixth Edition is designed to meet this preference.

We are particularly grateful to Arthur G. Spence, Esq., Associate General Counsel of City National Bank of Beverly Hills, California, and to the Bank for allowing us to use several of the Bank's forms. The cooperation of Mr. Spence and others at the Bank in sharing their experience with law students through the use of their forms has been outstanding.

We regret that Robert Jordan, whose name this book has borne since the First Edition in 1983, did not participate in this edition. However, evidence of his keen analytical mind and precise draftsmanship is still seen throughout this volume, as well as in Revised Articles 3, 4, and new Article 4A, for which he served as a Reporter.

We are deeply grateful to Tal Grietzer and his staff for their skill and dedication in formatting and preparing the manuscript for publication. We also thank Robert Abiri, UCLA School of Law, Class of 2005, for his editorial assistance and research.

WILLIAM D. WARREN
STEVEN D. WALT

April 2004

*

iii

ACKNOWLEDGMENTS

We gratefully acknowledge the permission extended to reprint excerpts from the following works:

The American Law Institute has given permission to reprint the following materials:

> Restatement (Third) of Property (Mortgages) § 5.5 (1996). Copyright © 1997 by the American Law Institute.

City National Bank. All forms in this book are reprinted with permission of City National Bank, a national banking association, of Beverly Hills, California.

Grant Gilmore, Formalism and the Law of Negotiable Instruments, 13 Creighton Law Review 441, 446-450 (1979). Copyright © 1979 Creighton University School of Law. Reprinted from the Creighton Law Review by permission.

Albert J. Rosenthal, Negotiability – Who Needs It?, 71 Colum. L. Rev. 375, 378-381, 283-385 (1971). Copyright © 1971 by the Directors of the Columbia Law Review Association, Inc. All Rights Reserved. This article originally appeared at 71 Colum. L. Rev. 375 (1971). Reprinted with permission.

*

SUMMARY OF CONTENTS

*

TABLE OF CONTENTS

TABLE OF CASES

Principal cases are in bold type. Non-principal cases are in roman type. References are to Pages.

TABLE OF STATUTES

PAYMENTS AND CREDITS

*

CHAPTER 1

NEGOTIABILITY AND HOLDERS IN DUE COURSE

A. INTRODUCTION

We introduce the materials on payments and credits by a treatment in this chapter of two traditional doctrines unique to negotiable instruments. We will refer to these as the merger doctrine (the instrument reifies the obligation to pay; the holder of the instrument is entitled to payment) and the holder-in-due-course doctrine (the holder of an instrument may take free of claims and defenses on the instrument). As we shall see, the holder-in-due-course doctrine, conceived long ago under different social and economic conditions, has been under attack for years by courts, legislatures and commentators. The policy justification for this harsh doctrine is so questionable that there was debate on whether what now remains of the doctrine should be retained in Revised Article 3. However, under the drafting-by-consensus regime that prevails in the writing of uniform state laws the doctrine was retained. In recent years the merger doctrine has come under criticism for the results it yields in real estate transactions that participants in that field believe are unjust. We will inquire throughout this chapter whether the decision to retain these doctrines in Revised Article 3 was sound. Whatever the merit of these rules, an understanding of them is essential to those planning and executing payment and credit transactions, and we treat them in this chapter. A review of the cases decided under Revised Article 3 shows a surprising number raising holder-in-due-course issues. Since adoption of Revised Articles 3 and 4 has been widespread, citation of the provisions of these articles in the text of the following chapters will not be prefaced by "revised." Citation of the provisions of the pre-revision statutes will be prefaced by "former."

The law of negotiable instruments is based in large part on common law doctrines developed primarily in the last half of the eighteenth century and the first half of the nineteenth century. This law was codified in Great Britain in 1882 in the Bills of Exchange Act and in 1896 in the United States in the Uniform Negotiable Instruments Law, usually referred to as the NIL. In 1952 the American Law Institute and the National Conference of Commissioners on Uniform State Laws promulgated the Uniform Commercial Code. Article 3 of the Code eventually displaced the NIL as the primary statute governing negotiable instruments. Article 4 of the Code complements Article 3 with respect to collection of negotiable instruments by banks and also governs the bank-customer relationship with respect to some matters relating to instruments. In 1990 Revised Article 3 was

1

promulgated to take the place of the original Article 3. At the same time conforming amendments to Articles 1 and 4 were promulgated. Revised Article 3 and the conforming amendments to Articles 1 and 4 have been enacted in all but one state. In 2002 several amendments to these Articles were promulgated. Revised Article 3 is not a radical departure from the earlier statute; the principal concepts of traditional negotiable instruments law have been preserved. But Revised Article 3 differs from former Article 3 with respect to a number of important substantive areas. In addition, no attempt was made to preserve the language of former Article 3. As a result, the drafting style reflected in Revised Article 3 is quite different from that of the previous statute.

We have included a number of cases interpreting Revised Articles 3 and 4, but in those negotiable instruments cases decided under former Article 3 or 4, we include the text of the particular section involved to the extent reference to the statutory language is necessary to understand the point at issue. Revised Article 3 is accompanied by a "Table of Disposition of Sections in Former Article 3" that indicates the section of Revised Article 3 governing the issue addressed by a section of former Article 3. In reading cases reprinted in this book, this table should be consulted because the result reached in the case may be different if the same facts are governed by Revised Article 3.

B.   CONCEPT OF NEGOTIABILITY

1.   HISTORICAL ORIGIN

Professor Gilmore sketches the background of negotiable instruments law in the following quotation from his article "Formalism and the Law of Negotiable Instruments," 13 Creighton L. Rev. 441, 446–450 (1979):

> "Our law of negotiable instruments dates from the late eighteenth century. * * * Lord Mansfield and his colleagues in the late eighteenth century were faced with radically new problems for which they devised radically new solutions.
>
> The radically new problems all stemmed from the industrial revolution and the vastly increased number of commercial transactions which it spawned. When goods were shipped, they had to be paid for. The idea that the payments could be made in metallic currency, chronically in short supply, was ludicrous. The primitive banking system could not cope with the situation: the bank check which—a hundred years later—became the universal payment device was unknown. In effect the merchants and the bankers invented their own paper currency. The form which they used was an old one: the so-called bill of exchange which was an order issued by one person (the drawer) to a second person (the drawee) directing the drawee to pay a specified sum of money at a specified time to a third person (the holder). Frequently these bills, drawn by sellers on buyers, represented the purchase price of goods sold. In a more sophisticated and somewhat later variant a

mercantile banking house issued what came to be called a letter of credit to a customer. The letter authorized the customer to draw on the bankers for the purchase price of goods which he intended to buy: Through the first half of the nineteenth century Yankees trading out of Boston, armed with their letters of credit which were frequently issued by English houses, roamed the Far East assembling their precious and fabulously profitable cargoes of silks and teas and spices, paying for them with drafts on London. For half a century these bills or drafts were an indispensable supplement to the official currencies and were indeed used as currency: the bills which showed up in litigation had, as the case reports tell us, passed from hand to hand in a long series of transactions. And a draft on a ranking London house was a much safer as well as a much more convenient thing to have than a bag-full of clipped Maria Theresa dollars. These bills moved in a world-wide market, typically ending up in the possession of people who knew nothing about the transaction which had given rise to the bill, had no way of finding out anything about the transaction and, in any case, had not the slightest interest in it.

Against that background, the courts, English and American, put together, in not much more than half a century, the law of negotiable instruments almost exactly as we know it today. Indeed anyone who has mastered the current American formulation of the subject in Article 3 of the Uniform Commercial Code will have a startling sense of *deja vu*—I suppose this is *deja vu* in reverse—if he then goes back to the mid-nineteenth century treatises: time seems to have been suspended, nothing has changed, the late twentieth century law of negotiable instruments is still a law for clipper ships and their exotic cargoes from the Indies. The *deja vu* is false, a sort of floating mirage—but I will return to that later.

In putting together their law of negotiable instruments, the courts assumed that the new mercantile currency was a good thing whose use should be encouraged. Two quite simple ideas became the foundation pieces for the whole structure. One was the good faith purchase idea. The stranger who purchased the bill in the market was entitled to do so without inquiry into the facts of the underlying transaction or of previous transfers of the bill and without being affected by them: if he bought the bill for value, in good faith and in the ordinary course of business, he held it free both of underlying contract defenses and of outstanding equities of ownership. The other idea which, the first time you run into it, sounds like nonsense—the legal mind at its worst—was even more basic to the structure and indeed was what gave the completed edifice its pure and almost unearthly beauty. That was the idea that the piece of paper on which the bill was written or printed should be treated as if it—the piece of paper—was itself the claim or debt which it evidenced. This idea came to be known as the doctrine of merger—the debt was merged in the instrument. At one stroke it drastically simplified the law of negotiable instruments, to the benefit of both purchasers and the people required to pay the instruments.

The bills of exchange were used as currency and exchanged many hands. Usually the bills would swap many hands so the holder wouldn't have notice of its origin.

① One theme: the good faith purchaser can buy the bill w/o knowing the original transaction and not be affected by it. If bought for value and in good faith, he is free of contract defenses and outstanding equities of ownership.

② The piece of paper itself is the claim or debt which is evidenced. (merger).

The only way to transfer the debt was by physical delivery of the bill itself. It also had to be endorsed.

Under merger theory the only way of transferring the debt represented by the bill was by physical delivery of the bill itself to the transferee. The courts also worked out an elaborate set of rules on when the transferor was required to endorse, as well as deliver, the bill and on what liabilities to subsequent parties he assumed by endorsing. When these formalities—delivery and endorsement—had been accomplished—but not until then—the transfer became a negotiation and the transferee a holder. Only the holder—the person physically in possession of the bill under a proper chain of endorsements—was entitled to demand payment of the bill from the party required to pay it; only payment to such a holder discharged the bill as well as the underlying obligation. Merger theory was also of immense importance from the point of view of the paying party: not only did he know whom he was supposed to pay—the holder—but, under another aspect of the theory, he was entitled to pay (and get his discharge) even if he knew, to state an extreme case, that the holder he paid had acquired the bill by fraud or trickery from a previous holder. Parties with claims adverse to the holder were required to fight their own battles; they could not involve the payor by serving notice on him not to pay.

See also James S. Rogers, The Early History of the Law of Bills and Notes (1995).

A 21st century business or consumer lawyer is wise to consider the doctrine of negotiability to be a legal landmine. In the next two chapters, we will learn how to protect your clients from it. In Grant Gilmore's sketch on the background of negotiability, we learn that it emerged centuries ago as a substitute for money. There surely is no shortage of money in circulation now, but when the law of payments was restated in 1990 in UCC Articles 3 and 4, the ancient doctrine of negotiability survived—limited somewhat but still around. And, as we will see, causing a lot of trouble.

We need a few preliminary working definitions in order to communicate.

A note — is a promise to pay another person

A "note," often referred to as a "promissory note," is *promise* to pay another person, a "payee." 3–104(e). This is a two-party transaction. A note is a negotiable instrument if it complies with the requirements of 3–104(a) (unconditional promise to pay money to a bearer or order, etc.).

A draft is an order by a drafter to a drawee to pay a payee. Ex. A check. The person signing the check is the drawer. The bank is the drawee.

A "draft" is an *order* by a "drawer" (3–103(a)(5)) to a "drawee" (3–103(a)(4)) to pay a payee. 3–104(e). This is a three-party transaction. A "check" is the most common form of draft. 3–104(f). The person signing the check is the drawer and the bank on which the check is drawn is the drawee.

Holder — possessor of an instrument.

In most cases, a "holder" is the possessor of an instrument that is either payable to that person or indorsed to that person. But the possessor of a bearer instrument is also a holder. This is a very important definition because we will be dealing with the rights of holders in due course, and a person must be a holder before it can be a holder in due course. 1–201(b)(21).

2. MERGER DOCTRINE

a. NEGOTIATION AND TRANSFER

(1) NEGOTIATION

The merger doctrine described by Professor Gilmore determines two important issues: (i) who can enforce the instrument against the obligor, and (ii) whom does the obligor pay to be discharged on the instrument. We discuss the first of these issues in this section on "Negotiation and Transfer," and the second in the next section on "Discharge."

The basic rule on enforcement is stated in 3–301:

"[P]erson entitled to enforce" an instrument means (i) the holder of the instrument, (ii) a nonholder in possession of the instrument who has the rights of a holder, or (iii) a person not in possession of the instrument who is entitled to enforce the instrument pursuant to Section 3–309 [lost instrument] or 3–418(d) [dishonored instrument]. A person may be a person entitled to enforce the instrument even though the person is not the owner of the instrument or is in wrongful possession of the instrument.

Rule! — A holder in possession of instru. can enforce

A person who is not an owner yet in possession can still enforce.

This provision implements the merger doctrine as described by Professor Gilmore by stating that, with minor exceptions, the right to enforce an instrument belongs to the holder of the instrument. The following elementary cases illustrate 3–301 and some basic concepts and terminology regarding negotiation and transfer of instruments.

Case #1. John signs a note and delivers it to Rachel. The note reads as follows:

John promises to pay Rachel. → $1K on 4/1/04. John is the maker of the note.

I promise to pay $1,000 on April 1, 2004 to the bearer of this note.

The note is "issued" by John, the "maker," when it is delivered to Rachel. 3–105(a) and 3–103(a)(5). The note is "payable to bearer." 3–109(a). When Rachel receives possession, she becomes the bearer of the note as well as its holder. 1–201(5) and (20). Normally, Rachel is also the owner of the note. But the right of Rachel to receive or enforce payment is based on the fact that Rachel is the holder of the note, not on Rachel's ownership. 3–301.

Bearer — the person the note is payable to.

Suppose Rachel loses the note and it is found by Peter who takes possession of it. By obtaining possession Peter does not become the owner of the note, but he becomes the holder of the note and thereby obtains the right to enforce it. 3–301. The transfer of possession which resulted in Peter's becoming a holder is described in 3–201(a) as "negotiation" of the note. Typically, negotiation is the result of a voluntary transfer of possession, but 3–201(a) applies to any transfer of possession, voluntary or involuntary.

Negotiation — is the result of a voluntary transfer of possession, but it could be involuntary transfer too.

Case #2.   John signs a note and delivers it to Rachel. The note reads as follows:

I promise to pay $1,000 on April 1, 2004 to the order of Rachel.

In this case the note is not payable to bearer. Rather, it is "payable to order" because it is "payable to the order of an identified person." 3–109(b). Upon delivery of the note to Rachel, she becomes its holder because she has possession and she is the person identified in the note as its payee. 1–201(20). In Case #1 we saw that a finder or thief can obtain the right to enforce a note payable to bearer simply by obtaining possession of it. That rule does not apply if an instrument is payable to an identified person. Negotiation of such an instrument also requires transfer of possession, but an indorsement by the holder is necessary as well. 3–201(b). (Note the UCC spelling, or misspelling, of indorse.) Thus, the note payable to Rachel cannot be negotiated unless she indorses it; no one else can become its holder until then.

Suppose Rachel does not lose the note. Rather, she sells it to Peter for cash and delivers the note to him. In this case no negotiation to Peter occurs unless Rachel indorses the note. Indorsement is defined in 3–204(a) and can be made for several purposes. The most important purpose is to negotiate the instrument. An indorsement is normally made on the reverse side of the instrument and can consist of a signature alone or a signature accompanied by other words. An indorsement by Rachel consisting of her signature preceded by the words "Pay to Peter" identifies a person to whom it makes the note payable and is called a "special indorsement." 3–205(a). An indorsement by Rachel consisting solely of her signature does not identify a person to whom the note is payable and is called a "blank indorsement." 3–205(b). The effect of a blank indorsement is to make the note payable to bearer. 3–205(b) and 3–109(c). If either indorsement is made, Peter becomes the holder when he obtains possession of the note (1–201(20)) and may enforce the note as holder. If Rachel indorses in blank, Peter can negotiate the note to somebody else either by delivery alone or by delivery plus Peter's indorsement. 3–205(b) and 3–109(c). If Rachel indorses specially, Peter must indorse the note in order to negotiate it and may indorse either specially or in blank. 3–205(a).

By way of a reality check, we will see that the fact that a finder or a thief may be the correct person to sue on a note doesn't necessarily mean that this person will recover. If the maker can prove that the instrument was lost or stolen, she has a valid defense under 3–305(c) unless the person suing on the note can prove holder-in-due-course status. 3–302.

(2) TRANSFER

Although the right to enforce an instrument is normally obtained as a result of negotiation, the right to enforce an instrument can also be obtained in some transactions in which negotiation does not occur. Suppose Rachel delivers the note in Case #2 to Peter without indorsing it. What rights does Peter obtain? Because Rachel's purpose in delivering the note is to give Peter the right to enforce it, Rachel has "transferred" the note to Peter. 3–203(a). Transfer means that there has been a conveyance by the transferor to the transferee of the transferor's right to enforce the instrument. This transfer can occur only by "delivery," a voluntary transfer of possession (1–201(b)(15)), plus an intent by the transferor to give to the transferee the right to enforce. Since the note was not indorsed by Rachel, Peter cannot enforce the note in his own right as holder and cannot negotiate the note to somebody else. But as a result of the transfer from Rachel, Peter obtains Rachel's right as holder to enforce the note. 3–203(b). This result is commonly referred to as the "shelter doctrine." Armed with that right and possession of the note, Peter becomes a person entitled to enforce the note under clause (ii) of the first sentence of 3–301. In addition Peter, as a buyer of the note for value, obtains a specifically enforceable right to have Rachel indorse the note so that Peter can become its holder. 3–203(c).

If, by transfer, Peter acquires Rachel's right as holder to enforce the note, why is it important whether Peter, in enforcing the note, is asserting his own right as holder or a right to enforce derived from Rachel's right as holder? The answer is burden of proof under 3–308, as illustrated in Problem 1 below. Read Comments 2 through 4 to 3–203 as well as 3–308(b) and the first two paragraphs of Comment 2 to 3–308.

[handwritten margin notes:]
3-203
Shelter
Doctrine.
But, even
if Rachel
doesn't endorse
(typically note
couldn't be
negotiated), Peter
can still enforce
it as holder. B/c
Rachel transfered
the note to him
So she had an
intent to transfer
her right to
enforce it.
So Peter can enforce it
this way, or enforce as
a holder in due course.

PROBLEMS

[handwritten:] 3-203(b) - Can't take
note if by fraud if had notice of it,
even if in possession

1. Mark signed a note and delivered it to Patricia for value; she, in turn, delivered it to Teresa for value. The note reads as follows:

I promise to pay $1,000 to the order of Patricia on November 1, 2004.

[handwritten:] Mark → Patricia → Teresa
"to order of Patricia"

Mark defaulted on the note and Teresa brought an action to enforce the note against him. In his pleadings Mark did not deny the authenticity of his signature or raise any defense to his liability on the note. Teresa introduced the note into evidence and rested. Mark sought a directed verdict. Is he entitled to one under 3–203, 3–301 and 3–308 if the following facts obtained:

   a. When Patricia delivered the note to Teresa she indorsed the instrument? *[handwritten:]* No. The note was given a specific endorsement to Patricia. She signed it and it was negotiable to Teresa.

   b. When Patricia delivered the note to Teresa she intended to pass ownership to Teresa but failed to indorse the instrument? *[handwritten:]* No. Teresa may enforce it b/c even if not indorsed Patricia still intended to transfer the right of enforcement → Shelter doctrine.

White & Summers, Uniform Commercial Code § 13–4b (burden of proof) (5th ed. 2000).

2. Pete fraudulently induced Maria to issue a note to him. The note reads as follows:

I promise to pay $1,000 to the order of Pete on July 1, 2004.

In May 2004 Pete indorsed and delivered the note to Helen who gave value, was in good faith and had no notice of any claims or defenses on the

[handwritten:] Maria → Pete → Helen → David
"to order of Pete" (indorsed) notice of fraud.
by fraud

[handwritten left margin: Helen bought in good faith. Maria notified Helen of the fraud later on. Helen had notice of fraud, gave it to David. He knew of the fraud.]

instrument. In June Maria discovered that she had been defrauded, notified Helen of the fraud, and stated her intention to refuse payment of the note. Helen, a busy executive, had no interest in incurring the litigation expenses needed to enforce the note, and, in August 2004, out of sympathy, gave the note, without indorsement, to her former husband, David, now an impecunious law student and desperate for money. She told him the circumstances surrounding the note and said that if he could recover anything on the note he could keep the recovery "for old time's sake." May David recover on the note from Maria free of her defense of fraud? 3–203(b). What policy is furthered by Article 3 in this case? Comment 2 to 3–203.

[handwritten: Ans: No David can't get the note (3-203(b) b/c he has notice of the fraud.]

b. DISCHARGE

A corollary to the merger doctrine that the right to enforce an instrument is the exclusive right of the holder is that the person obliged to pay the instrument discharges the obligation only by paying the holder. Until 2002, Revised Article 3 reflected this corollary in 3–602. The obligor who pays the holder is assured that nobody else can obtain a right to enforce the instrument if the obligor obtains surrender of the instrument from the holder at the time of payment. 3–501(a) and (b)(2). But there is also a corollary to the discharge rule: payment to a person who is not the holder might not result in discharge. This result raised the issue that caused the real property finance industry to vigorously challenge the traditional discharge rule.

[handwritten left margin: 3-501(a) One may only discharge the obligation by paying the holder. But, payment to a person who is not the holder might not result in discharge.]

PROBLEM

[handwritten left margin: Debtor Seller Bank]

Debtor bought a home from Seller in part with money that she borrowed from Bank. In order to secure her $100,000 obligation, evidenced by a negotiable promissory note, she granted Bank a mortgage on the property. The agreement was that payments on the note would be made to Bank each month. Bank immediately negotiated the note and assigned the mortgage to Assignee. Neither Bank nor Assignee notified Debtor about the assignment. Bank deliberately withheld notice for the purpose of defrauding Debtor by continuing to receive Debtor's payments after the assignment. After a number of payments were made to Bank, Assignee notified Debtor that she was in default and that unless she cured her default Assignee would initiate foreclosure proceedings. Bank has "suspended payments" (closed) and its owners have absconded. Should Debtor receive credit for the payments made to Bank after it had negotiated the note and assigned the mortgage to Assignee? What result under 3–602(a) before the 2002 amendment? How could Debtor have protected herself in this case? Should she have demanded to see her note each month before making her payment?

[handwritten left margin: Bank doesn't tell debtor it assigned Note, so debtor still keeps paying original bank. Can payments to original bank be credited]

[handwritten bottom: Seller → Debtor → Bank → Assignee / note / mortgage]

[handwritten right margin: Yes, Comment? says bank could be seen as an agent. Ask for a yearly accounting Demand to see note]

[handwritten: 3602a]

The traditional doctrine of former 3–602 that payment had to be made to the holder to achieve discharge was disapproved in Restatement (Third) of Property (Mortgages) § 5.5 (1996). It states:

§ 5.5   Effect of Performance to the Transferor After Transfer of an Obligation Secured by a Mortgage

[A]fter transfer of an obligation secured by a mortgage, performance of the obligation to the transferor is effective against the transferee if rendered before the obligor receives notice of the transfer.

The effect of former 3–602 was to impose the burden on the mortgagor to be sure that payments go to the note holder or its agent. This may be appropriate in commercial cases, but the Restatement view has much to commend it in cases involving mortgages on residential real estate. In these cases, as the Restatement commentary points out, it is unrealistic to require that consumer mortgagors ascertain the identity of the holder of their notes, either in the case of periodic payments or even for the final payment, given the practice in the industry of notifying the mortgagor at the time of payoff that the note and mortgage will be returned a month or six weeks later. Imposing the burden on the transferee of the mortgage note to notify the mortgagor of the transfer in these cases seems fair.

Virtually all real estate mortgage notes are immediately assigned by the loan originator (a bank, savings and loan association, or the like) and eventually are securitized. That is, an entity pools large numbers of mortgage notes and issues bonds secured by the mortgage receivables, i.e., the rights to future payments. The proceeds of the bond issue are then used to buy more mortgages. Fanny Mae (Federal National Mortgage Association) and Freddie Mac (Federal Home Loan Mortgage Corporation), among others, are in the business of arranging for pooling of mortgages. So, you might expect that the issue raised in the Problem is an important one. Actually, the issue hasn't caused much trouble. First, the real property finance industry is scrupulously careful to see that the mortgagor is notified of any assignment; assignees have great incentive to make sure that they receive their payments. Second, the loan originator usually becomes the agent of the assignee to "service" the loan, that is collect the payments and remit them to the assignee. In the Problem, Bank would usually be Assignee's agent and any payments made to Bank would be treated as though they had gone to Assignee. Nevertheless, in cases that fall outside the standard institutional loan transactions, litigation does arise, e.g., Lambert v. Barker, 348 S.E.2d 214 (Va. 1986).

After a decade of debate, the Permanent Editorial Board, charged with oversight of the UCC, promulgated in 2002 an amended version of 3–602, set out below, which revokes the traditional rule that only payments to a holder discharge instruments. This change is a broad rejection of the discharge rule that prevailed for hundreds of years: it is not restricted to real estate, and applies to commercial as well as consumer transactions.

Section 3–602.

[handwritten in margin: 3-602]

(a) Subject to subsection (e), an instrument is paid to the extent payment is made by or on behalf of a party obliged to pay the instrument, and to a person entitled to enforce the instrument.

(b) Subject to subsection (e), a note is paid to the extent payment is made by or on behalf of a party obliged to pay the note to a person that formerly was entitled to enforce the note only if at the time of the payment the party obliged to pay has not received adequate notification that the note has been transferred and that the payment is to be made to the transferee. A notification is adequate only if it is signed by the transferor or the transferee; reasonably identifies the transferred note; and provides an address at which payments subsequently are to be made. Upon request, a transferee shall seasonably furnish reasonable proof that the note has been transferred. Unless the transferee complies with the request, a payment to the person that formerly was entitled to enforce the note is effective for purposes of subsection (c) even if the party obliged to pay the note has received a notification under this paragraph.

[handwritten in left margin: Must receive adequate notification. A notification is adequate only if it is signed by the transferor or the transferee; reasonably identifies the transferred note and provides an address at which payments should be made.]

(c) Subject to subsection (e), to the extent of payment under subsections (a) and (b), the obligation of the party obliged to pay the instrument is discharged even though payment is made with knowledge of a claim to the instrument under Section 3–306 by another person.

(d) Subject to subsection (e), a transferee, or any party that has acquired rights in the instrument directly or indirectly from a transferee, including any such party that has rights as a holder in due course, is deemed to have notice of any payment that is made under subsection (b) after the date that the note is transferred to the transferee but before the party obliged to pay the note receives adequate notification of the transfer.

The traditional rule worked well if the transferor and transferee were honest parties. When they were not, obligors, particularly consumer obligors could be damaged. Does the new rule adequately protect obligors against dishonest parties? See Problem (b) below.

PROBLEM

Maker issued a note payable to the order of Payee, which Payee indorsed and delivered to Transferee. The note was payable in 60 monthly installments.

[handwritten in left margin: Maker Payee transferee 3-602]

(a) Neither Payee nor Transferee notified Maker of the transfer and Maker made six payments to Payee after the transfer before discovering that Payee no longer held the note. Must Transferee credit Maker for the amount of the six payments made to Payee? If so, is Payee liable to Transferee for the payments under this statute?

[handwritten in left margin: Yes, Transferee must credit Maker b/c he was not given the payments for the notification of the transfer. Yes, Payee is liable as transferee's agent.]

(b) Payee did not notify Maker of the transfer but Transferee gave adequate notification to Maker. Maker, a financially unsophisticated per-

[handwritten at bottom: Note Maker → Payee indorse → transferee]

Facts: Payee didn't notify Maker
Transferee did notify Maker
Maker doesn't trust transferee
Payee told Maker to keep making payments
+ it b/c it was transferee's agent.

CHAPTER 1 NEGOTIABILITY AND HOLDERS IN DUE COURSE **11**

son, was not familiar with Transferee, and, since she had heard nothing from Payee, was suspicious about sending any money to Transferee. Maker first phoned, then wrote Payee asking what she should do. Payee, a crook, told Maker to continue making payments to it because it was Transferee's agent for collection. Must Transferee credit Maker for the payments made to Payee after its notice to Maker?

I would say no, that it gave adequate notice and it Maker didn't trust Transferee, the transferee could have produced proof of the transfer, if he had asked.

3. HOLDER IN DUE COURSE: FREEDOM FROM CLAIMS AND DEFENSES

The most dramatic aspect of negotiability is the holder-in-due-course rule. The Restatement (Second) of Contracts § 336(1) (1981) provides that the assignment of a contract gives the assignee rights against the obligor "only to the extent that the obligor is under a duty to the assignor." And § 336(2) provides that the right of an assignee is subject to any defense or claim that the obligor had against the assignor. In other words, when the obligee of an ordinary contract assigns the contract, assignee gets only the rights of the obligee. Why has a different rule prevailed for negotiable instruments for centuries? Under Article 3, a holder in due course (3–302) takes free of some defenses of the obligor (3–305(b)) as well as claims of ownership (3–306). As a counselor, you cannot assume that either your business or consumer clients understand what a negotiable instrument is, much less how much trouble they can get into by becoming a party to one in any of several different capacities. The holder-in-due-course rule is counter-intuitive and difficult to justify to an irate client that has been victimized by it. We see it in action in a contemporary setting in the following Problem.

In ordinary contract cases, when the obligee of a contract assigns the contract, assignee gets only the rights of the obligee.

A holder in due course takes free of some defenses of the obligor (3-305b) and claims of ownership (3-306)

PROBLEM

Mark is one of 20 limited partners of a limited partnership (LP) in which Parker is the general partner. At the inception of the partnership, each limited partner contributed $100,000 in cash and gave Parker a negotiable promissory note for another $50,000, payable on demand. The understanding was that Parker would hold these notes until LP needed more funds and then would request each limited partner to contribute $50,000 more. Upon receipt of the money from each partner, Parker would return the note to the partner. The notes were made payable to the order of LP, and Parker had express authority to receive and indorse all instruments made payable to the LP. Without informing the limited partners of his intentions, which were entirely fraudulent, Parker indorsed the notes of all the limited partners to Bank and delivered them to Bank, which knew nothing of Parker's fraud and purchased the notes for 85% of the face value of each note. Parker took the money and ran. Mark calls you when Bank demands payment of his note. He heatedly informed Bank that Parker had no authority to do what he did and that Bank was at fault in dealing with a crook, therefore Bank should take the loss. Bank disagreed, explaining that

Is it a negotiable note.

- Mark is a limited partner in LP.
- He contributed $100K and a note worth $50 like the other partners.
- Parker is gen. partner.

, Parker indorsed all notes, sold them to Bank, and ran w/ money. Bank now demands payment on notes.

[Handwritten margin notes:
Maybe Note → Maker
[asks → for Payee]
[for Payee]
Bank

a)
The UCC imposes the loss on Mark. The policy reason for this is to allow instruments to be treated like money and to keep bona fide parties from having to trace where the note came from.]

before it bought the notes it had diligently inquired into the creditworthiness of the general and limited partners.

(a) On which party does the UCC impose the loss, Mark or Bank? What is the policy basis for this result? Why wouldn't the rules of Restatement § 336(1) and (2) serve as well in this case?

(b) How does Mark discover whether he is dealing with a negotiable note? See 3–104(a) (formalities). If by any chance you didn't know about these formal requirements before you took this course, why is Mark expected to know about them under the UCC? Should negotiable instruments bear legends warning of the consequences of negotiability? See our discussion of formalities later.

[Handwritten margin notes:
b) He looks at the formalities on the paper → it's a promise to pay, it has an amount, it's payable to bearer, payable on demand]

We will first examine the claims and defenses that holders in due course take free of, and then we will go into detail on the issue of who qualifies as a holder in due course.

a.   CLAIMS OF OWNERSHIP

Lord Mansfield created the doctrine that a good faith purchaser for value takes better rights than its assignor in two seminal 18th century cases involving claims of ownership: Miller v. Race, 1 Burr. 452, 97 Eng. Rep. 398 (K.B. 1758), and Rhodes v. Peacock, 99 Eng. Rep. 402 (1781). In the latter case, he said: "The holder of a bill of exchange [a draft], or promissory note, is not to be considered in the light of an assignee of the payee. An assignee must take the thing assigned, subject to all the equity to which the original party was subject. If this rule applied to bills and promissory notes, it would stop their currency. The law is settled, that a holder, coming fairly by a bill or note has nothing to do with the transaction between the original parties * * *." The doctrine was later applied to defenses.

[Handwritten margin notes:
A holder coming into possession of a note fairly should not have to think about the transaction b/w original parties).]

Lord Mansfield's doctrine on claims of ownership is found in 3–306. Defenses and claims of recoupment arise between the original parties to the instrument, e.g., between the maker of a note and the payee. Claims of ownership arise between the owner of the instrument and subsequent transferees, e.g., between the payee and a subsequent takers of the instrument. The Comment to 3–306 construes "claims" broadly, so that claims to the instrument includes a lien or a possessory right in it. Thus, 3–306's rule applies to these interests in the instrument as well.

[Handwritten margin notes:
Defenses and claims of recoupment arise only b/w the original parties to the instrument. Ex. Maker of note & payee.]

PROBLEM

In October 2002, for valuable consideration, Maurice made and delivered a negotiable promissory note to Patricia for $25,000, payable in annual installments of $5,000, at 10% interest. The first payment was due in October 2003. Patricia, a member of the Ohio National Guard, was called for active duty in January 2003, and requested that Alice, a family friend, hold the note and collect the payments until Patricia returned from abroad. In order to allow Alice to make the collections, Patricia indorsed the note to Alice by writing "Pay to Aliee" on the back of the note. Alice was down on her luck and, in breach of her agreement with Patricia, wrongfully indorsed and delivered the note to Harry in February 2003, who paid 85% of the face amount of the note to Alice. When Patricia returned from duty in 2004, she learned of Alice's wrongdoing, and sued Harry to retake possession of the note and to recover the $5,000 payment that Harry had collected from Maurice in October 2002. If Harry is a holder in due course, does he take free of Patricia's claim of ownership with respect to the note? With respect to the $5,000? See 3–306 and its Comment.

b.   ORDINARY DEFENSES

The extent to which a holder takes free of defenses is governed by 3–305(a) and (b). Subsection (a) states that the right to enforce an instrument is subject to defenses described in paragraphs (1) and (2) of that subsection and claims in recoupment described in paragraph (3). Subsection (b) of 3–305 is a limitation on subsection (a). The right of a holder in due course to enforce an instrument is subject to the defenses stated in subsection (a)(1)—the so-called "real defenses"—but is not subject to the "ordinary" defenses stated in subsection (a)(2) or claims in recoupment described in subsection (a)(3).

Section 3–305(a)(2) refers to defenses that are specifically stated in other sections of Article 3. Those defenses and the sections in which they are found are listed in the first paragraph of Comment 2 to 3–305. Subsection (a)(2) also refers to the common law defenses applicable to simple contracts which are not enumerated. The principal common law defenses are fraud, misrepresentation, and mistake in the issuance of the instrument.

c.   REAL DEFENSES

Section 3–305(a)(1) lists the defenses that may be asserted against even a holder in due course. These defenses are discussed in Comment 1 to 3–305. With the exception of the defense of discharge in bankruptcy, all of the real defenses refer to an instrument that is made unenforceable in order to carry out some public policy of the state not related to the law of negotiable instruments (illegality), or to an instrument that does not represent a contract of the person who signed the instrument (infancy, duress, fraud in the factum).

d.   CLAIMS IN RECOUPMENT

Restatement (Second) of Contracts § 336(2) (1981) states: "The right of an assignee is subject to any defense or claim of the obligor which accrues before the obligor receives notification of the assignment, but not to defenses or claims which accrue thereafter * * *." Suppose A promises

[Handwritten margin notes at top: A → B (pay $1K) → C (assigns the right to get $1K); B will deliver goods; A gets no notice of assignment.]

[Handwritten margin note: A has a defense against C, b/c no notification]

to pay $1,000 to B in return for a promise by B to deliver goods to A. B assigns to C the right of B to receive $1,000 from A. A receives no notification of the assignment. If A's promise to pay B was induced by B's fraud or if B failed to deliver the goods as promised, A has a defense to the obligation to pay B. The defense can be asserted against C, the assignee. Change the facts. Suppose there was no fraud by B and B tendered the goods to A, who accepted them. A has no defense to the obligation to pay for the goods. But suppose A has a claim against B to receive $600. If C demands payment of $1,000 from A, A can assert the $600 claim as a reduction of the amount owing to C from $1,000 to $400.

If A's promise to pay is a negotiable instrument and the instrument is negotiated to C, 3–305 rather than the Restatement governs the rights of A and C. Subsection (a)(2) of 3–305 applies to the defense of fraud or failure to deliver the goods. Subsection (a)(3) applies to A's $600 claim against B if A's claim arose from the transaction that gave rise to the instrument and is therefore a claim in recoupment. Furthermore, the rights of C depend upon whether C is a holder in due course. 3–305(b). Claims in recoupment are discussed in Comment 3 to 3–305.

PROBLEM

[Handwritten: assign → Finance Co.]

[Handwritten diagram: Plumber → Merchant; note $10K; Plumber then did work for Merchant in amount of $8K; + $4K of goods were defective. So Merchant owes him 12K (services & defects) − 10K note = $2K]

Merchant sold and delivered goods to Plumber who accepted them and, as payment of the price, delivered to Merchant a negotiable note of Plumber to pay $10,000 to the order of Merchant. The note was payable one year after the date it was issued. Merchant immediately negotiated the note to Finance Co. A month after the sale and delivery of the goods by Merchant, Plumber, at the request of Merchant, repaired and replaced water pipes and plumbing fixtures at Merchant's place of business. Plumber's bill for this work was $8,000. When Plumber's note became due, Finance Co. demanded payment. Plumber refused to pay for the following reasons: (1) Merchant had not paid the $8,000 owed for the work performed by Plumber; (2) some of the goods sold by Merchant to Plumber were defective and, as a result of the defects, Plumber incurred losses of over $4,000. How much is Finance Co. entitled to recover from Plumber if Finance Co. is a holder in due course? How much is Finance Co. entitled to recover if Finance Co. is not a holder in due course?

[Handwritten: If not a holder in due course, b/c Plumber received no notification of assignment, then doesn't owe Finance anything. If Finance is holder in due course, then gets $10K]

C.   FORMAL REQUISITES OF NEGOTIABLE INSTRUMENTS

The consequences of the use of negotiable instruments vary greatly from those of ordinary contracts. What kinds of contracts qualify for the special treatment accorded negotiable instruments? Under Article 3, as under the common law, form follows function.

Merger theory and the ability of a good faith purchaser for value to take free of claims and defenses with respect to the instrument were based on a separation of the right to payment represented by the instrument from the underlying transaction giving rise to the instrument. But merger theory assumed that the terms of the instrument were not inconsistent with separation from the underlying transaction, and that the terms of the right to receive payment could be determined simply by examination of the instrument itself. Thus, the consequences of negotiability were applied by the common law courts only if the instrument met certain criteria that satisfied these assumptions. The definition of negotiable instrument is found in Article 3 in 3–104(a), and this definition differs only slightly from the requisites for negotiability stated in the NIL and the original Article 3.

The definition of "negotiable instrument" in 3–104 defines the scope of Article 3. 3–102(a). The most important elements of that definition can be briefly described. Only an "order" or "promise" can qualify as a negotiable instrument. "Order" is defined in 3–103(a)(6) as a written instruction to pay money signed by the person giving the instruction. "Promise" is defined in 3–103(a)(9) as a written undertaking to pay money signed by the person undertaking to pay. Thus, a negotiable instrument is always a signed writing that promises or orders payment of money. Negotiable instruments fall into two categories: drafts and notes. An instrument is a draft if it is an order and is a note if it is a promise. 3–104(e). Checks are the most common examples of drafts. 3–104(f). Certificates of deposit are considered to be notes. 3–104(j). Representative simple Note Forms are set out at the end of this chapter. More complex Forms are found in Appendix III.

Because the rules applicable to negotiable instruments and the rules applicable to ordinary contracts can produce dramatically different results in some cases, it is imperative that both the person issuing a promise or order to pay money and the person to whom the promise or order is issued be able to know in advance whether Article 3 or ordinary contract law will apply. The various requirements of 3–104(a) are designed to provide mechanical tests to allow that determination to be made. One particularly important requirement is that the order or promise be "payable to bearer or to order," a term explained in 3–109. Thus, a technical and wholly formal distinction is made between a promise to pay "to John Doe" and a promise to pay "to the order of John Doe." The second promise may be a negotiable instrument if it otherwise qualifies under 3–104. The first promise cannot be a negotiable instrument. Because of this distinction, the issuer of a promissory note payable to an identified person can easily avoid the consequences of negotiability by avoiding use of the words of negotiability: "to order" or "to bearer," sometimes called the "magic words." Another device for avoiding the effects of Article 3 is provided by 3–104(d). These devices for excluding an order or promise from Article 3 are discussed in Comments 2 and 3 to 3–104.

Three of the requisites of a negotiable instrument relate to the certainty of the obligation to pay. First, the order or promise to pay must be "unconditional," a term explained in 3–106. An examination of that provision discloses that some promises or orders that are in fact conditional are deemed to be unconditional while others that are in fact unconditional are deemed to be conditional for the purposes of 3–104(a). The Comment to 3–106 is a guide to the rather arbitrary distinctions and refinements of 3–106. Second, the order or promise must be payable on demand or at a definite time, a requirement explained in 3–108. Third, the order or promise must be to pay a "fixed amount of money, with or without interest or other charges described in the promise or order." 3–104(a). The quoted language differs from 3–104(1)(b) of the original Article 3, which used the phrase "sum certain in money." *Taylor v. Roeder*, which follows, discusses the problem of variable interest rates under the original Article 3. It is fair to say that this case and several others like it shook the real property finance world. How is this issue resolved under Revised Article 3? 3–112(b).

Taylor v. Roeder

Supreme Court of Virginia, 1987.
234 Va. 99, 360 S.E.2d 191.

■ RUSSELL, JUSTICE.

The dispositive question in this case is whether a note providing for a variable rate of interest, not ascertainable from the face of the note, is a negotiable instrument. We conclude that it is not.

The facts are undisputed. VMC Mortgage Company (VMC) was a mortgage lender in Northern Virginia. In the conduct of its business, it borrowed funds from investors, pledging as security the notes secured by deeds of trust which it had obtained from its borrowers. Two of these transactions became the subject of this suit. Because they involve similar facts and the same question of law, they were consolidated for trial below and are consolidated in a single record here * * *.

In the first case, Olde Towne Investment Corporation of Virginia, Inc., on September 11, 1979, borrowed $18,000 from VMC, evidenced by a 60–day note secured by a deed of trust on land in Fairfax County. The note provided for interest at "[t]hree percent (3.00%) over Chase Manhattan Prime to be adjusted monthly." The note provided for renewal "at the same rate of interest at the option of the makers up to a maximum of six (6) months in sixty (60) day increments with the payment of an additional fee of [t]wo (2) points." The note was renewed and extended to November 11, 1980, by a written extension agreement signed by Olde Towne and by VMC.

In May 1981, Frederick R. Taylor, Jr., as trustee for himself and other parties, entered into a contract to buy from Olde Towne the land in Fairfax County securing the $18,000 loan. Taylor's title examination revealed the VMC deed of trust. He requested the payoff figures from VMC and forwarded to VMC the funds VMC said were due. He never received the cancelled Olde Towne note, and the deed of trust was not released.

In the second case, Richard L. Saslaw and others, on December 31, 1979, borrowed $22,450 from VMC evidenced by a 12–month note secured by deed of trust on Fairfax County land. This note also bore interest at

Handwritten top margin: ② Richard Saslaw borrows money from VMC evidenced by a note secured by a deed of trust in Fairfax land. Then ~~Barbara~~ Puris decide to buy land from Saslaw

Handwritten left margin: Saslaw ← loan VMC —→ Pruitt note / note · Puris want land

"3% over Chase Manhattan prime adjusted monthly." Interest was to be "payable quarterly beginning April 1, 1980." In November 1980, Virender and Barbara Puri entered into a contract to purchase from Saslaw, et al., the land subject to the last-mentioned deed of trust. The Puris designated the same Frederick R. Taylor, Jr., as their settlement attorney. Taylor's title examination revealed VMC's deed of trust. Taylor again requested a payoff figure from VMC. At settlement, Saslaw objected to the figure, communicated with VMC and received VMC's agreement to an adjusted figure. Taylor paid the adjusted amount to VMC. Again, Taylor failed to receive the cancelled Saslaw note, and the Saslaw deed of trust was not released.

Cecil Pruitt, Jr., was a trustee of a tax-exempt employees' pension fund. He invested some of the pension fund's assets with VMC, receiving as collateral pledges of certain secured notes that VMC held. The Saslaw note was pledged and delivered to him on January 25, 1980; the Olde Towne note was pledged and delivered to him on September 12, 1980. No notice was given to the makers, or to Taylor, that the notes had been transferred, and all payments on both notes were made to and accepted by VMC.

VMC received and deposited in its account sufficient funds to pay both notes in full, but never informed Pruitt of the payments and made no request of him for return of the original notes. In February 1982, VMC defaulted on its obligation to Pruitt for which both notes had been pledged as collateral. In May 1982, VMC filed a bankruptcy petition in federal court.

Learning that the properties securing both notes had been sold, Pruitt demanded payment from the respective original makers as well as the new owners of the properties, contending that he was a holder in due course. The makers and new owners took the position that they had paid the notes in full. Pruitt caused William F. Roeder, Jr., to qualify as substituted trustee under both deeds of trust and directed him to foreclose them. Taylor and the Puris filed separate bills of complaint against Roeder, trustee, seeking to enjoin the foreclosure sales. The chancellor entered a temporary injunction to preserve the *status quo* and heard the consolidated cases *ore tenus*. By letter opinion incorporated into a final decree entered February 3, 1984, the chancellor found for the defendant and dissolved the injunctions. We granted the complainants an appeal. The parties have agreed on the record that foreclosure will be withheld while the case is pending in this Court.

Under the general law of contracts, if an obligor has received no notice that his debt has been assigned and is in fact unaware of the assignment, he may, with impunity, pay his original creditor and thus extinguish the obligation. His payment will be a complete defense against the claim of an assignee who failed to give him notice of the assignment. * * *

Under the law of negotiable instruments, continued in effect under the Uniform Commercial Code, the rule is different: the makers are bound by their contract to make payment to the *holder*. * * * Further, a holder in due course takes the instrument free from the maker's defense that he has

Handwritten right margin: Once again the Puris designated Taylor to go get a figure of how much they owed VMC to pay off note. ~~Taylor~~ They paid off note, but received no cancelled note.

✗ Then VMC pledges and delivers both paid off notes to Cecil Pruitt. No notice was given to makers or to Taylor about transfer → of notes as collateral. VMC went bankrupt.

Pruitt demanded payment – saying he was a holder in due course. He sued makers and owners of the land.

Foreclosure was withheld until settlement of case.

Rule: Under contract law, if an obligor didn't receive notice of assignment of debt and he paid original creditor, he would still be released.

Handwritten bottom margin: Rule: But, under negotiability, the makers must pay the holder. So a holder in due course, takes free from the maker's defense he paid it to original creditor.

made payment to the original payee, if he lacks notice of the payment and has not dealt with the maker. UCC § 3–305. Thus, the question whether the notes in this case were negotiable is crucial.

UCC § 3–104(1) provides, in pertinent part:

Any writing to be a negotiable instrument within this title must

* * *

(b) contain an unconditional promise or order to pay a sum certain in money....

The meaning of "sum certain" is clarified by UCC § 3–106:

(1) The sum payable is a sum certain even though it is to be paid

(a) with stated interest or by stated installments; or

(b) with stated different rates of interest before and after default or a specified date; or

(c) with a stated discount or addition if paid before or after the date fixed for payment; or

(d) with exchange or less exchange, whether at a fixed rate or at the current rate; or

(e) with costs of collection or an attorney's fee or both upon default.

(2) Nothing in this section shall validate any term which is otherwise illegal.

Official Comment 1, which follows, states in part:

It is sufficient [to establish negotiability] that at any time of payment the holder is able to determine the amount then payable *from the instrument itself* with any necessary computation.... The computation must be one which can be made *from the instrument itself without reference to any outside source,* and this section does not make negotiable a note payable with interest "at the current rate."

(Emphasis added.) UCC § 3–107 provides an explicit exception to the "four corners" rule laid down above by providing for the negotiability of instruments payable in foreign currency.

We conclude that the drafters of the Uniform Commercial Code adopted criteria of negotiability intended to exclude an instrument which requires reference to any source outside the instrument itself in order to ascertain the amount due, subject only to the exceptions specifically provided for by the U.C.C. * * *

The appellee points to the Official Comment to UCC § 3–104. Comment 1 states that by providing criteria for negotiability "within this Article," * * * "leaves open the possibility that some writings may be made negotiable by other statutes or by judicial decision." The Comment continues: "The same is true as to any new type of paper which commercial

[handwritten margin notes:]

Rule:

3-104 says the instrument itself must show an amount payable, for it to be negotiable, it has to indicate this (you don't have to look at any outside source to see how much to pay). So

Variable interest loans fluctuate and don't have a definite set amount so can't be negotiable.

practice may develop in the future." The appellee urges us to create, by judicial decision, just such an exception in favor of variable-interest notes.

Appellants concede that variable-interest loans have become a familiar device in the mortgage lending industry. Their popularity arose when lending institutions, committed to long-term loans at fixed rates of interest to their borrowers, were in turn required to borrow short-term funds at high rates during periods of rapid inflation. Variable rates protected lenders when rates rose and benefitted borrowers when rates declined. They suffer, however, from the disadvantage that the amount required to satisfy the debt cannot be ascertained without reference to an extrinsic source—in this case the varying prime rate charged by the Chase Manhattan Bank. Although that rate may readily be ascertained from published sources, it cannot be found within the "four corners" of the note.

Other courts confronted with similar questions have reached differing results. See, e.g., A. Alport & Son, Inc. v. Hotel Evans, Inc., 65 Misc.2d 374, 376–77, 317 N.Y.S.2d 937, 939–40 (1970) (note bearing interest at "bank rates" not negotiable under U.C.C.); Woodhouse, Drake and Carey, Ltd. v. Anderson, 61 Misc.2d 951, 307 N.Y.S.2d 113 (1970) (note providing for interest at "8½% or at the maximum legal rate" was not usurious. Inferentially, the note was negotiable.); Farmers Production Credit Ass'n v. Arena, 145 Vt. 20, 23, 481 A.2d 1064, 1065 (1984) (variable-interest note not negotiable under U.C.C.).

The U.C.C. introduced a degree of clarity into the law of commercial transactions which permits it to be applied by laymen daily to countless transactions without resort to judicial interpretation. The relative predictability of results made possible by that clarity constitutes the overriding benefit arising from its adoption. In our view, that factor makes it imperative that when change is thought desirable, the change should be made by statutory amendment, not through litigation and judicial interpretation. Accordingly, we decline the appellee's invitation to create an exception, by judicial interpretation, in favor of instruments providing for a variable rate of interest not ascertainable from the instrument itself.

In an alternative argument, the appellee contends that even if the notes are not negotiable, they are nevertheless "symbolic instruments" which ought to be paid according to their express terms. Those terms include the maker's promises to pay "to VMC Mortgage Company *or order*," and in the event of default, to make accelerated payment "at the option of the *holder*." The emphasized language, appellee contends, makes clear that the makers undertook an obligation to pay any party who held the notes as a result of a transfer from VMC. Assuming the abstract correctness of that argument, it does not follow that the makers undertook the further obligation of making a monthly canvass of all inhabitants of the earth in order to ascertain who the holder might be. In the absence of notice to the makers that their debt had been assigned, they were entitled to the protection of the rule in *Evans v. Joyner* in making good-faith payment to the original payee of these non-negotiable notes.

[handwritten margin notes at top: for permanent injunction seeking payment for note and foreclosure.]

[handwritten left margin: So case remanded]

Accordingly, we will reverse the decree and remand the cause to the trial court for entry of a permanent injunction against foreclosure.

■ COMPTON, JUSTICE, dissenting.

The majority views the Uniform Commercial Code as inflexible, requiring legislative action to adapt to changing commercial practices. This overlooks a basic purpose of the Code, flexibility and adaptability of construction to meet developing commercial usage.

[handwritten left margin: Dissent says judicial action should be taken to make an exception b/c Code requires liberal flexibility in a changing marketplace.]

According to § 1–102(1), the UCC "shall be liberally construed and applied to promote its underlying purposes and policies." One of such underlying purposes and policies is "to permit the continued expansion of commercial practices through custom, usage and agreement of the parties." § 1–102(2)(b). Comment 1 to this section sets out clearly the intention of the drafters:

> "This Act is drawn to provide flexibility so that, since it is intended to be a semi-permanent piece of legislation, it will provide its own machinery for expansion of commercial practices. *It is intended to make it possible for the law embodied in this Act to be developed by the courts in light of unforeseen and new circumstances and practices.* However, the proper construction of the Act requires that its interpretation and application be limited to its reason." (Emphasis added).

The majority's rigid interpretation defeats the purpose of the Code. Nowhere in the UCC is "sum certain" defined. This absence must be interpreted in light of the expectation that commercial law continue to evolve. The § 3–106 exceptions could not have been intended as the exclusive list of "safe harbors," as the drafters anticipated "unforeseen" changes in commercial practices. Instead, those exceptions represented, at the time of drafting, recognized conditions of payment which did not impair negotiability in the judgment of businessmen. To limit exceptions to those existing at that time would frustrate the "continued expansion of commercial practices" by freezing the Code in time and requiring additional legislation whenever "unforeseen and new circumstances and practices" evolve, regardless of "custom, usage, and agreement of the parties."

> "The rule requiring certainty in commercial paper was a rule of commerce before it was a rule of law. It requires commercial, not mathematical, certainty. An uncertainty which does not impair the function of negotiable instruments in the judgment of business men ought not to be regarded by the courts.... The whole question is, do [the provisions] render the instruments so uncertain as to destroy their fitness to pass current in the business world?" *Cudahy Packing Co. v. State National Bank of St. Louis,* 134 F. 538, 542, 545 (8th Cir.1904).

[handwritten left margin: It's custom and usage to transact w/ variable interest loans now.]

Instruments providing that loan interest may be adjusted over the life of the loan routinely pass with increasing frequency in this state and many others as negotiable instruments. This Court should recognize this custom and usage, as the commercial market has, and hold these instruments to be negotiable.

The majority focuses on the requirement found in Comment 1 to § 3–106 that a negotiable instrument be self-contained, understood without reference to an outside source. Our cases have interpreted this to mean that reference to terms in another agreement which materially affect the instrument renders it nonnegotiable. See, e.g., McLean Bank v. Nelson, Adm'r, 232 Va. 420, 350 S.E.2d 651 (1986) (where note was accepted "pursuant" to a separate agreement, reference considered surplusage and the note negotiable); Salomonsky v. Kelly, 232 Va. 261, 349 S.E.2d 358 (1986) (where principal sum payable "as set forth" in a separate agreement, all the essential terms did not appear on the face of the instrument and the note was nonnegotiable).

The commercial market requires a self-contained instrument for negotiability so that a stranger to the original transaction will be fully apprised of its terms and will not be disadvantaged by terms not ascertainable from the instrument itself. For example, interest payable at the "current rate" leaves a holder subject to claims that the current rate was established by one bank rather than another and would disadvantage a stranger to the original transaction.

The rate which is stated in the notes in this case, however, does not similarly disadvantage a stranger to the original agreement. Anyone coming into possession could immediately ascertain the terms of the notes; interest payable at three percent above the prime rate established by the Chase Manhattan Bank of New York City. This is a third-party objective standard which is recognized as such by the commercial market. The rate can be determined by a telephone call to the bank or from published lists obtained on request. * * *

Accordingly, I believe these notes are negotiable under the Code and I would affirm the decision below.

NOTES

1. See 3–104(a), 3–112(b) and Comment 1 to 3–112.

2. Since the scope of Article 3 (3–102(a)) is determined by the definition of negotiable instrument in 3–104, it is not surprising that this definition was the subject of a great deal of debate in the revision of Article 3. There were a number of proposals either to restrict or enlarge the kinds of instruments to which the harsh doctrine of negotiability would apply by changes in the definition of negotiable instrument. At one extreme was the view that the concept of negotiability was no longer needed; let the parties contract for whatever terms they can agree on for credit and payment instruments. A recurring suggestion for reform was to discard the "magic words"—"order" and "bearer"—as prerequisites of negotiability. Then too, a number of proposals were made to junk the traditional formal requirements of negotiability in favor of a functional test along the lines of that suggested in Fred H. Miller and Alvin C. Harrell, The Law of Modern Payment Systems 2.01, at [2][c] (2003):

[handwritten margin notes:]

To be negotiable it must

① be signed by maker or drawer

② must be for payment of money.

③ must be by delivery w/ necessary endorsement or assignment

The Mechanical tests remain in effect today. The formal requirements are supported by the fact that they provide a bright line to know when you have a negotiable instrument

(1) Any writing to be a negotiable instrument within this article must be

(a) signed by the maker or drawer;

(b) for the payment, or evidence a right to the payment, of money; and

(c) of a type which in the ordinary course of business is transferred by delivery with any necessary endorsement or assignment.

This is similar to the definition of "instrument" in 9–102(a)(47).

After five years of discussion, the Drafting Committee decided to retain the traditional, somewhat mechanical tests similar to those developed at common law and codified in both the NIL and the 1962 version of Article 3. The strongest reason for this was the elusive quest for a "bright line." Comment 2 to 3–104 explains:

Total exclusion from Article 3 of other promises or orders that are not payable to bearer or order serves a useful purpose. It provides a simple device to clearly exclude a writing that does not fit the pattern of typical negotiable instruments and which is not intended to be a negotiable instrument. If a writing could be an instrument despite the absence of "to order" or "to bearer" language and a dispute arises with respect to the writing, it might be argued that the writing is a negotiable instrument because the other requirements of subsection (a) are somehow met. Even if the argument is eventually found to be without merit it can be used as a litigation ploy. Words making a promise or order payable to bearer or to order are the most distinguishing feature of a negotiable instrument and such words are frequently referred to as "words of negotiability." Article 3 is not meant to apply to contracts for the sale of goods or services or the sale or lease of real property or similar writings that may contain a promise to pay money. The use of words of negotiability in such contracts would be an aberration. Absence of the words precludes any argument that such contracts might be negotiable instruments.

3. Why then is a check that says "Pay to Payee" a negotiable instrument under 3–104(c) while a promissory note with this language is not? The reason for this distinction is that, as we shall see, banks deal with the billions of checks issued each year almost entirely on an automated basis. They pay checks drawn on them largely on the basis of machine-readable information encoded on the bottom of the check. Virtually all checks are printed with the words "Pay to the order of." If a drawer scratches out the word "order," the depositary and drawee banks have no feasible way of detecting that they are taking a nonnegotiable instrument. Section 3–104(c) largely relieves them of the burden of having to look at the face of each check to know whether it is negotiable. Comment 2 to 3–104.

4. The justification for retaining the "words of negotiability"—"bearer" or "order"—stated in Note 2 is that they describe a bright line test for negotiability. Certainly most creditors know what these words mean, but is this true of most debtors? There is nothing about this 18th century formalism that would indicate to an unsophisticated debtor that its inclusion means a debtor who is defrauded by a payee is, nevertheless, liable to a good faith purchaser of the instrument. This is a harsh consequence to visit upon a debtor who has no way of learning what these words mean short of consulting a lawyer. During the Drafting Committee discussions, a strong view was pressed that if the doctrine of negotiability was to be retained (and not all were in favor of doing so), then any note that purported to be negotiable should bear a legend warning of the consequences of negotiability. Such a provision was carried in a number of drafts until late in the drafting process. When it was finally dropped in the last year of the project, the justification for doing so was that business debtors should be held to know what business documents mean and, as we shall see, the doctrine of negotiability has been severely circumscribed in consumer transactions.

D. REQUIREMENTS FOR HOLDER IN DUE COURSE

Section 3–302. Holder in Due Course

(a) * * * "[H]older in due course" means the holder of an instrument if:

> (1) the instrument when issued or negotiated to the holder does not bear such apparent evidence of forgery or alteration or is not otherwise so irregular or incomplete as to call into question its authenticity; and

> (2) the holder took the instrument (i) for value, (ii) in good faith, (iii) without notice that the instrument is overdue or has been dishonored or that there is an uncured default with respect to payment of another instrument issued as part of the same series, (iv) without notice that the instrument contains an unauthorized signature or has been altered, (v) without notice of any claim to the instrument described in Section 3–306, and (vi) without notice that any party has a defense or claim in recoupment described in Section 3–305(a).

1. GOOD FAITH AND NOTICE

To qualify as a holder in due course under 3–302 a holder must, among other requirements, have taken the instrument in good faith and without notice of any defense against or claim to it on the part of any person. The meaning of good faith as applied to negotiable instruments has varied over the years. The law prior to the adoption of the NIL is traced by the Court in Howard National Bank v. Wilson, 96 Vt. 438, 120 A. 889 (1923):

> Prior to the Negotiable Instruments Act, two distinct lines of cases had developed in this country. The first had its origin in Gill v. Cubitt, 3 B. & C. 466, 10 E.C.L. 215, where the rule was distinctly laid down by the court of King's Bench that the purchaser of negotiable paper must exercise reasonable prudence and caution, and that, if the circumstances were such as ought to have excited the suspicion of a prudent

and careful man, and he made no inquiry, he did not stand in the legal position of a bona fide holder. The rule was adopted by the courts of this country generally and seem to have become a fixed rule in the law of negotiable paper. Later in Goodman v. Harvey, 4 A. & E. 870, 31 E.C.L. 381, the English court abandoned its former position and adopted the rule that nothing short of actual bad faith or fraud in the purchaser would deprive him of the character of a bona fide purchaser and let in defenses existing between prior parties, that no circumstances of suspicion merely, or want of proper caution in the purchaser, would have this effect, and that even gross negligence would have no effect, except as evidence tending to establish bad faith or fraud. Some of the American courts adhered to the earlier rule, while others followed the change inaugurated in Goodman v. Harvey. The question was before this court in Roth v. Colvin, 32 Vt. 125, and, on full consideration of the question, a rule was adopted in harmony with that announced in Gill v. Cubitt, which has been adhered to in subsequent cases, including those cited above. Stated briefly, one line of cases including our own had adopted the test of the reasonably prudent man and the other that of actual good faith. It would seem that it was the intent of the Negotiable Instruments Act to harmonize this disagreement by adopting the latter test. That such is the view generally accepted by the courts appears from a recent review of the cases concerning what constitutes notice of defect. Brannan on Neg.Ins.Law, 187–201. To effectuate the general purpose of the act to make uniform the Negotiable Instruments Law of those states which should enact it, we are constrained to hold (contrary to the rule adopted in our former decisions) that negligence on the part of the plaintiff, or suspicious circumstances sufficient to put a prudent man on inquiry, will not of themselves prevent a recovery, but are to be considered merely as evidence bearing on the question of bad faith. 96 Vt. at 452–453, 120 A. at 894.

The definition of "good faith" in former Article 3 was purely subjective: "honesty in fact." In Revised Article 3, the definition was changed to "honesty in fact and observance of reasonable commercial standards of fair dealing." This definition is now found in 1–201(b)(20) and applies to all Articles except Article 5. There is no definition of "fair dealing." Section 3–302(a)(2) continues the previous Article 3 requirement that the instrument be taken both in good faith and without notice of claims or defenses. "Notice" is defined in 1–202(a):

(a) * * * [A] person has "notice" of a fact if the person

(1) has actual knowledge of it:

(2) has received a notice or notification of it; or

(3) from all the facts and circumstances known to the person at the time in question, has reason to know that it exists.

Clearly, there are aspects of both subjectivity and objectivity in the standards Article 3 requires for holder-in-due-course status. We include two opinions in this section. The first, *Kaw Valley*, decided under the former statute, is one of the few decisions in which a court discusses the difference between good faith and notice. It also involves a very common transaction, inventory financing. The second, *Maine Family Federal*, is one of the first cases to consider the meaning of "fair dealing" in the amended definition of good faith in Revised Article 3. It is a much discussed opinion.

Kaw Valley State Bank & Trust Co. v. Riddle

Supreme Court of Kansas, 1976.
219 Kan. 550, 549 P.2d 927.

■ FROMME, JUSTICE.

This action was brought by The Kaw Valley State Bank and Trust Company (hereinafter referred to as Kaw Valley) to recover judgment against John H. Riddle d/b/a Riddle Contracting Company (hereafter referred to as Riddle) on two notes and to determine the priority of conflicting security agreements. The two notes were covered by separate security agreements and were given to purchase construction equipment. The Planters State Bank and Trust Company (hereinafter referred to as Planters) held a note and security interest on the same and other construction equipment acquired by Riddle. Kaw Valley had acquired the two notes and the security agreements by assignment from Co–Mac, Inc. (hereinafter referred to as Co–Mac), a dealer, from whom Riddle purchased the construction equipment.

In a trial to the court Kaw Valley was found not to be a holder in due course of one of the notes. Its claim on said note, totaling $21,904.64, was successfully defended on the grounds of failure of consideration. It was stipulated at the trial that none of the construction equipment for which the note was given had ever been delivered by Co–Mac. Kaw Valley has appealed.

* * *

Prior to the transactions in question Riddle had purchased construction equipment and machinery from the dealer, Co–Mac. A number of these purchases had been on credit and discounted to Kaw Valley by Co–Mac. Including the Riddle transactions, Kaw Valley had purchased over 250 notes and security agreements from Co–Mac during the prior ten year period. All were guaranteed by Co–Mac and by its president personally.

In May, 1971, Riddle negotiated for the purchase of a model 6–c Caterpillar tractor, a dozer and a used 944 Caterpillar wheel tractor with a two yard bucket. Riddle was advised that this machinery could be delivered but it would first be necessary for Co–Mac to have a signed note and security agreement to complete the transaction. An installment note, security agreement and acceptance of delivery of the machinery was mailed to Riddle. These were signed and returned to Co–Mac. Ten days later, the machinery not having been delivered, Riddle called Co–Mac and inquired about purchasing a D–8 Caterpillar and a #80 Caterpillar scraper in place of the first machinery ordered. Co–Mac agreed to destroy the May 11, 1971 papers and sell this larger machinery to Riddle in place of that previously ordered.

The sale of this substitute machinery was completed and the machinery was delivered after the execution of an additional note and security agreement. However, the May 11, 1971 papers were not destroyed. The note had been discounted and assigned to Kaw Valley prior to the sale of the substitute machinery. Thereafter Co–Mac, who was in financial trouble, made regular payments on the first note to Kaw Valley. The note was thus kept current by Co–Mac and Riddle had no knowledge of the continued existence of that note. The 6–c Caterpillar tractor, dozer and the used 944 Caterpillar wheel tractor were never delivered to Riddle. Riddle received no consideration for the May 11, 1971 note and no lien attached under the security agreement because the machinery never came into possession of Riddle. (See UCC § 9–204.) The debtor never had rights in any of the collateral.

On February 24, 1972, representatives of Riddle, Co–Mac and Kaw Valley met for the purpose of consolidating the indebtedness of Riddle on machinery notes held by Kaw Valley and guaranteed by Co–Mac. Riddle was behind in some of his payments and wanted to consolidate the notes and reduce his monthly payments to $4,500.00. Kaw Valley disclosed eight past due machinery notes, each representing separate purchase transactions by Riddle. Riddle objected to one of these notes dated July 16, 1971, because the machinery purchased under this particular transaction had been previously returned to Co–Mac.

It was agreed by Kaw Valley that Riddle did not owe for this machinery because of the previous settlement between Co–Mac and Riddle. Kaw Valley cancelled the $5,000.00 balance shown to be due from Riddle.

Thereupon a renewal note and security agreement for $44,557.70 dated February 24, 1972, was drawn consolidating and renewing the seven remaining notes. Riddle then asked Kaw Valley if this was all that it owed the bank and he was assured that it was. The renewal note was then executed by Riddle.

It was not until March 12, 1972, that Riddle was advised by Kaw Valley that it held the note and security agreement dated May 11, 1971, which Riddle believed had been destroyed by Co–Mac. This was within a week after a receiver had been appointed to take over Co–Mac's business affairs. Riddle explained the machinery had never been delivered and Co–Mac promised to destroy the papers. No demand for payment of the May 11, 1971 note was made on Riddle until this action was filed.

Prior to the time this action was filed, Riddle executed a note and granted a security agreement in all of its machinery and equipment to Planters. This included the machinery covered in the previous consolidation transaction of February 24, 1972, with Kaw Valley and Co–Mac.

Subsequently Kaw Valley obtained possession of the machinery covered by the February 24 transaction by court order. Thereupon by agreement in

[handwritten margin note top: Kaw Valley obtained possession of equipment by ct. order.]

writing between Kaw Valley, Planters and Riddle an immediate sale of the collateral covered in the February 24 transaction was held. By the terms of this agreement the first $22,200.00 in proceeds was to be paid to Kaw Valley in full satisfaction of the note of February 24, 1972. The money received from the sale in excess of this amount was to be paid to the Merchants National Bank to hold as escrow agent, awaiting a determination of entitlement by the court.

At the time of the trial the $22,200.00 had been received by Kaw Valley and the balance of the proceeds of the agreed sale amounting to $25,371.15 was in the hands of the escrow agent.

In the court's memorandum of decision filed November 19, 1974, the court found:

[handwritten margin note: Kaw Valley wanted to sell equipment and use proceeds to pay note. Some proceeds paid $25K, but Kaw sd it was also owed money on other note (Riddle thought was destroyed).]

"That the proceeds remaining in plaintiff's possession from the agreed equipment sale are $25,371.15. The plaintiff claims $21,904.64 of same is due on the transaction of May 11, 1971. The parties agree that the excess of $3,466.51 should be paid to defendant Planters State Bank to apply on its August 28, 1972 claim;"

On December 20, 1974, the court entered the following pay-out order:

"TO THE CLERK OF THE DISTRICT COURT:

"Now on this 20th day of December 1974, you are ordered to pay to The Planters State Bank and Trust Company the sum of $3,466.51 now in your hands, having been paid by the Kaw Valley State Bank and Trust Company, pursuant to the Journal Entry of Judgment entered herein on November 19, 1974."

[handwritten margin note: Riddle was forced to pay Planters $3,466.]

Although it does not appear who initiated the order, the $3,466.51 was paid to and accepted by Planters leaving the disputed proceeds of the sale ($21,904.64) in the hands of either the escrow agent or the court.

* * *

The primary point on appeal questions the holding of the trial court that Kaw Valley was not a holder in due course of the note and security agreement dated May 11, 1971.

[handwritten margin note: Issue: whether Kaw Valley was a holder in due course of the note and Sec. agmt. dated May 11, 1971 (first note that Co-Mac sd it would destroy).]

UCC § 3–306 provides that unless a holder of an instrument is a holder in due course he takes the instrument subject to the defenses of want or failure of consideration, nonperformance of any condition precedent, nondelivery or delivery for a special purpose. It was undisputed in this case that Riddle received no consideration after executing the note. The machinery was never delivered and he was assured by Co–Mac that the papers would be destroyed. The parties so stipulated. If Kaw Valley was not a holder in due course the proven defense was a bar to recovery by Kaw Valley.

UCC § 3–302 states that a holder in due course is a holder who takes the instrument (1) for value, (2) in good faith and (3) without notice of any defense against it. It was not disputed and the court found that Kaw Valley

[handwritten margin note: Riddle got no consideration after executing note – equipment didn't come.]

took the note for value so the first requirement was satisfied. The other requirements were subject to dispute. The trial court concluded:

> "Kaw Valley State Bank and Trust Company is not a holder in due course of the note and security agreement, dated May 11, 1971 for the reason that it did not establish in all respects that it took said instruments in good faith and without notice of any defense against or claimed to it on the part of John H. Riddle, and Kaw Valley State Bank and Trust Company therefor took said instruments subject to the defense of failure of consideration. [Citations omitted.]"

So we are confronted with the question of what is required for a holder to take an instrument "in good faith" and "without notice of defense." We will consider the two parts of the question in the order mentioned.

"Good faith" is defined in UCC § 1–201(19) as "honesty in fact in the conduct or transaction concerned." The first draft of the Uniform Commercial Code (U.C.C.) as proposed required not only that the actions of a holder be honest in fact but in addition it required the actions to conform to *reasonable commercial standards.* This would have permitted the courts to inquire as to whether a particular commercial standard was in fact reasonable. (See Uniform Commercial Code, Proposed Final Draft [1950], § 1–201, 18, p. 30.) However, when the final draft was approved the test of reasonable commercial standards was excised thus indicating that a more rigid standard must be applied for determining "good faith." * * *

From the history of the Uniform Commercial Code it would appear that "good faith" requires no actual knowledge of or participation in any material infirmity in the original transaction.

The second part of our question concerns the requirement of the U.C.C. that a holder in due course take the instrument without notice of any defense to the instrument. UCC § 1–201(25) provides:

> "A person has 'notice' of a fact when

> "(a) he has actual knowledge of it; or

> "(b) he has received a notice or notification of it; or

> "(c) from all the facts and circumstances known to him at the time in question he has reason to know that it exists. A person 'knows' or has 'knowledge' of a fact when he has actual knowledge of it. 'Discover' or 'learn' or a word or phrase of similar import refers to knowledge rather than to reason to know. The time and circumstances under which a notice or notification may cease to be effective are not determined by this act."

As is apparent from reading the above statute the standard enunciated is not limited to the rigid standard of actual knowledge of the defense. Reason to know appears to be premised on the use of reasonable commercial practices. * * * Since "good faith" and "no notice of defense" are both required of a holder to claim the status of a holder-in-due course it would appear that the two standards are not in conflict even though the standards of conduct may be different.

There is little or no evidence in the present case to indicate that Kaw Valley acted dishonestly or "not in good faith" when it purchased the note of May 11, 1971. However, as to "notice of defense" the court found from all the facts and circumstances known to Kaw Valley at the time in question it had reason to know a defense existed. The court found:

"During the period 1960 to May, 1971, plaintiff purchased from Co–Mac over 250 notes and secured transactions and held at any given time between $100,000.00 and $250,000.00 of such obligations. All of which were guaranteed by Co–Mac and personally guaranteed by D. J. Wickern, its president. Conant Wait personally handled most if not all of such transactions for plaintiff. Mr. Wait was aware that Co–Mac was making warranties and representation as to fitness to some purchasers of new and used equipment. Mr. Wait further knew that some transactions were in fact not as they would appear to be in that the money from Kaw Valley would be used by Co–Mac to buy the equipment that was the subject matter of the sale. Further, that delivery to the customer of said purchased equipment was sometimes delayed 60 to 90 days for repairing and/or overhauling of same. The plaintiff obviously on many transactions was relying on Co–Mac to insure payment of the obligations and contacted Co–Mac to collect delinquent payments. Some transactions involved delivery of coupon books to Co–Mac rather than the debtor so Co–Mac could bill service and parts charges along with the secured debt. Co–Mac collected payments directly from debtors in various transactions and paid plaintiff. Plaintiff did not concern itself with known irregularities in the transactions as it clearly was relying on Co–Mac;

"The coupon book on the May 11, 1971 transaction was not sent to defendant Riddle; no payments on same were made by defendant Riddle; the payments were made by Co–Mac until January 25, 1972; prior to early March, 1972, defendant Riddle did not know plaintiff had the May 11, 1971 secured transaction; knowledge of said transaction came to defendant Riddle on March 12, 1972 when Mr. Wait contacted defendant Riddle's manager; that Co–Mac had shortly before been placed in receivership; that no demand for any payment on said transaction was made by plaintiff to defendant Riddle until September 1972."

To further support its holding that Kaw Valley had reason to know that the defense existed the court found that when Kaw Valley, Co–Mac and Riddle met on February 24, 1972, to consolidate all of Riddle's past due notes Kaw Valley recognized Co–Mac's authority to act for it. Co–Mac had accepted return of the machinery on one of the eight transactions and Kaw Valley recognized its authority as their agent to do so and cancelled the $5,000.00 balance remaining due on the note held by the bank.

The cases dealing with the question of "reason to know a defense exists" seem to fall into four categories.

The first includes those cases where it is established the holder had information from the transferor or the obligor which disclosed the existence of a defense. In those cases it is clear if the holder takes an instrument having received prior or contemporaneous notice of a defense he is not a holder-in-due course. (Billingsley v. Mackay, 382 F.2d 290 [5th Cir. 1967].) Our present case does not fall in that category for there is no evidence that Co–Mac or Riddle informed Kaw Valley that the machinery had not been delivered when the note was negotiated.

The second group of cases are those in which the defense appears in an accompanying document delivered to the holder with the note. For example, when a security agreement is executed concurrently with a note evidencing an indebtedness incurred for machinery to be delivered in the future. In such case the instrument may under certain circumstances disclose a defense to the note, such as nondelivery of the machinery purchased. (See also Commerce Trust Company v. Denson, 437 S.W.2d 94 [Mo. App. 1968], and HIMC Investment Co. v. Siciliano, 103 N.J. Super. 27, 246 A.2d 502, for other examples.) Our present case does not fall in this category because Riddle had signed a written delivery acceptance which was handed to Kaw Valley along with the note and security agreement.

A third group of cases are those in which information appears in the written instrument indicating the existence of a defense, such as when the note on its face shows that the due date has passed or the note bears visible evidence of alteration and forgery or the note is clearly incomplete. (See E. F. Corporation v. Smith, 496 F.2d 826 [10th Cir. 1974]; Srochi v. Kamensky, 118 Ga. App. 182, 162 S.E.2d 889; and Winter & Hirsch, Inc. v. Passarelli, 122 Ill. App.2d 372, 259 N.E.2d 312.) In our present case the instrument assigned bore nothing unusual on its face and appeared complete and proper in all respects.

In the fourth category of cases it has been held that the holder of a negotiable instrument may be prevented from assuming holder in due course status because of knowledge of the business practices of his transferor or when he is so closely aligned with the transferor that transferor may be considered an agent of the holder and the transferee is charged with the actions and knowledge of the transferor.

Under our former negotiable instruments law containing provisions similar to the U.C.C. this court refused to accord holder in due course status to a machinery company receiving notes from one of its dealers because of its knowledge of the business practices of the dealer and the company's participation and alignment with the dealer who transferred the note. (International Harvester Co. v. Watkins, 127 Kan. 50, Sly. & 3, 272 P. 139, 61 A.L.R. 687.)

In Unico v. Owen, 50 N.J. 101, 232 A.2d 405, the New Jersey court refused to accord holder in due course status to a financing partnership which was closely connected with the transferor and had been organized to finance the commercial paper obtained by the transferor and others. The financing partnership had a voice in setting the policies and standards to be followed by the transferor. Under such circumstances the court found that the holder must be considered a participant in the transaction and subject to defenses available against the payee-transferor. In United States Finance

Company v. Jones, 285 Ala. 105, 229 So.2d 495, it was held that a finance company purchasing a note from a payee for fifty percent of its face value did not establish holder in due course status and must be held subject to defenses inherent in the original transaction. Other jurisdictions have followed the rationale of Unico. See American Plan Corp. v. Woods, 16 Ohio App.2d 1, 240 N.E.2d 886, where the holder supplied forms to the payee, established financing charges and investigated the credit of the maker of the note; Calvert Credit Corporation v. Williams, 244 A.2d 494 (D.C.App. 1968), where the holder exerted total control over payee's financial affairs; and Jones v. Approved Bancredit Corp., 256 A.2d 739 (Del.1969), where ownership and management of the holder and payee were connected.

In the present case Kaw Valley had worked closely with Co–Mac in over 250 financing transactions over a period of ten years. It knew that some of these transactions were not for valuable consideration at the time the paper was delivered since the bank's money was to be used in purchasing the machinery or equipment represented in the instruments as already in possession of the maker of the note. Kaw Valley had been advised that delivery to Co–Mac's customers was sometimes delayed from 60 to 90 days. Kaw Valley continued to rely on Co–Mac to assure payment of the obligations and contacted it to collect delinquent payments. Some of these transactions, including the one in question, involved the use of coupon books to be used by the debtor in making payment on the notes. In the present case Kaw Valley did not notify Riddle that it was the holder of the note. It delivered Riddle's coupon book to Co–Mac as if it were the obligor or was authorized as its collection agent for this transaction. Throughout the period from May 11, 1971, to February 25, 1972, Kaw Valley received and credited the monthly payments knowing that payments were being made by Co–Mac and not by Riddle. Then when Riddle's loans were consolidated, the May 11, 1971 transaction was not included by Kaw Valley, either by oversight or by intention, as an obligation of Riddle. Co–Mac occupied a close relationship with Kaw Valley and with its knowledge and consent acted as its agent in collecting payments on notes held by Kaw Valley. The working relationship existing between Kaw Valley and Co–Mac was further demonstrated on February 24, 1972, when the $5,000.00 balance due on one of Riddle's notes was cancelled when it was shown that the machinery for which the note was given had previously been returned to Co–Mac with the understanding that no further payments were due. UCC § 3–307(3) provides:

"After it is shown that a defense exists a person claiming the rights of a holder in due course has the burden of establishing that he or some person under whom he claims is in all respects a holder in due course."

In the present case the court found that the appellant, Kaw Valley, had not sustained its burden of proving that it was a holder in due course. Under the evidence in this case the holder failed to advise the maker of the note of its acquisition of the note and security agreement. It placed the payment coupon book in the hands of Co–Mac and received all monthly payments from them. A close working relationship existed between the two

companies and Co–Mac was clothed with authority to collect and forward
all payments due on the transaction. Agency and authority was further
shown to exist by authorizing return of machinery to Co–Mac and terminating balances due on purchase money paper. We cannot say under the
facts and circumstances known and participated in by Kaw Valley in this
transaction it did not at the time in question have reason to know that the
defense existed. This was a question of fact to be determined by the trier of
fact which if supported by substantial competent evidence must stand.

The judgment is affirmed.

NOTE

Is the court telling us that the doctrine of holding in due course
performs no legitimate function in inventory and sales financing?

PROBLEMS

1. On October 16, 1969, $8,000,000 of United States Treasury Bills in
bearer form were stolen from Morgan Bank. On October 28, 1969, when
the theft was discovered, Morgan Bank sent a "notice of lost securities,"
describing the stolen bills by serial number, to bankers and brokers
throughout the country. Third Bank, upon receiving the notice, placed the
notice in its lost securities file. On January 30, 1970 Third Bank made
loans totaling $82,000 to Bialkin. As collateral for the loans it took two
treasury bills each with a face amount of $50,000. The two bills were
among those stolen from Morgan Bank and were listed in the notice of lost
securities. The officer of Third Bank who approved the loan to Bialkin did
not check the lost securities file of Third Bank. He testified that he was not
aware of its existence. Third Bank later discovered that the treasury bills
had been stolen and reported it to law enforcement authorities. Morgan
Bank then sued to recover the bills.

Treasury bills come within the definition of "security" (8–102(a)(15))
that are governed by Article 8 of the UCC rather than Article 3. 3–102(a).
In this case Third Bank would defeat the claim of Morgan Bank if it
qualified as a "protected purchaser." 8–303. The treasury bills in this case
are now known as "security certificates." 8–102(d)(16). A protected purchaser of a security certificate is essentially the same as a holder in due
course of a negotiable instrument. Although he 1995 revision of Article 8
changed the notice test under that statute (8–105), would Third Bank have
notice of the claim of Morgan Bank under 1–202? This problem is based on
the facts, slightly modified, of Morgan Guaranty Trust Co. of New York v.
Third National Bank of Hampden County, 529 F.2d 1141 (1st Cir.1976).

2. In December 1957 Fazzari was induced by fraud to sign a promissory note for $400 payable to the order of Wade. After discovering the
fraud, in January 1958, Fazzari notified all of the local banks of the fraud.

of the frauds. He personally told cashier of Odessa Bank and advised him not to purchase the note. Later Odessa Bank bought the note, through cashier. He said he forgot Fazzari **33** *told him.*

CHAPTER 1 NEGOTIABILITY AND HOLDERS IN DUE COURSE

He personally spoke to the cashier of Odessa Bank and advised him not to purchase the note because he had been "tricked" by Wade. Three months later Odessa Bank, acting through its cashier, purchased the note. The cashier admitted that Fazzari had told him about the note in January but testified that at the time the note was purchased in April he had forgotten the incident. Did Odessa Bank take the note as a holder in due course? See 1–202. In the Comment to that provision, under the heading "Changes from former law," the following sentence appears: "The reference to the 'forgotten notice' doctrine has been deleted." The statement refers to a sentence in the former definition of "notice" that said: "The time and circumstances under which notice or notification may cease to be effective are not determined by this Act." The Comment to that section explained there was no intention of overruling a 1935 Supreme Court holding that notice that is forgotten is no longer notice. This problem is based on the facts of First National Bank of Odessa v. Fazzari, 10 N.Y.2d 394, 223 N.Y.S.2d 483, 179 N.E.2d 493 (N.Y. 1961).

Odessa Bank is not a holder in due course, it had notice of the fraud.

Rule: Notice that is forgotten is no longer notice, so maybe Odessa Bank was a holder in due course.

Maine Family Federal Credit Union v. Sun Life Assurance Co.

Supreme Judicial Court of Maine, 1999.
727 A.2d 335.

■ SAUFLEY, J.

We are called upon here to address the concept of "holder in due course" as defined by recent amendments to the negotiable instruments provisions of the Maine Uniform Commercial Code. We conclude that, pursuant to those amendments, the Superior Court (Cumberland County, Calkins, J.) did not err when it entered a judgment based on the jury's finding that the Maine Family Federal Credit Union was not a holder in due course. * * *

Maine Family Credit Union was not a holder in due course.

I. FACTS

Daniel, Joel, and Claire Guerrette are the adult children of Elden Guerrette, who died on September 24, 1995. Before his death, Elden had purchased a life insurance policy from Sun Life Assurance Company of Canada, through Sun Life's agent, Steven Hall, and had named his children as his beneficiaries. Upon his death, Sun Life issued three checks, each in the amount of $40,759.35, to each of Elden's children.[1] The checks were drawn on Sun Life's account at Chase Manhattan Bank in Syracuse, New York.[2] The checks were given to Hall for delivery to the Guerrettes.

Daniel, Joel and Claire got life insurance checks from Sun Life Assurance after father died.

Steven Hall was Sun's agent and supposed to deliver checks to family.

1. " 'Issue' means the first delivery of an instrument by the maker or drawer, whether to a holder or nonholder, for the purpose of giving rights on the instrument to any person." § 3–105(a).

2. Accordingly, Sun Life was the drawer of the checks. " 'Drawer' means a person who signs or is identified in a draft as a person ordering payment." § 3–103(a)(3). Chase Manhattan was the "drawee." " 'Drawee' means a person ordered in a draft to make payment." § 3–103(a)(2). More specifically, Chase Manhattan was also the "pay-

The parties have stipulated that Hall and an associate, Paul Richard, then fraudulently induced the Guerrettes to indorse the checks in blank and to transfer them to Hall and Richard, purportedly to be invested in "HER, Inc.," a corporation formed by Hall and Richard.[3] Hall took the checks from the Guerrettes and turned them over to Richard, who deposited them in his account at the Credit Union on October 26, 1995.[4] The Credit Union immediately made the funds available to Richard.

The Guerrettes quickly regretted having negotiated their checks to Hall and Richard, and they contacted Sun Life the next day to request that Sun Life stop payment on the checks. Sun Life immediately ordered Chase Manhattan to stop payment on the checks.[5] Thus, when the checks were ultimately presented to Chase Manhattan for payment, Chase refused to pay the checks, and they were returned to the Credit Union.

The Credit Union received notice that the checks had been dishonored on November 3, 1995, the sixth business day following their deposit.[6] By that time, however, Richard had withdrawn from his account all of the funds represented by the three checks. The Credit Union was able to recover almost $80,000 from Richard, but there remained an unpaid balance of $42,366.56, the amount now in controversy.

The Credit Union filed a complaint against Sun Life alleging that Sun Life was liable as drawer of the instruments, and that Sun Life had been unjustly enriched at the Credit Union's expense. * * *

The Credit Union moved for summary judgment. The Superior Court held, as a matter of law, that Daniel Guerrette had raised a "claim of a property or possessory right in the instrument or its proceeds," § 3–306,

or bank." " 'Payor bank' means a bank that is the drawee of a draft." § 4–105(3).

3. " 'Indorsement' means a signature, other than that of a signer as maker, drawer or acceptor, that alone or accompanied by other words is made on an instrument for the purpose of: (a) Negotiating the instrument; (b) Restricting payment of the instrument; or (c) Incurring indorser's liability on the instrument." § 3–204(a).

4. Maine Family Federal Credit Union is a "federally chartered credit union," regulated by the National Credit Union Administration. See 12 U.S.C.A. § 1752a (Law.Co-op.1996). It qualifies as an "insured credit union" under the Federal Credit Union Act, 12 U.S.C.A. §§ 1751–1795k (Law. Co-op.1996 & Supp.1998), and is therefore subject to the provisions of Regulation CC. 12 C.F.R. § 229 (1998).

By accepting the checks for deposit, Maine Family Federal Credit Union became the "depositary bank." Under Maine law, " '[d]epositary bank' means the first bank to

take an item ... unless the item is presented for immediate payment over the counter." § 4–105(2).

5. "A customer ... may stop payment of any item drawn on the customer's account ... by an order to the bank describing the item or account with reasonable certainty received at a time and in a manner that affords the bank a reasonable opportunity to act on it before any action by the bank with respect to the item...." § 4–403(a). Thus, Sun Life, as the customer of Chase Manhattan Bank, had the right to order Chase Manhattan to stop payment on the three checks deposited by Paul Richard at the Maine Family Federal Credit Union.

6. "Notice of dishonor may be given by any person and by any commercially reasonable means, including an oral, written or electronic communication, and is sufficient if it reasonably identifies the instrument and indicates that the instrument has been dishonored or has not been paid or accepted." § 3–503(b).

and therefore that Sun Life was entitled to assert that claim as a "defense" against the Credit Union. See § 3–305(c). The court found, however, that a genuine issue of material fact remained as to whether the Credit Union had acted in "good faith" when it gave value for the checks—a fact relevant to determining whether the Credit Union was a holder in due course. See § 3–302(a)(2)(ii). Accordingly, the court denied the Credit Union's motion for summary judgment, and the matter proceeded to trial.

At trial, the only issue presented to the jury was whether the Credit Union had acted in "good faith" when it gave value for the checks, thus entitling it to holder in due course status.[10] At the close of evidence, the Credit Union made a motion for a judgment as a matter of law, which the Superior Court denied. The jury found that the Credit Union had not acted in good faith and therefore was not a holder in due course. Therefore, the Superior Court entered judgment in favor of Sun Life * * * against the Credit Union. The court denied the Credit Union's renewed motion for judgment as a matter of law and motion to amend the judgment, and the Credit Union filed this appeal.

II. OBLIGATIONS OF THE PARTIES

At the heart of the controversy in this case is the allocation of responsibility for the loss of the unpaid $42,366.56, given the fact that Paul Richard and Steven Hall, the real wrongdoers, appear to be unable to pay. Maine, like the other forty-nine states, has adopted the Uniform Commercial Code. Under the Maine U.C.C., Articles 3 and 4 deal with "Negotiable Instruments" and "Bank Deposits and Collections." * * * It is these statutes that govern the parties' dispute.

Pursuant to Article 4 of the Maine U.C.C., the Credit Union, as a depositary bank, is a "holder" of the instruments, see § 4–205(1),[12] making it a "person entitled to enforce" the instrument under § 3–301(i). Upon producing an instrument containing the valid signature of a party liable on the instrument, a person entitled to enforce the instrument is entitled to payment, unless the party liable proves a defense or claim in recoupment, see § 3–308(b), or a possessory claim to the instrument itself. See § 3–306.

---

10. The parties stipulated to the fact that Daniel, Joel, and Claire were defrauded by Hall and Richard, and Paul Richard consented to the entry of judgment against him in the amount of $42,366.56 on the Credit Union's cross-claim against him. In addition, the parties stipulated that the Credit Union had incurred damages in the amount of $42,366.56. The parties' cooperation in crafting the stipulations appropriately allowed the court and the jury to focus on the only issue in dispute.

12. § 4–205(1) provides that a depositary bank becomes a holder of an item if the item was deposited by a customer who was also a holder. The Credit Union's customer, Paul Richard, became a holder of the checks when Daniel, Joel, and Claire indorsed them in blank and transferred them to Richard and Hall. See § 3–201(a) (" 'Negotiation' means a transfer of possession, whether voluntary or involuntary, of an instrument by a person other than the issuer to a person who thereby becomes its holder."); § 3–202(a)(ii) ("Negotiation is effective even if obtained ... [b]y fraud.").

Because their signatures appear on the backs of the checks, Daniel, Joel, and Claire are "indorsers" of the checks. See § 3–204(a), (b). As indorsers, they are obligated to pay the amounts due on each dishonored instrument "[a]ccording to the terms of [each] instrument at the time it was indorsed." § 3–415(a)(i). This obligation is owed "to a person entitled to enforce the instrument or to a subsequent indorser who paid the instrument under this section." § 3–415(a).

As drawer of the checks, Sun Life is obligated to pay each dishonored instrument "[a]ccording to its terms at the time it was issued." § 3–414(b)(i). Again, this obligation is owed to a person entitled to enforce the instrument or to an indorser who paid the draft under § 3–415. See § 3–414(b). Chase Manhattan, as drawee of these checks, was not obligated to accept them for payment, see § 3–408, and therefore has not been made a party to this action.

Unless the Credit Union is a holder in due course, its right to enforce the obligations of the drawer and indorsers of the instruments is subject to a variety of defenses, including all those defenses available "if the person entitled to enforce the instrument[s] were enforcing a right to payment under a simple contract." See § 3–305(a)(2). In addition, its right to enforce is subject to any claims in recoupment, see § 3–305(a)(3), or claims to the instruments themselves. See § 3–306. If, however, the Credit Union establishes that it is a "holder in due course," it is subject to only those few defenses listed in § 3–305(a)(1). See § 3–305(b). None of those specific defenses is applicable here. Thus, the Credit Union argues that because it is entitled as a matter of law to holder in due course status, it is entitled to enforce the instruments against the Guerrettes and Sun Life.

III.   HOLDER IN DUE COURSE

A.   Burden of Proof and Standard of Review

A holder in due course is a holder who takes an instrument in good faith, for value, and without notice of any claims or defenses. See § 3–302(a).

* * *

The Credit Union argues that the court erred in failing to find, as a matter of law, that it was a holder in due course. * * * The question before us, therefore, is whether any reasonable view of the evidence, along with any justifiable inferences therefrom, can possibly support the jury's conclusion that the Credit Union did not act in good faith and therefore was not a holder in due course. Alternatively stated, the question is whether the evidence compelled a finding that the Credit Union was a holder in due course. If there is any rational basis for the jury's verdict, we must affirm the judgment.

B.   Good Faith

We therefore turn to the definition of "good faith" contained in Article 3 of the Maine U.C.C. In 1990, the National Conference of Commissioners

[handwritten margin note: Rule: A holder in due course is a holder who takes an instrument in good faith, for value, and w/o notice of any claims or defenses.]

on Uniform State Law recommended substantial changes in the U.C.C. The Maine Legislature responded to those recommendations in 1993 by repealing the entirety of Article 3 and enacting a new version [of Article 3], which contains a new definition of "good faith." While the previous version of the good faith definition only required holder to prove that it acted with "honesty in fact," the new definition provides:

> "Good faith" means honesty in fact *and the observance of reasonable commercial standards of fair dealing*.

§ 3–103(a)(4) (emphasis added). Because the tests are presented in the conjunctive, a holder must now satisfy both a subjective and an objective test of "good faith."

1. Honesty in fact

Prior to the changes adopted by the Legislature in 1993, the holder in due course doctrine turned on a subjective standard of good faith and was often referred to as the "pure heart and empty head" standard. See M.B.W. Sinclair, Codification of Negotiable Instruments Law: A Tale of Reiterated Anachronism, 21 U. TOL. L. REV. 625, 654 (1990); see also Seinfeld v. Commercial Bank & Trust Co., 405 So.2d 1039, 1042 (Fla.Dist.Ct.App.1981) (noting that the U.C.C. "seem[s] to protect the objectively stupid so long as he is subjectively pure at heart"). That standard merely required a holder to take an instrument with "honesty in fact" to become a holder in due course.

Courts interpreting this language have routinely declared banks to be holders in due course, notwithstanding the failures of these banks to investigate or hold otherwise negotiable instruments, when they took the instruments with no knowledge of any defects, defenses, or stop payment orders. See, e.g., UAW–CIO Local #31 Credit Union v. Royal Ins. Co., 594 S.W.2d 276, 279 (Mo.1980) (en banc); Bank of New York v. Asati, Inc., 15 U.C.C. Rep. Serv.2d (CBC) 521, 1991 WL 322989 (N.Y.Sup.Ct. July 8, 1991). This approach has been understood to promote the negotiability of instruments, particularly checks, in the stream of commerce. Rejecting a contrary approach, one court put it bluntly:

> The requirement urged by defendant would bring the banking system to a grinding halt. A stop payment order issued by the drawer to the drawee which is unknown to the paying-collecting bank cannot fasten upon the paying bank any legal disability; particularly it cannot reduce the status of the collecting bank to a mere assignee of the instrument or a holder of a non-negotiable instrument, or a mere holder of a negotiable instrument.

Mellon Bank, N.A. v. Donegal Mutual Ins. Co., 29 U.C.C. Rep. Serv. (CBC) 912, 1980 WL 98414 (Pa. Ct. C.P. Alleghany County, Jan. 8, 1980).

Although courts were often urged to engraft an objective reasonableness standard onto the concept of "honesty in fact," most refused to do so. Their refusals recognized that: "[T]he check is the major method for transfer of funds in commercial practice. The maker, payee, and endorsers of a check naturally expect it will be rapidly negotiated and collected.... The wheels of commerce would grind to a halt [if an objective standard were adopted].'' Bowling Green, Inc. v. State St. Bank & Trust, 425 F.2d 81, 85 (1st Cir.1970).

Moreover, under the purely subjective standard, a bank was not expected to require the presence of offsetting collected funds in the customers' account in order to give value on newly deposited checks: ''A bank's permitting its customers to draw against uncollected funds does not negate its good faith.'' Asati, Inc., 15 U.C.C. Rep. Serv.2d at 521; accord * * *.

Application of the ''honesty in fact'' standard to the Credit Union's conduct here demonstrates these principles at work. It is undisputed that the Credit Union had no knowledge that Richard obtained the Sun Life checks by fraud. Nor was the Credit Union aware that a stop payment order had been placed on the Sun Life checks. The Credit Union expeditiously gave value on the checks, having no knowledge that they would be dishonored. In essence the Credit Union acted as banks have, for years, been allowed to act without risk to holder in due course status. The Credit Union acted with honesty in fact.

Thus, had the matter at bar been decided before the Legislature's addition of the objective component of ''good faith,'' there can be little question that the Credit Union would have been determined to have been a holder in due course. Because it took the instruments without notice of any possible dishonor, defect, fraud, or illegality, it could have given value immediately and yet have been assured of holder in due course status. * * * Today, however, something more than mere subjective good faith is required of a holder in due course.

2.   Reasonable commercial standards of fair dealing

We turn then to the objective prong of the good faith analysis. The addition of the language requiring the holder to prove conduct meeting ''reasonable commercial standards of fair dealing'' signals a significant change in the definition of a holder in due course.[19] While there has been little time for the development of a body of law interpreting this new objective requirement, there can be no mistaking the fact that a holder may no longer act with a pure heart and an empty head and still obtain holder in due course status.[20] The pure heart of the holder must now be accompanied by reasoning that assures conduct comporting with reasonable commercial standards of fair dealing.

---

19. ''The new definition of good faith *substantially affects* ... the requirements for holder in due course status.'' Hawkland & Lawrence UCC Series § 3–103:05 (Rev. Art. 3) (emphasis added).

20. The objective requirement, however, has generated a number of articles and commentaries on the reason, meaning, and anticipated interpretations of the changes.

See, e.g., Patricia L. Heatherman, Comment, Good Faith in Revised Article 3 of the Uniform Commercial Code: Any Change? Should There Be? 29 WILLAMETTE L. REV. 567 (1993); Kerry Lynn Macintosh, Liberty, Trade, and the Uniform Commercial Code, When Should Default Rules be Based on Business Practices? 38 WM. & MARY L. REV. 1465, 1466 (1997).

The addition of the objective element represents not so much a new concept in the doctrinal development of holder in due course status, but rather a return, in part, to an earlier approach to the doctrine. See JAMES J. WHITE & ROBERT S. SUMMERS, UNIFORM COMMERCIAL CODE § 14–6, at 628–29 (3d ed. 1988) (discussing the objective test of good faith in England, first applied by the King's Bench in Gill v. Cubitt, 3 B & C 466, 107 Eng.Rep. 806 (K.B. 1824)). The concept of an objective component of good faith has been part of the discussion regarding the holder in due course doctrine since the first enactment of the U.C.C. See id. (noting that "[t]he good faith requirement has been the source of a continuing and ancient dispute"). The early drafters debated the need and wisdom of including such an objective component and ultimately determined *not* to include it in the definition of good faith because of its potential for freezing commercial practices. * * * The "new" element of good faith requiring the holder to act according to reasonable commercial standards of fair dealing is actually a more narrow version of the "reasonable person" standard considered and rejected by the drafters of the 1962 Code.

The new objective standard, however, is not a model of drafting clarity. Although use of the word "reasonable" in the objective portion of the good faith test may evoke concepts of negligence, the drafters attempted to distinguish the concept of "fair" dealing from concepts of "careful" dealing:

> Although fair dealing is a broad term that must be defined in context, it is clear that it is concerned with the fairness of conduct rather than the care with which an act is performed. Failure to exercise ordinary care in conducting a transaction is an entirely different concept than failure to deal fairly in conducting the transaction.

U.C.C. § 3–103 cmt. 4 (1991).

Unfortunately, the ease with which the distinction between "fair dealing" and "careful dealing" was set forth in the comments to the U.C.C. revisions belies the difficulty in applying these concepts to the facts of any particular case, or in conveying them to a jury. The difficulty is exacerbated by the lack of definition of the term "fair dealing" in the U.C.C.[21] The most obvious question arising from the use of the term "fair" is: fairness to whom? Transactions involving negotiable instruments have traditionally required the detailed level of control and definition of roles set out in the U.C.C. precisely because there are so many parties who may be involved in a single transaction. If a holder is required to act "fairly," regarding all parties, it must engage in an almost impossible balancing of rights and interests. Accordingly, the drafters limited the requirement of fair dealing to conduct that is reasonable in the commercial context of the transaction at issue. In other words, the holder must act in a way that is fair according to commercial standards that are themselves reasonable.

21. One commentator has suggested that fair dealing refers to "playing by the rules." See Heatherman, supra, at 585. Yet "the rules" ordinarily define the parameters of reasonable conduct, a concept which sounds much like a negligence analysis.

The factfinder must therefore determine, first, whether the conduct of the holder comported with industry or "commercial" standards applicable to the transaction and, second, whether those standards were reasonable standards intended to result in fair dealing. Each of those determinations must be made in the context of the specific transaction at hand. If the factfinder's conclusion on each point is "yes," the holder will be determined to have acted in good faith even if, in the individual transaction at issue, the result appears unreasonable. Thus, a holder may be accorded holder in due course status where it acts pursuant to those reasonable commercial standards of fair dealing—even if it is negligent—but may lose that status, even where it complies with commercial standards, if those standards are not reasonably related to achieving fair dealing.

Therefore the jury's task here was to decide whether the Credit Union observed the banking industries' commercial standards relating to the giving of value on uncollected funds, and, if so, whether those standards are reasonably designed to result in fair dealing.

The evidence produced by the Credit Union in support of its position that it acted in accordance with objective good faith included the following: The Credit Union's internal policy was to make provisional credit available immediately upon the deposit of a check by one of its members. In certain circumstances—where the check was for a large amount and where it was drawn on an out-of-state bank—its policy allowed for a hold to be placed on the uncollected funds for up to nine days. The Credit Union's general written policy on this issue was reviewed annually—and had always been approved—by the National Credit Union Administration, the federal agency charged with the duty of regulating federal credit unions. See 12 U.S.C.A. § 1752a (Law. Co-op. 1996). In addition, the policy complied with applicable banking laws, including Regulation CC. See 12 C.F.R. §§ 229.12(c), 229.13(b) (1998).

The Credit Union also presented evidence that neither Regulation CC nor the Credit Union's internal policy *required* it to hold the checks or to investigate the genesis of checks before extending provisional credit. It asserted that it acted exactly as its policy and the law allowed when it immediately extended provisional credit on these checks, despite the fact that they were drawn for relatively large amounts on an out-of-state bank.[22] Finally, the Credit Union presented expert testimony that most credit unions in Maine follow similar policies.

In urging the jury to find that the Credit Union had not acted in good faith, Sun Life and the Guerrettes argued that the Credit Union's conduct did not comport with reasonable commercial standards of fair dealing when it allowed its member access to provisional credit on checks totalling over $120,000 drawn on an out-of-state bank without either: (1) further investigation to assure that the deposited checks would be paid by the bank upon

22. The Credit Union could also have withheld provisional credit under the law and its own internal policy if there were other reasons to doubt the validity of the checks. See 12 C.F.R. § 229.13(e) (1998).

which they were drawn, or (2) holding the instruments to allow any irregularities to come to light.

The applicable federal regulations provide the outside limit on the Credit Union's ability to hold the checks. Although the limit on allowable holds established by law is evidence to be considered by the jury, it does not itself establish reasonable commercial standard of fair dealing. The factfinder must consider all of the facts relevant to the transaction. The amount of the checks and the location of the payor bank, however, are relevant facts that a bank, observing reasonable commercial standards of fair dealing, takes into account when deciding whether to place such a hold on the account. The jury was entitled to consider that, under Regulation CC, when a check in an amount greater than $5,000 is deposited, or when a check is payable by a nonlocal bank, a credit union is permitted to withhold provisional credit for longer periods of time than it is allowed in other circumstances. See 12 C.F.R. § 229.13(b), (h) (1998). Therefore, the size of the check and the location of the payor bank are, under the objective standard of good faith, factors which a jury may also consider when deciding whether a depository bank is a holder in due course.

The Credit Union's President admitted the risks inherent in the Credit Union's policy and admitted that it would not have been difficult to place a hold on these funds for the few days that it would normally take for the payor bank to pay the checks. He conceded that the amount of the checks were relatively large, that they were drawn on an out-of-state bank, and that these circumstances "could have" presented the Credit Union with cause to place a hold on the account. He also testified to his understanding that some commercial banks followed a policy of holding nonlocal checks for three business days before giving provisional credit.[23] Moreover, the Credit Union had no written policy explicitly guiding its staff regarding the placing of a hold on uncollected funds. Rather, the decision on whether to place a temporary hold on an account was left to the "comfort level" of the teller accepting the deposit. There was no dispute that the amount of the three checks far exceeded the $5,000 threshold for a discretionary hold established by the Credit Union's own policy.

On these facts the jury could rationally have concluded that the reasonable commercial standard of fair dealing would require the placing of a hold on the uncollected funds for a reasonable period of time and that, in giving value under these circumstances, the Credit Union did not act according to commercial standards that were reasonably structured to result in fair dealing.

We recognize that the Legislature's addition of an objective standard of conduct in this area of law may well have the effect of slowing the "wheels of commerce."[24] As one commentator noted:

23. There was evidence that, on the second business day after he deposited the checks, Paul Richard notified the Credit Union that there may have been a problem with his deposit.

24. The new definition of "good faith" has been forecasted by some to bring possible

Historically, it was always argued that if negotiable instruments were to be usefully negotiable a subsequent holder should not have to investigate the transaction giving rise to the paper. The paramount necessity of negotiability has dominated thinking and legislation on negotiable instruments law. Drafts and promissory notes, it has been believed, must be able to change hands freely, without investigation beyond the face of the instrument, and with no greater requirement than the indorsement of the holder.

Sinclair, supra, at 630 (footnotes omitted). Notwithstanding society's oft-cited need for certainty and speed in commercial transactions, however, the Legislature necessarily must have concluded that the addition of the objective requirement to the definition of "good faith" serves an important goal. The paramount necessity of unquestioned negotiability has given way, at least in part, to the desire for reasonable commercial fairness in negotiable transactions.

* * *

NOTES

1. Is the court's interpretation of "fair dealing" consistent with Comment 4 to 3–103? As we will see later, the purpose of Regulation CC is to allow depositors to withdraw funds from their bank accounts more rapidly. However, it permits depositary banks to place holds on checks in specified cases to protect the banks. In this case the credit union could have placed a nine-day hold on the check, but Reg. CC does not require that banks place maximum holds on checks, and we will find that in most cases banks allow their depositors to withdraw the proceeds of checks much more quickly as a convenience. If a check is dishonored and the drawer later raises defenses on the check, banks have been able to recover from the drawer as holders in due course.

In *Maine Family Federal*, everything on the face of the checks paid by the credit union (CU) was regular ("in order," as bankers say). They were drawn by a large insurance company, Sun Life, on one of the largest banks in the world at that time, Chase, payable to the beneficiaries of an insurance policy in satisfaction of legitimate claims. The payees properly indorsed the checks and they were deposited by a customer of CU, Paul Richard, in his account. There was no basis for CU to have the slightest suspicion about the transaction. The fraud giving rise to the beneficiaries' claim of ownership arose entirely from activities about which CU knew nothing. CU got into trouble when it accommodated the wishes of its customer by allowing him to draw on the checks on the date of deposit. The strongest argument Sun Life had was that CU acted imprudently because these were checks of substantial amounts. But large checks from insurance

"undesirable changes" to the law of negotiable instruments. See Henry J. Bailey, New 1990 Uniform Commercial Code: Article 3, Negotiable Instruments, and Article 4, Bank Deposits and Collections, 29 WILLAMETTE L. REV. 409, 415 (1993).

companies are not unusual, and the fact they were drawn on an out-of-state bank in no way makes them appear unreliable; this would probably be normal for insurance checks. How this arguably imprudent conduct led the court to hold that the jury could have rationally concluded that CU did not act according to commercial standards of fair dealing is a stretch. CU dealt only with its customer, Richard, and whether its accommodation to him constituted dealing unfairly is highly problematic.

What effect will *Maine Family Federal* have on the practice of granting early withdrawal privileges to bank customers that has proved so popular? If this case is followed, where will courts draw the line on the size of checks that can be paid out by the depositary bank promptly? Will every payment by a depositary bank on an uncollected check be subject to scrutiny on fair-dealing grounds. The Clarks in Bank Deposits and Payments Monthly, Vol.7, No.10 (April 1999), describe the Maine decision as "dead wrong." But some cases purport to have adopted its analysis, e.g., Any Kind Checks Cashed, Inc. v. Talcott, 830 So.2d 160 (4th Dist.Fla.App. 2002). Others do not, e.g., Wachovia Bank, N.A. v. Federal Reserve Bank of Richmond, 338 F.3d 318 (4th Cir. 2003) ("To determine whether Wachovia acted in conformity with reasonable commercial standards of fair dealing, we consider the fairness of Wachovia's actions, rather than any negligence on its part." 338 F.3d at 323); State Bank of the Lakes v. Kansas Bankers Surety Co., 328 F.3d 906 (7th Cir. 2003) (["G]ood faith is in a different phylum from 'due care.' * * * Article 3 of the UCC, which contains a definition of 'good faith' * * * links commercial reasonableness to 'fair dealing.' Avoidance of advantage-taking, which this section is getting at, differs from due care." 328 F.3d at 909.).

2. The fair-dealing prong of good faith was enshrined in American contract law by Restatement (Second) Contracts § 205 (1981), which provides: "Every contract imposes upon each party a duty of good faith and fair dealing in its performance and its enforcement." Comments b. and d. draw an important distinction in the application of fair dealing between good faith purchase cases and those involving the performance of contracts. They explain that in determining whether one is a good faith purchaser the focus is on the honesty of the purchaser but in cases of performance of contracts fair dealing may require more than honesty. Thus, in performing a contract, one party may not take unfair advantage of another. Since the principal use of the good faith definition in Article 3 involves whether the taker of an instrument is, in effect, a good faith purchaser, should Article 3 have omitted the fair-dealing prong of the good faith definition? Cf. Comment 3 to 5–102, in which the drafters explain why they rejected the fair-dealing prong of the good faith definition with respect to letters of credit.

2. OVERDUE OR IRREGULAR INSTRUMENTS

PROBLEM

In payment of goods, Maker signed a negotiable note in the amount of $10,000 and mailed it to Payee. The note should have been payable in the

[Top margin diagram: Maker → (goods) Payee ← ($) Holder; note $10k; note]

amount of $20,000. Payee noticed the discrepancy and called Maker's attention to it. Maker told Payee to change the $10,000 to $20,000. Payee did so by erasing and typing over. The alteration was crudely done and very obvious. Payee then sold the note to Holder. Holder noticed the alteration but accepted Payee's truthful explanation of the circumstances under which it was made. When Holder demanded payment Maker refused, stating that Payee failed to deliver the goods for which the note was given. Assuming that Maker had a valid defense against Payee under 3–305(a)(2) relating to Payee's failure to perform the contract, is Holder subject to the defense? Suppose Holder, before completing the transaction, had called Maker and that Maker had verified that the $20,000 figure was correct. How does this affect your answer? See 3–302(a)(1) and Comment 1 to 3–302.

_____

Section 3–302(a) incorporates two traditional rules: holder-in-due-course status cannot be attained if the instrument is taken with notice that it is overdue or if the instrument is so irregular or incomplete as to call into question its authenticity. These doctrines are rooted in the law of good faith and may be viewed as special applications of the suspicious circumstances rule of Gill v. Cubitt. But for a long time they have enjoyed independent status, and NIL § 52 adopted them as separate requirements for holder-in-due-course status in addition to the good faith requirement.

Under the common law view, the fact that an instrument was overdue or irregular or incomplete was notice that something was wrong. But the fact that an instrument is overdue does not point to any particular defense or claim or, for that matter, to the existence of any defense or claim at all. Most notes are probably overdue because the makers can't pay them. Most checks that are still out more than 90 days (3–304(a)(2)) have not been collected because the holder hasn't deposited them. In the range of possibilities raised in the mind of one purchasing an overdue instrument, it is doubtful that the likelihood of a defense rises very high or that the possibility of a claim of ownership by a prior party is considered at all. The fact that an instrument bears an obvious alteration does warn a taker of the possibility of a fraudulent alteration but not of defenses or claims wholly unrelated to the alteration.

Why shouldn't a purchaser who is willing to pay good money for an overdue or irregular or incomplete instrument be entitled to holder-in-due-course-status? Perhaps the question is better phrased in terms of why such a purchaser should be accorded that status. The answer to these questions may depend upon whether one looks upon holder-in-due-course status to be the norm or whether it should be seen as something unusual to be given only when a clear commercial benefit is achieved. If negotiability is a doctrine to promote the free flow of instruments, what social or economic gain is achieved by encouraging the currency of stale, irregular or incomplete instruments?

[Handwritten marginal notes:
Left margin top: Maker made a note for $10K that should have been $20K. Payee brought this to the notice of Maker. The payee changed it from $10K to $20K but it was crudely done and obvious. Payee then sold note to Holder. Holder noticed the change but accepted it. When Holder demanded payment, saying payee never gave him his goods. Maker refused.
Center: Holder demanded payment, payee never gave him his goods.
Right top: Holder is not a holder in due course - b/c hasn't taken in good faith - standard probably is to issue a new note w/ new price. There is notice the instrument is incomplete.
Left middle: § Holder in due course status cannot be attained if the instrument is taken w/ notice that it's overdue or if the instrument is so irregular or incomplete as to call into question its authenticity.
Bottom left: Some would say most instruments are past due anyways, so shouldn't bar holder in due course status to those who buy it. After all, if we want negotiability to continue we can't look behind our books each time an instrument is sold.]

PROBLEMS

1. S agreed to sell real property to B for $58,000, of which $6,500 was to be a down payment. When making the down payment, B insisted that S execute a promissory note to B's order for the amount of $6,500 as evidence of indebtedness for any sums B might be called upon to expend to pay off any claims or liens with respect to the property of which B was not aware. In time B expended $4,244 in paying these claims. The note, which was executed by S on March 25 and due 75 days after date, was indorsed without recourse to Plaintiff on September 1 for a total consideration of $3,067. S refused to pay the note and Plaintiff brought suit. How much is Plaintiff entitled to recover—$6,500, $4,244, or $3,067? See 3–203(b), 3–302(a), 3–117, and 3–305(a). See also Brock v. Adams, 79 N.M. 17, 439 P.2d 234 (1968).

2. Payee sold a house to Maker and as partial payment of the price took a promissory note for $5,000 payable in monthly installments over a five-year period. When Payee's reserve army unit was called to active duty Payee asked Banker to collect the note during Payee's indefinite absence. Banker insisted that Payee indorse the note in blank and turn over possession of both the note and mortgage. Later Maker fell in default on the payments and Banker, who was also in financial difficulties, sold the note to Purchaser for value. Purchaser knew that four payments had not been made but had no knowledge of the circumstances under which Banker had taken the note. After Payee returned and learned of Banker's actions, Payee asserted a claim of ownership against Purchaser and sued to retake possession of the note. What result? Justice v. Stonecipher, 267 Ill. 448, 108 N.E. 722 (1915). See 3–304(b)(1) and 3–306.

3. NEGOTIABILITY IN CONSUMER TRANSACTIONS

a. INTRODUCTION

Universal C.I.T. Credit Corp. v. Ingel

Supreme Judicial Court of Massachusetts, Worcester, 1964.
196 N.E.2d 847.

■ SPIEGEL, JUSTICE.

This is an action of contract on a promissory note by the assignee of the payee against the maker. The case was first tried in the District Court of Fitchburg, to which it had been remanded by the Superior Court. There was a finding for the plaintiff in the sum of $1,630.12. At the request of the defendants, the case was retransferred to the Superior Court for trial by jury. Upon conclusion of the evidence the court allowed a motion by the plaintiff for a directed verdict to which the defendants excepted. They also excepted to the exclusion of certain evidence.

At the trial the plaintiff introduced in evidence the note,[1] a completion certificate signed by the defendants, and the District Court's finding for the plaintiff. The defendants admitted the authenticity of the signatures on the

1. "This Is A Negotiable Promissory
Note

note and the completion certificate. As a witness for the defendants, one Charles D. Fahey testified that he was the plaintiff's Boston branch manager at the time the defendants' note was purchased, and that the plaintiff purchases instalment contracts regarding automobile and property improvement purchases. He described the procedures by which purchases of commercial paper are arranged by the plaintiff; these procedures included a credit check on the "customer," i. e., the maker of the note which the plaintiff is planning to purchase. The defendants attempted to introduce through Fahey a credit report obtained by the plaintiff on Allied Aluminum Associates, Inc. (Allied), the payee of the note. The defendants excepted to the exclusion of this evidence. They offered to prove that the excluded report, which was dated "3–31–59," contained the following statement: "The subject firm is engaged in the sale of storm windows, doors, roofing, siding, and bathroom and kitchen remodeling work. The firm engages a crew of commission salesmen and it is reported they have been doing a good volume of business. They are reported to employ high pressure sales

$1890.00 (Total Amount of Note)

Fitchburg, Mass., (City, State)

6/22, 1959 (Date)

I/WE JOINTLY AND SEVERALLY PROMISE TO PAY TO ALLIED ALUMINUM ASSOCIATES, INC. OR ORDER THE SUM OF EIGHTEEN HUNDRED NINETY DOLLARS IN 60 SUCCESSIVE MONTHLY INSTALMENTS OF $31.50 EACH, EXCEPT THAT THE FINAL INSTALMENT SHALL BE THE BALANCE THEN DUE ON THIS NOTE. COMMENCING THE 25 DAY OF JULY, 1959, AND THE SAME DATE OF EACH MONTH THEREAFTER UNTIL PAID, with interest after maturity at the highest lawful rate, and a reasonable sum (15% if permitted by law) as attorney's fees, if this note is placed in the hands of any attorney for collection after maturity. Upon nonpayment of any instalment at its maturity, all remaining instalments shall at the option of the holder become due and payable forthwith. Charges for handling late payments, of 5¢ per $1 (maximum $5), are payable on any instalment more than 10 days in arrears. * * * *Notice of Proposed Credit Life Insurance:* Group credit life insurance will be obtained by the holder of this instrument, without additional charge to customer, subject to acceptance by the insurer, Old Republic Life Insurance Company, Chicago, Illinois. Such insurance will cover only the individual

designated and signing below as the person to be insured (who must be an officer if customer is a corporation, a partner if partnership), except that no individual 65 years of age or older on the date the indebtedness is incurred will be eligible for such insurance. Such insurance will become effective, upon acceptance by the insurer, as of the date the indebtedness is incurred, and will terminate when the indebtedness terminates or upon such default or other event as terminates the insurance under the terms of the group policy. The amount of such insurance will be equal to the amount of customer's indebtedness hereunder at any time but not to exceed $10,000; proceeds will be applicable to reduction or discharge of the indebtedness. The provisions of this paragraph are subject to the terms of the group policy and the certificate to be issued.

PLEASE PRINT MAILING ADDRESS

Customer acknowledges receipt of a completed copy of this promissory note, including above Notice.

ALBERT T. INGEL

Customer (Person on whose life group credit life insurance will be obtained, if applicable.)

DORA INGEL

(Additional Customer, if any)

ORIGINAL"

methods for the most part. They have done considerable advertising in newspapers, on radio, and have done soliciting by telephone. They have been criticized for their advertising methods, and have been accused of using bait advertising, and using false and misleading statements. The Boston Better Business Bureau has had numerous complaints regarding their advertising methods, and have reported same to the Attorney General. *FHA has had no complaints other than report of this from Better Business Bureau and have warned the firm to stop their practice.*"

The defendants excepted to the exclusion of testimony by the defendant Dora Ingel concerning certain of her negotiations with Allied. An offer of proof was made which indicates that this testimony might have been evidence of fraud or breach of warranty on the part of Allied. They also excepted to the exclusion of a letter[2] from the plaintiff to the defendant Albert.

I.

The defendants contend that the note was nonnegotiable as a matter of law and, therefore, any defence which could be raised against Allied may also be raised against the plaintiff. * * *

We thus conclude that the note in question is a negotiable instrument.

II.

* * * The defendants' answer denies that the plaintiff is "a holder in due course" of the note on which the action is brought; accordingly, this must be regarded as a matter "put in issue by the pleadings." We are satisfied that the finding of the District Court was prima facie evidence that the plaintiff took the note for value and without notice, and * * * the burden was on the defendants to rebut the plaintiff's prima facie case.

III.

The trial judge correctly excluded the evidence offered by the defendants to show that the plaintiff and Allied had worked together on various

2. "October 27, 1959 Identification 'B'

Mr. Albert Ingel

115 Belmont

Fitchburg, Massachusetts

Re: 200–12–51767

Dear Sir.

We are sorry to learn that the Aluminum Siding on which we hold your promissory note, is giving you cause for complaint. Our part in the transactions consisted of extending the credit which you desired, and arranging to accept prepayment of the advance on terms convenient to you. We did not perform any of the work, and any questions in connection with materials and workmanship should be adjusted with the dealer from whom you made your purchase. Therefore, we have passed your report along to Allied Aluminum and we are confident that everything reasonably possible will be done to correct any faulty conditions which may exist.

In the meantime, we shall appreciate your continuing to make payments on your note as they fall due so that your account may be kept in current condition.

Very truly yours,

UNIVERSAL C. I. T. CREDIT CORPORATION

C. KEVENY Collection Man"

*The actual transaction
has to be false. (Not the reputation of the company.*

48   CHAPTER 1 NEGOTIABILITY AND HOLDERS IN DUE COURSE

aspects of the financing and that the plaintiff was aware of complaints against Allied by previous customers. We are of opinion that there was nothing in this evidence by which the plaintiff had "reason to know" of any fraud. The letter of October 27, 1959, from the plaintiff to the defendant Albert was also properly excluded; it is immaterial that the plaintiff may have found out about Allied's alleged fraudulent representations after the note had been purchased.

Exceptions overruled.

NOTE

This is basically the only case where a consumer financier was found to be a holder in due course.

This 1964 case is the most recent authoritative opinion that we can find holding a consumer financer to be a holder in due course. Since this opinion, all courts have found some basis for denying financers that status. If you were representing the consumers in this case, what arguments would you make on Universal C.I.T.'s status as a holder in due course? Why has the doctrine of holding in due course disappeared from consumer credit transactions? For a broad indictment of the holder-in-due-course doctrine in consumer cases, based on public policy and the outrage of the Supreme Court of New Jersey, see Unico v. Owen, 232 A.2d 405 (N.J. 1967).

Holder in due course has disappeared from consumer credit transactions.

———————

Whether the doctrine of negotiability in all its vigor is necessary or even desirable when applied to modern negotiable instruments such as promissory notes and checks has been challenged in Grant Gilmore, The Good Faith Purchase Idea and the Uniform Commercial Code: Confessions of a Repentant Draftsman, 15 Ga. L. Rev. 605 (1981). Consider the following observations of Professor Albert J. Rosenthal taken from his article, "Negotiability—Who Needs It?," 71 Colum. L. Rev. 375, 378–381 (1971):

The negotiable promissory note of today is quite a different instrument, serving different purposes, and the consequences of its negotiability are quite different in impact. By far the most commonly employed variety of the species today is the note given by the install-ment purchaser of goods to reflect the unpaid portion of the purchase price. Typically, such a note is transferred just once, from the dealer to the lender (usually either a finance company or a bank), and thereafter remains in the possession of the latter or its lawyers until it is either paid off or offered in evidence in court. Its negotiable character is of no importance with respect to claims of ownership, as it is unlikely to be lost or stolen. Even if it is, the last indorsement will have been a special indorsement to the order of the lender; without the genuine further indorsement of the latter there can be no subsequent holder, much less a holder in due course.

The only significant consequence of the negotiability of such a note is that it cuts off the defenses of the maker. If, for example, the

& claims

purchaser gives the note in payment for a refrigerator, the finance company is entitled to full payment regardless of whether the refrigerator fails to work or whether its sale was accomplished through fraudulent misrepresentations or, indeed, whether it was ever delivered at all. And it may be small comfort to the buyer, forced to pay the finance company in full, to know that he has a cause of action against the seller, which may at best be collectible with difficulty and may in many cases be worthless because the seller is insolvent or has left town.

A promissory note of this kind, and a consequence of negotiability that works in this fashion, are a far cry from the stolen Bank of England note, and the protection accorded its purchaser, in Miller v. Race. Whether the finance company should be allowed to prevail free of the maker's defenses raises questions that ought to be decided on their own merits, and not merely through the absent-minded application of a doctrine created to meet an entirely different situation.

The social evils flowing from negotiability in this circumstance have become manifest, and there has been a clear trend in both the courts and the legislatures toward amelioration of its consequences. In particular, the unfairness to the poorest members of the community of the law governing consumer installment purchases has generated a reaction that is giving rise to a major alteration in it. This departure is being accomplished, not by modification of the provisions of Article 3 of the Code, but by legislative action forbidding the use of negotiable instruments in consumer installment transactions and by judicial attempts to stretch the facts to deny holder in due course status to finance companies. Since the installment buyer can be similarly harmed even without a negotiable instrument if there is a clause in his purchase contract waiving, as against an assignee of his obligation, any defenses on the contract that he may have, legislatures and courts have also been moving in the direction of declaring such clauses invalid.

It is not clear whether the apparent weakness in the opposition to these changes springs from a lack of genuine need on the part of sellers or lenders for continuation of the power to cut off buyers' defenses. While there has been ground to believe that where this protection is denied, credit nevertheless will remain available, a recent study suggests that this may not be so.

If an exception is carved out, should it be limited to consumer paper, or should it be applied to promissory notes across the board? Thus far, the demand for reform has been confined largely to the former. While there may be small commercial purchasers also in need of similar protection, and while there may be other situations in which unfair advantage seems to be taken of makers of promissory notes, there does not appear in such cases to be a resulting social problem of comparable dimension. On the other hand, we need to know more about the range of other uses to which promissory notes are put in today's economy, and about the circumstances in which the cutting off of claims and defenses in connection with such notes serves legitimate needs or works undue hardship.

* * *

The drafters of former Article 3 could not agree on a suitable consumer exception to the holder-in-due-course rule, and the solution to the issue eventually agreed upon in the UCCC after years of debate was not widely enacted. However, by the time Revised Article 3 was drafted there was a large body of state statutory and case law restricting the use of the holder-in-due-course doctrine in consumer transactions, and the drafting commit-tee finally settled on 3–302(g), which has the effect of subordinating Article 3 to that law, and not only to existing law but to similar law that may evolve in the future. See Comment 7 to 3–302.

[handwritten margin note: There is now a large body of state statutory and case law restricting the use of holder in due course doctrine in consumer transactions.]

b.   THE LEGISLATIVE RESPONSE

(1)   CONSUMER CREDIT SALES

By the early 1960s the handwriting was on the wall with respect to the judicial enforceability of notes against consumers who had valid defenses. One way or another, courts allowed consumers to assert their defenses. Indeed, many creditors had long since given up the use of negotiable instruments and contract clauses cutting off defenses upon assignment. Nevertheless, the issue of negotiability occupied more time and caused more rancor in the drafting of the Uniform Consumer Credit Code (1964–74) than any other issue. Creditor representatives saw negotiability as an issue of freedom of contract and wanted the UCCC to turn back the clock. To consumer advocates negotiability was a symbol of creditor overreaching, and they saw the UCCC as the instrumentality for finally driving a stake through the heart of negotiability in consumer cases. As we see below, the consumers won, but not before years of wrangling and equivocation. While these bitter debates were going on as late as the early 1970s, consumer credit was being revolutionized by the growth of the bank credit card which, in all but larger consumer purchases, replaced promissory notes and rendered the negotiability issue largely irrelevant.

Consumer credit sales are regulated in most states by statute. Most states have taken the position that the holder-in-due-course doctrine should be abrogated with respect to notes given by buyers to sellers of consumer goods or services. One approach taken is to prohibit the taking of a negotiable note from the buyer and to invalidate waiver of defenses clauses in the installment sale contract. The Uniform Consumer Credit Code, in effect in 11 jurisdictions, is an example of this kind of legislation. The 1974 Official Text provides as follows:

Section 3.307   [Certain Negotiable Instruments Prohibited]

With respect to a consumer credit sale or consumer lease, [except a sale or lease primarily for an agricultural purpose,] the creditor may not take a negotiable instrument other than a check dated not later than ten days after its issuance as evidence of the obligation of the consumer.

Section 3.404   [Assignee Subject to Claims and Defenses]

(1) With respect to a consumer credit sale or consumer lease [, except one primarily for an agricultural purpose,] an assignee of the rights of the seller or lessor is subject to all claims and defenses of the consumer against the seller or lessor arising from the sale or lease of property or services, notwithstanding that the assignee is a holder in due course of a negotiable instrument issued in violation of the provisions prohibiting certain negotiable instruments (Section 3.307).

(2) A claim or defense of a consumer specified in subsection (1) may be asserted against the assignee under this section only if the consumer has made a good faith attempt to obtain satisfaction from the seller or lessor with respect to the claim or defense and then only to the extent of the amount owing to the assignee with respect to the sale or lease of the property or services as to which the claim or defense arose at the time the assignee has notice of the claim or defense. Notice of the claim or defense may be given before the attempt specified in this subsection. Oral notice is effective unless the assignee requests written confirmation when or promptly after oral notice is given and the consumer fails to give the assignee written confirmation within the period of time, not less than 14 days, stated to the consumer when written confirmation is requested.

* * *

(4) An agreement may not limit or waive the claims or defenses of a consumer under this section.

The Federal Trade Commission has promulgated rules (16 C.F.R. Part 433—Preservation of Consumers' Claims and Defenses) (the "Holder Rule") designed to negate the holder-in-due-course doctrine in sales of consumer goods or services. The rules also apply to leases of consumer goods. References to "seller" also include a lessor. Any "consumer credit contract," a term which includes a promissory note, arising out of such a sale or lease must contain a bold-faced legend stating in effect that any holder of the contract is subject to all claims and defenses that the debtor has against the seller of the goods or services. The effect of the legend is to cause any assignee of the note or sales contract to take subject to the buyer's claims and defenses against the seller. Failure by a seller to include the legend is an unfair or deceptive act or practice under Section 5 of the Federal Trade Commission Act. Under that Act, the seller is subject to a civil suit by the FTC in which the court may "grant such relief as the court finds necessary to redress injury to consumers * * * resulting from the rule violation * * *. Such relief may include, but shall not be limited to, rescission or reformation of contracts, the refund of money or return of property, the payment of damages, and public notification respecting the rule violation * * * except that nothing in this subsection is intended to authorize the imposition of any exemplary or punitive damages." 15 U.S.C. § 57b(b). Under Revised Article 3, a promissory note bearing the FTC legend can be a negotiable instrument if it otherwise complies with 3–104(a) but there cannot be a holder in due course of the note. 3–106(d) and Comment 3 to 3–106.

(2) PURCHASE MONEY LOANS

Under traditional law, a financer who lends money to a buyer for the purpose of buying goods or services is not subject to claims or defenses the buyer may have against the seller. However, the purchase money loan transaction bears a close functional resemblance to the assigned paper transaction discussed above. In both cases the seller desires to be paid as soon as possible; the buyer chooses not to pay cash; and the financer is willing to provide the money. In the purchase money loan, the financer makes a loan to the buyer; in the assigned paper case, the seller retains a security interest in the goods sold and the financer buys the buyer's credit contract from the seller. Customs differ among the states: in some, consumer goods financing is done by purchase money loans, but in most the assigned-paper transaction predominates.

If financers are subject to consumer defenses in assigned-paper transactions, an incentive is present to convert to purchase money loans to free financers of consumer defenses. By the latter part of the 1960s consumer representatives began to advocate subjecting purchase money lenders to consumer claims and defenses in situations in which there was a sufficiently close relationship between the seller and the lender to warrant doing so. But how close must this relation be? The task of defining the requisite relationship has been difficult.

Under the FTC rule referred to above the seller is guilty of an unfair or deceptive act if it accepts the proceeds of a purchase money loan (§ 433.2(b)) unless the loan agreement between the debtor and the purchase money lender contains the requisite notice. If the loan agreement contains the notice, the lender thereby subjects itself to defenses arising out of the sale. Section 433.1(d) defines purchase money loan to include two cases: (1) the seller refers the buyer to the lender, or (2) the seller is affiliated with the lender by common control, contract or business arrangement (defined in Section 433.1(g) as "[a]ny understanding, procedure, course of dealing, or arrangement, formal or informal, between a creditor and a seller, in connection with the sale of goods or services to consumers or the financing thereof"). It is not at all clear what constitutes affiliation by business arrangement. In the very common case of the secured loan, the loan is made for a particular purpose and the lender will be aware that a particular seller is involved in the transaction, but, without more, this should not mean that the lender's right to repayment is subject to any defenses that the borrower has against the seller. There is no problem in the case in which the seller steers the buyer to the lender or the case in which the lender will make loans only if the proceeds are used to purchase from the particular seller. Suppose the buyer of an automobile from a dealer shows that the lender has made numerous loans to borrowers who used the proceeds to purchase automobiles from the same dealer. Have the lender and the dealer become affiliated by an informal course of dealing? Must the seller in each case inquire about the buyer's source of funds to determine whether the required legend was required and was in fact made? 2 White & Summers, Uniform Commercial Code § 17–9 b. (4th Prac. ed. 1995).

Compare the following provision of the Uniform Consumer Credit Code (1974 Official Text) dealing with the same problem. *1974 Uniform Consumer Credit Code (enacted in 11 states)*

Section 3.405 *[Lender Subject to Claims and Defenses Arising from Sales and Leases]*

(1) A lender, except the issuer of a lender credit card, who, with respect to a particular transaction, makes a consumer loan to enable a consumer to buy or lease from a particular seller or lessor property or services [, except primarily for an agricultural purpose,] is subject to all claims and defenses of the consumer against the seller or lessor arising from that sale or lease of the property or services if:

> (a) the lender knows that the seller or lessor arranged for the extension of credit by the lender for a commission, brokerage, or referral fee;
>
> (b) the lender is a person related to the seller or lessor, unless the relationship is remote or is not a factor in the transaction;
>
> (c) the seller or lessor guarantees the loan or otherwise assumes the risk of loss by the lender upon the loan;
>
> (d) the lender directly supplies the seller or lessor with the contract document used by the consumer to evidence the loan, and the seller or lessor has knowledge of the credit terms and participates in preparation of the document;
>
> (e) the loan is conditioned upon the consumer's purchase or lease of the property or services from the particular seller or lessor, but the lender's payment of proceeds of the loan to the seller or lessor does not in itself establish that the loan was so conditioned; or
>
> (f) the lender, before he makes the consumer loan, has knowledge or, from his course of dealing with the particular seller or lessor or his records, notice of substantial complaints by other buyers or lessees of the particular seller's or lessor's failure or refusal to perform his contracts with them and of the particular seller's or lessor's failure to remedy his defaults within a reasonable time after notice to him of the complaints.

Constitutes a close connection

* * *

(3) NEW SUBSECTION 3–305(e)

Commentators conclude that compliance with the FTC rule by lenders in including the legend on their notes has been poor. Clarks' Secured

Transactions Monthly, Vol. 18, No. 5, p.2 (July 2002). One of the reasons for this is uncertainty over whether the lender in question qualifies as a purchase money lender under the FTC rule. The following case addresses the effect of omission of the legend by a lender. The first part of the opinion contains a good description of a purchase money lending transaction.

Gonzalez v. Old Kent Mortgage Company

United States District Court, E.D. Pennsylvania, 2000.
2000 WL 1469313.

■ HART, MAGISTRATE J.

Old Kent Mortgage Company has filed a Motion to Dismiss several of the counts of the Amended Complaint. * * * For the reasons that follow, Old Kent's Motion will be granted in part and denied in part.

I.   COUNT FIVE—VIOLATION OF PENNSYLVANIA'S HOME IMPROVEMENT FINANCE ACT

According to the amended complaint, the plaintiff contacted Quality Builders concerning certain home improvements for which she wanted to contract. Quality Builders also promised to obtain financing for the $14,900 worth of work. Quality Builders contacted Accelerated Mortgage, who, in turn, contacted Old Kent to arrange financing for the plaintiff. Rather than entering a contract for the $14,900 worth of work, the plaintiff entered into a consumer credit transaction giving Old Kent a mortgage on her home in the amount of $36,000 at 11.75% interest for 360 months. The mortgage consolidated several other debts and included various fees and origination costs.

In the fifth count of the Amended Complaint, the plaintiff contends that the loan into which she entered was a "home improvement install-ment contract" within the meaning of the Home Improvement Finance Act, ("HIFA"), and that the inclusion of certain fees, costs, and commis-sions was violative of HIFA. Therefore, plaintiff claims she is entitled to three times the amount of the excess charges pursuant to the Pennsylvania Loan Interest and Protection Law, 41 P.S. §§ 101, et seq., ("Act 6"), the provision providing the remedies for a violation of HIFA.

Old Kent contends that the loan at issue was not a "home improve-ment installment contract" because it was a direct loan between the retail buyer and the lender. HIFA includes a direct loan exception. According to 73 P.S. § 500–102(10), the term "home improvement installment contract" does not apply when "the loan is contracted for or obtained directly by the retail buyer from the lending institution, person or corporation." To support their argument, Old Kent relies on ¶ 25 of the Amended Complaint.

25.   As a consequence of this settlement, Plaintiff entered into a consumer credit transaction with Old Kent in which Old Kent extend-

A home improvement installment contract does not apply when the loan is contracted directly by the retail buyer from lending institution.

CHAPTER 1   NEGOTIABILITY AND HOLDERS IN DUE COURSE   **55**

ed consumer credit which was subject to a finance charge and which was initially payable to Old Kent.

They also present the court with the signed promissory note in which the plaintiff is identified as the borrower and Old Kent as the lender.

The plaintiff responds that Old Kent's definition of a "direct loan" is much too broad. "The 'direct loan' exception would be superfluous if the basic definition did not cover any home improvement financing payable to an independent lender." Here, the plaintiff contends that the contractor promised to obtain financing for her home improvements. Quality Builders contacted Accelerated Mortgage who contacted Old Kent to arrange for financing. Quality Builders participated in obtaining financing by forwarding the work order and Plaintiff's loan application to Old Kent. Representatives of Quality Builders, Accelerated Mortgage, and Old Kent were present at the settlement. In a "Mortgage Loan Origination Agreement," attached to the Amended Complaint, Accelerated Mortgage Company identified itself as an independent contractor who distributes loan products. Accelerated's compensation for their services is included in the interest rate, total points, and fees, according to the agreement. Finally, at the settlement, Quality Builders was issued a check for $10,769.08 directly from Old Kent.

Considering these facts, alleged in the Amended Complaint, we find it difficult to call this a direct loan. The Honorable David A. Scholl of the Bankruptcy Court of this District held that a similar loan fell within the definition of a "home improvement installment contract." *Brown v. Courtesy Consumer Discount Co.*, 134 B.R. 134, 140–41 (Bankr.E.D.Pa.1991). Judge Scholl found the Debtor's lack of effort to obtain the loan dispositive of the question.

The only difficult issue is whether the contractor's ubiquitous presence in the transaction eliminates the exception for direct loans, contained in 73 P.S. § 500–102(10)(v). We hold that it does, since the Debtor made no effort whatsoever to obtain or contract for a loan directly from Courtesy or any other lender.

Brown, at 141. Here, the only effort made by the plaintiff to obtain financing was to complete the credit application supplied by the Quality Builders representative. Judge Scholl described the actions of the home improvement contractor who arranged for the financing as "dragging the body."[1]

If such a transaction is allowed to stand as a "legitimate" ... loan which is beyond the reach of HIFA, then the purported broad scope and limited exceptions of the HIFA would effectively be punctured with a gaping loophole, which would allow lenders and contractors to choose when they wished to allow the HIFA to apply to a transaction.

---

1. "Dragging the body" was also used by the Honorable Edmond B. Spaeth, Jr. to describe the actions of an automobile dealer who drags the consumer to a discount financ- ing company. In return, the dealer receives an economic benefit because the consumer is then able to purchase the car. *Anderson v. Automobile Fund*, 258 Pa.Super 1, 15 (1978).

The loan in this case does not fall into the direct loan exception.

Brown, at 141. Similarly, we find that the loan in this case does not fall into the direct loan exception of HIFA.

II. COUNT SEVEN—BREACH OF CONTRACT

In Count 7 of the Amended Complaint, the plaintiff alleges that, pursuant to the FTC Holder Rule, Old Kent is liable for the claims that the plaintiff has against Quality Builders. Old Kent makes three arguments against this proposition. First, it argues that there is simply no contract in existence between itself and the plaintiff under which the plaintiff can hold Old Kent liable for any damages caused by Quality's conduct. Second, Old Kent claims that the FTC Holder Rule would not apply to this set of facts, even if a contract based on the Holder Rule did exist. Finally, Old Kent argues that the Holder Rule does not authorize the type of relief sought by the plaintiff. On all three counts, Old Kent is incorrect.

There is a contract here b/w Old Kent and π. It consisted of the loan agmt. and the promissory note. Old Kent failed to include in the Notice of Preservation of Claims and Defenses required by the FTC.

First and foremost, there is a contract here between Old Kent and the plaintiff. That contract consists of the loan agreement and promissory note themselves. Plaintiff alleges (and for Rule 12(b)(6) purposes we must presume this allegation to be correct) that "Old Kent failed to include in its promissory note the Notice of Preservation of Claims and Defenses required by the Federal Trade Commission regulation, 16 C.F.R. § 433.2 (the 'FTC Holder Rule') a *per se* unfair or deceptive practice." That notice, had it been included, would have stated as follows:

NOTICE

ANY HOLDER OF THIS CONSUMER CREDIT CONTRACT IS SUBJECT TO ALL CLAIMS AND DEFENSES WHICH THE DEBTOR COULD ASSERT AGAINST THE SELLER OF GOODS OR SERVICES OBTAINED PURSUANT HERETO OR WITH THE PROCEEDS HEREOF. RECOVERY HEREUNDER BY THE DEBTOR SHALL NOT EXCEED AMOUNTS PAID BY THE DEBTOR HEREUNDER.

16 C.F.R. § 433.2(a).

Because this language does not appear, Old Kent argues that, as a matter of law, the plaintiff cannot establish the necessary elements to prove a breach of contract: (1) the existence of a contract; (2) a breach of that contract; and (3) resulting damages. Since the plaintiff is attempting to impose liability on Old Kent for the failures of Quality Builders and there are no terms in either contract to create such liability, Old Kent argues that this claim should be dismissed.

Plaintiff counters by arguing that "contract terms may be implied where public policy so requires" and the court should read the Holder Rule into the agreements. By doing so, the plaintiff argues, Quality's liability can be imputed to Old Kent.

In our view, plaintiff clearly has the high ground on this issue. Assuming, as we do for purposes of a 12(b)(6) Motion, that the Holder Rule should have appeared somewhere in the collection of documents that the plaintiff signed, and assuming further that this language would have, at least, given plaintiff a right to offset against monies claimed by Old Kent the value of any claims plaintiff may have against Quality, it would turn the law on its head to allow Old Kent to avoid the consequences of this language by its own failure—alleged by the plaintiff to be an illegal failure—to include the Holder Rule Notice in the loan documents.

Old Kent next argues that even if the Holder Rule Notice appeared in the note, it would not be applicable in the current circumstances because "[t]he rule does not expand a plaintiff's rights' it simply limits when a defendant, as an assignee of the contract, may rely on a particular defense (the holder-in-due-course defense)." Here again, Old Kent's argument is flawed.

Contrary to Old Kent's assertion, the language of the rule, the FTC commentary, and applicable case law support the use of the rule, if applicable, to preserve claims against the seller to defeat a creditor's right to be paid under the note.

The Holder Rule, itself, appears in a regulation entitled, "Preservation of Consumers' Claims and Defenses, Unfair or Deceptive Acts or Practices," and the required notice states, in pertinent part, "ANY HOLDER OF THIS CONSUMER CREDIT CONTRACT IS SUBJECT TO ALL CLAIMS AND DEFENSES WHICH THE DEBTOR COULD ASSERT AGAINST THE SELLER . . . ." 16 C.F.R. § 433.2(a). In addition, the FTC has stated that the purpose of the rule is:

> to preserve the consumer's legally sufficient claims and defenses so that they may be asserted to defeat or diminish the right of a creditor to be paid, where a seller who arranges financing for a buyer fails to keep his side of the bargain.

Armstrong v. Edelson, 718 F.Supp. 1372, 1379 (N.D.Ill.1989)(citing Guidelines on Trade Regulation Rule Concerning Preservation of Consumers' Claims or Defenses, 41 Fed.Reg. 20,023–024 (1976)).

In *Armstrong*, a case arising in the home improvement context, the district court found that the Holder Rule allowed a consumer to assert a fraud claim, arising from the actions of the contractor, against the assignees of his retail sales contract—a contract for certain home improvements. *Armstrong*, at 1378–79. Similarly, the district courts in *Boggess v. Lewis Raines Motors, Inc.*, 20 F.Supp.2d 979 (S.D.W.V.1998) and *Mayberry v. Said*, 911 F.Supp. 1393 (D.Kan.1995), held that car buyers could maintain their claims alleging violations of the Odometer Act against the banks holding the notes on the cars. Id., at 982. In doing so, the district courts again looked to the FTC's statement of the purpose of the rule.

> [The FTC holder rule] is directed at the preservation of consumer claims and defenses. It will require that all consumer credit contracts generated by consumer sales include a provision which allows the consumer to assert his sale-related claims and defenses against any holder of the credit obligation. From the consumer's standpoint, this means that a consumer can (1) defend a creditor suit for payment of an

obligation by raising a valid claim against the seller as a setoff, and (2) maintain an affirmative action against a creditor who has received payments for a return of monies paid on account. The latter alternative will only be available where a seller's breach is so substantial that a court is persuaded that rescission and restitution are justified.

Boggess, at 982 (quoting 40 Fed.Reg. 53524 (Nov. 18, 1975)).

Finally, Old Kent argues that even if the Holder Rule Notice was present in this case and applied to these facts, it would still not support a claim for affirmative relief. The problem with this argument its that it assumes plaintiff is seeking affirmative relief. There is nothing in plaintiff's complaint to suggest that she is seeking to hold Old Kent responsible for 100% of her claims against Quality, as opposed to using those claims simply as an offset against any attempt by Old Kent to collect on the note. As such, there is no practical significance to the argument that the Holder Rule can only be used as a defense to a holder in due course claim. Defeating the holder in due course status of a creditor simply allows a debtor to argue that it need not pay on the note; and that is all plaintiff seeks here. (Amended Complaint, at ¶ 91)("any holder of the consumer credit contract shall be liable for all claims the consumer has against the seller, *up to the amount of the contract*.") (emphasis added). * * *

An appropriate order follows.

ORDER

AND NOW, this 19 day of September, 2000, upon consideration of Old Kent's Motion to Dismiss Counts Five and Thirteen of the Amended Complaint and to Dismiss Old Kent from Counts Seven, Eight, and Ten of the Amended Complaint, the response, thereto, and the reply, IT IS HEREBY ORDERED that the Motion is GRANTED IN PART AND DENIED IN PART. Old Kent is DISMISSED from Count Ten of the Amended Complaint and Count Thirteen is DISMISSED in its entirety.

NOTE

Associates Home Equity Services, Inc. v. Troup, 778 A.2d 529 (N.J. Super. Ct. 2001), follows *Gonzalez* in applying the FTC holder rule to a direct lender's purchase money loan even when the lender's loan documents omit the FTC holder notice. In response to these cases, the following provision was added to 3–305 in 2002.

(e) In a consumer transaction, if law other than this article requires that an instrument include a statement to the effect that the rights of a holder or transferee are subject to a claim or defense that the issuer could assert against the original payee, and the instrument does not include such a statement:

(1) the instrument has the same effect as if the instrument included such a statement;

(2) the issuer may assert against the holder or transferee all claims and defenses that would have been available if the instrument included such a statement; and

(3) the extent to which claims may be asserted against the holder or transferee is determined as if the instrument included such a statement.

See Comment 6 to 3–305.

4. PAYEE AS HOLDER IN DUE COURSE ←

We don't usually think of a payee as being a holder in due course because the defenses that a maker or drawer raises are commonly based on the conduct of the payee such as fraud, misrepresentation, lack of consideration and the like. Since the payee perpetrated these wrongs on the obligor, the payee can hardly qualify as one who takes the instrument in good faith and without knowledge of the defense. But there are a few situations in which a payee should be allowed holder-in-due-course status; these involve more than two parties. Former 3–302(2) expressly stated: "A payee may be a holder in due course." This provision was omitted in the revision of Article 3. Comment 4 to 3–302 states: "Former Section 3–302(2) has been omitted in revised Article 3 because it is surplusage and may be misleading. The payee of an instrument can be a holder in due course, but use of the holder-in-due-course doctrine by the payee of an instrument is not the normal situation." We will look at two situations, one involving recoupment and one a defense.

Recoupment. Seller (S) sold goods to Buyer (B). B issued a promissory note payable to the order of S to evidence B's obligation to pay for the goods. At the time S took the note, it had no reason to believe that there were any defects in the goods. Later it was clear that the goods were defective and that B had a claim in recoupment against S for breach of warranty. S sued B on the note claiming that it had been in good faith at the time the note was taken and had no reason to believe at that time that there was anything wrong with the goods, and, therefore, was a holder in due course. It would be absurd in this case to allow S to take free of B's claim based on breach of warranty on the ground that S was a holder in due course. Section 3–305(b) states that the right of a holder in due course to enforce an obligation is not subject to "claims in recoupment * * * against a person other than the holder." Here the claim of recoupment can be asserted because it is against the holder. Comment 3 to 3–305 states: "It is obvious that the holder-in-due-course doctrine cannot be used to allow Seller to cut off a warranty claim that Buyer has against Seller."

Defenses. In Kane v. Kroll, 196 Wis.2d 389, 538 N.W.2d 605 (Wis.Ct. App.1995), the facts, somewhat altered, were these. Seller (S) sold cows to Buyer (B) on credit. B induced his Mother (M) to pay his debt to S by falsely representing to her that he was about to sell enough hay to come up with the money. M wrote a check to S for the debt. The next day B disclosed his fraud to M and she promptly stopped payment on the check.

When S presented the check to the drawee bank it was dishonored because of the stop order. S sued M on the check, claiming to be a holder in due course because S had no reason to know of the fraud that B had perpetrated on M.

Under the old law we would need more facts to decide the case. Former 3–305(2) provided that a holder in due course "takes the instrument free from all defenses of any party to the instrument with whom the holder has not dealt." Thus, if M had given the check to B and B had delivered the check to S, S would be a holder in due course because there were no dealings with M. But if M had delivered the check to S, S would most likely not be a holder in due course because S had dealt with M. This distinction makes no sense; in both cases S knew nothing of B's fraud on M. Why make a distinction based on an irrelevant fact, such as which party handed the check to S, determinative of S's status as a holder in due course?

Under Revised Article 3, the language in former 3–305(2) is deleted. Comment 2 to 3–305 explains: "The meaning of this language was not at all clear and if read literally could have produced the wrong result." Examples of cases in which payees may be holders in due course are set out in Comment 4 to 3–302. Case #1 is comparable to *Kane*. Comment 2 to 3–305 concludes: "The [holder-in-due-course] doctrine applies only to cases in which more than two parties are involved. Its essence is that the holder in due course does not have to suffer the consequences of a defense of the obligor on the instrument that arose from an occurrence with a third party." Although it is quite clear from the comments to 3–302 and 3–305 that payees can be holders in due course in three-party transactions coming within the ambit of the language quoted in the previous sentence, it is not so clear whether Article 3 offers specific guidance on cases in which payees cannot become holders in due course, other than the general rule that a taker with notice of a defense cannot qualify as a holder in due course. Comment 2 to 3–305 says that the "with whom the holder has not dealt" language of old 3–305(2) was dropped because "It is not necessary." White & Summers, Uniform Commercial Code § 14–9 (4th ed. 1995), contends that 3–305(b) serves the function of determining when payees cannot become holders in due course. It provides that the rights of a holder in due course are not subject "to defenses of the obligor stated in subsection (a)(2) or claims in recoupment stated in subsection (a)(3) against a person other than the holder." If the "against" clause at the end of the section applies to defenses as well as recoupment, the implication is that even if the payee is a holder in due course that person cannot take free of the defenses that a maker or drawer has against the payee-holder. This interpretation gives a sensible result, but nowhere do the voluminous comments to 3–302 and 3–305 refer to the "against" clause as applying in any case but recoupment.

5. TRANSACTIONS WITH FIDUCIARIES

Under 3–306 a holder in due course of an instrument takes free of "a claim of a property or possessory right in the instrument or its proceeds." For example, a claim to the instrument or its proceeds may arise if a

[handwritten top margin: 3-307 – shows negotiating instruments in breach of fiduciary duty. It states rules for determining when the person taking the instrument has notice of breach of fid. duty.]

fiduciary, in breach of fiduciary duty, negotiates the instrument for value. The negotiation of the instrument may be the means used by the fiduciary to misappropriate funds of the person to whom the fiduciary duty is owed. The claim of that person falls within the language of 3–306. Under 3–302(a)(2), the person to whom the instrument is negotiated cannot be a holder in due course if the instrument was taken with notice of the claim. Section 3–307 governs cases of negotiation of instruments in breach of fiduciary duty. It states rules for determining when the person taking the instrument has notice of breach of fiduciary duty. It also states that notice of breach of fiduciary duty is notice of the claim of the person to whom the fiduciary duty was owed. The scope of 3–307 is narrowed by (b)(ii) to cases in which "the taker has knowledge of the fiduciary status of the fiduciary." "Knowledge" is defined in 1–202(b) as actual knowledge, and Comment 2 to 3–307 points out that: "In many cases, the individual who receives and processes an instrument on behalf of the organization that is the taker of the instrument 'for payment or collection or for value' is a clerk who has no knowledge of any fiduciary status of the person from whom the instrument is received. In such cases, Section 3–307 doesn't apply because, under [1–202(f)], knowledge of the organization is determined by the knowledge of the 'individual conducting that transaction,' i.e., the clerk who receives and processes the instrument."

[handwritten right margin: Under 3-302 (a)(2), the person to whom the instrument is negotiated cannot be a holder in due course if the instrument was taken with notice of a claim.

Rule: Notice of breach of fiduciary duty is notice of the claim of the person to whom the fid. duty was owed. The taker has knowledge of the fid. Status of the fiduciary — must be actual knowledge. Instrument for the organization that is the taker of the instrument is a clerk who has no knowledge of any fiduciary Status of the person giving the instrument.

- Problem

- Fiscus is the guardian ad litem for Welty (child).
- A check was issued to Fiscus as guardian for Welty. It was Welty's $25K.]

PROBLEM

[handwritten: In most cases, the individ. who receives the]

Fiscus is the guardian ad litem for a minor child, Welty, who has won a judgment for $25,000 in a personal injury case. A check for this amount was issued payable to the order of "Fred Fiscus, Guardian ad Litem for Roy Welty." In which of the following cases does Bank have notice of a breach of fiduciary duty on the part of Fiscus under 3–307 (b)?

Case #1.   When Fiscus indorsed the check and delivered it to Bank, he requested that it be applied in partial payment of his overdue loan obligation to Bank. Bank followed his directions.

Case #2.   When Fiscus indorsed the check and delivered it to Bank, he completed a deposit slip directing that the check be credited to his personal account. His direction was carried out. It was on this issue, that pre-revision cases were divided. The different views are set out in *Smith v. Olympic Bank*, below, and *Matter of Knox*, discussed in the Note following the *Smith* opinion. Which view is adopted by 3–307(b)(2)? Why?

Case #3.   Fiscus delivered the check to Bank, indorsed "Fred Fiscus, Guardian ad Litem for Roy Welty," and deposited it in a guardianship account that he had opened in Bank for Welty earlier. A month later, Fiscus drew a check on the guardianship account, purporting to act in his fiduciary capacity, payable to the order of "Fred Fiscus." He deposited the check in his personal account in Bank and later misappropriated the proceeds of the check for his personal benefit.

[handwritten bottom: Case #1 – Yes, notice of breach of fiduciary duty 3-307 (b) (2) (i) – instrument is made payable to fiduciary and represented party and it B taken as payment for a personal debt of the fiduciary the taker knows it – in this case the bank loan

[left margin: Maybe be notice b/c deposited K for his own acct]

Case #2 – No, not notice, b/c doesn't meet reqmts of 3-307 (b)(2)(iii) – it was deposited to his own account, finally it has to be deposited into an acct other than fiduciary's]

Smith v. Olympic Bank

Supreme Court of Washington, 1985.

103 Wash.2d 418, 693 P.2d 92.

■ DORE, JUSTICE.

We hold that, where a bank allows a check that is made payable to a guardian to be deposited in a guardian's personal account instead of a guardianship account, the bank is not a holder in due course under the Uniform Commercial Code (UCC) because it has notice that the guardian is breaching his fiduciary duty.

Charles Alcombrack was appointed guardian for his son Chad Stephen Alcombrack who was then 7 years old and the beneficiary of his grandfather's life insurance policy. The insurance company issued a check for $30,588.39 made payable to "Charles Alcombrack, Guardian of the Estate of Chad Stephen Alcombrack a Minor". The attorney for the son's estate directed the father to take the check, along with the letters of guardianship issued to the father, to the bank and open up a guardianship savings and checking account. The father, however, did not follow the attorney's instructions. Instead, he took the check, without the letters of guardianship, to the bank and opened a personal checking and a personal savings account. The following was printed on the back of the check:

> By endorsement of this check the payee acknowledges receipt of the amount thereof in full settlement of all claims resulting from the death of Roy Alcombrack, certificate holder under Group Life Policy No. 9,745,632

/s/ Charles Alcombrack

Guardian of the Estate of Chad Stephen Alcombrack, a minor

Despite the above written notice that the check was payable to the father in his guardianship capacity, the bank allowed the father to place the entire amount in newly opened personal accounts. On the same day that the father opened his accounts, the attorney for the guardian called a trust officer from Olympic Bank and inquired as to the fees the bank charged for maintaining guardianship accounts. Responding to the attorney's questions, the trust officer wrote the attorney, specifically mentioning the "Estate of Chad Alcombrack".[1]

---

1. The following is the letter sent by the trust officer to the guardian's attorney:

"October 30, 1975

"Mr. Charles A. Schaaf, Attorney

"Reference: Estate of Chad Alcombrack

"Dear Mr. Schaaf:

"This is a follow up to our telephone conversation of October 28, 1975. The information you requested on the performance of our common trust funds will be available in about four weeks. October 31st is the end of our fiscal year. If this is not too long for you to wait, please let me know and I will send you a copy of our annual report.

"Our fee for handling a Guardianship account is, eight tenths (⁸⁄₁₀) of one percent (1%), minimum of $350.00 per year."

The father, and later his new wife, used all but $320.60 of the trust money for their own personal benefit. Bank records disclosed how the estate money was withdrawn: five withdrawals were made to cash or into the father's checking account (total—approximately $16,000); one withdrawal paid off an unsecured personal loan made by the bank to the father (approximately $3,000); seven debits to the account were made by the bank exercising its right of offset to make payments on or pay off personal loans by the bank to the father (total—approximately $12,500).

After the depletion of the son's estate, J. David Smith was appointed successor guardian. He received a judgment against the father and instituted this suit against the bank. The trial court granted summary judgment in favor of the bank. The Court of Appeals reversed and remanded, holding that the trial court should determine the factual issue whether the bank was a holder in due course.

Olympic Bank claims that it is a holder in due course (HIDC) and, as such, is not subject to the claims of the petitioner. In order to qualify as a HIDC, the bank must meet five requirements. It must be (1) a holder (2) of a negotiable instrument, (3) that took the instrument for value (4) in good faith and (5) without notice that it was overdue, dishonored, or of any defense or claim to it on the part of any person. * * * We need not decide whether the bank met the first four conditions as we hold that the bank took the check with notice of an adverse claim to the instrument and, therefore, is not a holder in due course. Consequently, the bank is liable to the petitioner.[4]

A purchaser has notice of an adverse claim when "he has knowledge that a fiduciary has negotiated the instrument in payment of or as security for his own debt or in any transaction for his own benefit or otherwise in breach of duty." UCC 3–304(2). Thus, the issue raised by this case is whether the bank had knowledge that the guardian was breaching his fiduciary duty when it allowed him to deposit a check, made payable to him in his guardianship capacity, into his personal accounts. As to this issue, Von Gohren v. Pacific Nat'l Bank, 8 Wash.App. 245, 505 P.2d 467 (1973) is persuasive and controlling. In *Von Gohren*, it was held that a bank had notice that an employee was breaching her fiduciary duty when it allowed her to deposit third-party checks payable to her employer in her personal account. The bank was put on notice despite the fact that the employer had authorized the employee to draw checks against his account and also to endorse checks made payable to him and deposit such checks into his account. The court held that notice need not always consist of actual knowledge of a breach of a fiduciary duty, but can be predicated upon reasonable commercial standards. The court concluded by stating:

4. UCC § 3–306 sets forth the liabilities of one who accepts a check and who is not a holder in due course.

"Unless he has the rights of a holder in due course any person takes the instrument subject to

"(a) all valid claims to it on the part of any person; and

"(b) all defenses of any party which would be available in an action on a simple contract; . . . "

It is our view that since defendant had notice of the claim by virtue of UCC § 3–304(2), and since it is undisputed that defendant did nothing to investigate Mrs. Martin's authority to negotiate checks payable to her employer, we must hold as a matter of law it did not act in accordance with reasonable commercial standards.

Von Gohren, at 255, 505 P.2d 467. The same conclusion is mandated in the present case.

Here, the bank knew it was dealing with guardianship funds. The check was payable to the father as guardian and not to him personally. The father endorsed it in his guardianship capacity. The bank received a call from the guardian's attorney inquiring about the fee the bank charged for guardianship accounts, and a trust officer for the bank replied in a letter referring to the "Estate of Chad Alcombrack".

Reasonable commercial practices dictate that when the bank knew that the funds were deposited in a personal account instead of a guardianship account, it also knew that the father was breaching his fiduciary duty. The funds lost the protection they would have received in a guardianship account when they were placed in a personal account. If the funds had been placed in a guardianship account, the bank would not have been allowed to exercise its set-off rights which amounted to approximately $12,500. * * * Nor would it have been permitted to accept a check, drawn on the guardianship account, from the father in satisfaction of the father's unsecured personal loan in the amount of approximately $3,000. Nor could the father, or bank, have authorized his new wife to write checks against the guardianship account without court approval. * * * A fiduciary has a duty to ensure that trust funds are protected. * * * Here, the father breached his duty.

While this is the first time, under the Uniform Commercial Code, that we have held a bank liable for allowing a guardian to deposit trust funds in a personal account, we have held a bank liable in a pre-Code case for allowing a trustee to breach his fiduciary duty. * * * In addition, other jurisdictions have held banks liable under similar circumstances using the Code * * * and without using the Code * * *. The policy reasons for holding a bank liable are compelling—especially in the situation presented in this case. The ward has no control of his own estate. He must rely on his guardian and on the bank for the safekeeping of his money. In order to protect the ward, the guardian and bank must be held to a high standard of care. For the guardian, this means that he must deposit guardian funds in a guardianship account. For the bank, it means that when it receives a check made payable to an individual as a guardian, it must make sure that the check is placed in a guardianship account. This will not place an undue burden on either banks or guardians and will have the beneficial effect of protecting the ward.

* * *

NOTE

In Matter of Knox, 64 N.Y.2d 434, 488 N.Y.S.2d 146, 477 N.E.2d 448 (1985), a pre-Revision case, rejects 9–307(b)'s imputation of notice when a bank allowed a guardian to deposit a check payable to him as guardian in his personal account. Knox involved a father who was guardian of the property of a minor son. Robert, the son, was injured when he was four years old. An action brought on behalf of Robert for damages was settled and a check was issued to the father as guardian of the property of the son. The check was negotiated to a bank and $11,000 of the proceeds of the check was deposited in the personal account of the father in the bank. The amount deposited in the account was eventually spent in the purchase of a house for the family and for other family expenses. The family included three other children besides Robert and the parents. The family was impoverished and the father stated that the money was spent to "give Robert as well as the rest [of the family] the same kind of normal life that any family enjoys." Eventually an action was brought against the father by a guardian ad litem appointed for Robert to recover the funds that had been misappropriated by the father. The bank was joined in the action and the trial court entered judgment against both. The bank appealed and the Appellate Division reversed the judgment against the bank. In affirming the Appellate Division, the Court of Appeals, one judge dissenting, stated:

> In Bradford Trust Co. v. Citibank, 60 N.Y.2d 868, 470 N.Y.S.2d 361, 458 N.E.2d 820, we held that "there is no requirement that a check payable to a fiduciary be deposited to a fiduciary account, and the fact that the instrument was not so deposited may not, without more, be relied upon as establishing a wrongful payment on the part of the depositary bank" * * *. Our decision was grounded upon the Uniform Commercial Code which provides that "[a]n instrument made payable to a named person with the addition of words describing him * * * as [a] fiduciary for a specified person or purpose is payable to the payee and may be negotiated, discharged or enforced by him" (Uniform Commercial Code § 3–117[b]), and that mere knowledge that the "person negotiating the instrument is or was a fiduciary" does not of itself give the purchaser of a negotiable instrument notice of any claims or defenses (Uniform Commercial Code § 3–304[4][e]). The conduct with which [the bank] is charged—having negotiated a check payable to [the father] in a fiduciary capacity without requiring deposit of the check in a fiduciary account—is thus permissible.
>
> In general, a bank may assume that a person acting as a fiduciary will apply entrusted funds to the proper purposes and will adhere to the conditions of the appointment * * *. A bank is not in the normal course required to conduct an investigation to protect funds from possible misappropriation by a fiduciary, unless there are facts—not here present—indicating misappropriation * * *. In this event, a bank may be liable for participation in the diversion, either by itself acquiring a benefit, or by notice or knowledge that a diversion is intended or being executed * * *. No facts are before this court suggesting that

Before revision Matter of Knox — rejected the rights that notice is given when a guardian deposits a check payable to him as guardian in his own personal account.

The family was impoverished and father used the funds to not only benefit the child, but entire family.

[the bank] had notice that [the father] intended to, or did in fact, use the settlement proceeds for improper purposes. Consequently, [the bank] cannot be charged with the misappropriation.

Section 3–307(b)(2)(iii) has been controversial. Some states did not enact it, e.g., Alabama, and others that enacted it repealed it a few years later, e.g., Missouri.

PROBLEM

Assume the same facts as set out in Case #2 in the Problem at the beginning of the section, except that Fiscus deposited the check in his personal account until he could open a guardianship account at a bank in another locality. Three days after Fiscus deposited the check in his account, he wrote a check on the account for the entire $25,000 amount and deposited the check in the guardianship account in the other bank. He subsequently used the proceeds of this account for his personal benefit in breach of his fiduciary duty. In Richards v. Seattle Metropolitan Credit Union, 68 P.3d 1109 (Wash. App. 2003), the court held that although Bank was liable in conversion for breach of its fiduciary duty by allowing the funds to be deposited in an account other than the fiduciary account, Bank's breach was not the proximate cause of the child's loss and no damages were assessed. The loss occurred when the funds were taken from a guardianship account in another bank. Do you agree with this result?

NOTE: UNIFORM FIDUCIARIES ACT

When the National Conference approved the final draft of Revised Article 3, the Commissioners did so knowing that 3–307 took positions contrary to those of another uniform act, the Uniform Fiduciaries Act, that had been promulgated by the National Conference in the 1920s and adopted in about half of the states. The inconsistency between the two acts was before the court in County of Macon v. Edgcomb, 274 Ill.App.3d 432, 654 N.E.2d 598 (Ill. App. Ct. 1995), in which a county treasurer, Edgcomb, embezzled over $400,000 in county funds by stealing checks made to the county, endorsing them and depositing them in his personal account in Bank. Under UFA § 9, Bank had no liability in the absence of knowledge of the breach of fiduciary obligation or bad faith, but under 3–307(b)(2) Bank would be liable. Conceding that when choosing between conflicting statutes the more recent enactment will prevail as the later expression of legislative intent, the court applied the UFA to the case because Revised Article 3 was not in effect at the time of the embezzlement and amendatory acts should be construed as prospective unless the act indicates otherwise. The National Conference has issued an "Addendum to Revised Article 3, Notes to Legislative Counsel. * * * 2. If Revised Article 3 is adopted in your state and the Uniform Fiduciaries Act is also in effect in your state, you may want to consider amending Uniform Fiduciaries Act § 9 to conform to

[Handwritten margin notes:]

Some states have not enacted 3-3-7(b)(2)(iii)

Say Fiscus deposits the trust money in his own account then days later transferred all the money into a new guardianship acct at different bank. He used the proceeds for his own benefit, subsequently. This is notice — he is transferring funds into a personal account — which is breach of fiduciary duty.

Revised Art. 3 and Uniform Fiduciaries Act were inconsistent w/ one another. If a guardian deposited trust funds in his personal acct, the bank would be liable under Art. 3, but not under Uniform Fiduciary Act.

Section 3–307(b)(2)(iii) and (4)(iii). See Official Comment 3 to Section 3–307.''

PROBLEM

Little Corporation has about 100 stockholders and conducts its manufacturing operations in Centerville, a small city. Little has a checking account in Centerville Bank. The agreement between Little and the bank provides that the bank is authorized to honor checks drawn on the account if signed in the name of Little by either the president or treasurer of Little. Della, the president of Little, was involved in the following transactions:

Case #1. Della's personal credit card was used to pay for automobile rentals, restaurant meals, and hotel accommodations. All of the credit card charges were incurred for her personal benefit and were not related to any business purpose of Little. Della wrote a check drawn on Little's checking account and sent it to Issuer of the credit card to pay the monthly bill that included the charges.

Case #2. Della bought a small but expensive rug from Merchant and paid for it by writing a check drawn on Little's checking account. The rug was delivered to Della at the store.

Case #3. Della went to Clothier's store and ordered several dresses that were to be custom made for her. Della paid by writing a check drawn on Little's checking account. Before accepting the check, Clothier asked her why a check of the corporation was being used to pay for the clothing. She answered, "The dresses are a present from a grateful employer for five years of faithful service by yours truly."

Case #4. Della wrote a $1,000 check drawn on Little's account payable to her. She indorsed the check in blank and deposited it to her account in Depositary Bank by delivering it to a teller who knew her personally and knew that she was president of Little.

In each of the foregoing cases, Della committed a breach of fiduciary duty to Little in writing the check on Little's account. When Little discovered the defalcations it brought actions to recover the proceeds of the checks written by Della and paid from Little's account. The actions were brought against Issuer of the credit card in Case #1, against Merchant in Case #2, against Clothier in Case #3, and against Centerville Bank in Case #4. State your opinion whether Little is entitled to recover in each case. 3–306, 3–307, 1–202(a) ("notice") and (b) ("knowledge"), and Comment 2 to 3–307.

6. VALUE

a. INTRODUCTION

If Thief steals a negotiable instrument from Owner and sells it to unsuspecting Holder, it may make sense to give Holder rights in the

[Handwritten margin notes:]

- Little has 100 stockholders
- It has a checking account in Centerville Bank.
- Little's president or treasurer can sign checks drawn on Little's account.

Case #1 – Little may recover. The Taker, Issuer of credit card, accepted the check for a personal debt of the fiduciary – so had notice. 3-307(b)(2)(i).

Case #2 – Little cannot recover

Case #3 – Little can recover – Clothier had notice b/c she asked and Della told her form it was from company. So facts and circumstances gave Clothier notice of a breach 1-202(a)(3).

Case #4
Little can recover. Other Bank accepted the check + company check and allowed it to be deposited for her personal benefit – so this is notice of a breach. 3-307(b)(2)(iii)

instrument at the expense of Owner. One or the other must bear a loss. Although each is equally innocent, the negotiability doctrine tips the scales in favor of Holder in order to carry out a policy objective of encouraging free commerce in instruments. But if Holder has paid nothing for the instrument, denial of the right to defeat Owner's title results in no loss to Holder except missing out on a windfall. Thus, if Thief makes a gift of the instrument to Holder it seems unfair to allow Holder to profit at the expense of Owner. Since it is not necessary to impose a loss on Owner in order to carry out the objective of encouraging free commerce in instruments, Holder loses. Section 3–302(a)(2)(i) provides that only a holder who takes the instrument for value can be a holder in due course. Taking for value is defined in 3–303(a). Although the requirement of taking for value can be explained in part by distinguishing between loss and windfall, this distinction is not always clearly apparent in the cases covered by 3–303(a). The elementary problems that follow illustrate some cases covered by that section. In each problem, and the cases that follow, you might ask yourself whether the holder-in-due-course doctrine is necessary to protect some interest of the holder or whether the doctrine simply confers on the holder a windfall. If there is a windfall, is the result justified by commercial necessity? You might also ask whether, if the doctrine did not exist, the taking of the instrument in the particular transaction would have been discouraged.

PROBLEMS

In each of the following problems make these assumptions: Maker gave to Payee a negotiable note in the amount of $1,000 payable on a stated date. Maker's issuance of the note was induced by Payee's fraudulent promise to deliver goods that were never delivered. In each case, Payee, prior to the due date, negotiated the note to Holder who had no notice of the fraud. On the due date Holder demanded payment of Maker who refused and asserted the defenses of fraud and failure of consideration.

1.   Payee negotiates the note to Holder in consideration of Holder's agreement to perform services for Payee. Before Holder is obligated to begin performance of the promised services the note falls due. Was there consideration for the transfer of the note from Payee to Holder? 3–303(b). Was the note taken for value by Holder? 3–303(a)(1).

2.   Payee negotiates the note to Holder who pays $900 cash for the note. Is Maker's defense good against Holder? What provision in 3–303(a) applies to this case? If Maker is liable, how much can Holder recover? 3–302(a)(2). Suppose Holder paid $600 cash for the note and promised to pay an additional $300 cash in 60 days. After paying the $600, Holder learned of the fraud and paid no more. How much can Holder recover? See O. P. Ganjo, Inc. v. Tri–Urban Realty Co., 108 N.J.Super. 517, 261 A.2d 722 (N.J. Super. Ct. Law Div. 1969). Comment 6, Case #5, to 3–302(d).

3.   Payee was indebted to Holder on a loan past due. Holder demanded payment but Payee was unable to pay. In order to forestall legal action by Holder, Payee negotiated Maker's note to Holder as collateral for payment of Payee's loan. When the note became due, Payee was still unable to repay the loan. Holder thereupon demanded payment of the note by Maker. Is Maker's defense good against Holder? 3–303(a)(3).

b.   RIGHTS OF DEPOSITARY BANK IN DEPOSITED CHECK

The material in this section examines one of the most common applications of the holder-in-due-course doctrine: when does a bank in which a check is deposited become a holder in due course of that check? Does it give value as soon as the depositor is given a provisional credit in the deposit account, or only when it pays out the proceeds of the check to the depositor? The answer to this question influences the bank's decisions on when to allow its depositors to draw on recently deposited checks. If the bank is a holder in due course, it takes free of any defenses between the drawer and the payee of the check, and if it is unable to recover from the depositor for money paid out on a check that the drawee bank refuses to pay, it can count on the liability of the drawer. As we explain below, Article 4 has its own rules for determining when a depositary or other collecting bank has given value for a check. These rules are stated in 4–210 and 4–211, and they complement 3–303; they do not displace it.

Checks are usually deposited by the payee in the payee's bank. That bank of first deposit is a "depositary bank." 4–105(2). The payee's bank is also referred to as a "collecting bank" if the check is not drawn on the payee's bank. 4–105(5). The depositary bank normally credits the account of the depositor for the amount of the check and forwards the check to the drawee for payment. The drawee is referred to in 4–105(3) as the "payor bank." The depositary bank is considered to be acting as the agent of the depositor in obtaining payment of the deposited check. 4–201. The credit to the depositor's account is normally provisional in nature. When the check is paid by the payor bank, this provisional credit becomes final, i.e., the credit represents a debt owed by the depositary bank to the depositor, 4–215(d). If the check is not paid by the payor bank, the depositary bank has the right to "charge back," i.e., cancel the provisional credit. 4–214(a).

Frequently, the depositary bank will also be a creditor of the depositor because of a past transaction such as a loan. If a debt owing by the depositor to the depositary bank is past due, the depositary bank may exercise a common law right to set off against the debt any amounts which the bank owes the depositor. For example, if the depositor owes the depositary bank $1,000 on a past-due loan and there is an $800 final credit balance in the depositor's checking account, the depositary bank may simply wipe out the $800 balance by applying it to reduce the $1,000 loan balance.[1] In addition to this right of setoff a depositary bank has a closely-related common law right known as a banker's lien. See Restatement, Security § 62.

---

1.   The bank's right of setoff may be limited by statute. For example, Calif. Financial Code § 864 limits setoffs with respect to   certain consumer-type installment debt owed to the bank.

Setoff
If a depositor owes a depositary bank $1K on a past due loan and deposits a check in the account, the depositary bank has a lien in the check as security for the debt.

The bank can collect the check and apply the proceeds to the debt owed.

Thus, the bank is taking for value (the check) so could be a HDC

There can be no present right of setoff with respect to an uncollected check until collected the check does not represent a debt.

So must collect to be considered taking for value on an antecedent debt

— For example, if the depositor owes the depositary bank $1,000 on a past-due loan and deposits a check to the depositor's account in the regular course of business, the depositary bank has a lien in the check as security for the $1,000 debt. Although the bank acts as agent for the depositor when it forwards the check to the payor for payment, it also has a property interest in the check represented by the lien. Thus, the depositary bank can collect the check and apply the proceeds to the debt owed by the depositor. Since the taking of an instrument for an antecedent debt is value, the depositary bank could attain the rights of a holder in due course. These two related but separate common law rights—setoff and banker's lien—are preserved under 1–103. Comment 1 to 4–210. The two common law rights are frequently confused. It is not uncommon for a court to refer to the banker's lien as a right of setoff or to refer to the right of setoff as a banker's lien. When a depositary bank is asserting a right in an uncollected check it is relying on a lien. A setoff can occur only if there are mutual debts. There can be no present right of setoff with respect to an uncollected check because until collected the check does not represent a debt of the depositary bank to the depositor. Restatement, Security § 62.

Depositary banks may acquire rights as holders in due course under other provisions of the UCC. Suppose there is no debt owing by the depositor when the check is deposited. Whether the depositary bank has given value for the check is determined under 4–211, which states that the bank has given value to the extent it has a security interest in the check. Section 4–210 states rules for determining when a security interest arises. This security interest is in addition to the bank's common law banker's lien. Comment 1 to 4–210. By virtue of 4–210 the depositary bank has a security interest under subsection (a)(1) if the check is deposited and the resulting credit is withdrawn, under subsection (a)(2) if the check is deposited and the depositor is given the right to withdraw the credit, and under (a)(3) if the bank makes a loan or cash payment based on the check. In these cases the bank is treated as though it were a lender to the depositor taking as security a security interest in the check. In the case in which the depositor is not allowed to withdraw the funds, the bank does not have a security interest and is not a holder in due course. It has committed no funds and is fully protected by its ability to charge back the depositor's account in the event the check is not paid by the payor bank.

In most cases the depositor has an existing credit balance in the account when a deposit is made and there may be a series of deposits and withdrawals from the account. In those cases, whether credit for a particular check has been withdrawn cannot be determined except by applying some mechanical tracing rule. Such a rule is provided by the last sentence of 4–210(b), which states that "credits first given are first withdrawn." This rule is usually referred to as the first-in-first-out or FIFO rule.

PROBLEM

The table shows debits and credits made to Depositor's checking account in Depositary Bank. Withdrawals were made by payment by

Depositary Bank of checks drawn by Depositor on the account. Deposits were made either in cash or by third-party checks payable to Depositor as indicated.

Date	Debit	Credit	Balance
Nov. 1	Existing balance		4,000
Nov. 2	Deposit by check	5,000	9,000
Nov. 3	Withdrawal	4,000	5,000
Nov. 4	Deposit in cash	6,000	11,000
Nov. 5	Withdrawal	5,000	6,000
Nov. 6	Received notice of dishonor of check deposited on Nov. 2		
Nov. 7 (A.M.)	Withdrawal	3,000	3,000
Nov. 7 (P.M.)	Charge-back of Nov. 2 credit	5,000	–2,000

The check deposited on November 2 was not paid by the payor bank because the drawer had stopped payment. 4–403(a). Depositary Bank received notice of dishonor of the check on November 6. Depositor is insolvent. Depositary Bank brings an action against the drawer of the November 2 check to recover the amount of the check. 3–414(b). The drawer defends by asserting that no consideration was given for the check. 3–303(b). Assume that Depositary Bank is a holder in due course if it gave value for the check. Did Depositary Bank give value? 4–210(a)(1) and (b). Is the result in this Problem consistent with the case discussed in Comment 2 to 3–303? That case is governed by 3–303(1)(a), under which the unperformed promise of performance is not value. The rationale is that until performance is made the promisor will not suffer any out-of-pocket loss and dishonor of the check excuses performance by the promisor. In this Problem, is holder-in-due-course status necessary to protect Depositary Bank against an out-of-pocket loss when Depositary Bank received notice of dishonor on November 6? 4–214(a).

Section 4–210(a)(1) refers not only to cases in which a credit has been withdrawn, but also to cases in which the credit has been "applied." The latter term refers to cases in which the credit has been used by the bank to pay an obligation to itself or to make a payment to a third party.

NOTE

Earlier, when we were discussing the concept of negotiability, we quoted from Professor Rosenthal's article questioning the desirability of the doctrine of negotiability. Here we include another section of that article in which he considers the negotiability of checks. This is from Albert J. Rosenthal, "Negotiability—Who Needs It?," 71 Colum. L. Rev. 375, 382–385 (1971). Bankers disagree with Professor Rosenthal's view on the importance of holder-in-due-course status as to checks.

To begin with, negotiability normally plays almost no part with respect to checks. While some checks are cashed at a grocery store or across the counter at a bank, the overwhelming majority of checks are

drawor - makar of the chak
payor - parson (bank) who pays the chak
payee - person who gats the chelk.

72   CHAPTER 1 NEGOTIABILITY AND HOLDERS IN DUE COURSE

Most of the time the
payee deposits the
check rather than
negotiates it. The
bank then sends the
check back to drawee
bank to get payment
If paid, the check is
marked and returned
to drawer. If it is
not paid, a slip
is attached as to
why and sent to
payee.

deposited by the payee for collection at his own bank, which, acting merely as the depositor's agent for that purpose, sends the check through banking channels to the drawee bank where it is presented for payment. If paid, the check is so marked and is ultimately returned to the drawer along with his monthly statement; if the check is dishonored, a slip setting forth the reason is attached to it and goes with it back through banking channels to the payee.

There is no holder in due course (except perhaps the payee himself) of such a check since, even though such other requirements as good faith and lack of notice may be met, the bank would not have given value for the check. Any dispute between drawer and payee will, therefore, simply be between themselves, with no one else in a position to assert special rights.

Let us now modify the case of a relatively poor buyer purchasing a refrigerator on installments, and substitute a middle-class consumer paying for it with his personal check. If the refrigerator fails to work properly, if its defect is immediately apparent, if the buyer's attempts to get redress from the seller prove unavailing, and if the buyer moves with sufficient alacrity, he can often stop payment on his check before it has cleared through his own bank. The buyer and seller will then be in a position themselves to resolve their dispute on the merits, with the buyer having the tactical advantage that the seller will have to bring suit in order to collect if the matter cannot be resolved without litigation.

Suppose, however, the bank in which the seller-payee deposits the check allows him to draw against it before it has been collected. This is not standard practice, but it does occur with some frequency. When the check is presented to the drawee bank for payment, it is dishonored because of the stop payment order. This time, however, the depositary bank is given the status of holder in due course "to the extent to which credit for the item has been withdrawn or applied," or "if it makes an advance on or against the item." To this extent, the drawer cannot assert against the bank the defense that the sale of the refrigerator was fraudulent. Although the stop payment order is effective, its utility to the drawer is defeated, since he is liable to the depositary bank.

* * *

If the depositary bank were to grant credit to the payee by allowing withdrawals before collection, and if it were to do this in reliance upon its knowledge of the *drawer's* financial standing or reputation, there might be good reason to protect the depositary bank in this fashion. Typically, however the depositary bank pays no attention to the identity of the drawer; in fact, it does not even know whether the drawer's signature is genuine. It will often allow or refuse to allow withdrawals against the check before collection solely on the basis of its relations with and knowledge of the creditworthiness of its own customer, the payee. If payment is stopped, and the depositary bank cannot recover its advances by charging the amount back against the payee's account, but is permitted to hold the drawer liable, the bank receives a windfall: in such cases, it picks up the liability of the drawer, which by hypothesis it had not counted upon when it made its decision to allow withdrawals before collection.

The fact that the depositary bank would not normally be relying upon the drawer's credit may be seen in the improbable combination of circumstances that have to coincide for the drawer's liability to matter. First, the bank's customer, the payee, must have allowed his account to drop to the point at which some of his withdrawals cannot be charged against other funds in the account but must be regarded as advances against the uncollected check. Second, the payee must be insolvent, or at least his assets must not be readily amenable to collection. Third, the drawer has to be solvent and available, and his signature genuine. Fourth, the check must be dishonored. Finally, for the doctrine to make any ultimate difference, the drawer must have a legitimate defense on the check that is good against the payee, but is not of a type that can be asserted against a holder in due course. Only if all of these elements coincide is the bank's position improved by virtue of its becoming a holder in due course. It must therefore be a rare case indeed in which the bank's decision to extend credit before the check is collected can be regarded as having been made in reliance upon its ability to cut off the defenses of the drawer. Neither banks specifically, nor commerce in general, seem to need the rule declaring the bank to be a holder in due course. Where the bank relies entirely on the identity and credit of the payee in allowing withdrawals, it should shock no one's conscience if the bank were limited to the payee as a source of reimbursement.

* * *

c. ARTICLE 9 SECURITY INTEREST AS VALUE

Those who have studied Article 9 know that much asset-based financing in which the collateral consists of inventory, accounts and their proceeds, which may include negotiable instruments, is done on what is called a "floating lien" basis. That is, a lender takes a security interest in all the debtor's personal property, now owned or thereafter acquired, to secure all present and future obligations of the debtor. As soon as the debtor acquires an item of collateral, the lender's security interest automatically attaches to it as security for the outstanding loan balance. In the following case, Bank had a floating lien on Bowl–Mor's assets and their proceeds. The SBA check was proceeds of Bowl–Mor's chattel paper collateral, and as soon as Bowl–Mor acquired the check, Bank's security interest attached. See footnote 1. Can it be that Bank's Article 9 security interest, which first attached when the check was in the possession of Bowl–Mor, is value within the meaning of 4–211 even though it does not comply with 4–210? See 3–303(a). If so, banks having Article 9 floating liens could become holders in due course of checks the instant they take possession on deposit because their security interest attached to the checks even before deposit. *Bowling Green* was the first authoritative holding on this issue.

Bowling Green, Inc. v. State Street Bank & Trust Co.

United States Court of Appeals, First Circuit, 1970.
425 F.2d 81.

■ COFFIN, CIRCUIT JUDGE.

On September 26, 1966, plaintiff Bowling Green, Inc., the operator of a bowling alley, negotiated a United States government check for $15,306 to Bowl–Mor, Inc., a manufacturer of bowling alley equipment. The check, which plaintiff had acquired through a Small Business Administration loan, represented the first installment on a conditional sales contract for the purchase of candlepin setting machines. On the following day, September 27, a representative of Bowl–Mor deposited the check in defendant State Street Bank and Trust Co. The Bank immediately credited $5,024.85 of the check against an overdraft in Bowl–Mor's account. Later that day, when the Bank learned that Bowl–Mor had filed a petition for reorganization under Chapter X of the Bankruptcy Act, it transferred $233.61 of Bowl–Mor's funds to another account and applied the remaining $10,047.54 against debts which Bowl–Mor owed the Bank. Shortly thereafter Bowl–Mor's petition for reorganization was dismissed and the firm was adjudicated a bankrupt. Plaintiff has never received the pin-setting machines for which it contracted. Its part payment remains in the hands of defendant Bank.

Plaintiff brought this diversity action to recover its payment from defendant Bank on the grounds that the Bank is constructive trustee of the funds deposited by Bowl–Mor. In the court below, plaintiff argued that Bowl–Mor knew it could not perform at the time it accepted payment, that the Bank was aware of this fraudulent conduct, and that the Bank therefore received Bowl–Mor's deposit impressed with a constructive trust in plaintiff's favor. The district court rejected plaintiff's view of the evidence, concluding instead that the Bank was a holder in due course * * * and was therefore entitled to take the item in question free of all personal defenses. Bowling Green, Inc., etc. v. State Street Bank and Trust Co., 307 F.Supp. 648 (D.Mass.1969).

* * *

Plaintiff's first objection arises from a technical failure of proof. The district court found that plaintiff had endorsed the item in question to Bowl–Mor, but there was no evidence that Bowl–Mor supplied its own endorsement before depositing the item in the Bank. Thus, we cannot tell whether the Bank is a holder within the meaning of § 1–201(20), which defines holder as one who takes an instrument endorsed to him, or to bearer, or in blank. But, argues plaintiff, once it is shown that a defense to an instrument exists, the Bank has the burden of showing that it is in all respects a holder in due course. This failure of proof, in plaintiff's eyes, is fatal to the Bank's case.

We readily agree with plaintiff that the Bank has the burden of establishing its status in all respects. UCC § 3–307(3), on which plaintiff relies to establish the defendant's burden, seems addressed primarily to cases in which a holder seeks to enforce an instrument, but Massachusetts courts have indicated that the policy of § 3–307(3) applies whenever a party invokes the rights of a holder in due course either offensively or defensively. Cf. Elbar Realty Inc. v. City Bank & Trust Co., 342 Mass. 262, 267–268, 173 N.E.2d 256 (1961). The issue, however, is not whether the Bank bears the burden of proof, but whether it must establish that it took the item in question by endorsement in order to meet its burden. We think not. The evidence in this case indicates that the Bank's transferor, Bowl–Mor, was a holder. Under UCC § 3–201(a), transfer of an instrument vests in the transferee all the rights of the transferor. As the Official Comment to § 3–201 indicates, one who is not a holder must first establish the transaction by which he acquired the instrument before enforcing it, but the Bank has met this burden here.

We doubt, moreover, whether the concept of "holder" as defined in § 1–201(20) applies with full force to Article 4. Article 4 establishes a comprehensive scheme for simplifying and expediting bank collections. Its provisions govern the more general rules of Article 3 wherever inconsistent. UCC § 4–102(1). As part of this expediting process, Article 4 recognizes the common bank practice of accepting unendorsed checks for deposit. * * * § 4–201(1) provides that the lack of an endorsement shall not affect the bank's status as agent for collection, and § 4–205(1) authorizes the collecting bank to supply the missing endorsements as a matter of course. In practice, banks comply with § 4–205 by stamping the item "deposited to the account of the named payee" or some similar formula. * * * We doubt whether the bank's status should turn on proof of whether a clerk employed the appropriate stamp, and we hesitate to penalize a bank which accepted unendorsed checks for deposit in reliance on the Code, at least when, as here, the customer himself clearly satisfies the definition of "holder". Section 4–209 does provide that a bank must comply "with the requirements of section 3–302 on what constitutes a holder in due course," but we think this language refers to the enumerated requirements of good faith and lack of notice rather than to the status of holder, a status which § 3–302 assumes rather than requires. We therefore hold that a bank which takes an item for collection from a customer who was himself a holder need not establish that it took the item by negotiation in order to satisfy § 4–209.

* * *

This brings us to plaintiff's final argument, that the Bank gave value only to the extent of the $5,024.85 overdraft, and thus cannot be a holder in due course with respect to the remaining $10,047.54 which the Bank credited against Bowl–Mor's loan account. Our consideration of this argument is confined by the narrow scope of the district court's findings. The

Bank may well have given value under § 4–208(1)(a) when it credited the balance of Bowl–Mor's checking account against its outstanding indebtedness. See Banco Espanol de Credito v. State Street Bank & Trust Co., 409 F.2d 711 (1st Cir.1969). But by that time the Bank knew of Bowl–Mor's petition for reorganization, additional information which the district court did not consider in finding that the Bank acted in good faith and without notice at the time it received the item. We must therefore decide whether the Bank gave value for the additional $10,047.54 at the time the item was deposited.

Resolution of this issue depends on the proper interpretation of § 4–209, which provides that a collecting bank has given value to the extent that it has acquired a "security interest" in an item. In plaintiff's view, a collecting bank can satisfy § 4–209 only by extending credit against an item in compliance with § 4–208(1). The district court, on the other hand, adopted the view that a security interest is a security interest, however acquired. The court then found that defendant and Bowl–Mor had entered a security agreement which gave defendant a floating lien on Bowl–Mor's chattel paper. Since the item in question was part of the proceeds of a Bowl–Mor contract, the court concluded that defendant had given value for the full $15,306.00 at the time it received the deposit.[1]

With this conclusion we agree. Section 1–201(37) defines "security interest" as an interest in personal property which secures payment or performance of an obligation. There is no indication in § 4–209 that the term is used in a more narrow or specialized sense. Moreover, as the official comment to § 4–209 observes, this provision is in accord with prior law and with § 3–303, both of which provide that a holder gives value when he accepts an instrument as security for an antecedent debt. Reynolds v. Park Trust Co., 245 Mass. 440, 444–445, 139 N.E. 785 (1923). Finally, we note that if one of the Bank's prior loans to Bowl–Mor had been made in the expectation that this particular instrument would be deposited, the terms of § 4–208(1)(c) would have been literally satisfied. We do not think the case is significantly different when the Bank advances credit on the strength of a continuing flow of items of this kind. We therefore conclude that the Bank gave value for the full $15,306.00 at the time it accepted the deposit.

We see no discrepancy between this result and the realities of commercial life. Each party, of course, chose to do business with an eventually irresponsible third party. The Bank, though perhaps unwise in prolonging its hopes for a prospering customer, nevertheless protected itself through security arrangements as far as possible without hobbling each deposit and

---

1. [Ed]s. The bank secured its loan to Bowl–Mor by a security interest in Bowl–Mor's installment sale contracts (defined as chattel paper by § 9–105(1)(b)). Its security interest applied not only to the chattel paper but also to any proceeds of the chattel paper. § 9–306. Bowling Green's check to Bowl–Mor, since it was in payment of the first installment of its sales contract, was proceeds. Under § 9–306 and § 9–203 the bank automatically obtained a security interest in this check as soon as Bowl–Mor obtained "rights" in the check, which in this case was when Bowl–Mor received the check.]

withdrawal. Plaintiff, on the other hand, not only placed its initial faith in Bowl–Mor, but later became aware that Bowl–Mor was having difficulties in meeting its payroll. It seems not too unjust that this vestige of caveat emptor survives.

Affirmed.

NOTES

1. The conclusion in *Bowling Green* that a depositary bank could become a holder in due course of a check which did not bear the indorsement of the depositor was very controversial and was not supported by the text of Article 3 and Article 4 then in effect. Some courts refused to follow *Bowling Green*. But Revised Article 4 follows *Bowling Green* in this regard. Section 4–205 states that a depositary bank receiving a check for collection becomes a holder when it receives the check if the customer was then a holder regardless of whether the check is indorsed by the customer. It goes on to state that the bank becomes a holder in due course if it satisfies the other requirements of 3–302.

2. Acquisition of a lien by a depositary bank does not depend upon the bank's making any accounting entries to "apply" the check to the outstanding debt. See Maryland Casualty Co. v. National Bank of Germantown & Trust Co., 320 Pa. 129, 182 A. 362 (1936). By contrast 4–210(a)(1) states that the bank gets a security interest in the deposited check at the time that credit given for it is "applied." In *Bowling Green* the court indicates that this refers to the time when Bowl–Mor's deposit account, which had been credited with the amount of the check, was charged $10,047.54 in reduction of the loan. Suppose a check payable to Customer was indorsed by Customer to Depositary Bank and delivered to one of its officers in reply to a demand by Depositary Bank to immediately cover an overdraft. Thereafter, but before the check was deposited to Customer's account, the drawer of the check told the officer handling the transaction that the check was issued without consideration. At what time was "credit given for the item * * * applied"? 4–210(a)(1). At what time did Depositary Bank take the instrument "as payment of, or as security for, an antecedent claim"? 3–303(a)(3). At what time did Depositary Bank acquire a "lien in the instrument other than a lien obtained by judicial proceeding"? 3–303(a)(2). Peoria Savings & Loan Association v. Jefferson Trust & Savings Bank of Peoria, 81 Ill.2d 461, 43 Ill.Dec. 712, 410 N.E.2d 845 (1980).

FORM. PROMISSORY NOTE–FIXED MATURITY

 **CITY NATIONAL BANK**

PROMISSORY NOTE - FIXED MATURITY

(INTEREST FIXED)

For value received, the undersigned, * ("Borrower"), promises to pay to the order of City National Bank, a national banking association ("CNB"), at its office in this city, in lawful money of the United States of America and in immediately available funds, the principal sum of * Dollars ($*), with interest thereon from the date of disbursement at the rate of * percent (*%) per year (computed on the basis of a 360–day year, actual days elapsed).

Interest accrued on this Note shall be payable on the * day of each *, commencing *, *. The minimum interest charge for the term of this Note shall in no event be less than One Hundred Dollars ($100.00).

Principal and any interest remaining unpaid shall be payable in full on *, *.

The occurrence of any of the following with respect to any Borrower or any guarantor of this Note or any general partner of such Borrower or guarantor, shall constitute an "Event of Default" hereunder:

1. The failure to make any payment of principal or interest when due under this Note;

2. The filing of a petition by or against any of such parties under any provisions of the *Bankruptcy Code*;

3. The appointment of a receiver or an assignee for the benefit of creditors;

4. The commencement of dissolution or liquidation proceedings or the disqualification of any such parties which is a corporation, partnership, joint venture or any other type of entity;

5. The death or incapacity of any of such parties who is an individual;

6. Any financial statement provided by any of such parties to CNB is false or misleading;

7. Any default in the payment or performance of any obligation, or any default under any provisions of any contract or instrument pursuant to which any of such parties has incurred any obligation for borrowed money, any purchase obligation or any other liability of any kind to any person or entity, including CNB;

8. Any sale or transfer of all or a substantial or material part of the assets of any of such parties other than in the ordinary course of business; or

9. Any violation, breach or default under any letter agreement, guaranty, security agreement, deed of trust or any other contract or instrument executed in connection with this Note or securing this Note.

Upon the occurrence of any Event of Default, the holder of this Note, at the holder's option, may declare all sums of principal and interest outstanding hereunder to be immediately due and payable without presentment, demand, protest or notice of dishonor all of which are expressly waived by each Borrower. Each Borrower agrees to pay all costs and expenses, including reasonable attorneys' fees, expended or incurred by the holder (or allocable to the holder's in-house counsel) in connection with the enforcement of this Note or the collection of any sums due hereunder and irrespective of whether suit is filed. Any principal or interest not paid when due hereunder shall thereafter bear additional interest from its due date at a rate of five percent (5.0%) per year higher than the interest rate as determined and computed above, and continuing thereafter until paid.

Should more than one person or entity execute this Note as a Borrower, the obligations of each such Borrower shall be joint and several.

This Note and all matters relating thereto, shall be governed by the laws of the State of California.

*, a

* corporation

BY: _____

ITS: _____

FORM. DEMAND NOTE

 CITY NATIONAL BANK   **DEMAND NOTE**
                                                 (INTEREST TIED TO PRIME)

On demand, or if no demand is made, then on *, *, for value received, the undersigned * ("Borrower"), promises to pay to the order of City National Bank, a national banking association ("CNB"), at its Office in this city, in lawful money of the United States of America and in immediately available funds, the principal sum of * Dollars ($*), plus interest thereon at a rate computed on the basis of a 360–day year, actual days elapsed, equal to the "Prime Rate" of CNB as it exists from time to time, plus * percent (*%) per year. "Prime Rate" shall mean the rate most recently announced by CNB at its principal office in Beverly Hills as its "Prime Rate." Any change in the Prime Rate shall become effective on the same business day on which the Prime Rate shall change, without prior notice to Borrower.

Interest accrued on this Note shall be payable on the * day of each *, commencing *, *. The minimum interest charge for the term of this Note shall in no event be less than One Hundred Dollars ($100.00).

In the event the interest is not paid as it becomes due, or in the event there occurs any material default in the payment or performance of any obligation owing by any Borrower to CNB, then the holder of this Note, at the holder's option, may declare all sums of principal and interest outstanding hereunder to be immediately due and payable without presentment, demand, protest or notice of dishonor all of which are expressly waived by each Borrower. If principal or interest is not paid on the agreed or accelerated date of maturity, then the interest rate provided for under this Note shall, at CNB's option, and without notice, be increased to an amount 5.0% per year higher than the interest rate as determined and computed above, effective from the day following the time that such payment of principal or interest became overdue and continuing thereafter until paid.

Each Borrower agrees to pay all costs and expenses, including reasonable attorneys' fees, expended or incurred by CNB (or allocable to CNB's in-house counsel) in connection with the enforcement of this Note or the collection of any sums due hereunder and irrespective of whether suit is filed.

Should more than one person or entity execute this Note as a Borrower, the obligations of each such Borrower shall be joint and several.

This Note and all matters relating thereto shall be governed by the laws of the State of California.

*, a

* corporation

By: ⸺

Its: ⸺

CHAPTER 2

LIABILITY OF PARTIES TO NEGOTIABLE INSTRUMENTS

A. LIABILITY OF MAKER

An understanding of the liability of the parties to negotiable instruments is essential to counseling clients in planning transactions as well at the litigation stage. The obligations of the parties are set out in four sections: the obligation of a maker in 3–412, of an acceptor in 3–413, of a drawer in 3–414, and of an indorser in 3–415.

The person primarily obliged to pay a promissory note is the maker, who has expressly agreed to do so. The relevant statutory provisions are: 3–103(a)(5), which defines "maker" as "a person who signs or is identified in a note as the person undertaking to pay;" 3–412, which states, "[t]he issuer of a note * * * is obliged to pay the instrument (i) according to its terms at the time it was issued * * *;" and 3–105(a), which defines "issue" as "the first delivery of an instrument by the maker or drawer, whether to a holder or nonholder, for the purpose of giving rights on the instrument to any person."

PROBLEM

New Movies Incorporated (NMI) produces films. It has rounded up 20 wealthy backers for a new motion picture, each of whom has agreed to contribute $1 million to the project. Now NMI wishes to obtain some bank financing before signing the talent for the film. In order to do this, NMI has persuaded all the backers to sign a single negotiable promissory note payable to NMI for $20 million that NMI can show banks and others to induce them to commit to the picture. Before production commenced, some of the backers wished to withdraw because of the economic recession. In order to keep them committed, NMI warned the backers that any signer of the note can be sued for the full amount of the note. Your client, a wealthy plastic surgeon, is one of the backers. She calls you and asks (1) whether NMI is correct is asserting that she can be sued for the full $20 million, and (2) if NMI is correct, what rights does she have against the other signers. What do you tell her (besides telling her to call you *before* she signs her name, not *after*)? See 3–412 and 3–116(a) and (b).

B. DRAWERS, DRAWEES AND ACCEPTORS

How do you answer the Problems below on the basis of the discussion in the text following these Problems? We use ordinary bank checks to illustrate the issues treated in this section.

PROBLEMS

Drawer signed and delivered a check for $1,000 to Payee in payment for goods purchased. The check was drawn on Drawee bank where Drawer maintains a deposit account.

1. When Payee presented the check to Drawee for payment, Drawee dishonored the check because Drawer had stopped payment on the check owing to its dissatisfaction with the goods delivered.

(a) Is Drawee liable on the check to Payee?

(b) Is Drawer liable on the check to Payee?

2. When Payee presented the check to Drawee for payment, Drawee dishonored the check even though no stop payment order had been received and Drawer had sufficient funds in its account to pay the check.

(a) Is Drawee liable on the check to Payee?

(b) Is Drawee liable to Drawer?

3. When Payee presented the check to Drawee for acceptance, Drawee certified the check. Later Payee presented the certified check to Drawee for payment. Drawee dishonored the check because after it had certified the check it received a stop order from Drawer.

(a) Is Drawee liable to Payee?

(b) Is Drawer liable to Payee?

4. When Payee presented the check to Drawee for acceptance, Drawee refused to certify the check, even though Drawer had sufficient funds in its account to cover the check. Is Drawee liable to Payee if Payee can show that when it presented the check to Drawee for payment ten days later, the check was dishonored because there were no longer funds in the account to pay the check?

When a drawer orders a drawee to pay an amount of money to the payee, nobody has expressly agreed to make the payment. A draft normally arises out of a pre-existing creditor-debtor relationship between the drawer and the drawee. For example, a seller ships goods to a buyer who is located in a distant market. The contract of sale provides for payment of the price of the goods by a draft drawn by the seller on the buyer or the buyer's bank acting on behalf of the buyer. The seller draws a draft ordering the drawee to pay to the order of a named payee a sum of money equal to the price of the goods. The named payee may be the seller's bank which buys the draft from the seller for the face amount less a discount to compensate the bank for its services. In that case, the draft is delivered to the bank, which then becomes its holder. The draft is then "presented" to the drawee for payment. "Presentment" is defined in 3–501(a). In this case, presentment is simply a demand made on the drawee to pay. Subsection (b) of 3–501 states rules regarding the place, time, and manner of presentment. In our example, presentment might be made by the bank named as payee of the draft, but often the draft will be negotiated to another bank located near the buyer and that bank will present the draft to the drawee for payment. When the draft is paid the buyer has discharged the obligation to the seller to pay the price of the goods.

The most common example of a draft is the ordinary check which is a draft drawn on a bank and payable on demand. 3–104(f). Payment of checks is also normally based on a creditor-debtor relationship. A check is drawn by a customer of a bank who has a checking account in the bank; the credit balance in the account represents a debt of the bank to the customer. When the bank pays the check, the bank's debt to the customer is reduced by the amount of the check.

Since the drawee of a draft has made no promise in the instrument to pay the payee or other holder, the holder has no action on the instrument against the drawee to enforce payment. 3–408. Sometimes the drawee will obligate itself, by a letter of credit or other separate contract, to pay a draft. In that case failure by the drawee to pay the draft may result in liability to the holder for breach of the letter of credit, but there is no liability based on an obligation created by the draft. In the absence of a separate contract of the drawee such as a letter of credit, payment by the drawee will normally depend upon the drawee's obligation to the drawer arising from an express or implied contract between them. For example, in opening a checking account for a customer, the bank incurs an obligation to the customer to pay properly payable checks drawn on the account. Failure to pay a properly payable check may result in liability to the customer for wrongful dishonor (4–402), but the holder of the check has no cause of action against the drawee bank. Before codification of negotiable instruments law by the NIL in the late 19th century, a minority of states took the view that a check created a direct liability on the part of the drawee bank to the holder. The theory was that a check amounted to an equitable assignment of the drawer's funds on deposit, but NIL § 189 took the majority view that the check is not itself an assignment. Article 3 follows the NIL in that respect.

Although a draft, by its stated terms, is simply an order of the drawer to the drawee to pay, it is also an obligation of the drawer to pay the draft if the draft is dishonored. 3–414(b). "Dishonor" occurs if the drawee fails to make timely payment when the draft is presented for payment. Dishonor of ordinary checks and drafts is defined in 3–502(b) and (e). The drawer of a draft other than a check can avoid liability under 3–414(b) if the signature of the drawer is accompanied by words that disclaim liability such as "without recourse." 3–414(e). Disclaimer of the drawer's liability is normally limited to documentary drafts. Comment 5 to 3–414. With respect to checks, disclaimer is not effective. 3–414(e). A relatively unimportant limitation on drawer's liability is provided by 3–414(f). This provision is explained in Comment 6 to 3–414.

Section 3–408 states that "the drawee is not liable on the instrument until the drawee accepts it." Section 3–409(a) defines "acceptance" as "the drawee's signed agreement to pay a draft as presented." The acceptance "must be written on the draft and may consist of the drawee's signature alone." A drawee that accepts a draft is known as the "acceptor" and is obliged to the holder to pay the draft. 3–413(a). To understand the concept of acceptance better, it is appropriate to distinguish between two types of drafts. The most common type of draft is the demand draft or "sight draft." It contemplates that the amount of the draft will be paid by the drawee upon presentation or "on sight." A draft that does not specify a time of payment is payable on demand. 3–108(a). A check is the most common example of a demand draft. Another type of draft, called a "time draft" does not contemplate immediate payment by the drawee. For example, suppose the draft reads as follows: "Pay $1,000 to the order of Jane Doe sixty days after presentment of this draft." Here, two steps are contemplated. Jane Doe, or some subsequent holder, will initially present the draft to the drawee to start the running of the 60 days, and when that period of time has passed a second presentment will be made for payment. The first presentment is known as a "presentment for acceptance." Its purpose is to allow the holder to know whether the drawee is agreeable to honoring the draft. Agreement of the drawee is manifested by acceptance, i.e., the drawee's signing of the draft with or without the addition of the word "accepted" or other words indicating an intention to accept. The date of acceptance is normally included but is not required. 3–409(a) and (c). The drawee's acceptance is equivalent to a promise to pay the amount of the draft to the holder. Thus, the obligation of an acceptor is like that of the maker of a note.

Another example of an accepted draft is the certified check. If the payee of an ordinary check wants assurance of payment, one way of getting it is to insist that the drawer obtain the acceptance of the drawee bank before the check is taken by the payee. This is done by the drawee bank's signing the check in much the same way as described in the case of a time draft. But the terminology differs. The bank's signature is called "certification" but it is identical to acceptance. 3–409(d). Certification is normally obtained by the drawer before delivery of the check to the payee, but in unusual cases the holder of an uncertified check may prefer to obtain the drawee bank's agreement to pay rather than payment itself. This can be done by asking the drawee bank to certify the check. The drawee of a check may certify it as a courtesy to the drawer or to the holder, but is not obliged to do so. Nor is refusal to certify a dishonor of the check. 3–409(d). Because certification of a check is treated by the bank as the equivalent of payment insofar as the drawer is concerned, the account of the drawer will

It allows the holder to know whether drawee will honor the draft.

When drawee has accepted the check — he will honor it. A certified check is an accepted draft — the bank will pay it. The bank's signature is a certification.

be debited in the amount of the check at the time of certification. The effect of certification is to transform the check, which originally represented an order to pay of the drawer, into a promise of the drawee to pay the amount of the check to its holder. This transformation is reflected in 3–414(c), which states that acceptance of a draft by a bank discharges the drawer's obligation to pay the draft.

PROBLEM

Seller contracted to sell real property to Buyer for $150,000 cash to be paid on the settlement date by a certified check. Buyer arrived at the settlement with an uncertified check drawn on her funds in Drawee Bank. When Seller refused to take the check, Buyer induced Seller to call Drawee Bank and inquire about the balance of her account. An authorized person at the bank assured Seller that there were funds in the account sufficient to cover the check. "But," Seller countered, "will there be funds there when the check is presented?" The bank representative replied in the affirmative, and when asked to confirm this in writing, sent an immediate fax to Seller stating: "This letter is to verify that the funds are available in Buyer's account. There is a hold on the funds for the check that was given you." When Seller presented the check for payment, Drawee Bank dishonored on the ground of insufficient funds in the account. The bank representative had mistakenly misstated the balance of the account. Is Drawee Bank liable to Seller on the check? The facts are based on those in Harrington v. MacNab, 163 F.Supp.2d 583 (D.Md. 2001).

C. LIABILITY OF INDORSER

In the previous chapter, we examined the function of an indorsement in the negotiation of an instrument. Indorsement also has the additional function of causing the indorser to incur liability on the instrument. The obligation of the indorser, stated in 3–415(a), is to pay the instrument if the instrument is dishonored, but indorser's liability may be avoided by appropriate words accompanying the signature that disclaim liability. The most commonly used words indicating disclaimer are "without recourse." 3–415(b). An indorsement containing such language is called a "qualified indorsement." As we see in Problem 2 below, indorser's liability can be an unpleasant surprise to holders who believe that they are indorsing merely to transfer the instrument.

Indorsement has the function of causing the indorser to incur liability on instrument.

3-415(a) — indorser must pay the instrument if instrument is dishonored, but liability may be avoided if there is a disclaimer — (without recourse).

PROBLEMS

1. Employer sent Peter his paycheck in the amount of $5,000, drawn on Bank One. Peter indorsed the check in blank and deposited it in his depositary bank, Bank Two. Bank Two gave Peter immediate credit for the check in his account, and Peter withdrew the amount of the credit before Bank Two learned that Bank One had dishonored the check because

Problem — Employer gave Peter $5K on Bank One check. He deposit and withdrew $5K. Bank Two gave him credit.

Employer → Peter → Bank Two (depositor bank)

Bank One ← ↓

dishonored

Employer had previously withdrawn all the money from the account. Employer went out of business, costing Peter his job, and several months later an impecunious Peter heard from Bank Two that it wanted $5,000 from him, long after Peter had closed his account in that bank. (i) If Bank Two chooses not to proceed against insolvent Employer on the check, is Peter personally liable to Bank Two for $5,000? (ii) If Peter has to pay, may he enforce the check against Employer? 3–414(b).

2. Seller sold residential real property to Buyer for the price of $100,000. Buyer was able to borrow $75,000 from a bank, secured by a first mortgage on the property. But Buyer didn't have enough cash to come up with the remaining $25,000. In order to make the sale, Seller agreed to take a second mortgage on the property from Buyer that secured a negotiable promissory note, payable in installments over ten years, in the amount of $20,000 made by Buyer to Seller. Buyer paid Seller the remaining $5,000 balance in cash. In State A, where the land was located, there is a secondary market for second mortgage notes, and Investor was willing to pay Seller $15,000 in cash for the note. Seller indorsed in blank the note to Investor and assigned the mortgage. Buyer defaulted on the payments on the $20,000 note, but under State A's real property anti-deficiency law Buyer is not personally liable on a purchase money note. Thus, Investor had no right to sue Buyer on the note, so it brought suit against Seller as an indorser. Is Seller liable to Investor on the note even though the maker, Buyer, was not liable? Had Seller talked to you before indorsing the note, what advice would you have given him? See 3–415(b).

Drafts

The obligation of the indorser to pay an instrument arises upon its dishonor. With respect to unaccepted drafts, dishonor usually requires presentment for payment and a failure of the drawee to pay. 3–502(b)(1) through (3). With respect to some time drafts, dishonor requires presentment for acceptance and failure of the drawee to accept. 3–502(b)(4). In some cases, dishonor can occur without presentment. 3–502(e) and 3–504(a).

The obligation of an indorser of an unaccepted draft is subject to discharge in two situations. First, if the draft is a check and collection of the check is not initiated within 30 days of the indorsement, the indorser is discharged. 3–415(e). Second, discharge can occur as the result of a failure to give timely notice of dishonor to the indorser. 3–415(c) and 3–503(a). The manner and time for giving notice are stated in 3–503(b) and (c). Notice of dishonor need not be given if it is excused. 3–504(b). Delay in giving notice may also be excused in some cases. 3–504(c).

Indorser's liability with respect to checks has very limited importance because most checks are deposited by the payee with a depositary bank for collection. The depositary bank gives the depositor provisional credit for the check. Under 4–214(a), if the check is dishonored, the depositary bank

---

Handwritten margin notes (left):

Bank one actually dishonored b/c Employer had withdrawn all the money from the account. Employer went out of business. Bank Two wanted $5k from Peter.

(i) Peter is not liable. Although the check was dishonored (3–502) and indorser (Peter) deposited check w/in 30 day to Bank (3–415) no notice of dishonor was given. 3–503(a). Peter heard from bank, not within 30 days, but several months later.

(b) Yes, 3–414(b) the obligation is owed to the indorser who paid the draft.

2. Seller sold property to Buyer. It was worth $100K. Buyer came up with $75K. Buyer still owed other $25K. A promissory note for $20K (he pd $5K already) was made by Buyer to Seller. Investor bought note from Seller for $15K. Seller indorsed the note. Buyer failed to pay. Investor brought suit against Seller.

Handwritten notes (bottom):

Seller as indorser is not liable b/c no dishonor was given. Notice was not given to Seller or return of the non-pd drafts was not given.

§ 84 The obligation of an indorser can be discharged if:
1) The draft is a check and collection of the check is not initiated w/in 30 days of the indorsement (3-415(c)
And 2) there is a failure to give timely notice of dishonor to indorser.

CHAPTER 2   LIABILITY OF PARTIES TO NEGOTIABLE INSTRUMENTS   87 ~~3-45~~

3-415(c)
3-503(a)

may revoke the credit or otherwise obtain refund from the depositor. Normally, the depositary bank will use this remedy rather than the remedy provided by 3–415(a).

Also, if a draft is accepted by a bank after the draft is indorsed, the indorser is discharged. 3-415(d)

If a draft is accepted by a bank after the draft is indorsed, the indorser is discharged. 3–415(d). The rule is similar to 3–414(c) with respect to the liability of a drawer. Thus, with respect to an accepted draft, an indorser has liability under 3–415(a) only if the indorsement is made after the acceptance or if the acceptor is not a bank. Rules with respect to dishonor of accepted drafts are stated in 3–502(d).

Notes

Dishonor of a note payable at a definite time does not normally require presentment unless the note is payable at or through a bank. 3–502(a)(2) and (3). In the case of notes that do not require presentment, indorser's liability under 3–415(a) arises automatically if the note is not paid when due. If a note is payable on demand, is payable at or through a bank, or the terms of the note require presentment, dishonor requires presentment and a failure to pay by the maker. But the requirements in 3–502(a) with respect to presentment can be waived. 3–504(a). Notice of dishonor required by 3–503(a) also can be waived, and waiver of presentment is also waiver of notice of dishonor. 3–504(b). Since most promissory note forms contain a clause waiving presentment and notice of dishonor, these formalities have little importance with respect to indorser liability in note cases. See the Promissory Note and Demand Note forms at the end of Chapter 11.

D.   LIABILITY OF TRANSFEROR

Work the following Problem on the basis of the discussion in the text following the Problem.

Maker   note for $1K→   Payee   →   Holder
         ←(indorsed w/o recourse)
         wants maker to pay.

First, Holder cannot sue payee or hold him obligated as an indorser b/c he indorsed w/o recourse. But, he may sue under implied warranties 3-416(a)(4) – he can sue for breach of warranty that the right to enforce is not subject to any claims as stated against transferor.

PROBLEM

Maker signed and delivered a promissory note for $1,000 payable to the order of Payee one year after date. Shortly after receiving the note, Payee, who had fraudulently induced Maker to issue the note, indorsed the note "without recourse" and sold it to Holder for $600. When Holder presented the note to Maker for payment, Maker refused to pay because she had learned that Payee had defrauded her. Does Holder have rights against Payee? See 3–415(b) and 3–416(a)(4). Comment 5 to 3–416.

In this case a claim of fraud is asserted.

For sales of goods, the law gives the buyer the benefit of certain warranties of the seller that implied in the sale, unless they are disclosed by the contract.

If goods are sold, the law gives to the buyer the benefit of certain warranties of the seller that are implied by reason of the sale and which apply unless they are disclaimed in the contract between the parties. For example, the seller warrants that the buyer is receiving good title to the

For example, the seller may warrant that buyer is receiving good title to the goods.

goods and, if the seller is a merchant, that the goods are fit for the ordinary purposes for which such goods are used. 2–312(1) and 2–314. If an instrument is sold the law gives to the buyer the benefit of implied warranties that are comparable to sale of goods warranties, but which are expressed in terms appropriate to what the buyer is buying—a right to receive payment from the person obliged to pay the instrument. These warranties are known as "transfer warranties" and are stated in 3–416(a).

Two of the transfer warranties relate to the authenticity of the instrument; the transferor warrants that all signatures are authentic and authorized, and the instrument has not been altered. 3–416(a)(2) and (3). The other three warranties relate to the enforceability of the instrument. Under 3–416(a)(1) there is a warranty that the transferor is a person entitled to enforce the instrument. If the transferor is a person entitled to enforce the instrument, transfer will give the transferee that right. 3–203(b). The 3–416(a)(1) warranty, in practice, serves as a warranty that there are no unauthorized or missing indorsements that prevent the transferor from giving to the transferee the right to enforce the instrument. Under 3–416(a)(4) there is a warranty that the right to enforce the instrument is not subject to defenses that can be asserted against the transferor. Finally, there is a warranty of no knowledge of bankruptcy or other insolvency proceedings initiated against the person obliged to pay the instrument. 3–416(a)(5).

The transfer warranties are of very limited importance because in most cases the transferor is also an indorser and, as such, guarantees payment of the instrument. 3–415(a). In those cases the transfer warranties are redundant because the guarantee of payment gives greater rights to the transferee than do the warranties. Thus, the transfer warranties are important only in cases in which the transfer is made without indorsement or there is an indorsement without recourse. If the payee of a note indorsed the note without recourse, the transferee is assured of receiving an authentic and enforceable instrument but takes the risk that the maker will be unwilling or unable to pay the note.

E. CASHIER'S CHECKS AND TELLER'S CHECKS

In this section we give detailed treatment to the rights of parties under cashier's checks and teller's checks. Our objective is to help you deal with one of the contemporary dilemmas facing business lawyers: how to take payment when the deal closes. Since the obligor side is not likely to lug sacks of money to the closing, the obligee should obtain agreement in advance on how payment is to be made. The ordinary uncertificated check leaves the payee vulnerable on several grounds: the drawer may stop payment on the check, thereby placing the burden on the payee to come after the drawer for payment; the drawer may have no money in its account in the bank; or, in rare cases, the bank on which payment is drawn may suspend payments before the check is paid because of insolvency, leaving the payee with a claim against the bank not covered by deposit

[Handwritten marginalia left column:]

If an instrument is sold the law gives to the buyer the benefit of implied warranties the right to receive payment from the person obliged to pay the instrument. Known as transfer warranties. 3–416(a).

Warranties:
① Warranty that all signatures are authentic and authorized and instrument has not been altered. 3–416(a)(2) + (3).
② 3–416(a)(1) – warranty that the transferor is a person entitled to enforce the instrument. Transferee will have same right.
③ 3–416(a)(1) – warranty that there are no unauthorized or missing indorsements that prevent transferor from giving the right to enforce.
④ 3–416(a)(4) – warranty that the right to enforce the instrument is not subject to defenses that can be asserted against first transferor.
⑤ 3–416(a)(5) – warranty of no knowledge of bankruptcy or insolvency.

In most cases the transferor is also an indorser who has to pay under 3–415(a).

[Handwritten marginalia bottom:]
The transfer warranties are important only in cases in which the transfer is made w/o indorsement or there is an indorsement w/o recourse.

The ordinary uncertified check leaves the payee vulnerable. 1) The drawer may stop payment on the check, thereby placing the burden on the payee to come after the drawer for payment. (And drawer may have no money in its account.

CHAPTER 2 LIABILITY OF PARTIES TO NEGOTIABLE INSTRUMENTS **89**

insurance because the bank has no liability on the check (3–408) and therefore the payee has no "deposit" insured by the Federal Deposit Insurance Act. 12 U.S.C. § 1813(*l*) ("deposit"). On the other hand, we will see that no one can stop payment under 4–403 on a cashier's check; the payee can be sure that a cashier's check will not be returned marked "not sufficient funds;" and, even if the bank fails, the holder of the check is protected, at least to the extent of $100,000, by federal deposit insurance. 12 U.S.C. § 1813(*l*)(4). So why is it that in some cases even when the parties are across the street from each other, the obligee will insist on a wire transfer, which we will study in a later chapter, instead of a cashier's check? But first we have more to learn about cashier's checks.

With a cashier's check the payee can usually be assured of payment. There will usually be funds.

1. USE IN PAYMENT OF OBLIGATIONS

In some transactions a creditor is unwilling to take the personal check of the debtor in payment of the obligation owed to the creditor. Instead, the creditor may insist on delivery by the debtor of the obligation of a bank as payment. The debtor can comply by delivering a cashier's check, a teller's check, or a check of the debtor that has been certified by the drawee. We have already discussed the certified check. Some banks have discontinued the practice of certifying checks. Cashier's checks and teller's checks have become the principal means of allowing a debtor to pay a debt with a bank obligation.

Sometimes a creditor will not take a personal check in payment of a debt. They instead require a certified check, cashier's check or teller's check.

A cashier's check is a rather strange instrument. It is always issued by a bank and is in the form of an ordinary check, except that the drawer and the drawee are the same bank. Thus, Bank A orders itself to pay a sum of money to the payee stated in the instrument. One can justly argue that an order to oneself to pay money is fundamentally different from an order by one person to another person to pay money. The liability of the "issuer" (3–105(c)) of a cashier's check is not stated in 3–414(b), which applies to drawers of drafts (3–414(a), but in 3–412, and is identical to the obligation of the maker of a note. However, 3–104(f) follows the universal banking practice of referring to a cashier's check as a check. This practice is also reflected in legislation other than Articles 3 and 4. Section 3–103(a)(6) defines "order" as a "written instruction to pay money" and artificially states that the "instruction may be addressed to any person, including the person giving the instruction." Thus, a cashier's check is an order and, under 3–104(e) and (f), is a draft and a check. The purpose of the artificiality in the definition of "order" was to allow references to drafts and checks in Article 3 to include cashier's checks.

This is paying a debt with a bank as the obligor.

Cashier's check — check issued by bank, except the drawer and drawee are the same bank. (The liability of the issuer is identical to the obligation of the maker of a note.)

A cashier's check is an order and under 3–104(e) d(f) is a draft and a check.

A teller's check, like a cashier's check, is always issued by a bank. The difference between the two is that a cashier's check is drawn on the issuing bank while a teller's check typically is drawn on another bank. In some cases a teller's check is drawn on a nonbank but is payable at or through a bank. 3–104(h). A typical use of teller's checks is the practice of credit unions or small banks of maintaining deposits in regional or city banks from which to make payments. The issuer of a teller's check is obliged to pay the check as drawer of the check. 3–414(b). If a teller's check is issued

Teller's check — issued by a bank. A cashier's check is drawn on the issuing bank while a teller's check is typically drawn on another bank. Usually used by credit unions. The issuer of the teller's check is obliged to pay the check as drawer of the check.

by Bank A and the check is drawn on Bank B, presentment for payment of the check is made to Bank B, the drawee. As in the case of the drawee of an ordinary check, Bank B as drawee of a teller's check has no obligation to the payee to pay the check. 3–408. If the check is dishonored, the remedy of the payee is against Bank A. Thus, a teller's check represents an obligation of the bank that issues the check, not of the bank on which it is drawn.

One of the aspects in which cashier's checks differ from ordinary checks is the effect of taking a check on the underlying obligation for which the check was given. Section 3–310(b)(1) provides that if an uncertified check is taken for an obligation, the obligation is suspended "until dishonor of the check or until it is paid or certified." If the check clears, the obligation is discharged; if it is dishonored, the payee has a choice whether to take action against the drawer on the check or on the underlying obligation. Usually, there is no advantage to the payee in being able to pursue the drawer on the underlying transaction, but in a few instances there may be. However, if the obligee takes a cashier's check for an obligation, the obligation is discharged (3–310(a)) and the payee is restricted to its rights on the check against the issuing bank. As we explained above, if the bank has failed, the holder is insured by federal deposit insurance to the extent of $100,000.

PROBLEM

Seller contracted to sell goods to Buyer with payment by cashier's check to be made at the time of delivery. Buyer purchased a cashier's check in the amount of $10,000 from Bank made payable to Seller. Bank delivered the check to Buyer who held it pending Seller's performance. Before delivering the cashier's check to Seller, Buyer learned that Seller did not intend to comply with the contract. Buyer asked Bank to return the money that it paid to Bank to issue the check, but Bank delayed in doing so. Is Buyer, the remitter, a person entitled to enforce the instrument under 3–301? The prevailing view in case law is that since a remitter is not a party to an instrument it cannot enforce the instrument under 3–301. The authorities are marshaled in Perrino v. Salem, Inc., 243 B.R. 550 (D. Me. 1999), which states that although Article 3 does not directly address the issue in the text, Comment 1 to 3–312 expressly says that a remitter is not a person entitled to enforce a check. How do you reconcile this Comment with the 2002 addition to the Comment to 3–301? What is the statutory basis for this language?

2. PAYMENT WITH NOTICE OF ADVERSE CLAIM

a. RIGHT TO STOP PAYMENT

The right of a buyer who has paid a seller with a cashier's check or a teller's check and who has either been defrauded or has received defective goods to stop payment on the check are considered in the following Problems and text.

[Handwritten marginalia:]

Example.
If teller's check is issued by Bank A and the check is drawn on Bank B (presentment for payment is made to Bank B, drawee)
In this case Bank B as drawee has no obligation to pay check. If check is dishonored the remedy of payee is against Bank A.

If the obligee takes a cashier's check for an obligation/the obligation is discharged and the payee is restricted to its rights on the check against the issuing bank.

Problem
Seller contracted to sell goods. Buyer to sell goods. Buyer got cashier's check from bank in amount of $10K. Buyer then learned Seller was not going to perform contract so did not give him check. Buyer wanted money it gave to Bank (back) in order that it would issue check. Bank delayed in doing so. Can Buyer enforce the instrument under 3–301? No, he is a remitter. IX used to be that since a remitter was not party to the instrument he can't enforce it. In 2002, this was amended. Now a remitter that has received an instrument from the issuer but has not given it (transferred) can enforce. Comment 3–301

PROBLEMS

1. Seller agreed to sell goods to Buyer but insisted on immediate payment by means of a cashier's check or teller's check. Buyer had an account in Bank A. At the request of Buyer, Bank A issued a cashier's check payable to the order of Seller and delivered it to Buyer. Bank A debited the account of Buyer in the amount of the cashier's check. Buyer delivered the check to Seller, but Seller failed to deliver the promised goods stating that they would be delivered as soon as they became available. Buyer, fearing fraud on the part of Seller, stated that Seller had promised immediate delivery and demanded return of the check but Seller refused. Buyer ordered Bank A to stop payment on the check. Since the funds to pay for the cashier's check were withdrawn from Buyer's account, must Bank A comply with Buyer's stop payment order under 4–403(a)?

2. Assume the same facts as in Problem 1 except that at the request Buyer, Bank A issued a teller's check drawn on Bank B payable to the order of Seller. Bank A debited the account of Buyer in the amount of the teller's check. Buyer delivered the check to Seller. Buyer ordered Bank B to stop payment of the check. Must Bank B comply with Buyer's stop payment order under 4–403(a)? What is Bank A's liability on the check?

Suppose a buyer pays for goods by delivering the buyer's uncertified personal check to the seller. Shortly after the goods are delivered, the buyer examines them and decides that they are unsatisfactory. The buyer seeks to return the goods to the seller and obtain return of the check. The seller denies that the goods are defective and refuses to return the buyer's check. Or, suppose there is a fraudulent sale. The seller took the buyer's check after promising to deliver the goods, but the seller had no intention of carrying out the promise. No goods were ever delivered to the buyer. In either of these two cases the best remedy of the buyer is to prevent the drawee of the check from paying the check. Without that remedy the buyer has the burden of bringing an action against the seller. If the buyer can prevent payment of the check, it is the seller who has the burden of bringing an action. The buyer can prevent payment of an uncertified check of the buyer if the buyer can act very quickly. The check issued by the buyer to the seller functions as an order by the buyer to the buyer's bank to pay money to the seller. Section 4–403 allows the buyer to countermand that order by what is referred to as a "stop-payment order," which is simply an instruction to the bank not to pay the check. A stop-payment order may be given orally or in writing and must describe the check with reasonable certainty so that the bank can identify the check. The bank is obliged to carry out the order if it is received in time to allow the bank a reasonable opportunity to act on the order before the check is paid. 4–403(a). Failure to carry out the order can give rise to an action for damages. 4–403(c).

The remedy provided by 4–403 is not available, however, if the buyer pays for the goods with a certified check, cashier's check, or teller's check. Section 4–403 applies only to an "item [check] drawn on the customer's [buyer's] account." What are the rights of the buyer under 4–403 if a certified check is delivered to the seller? A certified check, in form, is drawn on the customer's account, but it is not treated that way under 4–403(a). The right of a customer to stop payment of a check is conditioned upon receipt by the bank of a stop-payment order "before any action by the bank with respect to the item described in Section 4–303." One of the actions referred to in 4–303 is payment of the check. 4–303(a)(2). Another is certification. 4–303(a)(1). So far as the rights and obligations of the drawer are concerned, certification of a check is treated as the equivalent of payment. When the check is certified it is treated as an obligation of the certifying bank rather than an item drawn on the drawer's account. Thus, if the buyer delivers a certified check to the seller, no right to stop payment of the check ever arises.

If the buyer delivered a cashier's check or teller's check to the seller, the analysis under 4–403 is somewhat different. A cashier's check or teller's check is not drawn on the buyer's account even though the buyer may have bought the check from the buyer's bank which obtained payment for it by debiting the buyer's account. Section 4–403 allows the buyer to stop payment of a check of the buyer, but does not allow the buyer to stop payment of a check issued by the buyer's bank. Comment 4 to 4–403. Section 4–403 does not apply at all to a cashier's check because the obligation of the issuer is the same as the obligation of the issuer of a note. 3–412. There is no instruction by one person to another that can be countermanded. Section 4–403 does apply to a teller's check. The issuer of a teller's check is like the drawer of an ordinary check. The bank issuing the teller's check draws the check on the account of the issuer in the drawee bank. The issuer is a customer of the drawee bank. § 4–104(a)(5). Thus, under 4–403, the issuer of the teller's check has a right to stop payment by the drawee bank. But that right belongs only to the issuer of the check; the buyer has no right to stop payment.

b.   ISSUING BANK DELAYS PAYMENT

Cashier's checks are usually issued by banks at the request of customers of the bank. Some customers may be big institutions that provide a large volume of business for the bank. If a such a valued customer of an issuing bank wishes to have payment stopped on a cashier's check, a patient explanation by the bank of why it cannot stop payment on the check under the law may not satisfy the customer. "Just do it," the angry customer says as he slams down the receiver. The following Problem addresses this issue and Revised Article 3's solution.

PROBLEM

Seller agreed to sell goods to Buyer but insisted on immediate payment by means of a cashier's check before it would deliver the goods. Buyer had an account in Bank, and, at the request of Buyer, Bank issued a cashier's check payable to the order of Seller and delivered it to Buyer. Buyer delivered the check to Seller who promised shipment of the goods the following day. Overnight, Buyer developed a common commercial affliction known as "buyer's remorse," and pleaded with Seller to call the deal off and return the check. When Seller proved unreasonable, Buyer demanded that Bank not pay the check ("Just do it!"), promising to reimburse it for any litigation expenses if Seller pressed its claim. Buyer assured Bank that Seller probably didn't want a lawsuit and would just drop the whole matter. Assuming that Buyer is a very good customer of Bank, would you advise Bank that in view of passage of 3–411 Bank should go ahead and pay Seller? See 3–411(b) and Comment 2 to 3–411.

3. ISSUING BANK'S RIGHT TO RAISE OWN CLAIMS OR DEFENSES

In our inquiry into the question whether you would advise a client to accept a cashier's check in payment, we have seen that the person obtaining a cashier's check has no right to stop payment on the check under 4–403 and that the issuing bank cannot assert defenses of others (3–305(c)) unless payment has been enjoined (3–602(e)(1)). This leaves a third issue to be resolved: can the issuing bank raise its own claims or defenses when a cashier's check is presented to it for payment? Before enactment of Revised Article 3 there was a split of authority in the cases, as well as a lively disagreement among commentators, on the matter. The initial article on the subject was Lary Lawrence, Making Cashier's Checks and Other Bank Checks Cost–Effective: A Plea for Revision of Articles 3 and 4 of the Uniform Commercial Code, 64 Minn. L. Rev. 275 (1980), which advocated making cashier's checks "cash equivalents" by prohibiting issuing banks from raising any defenses to payment even against non-holders in due course. Flatiron Linen, Inc. v. First American State Bank, 23 P.3d 1209 (Colo. 2001), is a ringing affirmation of the cashier's-check-as-cash view. The cash equivalent theory found no support in Revised Article 3, and 3–411(c) allows the "obligated bank" to refuse payment with impunity if it "asserts a claim or defense of the bank that it has reasonable grounds to believe is available against the person entitled to enforce the instrument." The following case discusses the meaning of this language.

State Bank & Trust v. First State Bank of Texas

United States Court of Appeals, Tenth Circuit, 2000.
242 F.3d 390.

■ LUCERO.

Plaintiff-appellee State Bank & Trust, N.A. ("State Bank") sued defendant-appellant First State Bank of Texas ("Bank of Texas") to recover, under Texas law, the amount of a cashier's check issued by Bank of Texas and two documentary drafts issued by Bank of Texas customer Buzz Speer. Bank of Texas counterclaimed to recover, under Oklahoma law, the face amount of a cashier's check issued by State Bank and seven documentary drafts that appeared on their face to be issued by State Bank customer Ventura Classics. The trial court granted summary judgment to State Bank on its claims and in a non-jury trial held that State Bank was not liable on any of Bank of Texas's counterclaims. In the appeal on the merits, only Bank of Texas's counterclaims are at issue. The other appeal and cross-appeal concern the trial court's award of costs and attorneys' fees to State Bank.

These related appeals raise state law issues under Oklahoma and Texas law. Exercising jurisdiction pursuant to 28 U.S.C. § 1291, we affirm in part, reverse in part, and remand to the trial court for proceedings consistent with this opinion.

I

The banks' customers, Speer and Ventura Classics, sold used automobiles to one another. Typically, payment was accomplished by means of a documentary draft. The buyer of an automobile would prepare a documentary draft consisting of an envelope displaying payment information. The buyer would then send the draft to the seller who would place the title documents for the automobile being purchased inside the envelope and deposit the documentary draft with his own bank. The seller's bank would forward the draft and title document to the buyer's bank for payment or collection. Once a draft was received by the buyer's bank, the bank would call the buyer and ask him to inspect the draft. The buyer was required to verify the draft, determine whether the title documentation was in order, and instruct the bank either to pay the draft or to return the draft unpaid.

At issue in this appeal are seven documentary drafts drawn on Ventura's account and presented by Bank of Texas to State Bank for payment ("State Bank drafts"). On receipt of the first five drafts, totaling $87,750, Bank of Texas gave Speer immediate credit and Speer withdrew the funds *before* the drafts were presented to State Bank for payment or collection. When State Bank received the forwarded drafts, it called Ventura's representative, Goss, to verify the drafts. Goss did not authorize payment. Accordingly, State Bank returned the drafts to Bank of Texas unpaid. However, it did not do so until several days after the period stated on the drafts for payment or return.

On receipt of the returned drafts, Bank of Texas resubmitted the drafts to State Bank along with a handwritten note from Judy Massey, a vice president at Bank of Texas, stating "Dispute of Date of Return." The note was accompanied by several photocopied sections of the Uniform Commercial Code ("UCC") concerning a bank's payment deadlines. In response to the second receipt of the drafts, an employee of State Bank, Teresa Bray, issued a cashier's check in the amount of $87,750 to pay for the drafts. The check was mailed to Bank of Texas before the State Bank employee responsible for Ventura's account, Vice President Coy Gallatin, was made aware of the issuance of the check. He was thus prevented from retrieving the check from the mail.

The following day, State Bank informed Bank of Texas that the cashier's check had been issued mistakenly and sent without authorization and, consequently, that a stop payment order was being placed on the check. Bank of Texas claimed to have received the check and submitted it for payment prior to receipt of notice of the stop payment order. After receipt of the first five documentary drafts at issue, Bank of Texas received two additional drafts, totaling $36,800, for which it gave immediate credit to Speer's account followed by Speer's immediate withdrawal of the funds.

After a bench trial, the district court ruled that State Bank was not liable on Bank of Texas's claims. * * * Bank of Texas appeals the district court's ruling on its counterclaims.

The district court awarded State Bank $77,335.76 in attorneys' fees and $14,250.24 in costs. *See State Bank & Trust, N.A. v. First State Bank of Texas*, No. 97–CV–277–B, at *11–13 (N.D. Okla. Jun 21, 1999) ("*State Bank III*"). The court also awarded interest at the rate of 4.879% per annum. *See id.* Bank of Texas appealed these awards and State Bank cross-appealed arguing that the district court improperly denied the award of certain costs and fees.

II. STATE BANK'S COUNTER CLAIMS

* * *

E. The Cashier's Check

1. State bank's obligation to pay the cashier's check

Upon receipt of the drafts for the second time, State Bank, through its employee Teresa Bray, issued a cashier's check in payment of the drafts. When another employee of State Bank realized the cashier's check had been issued mistakenly, State Bank attempted, but failed, to retrieve the check from the mail. Consequently, the following day State Bank contacted Bank of Texas to inform Bank of Texas that the cashier's check had been issued mistakenly, without authorization, and thus a stop payment order had been placed on the check.

The trial court found State Bank was justified in issuing the stop payment under § 3–411(c)(ii) because the drafts were forged and Speer was attempting to perpetrate fraud. Section 3–411(c) provides, in relevant part, that damages are not allowed under the section "if the refusal of the obligated bank to pay occurs because ... the obligated bank asserts a claim or defense of the bank that it has reasonable grounds to believe is available against the person entitled to enforce the instrument."

Bank of Texas argues that § 3–411(c) only allows the issuer of a cashier's check to avoid damages, not to avoid payment of the check. This argument completely ignores § 3–305(a) which details general defenses an obliged party can assert to the payment of an instrument. Specifically, that section allows the obligated party to assert a defense ... stated in another section of this article or a defense ... that would be available if the person entitled to enforce the instrument were enforcing a right to payment under a simple contract.

§ 3–305(a)(2).

In support of the trial court's holding that State Bank was justified in stopping payment on the cashier's check, State Bank raises four arguments on appeal. First, State Bank claims Bank of Texas misrepresented material facts in its letter accompanying the drafts on their second return to State Bank. Second, State Bank argues it properly stopped payment due to the fact the check was issued by mistake. Third, it argues Bank of Texas did not give valid consideration for the cashier's check. Finally, State Bank argues Speer's underlying fraud vitiated the contracts, i.e., the drafts, and thus provided a defense to the enforcement of the contracts. Because we find State Bank's second defense to payment of the cashier's check sufficient to affirm the trial court's holding, we need not reach the other three arguments raised on appeal.

As discussed above, § 3–305(a)(2) allows an obliged party to assert defenses to payment of an instrument otherwise available under Article 3 of the Oklahoma Commercial Code. Section 3–418(b) provides "if an instrument has been paid or accepted by mistake ... the person paying or accepting may, to the extent permitted by the law governing mistake and restitution ... revoke the acceptance." Section 3–409 defines "acceptance" as the "drawee's signed agreement to pay a draft as presented." Thus, in the case at issue, State Bank had accepted the cashier's check.

Under Oklahoma law, mistake of fact

is a mistake not caused by the neglect of a legal duty on the part of the person making the mistake, and consisting in:

    1. An unconscious ignorance or forgetfulness of a fact past or present, material to the contract; or,

    2. Belief in the present existence of a thing material to the contract, which does not exist, or in the past existence of such a thing, which has not existed.

Okla.Stat.Ann.tit. 15, § 63. The commentary to Article 3 of the Oklahoma Commercial Code states that:

    [I]f money is paid under a mistake of fact—that is, on the mistaken supposition that a specific fact exists which would entitle the payee to the money—and when the money would not have been paid if the payor had known the fact was otherwise, then the money generally can be recovered. The basis for the rule is that money paid through misapprehension of facts belongs, in equity and good conscience, to the person who paid it.

Okla.Stat.Ann. tit. 12A, Commentary on Revised Uniform Commercial Code Articles 3 and 4 Negotiable Instruments and Bank Deposits and Collections, as Enacted in Oklahoma, Article 3, Recovery of Payment by Mistake (citations omitted).

Oklahoma Comments [handwritten margin note]

In the instant case, State Bank employee Bray mistakenly believed State Bank was authorized by its customer to issue the cashier's check, and thus she mistakenly issued the check. At trial, she testified she would not have issued the check had she known Goss had told State Bank not to pay for the drafts. Moreover, State Bank's behavior following the issuance of the cashier's check, i.e., the attempt to retrieve the check from the mail and the immediate placement of a stop order on the check, supports the conclusion that the bank mistakenly issued the check. Because of this mistake, State Bank had a viable defense to payment of the check and was able to revoke its acceptance under § 3–418(b). On this alternative ground, we affirm the district court's holding that State Bank was justified in stopping payment on the cashier's check.

> 2. Bank of Texas's immunity from State Bank's
> defenses to payment of the cashier's check

According to § 3–418(c), State Bank cannot successfully invoke mistake as a defense to payment of the cashier's check if Bank of Texas "took the [cashier's check] in good faith and for value." Under §§ 3–305(a) and (b), State Bank cannot successfully assert a common law contract defense or other defense listed in Article 3 of the Oklahoma Commercial Code if Bank of Texas was a holder in due course. Section § 3–302(a)(2) defines a holder in due course as one who took an instrument "(i) for value, (ii) in good faith, . . . and (vi) without notice that any party has a defense or claim in recoupment described in subsection (a) of Section 3–305 of this title." Section 3–303(a)(3) states that an instrument is taken for value if it is "issued . . . as payment of, or as security for, an antecedent claim against any person, whether or not the claim is due."

Bank of Texas argues that State Bank issued the cashier's check in payment of Bank of Texas's valid claim of late return. Therefore, under § 3–302(a)(2), the claim of late return was "value" transferred for the cashier's check.

Earlier in this opinion, we affirmed the trial court's finding of fact that State Bank issued the cashier's check to pay for the drafts and not in response to Bank of Texas's claim of late return. Because State Bank issued the cashier's check to pay for the drafts—which were worthless because Ventura refused to authorize payment—rather than to pay for Bank of Texas's claim of late return, Bank of Texas transferred no value for the cashier's check. For this reason, Bank of Texas is not immune under § 3–418 to State Bank's defense of mistaken payment of the check.

As with the issue of whether State Bank was justified in stopping payment of the cashier's check, the parties raise numerous arguments on appeal to support their positions concerning whether Bank of Texas was immune to State Bank's defense to payment of the check. Because we conclude Bank of Texas did not take the cashier's check for value, we affirm, albeit on alternate grounds, the district court's holdings that State Bank could stop payment on the cashier's check and that Bank of Texas was not a holder in due course. Our reasoning makes it unnecessary to consider the parties' other arguments.

III. COSTS AND FEES

* * *

A. State Bank's Cross Appeal

1. Attorneys' fees under Texas law

.... State Bank claims it can recover attorneys' fees under Tex.Civ.Prac. & Rem.Code Ann. § 38.001, Tex.Bus. & Com.Code Ann. § 4.103(e) and Tex. Bus. & Com.Code Ann. § 3.411(b). We address these arguments in turn.

* * *

C. Tex.Bus. & Com.Code Ann. § 3.411(B)

Section 3.411(b) provides that a person who enforces a right to a check "is entitled to compensation for expenses and loss of interest resulting from . . . nonpayment and may recover consequential damages." Section 3.411(c) provides that expenses or consequential damages are not recoverable if the obligated bank refused to pay because it had "reasonable grounds to believe [it had a claim or defense] . . . available against the person entitled to enforce the instrument."

The trial court denied recovery of attorneys' fees to State Bank under § 3.411 because it found that it "did not and [could not] . . . conclude that Bank of Texas had no reasonable basis for asserting the positions taken." *State Bank III*, at 7. We affirm the trial court and reject as frivolous State Bank's assertion that the trial court's finding "was inconsistent with the court's earlier finding that Bank of Texas had *no* viable defense to payment of that check under § 3–411(c)." (Appellee's Br. B at 39.) Although the court ultimately found Bank of Texas had no viable defense, that determination did not preclude the court from finding that Bank of Texas had a reasonable basis for asserting defenses to payment.

NOTE

The policy basis for the cashier's-check-as-cash view is stated in *Flatiron Linen*, cited in the preamble paragraph of this section: "[W]e look to and take guidance from the nature and usage of cashier's checks. The commercial world treats cashier's checks as the equivalent of cash. People accept cashier's checks as a substitute for cash because the bank, not an individual, stands behind it. By issuing a cashier's check, the bank becomes the guarantor of the value of the check and pledges its resources to the payment of the amount represented upon presentation. 'To allow the bank to stop payment on such an instrument would be inconsistent with the representation it makes in issuing the check. Such a rule would undermine the public confidence in the bank and its checks and thereby deprive the cashier's check of the essential incident which makes it useful.' " 23 P.3d at

1213. The court in *Flatiron Linen* states that its holding is in accord with the majority rule.

PROBLEM

Rolando requested that Bank One issue a cashier's check for $10,000, which he intended use to pay for goods that Parsons agreed to sell Rolando. Roland paid for the cashier's check by giving Bank One an ordinary check for $10,000 drawn on his account in Bank Two. When Bank One issued the cashier's check, Rolando delivered it to Parsons, who then delivered the goods to Rolando. When Parsons presented the cashier's check to Bank One for payment, it dishonored the check because Rolando's check was returned by Bank Two for insufficient funds. Bank One refused to pay the cashier's check on the ground that it had been fraudulently induced to issue the check and was protected from expenses or consequential damages by 3–411(c)(ii).

(a) Bank One, at Rolando's request, made the cashier's check payable to Rolando, who indorsed and delivered it to Parsons. Did Bank One have reasonable grounds to believe that it had a defense of fraud that it could assert against Parsons? Is Parsons entitled to collect the amount of the check from Bank One?

[handwritten margin note: No, it was a personal claim or defense that is not good against a HDC.]

(b) If Bank One, at Rolando's request, made the cashier's check payable to Parsons, to whom Rolando delivered the check, would your answers to the questions in (a) change? See Case #1, Comment 4, to 3–302.

4. LOST INSTRUMENTS   *[handwritten: – Will Try to Finish Entire Chapter on Monday]*

a. LOST INSTRUMENTS UNDER SECTION 3–309

We have seen that the person obliged to pay an instrument can obtain discharge by paying the holder even if some other person has a claim to the instrument. The discharge can be asserted against anyone other than a person with rights of a holder in due course who took the instrument without notice of the discharge. 3–601(b). If the instrument is surrendered when payment is made, there is no risk that the instrument will be negotiated to a holder in due course. But we have also seen that in some cases the person entitled to enforce the instrument is not in possession of the instrument. 3–301. Although payment to a person entitled to enforce who does not have possession results in discharge (3–602(a)), there is the possibility that the instrument is in existence and has or will come into the possession of a holder in due course. Section 3–309 deals with enforcement of lost instruments. Suppose the payee indorses the instrument in blank and then loses it. The payee can enforce the instrument, but 3–309(b) requires the court to find that the person required to pay the instrument is "adequately protected against loss that might occur by reason of a claim by another person to enforce the instrument." The predecessor of 3–309 was 3–804 of former Article 3, which provided that "[t]he court may require security indemnifying the defendant against loss by reason of further

[handwritten margin note: 3–309 deals with enforcement of lost instruments. Suppose payee indorses check then loses it. 3–309(b) – requires the court to find that the person required to pay the lost instrument is adequately protected against loss that might occur by reason of a claim by another person to enforce instr.]

claims on the instrument." The quoted language in 3–804 was not uniformly adopted. Some states, including New York, as we see in *Diaz* below,
changed the language in their versions of former Article 3.

The 2002 amendment to 3–309 is illustrated by the following case.

PROBLEM

Maker borrowed $100,000 from Bank and evidenced its loan by a
promissory note payable to the order of Bank. When Bank failed, the
Federal Deposit Insurance Corporation (FDIC) acquired the note when it
became receiver for Bank. FDIC sold the note in a batch of several hundred
notes to Pooler, which planned to securitize the notes and issue bonds
backed by the note pool. Later FDIC disclosed to Pooler that it had lost the
original of the note before the sale and that possession of the note had
never been delivered to Pooler. Pooler now brings suit against Maker on
the note under 3–309 as a lost note. Maker defended on the ground that
Pooler never had possession of the note and could not have lost it. What
does Pooler have to prove to recover under 3–309? The facts are suggested
by those in Dennis Joslin Company, LLC v. Robinson Broadcasting Corporation, 977 F.Supp. 491 (D. D. C. 1997).

NOTE

In the contemporary world in which notes are pooled by the FDIC and
sold in bulk to others for securitization, it is likely that the assignee's first
step on learning that it didn't receive the note would be to proceed against
the FDIC under warranties contained in the assignment to assure the
assignee that it received all the notes described in the assignment documents. Since in large portfolio purchases "due diligence" may not extend to
examining each file for a note, the transferee should bargain for a blanket
warranty that protects it if a note is missing by requiring the transferor to
repurchase the rights to missing notes. The transfer warranty of 3–416
does not apply because the note was not delivered under 3–203(a).

b. LOST CASHIER'S, TELLER'S OR CERTIFIED CHECKS UNDER SECTION 3–312

Although 3–309 and its predecessor, former 3–804, apply to any instrument, most lost instrument problems arise with respect to cashier's checks,
teller's checks, and certified checks. Section 3–312, which has no predecessor, applies only to these bank obligations and can be used as an alternative
to 3–309. But in some cases a person with rights under 3–312 does not have
rights under 3–309 because the person is not a person entitled to enforce
the instrument. In that category are remitters of cashier's checks or teller's
checks and drawers of certified checks who cannot enforce the lost check
but who can use 3–312 to obtain refund from the bank that issued or
certified the check. See Comment 1 to 3–312. Cf. Comment to 3–301.

Diaz, which follows, was decided under the New York version of 3–804 of the original Article 3. It involved loss of a certified check by the payee of the check. Section 3–312 was a direct response to the hardship suffered by people in the position of Ms. Diaz in the following case.

Diaz v. Manufacturers Hanover Trust Co.

New York Supreme Court, Queens County, Special Term, 1977.
92 Misc.2d 802, 401 N.Y.S.2d 952.

■ MARTIN RODELL, JUSTICE.

The petitioner moves by order to show cause to require the respondent Manufacturers Hanover Trust Company to pay the sum of $37,000 or in the alternative to require the respondent Al Newman to issue a new negotiable instrument to her in the same amount.

The facts are uncontroverted. The petitioner posted the sum of $37,000 as security for a bond in behalf of a defendant in a criminal proceeding. Said security was posted with the respondent Newman, a licensed bail bondsman.

The aforementioned criminal action was concluded on July 20, 1977. Subsequently, the petitioner made demand upon the respondent Newman for the sum of $37,000, which she had heretofore posted with him. On August 4, 1977 the respondent Newman dutifully delivered to the petitioner two certified checks, in the amounts of $12,000 and $25,000, drawn on the respondent Manufacturers Hanover Trust Company. Shortly thereafter, the petitioner lost, misplaced, or was criminally relieved of the said certified checks and has to this date been unable to locate them.

The petitioner notified the respondent Newman, who, in turn, requested that the respondent Manufacturers Hanover Trust Co. stop payment. To this date, the checks have not been presented to Manufacturers Hanover Trust Co. for payment.

The petitioner also contacted an unnamed officer of the respondent Manufacturers Hanover Trust Co., who informed her that the bank would not honor any replacement checks issued by the respondent Newman unless an indemnity bond was posted in twice the amount of the original checks. The petitioner avers that this is an onerous and unjust burden; justifiably so, as it would require the posting of $74,000 as security.

* * * When a bank certifies a check, it accepts that check and has the obligation to pay the amount for which it is drawn. * * * The bank in certifying a check obligates itself to an innocent holder in due course to pay the amount for which the check is drawn. Thus, the respondent Manufacturers Hanover Trust Co., through its act of certification, assumed liability on the instruments.

The owner of an instrument which is lost, whether by destruction, theft or otherwise, may maintain an action in his own name and recover from any party liable thereon upon due proof of his ownership, the facts which prevent his production of the instrument and its terms. The court shall require security, in an amount fixed by the court not less than twice the amount allegedly unpaid on the instrument, indemnifying the defendant, his heirs, personal representatives, successors and assigns against loss, including costs and expenses, by reason of further claims on the instrument, but this provision does not apply where an action is prosecuted or defended by the state or by a public officer in its behalf. L.1962, c. 553; amended L.1963, c. 1003, § 9, eff. Sept. 27, 1964 (Uniform Commercial Code, § 3–804.)

While it is clear that the petitioner has the right to recover the amount of the checks upon sufficient proof that in fact the checks did at one time exist, were payable to her and cannot be produced, the issue to be decided is presented to this court as follows:

May the court order payment on a lost negotiable instrument without requiring the payee to post security as required in Uniform Commercial Code, § 3–804? In 487 Clinton Avenue v. Chase Manhattan, 63 Misc.2d 715, 313 N.Y.S.2d 445 (1970, Supreme Court, Kings County), the payee of a certified check was robbed of same at gun point and offered to pay the proceeds into an account controlled by the certifying bank. The court held that it had discretion to fix the security and that the security offered by the plaintiff was adequate.

The court notes that no appeal has been taken from the above decision, and thus no Appellate Court guidance is available. However, the Supreme Court in New York County in Guizani v. Manufacturers Hanover Trust, N.Y.L.J. October 12, 1971, p. 2, col. 5, held that under New York's version of this section (Uniform Commercial Code, § 3–804), the furnishing of the security is mandatory and not discretionary.

The section, as drawn by the drafters of the Uniform Commercial Code, and found in the Official Text and Official Commentaries, made the requirement for security discretionary with the court by the use of the word "_may._" The Official Commentaries to the Uniform Commercial Code state as follows:

"There may be cases in which so much time has elapsed, or there is so little possible doubt as to the destruction of the instrument and its ownership that there is no good reason to require the security."

The court, in 487 Clinton Avenue v. Chase Manhattan, supra, predicated its decision on the above reasoning. However, the New York version of section 3–804 of the Uniform Commercial Code pointedly changed the word "may" to "shall," and the Legislature in 1964 further amended this section to fix the amount of security to be not less than twice the amount allegedly unpaid on the instrument. * * * Thus, our Legislature appears to have considered the matter and amended the statute to make the furnishing of security not only mandatory but has also set the minimal amount at not less than twice the amount allegedly unpaid on the instrument.

* * *

The New York Commission Commentaries on section 3–804 of the Uniform Commercial Code leave little doubt that the express purpose of the Legislature was to make the furnishing of security mandatory rather than discretionary and thus conform to section 333 of the old Civil Practice Act.

* * *

If the court is to have the authority to determine the amount of security to be furnished, it would seem on the basis of the legislative history of this section that the change must come from the Legislature.

The court notes additionally that this section, as enacted by our Legislature, while being most positive in regard to the requirement of security and the amount thereof, fails to set any limit whatsoever as to the amount of time the security shall remain posted. The problem of the longevity of a certified check no doubt rendered the Legislature unable to fix a time limit. There being no legislative scheme to either limit the life of a certified check or the duration of time for which a bond must be posted, an unfortunate gap exists into which the petitioner's prayer must fall. It is the opinion of this court that further revision of this section of the Uniform Commercial Code is mandated, or in the alternative, legislation dealing with the valid life of certified checks must be enacted. Simple justice cries out for remedial legislation at the next session of the Legislature. The petitioner is being deprived of her life savings; the bank receives no benefit from the funds which are necessarily frozen. Under the present posture of the law, the funds will remain in that condition until the end of time or it escheats to the state, whichever comes first.

In light of the above, the court is constrained to reject the petitioner's application for recovery without posting of security as required by section 3–804 of the Uniform Commercial Code.

* * *

PROBLEMS

How does 3–312 resolve the following problems? Comment 4 to 3–312.

Claimant lives in New York and has her life savings amounting to almost $100,000 in First Bank. She decided to retire and move to Miami Beach to be near her sister. In anticipation of the move she obtained a cashier's check, dated January 2, from First Bank for $90,000 payable to her order. Her deposit account was immediately debited for $90,000.

1. Thief stole Claimant's purse on January 5 and it contained the cashier's check. The check was not indorsed by Claimant. She immediately called First Bank and asked that payment be stopped. An employee explained to her that if she would come in and sign a form asserting a claim to the check she could get her money back 90 days after the date of the check, but if she wanted her money immediately she would have to provide a bond to protect the bank. 3–309. Having no resources to obtain a bond, Claimant went to First Bank on January 6 and signed a form asserting her rights under 3–312(b). Included in the form was a declaration of loss complying with 3–312(a)(3). Thief forged Claimant's signature as an indorsement of the cashier's check and deposited the check in his account in Second Bank on January 8. The check was promptly presented to First Bank for payment. First Bank paid the check. Thief withdrew the proceeds of the check from his account in Second Bank and absconded. Ninety days after the date of the check, Claimant demanded payment of $90,000 from First Bank. What are Claimant's rights against First Bank if it refuses to pay? If First Bank pays, what are its rights against Second Bank?

2. Change the facts in Problem 1. When First Bank issued the check to Claimant, she indorsed the check by writing her name on the back. She then mailed the check to her sister in Miami Beach who had agreed to deposit it in her account until Claimant could arrive and open her own account. The check was stolen from the mail by Thief who deposited it in his account in Second Bank. By January 10, Claimant realized that something had happened to the check. On that date she went to First Bank and requested that payment be stopped. She was given the same information that was given in Problem 1 and on January 10 executed the necessary form to claim her rights under 3–312(b). On January 11 Second Bank presented the check to First Bank for payment. First Bank paid the check. Ninety days after the date of the check, Claimant sought $90,000 from First Bank and it refused to pay. What are Claimant's rights against First Bank?

3. Change the facts in Problem 2 in one respect. The check was deposited by Thief in Second Bank on May 10. Second Bank promptly presented the check to First Bank for payment. At the time the check was presented for payment First Bank had already paid $90,000 to Claimant because 90 days had elapsed since the date of the check. First Bank dishonored the check. What are Second Bank's rights against First Bank and Claimant?

F. ACCOMMODATION PARTIES

1. LIABILITY OF ACCOMMODATION PARTY AND RIGHTS AGAINST ACCOMMODATED PARTY

a. ACCOMMODATED PARTY IS INDIVIDUAL

The issues raised in this basic Problem are discussed in the text following the Problem.

PROBLEM

Bank would lend Son the $25,000 that he needed to start his own business only if his Mother would "co-sign" the note. Mother reluctantly did so by signing her name on the face of the note in the lower right hand corner beneath that of Son. Bank advanced the money to Son. Mother was paid nothing by Son for her cooperation and she received none of the proceeds of the loan. When Son went into default in his payments on the note, Bank asked Mother to pay the note. Mother, who had broken with Son by this time, was reluctant to do so. When Bank threatened to sue her, she demanded that Bank sue Son first, and only if he could not pay the judgment should Bank be allowed to sue her. (1) Is Mother correct on this issue? In what capacity did Mother sign within the meaning of 3–419(b)? (2) If Mother pays the note, what are her rights against Son? (3) If Son pays the note, what are his rights against Mother?

————————

A creditor taking the promissory note of a debtor who is not a good credit risk may require that a third party act as guarantor of the debtor's obligation to pay the note. Sometimes this guaranty is expressly stated. In many cases, however, a person who intends to act as guarantor does not expressly state that intention and signs the note as co-maker or indorser. For example, Son wants to buy equipment from Dealer for use in Son's business venture. Dealer is willing to sell to Son on credit only if Mother signs the note as co-maker along with Son. Two people who sign a note as co-makers are jointly and severally liable to pay the note. 3–412 and 3–116(a). Thus, if the note is not paid at the due date, Dealer as holder can enforce payment for the full amount against either Son or Mother or both. If two people are jointly and severally liable to pay an obligation and one of the obligors pays the entire amount, the normal rule, in the absence of a contrary agreement between the two obligors, is that the burden is shared equally by the two obligors. This principle of equal sharing is expressed as a right of the obligor who pays the obligation to receive "contribution" from the other obligor. 3–116(b). The contribution rule is based on the assumption that the joint obligation was incurred for the joint benefit of the two obligors and that each should contribute equally in the payment of the obligation. But this assumption is not true if Mother did not have any property interest either in Son's business venture or in the equipment for which the note was given. There is a suretyship relationship between Son and Mother. Generically, Mother is referred to as the "surety" and Son is referred to as the "principal" or "principal debtor." In Article 3, the terminology is different. Mother is the "accommodation party," Son is the "accommodated party," and the note is signed by Mother "for accommodation." 3–419(a).

Mother, as accommodation party, has certain rights against Son. If Son doesn't pay the note when due and Mother has to pay, it is only fair that she be entitled to recover from Son the full amount that she paid. He got the full benefit of the transaction that gave rise to the note and therefore should have to bear the full burden. Otherwise, Son would be unjustly enriched at the expense of Mother. Instead of having the normal right of contribution from a co-obligor, Mother has a right of "reimbursement" for the amount she paid and has subrogation rights as well. By subrogation she succeeds to the rights that Dealer had against Son on the note. 3–419(e).

When she pays the note she can require its surrender by Dealer (3–501(b)(2)) and becomes the person entitled to enforce the note. 3–301. Thus, if a note is secured by a security interest in collateral, the accommodation party who pays the note succeeds to the rights of the creditor with respect to the security interest (9–618(a)) and is entitled to a formal transfer of the note and security interest. Reimann v. Hybertsen, 275 Or. 235, 550 P.2d 436 (1976).

If Son pays the note when due, Son has no right of contribution against Mother because she did not benefit from the transaction. 3–419(f) and 3–116(b).

Any type of instrument can be signed for accommodation, and an accommodation party could sign as maker, drawer, acceptor, or indorser. In the typical case the instrument is a note and the accommodation party signs either as maker or indorser. We have examined the function of indorsement in the negotiation of an instrument and that is its primary function, but an indorsement can also be made for the purpose of incurring liability on the instrument. 3–204(a). In most cases, the negotiation and liability purposes coincide, but in some cases only one is present. For example, if an instrument is payable to an identified person, negotiation requires indorsement by the holder. 3–201(b). But the holder can negotiate the instrument without incurring liability as an indorser by indorsing without recourse. 3–415(b). The purpose of the indorsement is negotiation, not liability. An indorsement for accommodation is the converse. Because it is not made by the holder of the instrument, it has no negotiation function and is referred to in 3–205(d) as an "anomalous indorsement." Its only purpose is to impose liability on the indorser.

PROBLEM

Bob and Ted borrowed money from Bank to set up their own business. Bank required that their wives, Carol (Bob) and Alice (Ted), and Bob's parents, Bill and Mildred, cosign the note. All signed the note in the lower right-hand corner. When Bob and Ted defaulted on the note, Bank demanded and received payment from Bill and Mildred. Neither Bill, Mildred, Carol nor Alice played any part in the business, and the property of the business was in the name of Bob and Ted. The facts in this Problem are based on Fithian v. Jamar, 410 A.2d 569 (Md. 1979).

(a) In a state that does not recognize community property, what are the rights of Bill and Mildred against Bob? Ted? Carol? Alice? See 3–116 and 3–419.

(b) Would your answer change in a community property state?

b. ACCOMMODATED PARTY IS BUSINESS ORGANIZATION

PROBLEM

X owned 50% of the capital stock of Corporation and was its President. Y and Z each owned 25%. Corporation needed money for working capital and borrowed it from Bank which insisted as a condition to the loan that X sign the note because of the precarious financial condition of Corporation. The note was signed as follows:

Corporation

By X, President

X, individually

The loan, which is unsecured, was made by crediting the entire principal amount to Corporation's account with Bank and was used entirely for corporate purposes. Corporation has defaulted on the loan. After Corporation's default on the loan to Bank, X paid Bank the entire unpaid balance amounting to $10,000. Is X an accommodation party? Is X entitled to reimbursement from Corporation for the $10,000 paid to Bank or are X's rights limited to a claim for contribution? Would X's rights be any different if X owned 100% of the stock of Corporation rather than 50%? What do you learn about these questions from the following case?

[handwritten margin note: No, he had property in company, he was benefitting from it. So signing note made him an obligor]

[handwritten note: No.]

Plein v. Lackey

Supreme Court of Washington, Third District, 2003.
149 Wash.2d 214, 67 P.3d 1061.

■ MADSEN, J.

Lee Cameron signed a promissory note both in his corporate capacity and individually, secured by a deed of trust, to purchase property from Sunset Investments for his corporation, Alpen Group, Inc. Later, Cameron paid off the Sunset note. He then sought to enforce the instrument and foreclose the deed of trust when Alpen defaulted. He claims he signed the note as an accommodation party and was therefore entitled to foreclose. We agree.... We reverse the Court of Appeals and reinstate the trial court's grant of summary judgment in favor of Cameron.

FACTS

In 1997, Paul Plein, Bruce White, and Lee Cameron formed Alpen Group Inc. to buy and sell real estate (the group formerly operated as a partnership). In April 1997, Alpen purchased a lot from Sunset Investments, issuing a promissory note for $75,000 to Sunset with the promise to pay stated: "For value received, ALPEN GROUP, INC., A WASHINGTON CORPORATION, promise(s) to pay to SUNSET INVESTMENTS...." The note was secured by a deed of trust naming Sunset as the beneficiary and Alpen as the grantor. It was signed by Cameron as "Secretary/Treasurer" and by White as "Vice–President". Cameron, his wife, Plein (who was president), and his wife each signed "individually."

Alpen also borrowed $136,500 from Columbia State Bank, executing a promissory note also secured by a deed of trust. Columbia loaned the money in part on Sunset's agreement to subordinate its interest in the property to Columbia's. Alpen commenced constructing a log home on the lot. However, more funds were needed, and Cameron advanced $30,000.

[handwritten margin note: Lee Cameron signed a note individually and in corp. capacity to purchase property from Sunset Investments for the corporation (Alpen). He paid off the note and then sought enforcement on the instrument for Alpen to pay him. He said he signed the note as an accommodation party.]

[handwritten margin note: Cameron was the Treasurer of Alpen. (Alpen was making the note to Sunset but all officers signed it.)]

The money was still insufficient to complete the project and trade creditors were owed an additional $45,000. Cameron declined to loan any more money to Alpen. The parties state that Plein, as president of Alpen, issued deeds of trust against the log home to secure the debt to the trade creditors.

At some point thereafter, Plein was ousted and Cameron became president. Alpen issued a promissory note for the $30,000 that Cameron had advanced to Alpen, secured by another deed of trust on the property. Then, one of the trade creditors sued Alpen in Thurston County Superior Court. The record does not contain any information about that suit beyond the parties' brief descriptions, but it evidently involved a number of claims and cross-claims resulting in payment to the creditor who sued and a judgment entered against Alpen in favor of Plein for $45,000, which Plein recorded. In addition, Cameron received all the stock in Alpen.

At this point, the creditors, in order of their secured interests in the log home property, were (1) Columbia, (2) Sunset, (3) the unpaid trade creditors, (4) Cameron, and (5) Plein. Any equity remaining in the property would be that of Alpen.

According to plaintiffs, "around the time the Thurston County suit was being litigated," the note to Columbia Bank came due and Columbia refused to extend the loan. Clerk's Papers (CP) at 105. In October 1998, Cameron paid the amount due to Columbia with his personal funds and Columbia endorsed the note to Cameron. In addition, Columbia assigned the beneficial interest in its deed of trust to Cameron. Then, in December 1998, the pivotal transaction in this case occurred. Cameron paid the amount due Sunset, Sunset endorsed the promissory note for this loan to Cameron, and Sunset assigned its beneficial interest in its deed of trust to Cameron.

By these two transactions, Cameron, as beneficiary of the two deeds of trust originally issued to Columbia Bank and Sunset, claimed secured interests in the property superior to all other secured interests. He also continued to have a secured interest junior to the trade creditors based on his loan of $30,000 to Alpen.

In October 1999, Cameron, as assignee of the Sunset note, hired attorney Chester Lackey to begin nonjudicial foreclosure proceedings as a result of Alpen's default on the Sunset note. All of the secured creditors received notice of the foreclosure informing them that the trustee's sale of the property would be held on March 31, 2000.

On February 7, 2000, Plein and the trade creditors (hereafter Plein) brought this suit against Cameron and Lackey (hereafter Cameron), seeking a permanent injunction barring the trustee's sale and a declaration that the deed of trust was void because the underlying debt had been paid, i.e., there was no default on the underlying debt. Plein did not seek a preliminary injunction or any other order restraining the sale. On March 28, three days before the scheduled sale, Plein filed a motion for summary judgment, claiming that undisputed facts showed that Cameron paid off the Sunset note on behalf of Alpen, thus extinguishing the debt. Plein further claimed that he was entitled to an order declaring that his and the trade creditors security interests were superior to Cameron's and that the foreclosure proceedings were void.

Plein did not obtain a preliminary injunction or restraining order restraining the sale, and on March 31, the trustee's sale occurred. Cameron, the only bidder, bought the property for $245,312.35 (approximately the total of the Columbia, Sunset, and Cameron notes).

[handwritten margin note: Trustee's sale did occur anyway. Cameron bought property for $245K.]

On May 1, 2000, Cameron filed a cross-motion for summary judgment. He argued there was no evidence supporting Plein's motion for summary judgment because Mr. Plein's declaration, the only material submitted by Plein, was not made on personal knowledge. Cameron also argued he was entitled to summary judgment because the evidence indisputably established that Cameron purchased the Sunset and Columbia notes and obtained valid assignments of the promissory notes and deeds of trust for his personal benefit, rather than paying on behalf of Alpen. Cameron also argued that Plein failed to timely and properly object to the sale, pointing out Plein did not seek a preliminary injunction or a restraining order in time to restrain the trustee's sale.

The trial court granted Cameron's motion and dismissed Plein's complaint. Plein appealed and the Court of Appeals reversed. That court reasoned that where a person is individually liable on a note and pays it, the individual cannot also foreclose because the debt has been extinguished. The court held that there are disputed facts regarding Cameron's personal liability on the Sunset note that preclude summary judgment. In addition, the Court of Appeals reasoned that if Cameron was personally liable on the note, then Plein's failure to obtain an order restraining the foreclosure sale would make no difference because the debt would have been extinguished, Cameron would have nothing on which to foreclose, and the trustee's sale would be null and void.

Cameron petitioned for review by this court; his petition was granted. For the first time, he specifically relies on RCW 62A.3-419, a provision in the Uniform Commercial Code, to argue that he signed the Sunset note as an accommodation party, and that as such he had the right, once he paid the note, to enforce the instrument against Alpen and to foreclose the deed of trust. * * *

[handwritten margin note: Cameron says he signed as an accommodation party only.]

ANALYSIS

Application of RCW 62A.3-419 resolves the first issue in this case, whether Cameron signed the Sunset note as an accommodation party. * * *

[handwritten margin note: Issue: Is Cameron an accommodation party.]

Section 3-419(1) provides that

[i]f an instrument is issued for value given for the benefit of a party to the instrument ("accommodated party") and another party to the instrument ("accommodation party") signs the instrument for the purpose of incurring liability on the instrument without being a direct

[handwritten margin note: 3-419(1)]

beneficiary of the value given for the instrument, the instrument is signed by the accommodation party "for accommodation."

The comments to the statute explain that "[a]n accommodation party is a person who signs an instrument to benefit the accommodated party either by signing at the time value is obtained by the accommodated party or later, and who is not a direct beneficiary of the value obtained." RCWA 62A.3–419, cmt. 1, at 161. The issue whether a party is an accommodation party is a question of fact, comment 3 to section 3–419, and the party asserting accommodation party status bears the burden of proof.

Comment 1 to section .3–419 gives an example of accommodation party status that parallels the facts of this case:

> For example, if X cosigns a note of Corporation that is given for a loan to Corporation, X is an accommodation party if no part of the loan was paid to X or for X's direct benefit. This is true even though X may receive indirect benefit from the loan because X is employed by Corporation or is a stockholder of Corporation, or even if X is the sole stockholder so long as Corporation and X are recognized as separate entities.[2]

Here, the promissory note states that for value received, *Alpen* promised to repay the borrowed amount. The direct beneficiary of the loan was the corporation. As a stockholder of Alpen, any benefit obtained by Cameron was derivative and indirect. *See* Neil B. Cohen, *Suretyship Principles in the New Article 3: Clarifications and Substantive Changes*, 42 ALA. L.REV. 595, 600 (1991). Thus, Cameron received no proceeds from and no direct benefit from the loan.

In addition to the direct/indirect benefit inquiry, another factor that serves to establish accommodation party status is that the lender would not have made the loan in the absence of the party's signature on the note giving rise to liability. *Hendel v. Medley*, 66 Wash.App. 896, 899, 833 P.2d 448 (1992) (decided under former UCC provisions regarding accommodation parties); 11 AM.JUR.2D *Bills and Notes* § 85 (2002) (two primary factors that indicate accommodation party status are that the party received no direct benefit from the proceeds of the instrument and that the loan would not have been made unless the party signed the instrument). Here, Plein's complaint itself asserts that Sunset would not have loaned the money to Alpen, which had no assets, unless the corporate officers signed individually, thus incurring personal liability. Plein repeats this factual statement in his appellate brief. ("[b]ecause Alpen had virtually no other assets, as is customary in the business, Sunset demanded and obtained the personal guaranties of Alpen's owners"). Plein has repeatedly insisted that Cameron was a personal guarantor of the loan.

Because there are no disputed material questions of fact as to Cameron's status, we conclude as a matter of law that Cameron signed the Sunset

2. There is no suggestion in this record or the briefing that Cameron and Alpen Group, Inc., were not separate entities.

[handwritten margin note at top: "Conclusion: Cameron is an accommodation party."]

note as an accommodation party.[3] Cameron obtained no direct benefit from the loan, and Plein has conceded that the loan would not have been made unless the individual stockholders were subject to personal liability on the note.

* * *

The Court of Appeals is reversed and the trial court's grant of summary judgment in favor of Cameron is reinstated.

2.   SURETYSHIP DEFENSES

A surety, in addition to having rights against the principal debtor, also has certain rights which can be asserted against the creditor seeking enforcement of the surety's obligation to pay the debt. These rights are usually referred to as "suretyship defenses." Suretyship defenses relate to changes in the obligation of the principal debtor without the consent of the surety. For example, a surety guarantees performance of the principal debtor as buyer under a contract of sale of coal to be supplied on credit by a seller. The seller and the principal debtor agree to amend the contract so that it refers to fuel oil rather than coal. The surety didn't agree to the amendment. If the principal debtor fails to pay for fuel oil purchased under the amended contract and the seller demands payment, the surety has a complete defense. The surety's obligation related to a contract of the principal debtor to buy coal not fuel oil. The seller and the principal debtor cannot impose a new contract on the surety.

However, in some cases it cannot be said that the creditor and the principal debtor have attempted to impose an entirely new contract on the surety. There might be only some modification of the contract. In those cases the existence of a defense may be justified only if the modification causes loss to the surety. A few examples illustrate the problem. The principal debtor borrows money from a lender. The debt is payable with interest and is secured by a security interest in personal property of the principal debtor. After the suretyship relationship arises, the lender agrees with the principal debtor to an amendment of the debt obligation as follows: (1) the amendment changes the interest rate; or (2) it extends the due date of the debt; or (3) it releases some of the collateral that secures the debt; or (4) it releases the principal debtor from any personal obligation to pay the debt. In each of these cases, if the surety does not agree to the change it may be unfair to allow the lender to enforce the surety's obligation to pay if, at the time the change was made, the lender had knowledge of the suretyship relationship. The suretyship defenses are

---

3. An accommodation party may be a maker, a drawer, an acceptor, or an indorser. Section .3–419(b). He or she is liable on the note in the capacity in which he or she signed, usually as a maker or indorser. Cmt. 4, § .3–419. However, the nature of the liability on the note does not dictate whether

Cameron was an accommodation party. Instead, the absence of direct benefit, and the fact that Sunset would not have made the loan without individual liability on the part of the stockholders dictate that he signed as an accommodation party.

intended to protect the surety by providing that in some cases a change in the terms of the debt may result in a total or partial discharge of the surety. See Restatement (Third) of Suretyship and Guaranty §§ 39–44 (1995).

Restatement § 4(1) provides that to the extent negotiable instruments law governs, it takes precedence over otherwise applicable rules in the Restatement. The suretyship defenses with respect to negotiable instruments are stated in 3–605. In 2002 this section was substantially rewritten to bring it into harmony with the principles of the Restatement. Readers of 3–605 will profit from having a copy of the Restatement at hand; frequent references are made to it in the Comments. However, 3–605 applies to some transactions beyond those covered in the Restatement, including indorsers of notes and checks, as well as co-makers, who are not accommodation parties.

We have eschewed an analysis of the complexities of 3–605 because suretyship defenses are almost always waived in instruments prepared by creditors. The most important provision in 3–605 is subsection (f), which authorizes waivers. Comment 9 says:

> The importance of the suretyship defenses provided in Section 3–605 is greatly diminished by the fact that the right to discharge can be waived as provided in subsection (f). The waiver can be effected by a provision in the instrument or in a separate agreement. It is standard practice to include such a waiver of suretyship defenses in notes prepared by financial institutions or other commercial creditors. Thus, Section 3–605 will result in the discharge of an accommodation party on a note only in the occasional case as in which the note does not include such a waiver clause and the person entitled to enforce the note nevertheless takes actions that would give rise to a discharge under this section without obtaining the consent of the secondary obligor.

Even general language "indicating that the parties waive defenses based on suretyship or impairment of collateral" will suffice. 3–605(f). However, some note forms do not contain such waivers. This omission may be explained by 3–605(e), which provides that certain suretyship defenses cannot be asserted unless the creditor has knowledge of the accommodation. If this knowledge is present, the creditor may ask the accommodation party to sign a separate guaranty contract that contains the waivers.

Section 3–605 applies to only a narrow category of transactions, those in which the payment obligation is a negotiable instrument and the secondary obligor is a party to the instrument, such as an indorser or co-maker. The separate guaranty contracts that are more common in most commercial lending are not covered. The implied suretyship in the familiar real property transaction in which a grantee assumes existing financing is not covered because the assuming grantee is not a party to the instrument. See Comment 2.

The Restatement is generally regarded as a major advance in modernizing and clarifying the law of suretyship. A case can be made for the 2002 revisions of 3–605 on the ground that the Restatement rules constitute the prevailing law of the great majority of suretyship transactions. Since 3–605 applies to only narrow segment of suretyship transactions, conformity with the Restatement, when appropriate, is a desirable simplification.

G. SIGNATURES BY REPRESENTATIVES

A person is not liable on an instrument unless the instrument is signed personally by that person or by a representative who is authorized to sign for that person. 3–401(a). Whether a representative is authorized to sign for a represented person is determined by general principles of the law of agency. 3–402(a). Consider this case: Employer, an individual, has a checking account in Bank that is used to pay obligations incurred in Employer's business. Employer follows the practice of personally signing all checks, except that Employer authorizes Employee to sign Employer's name to checks during extended absences of Employer. Bank has paid all checks drawn on Employer's account whether Employer's name was written in Employer's handwriting or that of Employee. Employer never objected to the payment by Bank of any check on which Employer's name was written by Employee. On one occasion Employer was about to leave town and instructed Employee to pay all invoices arriving during Employer's absence except invoices of John Doe. In violation of these instructions Employee writes a check on Employer's account to John Doe in payment of a bill that Doe submitted. Employee's act of signing Employer's name to that particular check is not authorized by Employer in the sense that Employer never assented to it, but Employer nevertheless may be bound by the signature. The question of whether the signature is binding on Employer is determined by the law of agency. In our example, the probable result under agency law is that Employer is bound because Employee, although lacking actual authority to sign the Doe check, had apparent authority to do so because Employee had general authority to sign checks. In that event, under 3–401(a) and 3–402(a), the signature by Employee is effective as the authorized signature of Employer.

Signatures by agents on behalf of principals occur most often with respect to the obligations of organizations such as corporations whose signatures are made by its officers or employees. Two problems arise: Whether the corporation is bound by the signature of the officer or employee and whether the officer or employee also becomes a party to the instrument by signing it on behalf of the principal. If it is clear that an agent is signing on behalf of a named principal, only the principal is bound. But sometimes it is not clear whether the agent's signature is in behalf of the principal or whether it is made to impose liability on the officer as an accommodation party.

1. LIABILITY OF AGENT ON NOTES

The problem of ambiguous signatures on notes by representatives is governed by 3–402(b). How does this provision resolve the cases in the following Problem?

[handwritten margin note at top: 3-402 — governs Signatures by representatives.]

PROBLEMS

Your client, Carolyn Park, has been appointed Treasurer of New Corp., Inc., a new enterprise. She is authorized to sign promissory notes on behalf of the company.

1. Before taking up her duties she consults you about <u>personal</u> liabilities that she might incur in her new position. Among these is her concern about signing her name on notes given to evidence substantial bank loans and other credit extensions made to the company. Her fear is that if later on her new employer should fail and have to file in bankruptcy, holders of these notes might come after her as personally liable on the notes. How should she sign the company's notes to gain full protection from personal liability under 3–402(b)?

2. Are the following signatures "unambiguous" within the meaning of 3–402(b)?

(a) New Corp. Inc., by Carolyn Park *[handwritten: ambiguous]*

(b) New Corp. Inc., Carolyn Park, Treasurer *[handwritten: unambiguous]*

(c) Carolyn Park, Treasurer *[handwritten: ambiguous]*

(d) New Corp. Inc., Carolyn Park

3. Carolyn signed a note authorized by New Corp. Inc. merely by writing her name, "Carolyn Park."

(a) Is New Corp. Inc. liable on this note? See 3–401(a).

(b) This signature is clearly ambiguous. What would she have to prove under 3–402(b)(2) to avoid personal liability on the note against a <u>non-holder in due course</u>?

4. In order to evidence a loan obligation incurred by New Corp. to Lender, Carolyn signed on the front of the note: "New Corp., Inc., by Carolyn Park, Treasurer." On the back of the instrument, she signed "Carolyn Park." When New Corp. filed in bankruptcy, Lender sued Carolyn as indorser of the note. The usual reason one signs on the back of the note is to guarantee payment. Are there any facts that could be admitted into evidence to save Carolyn from personal liability against a non-holder in due course? Comment 2 to 3–402.

2. LIABILITY OF AGENT ON CHECKS

Section 3–402(c) states a different rule for checks than we saw in the prior section for notes. Why was this done?

Medina v. Wyche

District Court of Appeal of Florida, Third District, 2001.
796 So.2d 622.

■ COPE, J.

Vincent Medina and Allied Transportation Resources, Inc. appeal a final judgment entered after non-jury trial. We affirm in part and reverse in part.

We affirm the judgment for rent, and double rent, pursuant to section 83.06, Florida Statutes, against Medina and Allied. There was conflicting evidence regarding the rent claims, and the trial court resolved the conflict. The judgment is supported by competent substantial evidence. *See Perez v. Marti,* 770 So.2d 284 (Fla. 3d DCA), *review denied,* 773 So.2d 56 (Fla.2000).

The trial court also entered judgment against Medina and Allied on account of a check for insufficient funds in the amount of $34,348. The check indicates on its face that it was written on the account of First Delta Financial, a family corporation owned and controlled by Medina.

Medina signed this check. His corporate title does not appear before his signature. Appellee James G. Wyche, the landlord, contended that Medina was personally liable because he signed the check without indicating his corporate capacity below his signature. Medina argues that he was not personally liable on account of having signed the check.

We conclude that Medina is not personally liable for the corporate check, which was written on September 9, 1998. Effective January 1, 1993, Florida adopted Revised Article 3 of the Uniform Commercial Code ("UCC"). Ch. 92–82, §§ 2, 60, 62, Laws of Fla. The revised statute provides, in part:

673.4021.   Signature by representative

. . . .

> (3) If a representative signs the name of the representative as drawer of a check without indication of the representative status and the check is payable from an account of the represented person who is identified on the check, the signer is not liable on the check if the signature is an authorized signature of the represented person.

§ 673.4021(3), Fla. Stat. (1997).

The official comment makes clear that the revision is intended to address the situation now before us:

> 3.   Subsection is directed at the check cases. It states that if the check identifies the represented person the agent who signs on the signature line does not have to indicate agency status. Virtually all checks used today are in personalized form which identify the person on whose account the check is drawn. In this case, nobody is deceived into thinking that the person signing the check is meant to be liable. This subsection is meant to overrule cases decided under former Article 3 such as *Griffin v. Ellinger,* 538 S.W.2d 97 (Texas 1976).[2]

19B Fla. Stat. Ann. 149 (1993).

---

2. The *Griffin* decision held that where a corporate officer signed a check on a corporate account without indicating his corporate capacity, he was personally liable. 538 S.W.2d at 98.

This UCC modification "puts the Code's legal stamp of approval on the obvious intent of the transaction-that the company's check binds only the company, even if an agent signs in her own name." 2 James J. White and Robert S. Summers, *Uniform Commercial Code* § 16–5, at 86 (4th ed.1995); *see* 1 Patricia F. Fonseca and John R. Fonseca, *The Law of Modern Commercial Practices* § 6.56, at 6–104 (2d rev. ed.2000).

The landlord relies on such cases as *BBD Elec. Distribs., Inc. v. Magid*, 673 So.2d 80 (Fla. 3d DCA 1996) and *Hind-Marsh v. Puglia*, 665 So.2d 1091 (Fla. 3d DCA 1995), but those cases involved checks written prior to January 1, 1993, which was the effective date of the new UCC provision. Ch. 92–82, § 62, Laws of Fla. We therefore reverse the judgment of $34,348 against Medina individually. * * *

Affirmed in part, reversed in part, and remanded for entry of a corrected judgment.

H. ACCORD AND SATISFACTION

Effectuating an accord and satisfaction of a disputed claim by a "full satisfaction" legend on a check is a cheap and fast way in which to settle a claim. Section 3–311(a) and (b) provide that, as a general rule, if the legend on the check is conspicuous and the claim is subject to a bona fide dispute, the claimant cannot receive payment of the check without agreeing to the accord and satisfaction. If the claimant wishes to avoid settlement for the amount of the check, it may not cash the check or deposit it for collection. However, accord and satisfaction is a two-edged sword. As Comment 1 to 3–311 points out, accord and satisfaction by use of notations on checks is useful to consumers in disputes about the quality of goods or services purchased, but it is also commonly employed by insurance companies to settle claims of insured parties.

Section 3–311(c)(1) addresses a problem encountered by organizations like large retailers and other high volume recipients of checks who find it burdensome and wasteful to conduct a visual search of tens of thousands of checks to see if a handful contain a proposed accord and satisfaction legend. This provision allows such an organization to notify its customers to send any communications concerning disputed debts, including checks containing full satisfaction legends, to a specified address at which these checks and other communications can be examined and decisions made with respect to whether to accept them as settlement of claims. This allows retailers to rapidly process other checks without sight examination to detect accord and satisfaction language. Section 3–311(c)(2) is an alternative to 3–311(c)(1), which is designed to ameliorate the consequences of an inadvertent accord and satisfaction. It is explained in Comment 6 to 3–311.

In the growing body of case law involving accord and satisfaction, the two most heavily litigated issues are whether the full-satisfaction language is conspicuous and whether the accord is tendered in good faith. We deal with the first of these issues in the case below and with the second in the Problem following this case.

Gelles & Sons, Inc. v. Jeffrey Stack, Inc.

Supreme Court of Virginia, 2002.
569 S.E.2d 406.

■ Opinion By JUSTICE ELIZABETH B. LACY.

Gelles & Sons General Contracting, Inc. (Gelles) appeals the trial court's final order, holding that its claim for additional monies allegedly due under its contract with Jeffrey Stack, Inc. (JSI) was barred by an accord and satisfaction pursuant to Code § 8.3A–311. Because we conclude that the trial court's factual determination, that a reasonable person would consider that JSI provided Gelles with a "conspicuous statement to the effect that the instrument was tendered as full satisfaction of the claim," was not clearly erroneous, we will affirm the judgment of the trial court.

Through a series of oral agreements, Gelles agreed to provide brick laying work on JSI's construction project. Gelles submitted invoices totaling $91,932 for its work. JSI paid Gelles $70,486. In response to Gelles' invoice for a balance of $26,175, JSI sent Gelles a schedule of account on December 8, 2000, reflecting a balance remaining of only $13,580 after adjustments made for work and materials provided by JSI "in order to properly complete the work." In a December 11 facsimile transmittal Gelles disagreed with JSI's statement of account and requested payment of the full amount invoiced. On December 13, 2000, JSI sent Gelles a letter detailing the deficiencies in Gelles' work. The final paragraph of the letter stated, "JSI Paving and Construction stands by its final amounts as stated on the latest correspondence dated December 8, 2000. Enclosed, please find a check in the amount of $13,580.00 representing final payment on the contract." Gelles negotiated JSI's check for that amount.

Gelles filed a motion for judgment against JSI and its bonding company, North American Specialty Insurance Company (NASIC), for $26,000 plus interest, asserting that it was entitled to the entire unpaid balance. JSI and NASIC filed a plea in bar, claiming that Gelles' action was barred by an accord and satisfaction pursuant to Code § 8.3A–311.

After an evidentiary hearing on the plea in bar, the trial court concluded that the requirements set out in Code § 8.3A–311(a)–(b) had been met, that there was an accord and satisfaction, and entered an order dismissing Gelles' motion for judgment. We awarded Gelles this appeal.

DISCUSSION

Code § 8.3A–311 provides in pertinent part:

(a) If a person against whom a claim is asserted proves that (i) that person in good faith tendered an instrument to the claimant as full satisfaction of the claim, (ii) the amount of the claim was unliquidated or subject to a bona fide dispute, and (iii) the claimant obtained payment of the instrument, the following subsections apply.

(b) ... the claim is discharged if the person against whom the claim is asserted proves that the instrument or an accompanying written communication contained a conspicuous statement to the effect that the instrument was tendered as full satisfaction of the claim.

Gelles maintains that the statement in JSI's December 13 letter that the check submitted by JSI represented "final payment on the contract" did not meet the requirements of Code § 8.3A–311(b) because it was neither conspicuous nor sufficiently clear to inform a reasonable person that cashing the check constituted a settlement of the claims between the parties.

Conspicuous, as defined in Code § 8.1–201(10), means a term or clause that a reasonable person "ought to have noticed." This definition describes a physical attribute of the statement, not the content or meaning conveyed by the statement. Therefore, the manner in which the statement is displayed is the focus of the inquiry. According to Code § 8.1–201(10), whether a term or clause is conspicuous, as required by Code § 8.3A–311(b), is a decision to be made by the court.

There is no statutory requirement, found in Code § 8.1–201(10) or elsewhere, that the term or clause must be displayed in specific type or in any other distinguishing manner. While asserting that the statement in issue is not conspicuous, Gelles presents little support for this assertion, suggesting rather that "[t]he most important question" is whether the statement adequately relayed JSI's intent to tender the check in full satisfaction of Gelles' claim. Under these circumstances, we find no basis for rejecting the trial court's determination that the statement at issue was "conspicuous" for purposes of Code § 8.3A–311(b).

The crux of Gelles' argument on appeal is that the language at issue would not clearly inform a reasonable person that the check was being offered in full satisfaction of the claim. As noted in the official comment, Code § 8.3A–311 "follows the common law" with only "minor variations to reflect current business conditions." Thus, common law principles regarding the nature of the offer are relevant to applying the doctrine of accord and satisfaction as codified in Code § 8.3A–311.

Under the common law, an accord and satisfaction requires both that the debtor intend that the proffered amount be given in full satisfaction of the disputed claim and that the claimant accept that amount in accordance with the debtor's intent. *Virginia-Carolina Elec. Works, Inc. v. Cooper,* 192 Va. 78, 80–81, 63 S.E.2d 717, 719 (1951). The acceptance need not be express, but may be implied. *Id.* at 80–81, 63 S.E.2d at 719. In *Mercury Insurance Co. v. Griffith,* 178 Va. 9, 18, 16 S.E.2d 312, 315 (1941), we explained that the giving and acceptance of a check is prima facie evidence that the check constituted "payment in full" of the disputed account and that acceptance of the check "merely placed the burden of proof upon the [claimant]." "The acceptance of a check on which appears 'in full of

---

Handwritten margin notes:

Rule: The claim is discharged if the person whom the claim is against proves the instrument or an accompanying communication contained a conspicuous statement that the instrument was tendered as full satisfaction of the claim.

Gelles says that the statement "final payment on the contract" — does not meet the regmts of an accord and satisfaction stmt. b/c it was neither conspicuous nor would inform a reasonable person that cashing the check would constitute settlement.

Conspicuous = a reasonable person ought to have noticed.

The statement was conspicuous — it shows intent to tender the check in full. Satisfaction of the claim.

Rule: An accord and satisfaction requires both that the debtor intend that the proffered amount be given in full satisfaction of the disputed claim and that the claimant accept the amount in accordance of with debtor's intent. The acceptance need not be express, but implied.

account,' or words of like import, does not in fact close the account unless it was accepted with intelligent appreciation of its possible consequences, coupled with knowledge of all relevant facts." *Id.* at 20, 16 S.E.2d at 316.

Code § 8.3A–311 codifies these principles in subsections (a) and (b). Thus, once the requirements of those subsections are met, an accord and satisfaction is presumed. The party challenging the accord and satisfaction may rebut this presumption. Unlike the common law, however, the statute requires the claimant to overcome the presumption by satisfying an objective rather than a subjective test, that is, would a reasonable person have considered that the "instrument was tendered as full satisfaction of the claim?" *See Webb Bus. Promotions, Inc. v. American Electronics & Entertainment Corp.*, 617 N.W.2d 67, 76 (Minn.2000) (applying the UCC and holding that the presumption is rebutted if the claimant shows that a reasonable person would not have understood that the payment meant to discharge the obligation).

We now turn to the application of these principles to the facts of this case. First, Gelles urges that this Court adopt "clear guidelines" for language that is sufficient to give rise to the presumption under the statute. The statute itself, however, by describing the required statement as one "to the effect" that the tender will satisfy the debt, necessarily contemplates that no specific language is required and that each case must be considered on its own merits. Additionally, if a claimant has any misgivings about the nature of the tender, Code § 8.3A–311(c)(2) allows the claimant to repay the creditor within 90 days and nullify the accord and satisfaction. This statutory scheme protects a claimant and is inconsistent with a requirement that only certain language will invoke the presumption.

The trial court concluded in this case that the evidence presented a prima facie case of an accord and satisfaction under the statute. In rejecting Gelles' arguments that the language at issue was ambiguous and would not lead a reasonable person to conclude that the tender of the check by JSI in its December 13 letter was intended as full satisfaction of Gelles' claim, the trial court properly looked at the circumstances of the transaction and the conduct of the parties. *See John Grier Constr. Co. v. Jones Welding & Repair, Inc.*, 238 Va. 270, 272–73, 383 S.E.2d 719, 721 (1989). The fact finder, in this case the trial court, found that a reasonable person could not have considered the language of the December 8 and 13 letters "was anything other than" an expression of JSI's intent that the check and letter proffered on December 13 was, "in effect, a drop-dead letter that says, 'This is it. This is what we're going to pay you.'" Further, the trial court specifically stated that Gelles' evidence that its president did not think the language meant full satisfaction of the claim was not credible. We cannot say that, on this record, these factual findings were clearly erroneous.

The record supports the trial court's finding that the entire course of conduct and communications between these parties made clear that JSI offered the $13,580 as the final payment that it intended to make and that JSI considered that amount to represent the proper accounting under the

[handwritten margin note: So JSI is discharged.]

contract. JSI's December 8 and December 13 letters to Gelles, taken together, made express JSI's position that it would pay no more under the contract than the $13,580 check that it included with the December 13 letter. Nothing in the language of the December 8 and 13 letters qualified JSI's decision to "stand[] by its final amounts."

Accordingly, for the reasons stated above, we will affirm the judgment of the trial court.

Affirmed.

PROBLEM

[handwritten margin note: Usually insurance companies will include an accord and satisfaction stmt. on check and make claimant sign a release of claim.]

If an insurance company is settling a claim it will usually include a full-satisfaction statement on the check and require the claimant to sign a release of all claims on an accompanying form. This Problem raises the issue of whether this practice is a good faith tender of an accord under 3–311(a)(i) in a case in which the claimant is not represented by counsel and has dealt only with the insurance company's claim adjuster.

[handwritten margin note: Insurance company sends Kathy out to help claimant file a claim. Kathy works for company. She urges them to settle and sign releases. They do, and cash check but then try to return money six weeks later.]

Claimant was injured in an automobile collision with a negligent driver, Dulles, whose liability insurance carrier was Security Insurance Company. The policy limit on Dulles' liability coverage was only $25,000. Security's claims adjuster, Kathy, met with Claimant and her husband while she was still in the hospital and offered her services to assist her in filing a claim with Security. Kathy was friendly and helpful to Claimant and her husband throughout. In time, Kathy sent Claimant a letter, a check and a release form. The letter described the terms of the settlement *and urged Claimant to sign the release form.* The release form said "RELEASE OF ALL CLAIMS," and the check for $25,000 had typed on it "FINAL SETTLEMENT OF ANY AND ALL CLAIMS ARISING FROM BODILY INJURY CAUSED BY ACCIDENT ON 11/21/02." Claimant signed the release form and cashed the check, but six months later attempted to return the money by sending Security a check for $25,000, which Security returned with a note saying that it considered the claim settled. The reason Claimant demanded to rescind the release was that Kathy had not disclosed to her the possible effect of the release in making the car manufacturer only severally liable for damages in any subsequent litigation.

Claimant knew that Kathy was an employee of Security, but Kathy made no effort to explain to her the conflict of interest involved in recommending that Claimant sign the release. Security's policy was to discourage their claimants from seeking counsel. Kathy told Claimant that if counsel were retained, she could no longer assist her. Claimant considered retaining counsel for some other claims that she had arising out of the collision against the auto manufacturer concerning a defective seat belt, but finally decided against doing so. Security conceded that it used this same legend on all settlement checks involving personal injuries in auto accidents.

In many instances for different reasons, claimants are not represented by counsel in insurance cases and deal only with claims adjusters. The facts in this Problem raise the important issue of whether an accord is tendered in good faith under 3–311(a)(i) if the claims adjuster does not disclose its conflict of interest and cautions the claimant to seek legal advice about the effect of the release. In a case on similar facts, Jones v. Allstate Insurance Company, 45 P.3d 1068 (Wash. 2002), the Supreme Court of Washington on a 5–4 decision held on summary judgment that there was no accord and satisfaction under 3–311(a)(i) because of lack of good faith.

(a) Assume that Security Insurance Company comes to you after this decision and seeks your advice on how they should change their operations to make their tendered accords "bullet proof" under 3–311(a)(i). What do you tell them?

(b) In *Jones*, the majority apparently believed that the insurance company's practice of using the same full-satisfaction language routinely on their settlement checks brought the case within the language in the first paragraph of Comment 4 to 3–311, the last sentence of which is: "Use of a check on which full satisfaction language was affixed routinely pursuant to such a business practice may prevent an accord and satisfaction on the ground that the check was not tendered in good faith under subsection (a)(i)." Do you believe this admonition relates to the facts in the Problem?

NOTES

1.   Before Revised Article 3, the UCC had no section on accord and satisfaction. One of the reasons for adding 3–311 was a deep division of authority over the meaning of 1–207 which provided that: "[a] party who, with explicit reservation of rights, performs or promises performance or assents to performance in a manner demanded or offered by the other party does not thereby prejudice the rights reserved. Such words as 'without prejudice', 'under protest' or the like are sufficient." The issue was whether under this section the recipient of a check marked "tendered in full satisfaction" could negate the effect of these words by merely writing "reserving all rights" or "under protest" on the check. The drafters of 3–311 took the position that the recipient of a full-satisfaction check could avoid an accord and satisfaction only by not cashing the check; words reserving rights were ineffective. This result was reached by adding a new subsection to 1–207: "(2) Subsection (1) does not apply to an accord and satisfaction." A new Comment 3 to 1–207 was added.

2.   The drafting of 3–311 was contentious; the final product is a series of compromises that can be detected by going through the section in the manner of an archeological dig. Stage 1. Subsections (a) and (b) codify the common law rule of accord and satisfaction. Ironically this was supported both by consumers, who saw it as the little person's way of settling disputes without having to litigate, as well as by insurance companies and other businesses who wanted to induce their customers to settle claims by sending them checks that they would be tempted to cash on the bird-in-the-

hand principle. Stage 2. Department stores, utilities and others who receive a huge volume of checks objected that the unadorned common law rule meant that they had to sift through thousands of checks each day to reach the few that contained the full-satisfaction legend. This was unduly expensive, and, in consequence, the drafters were urged to get rid of the archaic rule that contract disputes can be settled by legends on checks. The drafters addressed their concerns in subsection (c)(1) which allows these organizations to require that customers send checks intended to pay disputed claims to a special office where the staff is trained to look for and deal with full-satisfaction checks. Subsection (c)(2) was a concession to companies that did not wish to use the somewhat cumbersome subsection (c)(1). Inadvertent accord and satisfaction could be avoided by allowing the claimant that had mistakenly cashed a full-satisfaction check to tender the money back to the drawer of the check within 90 days after payment. Stage 3. Subsection (c) looked too pro-business to consumer representatives and they posed this case: Suppose Big Store sends out the notice under subsection (c)(1) that all checks for disputed claims must be sent to a certain post office box. Although Big Store complied fully with the requirements for notice under subsection (c)(1), Customer delivered her full-satisfaction check to the credit manager for the branch of Big Stores where she had always shopped. She had talked with him by telephone and he was aware of the dispute on the balance of her account. Big Store cashed her check and did not avail itself of the escape valve in subsection (c)(2). Do you mean to tell me, the consumer representatives asked, that there should be no accord and satisfaction in this case merely because Customer hadn't read all the periodic statements she received from Big Store (Do you read yours?), even though the person in charge of her account received the check bearing a conspicuous full-satisfaction legend and cashed the check? This was a persuasive argument and subsection (d) was added to address this concern. Reaching consensus on the wording of subsection (d) was very difficult.

[Handwritten margin notes:] The code 3-311 (c)(1) now requires that if someone wants to send a check w/ an accord and satisfaction of claim, they have to send it to a special office where the staff is trained in looking for these statements. (Dept of company.)

Inadvertent accord can be avoided by returning money back to drawer within 90 days.

CHAPTER 3

PAYMENT SYSTEMS: CHECKS AND CREDIT CARDS

A. CHECK COLLECTION

According to Fred R. Bleakley, Fast Money: Electronic Payments Now Supplant Checks at More Large Firms, Wall St. J., April 13, 1994, at A1, the following scene, reminiscent of Apocalypse Now, occurs nightly in Burbank, California: Helicopters swirl into the Burbank Airport, landing in rapid succession, carrying hundreds of pounds of bundled checks. Workers race around, hurling the bundles into carts which are run out to Flight 401, a Learjet, in order to meet its 10:30 p.m. flight time. The jet carries $600 million in corporate checks that must be delivered to banks in 46 out-of-state cities to meet an 8 a.m. deadline. Missing the deadline will delay payment of the checks a day, depriving the owners of the checks the use of $600 million for that period. The jet arrived on schedule (5:10 a.m.) at an Ohio airport used by U.S. Check Inc., the largest check courier, as the central clearing point. Waiting there were 18 jets and six propeller planes loaded with 25,000 pounds of checks totaling $20 billion which had come in on other flights. This fleet promptly took off, split up and headed for 46 cities, where they were met by courier trucks which delivered them to 150 banks by the 8 a.m. deadline. Whew!

Tons of checks are lugged around by trucks, helicopters and airplanes all over the nation. Some checks are stolen; others are lost. A courier plane carrying Bank of America deposits went down in the Pacific and some of the checks dredged up from the ocean had to be restored by hair dryers. In the age of computers, why can't the enormous cost of transporting and processing checks be greatly reduced by communicating the information on checks electronically or, better still, by getting rid of checks in favor of electronic payments? The so-called checkless society has been talked about for several decades. The United States continues to be a check society, though less so than in the past. Although checks' share in the total value of noncash payments is declining, it remains the most commonly used non-cash payment instrument in the United States. The average value of checks written has declined, however, from $1,544 in 1979 to $925 in 2000. This decline is partly explained by the decrease in the use of checks by businesses and governments. Geoffrey R. Geddes & Jack K. Walton II, Fed. Reserve Bull. 360, 362, 367 (August 2002). Americans still write eight times as many checks as Europeans and 122 times as many as Japanese! The United States is the only industrial country that relies heavily on paper checks to make payments. Lucinda Harper, Americans Won't Stop Writing Checks, Wall St. J., Nov. 24, 1998, at A2.

But times are finally changing. In Michelle Higgins, The Check Isn't in the Mail, Wall St.J., May 1, 2002, at D2, the author reported that the number of checks being written to pay for goods and services is finally declining, down 3% to 29.15 billion transactions in 2001 from its peak of 30.12 billion in 1996. Overall check transactions totaled 50.91 billion in 2000 and are expected to peak at 51.92 billion in 2002 and gradually decline thereafter. Credit and debit card use is believed to be the reason for the decline in checks. Even though debit card use is growing faster than credit card use, the latter is still growing briskly, from 14.63 billion transactions in 1995 to 21.05 billion transactions in 2001, with the prediction that there will be 24.72 billion transactions in 2005. Caution: these predictions have been notably inaccurate in the past.

1.   TIME CHECK IS PAID BY PAYOR BANK

Article 4 governs the rights and obligations of banks and their customers with respect to the collection of checks by the banking system. However, the Federal Reserve Board has always played a very important role in check collection. This role has been expanded by Regulation CC, 12 U.S.C. § 4001 et seq. We discuss the impact of Regulation CC later in this chapter.

The check collection process consists of the movement of the check from the depository bank to its presentation at the payor bank. 4–105(3), 4–105(2). Unsurprisingly, the process of returning the check operates in reverse: the check moves from the payor bank to the depository bank, and ultimately to the depositor. The check return process is important when the payor bank dishonors the check. To avoid liability for the check, the payor bank must return the dishonored check to the depository bank within a prescribed time. Article 4 sets a midnight deadline by which the payor bank must return the dishonored item. 4–104(a)(10). Section 4–301's midnight deadline applies when the payor bank has settled an item and wished to revoke settlement. In addition, 4–302(a)(1) requires the payor bank to return the item or make settlement by midnight of the banking day or receipt of the item, unless the bank is a depository bank. Failure to comply with the midnight deadline makes a settlement final. The amount paid can't be recovered. When settlement hasn't occurred timely, tardy settlement makes the payor bank liable ("accountable") for the face amount of the item.

a.   THE MIDNIGHT DEADLINE

Solve the following Problems on the basis of the text following the Problems and statutory provisions provided.

PROBLEMS

1.   Drawer wrote a check for $10,000 (Check) on its account in Bank A payable to the order of Payee who deposited it in its account in Bank B, the

[handwritten margin note: It used to be most transactions were done by checks, this has decreased, largely b/c of the use of credit and debit cards.]

"depositary bank" 4–105(2). Bank B gave Payee a provisional credit for the amount of Check and sent it to Bank A for payment. Check was presented to Bank A on Monday at 8:30 a.m. in a bundle of checks itemized in a cash letter, which listed each check and the total dollar amount for the bundle. Bank A provisionally settled for the checks by sending Bank B a Fedwire for the total amount of the cash letter on Monday afternoon. The checks in the bundle went through Bank A's reader-sorter computer on Monday afternoon.

(a) The reader-sorter selected out Check because Drawer's account balance was insufficient to pay it. On Tuesday morning, Bank A reviewed Drawer's account to ascertain whether Drawer had added funds sufficient to pay Check by that time. Finding none, Bank decided to dishonor Check and sent it to its check-return office on Tuesday afternoon, but owing to a mix-up Check was not returned until the 3:00 a.m. courier on Wednesday. Check reached Bank B on Wednesday afternoon, and on Thursday Bank B erased the provisional credit in Payee's account and delivered Check to Payee on Friday. Did Bank A revoke its settlement with Bank B under the time limits of 4–301(a)? Is Bank A accountable to Payee for the amount of the check under 4–302(a) even if Payee has suffered no damage?

(b) Check was selected out for visual inspection because of its relatively large amount. After Check was inspected, Bank A decided to pay it, and Drawer's account was debited for the amount of Check at 1:00 p.m. on Tuesday. Check was then routed to a filing clerk whose responsibility it was to place it with Drawer's other cancelled checks to be mailed to Drawer at the end of the monthly billing cycle. At 5:00 p.m. on Tuesday, Bank A learned that a mistake had been made and that Drawer's account was insufficient to cover the amount of Check, but the file clerk had left and the employees could not locate Check until 9:00 p.m., an hour after the 8:00 p.m. motor courier had left. They placed it in the mail at 10:00 p.m. addressed to the presenting bank, Bank B, where it arrived on Friday. Did Bank A revoke its settlement under 4–301(a) and (d)(2) or was Check finally paid at 1:00 p.m. on Tuesday under 4–215(a) when Bank A completed its processing? "Send" is defined in 1–201(b)(36).

(c) Change the facts in question (b) by having Bank A send the Fedwire to Bank B on Tuesday afternoon. Bank B's loss from the one-day delay in settlement was only one day's interest on the $10,000. Would this change your answer in (b)?

2. Drawer drew a check (Check) on its account in Bank payable to the order of Payee. Upon receipt of Check, Payee deposited it in its account, which was also in Bank, on Monday. Hence, Bank is both the payor and depositary bank. Bank gave Payee a provisional settlement in its account on Tuesday for the amount of Check. On Wednesday morning Bank discovered that Drawer's account was insufficient to pay Check. On Wednesday afternoon Bank erased the credit from Payee's account and returned Check to Payee. Did Bank properly revoke the credit in Payee's account under 4–301(a) and (b)? Is Bank liable to Payee for the amount of the check under 4–302(a)(1)?

The next case in this book discusses the issue of when, under Article 4, the bank on which a check is drawn is deemed to have paid the check. This issue is presented in its most simple form if the payee of a check takes it to the drawee bank and asks for payment in cash over the counter. The check is paid when the bank gives cash equal to the amount of the check to the payee. 4–215(a)(1). But that case is not at all typical. Most checks are not paid in cash but are deposited in a bank account of the holder of the check.

To understand how Article 4 applies to checks deposited in a bank, it is necessary to understand the concept of settlement in Article 4. 4–104(a)(11) and 4–213. Typically, in the check-collection process, each bank that takes a check pays for it at, or shortly after, the time that the check is taken. Article 4 uses the terms "settlement" and "settle" to refer to this act of paying for the check. But to say that a bank has settled or paid for a check is not the same as saying that the bank has paid the check. The bank on which a check is drawn is referred to in Article 4 as the payor bank. 4–105(3). Only a payor bank can pay the check; any other bank giving value for the check may be buying the check but is not paying it. And even in the case of the payor bank there is a distinction between the bank's settling for the check and paying the check. For example, suppose the payee of a check deposits it to the payee's account in Bank A. The drawer of the check also has an account in Bank A and the check is drawn on that account. In this case, Bank A is both the depositary bank with respect to the check and the payor bank. 4–105(2) and (3). Bankers refer to this kind of check as an "on us" item. At or shortly after the time Bank A receives the check from the payee, Bank A will credit the account of the payee for the amount of the check. By making that credit Bank A settles for the check. 4–104(a)(11) and 4–213(a)(2)(iii). This settlement, however, is provisional in nature because Bank A has the right to revoke it under certain circumstances.

At the time Bank A settles with the payee for the check, it usually does not know whether, as the payor bank, it should pay the check. For example, suppose the balance in the drawer's account in Bank A is not sufficient to cover the amount of the check. Bank A has no obligation to the payee of the check to pay the check (3–408) and, if Bank A is not assured of reimbursement from the drawer of the check, Bank A normally would refuse to pay the check. Under Article 4, Bank A is given a time-limited right to revoke or recover the payment that it made to the payee when the payee's account was credited. 4–301(a). The prescribed technique for accomplishing this result is to return the check to the payee and to debit ("charge-back") the payee's account in the amount of the check. As payor bank, Bank A "pays the check" if and when it has not exercised its right to recover a provisional payment that it has made and the right of recovery no longer exists. 4–215(a)(3) and 4–301(a). This practice of settle-first-take-back-later is in effect because it is operationally efficient. Since payor banks have reason to refuse payment with respect to only a tiny percentage of the vast number of checks that are processed each day for payment, it is sensible to pay for all checks as they are received ("settlement") and to deal later with the small number of checks that turn out to be bad by revoking the settlement and returning the checks. Although in Montana only one in every 192 checks is returned, in Los Angeles, where guilt is less oppressive, one in every 34 bounces. Roger Lowenstein, Behind the Teller Window, Wall St. J., Dec. 30, 1996, at A10.

A similar analysis applies with respect to the more common case in which the depositary bank is not also the payor bank. In that case the depositary bank is a "collecting bank" that acts as agent of the holder to obtain payment of the check. 4–105(5). The depositary bank will either present the check directly to the payor bank or it will negotiate the check to an "intermediary bank," which acts as a collecting bank to obtain payment of the check. 4–105(4) and (5). The intermediary bank is likely to be a Federal Reserve bank and often there is more than one intermediary bank. Each collecting bank will give provisional settlement to the bank from which the check is received. The last collecting bank will present the check for payment to the payor bank, which will give provisional settlement to the presenting bank.

In transactions between banks, settlement is often made by a credit to the Federal Reserve account of the bank receiving the settlement. The payor bank may refuse payment of the check by returning it to the presenting bank and recovering the amount of the check from that bank. 4–301(a). In turn the presenting bank and each collecting bank may return the check to the bank from which it received the check and recover the provisional payment. 4–214(a). As we will see, Regulation CC requires payor and collecting banks to expedite the return of checks and authorizes them to return checks directly to the depositary bank or to any bank that has agreed to handle the checks for expeditious return to the depositary bank. Any bank returning the check may obtain the amount of the check from the bank to which the check is transferred. When the depositary bank receives the returned check, it may recover the provisional payment given to the holder from whom it took the check for collection. 4–214(a).

Blake, which follows, describes in more detail the time-limited right that Article 4 gives to a payor bank to return a check and recover any provisional settlement given for the check or to avoid liability to pay the check under 4–302. It also deals with one of the more common excuses for failing to meet the midnight deadline, delays recognized by 4–109 (formerly 4–108).

Blake v. Woodford Bank & Trust Co.

Court of Appeals of Kentucky, 1977.
555 S.W.2d 589.

■ PARK, JUDGE.

This case involves the liability of * * * Woodford Bank and Trust Company on two checks drawn on the Woodford Bank and Trust Company and payable to the order of * * * Wayne Blake. Following a trial without a jury, the Woodford Circuit Court found that the bank was excused from meeting its "midnight deadline" with respect to the two checks. Blake appeals from the judgment of the circuit court dismissing his complaint. The bank cross-appeals from that portion of the circuit court's opinion relating to the extent of the bank's liability on the two checks if it should be determined that the bank was not excused from meeting its midnight deadline.

BASIC FACTS

The basic facts are not in dispute. On December 6, 1973, Blake deposited a check in the amount of $16,449.84 to his account at the Morristown Bank, of Morristown, Ohio. This check was payable to Blake's order and was drawn on the K & K Farm Account at the Woodford Bank and Trust Company. The check was dated December 3, 1973.

On December 19, 1973, Blake deposited a second check in the amount of $11,200.00 to his account in the Morristown Bank. The second check was also drawn on the K & K Farm Account at the Woodford Bank and Trust Company and made payable to Blake's order. The second check was dated December 17, 1973.

When Blake deposited the second check on December 19, he was informed by the Morristown Bank that the first check had been dishonored and returned because of insufficient funds. Blake instructed the Morristown Bank to re-present the first check along with the second check. Blake was a cattle trader, and the two checks represented the purchase price for cattle sold by Blake to James Knight who maintained the K & K Farm Account. Blake testified that he had been doing business with Knight for several years. On other occasions, checks had been returned for insufficient funds but had been paid when re-presented.

The two checks were forwarded for collection through the Cincinnati Branch of the Federal Reserve Bank of Cleveland. From the Federal Reserve Bank, the two checks were delivered to the Woodford Bank and Trust Company by means of the Purolator Courier Corp. The checks arrived at the Woodford Bank and Trust Company on Monday, December 24, 1973, shortly before the opening of the bank for business. The next day, Christmas, was not a banking day. The two checks were returned by the Woodford Bank and Trust Company to the Cincinnati Branch of the Federal Reserve Bank by means of Purolator on Thursday, December 27, 1973.

The two checks were received by the bank on Monday, December 24. The next banking day was Wednesday, December 26. Thus, the bank's "midnight deadline" was midnight on Wednesday, December 26. § 4–104(1)(h) [Revised § 4–104(a)(10)]. As the bank retained the two checks beyond its midnight deadline, Blake asserts that the bank is "accountable" for the amount of the two checks under § 4–302(1)(a) [Revised § 4–302(a)(1)].

HISTORY OF PAYOR BANK'S LIABILITY FOR RETAINING CHECK

Under the Uniform Negotiable Instruments Law a payor bank was not liable to the holder of a check drawn on the bank until the bank had accepted or certified the check. * * * Because of the payor bank's basic nonliability on a check, it was essential that some time limit be placed upon the right of the payor bank to dishonor a check when presented for payment. If a payor bank could hold a check indefinitely without incurring liability, the entire process of collection and payment of checks would be intolerably slow. To avoid this problem, a majority of courts construing § 136 and § 137 of the Uniform Negotiable Instruments Law held that a payor bank was deemed to have accepted a check if it held the check for 24 hours after the check was presented for payment. * * * Thus, in a majority of jurisdictions, the payor bank had only 24 hours to determine whether to pay a check or return it. However, in Kentucky and a few other jurisdictions, the courts held that § 136 and § 137 of the Uniform Negotiable Instruments Law applied only to checks which were presented for acceptance. * * * Consequently, the payor bank would be liable on the check only if it held the check "for an unreasonable length of time" and could thus be deemed to have converted the check.

In order to bring uniformity to the check collection process, the Bank Collection Code was proposed by the American Bankers' Association. The Bank Collection Code was adopted by Kentucky in 1930. Under § 3 of the Bank Collection Code, a payor bank could give provisional credit when a check was received, and the credit could be revoked at any time before the end of that business day. The payor bank became liable on the check if it retained the item beyond the end of the business day received. * * *

Banks had only a few hours to determine whether a check should be returned because of insufficient funds. Banks were required to "dribble post checks" by sorting and sending the checks to the appropriate bookkeepers as the checks were received. This led to an uneven workload during the course of a business day. At times, the bookkeeping personnel might have nothing to do while at other times they would be required to process a very large number of checks in a very short time. * * * Because of the increasingly large number of checks processed each day and the shortage of qualified bank personnel during World War II, it became impossible for banks to determine whether a check was "good" in only 24 hours. The banks were forced to resort to the procedure of "paying" for a check on the day it was presented without posting it to the customer's account until the following day. See First National Bank of Elwood v. Universal C.I.T. Credit Corporation, 132 Ind.App. 353, 170 N.E.2d 238, at 244 (1960). To meet this situation, the American Banking Association proposed a Model Deferred Posting Statute. * * *

Under the Model Deferred Posting Statute, a payor bank could give provisional credit for a check on the business day it was received, and the credit could be revoked at any time before midnight of the bank's next business day following receipt. A provisional credit was revoked "by returning the item, or if the item is held for protest or at the time is lost or is not in the possession of the bank, by giving written notice of dishonor, nonpayment, or revocation; provided that such item or notice is dispatched in the mails or by other expeditious means not later than midnight of the bank's next business day after the item was received." * * * If the payor bank failed to take advantage of the provisions of the deferred posting statute by revoking the provisional credit and returning the check within the time and in the manner provided by the act, the payor bank was deemed to have paid the check and was liable thereon to the holder. * * *

The Model Deferred Posting Statute was the basis for the provisions of the Uniform Commercial Code. Under § 4–301(1) [Revised § 4–301(a)] of the Uniform Commercial Code (UCC), a payor bank may revoke a provisional "settlement" if it does so before its "midnight deadline" which is midnight of the next banking day following the banking day on which it received the check. Under the Model Deferred Posting Statute, the payor bank's liability for failing to meet its midnight deadline was to be inferred rather than being spelled out in the statute. Under UCC § 4–302 [Revised § 4–302], the payor bank's liability for missing its midnight deadline is explicit. If the payor bank misses its midnight deadline, the bank is "accountable" for the face amount of the check. * * *

Like the Model Deferred Posting Statute, the Uniform Commercial Code seeks to decrease, rather than increase, the risk of liability to payor banks. By permitting deferred posting, the Uniform Commercial Code extends the time within which a payor bank must determine whether it will pay a check drawn on the bank. Unlike the Bank Collection Code or the Uniform Negotiable Instruments Law as construed by most courts, the Uniform Commercial Code does not require the payor bank to act on the day of receipt or within 24 hours of receipt of a check. The payor bank is granted until midnight of the next business day following the business day on which it received the check.

EXCUSE FOR FAILING TO MEET MIDNIGHT DEADLINE

UCC § 4–108(2) [Revised § 4–109(b)] provides:

"Delay by a * * * payor bank beyond time limits prescribed or permitted by this Act * * * is excused if caused by interruption of communications facilities, suspension of payments by another bank, war, emergency conditions or other circumstances beyond the control of the bank provided it exercises such diligence as the circumstances require."

The circuit court found that the bank's failure to return the two checks by its midnight deadline was excused under the provisions of UCC § 4–108.

The circuit court dictated its findings of fact into the record:

"From all of the evidence that was presented in this case, it would appear that there was no intentional action on the part of the bank to hold these checks beyond the normal course of business as an accommodation to its customer. In fact, the uncontroverted testimony of the bank officers was to the contrary. To say that the bank failed, through certain procedures, to return the checks by the midnight deadline does not, in the mind of this Court, imply or establish an intentional act on the part of the bank.

* * *

"In this instance we have the Christmas Holiday, which caused in the bank, as in all businesses, certain emergency and overloaded situations. This is not unique to the banking industry; but is true of virtually every business in a christian society, in which the holiday of Christmas is observed as the major holiday of the year. Special considerations are always given to employees as well as customers of these banking institutions.

" * * * On the Christmas Holiday, two machines were broken down for periods of time during this critical day in question. There was an absence of a regular bookkeeper."

Under CR 52.01, these findings of fact cannot be set aside by this court unless they are clearly erroneous. The foregoing findings are supported by the record, and are not questioned by Blake on the appeal.

After making findings of fact, the circuit court dictated the following conclusions into the record:

" * * * The entire cumulative effect of what happened would constitute diligence on the part of the bank, as circumstances required.

"It is the opinion of the Court and it is the Finding of the Court that the circumstances described by the banking officers, the standards of banking care, as described by expert witnesses, would bring the bank within 4–108(2), and the Court therefore, finds as a fact that there were circumstances here beyond the control of the bank, and that it exercised such diligence as those circumstances required."

When the circuit court concluded "that there were circumstances here beyond the control of the bank, and that it exercised such diligence as those circumstances required," the circuit court was doing no more than repeating the words of the statute. This court must determine whether the circuit court's findings of fact support these conclusions.

Before turning to the facts presented in this case, it is appropriate to discuss the only two cases involving the application of UCC § 4–108 to a payor bank's midnight deadline. In Sun River Cattle Co. v. Miners Bank of Montana, 164 Mont. 237, 521 P.2d 679 (1974), the payor bank utilized a computer in the adjacent town of Great Falls to process its checks. The checks were picked up at the Miners Bank by an armored car between 5:00 p.m. and 6:00 p.m. on the date of receipt. The checks would normally reach the computer center at Great Falls around 10:30 p.m. Ordinarily the checks would have been processed by 11:30 p.m., returned to the Miners Bank by 8:00 a.m. the next morning. The checks in question were received by the Miners Bank on May 11. On that day, the armored car broke down, and the checks did not reach the computer center at Great Falls until 1:30 a.m. the next morning, May 12. On that morning, the computer malfunctioned and the checks were not returned to the Miners Bank until 2:30 p.m. on May 12. There was no testimony as to what actually happened to the checks after they were received by the Miners Bank on the afternoon of May 12, but the Miners Bank failed to return the checks by midnight of May 12. The trial court held that the failure of the Miners Bank to meet its midnight deadline was excused by the provisions of UCC § 4–108(2). The Montana Supreme Court reversed, holding that the Miners Bank had failed to show the degree of diligence required under the circumstances. The Montana court pointed out that the Miners Bank had more than the normal interest in the activities in the account upon which the checks were drawn, and that due diligence could not be shown merely by following ordinary operating procedures.

In Port City State Bank v. American National Bank, 486 F.2d 196 (10th Cir.1973), the payor bank, American National, was changing from machine posting to computer processing of its checks commencing Monday, December 1, 1969. Two checks were in dispute. The first check arrived at American National on Friday, November 28, 1969. As Monday was the next banking day, the midnight deadline for the first check was December 1. The second check arrived on Tuesday, December 2, 1969, and the midnight deadline for that check was Wednesday, December 3. American National's new computer developed a "memory error" which rendered it unusable at 10:00 a.m. on December 1, the first day of computer operations. The computer manufacturer assured the bank that repairs would not take "too long." Unfortunately repairs and testing were not completed until the early hours of Tuesday, December 2. In the meantime, American National attempted to utilize an identical computer in a bank some two and a half hours away. Processing commenced at the other bank at 11:30 p.m. on December 1, and continued through the night. Although work proceeded to the point of "capturing" all of the items on discs, the backup computer was required by its owner, and the American National personnel returned to the bank to complete the printing of the trial balances. Another memory error developed in the new computer which again rendered the computer unusable. No further use could be made of American National's computer until a new memory module was installed on Thursday, December 4. The trial court held that the computer breakdown constituted a condition beyond the control of American National and that the bank had exercised due diligence. On appeal, the United States Court of Appeals affirmed, holding that the findings of the district court were not clearly erroneous.

* * *

The basic facts found by the circuit court can be summarized as follows: a) the bank had no intention of holding the checks beyond the midnight deadline in order to accommodate its customer; b) there was an increased volume of checks to be handled by reason of the Christmas Holiday; c) two posting machines were broken down for a period of time on December 26; d) one regular bookkeeper was absent because of illness.

Standing alone, the bank's intention not to favor its customer by retaining an item beyond the midnight deadline would not justify the application of § 4–108(2). The application of the exemption statute necessarily will turn upon the findings relating to heavy volume, machine breakdown, and absence of a bookkeeper.

The bank's president testified that 4,200 to 4,600 checks were processed on a normal day. Because the bank was closed for Christmas on Tuesday, the bank was required to process 6,995 checks on December 26. The bank had four posting machines. On the morning of December 26, two of the machines were temporarily inoperable. One of the machines required two and one half hours to repair. The second machine was repaired in one and one half hours. As the bank had four bookkeepers, the machine breakdown required the bookkeepers to take turns using the posting machines for a time in the morning. One of the four bookkeepers who regularly operated the posting machines was absent because of illness on December 26. This bookkeeper was replaced by the head bookkeeper who had experience on the posting machines, although he was not as proficient as a regular posting machine operator.

Because of the cumulative effect of the heavy volume, machine breakdown and absence of a regular bookkeeper, the bank claims it was unable to process the two checks in time to deliver them to the courier from Purolator for return to the Federal Reserve Bank on December 26. As the bank's president testified:

> "Because we couldn't get them ready for the Purolator carrier to pick them up by 4:00 and we tried to get all our work down there to him by 4:00, for him to pick up and these two checks were still being processed in our bookkeeping department and it was impossible for those to get into returns for that day."

* * *

The increased volume of items to be processed the day after Christmas was clearly foreseeable. The breakdown of the posting machines was not an unusual occurrence, although it was unusual to have two machines broken down at the same time. In any event, it should have been foreseeable to the responsible officers of the bank that the bookkeepers would be delayed in completing posting of the checks on December 26. Nevertheless, the undisputed evidence establishes that no arrangements of any kind were made for return of "bad" items which might be discovered by the bookkeepers after the departure of the Purolator courier. The two checks in question were in fact determined by Mrs. Stratton to be "bad" on December 26. The checks were not returned because the regular employee responsible for handling "bad" checks had left for the day, and Mrs. Stratton had no instructions to cover the situation.

Even though the bank missed returning the two checks by the Purolator courier, it was still possible for the bank to have returned the checks by its midnight deadline. Under UCC § 4–301(4)(b) [Revised § 4–301(d)(2)] an item is returned when it is "sent" to the bank's transferor, in this case the

Federal Reserve Bank. Under UCC § 1–201(38) an item is "sent" when it is deposited in the mail. 1 R. Anderson, Uniform Commercial Code § 1–201 pp. 118–119 (2d ed. 1970). Thus, the bank could have returned the two checks before the midnight deadline by the simple procedure of depositing the two checks in the mail, properly addressed to the Cincinnati branch of the Federal Reserve Bank.

This court concludes that circumstances beyond the control of the bank did not prevent it from returning the two checks in question before its midnight deadline on December 26. The circumstances causing delay in the bookkeeping department were foreseeable. On December 26, the bank actually discovered that the checks were "bad," but the responsible employees and officers had left the bank without leaving any instructions to the bookkeepers. The circuit court erred in holding that the bank was excused under § 4–108 from meeting its midnight deadline. The facts found by the circuit court do not support its conclusion that the circumstances in the case were beyond the control of the bank.

RE–PRESENTMENT OF CHECK PREVIOUSLY DISHONORED BY NONPAYMENT

On its cross-appeal, the bank argues that the circuit court erred in holding that there was no difference in the status of the two checks. The bank makes the argument that it is not liable on the first check which had previously been dishonored by nonpayment. Blake received notice of dishonor when the first check was returned because of insufficient funds. The bank claims that it was under no further duty to meet the midnight deadline when the check was re-presented for payment.

The bank relies upon the decision of the Kansas Supreme Court in Leaderbrand v. Central State Bank, 202 Kan. 450, 450 P.2d 1 (1969). A check drawn on the Central State Bank was presented for payment on two occasions over the counter. On both occasions, the holder of the check was advised orally that there were not sufficient funds in the account to honor the check. Later, the holder deposited the check in his own account at the First State Bank. The First State Bank did not send the check through regular bank collection channels, but rather mailed the check directly to the Central State Bank for purposes of collection. The check arrived at the Central State Bank on March 21 or March 22, and the check was not returned by the Central State Bank to the First State Bank until April 5. The Kansas Supreme Court held that there was no liability under § 4–302 of UCC for a check which had previously been dishonored when presented for payment.

Relying on the provisions of UCC § 3–511(4), the Kansas Supreme Court held that "any notice of dishonor" was excused when a check had been "dishonored by nonacceptance" and was later re-presented for payment. The Kansas Supreme Court specifically held that § 3–511(4) [See Revised § 3–502(f)] applied to a check which was dishonored when presented for payment, stating:

"While the language of 84–3–511(4), supra—'Where a draft has been dishonored by nonacceptance'—does not refer to a dishonor by nonpayment, we think reference to the dishonor of a 'draft' 'by nonacceptance' would, a fortiori, include the dishonor of a check by nonpayment."

The Kansas Supreme Court concluded that a payor bank was excused from giving any further notice of dishonor when a previously dishonored check was re-presented for payment and there were still insufficient funds in the drawer's account to cover the check.

* * *

The decision of the Kansas Supreme Court in the *Leaderbrand* case has been criticized. As UCC § 3–511(4) applies by its terms to a "draft" which has been "dishonored by nonacceptance," most of the criticism has been directed to the Kansas court's application of § 3–511(4) to a check which had been dishonored by nonpayment. As stated in B. Clark and A. Squillante, The Law of Bank Deposits, Collections and Credit Cards at 71–72 (1970):

"Use of this section to excuse retention under § 4–302 seems questionable, since the draftsmen are saying nothing more than dishonor by nonacceptance excuses notice of dishonor by nonpayment. If a time draft is not accepted, it is a useless act to present it for payment. On the other hand, sending a check through a second or third time often yields results, since the depositor may have had time to make a deposit to his account. It is presumably for this reason that the Code draftsmen limited the excuse rule of § 3–511(4) to 'nonacceptance' of 'drafts' and did not by express language indicate 'nonpayment' of 'checks.' "

See also Note, Uniform Commercial Code—Nonapplicability of Payor Banks "Midnight Deadline" to Re–Presented Checks, 18 Kan.L. Rev. 679 (1970).

Two courts have refused to follow the *Leaderbrand* decision. In Wiley, Tate and Irby v. Peoples Bank and Trust Company, 438 F.2d 513 (5th Cir.1971), the United States Court of Appeals for the Fifth Circuit held:

"We disagree with *Leaderbrand* and hold § 3–511(4) inapplicable here. Acceptance applies only to time items. It has nothing to do with demand items."

In Sun River Cattle Co. v. Miners Bank of Montana, supra, the Montana Supreme Court rejected the *Leaderbrand* decision and followed the decision of the United States Court of Appeals in the *Wiley, Tate and Irby* case. The Montana Supreme Court held that § 3–511(4) of the UCC was inapplicable to checks payable on demand.

* * *

A practical reason also exists for rejecting the *Leaderbrand* decision. In 1972, approximately 25 billion checks passed through the bank collection process. The Federal Reserve Banks handled 8 billion checks that year.

* * * An earlier study indicated that only one half of one percent of all checks were dishonored when first presented for payment. Of those initially dishonored, approximately one half were paid upon re-presentment. F. Leary, Check Handling Under Article Four of the Uniform Commercial Code, 49 Marq.L. Rev. 331, 333, n. 7 (1965). A significant number of previously dishonored checks are paid upon re-presentment in the regular course of the check collection process. Such checks are often presented through intermediate collecting banks, such as the Federal Reserve Bank in this case. Each collecting bank will have made a provisional settlement with its transferor, and, in turn, received a provisional settlement from the bank to which it forwarded the check. In this way, a series of provisional settlements are made as the check proceeds through the bank collection process.

Under UCC § 4–213(2) [Revised § 4–215(c)], final payment of a check "firms up" all of the provisional settlements made in the collection process. Under subsection (1)(d) of UCC § 4–213 [Revised § 4–215(a)(3)], a payor bank makes final payment of a check when it fails to revoke a provisional settlement "in the time and manner permitted by statute, clearing house rule or agreement." As to items not presented over the counter or by local clearing house, this means that a payor bank is deemed to have made final payment of a check when it fails to revoke a provisional settlement by its midnight deadline. See UCC § 4–213, Official Code Comment 6 [Comment 7 to Revised § 4–215]. In his article on check handling, Leary has described § 4–213 as the "zinger" section: "when provisional credit given by the payor bank becomes firm then—'zing'—all prior provisional credits are instantaneously made firm." Leary, op.cit., at 361. If a payor bank was not required to meet its midnight deadline with respect to previously dishonored items, then none of the other banks involved in the collection process could safely assume that the check had been paid. Consider the problems of the depository bank. It must permit its customer to withdraw the amount of the credit given for the check when provisional settlements have become final by payment and the bank has had "a reasonable time" to learn that the settlement is final. See UCC § 4–213(4)(a) [Revised § 4–215(e)(1)]. The depository bank will rarely receive notice that an item has been paid. In actual practice, the depository bank will utilize availability schedules to compute when it should receive the check if it is to be returned unpaid. Leary, op.cit., at 345–346. If a payor bank is not bound by its midnight deadline as to previously dishonored items, then there is no way for the depository bank to know whether a previously dishonored item has been paid upon re-presentment except by direct communication with the payor bank. Such a procedure would impose an unnecessary burden upon the check collection process.

This court concludes that the circuit court was correct in holding that there was no difference in the status of the two checks.

* * *

NOTES

1. The court deals with the question of whether the first check, which was re-presented on December 24, should be treated differently from the second check which was presented for the first time on that date. Woodford Bank argued that because that check had been properly returned the first time that it was presented, it had no duty to return it in a timely manner a second time. A previous case, *Leaderbrand*, discussed in the opinion, supported this argument. The court in *Leaderbrand* relied on Former 3–511(4). That provision was intended to apply to time drafts. It states the principle that if the draft is dishonored when presented for acceptance, it is not necessary to present it again for payment to charge secondary parties. Despite the clear language of Former 3–511(4) restricting the provision to dishonor by nonacceptance, the court in *Leaderbrand* applied it to a check dishonored when presented for payment. Revised Article 3 dropped former 3–511(4) and replaced it with 3–502(f), which does not contain the language relied on in *Leaderbrand*. *Leaderbrand* has been widely criticized and the court in *Blake* declined to follow it.

Re-presentment of checks is common, and about one half are paid when presented the second time. The typical case is that of a customer who writes a check to be covered by a check contemporaneously deposited in the customer's account or which will be deposited in the very near future. If the customer's check is presented for payment before the deposited check is collected, the customer's check may be dishonored because of a temporary insufficiency of funds in the account. If the check is re-presented, it must be treated as a check presented for the first time because, if the midnight deadline does not apply to such checks, the depositary bank would have no basis for making a judgment whether the check was paid. The depositary bank receives notice that a check has been dishonored either by return of the check or by a separate notice of dishonor. But it is not told that a check has been paid. The bank normally determines that a check has been paid by the fact that it didn't receive the returned check or notice of dishonor within the normal time for receiving the check or notice.

2. Taken together 4–301(a) and 4–302(a) provide that if a check arrives on Day 1, Payor Bank may avoid being held accountable for, meaning liable for, the amount of the check by returning it before its "midnight deadline" (midnight of Day 2, 4–104(a)(10)), only if it had settled for the check before midnight of Day 1. We discussed settlement briefly in the text preceding *Blake*. In Hanna v. First National Bank of Rochester, 87 N.Y.2d 107, 637 N.Y.S.2d 953, 661 N.E.2d 683 (N.Y. 1995), checks arrived at Payor Bank on November 12 and were returned on November 13, but Payor Bank was held accountable on the checks because it offered no proof that it had settled for the checks on November 12. Payor Bank objected to this result on the ground that it should not be liable for the full amount of the checks, $44,503, when Depositary Bank's loss was minimal. The court stated:

> Some commentators have questioned the wisdom of imposing liability under UCC 4–302(a) for a payor bank's failure to settle for the item on

the day it is received when the bank has dishonored or returned the item within the midnight deadline because if the item has been dishonored before payment of it has become final, the only apparent harm that results is that the depositary bank has been deprived of one day's interest on the amount of the item. They maintain that holding the payor bank accountable for the face value of the item in the light of such minimum damages is an unduly harsh penalty (see 6 Hawkland, Leary & Alderman, UCC Series, § 4–302:02). * * * We do not similarly view the matter.

661 N.E.2d at 688.

The unusual aspect of *Hanna* is how the issue of failure to settle on Day 1 ever arose. *Hanna* is the first reported case we have seen in which there was no settlement on the date of delivery. A large percentage of checks are presented by Federal Reserve banks, and, as to these checks, there is always settlement on the day of presentment. This is true because the Fed will not present a check to a payor bank unless that bank or its correspondent bank has an account in the Fed; this account will be promptly debited by the Fed. With respect to checks not presented by the Fed, settlement may be made by the payor bank's sending a Fedwire credit to the presenting bank's Fed account before the close of Fedwire (6:30 p.m. ET) on the day of delivery. If, as in *Hanna*, a check is presented through a clearing house, the banks that are members of the clearing house usually have agreements (4–213(a)) providing that as each member exchanges checks at the clearing with each other member, the amounts are netted out with debit balances to be paid that day by wire transfers to the account of the creditor bank in the Fed by an agreed time or by entries in accounts each of the members holds in the others. In short, in clearing house transactions, payor banks must settle for checks on the day the checks are delivered to it. The court has little to say about why this result didn't follow in *Hanna*, other than to observe, laconically, that the payor bank had presented no admissible evidence of settlement on November 12.

3. In the reference to the Wall Street Journal article at the beginning of this chapter describing the hectic pace of check collection, the deadline the courier service was trying to meet was to get the checks to the payor banks by 8 a.m. You don't find anything in the UCC about such a deadline because it is imposed by Federal Reserve regulations (12 CFR §§ 229.34(c), 229.39(d)) which take precedence over Article 4 requirements. 4–103(b). Section 4–213(a) expressly states that the medium and time of settlement may be prescribed by Federal Reserve regulations. Cash management people view the rule of 4–301 that settlement may be made at any time before midnight of the day of presentment as terribly lax. They want the balance of their accounts known earlier in the day so that they can invest unneeded funds in overnight money markets. In 1994 the Fed imposed "same-day settlement" (SDS) rules for checks not clearing through the Fed which give certain benefits (e.g., freedom from having to pay presentment fees to payor banks) to checks delivered to payor banks or their check processing facility by 8 a.m. For checks qualifying as SDS checks, settlement must be made by a credit to the presenting bank's Federal Reserve bank account, unless the presenting bank otherwise agrees, and must be made by the close of Fedwire. Failure to meet this deadline will make the payor bank accountable under 4–302. This rule does not apply to checks cleared through the Fed because payor banks are prohibited from charging the Fed presentment fees, and settlement is made intra-day by the Fed's debiting the payor bank's account in the Fed. In other words, the Fed does not need the same-day settlement rule to protect it. This settlement rule is discussed in 1 Clark & Clark, The Law of Bank Deposits, Collections and Credit Cards & 5.10 (Rev. ed. 1999) and Robert D. Mulford, New Federal Reserve Actions Modifying the UCC: Intraday Posting, Same–Day Settlement, and MICR Encoding Warranties, 26 UCC L.J. 99 (1993). In 1998 the Fed requested input from banks on their experience with SDS in preparation for possible changes. Clarks' Bank Deposits and Payments Monthly, Vol. 6, No. 12, June 1998. p.7. discusses the matter.

b.   WHAT IS A PAYOR BANK?

Under 4–302(a) presentment to the payor bank starts the running of the midnight deadline period. But in the branch banking system so common today, what is the payor bank? In a branch banking system, checks drawn by customers having accounts in a branch will usually not be sent to the branch for payment initially but will be routed through a processing center where the checks are run through a reader/sorter machine and drawers' balances are adjusted in the bank's electronic data storage system. Checks meeting the bank's standards for sight review of signatures (usually large balance checks) may then be delivered to the branch where the drawer has an account and signature cards are kept. Which is the payor bank for the purpose of the midnight deadline: any branch in the system, the branch where the drawer maintains its account whose address is on the check, or the processing center? Section 4–107 states: "A branch or separate office of a bank is a separate bank for the purpose of computing the time within which and determining the place at or to which action may be taken or notices or orders shall be given under this Article and under Article 3." Comment 1 suggests that this is the best the drafters can do given the infinitely varying practices in the huge banking industry, and the courts will have to sort out the proper results "on the basis of the facts of each case." See the extensive discussion on this issue in 2 White & Summers, Uniform Commercial Code 20–4c. (4th prac. ed. 1995).

PROBLEMS

1. Bank has 20 branches in and around a large city and a central processing center (Center) to which all checks drawn on any branch of Bank are automatically routed for processing by directions encoded on the bottom of the check. These directions are pursuant to 4–204(c) that allows the payor bank to designate the place where presentment should be made. The check in question is received by Center at noon on Day 1 and run through Bank's computers. Because the check is for an amount larger than $5,000, it is then delivered to Branch, whose address is on the check, at

8:00 a.m. on Day 2 for sight review of signature. Branch decided at noon on Day 2 to dishonor the check and delivered it to Center at 5:00 p.m. on Day 2. At 3:00 a.m. on Day 3, Center dispatched the check by motor courier to the presenting bank. Did Bank meet its midnight deadline?

2. Show–Me Bank (SMB) has 100 branches in Missouri; most are clustered around either St. Louis or Kansas City. SMB maintains separate processing centers (Centers) in St. Louis for the eastern area (Eastern) and in Kansas City for the western area (Western). Checks drawn on eastern branches are routed to Eastern Center, and those drawn on western branches go to Western Center. Payee deposits a check drawn on an Eastern branch in her deposit account in a Western branch on Day 1. The check is delivered by Western branch to Western Center at 8 a.m. on Day 2, which sends it by air courier to Eastern Center where it arrives at noon on Day 3 and is run through that Center's computers. Because the check is for an amount larger than $5,000, at 8 a.m. on Day 4 the check is delivered to the Eastern branch whose address is on the check for sight review of the signature. Eastern Branch decided at noon on Day 4 to dishonor the check and returned it to Eastern Center at 5:00 p.m. on Day 4. At 11:00 p.m. on Day 4, Eastern Center dispatched the check by air courier to Western Center where it arrived at 1:00 a.m. on Day 5. Did SMB meet its midnight deadline?

c. CHECK KITING

The prevalence of check kiting scams in recent years has placed pressure on the strict accountability rule of 4–302(a). If a depositary bank, knowing that a kite is taking place, presents checks to a payor bank that doesn't know about the kite, is it fair to impose strict accountability on the payor bank that misses its midnight deadline on these checks? The depositary bank is trying to get paid before the kite crashes, while the payor bank ends up liable for the face amount of these "large item" checks that are drawn on uncollected, in fact, uncollectible, funds in the kiter's account. The following case is a good analysis of the problem under Revised Article 4. Check kiting is discussed in 1 Clark & Clark, The Law of Bank Deposits, Collections and Credit Cards, Chapter 9 (Rev. ed. 1999). In the 1990 revision of Article 4, after much discussion, a new defense to the accountability rule was added by 4–302(b): "The liability of a payor bank to pay an item pursuant to subsection (a) is subject to defenses based on * * * proof that the person seeking enforcement of the liability presented or transferred the item for the purpose of defrauding the payor bank." Comment 3 says: "A payor bank that makes a late return of an item should not be liable to a defrauder operating a check kiting scheme." Why didn't the court in the following case refer to 4–302(b) and the quoted Comment?

First National Bank in Harvey v. Colonial Bank

United States District Court, N.D. Illinois, 1995.
898 F.Supp. 1220.

■ GRADY, DISTRICT JUDGE.

Before the court are the parties' cross-motions for summary judgment. For the reasons explained, plaintiff First National Bank in Harvey's motion is granted in part and denied in part. Defendant Colonial Bank's motion is granted in part and denied in part. Defendant Federal Reserve Bank of Chicago's motion is granted.

Check kiting is a form of bank fraud. The kiter opens accounts at two (or more) banks, writes checks on insufficient funds on one account, then covers the overdraft by depositing a check drawn on insufficient funds from the other account.

> To illustrate the operation, suppose that the defrauder opens two accounts with a deposit of $500 each at the First National Bank and a distant Second National Bank. (A really successful defrauder will have numerous accounts in fictitious names at banks in widely separated states.) The defrauder then issues for goods or cash checks totaling $3000 against the First National Bank. But before they clear and overdraw the account, he covers the overdrafts with a check for $4,000 drawn on the Second National Bank. The Second National account will be overdrawn when the $4,000 check is presented; before that happens, however, the defrauder covers it with a check on the First National Bank. The process is repeated innumerable times until there is a constant float of worthless checks between the accounts and the defrauder has bilked the banks of a substantial sum of money.

John D. O'Malley, "Common Check Frauds and the Uniform Commercial Code," 23 Rutgers L. Rev. 189, 194 n. 35 (1968–69). By timing the scheme correctly and repeating it over a period of time, the kiter can use the funds essentially as an interest-free loan. Williams v. United States, 458 U.S. 279, 281 n. 1, 102 S.Ct. 3088, 3090 n. 1, 73 L.Ed.2d 767 (1982) (quoting Brief for the United States).

Check kiting is possible because of a combination of two rules found in Article 4 of the Uniform Commercial Code. Under § 4–208(a)(1) [4–210(a)(1)], a depositary bank may allow a customer to draw on uncollected funds, that is, checks that have been deposited but not yet paid. Second, under §§ 4–301 and 4–302, a payor bank must either pay or dishonor a check drawn on it by midnight of the second banking day following presentment. Barkley Clark, The Law of Bank Deposits, Collections and Credit Cards & 5.03[5] (3d ed. 1990). Thus, when a kite is operating, the depositary bank allows the kiter to draw on uncollected funds based on a deposit of a check. The depositary bank presents that check to the payor bank, which must decide whether to pay or return the check before the midnight deadline. The check may appear to be covered by uncollected funds at the payor bank, and so the payor bank may decide to pay the check by allowing the midnight deadline to pass.

A kite crashes when one of the banks dishonors checks drawn on it and returns them to the other banks involved in the kite. Clark, supra. Usually, such a dishonor occurs when one bank suspects a kite. Id. However, an individual bank may have trouble detecting a check kiting scheme. "Until one has devoted a substantial amount of time examining not only one's own account, but accounts at other banks, it may be impossible to know whether the customer is engaged in a legitimate movement of funds or illegitimate kiting." James J. White & Robert S. Summers, Uniform Commercial Code § 17–1 (3d ed. 1988 & Supp. 1994). But each bank is usually able to monitor only its own account, and "[t]here is no certain test that distinguishes one who writes many checks on low balances from a check kiter." White & Summers, supra, § 17–2. Even if a bank suspects a kite, it might decide not to take any action for a number of reasons. First, it may be liable to its customer for wrongfully dishonoring checks. § 4–202. Second, if it reports that a kite is operating and turns out to be wrong, it could find itself defending a defamation suit. White & Summers, supra, § 17–1 (Supp. 1994). Finally, if it errs in returning checks or reporting a kite, it may risk angering a large customer. Id.

This case involves the fallout of a collapsed check kite. Two of the banks involved, First National Bank in Harvey ("First National") and Colonial Bank ("Colonial") are the parties to this litigation. The Federal Reserve Bank of Chicago (the "Reserve Bank"), through whose clearinghouse the relevant checks were processed, is also a party.

Shelly International Marketing ("Shelly") opened a checking account at First National in December 1989. The principals of Shelly also opened accounts at the Family Bank (a nonparty) in the names of Shelly Brokerage and Crete Trading around December 1990. On December 31, 1991, the principals of Shelly opened a checking account at Colonial Bank in the name of World Commodities, Inc. Shelly and World Commodities were related companies, with the same or similar shareholders, officers, and directors. The principals of Shelly and World Commodities began operating a check kiting scheme among the accounts at the three banks in early 1991.

The main events at issue in this case took place in February 1992. The checks that form the basis of this suit are thirteen checks totalling $1,523,892.49 for which First National was the depositary bank and Colonial was the payor bank (the "Colonial checks"). Also relevant are seventeen checks totalling $1,518,642.86 for which Colonial was the depositary bank and First National was the payor bank (the "First National checks").

On Monday, February 10, Shelly deposited the thirteen Colonial checks to its First National account. First National then sent those checks through the check clearing system. That same day, World Commodities deposited the seventeen First National checks to its Colonial account.

The next day, Tuesday, February 11, the Colonial checks were presented to Colonial for payment, and the First National checks were presented to First National for payment. That day, David Spiewak, an officer with First National's holding company, Pinnacle, reviewed the bank's records to determine why there were large balance fluctuations in Shelly's First National account. Spiewak began to suspect that a kite might be operating. He did not know whether Colonial had enough funds to cover the Colonial checks that had been deposited on Monday, February 10, and forwarded to Colonial for payment. Later that day, First National froze the Shelly account to prevent any further activity in it.

On the morning of Wednesday, February 12, Spiewak met with First National president Dennis Irvin and Pinnacle's chief lending officer Mike Braun to discuss the Shelly account. Spiewak informed the others of what he knew, and the three agreed that there was a possible kite. They concluded that further investigation was needed. The First National officers decided to return the First National checks to Colonial. First National says that the decision was made at this meeting, but Colonial says the decision was actually made the day before.

On Wednesday, First National returned the First National checks to Colonial. Under Regulation CC, a bank that is returning checks in excess of $2,500.00 must provide notice to the depositary bank either by telephone, actual return of the check, or Fed Wire before 4:00 p.m. on the second business day following presentment. First National notified Colonial by Fed Wire that it was returning the seventeen First National checks. Initially, the large item return form indicated that the reason for the return was "uncollected funds," but Spiewak changed that reason to "refer to maker."

Colonial received the Fed Wire notices at approximately 2:45 p.m. on Wednesday and routed them to its cashier, Joanne Topham. Randall Soderman, a Colonial loan officer, was informed of the large return, and immediately began an investigation. He realized that if the Colonial checks were not returned by midnight that same day, Colonial would be out the money. Returning the Colonial checks before midnight would protect Colonial from liability, but it would risk disappointing the customer. Anthony Schiller, the loan officer in charge of the World Commodities account, called World Commodities comptroller Charles Patterson and its attorney Jay Goldstein. Both assured Schiller that the First National checks were good and should be redeposited. Ultimately, Richard Vucich, Colonial's president, and Joanne Topham, Colonial's cashier, decided not to return the Colonial checks on Wednesday. They decided instead to meet on Thursday morning with Schiller to discuss the matter.

Schiller, Topham, and Vucich met on the morning of Thursday, February 13. At the conclusion of the meeting, they decided to return the thirteen Colonial checks to First National. At about 10:45 a.m., Colonial telephoned First National to say that it intended to return the Colonial checks. Colonial sent the Colonial checks back through the Reserve Bank as a return in a return cash letter. The Reserve Bank debited First National's Reserve Bank account in the amount of the Colonial checks. First National received the returned Colonial checks on Friday, February 14.

First National then resorted to the Fed's "challenge procedure" to contest the return of the Colonial checks after the midnight deadline. First National prepared and submitted to the Reserve Bank a "Sender's Claim of Late Return" form for each of the Colonial checks. The Reserve Bank processed the claim forms and credited the Reserve Bank account of First National $1,523,892.49 and debited the Reserve Bank account of Colonial in the same amount. On February 24, Colonial prepared and filed a "Paying Bank's Response to Claim of Late Return" form for each of the thirteen Colonial checks. As a consequence of the processing of the response forms, the Reserve Bank reversed the credit given to First National and the debit made to Colonial.

First National then filed this suit against Colonial and the Reserve Bank, alleging that Colonial wrongfully returned the Colonial checks after the midnight deadline and the Reserve Bank wrongfully accepted the late return. * * * Count V against Colonial alleges breach of UCC § 4–302 for Colonial's failure to return the checks by the midnight deadline. * * *

First National moved for partial summary judgment as to Count V. On August 27, 1993, this court denied the plaintiff's motion. First Nat'l Bank in Harvey v. Colonial Bank, 831 F.Supp. 637 (N.D.Ill.1993). The parties now have each moved for summary judgment on all counts. Along with deciding the remaining counts, today's opinion reconsiders portions of our earlier ruling on Count V. * * *

* * *

I. COUNT V: BREACH OF UCC § 4–302 AGAINST COLONIAL

A. Accountability

Article 4 of the Uniform Commercial Code adopts a policy of "final payment"; that is, a check is considered to be finally paid at some specific and identifiable point in time. § 4–215 Comment 1. Final payment is the "end of the line" in the check collection process. Section 4–301 sets up the "midnight deadline" in the process: a payor bank which intends to return a check presented to it must do so before midnight of the next banking day following receipt of the check. §§ 4–301(a), 4–104(a)(10). If a payor bank fails to return a check before the midnight deadline, final payment occurs. * * *

Section 4–302 spells out the payor bank's liability for its late return of an item, that is, return after the midnight deadline:

(a) If an item is presented to and received by a payor bank, the bank is *accountable* for the amount of:

(1) a demand item, other than a documentary draft, whether properly payable or not, if the bank ... does not pay or return the item or send notice of dishonor until after its midnight deadline....

§ 4–302 (emphasis added). The operative word in this section is "accountable." Courts interpreting this section have nearly unanimously concluded that § 4–302 imposes strict liability on a payor bank for failing to adhere to the midnight deadline, and makes the measure of damages the face amount of the check. In an early decision, the Illinois Supreme Court held that "accountable" means "liable" for the amount of the item. Rock Island Auction Sales, Inc. v. Empire Packing Co., 32 Ill.2d 269, 204 N.E.2d 721, 723 (Ill. 1965). The Rock Island court contrasted the "accountability" language in § 4–302 with the language used to specify the measure of damages in what is now § 4–103(e). Section 4–103(e) makes a bank liable for failing to exercise ordinary care in the handling of a check in "the amount of the item reduced by an amount that could not have been realized by the exercise of ordinary care." § 4–103(e). The Official Comment to this section explains: "When it is established that some part or all of the item could not have been collected even by the use of ordinary care the recovery is reduced by the amount that would have been in any event uncollectible." In other words, § 4–103(e) imposes liability in the amount of the loss caused by the negligence, while § 4–302(a) imposes strict liability in the face amount of the check.

The *Rock Island* court reasoned that the special role of the payor bank in the check collection system justifies the imposition of liability regardless of negligence. The midnight deadline requires the payor bank—the bank in the best position to know whether there are funds available to cover the check—to decide whether to pay or return the check:

> The role of a payor bank in the collection process . . . is crucial. It knows whether or not the drawer has funds available to pay the item. The legislature could have considered that the failure of such a bank to meet its deadline is likely to be due to factors other than negligence, and that the relationship between a payor bank and its customer may so influence its conduct as to cause a conscious disregard of its statutory duty.

Rock Island, 204 N.E.2d at 723.

The overwhelming majority of courts that have considered the meaning of § 4–302(a) have followed the *Rock Island* court in concluding that the liability of a payor bank that fails to return a check by the midnight deadline is strict and is in the face amount of the check. * * *

Even where the damage suffered by the payee is not caused by the lateness of the return, the midnight deadline still has been strictly enforced. For example, in Chicago Title Ins. Co. v. California Canadian Bank, 1 Cal. App. 4th 798, 2 Cal. Rptr.2d 422, 424 (Ct. App. 1991), the payor bank decided to return twenty-eight checks involved in a massive check fraud scheme. The checks left the bank before the midnight deadline, but did not arrive at the clearinghouse until the next day—after the midnight deadline had passed. The court held that the bank's return was late. It held the bank strictly accountable for the face amount of the checks, reasoning that the bank " 'may be held strictly liable for its failure to return the checks by the applicable deadlines, regardless whether [the other party] demonstrated it suffered actual damage solely as a result of [the Bank's] omission.' " Id. at 426–29 (quoting Los Angeles Nat'l Bank v. Bank of Canton, 229 Cal. App.3d 1267, 280 Cal. Rptr. 831, 838 (Ct. App. 1991)); see also American Title Ins. Co. v. Burke & Herbert Bank & Trust Co., 813 F.Supp. 423, 426 (E.D.Va.1993) ("[L]iability for the face amount of the check is imposed without regard to whether any damages have been sustained as a result of the payor bank's failure to make a timely return."), aff'd, 25 F.3d 1038 (4th Cir.1994).

* * *

But is it appropriate to enforce the accountability provision of § 4–302 where a check kiting scheme is involved? The Minnesota Supreme Court did in Town & Country State Bank v. First State Bank, 358 N.W.2d 387, 393–95 (Minn.1984). There, the court held that two payor banks that held kited checks beyond the midnight deadline made "final payment" on the checks and were therefore accountable for the amounts of those checks. * * *

* * *

This court's prior opinion held that First National could not recover under the accountability provision of § 4–302 if it would be unjustly enriched by the recovery. § 1–103; 831 F.Supp. at 641. On the undisputed evidence presented by First National on the present motion, however, we now see that it did suffer a loss. At some point during the check kiting scheme, funds were siphoned out of the banking system, causing a deficit in First National's assets. The important point is that First National will not be unjustly enriched by recovering from Colonial. It has suffered a loss at some point, and will not experience a windfall if it recovers from Colonial.

Therefore, we conclude that Colonial is absolutely liable in the face amount of the Colonial checks for missing the midnight deadline. This does not end the analysis, however, because Colonial raises the defenses of good faith and mistaken payment to defeat strict accountability.

B.   Good Faith

The general provisions of the Uniform Commercial Code state: "Every contract or duty within this Act imposes an obligation of good faith in its performance or enforcement." § 1–203 [1–304]. The Code defines "good faith" as "honesty in fact in the conduct or transaction concerned." § 1–201(19) [1–201(b)(20)]. Colonial argues that First National's lack of good faith defeats its § 4–302 claim of accountability, contending that First National orchestrated the events of the week of February 10 in order to cause Colonial to miss the midnight deadline for returning the Colonial checks.

The first question is whether we should even consider bad faith in this check kiting case. First National urges us to refrain from injecting notions of bad faith to reallocate the loss here. It contends that introducing the concept of bad faith will muddy the concepts of certainty and finality, which are central to the treatment of kites by Article 4. However, the UCC itself, in § 1–103, injects notions of good faith into every transaction covered by it, and we cannot simply ignore the statute.

Colonial charges that First National returned the seventeen First National checks to Colonial on Wednesday, February 12, under circumstances amounting to bad faith. Colonial argues that First National deliberately caused confusion in returning the First National checks, which caused Colonial to miss the midnight deadline for the Colonial checks.

Colonial offers the following facts to show First National's bad faith. On Tuesday, February 11, Spiewak thought that a kite was taking place and together with other First National officers decided that the First National checks would be dishonored and returned to Colonial. First

National returned the checks the next day, Wednesday, a day on which it is closed for business. It also notified Colonial of the return late in the day (2:45 p.m.) by Fed Wire rather than by telephone, a practice that is rarely used and less desirable than telephone notice because a wire notice may not be picked up by an employee for some time, while telephonic notice is received directly by a bank employee who can take immediate action. Finally, First National changed the reason for the return from "uncollected funds" to "refer to maker." When Colonial received the wire transmittal, it attempted to contact First National to determine why First National returned the checks "refer to maker." No one at Colonial was able to talk to anyone at First National, however, because a recorded message informed Colonial employees that First National was closed on Wednesdays. First National's endorsement stamp contains only its general telephone number, not any other telephone number that would allow telephone calls to be made even when the switchboard is closed, as is the practice at most Chicago area banks.

In short, Colonial argues that First National's failure to advise Colonial of the kite, its delay in giving notice of the return, its use of Fed Wire to give notice of the return, its return of the checks marked "refer to maker," and its return of the checks on a day when it was closed for business caused Colonial to miss the midnight deadline for the Colonial checks. These facts amount to bad faith, Colonial contends; consequently First National may not recover any losses it suffered in the kite. And, in any event, whether First National's acts constitute bad faith is an issue of fact that precludes summary judgment in favor of First National.

Colonial's argument raises specific questions about whether First National's conduct amounts to bad faith. But it also raises more general questions about banks' conduct in check kiting schemes: Does a depositary bank that suspects a kite have a good faith duty to disclose its suspicions to the payor bank? Furthermore, does a bank act in bad faith if it discovers or suspects a kite and attempts to shift the loss to the other bank by returning checks drawn on it while at the same time forwarding checks that have been deposited with it for payment?

Courts that have dealt with these issues usually take the latter two questions together, and most have concluded that a bank has no good faith obligation to disclose a suspected kite or to refrain from attempting to shift the kite loss. These were the conclusions of the Mississippi Supreme Court in the leading case of Citizens Nat'l Bank v. First Nat'l Bank, 347 So.2d 964 (Miss.1977). In *Citizens*, a check kite was operating through accounts at Citizens National Bank and at First National Bank. First National discovered the kite, and returned all checks drawn on its account that Citizens had presented. At the same time, First National presented checks to Citizens that the kiter had drawn on Citizens and deposited with First National. First National also accepted deposits by the kiter and payments by Citizens. After the kite crashed, Citizens sued First National, charging that First National converted funds belonging to Citizens.

The Mississippi Supreme Court upheld the dismissal of the complaint, agreeing with the chancellor's opinion which stated, "I cannot find where FNB has been charged with doing anything other than acting as a prudent and careful bank should act." Id. at 967, 969. In holding that there was no duty on the part of First National to notify Citizens of its conviction that their mutual customer was kiting checks, the court reasoned:

> [T]hese two banks were competitors in the banking field and ordinarily banks deal with each other at arm's length. The bill does not allege any circumstances or facts that tend to show that a confidential or fiduciary relationship existed between these two banks, neither does it show that there is any requirement in the banking field that one bank notify another of its discovery of a customer kiting checks. In the absence of a fiduciary or confidential relationship, or some other legal duty, First National Bank had no duty to inform Citizens National Bank that Duran was kiting checks. This being true, we are of the opinion that First National Bank had the legal right to continue to accept for deposit checks drawn by Duran on accounts at Citizens National Bank and present those checks for payment. At the same time, First National Bank had the legal right to refuse to pay checks drawn by Duran on accounts in First National Bank and deposited in Citizens National Bank.

Id. at 967.

In a more recent case, the district court in Connecticut similarly concluded that a bank's failure to tell another bank about a suspected kite, while returning checks drawn on it and accepting checks drawn on the other bank, is not bad faith. Cumis Ins. Society, Inc. v. Windsor Bank & Trust Co., 736 F.Supp. 1226, 1231–34 (D.Conn.1990). In *Cumis*, the insurer of a credit union that sustained a kite loss sued the winning bank. The facts are similar: the bank suspected a kite and began to dishonor checks drawn against it while continuing to collect on checks drawn on the credit union and deposited with the bank. The bank had even instituted an expedited check clearing procedure specifically to handle drafts drawn on the credit union. Id. at 1230. The court refused to impose a good faith duty to disclose the kite:

> There is thus no duty between competing institutions to inform one another of the existence of a check kiting scheme because these institutions deal at arms length, have their own means of detecting check kiting, and, realistically, need no protection from other institutions.

Id. at 1233. The court identified several exceptions to this general rule: (1) where a fiduciary or confidential relationship exists; (2) where a contractual relationship exists; (3) where there is a duty created by law; and (4) where there was fraud or misrepresentation by the defendant bank. * * *

* * *

The facts here amount to, at most, an attempt by First National to shift the kite loss to Colonial. First, as First National points out, wire notice is a legally permissible method of notifying another bank of a large return. 12 C.F.R. § 229.33(a). In addition, First National has presented evidence that notifying other banks of large returns by wire rather than by telephone was its usual practice.

Although Colonial makes much of the fact that First National returned the First National checks marked "refer to maker" rather than "uncollected funds," the parties agree that "refer to maker" is a legally permissible reason for returning a check. And Colonial had contacted the maker, World Commodities, and its counsel, receiving assurances that the checks were good. As to First National's delay in informing Colonial of the return, it is undisputed that First National notified a Colonial employee at 9:30 a.m. on Wednesday, February 12, that it would be returning certain checks, although it notified the wrong employee and did not specify the number or dollar amounts of those checks. But First National sent the wire notice later the same day stating that seventeen checks totalling $1,518,642.86 were being returned "refer to maker." Even if, as Colonial contends, First National officers decided to return the checks on Tuesday rather than Wednesday, Colonial had notice more than twelve hours before the midnight deadline that checks drawn on the Shelly account were being returned. And even though Colonial was not able to contact First National on Wednesday, Colonial knew on that day that the First National checks were being returned and that the midnight deadline for the Colonial checks was rapidly approaching.

All of First National's conduct regarding the First National checks was proper under the applicable laws. First National had the right to present the Colonial checks for payment and the right to return the First National checks. At most, First National took advantage of these laws and regulations to attempt to shift the kite loss onto Colonial. But even if this is what happened, such conduct does not constitute bad faith.

First National and Colonial were faced with the same dilemma at the same time: a number of checks totaling a goodly sum of money drawn on the account of a customer with low collected funds balances. First National chose to return the checks unpaid, but Colonial chose to trust its customer to cover the checks. By the time Colonial realized that its decision was wrong, it was too late—the midnight deadline had passed and the checks were paid. Each bank made a business decision; First National's turned out to be the correct one.

* * *

For the reasons explained, plaintiff First National's motion for summary judgment is granted as to Count V of the first amended complaint * * *. Colonial's motion for summary judgment is * * * denied as to Count V.

NOTES

1. The principal case states the prevailing rule, but Oregon courts have taken the view that a depositary bank may be in bad faith if it presents checks knowing of a check kite while dishonoring checks drawn on it. *Farmers & Merchants State Bank v. Western Bank*, 841 F.2d 1433 (9th Cir.1987), applies Oregon law and reviews the state court authorities. 1 Clark & Clark, The Law of Bank Deposits, Check Collections and Credit Cards & 9.03 (Rev. ed. 1999). Should the "fair dealing" prong of the definition of "good faith" in 1–201(b)(20) have any effect on facts like those in *First National Bank in Harvey*?

2. In the text before the principal case we asked why the court didn't refer to 4–302(b) and the reference to check kiting in Comment 3 to 4–302. What is your answer? Is the reference to check kiting in Comment 3 to 4–302 consistent with the reference to check kiting in Comment 3 to 3–418? White & Summers, Uniform Commercial Code § 17–3 (4th ed. 1995). In In re Spring Grove Livestock Exchange, Inc., 205 B.R. 149 (Bankr.D.Minn. 1997), the trustee in bankruptcy of the check kiter attempted to enforce the midnight deadline of former 4–302 against the payor bank. Conceding that in contests between banks in check kiting cases the courts usually allocate the loss to the payor bank, the court held in favor of the payor bank in this case, observing that: "[N]o court has allowed a check kiter, in his individual capacity, to enforce the midnight deadline against a defrauded bank." 205 B.R. at 159 n.15. It noted that this case would have been covered by the fraudulent presentment language of Revised 4–302(b) had that provision been in effect.

d.   EFFECT OF REGULATION CC ON THE MIDNIGHT DEADLINE

Regulation CC, 12 CFR pt. 229, § 229.30(c), is a major modification of the Article 4 midnight deadline. In this regulation the Fed attempts to speed the return of checks by extending the midnight deadline. How does this make returns swifter? The regulation is set out below.

(c) Extension of deadline. The deadline for return or notice of nonpayment under the U.C.C. * * * is extended to the time of dispatch of such return or notice of nonpayment where a paying bank uses a means of delivery that would ordinarily result in receipt by the bank to which is sent

(1) On or before the receiving bank's next banking day following the otherwise applicable deadline [the UCC midnight deadline], for all deadlines other than those described in paragraph (c)(2) of this section; this deadline is extended further if a paying bank uses a highly expeditious means of transportation, even if this means of transportation would ordinarily result in delivery after the receiving bank's next banking day; or

(2) Prior to the cut-off hour for the next processing day (if sent to a returning bank), or on the next banking day (if sent to the depositary bank), for a deadline falling on a Saturday that is a banking day (as defined in the applicable U.C.C.) for the paying bank.

An example of how these provisions operate is found in the following case.

Oak Brook Bank v. Northern Trust Company

United States Court of Appeals, Seventh Circuit, 2001.
256 F.3d 638.

■ POSNER, CIRCUIT JUDGE.

A bank that dishonors a check presented to it for payment must return the check to the bank in which the check had been deposited (the "depositary" bank), either directly or via a "returning bank," which acts as a transmitting agent. (The bank to which the check is presented for payment is called, even if it dishonors the check, the "payor" bank—a confusing usage in this context since it has *refused* to pay the check.) Like the other federal reserve banks, the Federal Reserve Bank of Chicago is a returning bank; indeed, returning checks is the major conventional banking activity in which federal reserve banks engage. In the case at hand, a check kiter who had accounts in both Oak Brook Bank and Northern Trust Company deposited in his Oak Brook account checks (none for less than $2,500) totaling some $450,000 drawn on his Northern account, which had only a minute balance (exactly how much, the record does not disclose). The checks were presented to Northern for payment the next day, February 11, 1998. On February 13, Northern decided to dishonor them and it informed Oak Brook of that decision by phone shortly before 4 p.m. By that time, however, Oak Brook had credited the kiter's account and he had withdrawn all but about $7,000 of the money in the account. At 4:30 p.m., Northern sent the dishonored checks by courier to the Federal Reserve Bank, which received them sixteen minutes later.

Oak Brook sued the kiter and the kiter's company in federal district court under RICO and added a claim under the supplemental jurisdiction of the district court against Northern, charging that the dishonor was ineffective because the return of the checks was untimely and concluding that therefore Northern must make good Oak Brook's loss. The district court granted summary judgment for Northern and entered a Rule 54(b) judgment enabling Oak Brook to take an immediate appeal. The claim against the kiter and his company remain pending in the district court. The issue in this appeal, a novel one, is the meaning of "banking day" in regard to federal reserve banks.

The banking article of the Uniform Commercial Code requires the payor bank that wishes to dishonor a check to dispatch it (for example by putting it in the mail), either to the depositary bank or to a "returning" bank for forwarding to the depositary bank, by midnight on the next banking day after the banking day on which the payor bank had received the check; and failure to make the deadline requires the payor bank to pay the check. UCC §§ 4–104(a)(10), 4–302(a)(1). Northern missed this deadline, for remember that it received the checks on February 11 but didn't dispatch them to the Federal Reserve Bank until the thirteenth. No matter.

In 1987, concerned about delay in depositors' access to funds that they deposited by check, Congress, in the Expedited Funds Availability Act, 12 U.S.C. §§ 4001–10, shortened the "hold period" of depositary banks, that is, the period after a check is deposited before the depositor can withdraw the money from his account. 12 U.S.C. § 4002. The shortening of the hold period increased the risk of nonpayment to these banks, and to deal with that problem the Act authorized the Federal Reserve Board to issue regulations governing the system of bank payments. 12 U.S.C. § 4008(c)(1). Pursuant to this grant of authority the Board issued Regulation CC, 12 C.F.R. pt. 229, which contains two provisions that bear on this case. The first requires prompt notice of dishonor in the case of any check for more than $2,500, such as the kiter's checks that Northern dishonored. 12 C.F.R. § 229.33(a). It is conceded that this provision was satisfied by Northern's phone call to Oak Brook on the thirteenth. But second—and this is critical—the regulation extends the UCC's deadline from midnight to when the payor bank dispatches the dishonored check on its return journey, provided the bank "uses a means of delivery that would ordinarily result in receipt by the bank to which it is sent . . . on or before the receiving bank's next banking day following the otherwise applicable deadline." 12 C.F.R. § 229.30(c)(1).

It may seem odd that delay in returning the checks should make the payor bank have to pay them in a case such as this, when it had notified the depositary bank that the checks had been drawn against insufficient funds in time for that bank to prevent any money from being withdrawn. Oak Brook seems to have been careless in allowing the kiter to withdraw "his" money so fast. Of course it didn't know he was a kiter. But because of the size of the deposit, it could have refused withdrawal for seven business days, see 12 C.F.R. §§ 229.13(b), (h)(1), (h)(4), and thus until February 20; and had it done so it wouldn't have been left holding the bag, since it received notice of the dishonor on the thirteenth and the checks themselves back on the seventeenth. But all that is irrelevant. If Northern missed the extended deadline in Regulation CC, it must pay the checks. The reason for this severe sanction is that the depositary bank could get into serious trouble if it refused to allow a depositor to withdraw his money, or took other action against a depositor, without proof that the depositor had no right to the money. See UCC § 4–402.

And now we come at last to the nub of the case. The provision that we quoted from Regulation CC extending the deadline requires that the method of delivery used be calculated to get the check to the depositary or, as here, the returning bank by that bank's "next banking day following the otherwise applicable deadline." The "otherwise applicable deadline" was the UCC's deadline of midnight on February 12, the day after Northern received the checks. The "next banking day" was the thirteenth, and so Northern had to get the checks to the Federal Reserve Bank, the returning bank, by the end of the Federal Reserve Bank's "banking day" on the thirteenth; and the question is whether it made this deadline.

Regulation CC defines "banking day" as "that part of any business day on which an office of a bank is open to the public for carrying on *substantially all of its banking functions.*" 12 C.F.R. § 229.2(f) (emphasis added). (The UCC's definition of "banking day" is materially identical. See UCC § 4–104(a)(3).) Oak Brook argues that by 4:46 p.m. on February 13, the Federal Reserve Bank of Chicago was no longer carrying on "substantially all of its banking functions." More precisely, it argues that whether it was or not is a contestable issue and so the grant of summary judgment for Northern was premature.

The Federal Reserve Bank of Chicago is open 24 hours a day, but that is neither here nor there. Federal reserve banks perform many functions for the banking system that are not banking functions. The question is whether at 4:46 p.m. on February 13, 1998, it was still carrying on substantially all of its banking functions. The bank's main banking function is check processing (including returns) for other banks—and it turns out that we need not consider what if any other banking functions the Federal Reserve Bank of Chicago, or any other federal reserve bank, performs. For that matter, it is of no significance that check processing is the Chicago reserve bank's main banking activity. Regulation CC states that a federal reserve bank is a bank within the meaning of the regulation only insofar as it is a "paying bank," the definition of which, so far as pertains to federal reserve banks, appears to be limited to a bank that processes checks. See 12 C.F.R. §§ 229.2(e), (z). Given that definition and the fact that Regulation CC is concerned solely with check processing, we think that for purposes of the regulation "all of [a federal reserve bank's] banking functions" means check processing. For it is irrelevant to the purpose of the regulation whether the bank is performing some other banking function on a particular day or at a particular time of day; and it would impair the utility of the extended deadline if a payor bank (Northern here), in order to determine what the deadline was, had to familiarize itself with the daily schedule of a bank's banking operations unrelated to check processing. This point is not logically limited to federal reserve banks, but we need not decide its applicability to banks that provide a broader range of conventional banking services and, unlike federal reserve banks, are not defined in the regulation as limited-purpose banks.

So the issue narrows to whether the Federal Reserve Bank of Chicago was open to the public (Oak Brook concedes that this means to other banks, which are a federal reserve bank's only "public") at 4:46 p.m. on February 13 for processing checks. The bank's check-processing department employs about 100 persons, with half or even more working during the peak hours of midnight to 9 a.m. Between 4 and 5 on a Friday afternoon, however (February 13, 1998, was a Friday), only one or two persons are on duty in the department. The processing of returned checks includes receipting the checks, sorting them by type and region, dispatching them to the depositary bank, and confirming the amount returned. When only one or two employees are on duty in the department, only receipting is completed; sorting is begun but not completed; dispatching, crediting, and, of course, confirming are not even begun. If, therefore, as Oak Brook argues, all these are separate functions, it cannot be said that the Federal Reserve Bank of Chicago performs substantially all of its banking functions on Friday afternoons after 4, and therefore Northern missed the deadline and must pay the checks.

We reject the argument, primarily on practical grounds. It would be impractical for payor banks to monitor the internal operations of returning banks in order to make sure that sending a check by courier at a given hour on a given day would be an occurrence that was within the returning bank's "banking day." It is telling in this regard that Oak Brook's lawyer was unable to pinpoint the end of the Federal Reserve Bank's banking day on February 13, 1998. The end was earlier than 4:46 p.m., he told us, but he was unable to say how much earlier, though he thought it might have been at 2 p.m. To fix the precise time would require, he told us, an in-depth inquiry, and therefore a trial.

Faced with such uncertainty, payor banks would tend to go back to the old UCC deadline, which Regulation CC does not supersede but merely supplements. Had Northern placed Oak Brook's checks in the mail to the Federal Reserve Bank of Chicago shortly before midnight on February 12 (the old UCC deadline), the checks probably wouldn't have gotten to that bank until the seventeenth (Monday the sixteenth was a federal holiday), and processing would have begun then rather than been completed then and therefore Oak Brook might not have received the checks as soon as it did. The added delay would have made no difference in this case but could make a difference in other cases.

We hold, therefore, that a federal reserve bank is open to the public for substantially all of its banking functions whenever the check-processing department is open for the receipt of checks, which in the case of the Federal Reserve Bank of Chicago is 24 hours of every day that the bank is open. The few cases dealing with the meaning of "banking day" under the materially identical definition of the term in the UCC are in accord with our position * * * Northern's employment of a means of delivery calculated to get the checks to the Federal Reserve Bank by any time up to midnight on February 13 therefore beat the deadline, and so summary judgment in Northern's favor was rightly granted. We leave open the implications of our analysis for returning banks other than federal reserve banks, which we were told dominate the check-return function.

AFFIRMED.

NOTES

1. Judge Posner leaves open the meaning of banking day for returning banks other than Federal Reserve banks. Comment 2 to 4–104 speaks to this issue: "Under [the definition of banking day in 4–104(a)(3)] that part of a business day when a bank is open only for limited functions, e.g., to receive deposits and cash checks, but with loan, bookkeeping and other departments closed, is not part of a banking day."

2. In determining whether a payor bank has returned an item by its midnight deadline, 4–301(d)(2) focuses on when the item was "sent or delivered" rather than on when it arrived. If an item is mailed to the presenting bank just before the midnight deadline, the payor bank has revoked settlement under 4–301(a) and is not accountable under 4–302(a)(1), even though the item may not arrive for a week. In an effort to speed up returns, Reg. CC added an additional day for return of the item to allow the payor to use a more expeditious means of return, such as an early morning courier, that would get the check back much faster than mail dispatched before the midnight deadline. *Oak Brook Bank* is an example of what the Fed had in mind in expediting returns.

2. RIGHT OF COLLECTING BANK TO REVOKE SETTLEMENT ON DISHONORED CHECK

We saw in the preceding section that a payor bank may inadvertently pay a check by failing to return the check within its midnight deadline. A collecting bank, including a depositary bank, is also subject to a midnight deadline in the case of return of a dishonored check to the bank. If a check forwarded to the payor bank is not paid, the depositary bank may revoke the provisional credit that it gave to its customer with respect to the check. 4–214(a). But the depositary bank is required either to return the check to its customer or to give notice of dishonor to the customer before the bank's midnight deadline. The case below discusses the Revised Article 4 provisions on notice of dishonor and the consequences of the failure of the depositary bank to act within its deadline.

Essex Construction Corporation v. Industrial Bank of Washington, Inc.

United States District Court, D. Maryland, 1995.
913 F.Supp. 416.

■ MOTZ, CHIEF JUDGE.

Plaintiff Essex Construction Corporation (Essex) claims violations of the * * * District of Columbia banking laws. Essex alleges that Defendant Industrial Bank of Washington, Inc. (Industrial) * * * failed to provide timely notice that the check had been dishonored. Plaintiff seeks the amount of the check as damages. Defendant moves to dismiss or for summary judgment, and plaintiff cross-moves for default or summary judgment.

The relevant facts are not in dispute. On March 31, 1995, plaintiff deposited into its account at Industrial a check in the amount of $120,710.70 from East Side Manor Cooperative Association (East Side). East Side's check was drawn against its account at Signet Bank (Signet). At the time of the deposit, Industrial provisionally credited Essex's account but provided written notice that all but $100 of the funds would not be available for withdrawal until April 6, 1995.

On April 6, Signet notified Industrial that East Side had stopped payment on the check. Industrial placed a permanent hold on the $120,710.70 deposit, effectively revoking the provisional credit to Essex's account. On April 7, Industrial mailed written notice (including the returned check itself) to Essex.

On April 7, Essex wrote two checks in the amount of $21,224 and $18,084.60 against the funds it thought were available in its account at Industrial. Essex received Industrial's written notice of dishonor on April 11.

* * * [A] depository bank's right to revoke or charge back an uncollectible deposit * * * must comply with applicable state law. The District of Columbia has adopted the Uniform Commercial Code's system for regulating check processing transactions. The U.C.C. observes a fundamental distinction between "payor" and "collecting" banks. A payor bank is the bank maintaining the account against which a check is drawn, in this case Signet. See § 4–105(3). A collecting bank is a bank handling a check for collection from the payor, in this case Industrial. See § 4–105(5).

Payor and collecting banks have distinct obligations. A payor bank must decide whether to reject a check by midnight on the day it receives a check for collection. Failure to respond by midnight constitutes "final payment," making the payor bank strictly liable for the amount of the check. See First Nat'l Bank in Harvey v. Colonial Bank, 898 F.Supp. 1220, 1226 (N.D.Ill.1995) (discussing U.C.C.'s "final payment" system and role of payor banks); see also § 4–302(a). A collecting bank, in contrast, retains the right to revoke or charge back funds that are provisionally credited to a customer until the collecting bank's settlement with the payor bank becomes final. See § 4–214(a). It is at the moment of "final payment" by the payor bank that the respective liabilities for a check become fixed: the payor bank is strictly liable to the collecting bank for the amount of the check, see § 4–302(a), and the collecting bank loses the ability to revoke a provisional settlement or charge back withdrawn funds. See §§ 4–215(d), 4–214(a).

Essex argues that on April 6 Industrial's provisional credit to its account became a final and irrevocable payment under § 4–215(a). This contention misunderstands the difference between payor and collecting banks. As discussed, a final payment occurs when a payor bank accepts or fails to promptly reject a check presented for collection by a collecting bank. Industrial was the collecting bank in this transaction. Essex's reliance on § 4–215(a) therefore is misplaced. See § 4–215(a) ("An item is finally paid by a *payor* bank when the bank has first done any of the following. . . .") (emphasis added). Essex's right to the provisionally credited funds became irrevocable only upon "final payment" by Signet to Industrial, a condition that Essex does not allege occurred.

Essex also argues that Industrial's mailing of the returned check via first class mail on April 7 did not constitute timely notice of dishonor under D.C. law. § 4–214 provides in relevant part:

> § 4–214 Right of charge-back or refund; liability of collecting bank; return of item.

(a) If a collecting bank has made a provisional settlement with its customer for an item and fails by reason of dishonor ... to receive settlement for the item which is or becomes final, the bank may revoke the settlement given by it, charge back the amount of any credit given for the item to its customer's account, or obtain refund from its customer ... if by its midnight deadline or within a longer reasonable time after it learns the facts it returns the item or sends notification of the facts....

There is no dispute that Industrial failed by reason of dishonor to receive a final payment from Signet, the payor bank. Section 4–214(a) therefore provides that Industrial could revoke the provisional credit "if by its midnight deadline or within a longer reasonable time after it learn[ed] the facts it return[ed] the item or sen[t] notification of the facts." A bank's "midnight deadline" is defined as "midnight on its next banking day following the banking day on which it receives the relevant item or notice." § 4–104(a)(10); see also § 3–503(c)(i) ("[W]ith respect to an instrument taken for collection by a collecting bank, notice of dishonor must be given by the bank before midnight of the next banking day following the banking day on which the bank receives notice of dishonor of the instrument."). The parties do not dispute that Industrial received notice of dishonor from Signet on April 6, that Industrial mailed the returned check to Essex before midnight on April 7 via first class mail, but that Essex did not receive it until April 11.

Essex argues that merely mailing the notice of dishonor before midnight on April 7 was insufficient. Industrial attempts to rely on § 3–508(4) for the proposition that "[w]ritten notice is given when sent although it is not received." However, the District of Columbia Council repealed § 3–508 effective March 27, 1995. See An Act to revise Articles 3 and 4 of the Uniform Commercial Code, 1994 D.C.Laws 10–249. Industrial's position finds alternative support, however, in § 4–214. Section 4–214(a) requires a bank to "*send* notification of the facts" or "*return*" the dishonored item. (emphasis added). Section 4–214(b) defines an item as "returned" "when it is *sent* or delivered to the bank's customer." In addition, § 3–503(b) provides that notice of dishonor may be given by "any commercially reasonable means, including an oral, written, or electronic communication." Industrial did not unduly delay notifying Essex, but instead took the reasonable step of promptly mailing the returned check. Although immediately telephoning Essex may have constituted better customer service, Industrial complied with D.C. notice requirements by mailing the returned check to Essex on April 7.

Moreover, even were I to find that Industrial's method of notice was not sufficient, Essex would not be entitled to the damages it seeks. In a case involving directly analogous provisions of the U.C.C. as enacted in Illinois, the Seventh Circuit has held that a depositor is entitled only to the damages actually resulting from a bank's failure to provide timely notice of dishonor. See Appliance Buyers Credit Corp. v. Prospect Nat'l Bank, 708 F.2d 290, 292–95 (7th Cir.1983). Furthermore, although the Appliance

Buyers court reached this well-reasoned conclusion by interpreting an Illinois statute that was silent as to damages,[4] here the D.C. provision contains additional language which expressly so limits a depositor's remedies: a bank that fails to provide timely notice retains its right to charge back dishonored deposits "but is liable for any loss *resulting from the delay*." § 4–214(a) (emphasis added).[5] Plaintiff therefore may have been able to assert a claim for the bank charges associated with the two checks written on April 7, or for other foreseeable damages.[6] Essex, however, has made no showing of damages actually suffered.

A separate order granting defendant's summary judgment motion and entering judgment on its behalf is being entered herewith.

NOTE

In Gordon v. Planters & Merchants Bancshares, Inc., 935 S.W.2d 544 (Ark.1996), a collecting bank charged back against a customer's account a check for which it had received final settlement in violation of 4–215(d). The customer sued for punitive damages and the trial court granted the bank a directed verdict. The Supreme Court of Arkansas (4 to 3) reversed and remanded for a new trial. In its view the customer had shown substantial evidence that the bank had acted in a willful or malicious manner, and the "other rule of law" language 1–106(1) [1–305(a)] allows punitive damages even if not specifically provided for in the UCC. The court noted the "bad faith" language in 4–103(e). The dissenting judges were outraged; two judges didn't participate.

3.   CHECK ENCODING

The conservatism of the banking profession is snickered at by the following oft-told anecdote: When a retiring banker was asked what the

---

4. In *Appliance Buyers*, the Seventh Circuit noted that because the charge-back provision at issue in that case did not expressly address damages—in contrast to other U.C.C. provisions that expressly do hold banks "accountable" for the amount of the check—the drafters could not have intended "that banks should be held strictly liable for the face value of dishonored checks." 708 F.2d at 293. Instead, the *Appliance Buyers* court turned to Illinois' general damages provision, which provided only for actual damages and which was identical to D.C.'s current provision. Compare § 4–103(e) with 708 F.2d at 293 (quoting Ill. Rev.Stat. ch. 26 § 4–103(5)).

5. In fact, prior to revisions that became effective on March 27, 1995, the predecessor to § 4–214(a) was largely identical to the Illinois statute at issue in *Appliance Buyers*. In 1995, however, the D.C. Council re-

vised its U.C.C. provisions to add, among other changes, the above-quoted language that expressly limits recovery to actual loss. See 1994 D.C.Laws 10–249.

6. To recover the $120,710.70 from Industrial, therefore, Essex would have had to show that, absent the delay from April 7 to April 11, it would have been able to take action to collect from East Side. See Alioto v. United States, 593 F.Supp. 1402, 1416–17 (N.D. Ill. 1984) (discussing cases). The record indicates, however, that East Side stopped payment on the check because of its ongoing dispute with Essex, not that East Side lacked funds on April 11 (or any time thereafter) that it had on April 7. In addition, defendant points out that in a separate proceeding East Side has alleged that it directly informed Essex of the stop payment order on April 6, the same day Signet notified Industrial.

single biggest change in banking had been during his long career, he replied: "air conditioning." In the 20th century, the biggest change in check collection to have gained wide-spread acceptance was an elementary technology invented in 1956 and known as Magnetic Ink Character Recognition (MICR) encoding. In order to permit electronic processing of checks for presentment for payment, almost all checks in use today are preprinted with a row of numerals and symbols along the bottom of the check (the "MICR line") that can be read by machines that process the checks for payment. The preprinted MICR encoding identifies the payor bank, the Federal Reserve district in which the bank is located, the Federal Reserve Bank or branch that serves the payor bank, the number of the check, and the number of the account at the payor bank on which the check is drawn. When the check is deposited, either the depositary bank or the next collecting bank that has encoding equipment will add to the MICR line numerals that indicate the amount of the check. In some cases the encoding of the amount of the check will be done by the payee of the check before the check is deposited in the depositary bank. This can occur if the payee is a person receiving a very large volume of checks that are processed in processing centers operated by the payee. Examples of such payees are public utilities, insurance companies, and large retailers.

Most checks that have been encoded with the amount of the check will be processed by automated equipment by the payor bank and by collecting banks on the basis of the encoded information without any examination of the check by a human being. What happens if a check is payable in the amount of $123.45 but the person encoding the amount of the check erroneously encodes the amount as $12,345? The misencoding does not change the amount of the check. There has been no alteration of the check. But if the check is read by machines on the basis of the encoded amount, the bank that processes the check will treat it as a check in the amount of $12,345. If the payor bank pays the check, it has paid out the encoded amount to the presenting bank but will be entitled to debit the account of the drawer of the check only for the actual amount of the check. Or, the payor bank might wrongfully dishonor the check because the balance in the drawer's account, although large enough to cover the actual amount of the check, is not enough to cover the encoded amount. Before the 1990 revision, Article 4 did not address the problem of misencoding because MICR encoding did not exist when Article 4 was drafted. Section 4–209 now addresses the consequences of misencoding.

PROBLEM

Drayton drew a check on Bank One for $10,000 payable to the order of Park Company. Park deposited the check in its account in Bank Two and was given a provisional credit for the amount of the check. Bank Two forwarded the check to Bank One for payment; it arrived on May 1.

(a) Bank Two misencoded the check for $1,000, and on May 1 Bank One sent Bank Two a wire transfer for $1,000 intended as provisional settlement. Bank One debited Drayton's account for that amount and retained the check for mailing to Drayton at the end of the billing cycle with her other cancelled checks. When Bank Two received only $1,000 for the check, it reduced the credit in Park's account to that amount. Park complained to Bank Two about its failure to give $10,000 final credit for check. What are Bank Two's rights against Bank One under 4–302(a)? What are Bank One's rights against Bank Two under 4–209(a)? If Drayton's account exceeds $10,000, has Bank One suffered a loss under 4–209(c)? See Comment 2 to 4–209.

(b) The check was misencoded for $100,000. On May 1, Bank One provisionally settled for the check by sending Bank Two a wire transfer for $100,000.

(i) Drayton had more than $100,000 in her account and Bank One debited her account for $100,000. What are Drayton's rights against Bank One? 4–401(a). Bank One's rights against Bank Two? 4–209(a) and (c).

(ii) On May 2, Bank One discovered that Drayton had only $25,000 in her account and dishonored the check by returning it to Bank Two before midnight on that date. Does Drayton have rights against Bank One for wrongful dishonor under 4–402? If Bank One is liable for damages to Drayton, what is its recourse under 4–209(a) against Bank Two?

The following case concerns an under-encoding error of major proportions.

First Union National Bank v. Bank One, N.A.

United States District Court, E.D. Pa., 2002.
47 UCC Rep.Serv.2d 645, 2002 WL 501145.

■ BUCKWALTER, J.

[Eds. First Union, the depository bank, under-encoded in the amount of $0.00 a check with a face amount of $507,598.30 and presented the check to Mellon, the intermediate collecting bank, for collection. Mellon in turn presented the check to Bank One, the payor bank, for payment. After settling with Mellon in the amount of $0.00, Bank One discovered the under-encoding error and paid Mellon the $507,598.30 face amount of the check. Mellon did not remit the amount to First Union. Later, after First Union presented Bank One with a photocopy of the check, Bank One paid it the face amount of the check. On Bank One's behalf, First Union sought to recover from Mellon Bank One's payment to it (Mellon).]

* * * [T]he Court is presented with two separate but related sets of questions. The first is the liability of Mellon, as an intermediary collecting bank, for having remitted $0.00 to the depository bank when the face amount of the Check was $507,598.30, and the effect of First Union's encoding error on that liability. * * *

B. MELLON'S LIABILITY TO FIRST UNION

Plaintiff, First Union, moves for partial summary judgment against Mellon on Counts III and V of its complaint. Count III alleges breach of a collecting bank's duty to account to its customer under Article 4 of the UCC. Count V alleges unjust enrichment.

* * *

Section 4–215(d) of the UCC provides:

If a collecting bank receives a settlement for an item which is or becomes final, the bank is accountable to its customer for the amount of the item and any provisional credit given for the item in an account with its customer becomes final.

First Union's argument is straightforward. Bank One, the drawee bank, made final payment on the subject Check, an item in the amount of $507,598.30. Final payment triggered accountability along the chain of collection. Therefore, Mellon, the collecting bank that received settlement for an item which became final, is accountable to First Union, its customer, for the amount of the item, $507,598.30. The fact that First Union encoded the item in the wrong amount is irrelevant, because once final payment occurred, the drawee bank and each collecting bank along the chain of collection is strictly accountable to its respective customer for the amount of the item, here $507,598.30.

Mellon argues that for purposes of § 4–215(d) the "amount of the item" for which a collecting bank is accountable is the encoded amount of the check, as long as the encoded amount is less than the face amount of the check or, alternatively, whichever is less. Therefore, because Bank One made final payment on the under-encoded check in the amount of $0.00 on January 13, 1998, that is the amount for which Mellon is accountable. Mellon further argues that the fact that Bank One subsequently issued an unexplained adjustment to Mellon does not alter the fact that final payment was made prior to that time and in an amount which valued the Check as $0.00.

Mellon finds support for its position in *First Nat'l Bank of Boston v. Fidelity Bank, N.A.,* 724 F.Supp. 1168 (E.D.Pa.1989). In that case, plaintiff bank under-encoded a $100,000 check as a $10,000 check. The defendant, the payor bank, charged the drawer's account in the lesser amount, and remitted that sum to plaintiff. When plaintiff bank made demand upon defendant bank for the $90,000 deficit, the drawer's account was insufficient to cover it. The *First Nat'l Bank of Boston* court held that "as between the encoding bank and all other banks in the collecting process, . . . the encoder is estopped from claiming more than the encoded amount of the check." *Id.* at 1172.

This appears to support Mellon's position, however, the court reasoned that this equitable defense was available "where plaintiff's encoding error caused the payor bank to suffer a loss which it could not avoid by charging its customer's account." *Id.* at 1171. In the case at bar, the drawee bank,

Bank One, successfully charged its customer's account for the face amount of the Check and remitted that amount to Mellon, albeit without proper documentation. Mellon, in turn, held onto the funds relying on the fact that Bank One had made "final payment" the prior day in the encoded amount of $0.00. The holding of *First Nat'l Bank of Boston,* does not entitle Mellon to hold onto funds properly debited from the maker of a check midway along the chain of collection because of an encoding error made by the depository bank.

The equitable defense described in *First Nat'l Bank of Boston,* would only come into play if (1) Bank One charged its customer, LCI, the under-encoded amount; (2) Bank One remitted the under-encoded amount along the chain of collection to Mellon; and (3) upon First Union's demand to collect the higher, face amount of the check from either Mellon or Bank One, the maker of the check, LCI, had insufficient funds in its account to cover that higher amount. In this fictional scenario, First Union would be estopped from collecting the face amount of the check under *First Nat'l Bank of Boston* because First Union's encoding error caused the loss which could not be avoided by charging the drawer's account.

Mellon's reliance on Bank One's final payment on the encoded amount within the midnight deadline does not change the analysis under § 4–215(d). The midnight deadline provisions of § 4–302 and the final payment provisions of § 4–215(a) are only relevant with respect to the time at which a bank's accountability for the retained check is triggered. The rules of final payment and the midnight deadline do not dictate whether "the amount of the check" for purposes of § 4–215(d) is the encoded amount or the face amount when those two differ. As the case relied on by Mellon points out, there is no support for the broad proposition that final payment of the amount of an item for § 4–215 purposes is the encoded amount, rather than the face amount of the check. *See First Nat'l Bank of Boston,* 724 F.Supp. at 1172.

In another leading under-encoding case, which provides guidance, the Georgia Court of Appeals held that a depository bank could recover the amount of the deficiency from the drawee bank where the latter debited its customer's account only the encoded amount of an under-encoded check mis-encoded by the depository bank. *Georgia Railroad Bank & Trust Co. v. First Nat'l Bank & Trust Co. of Augusta,* 139 Ga.App. 683, 229 S.E.2d 482 (Ga.Ct.App.1976), *aff'd* 238 Ga. 693, 235 S.E.2d 1 (Ga.1977). In that case, plaintiff bank erroneously encoded a $25,000 check as a $2,500 check. The defendant, the drawee bank, charged the drawer's account in the lesser amount, and remitted that sum to plaintiff. The error was not discovered for several weeks, by which time the cancelled check had already been returned to the maker. When plaintiff made demand upon the defendant for the deficiency, the defendant brought the error to the maker's attention, but the latter refused to allow the defendant to charge his account the additional $22,500, despite the fact that sufficient funds existed in the account. The Georgia court held, without extended discussion, that the defendant was liable to the plaintiff for the face amount of the check. The court first reasoned that the defendant bank was accountable to the plaintiff bank for the amount of the item pursuant to two code sections: (1) under § 4–213(1),[2] defendant bank was accountable because it had made "final payment" by charging the maker's account, albeit in the wrong amount; and (2) under § 4–302, defendant bank was strictly accountable by retaining the check beyond the midnight deadline without completely settling for it. Thus, because the defendant was accountable to plaintiff for the item and, more significantly, because the drawer's account contained sufficient funds to cover the face amount of the check, which would allow the loss to be shifted from the shoulders of the drawee bank, the Georgia court held the defendant drawee bank liable to the plaintiff collecting bank for the full amount of the check and not the under-encoded amount.

The common denominator between *First Nat'l Bank of Boston* and *Georgia R.R. Bank and Trust Co.,* is the principle that ultimate liability for encoding errors should rest on the shoulders of the depository bank that makes the error when deciding who should bear the loss between the depository bank, the collecting bank and the drawee bank. However, in the usual case, such as the case at bar, the parties can be put back into their original positions, with no party sustaining a loss. In the instant case, the payee has been credited with the face amount of the check by the depository bank, which is awaiting to collect the funds through the collection chain. The drawer has been debited by the drawee bank in the face amount of the check. The drawee bank has remitted the face amount of the check to the intermediary collecting bank. All that is needed to complete the chain is for the intermediary collecting bank to remit the funds to the depository bank.

The Court finds that Mellon did not properly account to First Union after receiving final settlement on the face amount of the check in violation of § 4–215(d) and Orders Mellon to remit $507,598.30 to First Union. Because the Court has found Mellon liable for the face amount of the Check pursuant to § 4–215(d), it does not address First Union's claim of unjust enrichment.

*   *   *

NOTE

Although the court relied on the two cases that formed the basis for the drafting of 4–209(a), it didn't rely on the statute for its decision? Was this merely an oversight? Would it have changed the result? The analysis?

4.   ELECTRONIC PRESENTMENT

a.   UNDER UCC

With respect to collection of checks by a depository bank, the present system depends upon transportation of checks through the banking system from the depository bank to the payor bank. Substantially more than one

---

2.   Section 4–213 is the predecessor code section to 4–215.

billion checks a week are processed by the banking system; the transportation of this volume of paper to the payor bank is very expensive and, as we will see, delays payment. In Lucinda Harper, Americans Won't Stop Writing Checks, Wall. St. J., Nov. 24, 1998, at A2, the cost of transporting and processing checks is estimated at more than $181 billion per year. Even though check collection is highly automated, Ms. Harper estimates that each paper check passes through the hands of at least a dozen people.

It is not surprising that the banking system, which has been aggressively seeking methods of cutting costs, has considered alternatives to flying and trucking tons of checks across the nation each day. One method discussed is often referred to by bankers as "truncation," but this is a confusing term because it is used to describe two quite different transactions. One use of the term describes the practice of payor banks of retaining checks after payment rather than returning them to the drawers who wrote them. Some banks are attempting to persuade their customers through differential pricing to agree to this practice. We will discuss this matter later.

It is the second use of the term, sometimes described as "radical truncation," that we are concerned with at this point. In order to avoid confusing it with the other meaning of truncation, Revised Articles 3 and 4 refer to this process as "electronic presentment." 4–110. Under this process most checks would be retained by the depositary bank for destruction after a relatively short period of time. Presentment for payment of a check would be made to the payor bank by electronic transmittal of essential information describing the check rather than by delivery of the check. After the check is destroyed, an image of the check would be stored electronically so that a copy of the check could be produced if needed at some later time.

Although under the present system the check itself is normally transported to the payor bank, most checks are not examined by anybody in the payor bank's process of payment. In these cases the check serves only as the carrier of the electronic encoding on the MICR line, which is read by the automated machinery of the payor bank. Use of the paper check itself to convey the information contained on the MICR line is both inefficient and unnecessary. It is technologically feasible to provide this information to the payor bank by electronic transmission. Since a system of electronic presentment was believed to be a possible solution to the banking industry's difficulties with the present check payment system, much discussion during the drafting of Revised Articles 3 and 4 centered around how the revision should deal with electronic presentment. The agreement reached was that it was not the role of the UCC to mandate business practices in the banking industry. Electronic presentment, if found economically feasible, should come by inter-bank agreements or through the Federal Reserve pursuant to its broad regulatory authority. Articles 3 and 4 should be revised to remove any legal barriers to a regime of electronic presentment. The assumptions under which the Drafting Committee proceeded are set out in Comments 2 and 3 to 4–110. The changes made in Articles 3 and 4 to accommodate electronic presentment are explained in the following paragraphs.

With respect to collection of checks, presentment is simply a demand made to the drawee to pay the check. 3–501(a). The demand may be made by an electronic communication. 3–501(b)(1). But Revised Article 3 follows the pre–1990 law in preserving the right of the drawee to demand exhibition of the check and its surrender as a condition to payment. 3–501(b)(2). This right of the drawee to require exhibition and surrender of the check is subject, however, to rules stated in Article 4 and may be waived by the drawee by agreement. Section 4–110 permits electronic presentment by means of a "presentment notice" which is defined as "transmission of an image of an item or information describing the item." The presentment notice is in lieu of delivery of the check itself. Presentment under 4–110 requires an "agreement for electronic presentment" which provides for the presentment notice. The quoted term includes not only an agreement between the drawee and the presenting bank, but also a clearing-house rule or Federal Reserve regulation or operating circular providing for electronic presentment.

Electronic presentment raises a number of problems. The payor bank will not be able to examine the signature of the drawer to detect a possible forgery, but this problem exists under current practice as well, because most checks are not examined for forgery. Under the current practice, payor banks look at the drawer's signature only on some checks such as those in large dollar amounts. This practice could continue under a regime of electronic presentment by a requirement that large checks be excluded from electronic presentment. Or, presentment of some checks might be made by transmitting an image of the check rather than information describing the check to allow examination of the drawer's signature. Current imaging technology allows depositary banks to send to payor banks miniature digitized images of checks, 15 or 20 to a page. The process, encouraged by 4–110(a), is described in 2 Clark & Clark, The Law of Bank Deposits, Check Collections and Credit Cards & 16.02[1] (Rev. ed. 1999). Imaging gives more information than that contained on the MICR line; the drawer's signature appears as well as the name of the payee.

The agreement for electronic presentment would also have to provide for retention and destruction of the check in order to protect the drawer of the check against further negotiation of the check. Under present practice many payor banks return all cancelled checks to the drawer after the checks are paid. This will not be possible with respect to checks paid pursuant to electronic presentment. But this practice of returning checks to the drawer has become less prevalent in recent years. Many banks have induced customers to opt for checking-account plans in which cancelled checks are not returned and instead the customer is given a statement describing the checks paid. Under electronic presentment the payor bank would be able to obtain, at the request of a customer, a copy of any check paid for the customer's account for which the customer may have a particular need. The agreement for electronic presentment would provide for electronic storage of copies of checks presented electronically and would impose a duty on the storing bank to provide a copy of a check on request of the payor bank. 4–406(a) and (b).

b. UNDER FEDERAL LAW: "THE CHECK 21 ACT"

In the late 1980s the prospects of electronic presentment seemed bright. The Expedited Funds Availability Act, discussed in the next section, mandated that the Fed "shall consider * * * requiring by regulation, that * * * the Federal Reserve banks and depositary institutions provide for check truncation." 12 U.S.C. § 4008(b). The Fed has the power to mandate electronic presentment with no further authorization from Congress because 12 U.S.C. § 4008(c) gives the Fed the power to regulate any aspect of the payment system with respect to checks in order to carry out expedited funds availability. But after its 1988 post-EFTA study, the Fed declined to mandate electronic presentment. Although it conceded that electronic presentment was feasible given the technology current at that time, the study concluded that the benefits of mandatory electronic presentment would be outweighed by the potential risks borne by the paying banks. It concluded that the matter should be left up to banks to choose to participate in voluntary inter-bank or multi-bank electronic presentment agreements with Reserve banks or other presenting banks.

Fifteen years later Congress acted on its own. On October 28, 2003, President Bush signed into law the Check Clearing for the 21st Century Act ("The Check 21 Act" or "Check 21"), with an effective date one year later. Pub. L. No. 108–100, 117 Stat. 1177 (2003). Check 21 allows the use of electronic presentment and return of checks without electronic truncation agreements between banks. It does so by creating a new type of negotiable instrument: a "substitute check." A "substitute check" is a paper reproduction created from an electronic image of the original check and suitable for automated processing in the same manner as the original check. Sec. 3(16). A substitute check is the legal equivalent of the original check for all purposes if it accurately represents the information on the original check and contains the requisite legend ("This is a legal copy of your check. You can use it in the same way you would use the original check."). Sec. 4(b). Check 21 requires a bank to handle a substitute check if warranties created by the legislation cover the check. Sec. 4(a). Banks are not required to accept presentation of checks in electronic form, unless required to do so under an electronic truncation agreement.

Check 21 imposes a nondisclaimable warranty on a bank's use of a substitute check. Secs. 5, 8. The bank warrants to downstream parties handling the check that the check is the legal equivalent of the original check and that they will not receive requests to pay the original or substitute check already paid. The warranty continues to apply even if the substitute check is converted into electronic form or reconverted back from an electronic form into another substitute check. Sec. 5. Further, because the substitute check is the legal equivalent of the original check, any warranties that apply to the original check carry over to the substitute check. Check 21 also requires a bank transferring a substitute check to indemnify subsequent transferees for loss due to receipt of a substitute rather than original check. Sec. 6. The legislation contains some consumer protection provisions which require expedited recrediting of consumer deposit accounts. Clarks' Bank Deposit and Payments Monthly, Vol. 12, No. 5, Oct. 2003. The Federal Reserve Board introduced proposed implementing regulations, to be included as part of Regulation CC. Availability of Funds and Collection of Checks, 69 Fed. Reg. 1470 (12 CFR pt. 229) (proposed January 8, 2004).

Check 21's intended purpose is obscured by its provisions governing substitute checks. The legislation aims to facilitate electronic presentment without biasing the form check truncation might take. Sec. 2(a)(3). Electronic presentment transfers electronic images of checks without the physical transfer of checks themselves. See House Comm. On Fin. Serv., 108 Congr. 108–32 (Background and Need for Legislation). This does not require the creation and transfer of substitute checks. Check 21 facilitates electronic presentment merely by removing legal or contractual barriers that require transfer of original checks. It does this by giving substitute checks the same legal status as original checks. The legislation does not require banks to truncate checks electronically. Sec. 2(b)(2). Nor does it require banks to create or transfer substitute checks. Check 21 simply requires banks to accept substitute checks when created and sent for collection or return, if a bank has made substitute check warranties as to it. Sec. 4(a). In this way the legislation is consistent with the demand for medium-neutrality required by other recent federal legislation (e.g., The Electronic Signatures in Global and National Commerce Act).

Electronic presentment can proceed without the creation or transfer of a substitute check. A substitute check is useful only when an individual or bank prefers (and pays) to create or receive a paper check. For instance, a substitute check can be created from an electronic image of an original check and presented to a payor bank without an inter-bank electronic presentment agreement. After payment the payor bank can return the substitute check to the drawer with other cancelled checks. The same process can be used to return dishonored checks to the depository bank when the bank or the depositor insists on a paper check. Check 21 allows for the possibility that a demand for paper checks might remain as part of a market for electronic presentment. Its regulation of substitute checks is a way of accommodating this preference without interfering with the market for electronic presentment of checks. The unit cost of processing paper checks increases as the volume of paper checks processed declines. For banks and their customers who still want paper checks, substitute checks are cheaper to process than original checks. Electronic truncation has lower unit processing costs than both substitute and original (paper) checks, because it avoids use of paper checks entirely. Check 21 leaves to market participants the decision as to the optimal mix of electronic presentment and substitute checks.

Check 21's impact on the market for electronic presentment of checks is likely to be significant. By facilitating the settlement and return of checks electronically, the legislation reduces the time in which payees are denied access to deposited funds. Two other effects are predicted within the next few years. One is the development of check imaging technologies and applications to better detect check fraud. A second effect is to bring forward to the point of sale or deposit check imaging applications. These can allow a merchant to capture a digital image of the customer's original check and transmit it to the payor bank in real time. A similar forward movement allows scanning and transmitting upon deposit in ATM machines, increasing revenues generated by their use. Will Wade, Gauging the Long–Term Opportunities in Check 21, Amer. Banker, Oct. 31, 2003, Pg. 13.

5.   FUNDS AVAILABILITY AND REGULATION CC

Suppose Father living in Sacramento, California, mails a check for $1,000, drawn on First Bank in Sacramento, to Daughter, attending school in College Town, New York, 80 miles from New York City. The check arrives on Monday morning. Daughter takes it to Second Bank's College Town branch and deposits it in her account. On Monday night the check is driven by a courier to Second Bank's central check processing center in New York City and is run through a reader-sorter machine. On Tuesday morning it is taken to the New York Fed where it goes through another reader-sorter and is sent by air courier on Tuesday night to the San Francisco Fed where it arrives early Wednesday morning. There it goes through a reader-sorter machine, and on Wednesday afternoon is driven by courier to First Bank in Sacramento. By early Thursday morning the check has been posted by automation to Father's account, which was then debited. When Daughter deposited the check in Second Bank she asked when she could withdraw her money; she was told it would be available for her in two weeks. She needed the money earlier and called Father to describe her plight. He was irritated to learn that although the banking system had withdrawn the amount of the check from his account on Thursday morning, Daughter would not be able to withdraw the funds until several days later.

Second Bank's action in placing a two-week "hold" period on Daughter's check was thought necessary to protect itself from the possibility that the check would not be paid by First Bank, owing to insufficient funds in the account, entry of a stop-payment order or other reasons. Relatively long hold periods were thought to be necessary because of the slow and inefficient system banks use for returning checks that have been dishonored. Second Bank may not learn whether the check has been dishonored until the unpaid check is physically returned to it. The forward collection of the check in this case from College Town to Sacramento was fairly prompt because the MICR line enabled the collecting banks to utilize an automated system for sorting checks and directing them to the banks on which they are drawn. But there is no automated system for the return of checks. Each must be processed manually by clerks who must attempt to return the check to the proper bank by deciphering the sometimes unintelligible indorsements on the back of the check. Moreover, before institution of the reforms discussed below, the system of provisional credits made it desirable to send the check back through the same chain of banks as in the forward collection of the check. Thus, had First Bank dishonored the check that arrived there after that bank's 2:00 p.m. cutoff hour on Wednesday, it could have waited until its Friday night midnight deadline to send the check back to the San Francisco Fed. That bank would probably need a second banking day after the banking day of receipt for the manual processing of the check. The same is true for the New York Fed. Although the check would probably be returned by truck and air courier services, returning banks could slow the process down even more by mailing the returns back. One study found that although the forward collection process for checks averaged 1.6 days, the return averaged 5.2 days. Barkley Clark & Barbara Clark, Regulation CC: Funds Availability and Check Collection 1–4 (1988).

(1) FUNDS AVAILABILITY

Banks met the growing chorus of customer complaints about what seemed to be excessive hold periods by justifying their actions as necessary to protect them from bad check losses. But in the 1980s several states passed laws limiting hold periods, and in 1987 Congress enacted the Expedited Funds Availability Act of 1987, 12 U.S.C. § 4001 et seq. The Board of Governors of the Federal Reserve System implemented this statute by promulgating Regulation CC in 1988, 12 C.F.R. Pt. 229. Subpart B of Regulation CC prescribes mandatory availability schedules. Next day availability is required for "low risk" deposits for which a hold period is not needed to protect the depositary bank from risk. Examples are cashier's checks, certified checks, teller's checks, electronic payments (wire transfers and ACH credits), "on us" items, Treasury and state and local government checks. § 229.10. For local checks the funds must be made available to the depositor not later than the second day after the banking day of deposit. § 229.12(b). For nonlocal checks funds must be made available not later than the fifth business day following the banking day of deposit. § 229.12(c). But a depositor is allowed to withdraw up to $100 on the next banking day after deposit of either local or nonlocal checks. § 229.10(c). Section 229.13 sets out exceptions to these mandatory availability schedules with respect to new accounts, large deposits, redeposited checks, repeated overdrafts, and cases in which there is reasonable cause to doubt collectibility.

For some time the Fed has been considering shortening the five-day period for nonlocal checks to four days. According to the Fed, paper checks are moving more rapidly now. In 1999 it estimated that about 83% of checks arrive back at the payor bank on which they were drawn within five business days. This is up from 73% in 1990. Rick Brooks, High–Tech Tactics Let Banks Keep the "Float", Wall. St. J., June 3, 1999, at B1. This article contends that banks are sometimes given such wide latitude by the special exceptions to the mandatory availability schedules that customers, counting on a normal period of float, find themselves with bounced checks on which high fees can be charged. We will discuss the issue of dishonored checks in a later chapter.

A 1994 American Bankers Association study showed that banks were generally making funds available to depositors earlier than Regulation CC requires. For local checks drawn on consumer demand accounts, over 90% of the banks surveyed reported that they were making funds available on either the day of deposit or the next day. And over 50% of the banks were following the same practice for nonlocal checks on these accounts. 1 Clark & Clark, The Law of Bank Deposits, Collections and Credit Cards & 10.01[7] (Rev. ed. 1999). Anecdotal evidence indicates that these percentages are probably higher today. The reasons given for the banks' early availability policy are customer service and competition. Clark & Clark, supra. The operational difficulties of dealing with the multiple availability schedules of Regulation CC may be another factor. Moreover, as indicated above, in cases in which a bank has reason to question the collectibility of a check it can protect itself by withholding payment.

(2) CHECK COLLECTION AND RETURN

Today the law of check collection and return is found in Regulation CC as well as in Article 4, to the extent that its provisions are not preempted by Regulation CC. Consideration in the revision of Article 4 was given to redrafting Article 4 in order to make it compatible with Regulation CC. This approach was rejected because of the likelihood that Regulation CC will continue to evolve, leaving inconsistencies between Article 4 and Regulation CC. Compatibility was again considered in the amending process that yielded the 2002 amendments to Articles 3 and 4, and was again rejected.

To allow the banking system to meet the funds availability standards set by Regulation CC without exposing depositary banks to excessive bad check losses, it was necessary to expedite the return system. Subpart C of Regulation CC sets out a sweeping revision of the law of check collection and return in order to speed the return of dishonored checks, thereby preempting portions of Article 4.

In the early stages of the revision of Article 4, before the EFAA had been passed, the drafters had proposed several provisions designed to speed the return of dishonored checks. These provisions included: facilitating direct return of dishonored checks to depositary banks; reducing the number of returned checks by extending the payor bank's midnight deadline for checks under $100 (thus giving the drawer time to put enough money in the account to pay the check); requiring compliance with uniform indorsement standards governing the content and placement of bank indorsements; commencing the running of the midnight deadline for return from the time of delivery of checks to central bank processing centers; and imposing on payor banks the duty to give prompt notice of the nonpayment of items of $2,500 or more. Regulation CC incorporated all these provisions except the extension of the midnight deadline for small checks, which was not included in Regulation CC and dropped from later drafts of Article 4 because of the belief that it would slow the collection of checks; hence, all these provisions were deleted from Article 4.

But Regulation CC went far beyond these modest steps. In sections 229.30 and 229.31, it authorizes a payor or returning bank to return a check directly to the depositary bank or to any returning bank agreeing to handle the returned check for expeditious return to the depositary bank, regardless of whether the returning bank had handled the check for forward collection. The contemplation was that the banks most likely to agree to handle a returning check expeditiously were the regional Federal Reserve banks. The consequences of allowing a check presented by one bank to be returned by the payor bank to a different bank undermined the usual methods of interbank settlements. Under these methods, the payor bank gives the presenting bank a provisional settlement, which it revokes when it returns the dishonored check to that bank. If the payor bank returns the check to a bank that was not the presenting bank, the payor bank cannot obtain settlement for the returned check by revoking the settlement with the presenting bank. Rather, it must recover settlement from the bank to which it returned the check. But in order to give banks incentive to make expeditious returns, even if the payor bank does return the dishonored check to the presenting bank, § 229.31(c) forbids a payor bank to obtain settlement for the check by charging back against a credit it had previously given the presenting bank. The payor bank cannot recover settlement from a bank to which it has returned a check until the check has reached the returning bank, as though in forward collection. In harmony with these two provisions, section 229.36(d) provides that all settlements between banks for the forward collection of checks are final when made.

The inter-bank settlement provisions of Article 4 are stated in terms of provisional settlements. 4–201(1). Bank credit given by a settling payor or collecting bank is provisional in the sense that it can be revoked upon return of the item. The Fed's decision in Regulation CC to make all settlements final meant that now the conceptual approach of Article 4 to inter-bank settlements differed from that of Regulation CC, though, at least with respect to the issues addressed by Article 4, there is little functional difference between the two laws. The fact that under Regulation CC any credit given for a check is final rather than provisional was not intended by the drafters of Regulation CC to limit the right of a payor or collecting bank to return a check and recover the amount of the check from the bank to which it was returned. After stating that settlement under Regulation CC is final rather than provisional, the commentary to section 229.36(d) of Regulation CC explains: "Settlement by a paying bank is not considered to be final payment for the purposes of U.C.C. [§ 4–215(a)], because a paying bank has the right to recover settlement from a returning or depositary bank to which it returns a check under this subpart." Appendix Commentary, 53 Fed. Reg. 19,372, 19,486 (1988). The check collection aspects of Regulation CC are discussed in detail in 1 Clark &

Clark, Bank Deposits, Collections and Credit Cards, Chapter 8 (Rev. ed. 1999).

B. CREDIT AND DEBIT CARDS

1. INTRODUCTION

a. CREDIT CARDS

(1) HOW CREDIT CARDS FUNCTION

Credit cards fall into two broad categories: "restricted use" and "universal" cards. In the first category are credit cards issued by a merchant as a means of identifying customers who have charge accounts with the merchant. They are particularly convenient for merchants who have numerous retail outlets located over a large geographical area. These cards originally could be used to make purchases only from the merchant that issued the card, but in some cases use of the card to purchase from a limited number of other merchants is also permitted. "Restricted use" cards include cards issued by oil companies for use at affiliated or independently owned service stations that sell products of the company that issued the card. The most important characteristic of this category of credit card is that the primary purpose of the issuer is to facilitate sales of goods or services of the issuer. Financial institutions have become involved in the merchant credit business by issuing "private-label" credit cards that appear to be issued by the merchant. The so-called co-branded card, bearing the names of both the merchant and the financer, have also become common.

"Universal" credit cards comprise cards issued by financial institutions that provide short-term credit, usually unsecured, to cardholders to allow them to make purchases from a multitude of merchants and other sellers of goods and services who are not related to the issuer of the card. These used to be called travel and entertainment cards; more often today they are referred to as bank cards because of the prominence of Visa and Master-Card in this category. This category of credit card has emerged as an important substitute for cash or personal checks in paying for goods or services. A merchant who accepts this type of credit card as the payment mechanism is party to a preexisting arrangement either directly with the issuer of the card or with an interbank system to which the issuer belongs, such as Visa USA or MasterCard International. Pursuant to this arrangement the merchant can obtain payment from the issuer for purchases made by use of the card. In a face-to-face purchase, the cardholder signs a credit card slip indicating the amount of the purchase and containing the card number and other information taken from the card.

The merchant is faced with several risks in honoring a credit card. First, the person using the card may not be a person authorized to use the card. Second, the card may have been revoked by the issuer. One common reason for revocation is a report to the issuer that the card has been lost or stolen. Third, the amount of credit given by the issuer to the cardholder may not be sufficient to cover the amount of the purchase. The merchant can normally avoid the last two risks. At the time a purchase is to be made, the merchant can determine, through telephonic or electronic access to a computer center having a record of the card, whether the card is valid and whether the charge is within the cardholder's line of credit. Through this process the merchant obtains approval of the charge before the purchase is made and has assurance of receiving payment in accordance with the arrangement to which the issuer and merchant are parties. Normally the merchant receives the amount of the charge less a discount to compensate the issuer for financing the purchase. The issuer obtains this compensation by obtaining payment of the full amount of the charge from the cardholder. Thus, the credit risk of nonpayment by the cardholder is taken by the issuer. The issuer normally sends a monthly statement of charges to the cardholder. Under most plans, the cardholder has the option of paying the full amount by a specified date without an interest charge or of making payment in installments with an interest charge. Estimates are that 60% of cardholders carry monthly balances in their credit card accounts. Holman W. Jenkins, Jr., Credit Crunch? Let's Sue Visa and MasterCard, Wall St. J., Oct. 14, 1998, at A23.

The growth of credit cards issued by financial institutions has been phenomenal. The Bank of America first issued its BankAmericard in the 1950s. A consortium of banks formed an association to issue a competing card, MasterCharge, in 1960. The BankAmericard was later taken over by an association of banks, Visa USA. and renamed the Visa card. MasterCharge became MasterCard; its bank association is MasterCard International. These companies are owned and funded by their thousands of member banks. Formerly, many American banks issued both cards, but increasingly banks are required to choose between them. In 2003 Visa USA passed the $1 trillion mark in transactions per year; it had reached the $1 billion level in 1971. Eileen Alt Powell, Use of "Plastic" Changing Rapidly, LA Times, Aug. 29, 2003, at C2. In mid–2003, Visa had 45% of the market, MasterCard had 33%, and American Express had 15%. Jathon Sapsford, American Express May Reap Rewards in Credit Card Suit, Wall St. J., July 7, 2003, at C1. According to Ron Lieber, A Bonus for Blowing Off Your Bills, Wall St. J., Sept. 16, 2003, at D1: 61% of Americans carry balances on their credit cards and pay an average of 13% interest on these balances; the 51 million households that carry balances on their credit cards have balances averaging $11,944; and two-thirds of the revenue of card companies comes from interest charges.

Visa USA and MasterCard International do not issue credit cards. They set up the network of participating banks and handle the clearing and settlement of credit card debts. The usual procedure is that a merchant, authorized to honor Visa cards or MasterCards, will present to a "merchant bank," a member of the Visa or MasterCard network, the credit card slips signed by cardholders at the time of purchase and receive immediate credit for the amount of the slips, less discount, in its account with the merchant bank. The merchant bank then sends the slips through the Visa or

MasterCard clearing system to the various "issuing banks," which issued the credit cards to the cardholders. The issuing banks then transfer funds for the slips to the merchant bank through the credit card settlement process of Visa or MasterCard and bill the cardholders for their purchases. If the cardholder returns goods, the issuing bank credits the cardholder's account and charges back this amount against the merchant bank.

(2) The Perils of Success

Credit cards have been so wildly successful in expanding the volume of consumer credit that they are often viewed, particularly in the bankruptcy context, as posing a serious social problem for consumers. In little more than 40 years bank cards have completely replaced the traditional, highly inefficient, system in which merchants made their own decisions on the creditworthiness of their customers, relying on the often sketchy information the local credit bureau was able to gather on the prospective customer. For bank credit cards, the creditworthiness of the cardholder is determined by a professional credit grantor, the bank, at the time it issues the credit card, and it can impose spending limits consistent with the cardholder's credit record. The merchant is safe in relying on that decision of the bank and can devote its resources to selling rather than credit evaluation. The system is cheap and efficient.

At the beginning bank credit cards were restricted to middle or upper income groups, but over the years aggressive competition for market share led card issuers to lower their credit standards, sometimes with disastrous results for both card issuer and cardholder. Even the sub-prime market became a target of credit card issuers. Direct mail solicitation with low temporary teaser rates (sometimes zero), followed by much higher regular rates, became standard, as did "pre-approved" card offers. In a recent year a Moody's report estimated that approximately 3.5 *billion* pieces of mail were sent out offering credit cards to recipients. Teaser rates promoted card-surfing, that is moving balances from old cards to new ones to take advantage of the lower introductory rates. BNA Bankruptcy Law Reporter, Vol.11, No.20, p. 448 (May 1999). Horror stories abound of bankrupts with 15 or 20 credit cards, all maxed out, seeking discharge of debt totals far exceeding annual income. Card issuers frequently opposed bankruptcy discharges in such cases by alleging fraud under Bankruptcy Code § 523(a)(2)(A). Cardholders fought back by asserting that card issuers could not have justifiably relied on the cardholder's representation of intent to repay because of inadequate inquiry into the cardholder's financial position. For a good discussion of the issue, see In re Ellingsworth, 212 B.R. 326 (Bankr.W.D.Mo.1997). The abuse by some cardholders in excessive use of their cards was matched by the unwarranted lowering of credit standards by some card issuers in their relentless pursuit of market share. No resolution of the bankruptcy issue has made it through Congress as yet.

b. DEBIT CARDS

Debit and credit cards transfer funds in different ways and can be subject to different regulations. A working definition of the difference between a debit and credit transfer is found in Comment 4 to 4A–104: "In a credit transfer the instruction to pay is given by the person making the payment. In a debit transfer the instruction to pay is given by the person receiving the payment." Thus, a debit transfer may be an order from a creditor, authorized by the debtor, to the debtor's bank to pay the creditor. As it is sometimes put, debit transfers "pull" funds from the account of the payor (e.g., the debtor) to the payee (e.g., the creditor) on instruction by the payee. A common example is the authorization given by an insured person to the insurer to periodically withdraw premiums from the insured's bank account. Mortgage payments and many other periodic payments are made in this way. In contrast, credit transfers, such as payment by check, "push" funds from the payor's account to the payee on instruction by the payor. Article 4A does not cover debit wire transfers. 4A–103(a)(1) ("payment order"). But several kinds of consumer debit transfers are covered by the Electronic Fund Transfer Act, 15 U.S.C. § 1693 et seq. Regulation E, which implements the EFTA, defines "electronic fund transfer" as including "[t]ransfers resulting from debit card transactions, whether or not initiated through an electronic terminal." 12 CFR § 205.3(b)(5).

Debit cards have two common uses: to deposit and withdraw money from accounts and to transfer funds to a merchant as payment. The most popular use of debit cards is in the ubiquitous automated teller machine (ATM) system, as a means of depositing and withdrawing funds. These terminals are located in all manner of places convenient to customers: street corners, supermarkets, and, for safety, even in police stations. Their utility to customers is greatly enhanced by their around-the-clock availability. The customer can use the access card and a personal identification number (PIN) to make deposits and withdrawals from the customer's account in a bank or other financial institution. The cost of human teller-handled deposits and withdrawals is far more than the cost of deposits and withdrawals made by ATM.

One method by which debit cards are used to transfer funds as payment is the point-of-sale (POS) retail transaction. Here the buyer pays for goods or services by using a plastic coded card, called an access or debit card, inserted into an electronic terminal on the merchant's premises, which is linked to the banks of both the merchant and the cardholder, usually by means of an inter-bank network. The debit card contains a machine-readable identification of the buyer's bank account. When the card is inserted into the terminal, the amount of the transaction and the buyer's personal identification number (PIN) are also entered. The result is that the buyer's account is debited and the merchant's account is credited in that amount at the same time.

As the language quoted above from Regulation E indicates, debit cards may also be used in transactions with merchants who do not maintain electronic terminals. The card authorizes the merchant to draw on the buyer's account in the issuing bank for the amount of the sales price. The cardholder signs for the transaction, as in a credit card transaction, rather than using a PIN in an electronic terminal. If the debit card used is a Visa card or MasterCard in signature cases, the merchant sends the debit card slip through the more expensive Visa or MasterCard credit card clearing and settlement network to the issuing bank which immediately debits the cardholder's account, instead of billing as is done for credit cards. PIN-based clearing systems, like those operated by First Data Corporation, are cheaper. Jathon Sapsford, First Data Deal is Start of Fight in Debit Cards, Wall St. J., April 3, 2003, at C1. Estimates are that retailers pay about 15 cents for each PIN transaction but 60 cents for each signature transaction. Thus, the bank takes a larger inter-change fee (discount) from the merchant's sale price in signature cases. For this reason merchants challenged the requirement of Visa USA and MasterCard that all merchants authorized to accept credit cards must also accept their debit cards, and, in a class-action antitrust suit, won a settlement freeing them from this rule in 2003. Jathon Sapsford & Kara Scannell, Visa, MasterCard to Pay Share of $3 Billion Pact Over 10 Years, Wall St. J., May 2, 2003, at C9.

The market for debit cards is growing faster than that for credit cards. Although the volume of the credit card market is still much larger than that for debit cards because the size of the transactions financed is greater, according to Jathon Sapsford's First Data article, cited above, debit card purchases are increasing 24% per year while credit card purchases were going up only 7%. According to Visa USA, 60% of those surveyed used debit cards so they could carry less cash, and 70% said that use of debit cards gave them a better sense of how they spend their money. Calmetta Coleman, Debit Cards Look to Give Credit Cards a Run for Consumers' Money, Wall St. J., Dec. 3, 2001, at B1. One factor in the debit card/credit card competition is that one doesn't need a bank account to have a credit card but must have one to be accessed for a debit card, which are increasingly being called "check cards" by issuers. Michelle Higgins estimates that the average number of cards in the wallet of those who carry plastic is eight. Prepaid Credit Cards Find New Niche, Wall St. J., Dec. 31, 2002, at D2. If this is true, most of those must be credit cards.

2.   LIABILITY FOR UNAUTHORIZED USE OF CARDS

a.   CREDIT CARDS

Hurried retail cashiers have little time to examine credit cards to be sure that the person presenting them is the true cardholder or that the card is genuine rather than counterfeit. Billions of dollars of payments for gasoline are made each year by running credit cards through strip-reading devices on the pumps with no human examination of the credit card or its bearer. A thief or counterfeiter has a good chance of not being caught. Credit card fraud was estimated to cause $1.8 in losses in 2002, with 41% of that owing to lost or stolen credit cards. Paul Beckett & Jason Sapsford, As Credit–Card Theft Grows, A Tussle Over Paying to Stop It, Wall St. J., May 1, 2003, at A1. How should the loss be allocated in unauthorized credit card cases: on the careless merchant, on the card owner who is slow in reporting the loss or theft, or on the highly profitable credit card industry that has monitoring capacities that can stop multiple uses of lost, stolen or counterfeit cards?

In 1970 Congress decisively resolved this issue in the following statute. The provisions on credit cards are found in the Truth-in-Lending Act (TILA), 15 U.S.C. §§ 1601–1667(e), which is a grab-bag of consumer protection provisions. In § 1602(k) "credit card" is defined as "any card, plate, coupon book or other credit device existing for the purpose of obtaining money, property, labor, or services on credit." An "accepted credit card" means one "which the cardholder has requested and received or has signed or has used, or authorized another to use for the purpose of obtaining money, property, labor or, services on credit." § 1602(*l*). "The term 'cardholder' means any person to whom a credit card is issued or any person who has agreed with the card issuer to pay obligations arising from the issuance of a credit card to another person." § 1602(m). "The term 'unauthorized use,' as used in section 133 [§ 1643], means a use of a credit card by a person other than the cardholder who does not have actual, implied, or apparent authority for such use and from which the cardholder receives no benefit." § 1602(*o*).

Section 1643. Liability of Holder of Credit Card

(a)(1) A cardholder shall be liable for the unauthorized use of a credit card only if

(A) the card is an accepted credit card;

(B) the liability is not in excess of $50;

(C) the card issuer gives adequate notice to the cardholder of the potential liability;

(D) the card issuer has provided the cardholder with a description of a means by which the card issuer may be notified of loss or theft of the card, which description may be provided on the face or reverse side of the statement required by section 1637(b) or on a separate notice accompanying such statement;

(E) the unauthorized use occurs before the card issuer has been notified that an unauthorized use of the credit card has occurred or may occur as the result of loss, theft, or otherwise; and

(F) the card issuer has provided a method whereby the user of such card can be identified as the person authorized to use it.

PROBLEMS

1. Oscar paid for his meal at a restaurant by use of his credit card. The waiter surreptitiously copied the information on Oscar's card by a device that he concealed in his belt and sold this information to an enterprise that fraudulently produced plastic cards that were replicas of Oscar's card. These cards were used to make purchases at retail establishments. When these purchases appeared on Oscar's monthly statement, he protested to the credit card issuer that he had not made the purchases.

How does § 1643(a) apply to this Problem? How can fraud loss be reduced in cases such as this?

2. Oscar is absent minded, and his condition worsened in the months before his bar examination. He had obtained a credit card from Bank A but had forgotten to sign the back of the card. He used it only a couple of times by inserting it in the slot on gasoline pumps to buy gas; the mechanism on the pump did not search for the presence of a signature. He left the card unsigned on the top of a table in his bedroom in the house where he roomed. He wasn't aware that it had disappeared even though he was billed monthly for purchases that he had not made. The cause of his inattention was that he was so preoccupied in the weeks immediately before his exam that he had stopped opening his mail. After his exam, he discovered that the card had been stolen and that Bank A was demanding payment of $5,000 for purchases made on the card, some as long as three months after disappearance of the card, all of which were noted on Bank A's statements that Oscar had received. Not until then did Oscar notify Bank A of the unauthorized use of his card. How would this case be resolved under statute set out above? See § 1643(d).

————————

What policy was Congress implementing in adopting the drastic limitation in § 1643(a) on the liability of cardholders? What incentive does a cardholder have to report the loss or theft of a credit card? Does the fact that the $50 limit on liability has not been changed since 1970 give you some insight on what Congress had in mind? For a discussion of a variety of explanations of the TILA's allocation of risk between cardholder and card issuer, see Clayton P. Gillette, Rules, Standards, and Precautions in Payment Systems, 82 Va. L. Rev. 181 (1996).

b.   DEBIT CARDS

Debit cards are governed by the Electronic Fund Transfer Act (EFTA). 15 U.S.C. § 1693(a)–(r). Definitions appear in § 1693a and consumer liability is covered by 1693(g), which affords debit cardholders much less protection than the TILA gives credit cardholders. If the debit cardholder notifies the card issuer of loss or theft of the card within two days of learning of the loss, liability for unauthorized use is limited to $50, otherwise liability may go as high as $500. However, there is no limit for liability for an unauthorized charge if the cardholder fails to report the unauthorized charge appearing on a periodic statement within 60 days of transmittal of the statement. Why is the EFTA's limitation of the debit card liability different from, and less generous than, the TILA's limitation of the credit cardholder's liability? Questions have arisen about which statute applies in cases in which the same card may be used as both a debit and credit card. Regulation E addresses the issue in 12 CFR § 205.12, which provides that if an electronic fund transfer is involved the EFTA provisions apply; TILA applies if the card is used as a credit card without an electronic fund transfer. 2 Clark & Clark, The Law of Bank Deposits, Collections and Credit Cards, & & 15.03[2][c], 16.06[2] (Rev. ed. 2003). The problem has been alleviated by the pledge on the part of both Visa and MasterCard in 1997 that they would voluntarily apply the $50 limit to the unauthorized use of both cards.

PROBLEM

How would the case posed in the Problem 2 above be resolved if Oscar's debit card had been stolen? Concerned that owing to his stressful preparation for the bar exam he would forget his PIN, Oscar had copied it on a post-it stuck to the card where it remained at the time of the theft.

A cardholder whose debit card is lost, stolen or counterfeited is in a somewhat less advantageous position than a credit card holder in comparable circumstances because the money has already been removed from the cardholder's account, with bounced checks as a possible consequence, and what can be a prolonged period before the card issuing bank restores the money taken. Despite bank promises of "zero liability" for customers victimized by ATM fraud, E. Scott Reckard reports that banks take a tough stance on refunds in cases in which there is no hard evidence of fraud. Consumers, Banks Clash as ATM Fraud Escalates, LATimes, April 15, 2003, at C1. During the delay, cardholders can be deprived of necessary funds. On the other hand, in the case of a lost, stolen or counterfeited credit card, the cardholder can merely refuse to pay for fraudulent transactions charged on her account until the issue is resolved.

3. WHEN IS USE AUTHORIZED?

As we have seen, TILA's imposition of a $50 limit on liability shifts most of the risk of losses owing to unauthorized uses of credit cards from cardholders to card issuers. A use is unauthorized for the purpose of § 1643 if the card user lacks actual, implied or apparent authority to make a purchase with the card. § 1602(*o*). The card issuer bears the burden of proof as to unauthorized use. § 1643(b). The TILA allows state law to be more protective of cardholders, reducing their liability in such cases below $50. § 1643(c). Because the cardholder remains fully liable for charges from authorized use, it is no surprise that litigation focuses on whether card use is authorized.

Most unauthorized use cases raise issues of apparent authority rather than of actual or implied authority. The card issuer contends that the card user had apparent authority to make purchases on the cardholder's account owing to the user's status as a member of the cardholder's family or, as in the following case, as an employee of the cardholder. In the case below, the court allows for "apparent authority created through the cardholder's negligence." Does the court allow for liability based on authorized use under the TILA or instead on the cardholder's grossly negligent behavior? In other words, does the court carefully distinguish between negligence by a cardholder which creates apparent authority for someone else's use of the credit card and negligent acts that enable someone else to use the credit card whether or not apparent authority existed?

Minskoff v. American Express Travel Related Services Company, Inc.

United States Court of Appeals, Second Circuit, 1996.
98 F.3d 703.

■ MAHONEY, CIRCUIT JUDGE.

Plaintiffs-appellants Edward J. Minskoff and Edward J. Minskoff Equities, Inc. ("Equities") appeal from a final judgment entered September 15, 1995 in the United States District Court for the Southern District of New York, Robert P. Patterson, Jr., Judge, that granted the motion of defendant-appellee American Express Travel Related Services Company, Inc. ("American Express") for summary judgment dismissing plaintiffs-appellants' complaint. The complaint asserted claims under 15 U.S.C. § 1643, a provision of the Truth in Lending Act, 15 U.S.C. § 1601 et seq. (the "TILA"), and New York General Business Law § 512 for recovery of $276,334.06 paid to American Express through checks forged by an Equities employee to cover charges incurred by that employee on American Express credit cards that were fraudulently obtained and used by the employee. * * * The complaint also sought a declaratory judgment that plaintiffs-appellants were not liable for the balance of the unpaid charges outstanding on those credit cards, but the district court granted American Express summary judgment in the amount of $51,657.71 on its counterclaim for that balance.

We vacate the judgment of the district court and remand for further proceedings.

BACKGROUND

Minskoff is the president and chief executive officer of Equities, a real estate holding and management firm. In 1988, Equities opened an American Express corporate card account (the "Corporate Account") for which one charge card was issued in Minskoff's name. Minskoff also maintained a personal American Express account, which was established in 1963.

In October 1991, Equities hired Susan Schrader Blumenfeld to serve as its assistant to the president/office manager. Blumenfeld was responsible for both the personal and business affairs of Minskoff, and her duties included screening Minskoff's mail, reviewing vendor invoices and credit card statements (including statements for the Corporate Account), and forwarding such invoices and statements to Equities' bookkeepers for payment. Prior to Blumenfeld's employment with Equities, Minskoff personally reviewed all Corporate Account statements; after hiring Blumenfeld, he no longer reviewed any of these statements.

In March 1992, defendant-appellee American Express received an application for an additional credit card to issue from the Corporate Account in Blumenfeld's name. The application had been pre-addressed by American Express and mailed to Minskoff at his business address. It had been completed and submitted by Blumenfeld without the knowledge or acquiescence of Equities or Minskoff. American Express issued the supplemental card and mailed it to Equities' business address. From April 1992 to March 1993, Blumenfeld charged a total of $28,213.88 on that card.

During this period, American Express sent twelve monthly billing statements for the Corporate Account to Equities' business address. Each statement listed both Blumenfeld and Minskoff as cardholders on the Corporate Account, and separately itemized Corporate Account charges for Minskoff and Blumenfeld. These twelve statements show a total of $28,213.88 in charges attributed to Blumenfeld and $23,099.37 in charges attributed to Minskoff, for a total of $51,313.25. Between April 1992 and March 1993, American Express received twelve checks, drawn on accounts maintained by Minskoff or Equities at Manufacturers Hanover Trust ("MHT"), in payment of these charges, with each check made payable to American Express and bearing Equities' Corporate Account number. Minskoff did not review any statements or cancelled checks received during 1992 and 1993 from either his personal account with MHT or the Equities account with MHT.

In July 1992, American Express sent Minskoff an unsolicited invitation to apply for a platinum card. Blumenfeld accepted the invitation on behalf of Minskoff, again without the knowledge or acquiescence of either Minskoff or Equities.[3] Blumenfeld also submitted a request for a supplemental card to issue from this new account (the "Platinum Account") in her name. When platinum cards arrived in both Minskoff's and Blumenfeld's names, Blumenfeld gave Minskoff his card, claiming that it was an unsolicited upgrade of his American Express card privileges. Minskoff proceeded to use his platinum card for occasional purchases, and Blumenfeld charged approximately $300,000 to the Platinum Account between July 1992 and November 1993.

Between August 1992 and November 1993, American Express mailed sixteen Platinum Account monthly billing statements to Equities' business address. Each statement named Blumenfeld and Minskoff as cardholders and itemized charges for each separately. These statements attributed a total of $250,394.44 in charges to Blumenfeld and $10,497.31 to Minskoff, for a total of $260,891.75. These bills were paid in full with checks drawn

---

3. It is not clear from the record whether the invitation to receive a platinum American Express card was directed to Minskoff in his individual capacity or in his official position as president of Equities. The solicitation was preprinted with Minskoff's home address, and the record does not reveal how it ended up in Blumenfeld's hands at the Equities office.

on the MHT accounts, made payable to American Express, and bearing the Platinum Account number.

In November 1993, Equities' controller, Steven Marks, informed Minskoff that MHT had called to inquire about a check made payable to American Express for approximately $41,000 that had been written on Equities' MHT account. Minskoff stopped payment on the check, initiated an internal investigation of Equities' accounts that revealed the full extent of Blumenfeld's fraudulent activities, and gave notice to American Express of Blumenfeld's unauthorized charges to the Platinum and Corporate Accounts. Blumenfeld subsequently stated in an affidavit that she had forged approximately sixty checks drawn on Equities' MHT account and Minskoff's personal MHT account, including at least twenty payments to American Express for charges to the Platinum and Corporate Accounts. Although some of these checks were used to pay legitimate obligations of plaintiffs-appellants, an accounting analysis attributed losses totalling $412,684.06 to Blumenfeld's theft. In January 1994, Blumenfeld agreed to repay $250,000 to Minskoff and Equities in return for their promise not to institute legal action against her.

Plaintiffs-appellants initiated this action in the United States District Court for the Southern District of New York on February 15, 1994. As previously noted, they sought (1) to recover $276,334.06 that had been paid to American Express in satisfaction of unauthorized charges by Blumenfeld, and (2) a declaration that they were not liable for the outstanding balances on the Platinum Account. The district court, however, dismissed their complaint and awarded American Express $51,657.71 on its counterclaim for that balance. The district court reasoned that the $50 limit on a cardholder's liability for the unauthorized use of the cardholder's credit card specified in 15 U.S.C. § 1643(a)(1)(B), see supra note 1, did not apply to plaintiffs-appellants because their negligence in failing to examine credit card statements that would have revealed Blumenfeld's fraudulent charges "resulted in an appearance of authority [to use the cards] in Blumenfeld."

This appeal followed.

DISCUSSION

* * *

Plaintiffs-appellants contend that because Blumenfeld obtained the platinum and corporate credit cards through forgery and fraud, her use of the cards is *per se* unauthorized under section 1643, see supra note 1, and plaintiffs-appellants' liability is therefore limited to $50 by section 1643(a)(1)(B). Section 1643 applies, however, only in the case of an "unauthorized use" of a credit card. See § 1643(a)(1), (d). The term "unauthorized use" is defined as "a use of a credit card by a person other than the cardholder who does not have actual, implied, or apparent authority for such use and from which the cardholder receives no benefit." 15 U.S.C. § 1602(*o*). In determining whether a use is unauthorized, "Congress apparently contemplated, and courts have accepted, primary reliance on background principles of agency law in determining the liability of cardholders for charges incurred by third-party card bearers." Towers World Airways v. PHH Aviation Systems, 933 F.2d 174, 176–77 (2d Cir.), cert. denied, 502 U.S. 823, 112 S.Ct. 87, 116 L.Ed.2d 59 (1991).

Under general principles of agency, the authority of an agent "is the power of the agent to do an act or to conduct a transaction on account of the principal which, with respect to the principal, he is privileged to do because of the principal's manifestations to him." Restatement (Second) of Agency (the "Restatement") § 7 cmt. a (1958). Such authority may be express or implied, but in either case it exists only where the agent may reasonably infer from the words or conduct of the principal that the principal has consented to the agent's performance of a particular act. See id. cmt. b.

Apparent authority is "entirely distinct from authority, either express or implied," id. § 8 cmt. a, and arises from the "written or spoken words or any other conduct of the principal which, reasonably interpreted, causes [a] third person to believe that the principal consents to have [an] act done on his behalf by the person purporting to act for him," id. § 27; see also Fennell v. TLB Kent Co., 865 F.2d 498, 502 (2d Cir.1989). Apparent authority, then, is normally created through the words and conduct of the principal as they are interpreted by a third party, and cannot be established by the actions or representations of the agent. See *Fennell*, 865 F.2d at 502 (collecting cases).

The existence of apparent authority is normally a question of fact, and therefore inappropriate for resolution on a motion for summary judgment. * * * However, a principal may be estopped from denying apparent authority if (1) the principal's intentional or negligent acts, including acts of omission, created an appearance of authority in the agent, (2) on which a third party reasonably and in good faith relied, and (3) such reliance resulted in a detrimental change in position on the part of the third party. See Restatement § 8– * * *.

Viewing the facts in the light most favorable to plaintiffs-appellants, it is clear that Blumenfeld acted without actual or implied authority when she forged the platinum card acceptance form and supplemental card applications. Accordingly, plaintiff-appellants cannot be held accountable for Blumenfeld's initial possession of corporate and platinum cards. As we stated in *Towers*:

> Though a cardholder's [voluntary] relinquishment of possession may create in another the appearance of authority to use the card, [15 U.S.C. §§ 1602(*o*) and 1643] clearly preclude[ ] a finding of apparent authority where the transfer of the card was without the cardholder's consent, as in cases involving theft, loss, or fraud. However elastic the principle of apparent authority may be in theory, the language of the 1970 Amendments [to the TILA] demonstrates Congress's intent that the category of cases involving charges incurred as a result of *involuntary* card transfers are to be regarded as unauthorized under sections 1602(*o*) and 1643.

Towers, 933 F.2d at 177.

This result is consistent with the underlying policy of the TILA to protect credit card holders against losses due to theft or fraudulent use of credit cards on the theory that the card issuer is in the better position to prevent such losses. * * * We accordingly disagree with the decision of the district court insofar as it imposed upon plaintiffs-appellants the entire burden of the unauthorized charges made by Blumenfeld to the Corporate and Platinum Accounts.

However, while we accept the proposition that the *acquisition* of a credit card through fraud or theft cannot be said to occur under the apparent authority of the cardholder, our statement in *Towers* should not be interpreted to preclude a finding of apparent authority for the subsequent *use* of a credit card so obtained. Under the rule urged by plaintiffs-appellants, a cardholder could disregard both credit card and bank statements indefinitely, or even fail to act upon a discovery that an employee had fraudulently obtained and was fraudulently using a credit card, and still limit his liability for an employee's fraudulent purchases to $50. Cf. Transamerica Ins. Co. v. Standard Oil Co., 325 N.W.2d 210, 215 (N.D.1982) ("[A]n unscrupulous cardholder could allow another to charge hundreds of dollars in goods and services and then attempt to limit his liability to 50 dollars."). Nothing in the TILA suggests that Congress intended to sanction intentional or negligent conduct by the cardholder that furthers the fraud or theft of an unauthorized card user. We therefore agree with the district court to the extent that it decided that the negligent acts or omissions of a cardholder may create apparent authority to use the card in a person who obtained the card through theft or fraud. Apparent authority created through the cardholder's negligence does not, however, retroactively authorize charges incurred prior to the negligent acts that created the apparent authority of the user.

Applying these principles to the case at hand, we address the district court's conclusion that plaintiffs-appellants' failure to examine credit card and bank statements amounts to negligence which created an appearance of authority in Blumenfeld to use the card. Under New York law, consumers are obligated to "exercise reasonable care and promptness to examine [bank] statement[s] . . . to discover [any] unauthorized signature or any alteration." § 4–406(1) * * *. This provision is derived from a common law obligation to examine bank statements and report forgeries or alterations, and it is based upon a determination that "the depositor [is] in the better position to discover an alteration of the check or forgery of his or her own signature." Woods v. MONY Legacy Life Ins. Co., 84 N.Y.2d 280, 284, 617 N.Y.S.2d 452, 453, 641 N.E.2d 1070, 1071 (1994) (extending application of § 4–406 to brokerage accounts).

This policy is no less applicable to credit card holders than it is to bank depositors. Once a cardholder has established a credit card account, and provided that the card issuer is in compliance with the billing statement disclosure requirements of 15 U.S.C. § 1637,[4] the cardholder is in a superior position to determine whether the charges reflected on his regular billing statements are legitimate. A cardholder's failure to examine credit card statements that would reveal fraudulent use of the card constitutes a negligent omission that creates apparent authority for charges that would otherwise be considered unauthorized under the TILA. * * *

It is undisputed that between April 1992 and November 1993, American Express mailed to Equities' business address at least twenty-eight monthly billing statements documenting charges made to the Platinum and Corporate Accounts. Each of those statements clearly lists Blumenfeld as a cardholder, and each specifically itemizes those charges attributable to her credit card. During that same period, MHT mailed to Equities' business address numerous bank statements showing that checks made payable to American Express had been drawn on Equities' business account and Minskoff's personal account to pay these American Express charges. Minskoff concedes that he failed to examine any of these statements until November 1993, and no other employee or agent of Equities (other than Blumenfeld) became aware of the disputed monthly payments to American Express prior to the inquiry by Bankers Trust in November 1993. These omissions on the part of plaintiffs-appellants created apparent authority for Blumenfeld's continuing use of the cards, especially because it enabled Blumenfeld to pay all of the American Express statements with forged checks, thereby fortifying American Express' continuing impression that nothing was amiss with the Corporate and Platinum Accounts.

Plaintiffs-appellants argue that summary judgment is inappropriate because they exercised reasonable care in the hiring and supervision of Blumenfeld and in the implementation and administration of internal accounting procedures designed to detect and prevent fraud. In this case, however, while American Express concedes that Equities employed bookkeepers who were responsible, *inter alia*, for reviewing credit card statements and arranging for their payment, as well as reviewing bank statements and cancelled checks, the inadequate manner in which these procedures were performed from April 1992 to November 1993 enabled Blumenfeld to acquire unauthorized American Express credit cards, run up more than $300,000 in invalid American Express charges, and pay for them with approximately twenty forged checks drawn on Equities' MHT account and Minskoff's personal MHT account, without detection.

A cursory review of any of the American Express statements would have disclosed charges by Blumenfeld made with an unauthorized credit card. A review of any MHT statement would have disclosed one or more

---

4. Section 1637(b) requires "[t]he creditor of any account under an open end consumer credit plan [to] transmit to the obligor, for each billing cycle at the end of which there is an outstanding balance in that account or with respect to which a finance charge is imposed, a statement setting forth," *inter alia*, the outstanding balance in the account at the beginning and end of the statement period, the amount and date of each extension of credit during the period, the amount of any finance charge added to the account, and the date by which payment must be made to avoid finance charges.

payments to American Express (or, if the cancelled checks had previously been removed by Blumenfeld, charges that could not be matched to cancelled checks) generally in amounts far exceeding Minskoff's habitual American Express charges. We are not dealing in this case with an occasional transgression buried in a welter of financial detail. In our view, once a cardholder receives a statement that reasonably puts him on notice that one or more fraudulent charges have been made, he cannot thereafter claim lack of knowledge. The district court was justified in determining that no reasonable jury could conclude that this standard had been satisfied as to plaintiffs-appellants on the record presented in this case, warranting summary judgment in favor of American Express to the extent that we have previously indicated.

In our view, the appropriate resolution in this case is provided by adapting the ruling in *Transamerica* to provide that

> [American Express] is liable for [Blumenfeld's] fraudulent purchases [as to each credit card] from the time the credit card was issued until [plaintiffs-appellants] received the first statement from [American Express] containing [Blumenfeld's] fraudulent charges plus a reasonable time to examine that statement. After that time, [plaintiffs-appellants are] liable for the remaining fraudulent charges.

325 N.W.2d at 216. We accordingly vacate the judgment of the district court and remand for further proceedings to make this determination. We leave it to the district court in the first instance to ascertain whether, as the record is developed on remand, any issues require submission to a jury.

NOTES

1. Most of the TILA's provisions govern only the consumer credit transactions, not business transactions. § 1603(1). An exception is the TILA's limitation on liability for unauthorized use, which applies to credit cards used for business purposes as well. § 1645. For business cardholders, the $50 limit on liability of § 1643(a) is a default rule. A business cardholder can assume greater liability for unauthorized card use by its employees if it does not impose liability on them for such use. See, e.g., American Express Travel Related Services Co. v. Web, Inc., 405 S.E.2d 652 (Ga.1991).

2. In defining "unauthorized use" to mean the lack of actual, implied or apparent authority, the TILA (and implementing federal regulations; see 12 C.F.R. § 226.12(b)(1) (1997)) employs concepts borrowed from the law of agency. See Mary Elizabeth Matthews, Credit Cards—Authorized and Unauthorized Use, 13 Ann. Rev. Bank L. 233 (1994). Agency law can work to restrict the efficient allocation of loss from unauthorized card use, as determined by a court. In such cases courts sometimes stretch agency principles or infer facts that make agency law consistent with efficient loss allocation. Apparent authority, for example, requires that the principal's acts create in third parties a reasonable belief that a designated person is acting on its behalf. See Restatement (Second) of Agency § 8 (1958). A finding of authorized credit card use by an agent therefore requires conduct by the cardholder that creates such beliefs in merchants. The question of whether the card issuer or the cardholder is in a superior position to control the designated person's conduct is not directly at issue. The *Minskoff* court took the cardholder's failure to examine its credit card statements as omissions which induced a belief that the charges were authorized. Stieger v. Chevy Chase Savings Bank, F.S.B., 666 A.2d 479 (D.C.App.1995), goes further, concluding that an employee had apparent authority to make charges when she signed her name only after the employer had authorized her to make other charges. The employers in both cases were in a superior position to control the use of their credit cards by employees. The TILA's incorporation of agency notions seems to demand more: conduct by the cardholder that leads a merchant to believe that the employee is authorized to act on the employer's behalf.

PROBLEM

When Wife married Husband, she opened a credit card account with Bank and requested that Bank issue a credit card to her and a duplicate card to Husband in his name. When the marriage broke up, Wife notified Bank that she would no longer pay for Husband's charges on the credit card. The credit card agreement that Wife signed provided that an account could be closed by returning all cards. Bank immediately revoked both cards and gave numerous notifications to both parties of revocation and requests that the cards be returned. Both Wife and Husband continued to make charges on the cards. Wife contended that with respect to Husband's charges made after her notification to Bank, her liability should be limited to $50; the card should be treated as a lost or stolen card since she had no power to make her ungrateful spouse return it. Bank sued her for the balance of her account. What result? Which party was in the better position to prevent Husband's improper use of the card, Wife or Bank? These facts are based on Walker Bank & Trust Co. v. Jones, 672 P.2d 73 (Utah 1983).

4. ASSERTION OF CARDHOLDER OF DEFENSES

In Chapter 11, with respect to a promissory note issued by a consumer to obtain goods or services, we saw that various doctrines of case law or provisions of statutory or administrative law have been used to allow the consumer to assert against a financial institution that holds the note defenses that the consumer has against the seller of the goods or services. If a consumer uses a bank credit card to buy goods and the goods are either never delivered or are defective, should the cardholder be allowed to refuse to pay the issuer of the credit card to the extent that the cardholder would have been excused from paying the seller of the goods if the sale had been a credit sale by the seller? This question was hotly debated at the state level in the late 1960s. Financial institutions that were issuers of credit cards argued that they had only the most tenuous relationship with retailers honoring their cards, and should not be subjected to claims and defenses arising out of sales made pursuant to their cards. The card issuer, it was contended, should be no more involved in the sale transaction financed by a credit card than should a drawee bank in a sale paid for by a check drawn on the bank. Moreover, would not subjecting card issuers to sales defenses ultimately restrict the acceptability of credit cards by retailers? The concern of the retailer was that the card issuer would insist on a right to charge back against the retailer debts as to which the cardholder raised claims or defenses. Would a retailer in Maine feel secure in honoring a credit card presented by a cardholder who lives in California knowing that if the cardholder claims the goods are defective the retailer may end up with an unsecured claim against the debtor three thousand miles away?

In 1974 Congress enacted an amendment to the Truth in Lending Act, known as the Fair Credit Billing Act, stating rights and obligations of the cardholder and the issuer of the credit card with respect to the correction of a billing error that the cardholder believes has been made in the billing statement received from the issuer. The statement of these rights and obligations now appears, in amended form, in "Correction of Billing Errors" in 15 U.S.C. § 1666. "Billing error" is defined in § 1666(b) and includes reflection on the statement of an extension of credit not made by the cardholder and reflection on the statement of goods or services not accepted by the cardholder or not delivered to the cardholder in accordance with the agreement made at the time of the sales transaction. The 1974 legislation covered a number of other aspects of the issuer-cardholder relationship in §§ 1666a–1666i. Section 1666i, addressed the issue of the extent to which the cardholder can assert, as a defense to the obligation to pay the issuer, claims and defenses of the cardholder arising from the transaction in which the credit card was used. It is set out below:

Section 1666i. Assertion by Cardholder Against Card Issuer of Claims and Defenses Arising Out of Credit Card Transactions

(a) Subject to the limitation contained in subsection (b), a card issuer who has issued a credit card to a cardholder pursuant to an open end consumer credit plan shall be subject to all claims (other than tort claims) and defenses arising out of any transaction in which the credit card is used as a method of payment or extension of credit if (1) the obligor has made a good faith attempt to obtain satisfactory resolution of a disagreement or problem relative to the transaction from the person honoring the credit card; (2) the amount of the initial transaction exceeds $50; and (3) the place where the initial transaction occurred was in the same State as the mailing address previously provided by the cardholder or was within 100 miles from such address, except that the limitations set forth in clauses (2) and (3) with respect to an obligor's right to assert claims and defenses against a card issuer shall not be applicable to any transaction in which the person honoring the credit card (A) is the same person as the card issuer, (B) is controlled by the card issuer, (C) is under direct or indirect common control with the card issuer, (D) is a franchised dealer in the card issuer's products or services, or (E) has obtained the order for such transaction through a mail solicitation made by or participated in by the card issuer in which the cardholder is solicited to enter into such transaction by using the credit card issued by the card issuer. * * *

PROBLEM

California tourist, Marcy Birkenstock, goes to Maine, loves the maple syrup, buys $1,500 of the precious stuff, pays with her Visa card, issued by a bank in South Dakota, has the syrup shipped to her LA home, but hates the stuff delivered to her. She is sure that she has been defrauded. First, she calls Seller who maintains that the syrup shipped was exactly what she sampled at his store in Maine and assures her that he won't take the syrup back if she returns it. In a surly mood Marcy calls your law office to find out what she can do. If the Seller won't take the syrup back, she doesn't want to have to pay the bank issuing the Visa card when she is billed. (1) What do you tell her? (2) What is the purpose of the same-state or 100–mile limitation in the statute? (3) Where did the sale take place in this case? (4) What if Marcy had ordered the syrup by telephone after she had returned home? Or bought it on the Internet?

Section 1666i regulates only the rights between the cardholder and card issuer. The credit card systems, e.g., Visa USA and MasterCard International, have agreements governing the relationships of merchants, merchant banks, and issuing banks. These agreements allow limited recourse by an issuing bank against a merchant in defective merchandise cases. The issuing bank sends a chargeback to the merchant bank, requiring it to refund the payment made to it by the issuing bank. The merchant bank then charges back against the merchant's account. If there are too many complaints against a merchant, the merchant may be required to adopt fair policies for adjustment and return of defective merchandise in order to be allowed to continue to accept credit cards. See 2 Clark & Clark, The Law of Bank Deposits, Collections and Credit Cards ¶ 15.07[2] (Rev. ed. 2003).

Izraelewitz v. Manufacturers Hanover Trust Co.

Civil Court, City of New York, Kings County, 1983.
120 Misc.2d 125, 465 N.Y.S.2d 486.

■ IRA B. HARKAVY, JUDGE.

As the texture of the American economy evolves from paper to plastic, the disgruntled customer is spewing its wrath upon the purveyor of the plastic rather than upon the merchant.

Plaintiff George Izraelewitz commenced this action to compel the Defendant bank Manufacturers Hanover Trust Company to credit his Mastercharge account in the amount of $290.00 plus finance charges. The disputed charge, posted to Plaintiff's account on July 16, 1981, is for electronic diagrams purchased by Plaintiff via telephone from Don Britton Enterprises, a Hawaii-based mail order business.

On September 9, 1981 Plaintiff advised Defendant bank, Manufacturers Hanover Trust Company (Trust Company), that the diagrams had been unsuitable for his needs and provided Defendant with a UPS receipt indicating that the purchased merchandise had been returned to Don Britton. Defendant's Customer Service Department credited Plaintiff's account and waived finance charges on the item. Trust Company subsequently proceeded to charge back the item to the merchant. The merchant refused the charge back through The 1st Hawaii Bank, and advised Defendant bank of their strict "No Refund" policy. Don Britton also indicated that Plaintiff, during the course of conversation, had admitted that he was aware of this policy. On April 1, 1982 Defendant advised Plaintiff that his account would be redebited for the full amount. At two later dates, Plaintiff advised Trust Company of said dispute, denied knowledge of the "No Refund" policy and stated that the goods had been returned. The Trust Company once again credited Plaintiff's account and attempted to collect from Don Britton. The charge back was again refused and Plaintiff's account was subsequently redebited.

Bank credit agreements generally provide that a cardholder is obligated to pay the bank regardless of any dispute which may exist respecting the merchandise. An exception to this rule arises under a provision in the Truth in Lending Law which allows claimants whose transactions exceed $50.00 and who have made a good faith attempt to obtain satisfactory resolution of the problem, to assert claims and defenses arising out of the credit card transaction, if the place of the initial transaction is in the same state or within 100 miles of the cardholder. Consumer Credit Protection Act, 15 U.S.C.A. § 1666i.

It would appear that Plaintiff is precluded from asserting any claims or defenses since Britton's location exceeds the geographical limitation. This assumption is deceiving. Under Truth in Lending the question of where the transaction occurred (e.g. as in mail order cases) is to be determined under state or other applicable law. Truth in Lending, 12 CFR, § 226.12(c). Furthermore, any state law permitting customers to assert claims and defenses against the card issuer would not be preempted, regardless of whether the place of the transaction was at issue. In effect, these federal laws are viewed as bare minimal standards.

In Lincoln First Bank, N.A. v. Carlson, 103 Misc.2d 467, 426 N.Y.S.2d 433 (1980), the court found that:

> "(T)he statement that a card issuer is subject to all defenses if a transaction occurred less than 100 miles from the cardholder's address, does not automatically presume a cardholder to give up all his defenses should the transaction take place at a distance of greater than 100 miles from the mailing address." Id. at 436.

The facts at bar do not warrant a similar finding. Whereas in *Lincoln,* supra, the cardholder's defense arose due to an alleged failure of the card issuer itself to comply with statutory rules, the Defendant herein is blameless. The geographical limitation serves to protect banks from consumers who may expose them to unlimited liability through dealings with merchants in faraway states where it is difficult to monitor a merchant's behavior. These circumstances do not lend the persuasion needed to cast-off this benefit.

Considering, arguendo, that under the Truth in Lending Act, Plaintiff was able to assert claims and defenses from the original transaction, any claims or defenses he chose to assert would only be as good as and no better than his claim against the merchant. Accordingly, Plaintiff's claim against the merchant must be scrutinized to ascertain whether it is of good faith and substantial merit. A consumer cannot assert every miniscule dispute he may have with a merchant as an excuse not to pay an issuer who has already paid the merchant.

The crux of Plaintiff's claim, apparently, is that he returned the diagrams purportedly unaware of merchant's "No Refund" policy. The merchant contends that Plaintiff admitted that he knew of the policy and nonetheless used deceptive means to return the plans; in that they were sent without a name so they would be accepted; were not delivered to an employee of the company; were not in the original box; and showed evidence of having been xeroxed.

"No Refund" policies, per se, are not unconscionable or offensive to public policy in any manner. Truth in Lending Law "(n)either requires refunds for returns nor does it prohibit refunds in kind." Truth in Lending Regulations, 12 CFR, § 226.12(e). Bank-merchant agreements, however, usually do contain a requirement that the merchant establish a fair policy for exchange and return of merchandise.

To establish the fairness in Don Britton's policy, the strength of the reasons behind the policy and the measures taken to inform the consumer of it must necessarily be considered. Don Britton's rationale for its policy is compelling. It contends that printing is a very small part of its business, which is selling original designs, and "once a customer has seen the designs he possesses what we have to sell." Britton's policy is clearly written in its catalog directly on the page which explains how to order merchandise. To compensate for not having a refund policy, which would be impractical considering the nature of the product, Britton offers well-advertised backup plans with free engineering assistance and an exchange procedure, as well, if original plans are beyond the customer's capabilities. The Plaintiff could have availed himself of any of these alternatives which are all presumably still open to him.

On the instant facts, as between Plaintiff and the Defendant bank, Plaintiff remains liable for the disputed debt, as he has not shown adequate cause to hold otherwise.

Judgment for Defendant dismissing the complaint.

NOTES

1. 15 U.S.C. § 1666i's geographic limitation on the cardholder's use of defenses to payment against the card issuer does not specify where the "initial transaction occurred." As the court in *Izraelewitz* points out, the determination instead is left to state law. In Plutchok v. European American Bank, 540 N.Y.S.2d 135 (N.Y.Dist.Ct.1989), the court determined that under New York state law a contract concluded by telephone occurs where the acceptance occurs. The *Izraelewitz* court raises but does not need to resolve the issue of where the transaction occurred because it finds that the cardholder did not have a defense to payment against the merchant in the first place.

2. *Izraelewitz* is representative of the trend in cases interpreting 15 U.S.C. § 1666i, in which courts resist invitations to ignore the plain meaning of the provision in favor of policy. Although an informal policy argument might prefer eliminating § 1666i's geographic limit, the case for doing so is far from decisive. A card issuer has an advantage over the cardholder at monitoring and gaining information about merchants who have accounts with it, wherever the merchant is located. Repeat business between the merchant and card issuer also reduces the merchant's incentive and ability to engage in sharp practice when it affects the issuer. These considerations favor always allowing the cardholder to use whatever defense it has against the merchant to resist paying the card issuer. Cf. Singer v. Chase Manhattan Bank, 890 P.2d 1305 (Nev.1995). Against this, sharp practice by cardholders in transactions in distant locations also must be considered. There is also the possibility that local merchants might be well positioned to share information about the patterns of behavior of remote cardholders purchasing in their locality. If cardholders tend to "misbehave" differently in transactions entered into far from home, where reputational constraints are slight and such transactions are sporadic enough to make monitoring by card issuers costly, for instance, eliminating the geographic limit increases the cost to remote merchants of accepting payment by credit card. Thus, the likely source of misbehavior (merchant or cardholder) as well as its costs do not unambiguously favor doing away with a limit.

5. INTERNET FRAUD

Most Internet sales are paid for by credit cards, and security problems are mounting. Losses resulting from lost or stolen credit cards are not nearly as great as those from: (1) counterfeit credit cards in which the information on the card (credit card number and name of cardholder) is stolen and a new plastic card is manufactured from that information that can be used in face-to-face transactions, or (2) use of fraudulently obtained information in telephone, Internet sales or other remote transactions in which no plastic card is required. How are losses in Internet sales allocated? The following Problem raises the issue in a common fact situation.

PROBLEM

Brentwood Books (BB) sells rare books all over the world on its Website. It accepts Visa, MasterCard and Amex in payment, but for sales over $250, BB checks with the relevant network to verify that a card bearing the name and number submitted by the buyer has in fact been issued to the buyer. BB received a $1,000 order on the Internet purportedly from Lin Jong in Hong Kong, China, a well known book dealer, which directed that the sale be charged to Lin Jong's Visa card, with the credit card number and expiration date stated. BB verified with Visa International that a card bearing the stated number and expiration date had been issued to Lin Jong. When BB shipped the goods, it sent a memorandum to Union Bank, its California merchant bank (MB), that a sale had been made to be charged to Lin Jong's Visa card; MB credited BB's account for the amount of the sale and sent a charge message through the Visa International network to Hong Kong Bank, Lin Jong's issuing bank (IB), which debited Lin Jong's account for the amount of the sale. When Lin Jong saw the $1,000 charge on his statement, he protested to IB that he had not purchased the goods and demanded a chargeback. IB complied and sent a chargeback to MB, which erased the credit for that amount in BB's account. It became apparent that someone had stolen the information from Lin Jong's credit card and had ordered the goods sent to a Hong Kong address different from that of Lin Jong's business. Who should bear the loss in this case? How can the parties avoid losses of this kind on Internet sales?

———

Brentwood Books' difficulty is that it can't prove that Lin Jong received the goods because they don't have his signature. A typical online sale is considered a "card-not-present" transaction as opposed to a "card-present" sale at a brick-and-mortar store, where shoppers sign receipts. Thomas E. Weber, What Do You Risk Using a Credit Card to Shop on the Net, Wall.St.J., Dec. 10, 2001, at B1, states the understanding to be: "When a consumer challenges a card-not-present charge, the merchant is liable for the loss." Julia Angwin, Credit–Card Scams Bedevil E–Stores, Wall St. J., Sept. 19, 2000, at B1, reports that more Internet transactions are charged back (1.25%) than catalog transactions by telephone (0.33%) or storefront retail transactions (0.14%). She notes that one survey of 156 of the largest retailers showed that 2.64% of their Internet transactions are charged back. She interviewed online retailers whose chargeback losses have driven them to require that all deliveries be made only to the address of the cardholder and, for larger orders, to telephone the cardholder to confirm the order. The assumption is that a large portion of Internet chargeback losses are caused by use of stolen credit card numbers. Software has been developed to spot potential fraud cases, and Visa and MasterCard have developed new systems, "Verified by Visa" and "MasterCard SureCode," under which the cardholder receives a password resembling a PIN that only the cardholder can use in online sales. These systems will be phased in over the next few years. The intent is to have the use of the password treated as the equivalent to the cardholder's signature. Paul Beckett & Jathon Sapsford, As Credit–Card Theft Grows, A Tussle Over Paying to Stop It, Wall St. J., May 1, 2003, at A1.

CHAPTER 4

PAYMENT SYSTEMS: ELECTRONIC TRANSFERS

A. ELECTRONIC FUNDS TRANSFERS

1. THE BASIC TRANSACTION COVERED BY ARTICLE 4A

Article 4A was promulgated by ALI and National Conference in 1989. By 1996 it had been enacted in all 50 states. Representatives of the Federal Reserve Board and of the New York Federal Reserve Bank were very active in the four-year drafting process of Article 4A, and, after Article 4A was completed, Regulation J, which governs Fedwire (described below), was revised by the Federal Reserve Board to bring it into conformity with Article 4A. 12 C.F.R. § 210.25 et seq. The Fed's stated policy in doing so was to provide a "level playing field" in which the rights and obligations of the parties in all funds transfers would be governed by essentially the same set of rules. Ernest T. Patrikis, Thomas C. Baxter, Jr. and Raj K. Bhala, Wire Transfers 140 (1993) (hereafter Patrikis et al., Wire Transfers).

Article 4A does not apply to the consumer electronic funds transfers governed by the Electronic Fund Transfer Act, 15 U.S.C. § 1693 et seq. 4A–108. Typical transactions covered by the EFTA are: point-of-sale transactions in which retail customers pay for purchases by use of an access or debit card inserted in a terminal at a retail store that allows the bank account of the customer to be debited; automated teller machine transactions; direct deposit of paychecks in consumer accounts and preauthorized withdrawals from consumer accounts to pay consumer obligations like insurance premiums. 15 U.S.C. § 1693a(6). "Small dollar" wire transfers by Western Union and its competitors are not covered by Article 4A because payment orders are defined in 4A–103 as orders to banks and Western Union and its competitors are not banks.

The typical funds transfer transaction covered by Article 4A is a large payment of money from one business or financial organization to another made through the banking system by electronic means. The average size of a wire transfer is measured in the millions of dollars. Although checks and credit cards account for 98% of the volume of payment transactions, domestic wire transfers amount to 85% of the value of all payments. Finance: Trick or Treat?, The Economist, October 23, 1999, at 91. A common wire transfer might be: Los Angeles Seller is selling $100 million in property to a New York Buyer. The closing is in Buyer's counsel's office in New York. When negotiations are concluded and the deal is made, Buyer calls its office and requests that an instruction be given to its bank, New

York Bank (NYB), to transfer $100 million to Seller's account in Seller's bank, Los Angeles Bank (LAB). Within a few hours, Seller receives a call from its office stating that it has been notified by LAB that the funds are now in Seller's account in LAB and available for withdrawal by Seller. The deal is done.

What went on behind the scenes to move $100 million from New York to Los Angeles in a few hours? Some of the alternative methods follow. These are described in detail in Patrikis et al., Wire Transfers, Chapter 2.

(a) *Two bank transfer.* Buyer, the "originator" (4A–104(c)), instructs NYB, the "originator's bank" (4A–104(d)), to send $100 million to LAB, the "beneficiary's bank" (4A–103(a)(3)), for the account of the Seller, the "beneficiary" (4A–103(a)(2)). The instruction is a "payment order" (4A–103(a)(1)) and it may be transmitted "orally [e.g., by telephone], electronically, or in writing." NYB "accepts" (4A–209(a)) the payment order when it "execute[s]" (4A–301(a)) that order by sending a payment order to LAB intended to carry out the payment order it received from Buyer. LAB accepts the payment order of NYB by crediting the Seller's account and notifying Seller of this fact. 4A–209(b)(1). When LAB accepted the payment order, the "funds transfer" (4A–104(a)) was completed. Since Seller has received payment, Buyer's obligation to pay Seller for the property is discharged. 4A–406.

This transaction involved two payment orders: the first, from Buyer to NYB and the second, from NYB to LAB. With respect to the first, Buyer is the "sender" (4A–103(a)(5)), and NYB is the "receiving bank" (4A–103(a)(4)). With respect to the second, NYB is the sender and LAB is the receiving bank. In crediting Seller's account, LAB was not sending a payment order.

It is important to understand that Article 4A prescribes the liability of the parties to a funds transfer. It does not mandate a mode of settlement. That is, when NYB accepted Buyer's payment order, Buyer, as sender, became liable to pay the amount of that payment order to NYB, the receiving bank. 4A–402(c). When LAB, the beneficiary's bank, accepted NYB's payment order, NYB became liable to pay the amount of the order to LAB. 4A–402(b). When LAB credited Seller's account and gave notice to Seller, LAB paid Seller and Seller can withdraw the funds.

How these debts are settled, that is, how the money changes hands, is not covered by Article 4A, which merely provides for a series of bank credits, usually ending in a credit in the beneficiary's account in the beneficiary bank. NYB became a creditor of Buyer when it accepted Buyer's payment order by sending its own order to LAB. Buyer will pay its debt to NYB either by having enough money in its account in NYB that NYB can debit to cover the payment or by depositing enough money into the account, usually by the end of the banking day, to cover the payment made on Buyer's behalf. If no satisfactory agreement has been reached in advance between Buyer and NYB to fund the payment order, NYB would probably not accept the order.

LAB became a creditor of NYB when it accepted NYB's payment order by crediting Seller's account. Unless NYB and LAB have some agreement on how NYB will pay this debt, LAB probably would not accept the payment order. Usually in two-bank cases, settlement will be accomplished either through "cross accounts" or a "common account." In a cross-account situation, each bank will have an account in the other. When NYB accepts Buyer's payment order, it will debit Buyer's account and credit LAB's account. When LAB accepts NYB's payment order, it will debit NYB's account and credit Seller's account. Common-account settlement is possible when both NYB and LAB have accounts in a common correspondent bank. The correspondent bank will debit NYB's account and credit that of LAB.

(b) *CHIPS*. If both NYB and LAB are participants in the Clearing House Interbank Payments System (CHIPS) of the New York Clearing House Association, they can utilize the CHIPS facilities for both transmission of the payment order and settlement of the ensuing obligations. CHIPS is one of the two major wire transfer systems in the nation; it handles a large volume of international transfers and a number of its participants are foreign banks. Under CHIPS, NYB will send its payment order to LAB through the central CHIPS clearing system. At the end of the day, CHIPS computers will net out the difference between the total value of payments orders NYB has sent to LAB on that day, and vice versa, and the net balance debtor will pay through Fedwire the amount of the debit balance to the CHIPS Settlement Account at the New York Federal Reserve Bank; the net balance creditor will receive the amount of the credit balance from this account through Fedwire sent by the FRBNY at the end of the day. Patrikis et al., Wire Transfers, Chapter 17.

(c) *Fedwire*. This system is owned and operated by the 12 Federal Reserve banks and is the other major wire transfer system. It can be used only by banks in privity with Reserve banks. These banks must have accounts in the Fed. However, other banks can use Fedwire through correspondent banks that are in privity with the Fed. If both LAB and NYB have access to Fedwire, the transaction would go like this: Buyer instructs NYB to send the funds to LAB for credit to Seller's account. NYB instructs the New York Fed to send the funds to LAB, for Seller. The NY Fed will instruct the San Francisco Fed to send funds to LAB for Seller's account. The SF Fed will instruct LAB to credit Seller's account. LAB will notify Seller that the money is available for withdrawal. In this case four payment orders have been sent: from Buyer to NYB, from NYB to NY Fed, from NY Fed to SF Fed, and from SF Fed to LAB.

Fedwire is not only a communication system that receives and sends payment orders, but, like CHIPS, it is also a settlement system. However, there is a difference. Under Fedwire, as soon as the NY Fed sends the instruction to the SF Fed, it debits NYB's Federal Reserve account and credits the Federal Reserve account of the SF Fed. As soon as the SF Fed sends the instruction to LAB, it debits the NY Fed's Federal Reserve account and credits the Federal Reserve account of LAB. As they say in the business, with Fedwire "the message is the money." By the time LAB receives the payment order, all prior payment orders are settled. No end-of-day settlement, as in CHIPS, is necessary. Each sender's payment order is settled for at the time of acceptance by the receiving bank by debiting the Federal Reserve account of the sender and crediting the Federal Reserve account of the receiving bank.

At the time Article 4A was being written, the United Nations Commission on International Trade Law (UNCITRAL) was drafting the Model Law on International Credit Transfers which is intended to be a model for any nation that wishes to have legislation on the subject. Advisers who had been active in the Article 4A project served as members of the U.S. delegation to the Working Group which constituted the drafting committee for the Model Law. Article 4A and the Model Law bear many similarities but there are differences as well. As yet no nation has adopted the Model Law and it is exceedingly unlikely the U.S. will do so. The Model Law is discussed extensively in Patrikis et al., Wire Transfers, Chapters 19–23.

2.   PAYMENT ORDERS

A funds transfer involves a series of payment orders, defined in 4A–103(a)(1) as meaning "an instruction of a sender to a receiving bank, transmitted orally, electronically, or in writing to pay, or cause another bank to pay, a fixed or determinable amount of money to a beneficiary * * *." What was wrong with the payment order in the following case?

Grossman v. Nationsbank, N.A.

United States Court of Appeals, Eleventh Circuit, 2000.
225 F.3d 1228.

■ PER CURIAM:

Plaintiff–Appellant Stephen Grossman appeals the district court's order dismissing his complaint for failure to state a claim upon which relief could be granted. Fed.R.Civ.P. 12(b)(6). This case arises out of Grossman's claims that Nationsbank improperly transmitted a fund transfer on his behalf through the Federal Reserve Wire Transfer Network ("Fedwire"). Grossman alleged that the improper transfer resulted in damages of over $200,000 to him. After review, we affirm.

I.   GROSSMAN'S COMPLAINT

We first review the allegations in Grossman's complaint. Grossman's complaint alleges that he entered into a joint venture agreement (the "JV agreement") with HMF Management ("HMF") in order to participate in an investment program. On October 7, 1996, in furtherance of the JV agreement, Grossman opened an account at First Union National Bank (the "HMF–Grossman JV account"). Grossman received instructions from HMF for the wire transfer of Grossman's investment funds into the HMF–Grossman JV account at First Union. Grossman attached to his complaint as Exhibit B a copy of the wire-transfer instructions as he received them from HMF. The wire transfer instructions read as follows:

WIRE TRANSFER INSTRUCTIONS

HMF–GROSSMAN JV

BANK NAME: AM SOUTH BANK

BANK ADDRESS: CLEARWATER, FLORIDA

ABA#: 063 210 112

ACCOUNT NAME: DIVERSIFIED VENTURES

ACCOUNT NUMBER: 3283155856

FOR FURTHER CREDIT TO:

BANK NAME: FIRST UNION

BANK ADDRESS: JACKSONVILLE, FLORIDA

ABA#: 063000021

ACCOUNT NAME: HMF–GROSSMAN JV

CAP ACCOUNT NUMBER: 9981575600 [handwritten]

The wire transfer instructions thus directed that the funds be wired to bank name "Am South Bank," account name "Diversified Ventures," account number 3283155856, and then "for further credit to" bank name "First Union," account name "HMF–Grossman JV," account number 9981575600.

On October 11, 1996, Grossman visited a Nationsbank branch office and requested assistance in effecting the wire transfer of his funds to the HMF–Grossman JV account. Grossman provided a copy of the wire-transfer instructions to an employee of Nationsbank. The employee prepared a "Request for Funds Transfer" form that Grossman signed. Grossman attached to his complaint at Exhibit C a copy of the funds transfer form. The funds transfer form contained the following information, in pertinent part (the printed form headings are underlined):

WIRE AMOUNT $250,000.00

RECEIVING BANK (Use ONLY if different from Beneficiary's Bank)

FINAL DESTINATION: FIRST UNION, JACKSONVILLE, FL R/T #06300021, HMF–GROSSMAN JV #9981575600

BENEFICIARY'S BANK

FIRST DESTINATION: AM SOUTH BANK, CLEARWATER, FL R/T/ #063 210 112 DIVERSIFIED VENTURES

BENEFICIARY NAME

AM SOUTH BANK

BENEFICIARY ACCOUNT NUMBER (REQUIRED)

3283155856

ORIGINATOR TO BENEFICIARY INFORMATION (SPECIAL INSTRUCTIONS, EX. ATTENTION, REFERENCE NUMBER, ETC.)

FINAL DESTINATION ADDRESS: FIRST UNION 2801 SOUTHWEST HIGH

MEADOWS AVE, PALM CITY, FL 34490

ORIGINATOR/BY ORDER OF

STEPHEN GROSSMAN METHOD OF PAYMENT: DBT ACCT #2010788969

On October 17, 1996, Grossman was again in the Nationsbank branch office. The employee who had prepared the funds transfer form asked Grossman if the transfer had gone well. Grossman replied that he assumed it had gone well because the funds had reached the HMF–Grossman JV account at First Union. The employee then told Grossman that the "wire transfer room" had told her that because both Nationsbank and First Union were "on line," there was no need to route the funds through Am South Bank. As a result, Nationsbank had wired the money directly to First Union for credit to the HMF–Grossman JV account.

Grossman then reviewed the joint-venture documents, and determined that the transfer directly from Nationsbank to the HMF–Grossman JV account "appeared to be inconsistent with the wiring instructions given to him." While the funds had reached the ultimate intended account, the HMF–Grossman JV account, the funds had gone to the account directly and not through Am South Bank and the Diversified Ventures account. On October 18, 1996, Grossman again contacted the Nationsbank branch office and requested that the "wire be sent in accordance with the instructions he had been provided and, in turn, had provided the bank." After the same Nationsbank employee consulted with the "wire room," she told Grossman that the funds would be recalled and resent in conformity with the instructions.

Within the next several days, Grossman received confirmation from both the "wire room" and the same Nationsbank employee that the funds had been recalled and resent. However, in early November, Grossman contacted First Union and learned that no deposit had been received to the HMF–Grossman JV account. Grossman immediately called Am South Bank to inquire as to why the funds had not been forwarded to the HMF–Grossman JV account as the wiring instructions had directed. Am South told Grossman that it could not provide him any information regarding an account to which he was not a signatory, and that he should contact the owner of the Diversified Ventures account at Am South to which Nationsbank had wired the funds.

Over the next several months, Grossman tried unsuccessfully to determine what had happened to the funds that were intended for deposit in the HMF–Grossman JV account at First Union. Nationsbank continued to insist that it had transferred the money to Am South according to Grossman's instructions, and that it was then Am South's responsibility to complete the transaction pursuant to the instructions that Nationsbank had forwarded to Am South with the funds. In March 1997, Am South informed Grossman that the Diversified Ventures account had been closed in February 1997.

HMF, the sole signatory to the Diversified Ventures account at Am South, initially told Grossman that the delay in forwarding the funds to the HMF-Grossman JV account at First Union had been due to a federal audit of Diversified Ventures. However, on March 6, 1997, HMF wired $50,000.00 to Grossman's Nationsbank account in return for an agreement from Grossman authorizing HMF to deduct $50,000.00 from the principal sum of the investment that it would soon transfer to the HMF–Grossman JV account. Grossman attached to his complaint at Exhibit D a copy of this agreement. * * *

* * * Grossman's complaint alleges damages in excess of $200,000.00 as a result of Nationsbank's "failure to complete the wire transfer transaction in accordance with the instructions Grossman had provided, or to advise Grossman that such transaction could not be completed as structured." * * *

IV. DISCUSSION

The district court held, and the parties agree, that the provisions of Regulation J exclusively apply to the fund transfer in this case because it was effected by the use of Fedwire, the Federal Reserve Banks' wire-transfer system. *See* 12 C.F.R. § 210.25–32. Regulation J applies U.C.C. Article 4A to wire transfers conducted using Fedwire. * * *

We address Nationsbank's duty under Regulation J and U.C.C. Article 4A once Grossman requested the fund transfer, so that we can determine whether Grossman's complaint sufficiently stated a claim that Nationsbank breached its duty under those provisions. * * *

Now we address whether Nationsbank complied with it's duty under Regulation J. Regulation J directs that Nationsbank's duty as a receiving bank was to issue a payment order that complied with the sender's (Grossman's), instructions:

> The receiving bank is obliged to issue, on the execution date, a payment order *complying with the sender's order and to follow the sender's instructions concerning (i) any intermediary bank* or funds-transfer system to be used in carrying out the funds transfer, or (ii) the means by which payment orders are to be transmitted in the funds transfer. If the originator's bank issues a payment order to an intermediary bank, the originator's bank is obliged to instruct the intermediary bank according to the instruction of the originator. An intermediary bank in the funds transfer is similarly bound by an instruction given to it by the sender of the payment order it accepts.

12 C.F.R. Part 210, Subpart B, App. B, § 4A–302(a)(1) (emphasis supplied).

After analyzing Nationsbank's duty under § 4A–302(a)(1), we conclude that Grossman could not prove a set of facts in support of his claim which would entitle him to relief. The instructions Grossman provided to Nationsbank did not identify the banks by the terms "intermediary bank" and "beneficiary's bank." The instructions were therefore non-specific. On appeal, Grossman argues that he instructed Nationsbank to send the funds to the HMF–Grossman JV account at First Union, using Am South as an intermediary bank. However, the instructions Grossman gave Nationsbank cannot be read as indicating a normal transfer using an intermediary bank, because funds traveling through an intermediary bank are not deposited in an individual account at the intermediary bank. 12 C.F.R. Part 210, Subpart B, App. B § 4A-105(a)(2). The instructions Grossman gave to Nationsbank specifically stated that the money was to reach the Diversified Ventures account at Am South, account number 3283155856. The next line of the instructions read "for further credit to" the HMF–Grossman JV account at First Union, which indicates that the funds were first intended to be credited to the Diversified Ventures account at Am South with instructions that the funds were "for further credit to the HMF–Grossman JV account at First Union." Indeed, Nationsbank first sent the money directly to the HMF–Grossman JV account at First Union, and Grossman told Nationsbank in no uncertain terms that was not what he had instructed.

Grossman may not have understood that once the funds were deposited in the Diversified Ventures account at Am South, neither he nor Nationsbank would have any control over the money. Nonetheless, Grossman's instructions told Nationsbank to wire the funds to the Diversified Ventures account at Am South with instructions to send the money on to the HMF–Grossman JV account at First Union. Nationsbank did exactly that. The payment order form prepared by Nationsbank, which Grossman signed, listed the "First Destination" as the Am South Diversified Ventures account, and instructed that the "Final Destination" was to be the HMF–Grossman JV account at First Union. If this is not the transaction Grossman desired, he has not alleged that he gave Nationsbank any additional instructions, or that Nationsbank had any other way of knowing that Grossman intended a different transaction. Because Nationsbank followed the instructions that Grossman provided, Nationsbank complied with its duty under Regulation J. Therefore, Grossman cannot state a claim for a violation of Regulation J, and the district court did not err in granting Nationsbank's Rule 12(b)(6) motion to dismiss.

AFFIRMED.

NOTE

An originator's payment order may instruct that a designated intermediary bank be used to carry out the funds transfer, and the receiving bank is obliged to follow the instruction. 4A–302(a)(1). An "intermediary bank" means "a receiving bank other than the originator's bank or the beneficiary's bank." Why wasn't Am South Bank an intermediary bank in this case? How should Grossman have written the payment order in this case?

PROBLEM

Company sent Bank One, where it maintained a deposit account, a "letter of instructions" to (1) retain a daily balance of at least $10,000 in the account and (2) transfer automatically by wire transfer all funds in the account in excess of $110,000 to Company's account in Bank Two. Bank One began transferring funds to Bank Two whenever the balance rose above $110,000. Later Bank One ceased making these transfers. Company now asserts that it has been damaged by Bank One's failure to move the money into the account in Bank Two paying higher interest. One of the issues in assessing Company's claim against Bank One is whether Article 4A applies to this transaction. If the letter of instructions is not a "payment order," Article 4A does not apply. Is it a payment order? See 4A–103(a)(1). The facts are based on Trustmark Insurance Co. v. Bank One, Arizona, N.A., 48 P.3d 485 (Ariz. App. 2002).

3.   ACCEPTANCE OF PAYMENT ORDER

By Receiving Bank. "Acceptance," defined in 4A–209, is a core concept of Article 4A. The rights and obligations of the participants to a funds transfer under Article 4A arise as a result of acceptance. A payment order instructs a receiving bank to accept the payment order, but the receiving bank may either accept or reject. If a receiving bank accepts a sender's payment order, the sender becomes liable to the receiving bank for the amount of the payment order, 4A–402(c), and the receiving bank is obliged to issue a payment order complying with the sender's payment order. 4A–302(a)(1). A receiving bank, other than the beneficiary's bank, accepts the sender's payment order by executing the order, 4A–209(a), that is, by issuing a payment order intended to carry out the payment order received by the bank. 4A–301(a). An originator is a sender and an originator's bank is a receiving bank. When the originator's bank executes the payment order by sending it to a receiving bank, the originator's bank becomes a sender.

By Beneficiary's Bank. The last receiving bank in the chain is the beneficiary's bank, the one identified in the payment order as the bank in which the account of the beneficiary is to be credited. 4A–103(a)(3). Section 4A–209(b) spells out when a beneficiary's bank accepts a payment order. In the most common case, this occurs when the beneficiary's bank credits the beneficiary's account and notifies the beneficiary that it may withdraw the credit. 4A–405(a). At this point the beneficiary's bank becomes liable for the amount of the payment order to the beneficiary. 4A–404(a). The beneficiary has bank credit in its account in the amount of the funds transfer—"money in the bank"—that it can withdraw. The purpose of the funds transfer has been achieved: the beneficiary is paid and the underlying obligation that the originator owed the beneficiary is discharged. 4A–

406(a) and (b). Bank credit has been transferred from the originator's bank to the beneficiary's bank. Settlement between the banks may occur later.

PROBLEM

Beneficiary's Bank (BB) received a payment order for $10,000 and credited Beneficiary's (B) account for that amount. A few hours later BB notified B that the credit had been received, but said nothing about its availability. However, the evidence was uncontradicted that B had been given immediate access to the funds in its account at the time the account was credited. The issue before the court was whether payment was made at the time of the credit or at the time of the notice. Section 4A–405(a) states that payment is made "when . . . (i) the beneficiary is notified of the right to withdraw the credit * * * or (iii) funds with respect to the order are otherwise made available to the beneficiary by the bank." The court in First Security Bank of New Mexico v. Pan American Bank, 215 F.3d 1147 (10th Cir. 2000), held that payment occurred as soon as B had immediate access to the funds under 4A–405(a)(iii) even though BB had not given B notice of its right to withdraw the funds. The only discussion in Article 4A of this provision appears in Comment 5 to 4A–209 and is not clearly on point. Do you agree with the court's decision? What position does *Aleo*, following, take on this issue?

4. RECEIVER FINALITY

In Chapter 10 we discussed why obligees might not choose to take payment in uncertified checks or even in cashier's checks. At that point we suggested that they might demand to be paid by wire transfer in order to provide maximum safety. In the following case we see why this is so.

Aleo International, Ltd. v. Citibank

Supreme Court, New York County, 1994.
160 Misc.2d 950, 612 N.Y.S.2d 540.

■ HERMAN CAHN, JUSTICE.

Defendant Citibank, N.A. ("Citibank") moves for an order, pursuant to CPLR 3212, granting it summary judgment dismissing the complaint.

Plaintiff Aleo International, Ltd. ("Aleo") is a domestic corporation. On October 13, 1992, one of Aleo's vice-presidents, Vera Eyzerovich ("Ms. Eyzerovich"), entered her local Citibank branch and instructed Citibank to make an electronic transfer of $284,563 US dollars to the Dresdner Bank in Berlin, Germany, to the account of an individual named Behzad Hermatjou ("Hermatjou"). The documentary evidence submitted shows that at 5:27 p.m. on October 13, 1992, Citibank sent the payment order to the Dresdner Bank by electronic message. Dresdner Bank later sent Citibank an electronic message: "Regarding your payment for USD 284.563,00 DD 13.10.92 [indecipherable] f/o Behzad Hermatjou, Pls be advised that we have credited A.M. beneficiary DD 14.10.92 val 16.10.92 with the net amount of USD 284.136,16." This information was confirmed by the Dresdner Bank by fax to Citibank on July 29, 1993: "Please be advised that on 14.10.92 at 09:59 o'clock Berlin time Dresdner Bank credited the account of Behzad Hermatjou with USD 284.136,16 (USD 284.563,00 less our charges)." It is undisputed that Berlin time is six hours ahead of New York time, and that 9:59 a.m. Berlin time would be 3:59 a.m. New York time. At approximately 9 a.m. on October 14, 1992, Ms. Eyzerovich instructed Citibank to stop the transfer. When Citibank did not, this action ensued.

Article 4A of the Uniform Commercial Code ("UCC") governs electronic "funds transfers." The Official Comment to UCC § 4A–102 states that the provisions of Article 4A

> are intended to be the exclusive means of determining the rights, duties and liabilities of the affected parties in any situation covered by particular provisions of the Article. Consequently, resort to principles of law or equity outside of Article 4A is not appropriate to create rights, duties and liabilities inconsistent with those stated in this Article.

Article 4A does not include any provision for a cause of action in negligence. Thus, unless Citibank's failure to cancel Ms. Eyzerovich's transfer order was not in conformity with Article 4A, plaintiff Aleo has failed to state a cause of action, and this action must be dismissed.

UCC 4A–211(2), which governs the cancellation and amendment of payment orders, provides that

> A communication by the sender cancelling or amending a payment order is effective to cancel or amend the order if notice of the communication is received at a time and in a manner affording the receiving bank a reasonable opportunity to act on the communication before the bank accepts the payment order.

"Acceptance of Payment Order" is defined by UCC 4A–209 (2), which provides that:

> a beneficiary's bank accepts a payment order at the earliest of the following times: (a) when the bank (i) pays the beneficiary ... or (ii) notifies the beneficiary of receipt of the order or that the account of the beneficiary has been credited with respect to the order ...

The documentary evidence shows that Hermatjou's account was credited on October 14, 1992 at 9:59 a.m. Berlin time. Thus, as of 3:59 a.m. New York time, the Dresdner Bank "paid the beneficiary" and thereby accepted the payment order. Because this payment and acceptance occurred prior to Ms. Eyzerovich's stop transfer order at 9 a.m. on that day, according to UCC 4A–211(2), Ms. Eyzerovich's attempt to cancel the payment order was ineffective, and Citibank may not be held liable for failing to honor it.

"Summary judgment is designed to expedite all civil cases by eliminating from the Trial Calendar claims which can properly be resolved as a matter of law. . . . [W]hen there is no genuine issue to be resolved at trial, the case should be summarily decided." Andre v. Pomeroy, 35 N.Y.2d 361, 364, 362 N.Y.S.2d 131, 320 N.E.2d 853.

Accordingly, defendant's motion is granted and this action is dismissed.

NOTES

1. The attractions of the wholesale wire transfer system, as regulated by Article 4A, are that it is cheap, fast and final. After LAB accepted the payment order in the hypothetical case at the beginning of the chapter by crediting Seller's account and notifying Seller of its right to withdraw, Buyer could not stop payment by canceling the payment order unless LAB agreed to do so, and then only in the four cases set out in 4A–211(c)(2). These are that the payment order was (i) unauthorized; (ii) a duplicate; (iii) made to the wrong beneficiary; or (iv) in an excessive amount. "Buyer's remorse" is not listed. Since LAB will have little incentive to antagonize its customer, Seller, by agreeing to the cancellation of the payment order and may not be sure whether any of the four events has actually occurred, it is unlikely that many beneficiary banks will agree to cancel.

2. A concern often expressed by banks during the process of drafting Article 4A was that a beneficiary bank might need protection against the insolvency of prior banks in the chain. If the payment order is sent through Fedwire, the beneficiary's bank is fully protected because "the message is the money," and the beneficiary's bank is paid as soon as it receives the Fedwire payment order. 4A–209(b)(2) and 4A–403(a)(1). But in most other cases, the beneficiary's bank will not receive settlement on the payment order until after it has received the order. If it turns the money over to the beneficiary as soon as it receives the credit, it faces the risk that a prior bank in the chain may suspend payments before it settles with the beneficiary bank. Some banks wanted to solve this problem by being allowed to make provisional payments to their customers that would allow the beneficiary's bank to grab back the money paid out to the beneficiary if a prior bank failed before settlement. Strong arguments were made against this view by both users of the wire transfer system and the Fed; they contended that once the beneficiary's bank had made the money available to the beneficiary, it should be able to keep it. Receiver finality should be the goal of Article 4A. The users won this argument. Section 4A–405(c) invalidates provisional payments to beneficiaries, except in case of ACH transfers (4A–405(d), Comment 3) or, with respect to CHIPS transfers, in case of a meltdown of the entire American banking system (4A–405(e)), an event that Comment 4 cheerfully assures us "should never occur."

3. If a beneficiary bank cannot protect itself against up-stream insolvencies by making provisional payments to its customers, what can it do to guard against this risk? Patrikis et al., Wire Transfers, Chapter 10. First, it can reject the payment order if it doubts the solvency of the sending bank. 4A–210. Second, it can notify the beneficiary that it will not be allowed to withdraw the funds until the bank receives settlement from the sender of the order. 4A–209(b)(1). Third, it can withhold the funds until an hour after the opening of business on the day after receipt, by which time, if it has not already received settlement, it must reject to avoid acceptance. 4A–209(b)(3). But the competitive pressure on beneficiary's banks to afford their customers prompt payment upon receipt of payment orders is great. This is particularly true with respect to CHIPS banks, which are in direct competition with the Fedwire system that offers beneficiaries of Fedwire payments immediate access to the incoming funds. By adoption of new rules after the completion of Article 4A, CHIPS has created a loss-sharing system that requires CHIPS banks to contribute funds to allow the system to settle for payment orders sent over the system during a given day in the event that one or more banks are unable to meet their settlement obligations. Patrikis et al., Wire Transfers, Chapter 18. The level playing field between CHIPS and Fedwire has been achieved with respect to the early release of funds to beneficiaries.

5. THE "MONEY-BACK GUARANTEE"

The general rule is that an originator owes the originator's bank the amount of the payment order when the bank accepts the payment order. 4A–402(c) (second sentence). But what if payment never reaches the beneficiary intended by the originator? That is, the "funds transfer" (4A–104(a)) is not completed. For example, the payment is made to the wrong beneficiary or not made at all. As between the originator and its bank, which should bear the risk of loss? The originator still owes the beneficiary, and, if it is liable to its bank as well, it may have to pay twice. We see that under the "money-back guarantee" rule of 4A–402(c) (last sentence), the policy decision is made that the originator is not liable to its bank, and, if it has already paid, it may recover the payment. 4A–402(d). But what if the originator designated that the transfer be made by the originator's bank through a specified intermediary bank, and it is that bank that is at fault or doesn't send the payment because it has suspended payments? The originator's bank is required by 4A–302 to follow the originator's instructions with respect to intermediary banks. See 4A–402(e). The following case is the first authoritative holding on these matters.

Grain Traders, Inc. v. Citibank, N.A.

United States Court of Appeals, Second Circuit, 1998.
160 F.3d 97.

■ JOHN M. WALKER, JR., CIRCUIT JUDGE.

Plaintiff Grain Traders, Inc., ("Grain Traders") appeals from the April 16, 1997, judgment granting summary judgment for defendant Citibank, N.A., ("Citibank") and dismissing Grain Traders's diversity action brought under Article 4A of New York's Uniform Commercial Code ("Article 4A") and principles of common law seeking a refund from Citibank for an alleged uncompleted electronic funds transfer.

BACKGROUND

Grain Traders, in order to make a payment of $310,000 to Claudio Goidanich Kraemer ("Kraemer"), initiated a funds transfer on December 22, 1994, by issuing a payment order to its bank, Banco de Credito Nacional ("BCN"), that stated

WE HEREBY AUTHORIZE YOU DEBIT OUR ACCOUNT NR. 509364 FOR THE AMOUNT OF US $310,000.00 AND TRANSFER TO:

BANQUE DU CREDIT ET INVESTISSEMENT LTD. ACCOUNT 36013997 AT CITIBANK NEW YORK IN FAVOUR OF BANCO EXTRADER S.A. ACCOUNT NR. 30114C–ENEFICIARY CLAUDIO GOIDANICH KRAEMER—UNDER FAX ADVISE TO BANCO EXTRADER NR. 00541–318 0057/318–0184 AT. DISTEFANO/M. FLIGUEIRA.

Thus the transfer, as instructed by Grain Traders, required BCN to debit Grain Traders's account at BCN in the amount of $310,000, and then to issue a payment order to Citibank. That payment order, in turn, was to require Citibank to debit $310,000 from BCN's account at Citibank and to credit that amount to the account that Banque du Credit et Investissement Ltd. ("BCIL") maintained at Citibank. Citibank, in turn, was to issue a payment order to BCIL instructing it to transfer, by unspecified means, $310,000 to Banco Extrader, S.A. ("Extrader"). Extrader was then to credit the $310,000 to the account maintained at Extrader by Kraemer.

BCN duly carried out Grain Traders's instructions. Citibank, in turn, executed BCN's payment order by debiting $310,000 from BCN's account at Citibank, crediting that amount to BCIL's account at Citibank, and issuing a payment order to BCIL concerning the further transfers.

Both BCIL and Extrader suspended payments at some point after Citibank executed the payment order. BCIL apparently began closing its offices on December 31, 1994, and its banking license was revoked in July of 1995. Similarly, Extrader became insolvent sometime in late December of 1994 or early January of 1995. On December 28, 1994, apparently at Grain Traders's request, BCN contacted Citibank and requested cancellation of its payment order and return of the amount of the payment order. The message sent by BCN stated:

REGARDING OUR PAYMENT ORDER FROM 12/22/94 FOR USD 310,000 TO BANCO EXTRADER S.A. ACCT. NO. 30114 F/O BANQUE DE CREDIT ET INVESTISSEMENT LTD. ACCT NO. 36013997 F/C TO CLAUDIO GOLDANICH [SIC] KRAEMER. PLEASE NOTE THAT WE ARE REQUESTING FUNDS BACK AS SOON AS POSSIBLE.

YOUR IMMEDIATE ATTENTION TO THIS MATTER IS APPRECIATED.

Citibank sought authorization from BCIL to debit the amount that had been credited to its account on December 22, 1994, and, after several unsuccessful attempts to contact BCIL, received a message on January 3, 1995, from BCIL that purportedly authorized the debit. Citibank asserts that it was at this juncture that it determined that BCIL had exceeded its credit limitations and placed the account on a "debit no-post" status, meaning no further debits would be posted to the account. Citibank refused BCN's request to cancel the payment order, stating:

RE: YOUR PAYMENT [ORDER] . . . WE ARE UNABLE TO RETURN FUNDS AS BNF [SIC] BANK HAS AN INSUFFICIENT BALANCE IN THEIR ACCOUNT. FOR FURTHER INFORMATION WE SUGGEST THAT YOU CONTACT THEM DIRECTLY. WE CLOSE OUR FILE.

In November of 1995, Grain Traders filed this action seeking a refund from Citibank pursuant to U.C.C. §§ 4A–402(d), 4A–209, 4A–301, 4A–305, and 1–203, as well as common law theories of conversion and money had and received. Grain Traders alleges that the transfer was never completed—i.e., Extrader never credited Kraemer's account for the $310,000. Grain Traders further claims that the reason the transfer was not completed was because Citibank had already placed BCIL's account on a "hold for funds" status before it credited the $310,000 intended for Kraemer to BCIL's account. By making the credit to BCIL's allegedly frozen account, Grain Traders contends, Citibank improperly used the funds to offset BCIL's indebtedness to it and prevented BCIL from withdrawing the funds to complete the transfer.

Grain Traders moved for summary judgment on its Article 4A claim. Citibank cross-moved for summary judgment on the grounds that Grain Traders had failed to state a claim under Article 4A, could not establish its common law claims, and that its common law claims were, in any event, pre-empted by Article 4A. The district court denied summary judgment to Grain Traders and granted summary judgment in favor of Citibank. Grain Traders now appeals.

DISCUSSION

In its opinion, the district court held that (1) Section 402 of Article 4A established a cause of action only by a sender against its receiving bank, thus Grain Traders, who was a sender only with respect to BCN, had sued the wrong bank; (2) Sections 4A–209, 4A–301, 4A–305, and 1–203 of the U.C.C. did not create causes of action; and (3) Grain Traders could not establish elements necessary to its common law claims of conversion and money had and received. See Grain Traders, Inc. v. Citibank, N.A., 960 F.Supp. 784, 789, 792–93 (S.D.N.Y.1997). The district court did not reach Citibank's argument that the common law claims were pre-empted by Article 4A. Id. at 793 n. 8. On appeal, Grain Traders argues that the district court erred in dismissing its claim under § 4-A–402 and its common law claims. * * * Grain Traders does not appeal the dismissal of its claims under Sections 4A–209, 4A–301, 4A–305, and 1–203 of the U.C.C., and thus these claims are not a subject of this opinion. For the following reasons, we affirm the district court's judgment.

* * *

II. Article 4A Claims

Article 4A of the U.C.C. governs the procedures, rights, and liabilities arising out of commercial electronic funds transfers. A funds transfer is defined as a

> series of transactions, beginning with the originator's payment order [and] includes any payment order issued by the originator's bank or an intermediary bank intended to carry out the originator's payment order.

§ 4A–104(a). A "payment order" is defined as

> an instruction of a sender to a receiving bank ... to pay, or to cause another bank to pay, a fixed or determinable amount of money [where] the receiving bank is to be reimbursed by debiting an account of, or otherwise receiving payment from, the sender, and ... the instruction is transmitted by the sender directly to the receiving bank.

§ 4A–103(a)(1). Thus, as noted by the district court, "funds are 'transferred' through a series of debits and credits to a series of bank accounts." *Grain Traders*, 960 F.Supp. at 788. A "sender" is defined as "the person giving the instruction [directly] to the receiving bank," and a "receiving bank" is defined as "the bank to which the sender's instruction is addressed." There are other defined roles in a given funds transfer for the senders, receiving banks, or other participants, including the "originator" of the funds transfer (here Grain Traders), the "originator's bank" (here BCN), the "beneficiary" (here Kraemer) and the "beneficiary's bank" (here Extrader). For any given funds transfer, there can be only one originator, originator's bank, beneficiary, and beneficiary's bank, but there can be several senders and receiving banks, one of each for every payment order required to complete the funds transfer. See § 4A–103.

A. Grain traders's refund claim under § 4A–402

Section 4A–402 ("Section 402") covers the obligation of a sender of a payment order to make payment to the receiving bank after the order has been accepted as well as the obligation of a receiving bank to refund payment in the event the transfer is not completed. It provides, in relevant part,

> (c) ... With respect to a payment order issued to a receiving bank other than the beneficiary's bank, acceptance of the order by the receiving bank obliges the sender to pay the bank the amount of the sender's order.... The obligation of that sender to pay its payment order is excused if the funds transfer is not completed....

> (d) If the sender of a payment order pays the order and was not obliged to pay all or part of the amount paid [because the funds transfer was not completed], the bank receiving payment is obliged to refund payment to the extent the sender was not obliged to pay.

§ 4A–402(c), (d). Thus, under Section 402(c), the sender's obligation to pay the receiving bank is excused in the event that the transfer is not completed. If payment has already been made, a sender can seek a refund from the bank it paid under Section 402(d). It was this so-called "money-back guarantee" provision that Grain Traders invoked to obtain a refund from Citibank.

The district court held that Grain Traders's refund action against Citibank, an intermediary bank for the purposes of Grain Traders's funds transfer, was barred because a Section 402 refund action could only be maintained by a "sender" against the receiving bank to whom the sender had issued a payment order and whom the sender had paid. Thus, because Grain Traders was a "sender" only with respect to the payment order it issued to BCN, Grain Traders could look only to BCN, the receiving bank, for a refund.

In reaching its conclusion, the district court relied on the plain language of Section 402(d) as well as other provisions of Article 4A. It found that the language of Section 402(d) establishes a right of refund only between a sender and the receiving bank it paid. BCN, not Grain Traders, was the sender that issued the payment order to Citibank and paid Citibank by having its account debited in the amount of $310,000. Grain Traders argues that the fact that Section 402(d) does not use the words "receiving bank" but instead refers to "the bank receiving payment" means that the sender can sue any bank in the chain that received payment. We agree with Citibank that because the words "receiving bank" are defined as the bank that receives a payment order, Section 402(d)'s use of the words "bank receiving payment" simply clarifies that the right to a refund arises only after the sender has satisfied its obligation to pay the receiving bank.

The Official Comment to § 4A–402 supports this interpretation. It states, in relevant part:

> [t]he money-back guarantee [of § 4A–402(d)] is particularly important to Originator if noncompletion of the funds transfer is due to the fault of an intermediary bank rather than Bank A [the Originator's bank]. *In that case Bank A must refund payment to Originator, and Bank A has the burden of obtaining refund from the intermediary bank that it paid.*

§ 4A–402, cmt. 2 (emphasis added). We think this comment makes plain the intent of the Article 4A drafters to effect an orderly unraveling of a funds transfer in the event that the transfer was not completed, and accomplished this by incorporating a "privity" requirement into the "money back guarantee" provision so that it applies only between the parties to a particular payment order and not to the parties to the funds transfer as a whole.

The district court also relied on the express right of subrogation created by Section 402(5), which applies when one of the receiving banks is unable to issue a refund because it has suspended payments. Section 402(5) provides that:

If a funds transfer is not completed as stated in subsection (3) and an intermediary bank is obliged to refund payment as stated in subsection (4) but is unable to do so because not permitted by applicable law or because the bank suspends payments, a sender in the funds transfer that executed a payment order in compliance with an instruction, as stated in [§ 4–A–302(1)(a)] to route the funds transfer through that intermediary bank is entitled to receive or retain payment from the sender of the payment order that it accepted. The first sender in the funds transfer that issued an instruction requiring routing through that intermediary bank is subrogated to the right of the bank that paid the intermediary bank to refund as stated in subsection (4).

Where a right to refund has been triggered because a transfer was not completed, but one of the banks that received payment is unable to issue a refund because it has suspended payments, the orderly unraveling of the transfer is prevented and the risk of loss will be borne by some party to the transfer. Article 4–A allocates that risk of loss to the party that first designated the failed bank to be used in the transfer. *See* N.Y.U.C.C. § 4–A–402, cmt. 2 (where "Bank A [the sender] was required to issue its payment order to Bank C [the insolvent bank] because Bank C was designated as an intermediary bank by Originator[,] . . . . Originator takes the risk of insolvency of Bank C"). Under Section 402(5), all intervening senders are entitled to receive and retain payment and the party that designated the failed bank bears the burden of recovery by being subrogated to the right of the sender that paid the failed bank. We agree with the district court that

> the subrogation language of § 4–A–402(5) demonstrates that the originator does not, as a general matter, have a right to sue all the parties to a funds transfer. . . . [and] makes clear . . . that under § 4–A–402(4) no right to a refund otherwise exists between the originator and an intermediary bank. This is evident because there would be no need for the subrogation language of subsection (5) if the originator (as the first sender) already had a right to assert a refund claim directly against all intermediary banks.

960 F.Supp. at 790.

In sum, we agree with the district court's thoughtful analysis and conclude that § 4A–402 allows each sender of a payment order to seek refund only from the receiving bank it paid. Not only do the provisions of Article 4A support the district court's interpretation, there are sound policy reasons for limiting the right to seek a refund to the sender who directly paid the receiving bank. One of Article 4A's primary goals is to promote certainty and finality so that "the various parties to funds transfers [will] be able to predict risk with certainty, to insure against risk, to adjust operational and security procedures, and to price funds transfer services appropriately." § 4A–102, cmt. To allow a party to, in effect, skip over the bank with which it dealt directly, and go to the next bank in the chain would result in uncertainty as to rights and liabilities, would create a risk of multiple or inconsistent liabilities, and would require intermediary banks to investigate the financial circumstances and various legal relations of the other parties to the transfer. These are matters as to which an intermediary bank ordinarily should not have to be concerned and, if it were otherwise, would impede the use of rapid electronic funds transfers in commerce by causing delays and driving up costs. Accordingly, we affirm the district court's dismissal of Grain Traders's refund claim under Section 402(4).

B.   Common Law Claims

The district court also granted summary judgment to Citibank on Grain Traders's common law claims for conversion and money had and received, finding that Grain Traders could not establish essential elements of those claims. We do not address the district court's holding, however, because we agree with Citibank's argument, raised below but not reached by the district court, that even assuming Grain Traders could establish its claims, they are precluded by Article 4A.

Whether and to what extent Article 4A precludes common law actions is a matter of first impression for this court. Article 4A was enacted to correct the perceived inadequacy of " 'attempt[ing] to define rights and obligations in funds transfers by general principles [of common law] or by analogy to rights and obligations in negotiable instruments law or the law of check collection.' " Banque Worms v. BankAmerica Int'l, 77 N.Y.2d 362, 369, 568 N.Y.S.2d 541, 570 N.E.2d 189 (1991) (quoting Official Comment to § 4A–102). The Official Comment to Section 4A–102 states that the provisions of Article 4A represent a careful and delicate balancing of [competing] interests and are intended to be the exclusive means of determining the rights, duties, and liabilities of the affected parties in any situation covered by particular provisions of the Article. Consequently, resort to principles of law or equity outside of Article 4A is not appropriate to create rights, duties and liabilities inconsistent with those stated in this Article.

Similarly, Section 4A–212 states, in relevant part,

[l]iability based on acceptance arises only when acceptance occurs as stated in Section 4A–209, and liability is limited to that provided in this Article. A receiving bank is not the agent of the sender or beneficiary of the payment order it accepts, or of any other party to the funds transfer, and the bank owes no duty to any party to the funds transfer except as provided in this article or by express agreement.

We agree with those courts that have interpreted the above language to preclude common law claims when such claims would impose liability inconsistent with the rights and liabilities expressly created by Article 4 A. See, e.g., Banco de la Provincia de Buenos Aires v. BayBank Boston N.A., 985 F.Supp. 364, 369–70 (S.D.N.Y.1997) (for conversion claim to stand, it cannot be inconsistent with Article 4A); Centre–Point Merchant Bank Ltd. v. American Express Bank Ltd., 913 F.Supp. 202, 206 (S.D.N.Y.1996) (exclusivity of Article 4A is restricted to any situation covered by particular provisions of the Article and resort to common law must not be inconsistent); Sheerbonnet, Ltd. v. American Express Bank, Ltd., 951 F.Supp. 403,

407–08 (S.D.N.Y.1995) (same); see also Cumis Ins. Soc., Inc. v. Citibank, N.A., 921 F.Supp. 1100, 1110 (S.D.N.Y.1996) (claim for conversion failed because bank's actions expressly authorized by Article 4A); Aleo International, Ltd. v. Citibank, N.A., 160 Misc.2d 950, 612 N.Y.S.2d 540, 541 (Sup. Ct. 1994) (no claim for negligence unless conduct complained of was not in conformity with Article 4A). Because we determine that the liability sought to be imposed by Grain Traders's common law claims would be inconsistent with the provisions of Article 4A, we do not reach the issue of whether common law claims that concern matters expressly addressed by Article 4A would be precluded as duplicative even if consistent. See, e.g., Centre–Point, 913 F.Supp. at 208 (dismissing common law claims because "specific Article 4A provisions" applied to the transactions at issue).

* * *

CONCLUSION

We hold that Section 402 of Article 4A imposes a privity requirement such that a sender seeking a refund for an uncompleted funds transfer may look only to the receiving bank to whom it issued a payment order and payment. As a result, Grain Traders may look only to BCN for a refund. We also hold that Grain Traders's common law claims are precluded because they seek to impose liability on Citibank that would be inconsistent with the provisions of Article 4A.

The judgment of the district court is affirmed.

NOTES

1. The court refers to 4A–402(e) but does not discuss whether it applies to this case. That provision would deprive GT of its right to recover from BCN and grant GT, by subrogation, Citibank's right to recover from BCIL. See the last paragraph of Comment 2. Perhaps the court viewed 4A–402(e) as irrelevant to the issue before the court, GT's right to recover from Citibank. The district court addressed the question of the applicability of 4A–402(e) and concluded that it could not decide the matter because the record was unclear on whether BCIL had suspended payments. 960 F.Supp. at 791.

2. The issue of the degree to which Article 4A displaces common law principles has perhaps been the most widely litigated issue in wire transfer cases. Section 1–103(b) allows courts to invoke principles of law and equity to "supplement" the provisions of the Code, unless "displaced by the particular provisions of this [Act]." Anyone who has participated as a drafter of UCC provisions becomes familiar with the persistent gripe of advisors that something more specific than 1–103(b) should be drafted to deter courts from ignoring the Code provisions that the courts don't like in favor of judicial remedies such as restitution, negligence, money had and received, and the like, that empower courts to reach results more in keeping with their notions of justice. This is particularly true in cases involving consumers. But there are no consumers affected by Article 4A;

wire transfers amount to more than a trillion dollars a day. Hence, the final draft was a series of compromises made among powerful, well represented interests (money center banks, Board of Governors of Federal Reserve System, the New York Federal Reserve Bank, and giant corporate users, e.g., Exxon, General Motors), and these behemoths wanted some assurance that the bargained-for advantages that Article 4A gave them would not be taken away from them by courts using common law principles to change the intended meaning of the statute.

The result was the inclusion of Comment to 4A–102, quoted in part in *Grain Traders*. The plea by the drafters made in this Comment is that Article 4A is the result of long years of hard bargaining, and the final draft is a good faith attempt to balance the various competing interests. It will come as no surprise to learn that the success of this Comment in taking the pen out of the judge's hand in order to expand Article 4A's displacement of the common law has been spotty. Some commentators see it as manifesting a touch of hubris on the part of the drafters. Some courts believe that common law principles can be applied in wire transfer cases so long as they are not "inconsistent" with specific Article 4A provisions. The case law is fully analyzed in 2 Clark & Clark, Law of Bank Deposits, Collections and Credit Cards & 17.02[3] (Rev. ed. 1999). The authors conclude a long discussion by observing rather generously, in our view: "In all of these cases, the courts appeared to hold that (1) Article 4A does not preempt common-law causes of action in all cases, but that (2) preemption will be determined in each case by the extent to which the rules of Article 4A occupy the field covered by the particular common-law cause of action." The drafters did not expect more.

6. ERRONEOUS EXECUTION OF PAYMENT ORDERS

a. SENDING BANK'S ERRORS

A fertile field of litigation with respect to wire transfers is the case in which the receiving bank executes the sender's payment order by sending an erroneous payment order. In such cases the general principle adhered to by Article 4A is that the sender is liable for its own errors. The subject is discussed in Richard F. Dole, Jr., Receiving Bank Liability for Errors in Wholesale Wire Transfers, 69 Tul. L. Rev. 877 (1995).

For illustration, assume these facts. Originator (O) instructs its bank, Originator's Bank (OB), to send $100,000 to the account of Beneficiary (B) in Beneficiary's Bank (BB). OB executed O's payment order by instructing its correspondent bank, Intermediary Bank (IB) (4A–104(b)), to pay BB as indicated in the cases below. With respect to the payment order, O, OB and IB are senders and OB, IB and BB are receiving banks, and BB is also the beneficiary's bank. Thus, the funds transfer looks like this:

O———OB———IB———BB———B

Work through these elementary problems:

Case #1.   OB executed the payment order by instructing IB to pay BB $100,000 for the account of B. IB mistakenly instructed BB to pay $100,000 for the account of X.

    a.   Did IB execute the payment order of OB? 4A–301(a).

    b.   Is OB entitled to payment from O? 4A–402(c).

    c.   Is IB entitled to payment from OB? 4A–402(c).

    d.   Is BB entitled to payment from IB? 4A–402(b).

    e.   Is IB entitled to recover from X? 4A–303(c).

Case #2.   OB mistakenly instructed IB to pay BB $200,000 for B's account. IB executed OB's payment order by sending the same payment order to BB. BB deposited the funds in B's account and B withdrew the money. What are OB's rights against O and B under 4A–303(a)?

b.   DISCHARGE-FOR-VALUE RULE

Obligor instructed Bank A to pay $100,000 to Bank B for the account of X. Bank A mistakenly instructed Bank B to pay $100,000 for the account of Y. If Obligor owed a debt to Y in an amount in excess of $100,000, Y may claim that it is entitled to retain the funds under the discharge-for-value rule of the Restatement of Restitution § 14, under which a creditor is under no duty to make restitution even though the third party sent the money by mistake, so long as the creditor had no notice that the payment order was erroneously made. Some courts decline to follow the rule and hold that the money can be retained only if the recipient changed its position in reliance on the mistaken payment. The court in Banque Worms v. BankAmerica International, 568 N.Y.S.2d 541, 570 N.E.2d 189 (N.Y. Ct. App. 1991), adopted the discharge-for-value rule in a wire transfer transaction that went awry. Although the facts in that case occurred before enactment of Article 4A, the court viewed the rule as consistent with the policies of Article 4A. The court relied on Comment 2 to 4A–303 as showing that the drafters of Article 4A thought the discharge-for-value rule was appropriate in an analogous situation involving an erroneous payment order.

Finality of payment and the low cost of funds transfers are policy considerations that the *Banque Worms* court found support the discharge-for-value rule. Cf. Credit Lyonnais New York Branch v. Koval, 745 So.2d 837 (Miss.1999) (finality); General Electric Capital Corp. v. Central Bank, 49 F.3d 280 (7th Cir.1995) (finality and efficiency). Clearly, finality favors the rule. A beneficiary-creditor receiving funds can retain them as long as it received the funds without knowing or having notice that the payment was a mistake. Because detrimental reliance by the beneficiary is unnecessary, there are fewer occasions in which the transfer of funds will be disturbed than under a "mistake of fact" rule. In fact, finality favors allowing the recipient of a mistaken payment to keep it even if the recipient knew of the mistake.

Whether the discharge-for-value rule optimally lowers the cost of funds transfers compared to the "mistake of fact" rule is a closer question. A receiving bank issuing a payment order faces a risk that its sender will be unwilling or unable to reimburse it for the amount of the order. Both rules allocate this credit risk as between the receiving bank and the beneficiary, but they do so differently. The discharge-for-value rule increases the credit risk to the receiving bank as compared to the "mistake of fact" rule because there are fewer circumstances in which it can recover the funds from the beneficiary. Given this risk, the receiving bank can take precautions to avoid making mistaken payments or simply increase the price of executing a payment order. The "mistake of fact" rule shifts the receiving bank's credit risk to the beneficiary when the beneficiary does not detrimentally rely on the mistaken payment. This increases the cost to the beneficiary of dealing with the sender, and the increased cost presumably will be reflected in the price the beneficiary demands from it. The discharge-for-value rule optimally lowers the cost of funds transfers only if the marginal costs to the receiving bank associated with the rule are less than the marginal costs to the beneficiary associated with the "mistake of fact" rule. In estimating these costs, it is significant that the beneficiary in *Banque Worms* was a creditor who had entered into a revolving loan arrangement with the sender-debtor. Such arrangements almost always require the creditor to monitor its debtor. If so, the marginal costs to the beneficiary-creditor of detecting a mistaken payment might be slight.

7.   FAILURE OF RECEIVING BANK TO EXECUTE PAYMENT ORDER

Since payments of obligations in very large transactions are made through the wire transfer system, the potential for large consequential damages to flow from a receiving bank's failure to execute a payment order is great. One of the major policy decisions to be resolved in the drafting of Article 4A was whether receiving banks should be liable for consequential damages for failure to execute payment orders. Banking advisors saw this decision as crucial for their industry: they contended that they could not continue to offer cheap and fast service all over the world if they bore the risk of unlimited liability for consequential damages; imposition of such liability would force them to recast their industry in a form very different from the robust and flourishing enterprise it was at the time Article 4A was drafted. They relied for support of their position on the decision in Evra Corp. v. Swiss Bank Corp., 673 F.2d 951 (7th Cir. 1982).

In *Evra* Hyman–Michaels chartered a ship, the Pandora, from the ship's Owner under an agreement to make semi-monthly payments for hire in advance. If a payment was late, Owner could cancel the charter. Payments were to be made by deposit in the Banque de Paris in Geneva for the account of Owner. With the intention of making a periodic payment, Hyman–Michaels (Originator) issued a payment order to Continental (Chicago) to pay $27,000 to Banque de Paris in Geneva for the account of Owner. Continental (Chicago) executed the order by issuing a payment order to Continental (London) and debited the account of Hyman–Michaels in the amount of the order. Continental (London) executed the payment order of Continental (Chicago) by issuing a payment order to Swiss Bank in Geneva. Swiss Bank was instructed to issue a payment order to Banque de Paris to complete the funds transfer, but, for unknown reasons, failed to do so. Market conditions changed after the ship was chartered, and the hire payments required by the ship charter were below market rates. Because the beneficiary did not receive timely payment, Originator lost a valuable ship charter. The lower court awarded the Originator $2.1 million for lost profits even though the amount of the payment order was only $27,000. The appellate court reversed, in part on the basis of the common law rule of *Hadley v. Baxendale* that consequential damages may not be awarded unless the defendant is put on notice of the special circumstances giving rise to them. Swiss Bank did not have enough information to infer that if it lost a $27,000 payment order it would face liability in excess of $2 million.

PROBLEMS

1. How would this case be decided under Article 4A? Under Article 4A Hyman–Michaels is the originator of the funds transfer, Continental (Chicago) is the originator's bank, and Continental (London) and Swiss Bank are both "intermediary banks" (4A–104(b)). Each of the three banks is also a receiving bank with respect to the payment order it received. The duty of a receiving bank with respect to a payment order that it receives is stated in 4A–212. The duty of a receiving bank in executing a payment order is stated in 4A–302. The extent of liability of a receiving bank for late or improper execution or for failure to execute a payment order is stated in 4A–305. The right of the originator or other sender of a payment order to refund of amounts paid by them if the funds transfer is not completed is stated in 4A–402(c) and (d).

2. What is the policy basis of 4A–305's hard-hearted denial of consequential damages? Who is in the best position to evaluate the risk that a funds transfer will not be made on time and to manage that risk? See Comment 2 to 4A–305.

NOTE

Evra announces a default rule to the effect that a receiving bank is not liable for consequential damages resulting from its erroneous exclusion of a payment order, unless it has notice of the type or extent of damage at the time it executes the order. Thus, to avoid liability for consequential damages, receiving banks with such notice must contract around the rule. Section 4A–305(d) rejects that part of *Evra's* default rule allowing recovery when the bank has the requisite notice. Under 4A–305(d) consequential damages are recoverable from the receiving bank only "to the extent provided in an express written agreement." Comment 2 to 4A–305 judges that, to effect low-cost and speedy funds transfers, most receiving banks are in a comparatively poor position against their senders to reduce the risk of issuing erroneous payment orders. This may remain true even when the receiving bank has notice of special circumstances bearing on the type or extent of loss resulting from its erroneous execution of a payment order. See Comment 2 (paragraph 3) to 4A–305. If so, parties to most funds transfer therefore prefer to contract around *Evra*'s default rule. Section 4A–305(d) saves them the cost of having to do so because under it consequential damages aren't recoverable from the receiving bank without an express written agreement allowing recovery. Section 4A–305(d)'s default rule denying recovery of consequential damages therefore may optimally reduce contracting costs associated with funds transfers. Presumably to reduce proof and other litigation costs incurred in showing an agreement to opt out of 4A–305's default rule against consequential damages, 4A–305(d) requires that opting out be by "express written agreement."

8.   FRAUDULENT PAYMENT ORDERS

A wire transfer is a very efficient method of payment. Large amounts can be transferred in a short time at low cost. But this great efficiency also provides a highly efficient method for the theft of money. The thief might steal funds in a bank account by fraudulently inducing either the bank or the owner of the account to make a wire transfer of the funds to an account controlled by the thief in some other bank. For example, the thief might electronically transmit to the bank a payment order purporting to be that of the owner of the account. If the bank is unaware that its customer did not send the order, the fraud can succeed. If the bank executes the fraudulent payment order, it has transferred funds on behalf of the customer without authority of the customer to do so. Who takes the loss? Has the thief stolen funds of the customer or funds of the bank? Under Article 4A a receiving bank that executes a payment order is not acting as the agent of the sender. § 4A–212. But if the bank executes an order that it believes to be the order of its customer but which in fact was issued by a person not authorized to act for its customer, should the law of agency determine whether the customer is bound by the unauthorized payment order issued in its name? If agency law applies, the customer is not bound by the unauthorized order, the bank has no authority to debit the customer's account, and the bank takes the loss.

But the law of agency is not very useful in determining whether the risk of loss with respect to an unauthorized payment order transmitted electronically should fall upon the receiving bank's customer, the purported sender of the fraudulent payment order, or the receiving bank that accepted it. The agency doctrines of actual, implied, and apparent authority grew out of cases in which the person purporting to be the agent and the third party acting in reliance on the acts of the purported agent have some personal contact with each other. These doctrines do not work well in cases in which a commercial transaction normally is carried out in the name of a principal by a person who is anonymous and who has no direct contact with the third person. In the case of electronic transmission of a payment order, the receiving bank is acting on the basis of a message that appears on a computer screen. There is no way of determining the identity or authority of the person who caused the message to be sent. The receiving bank is not relying on the authority of any particular person to act for its customer. Instead, the receiving bank relies on a security procedure pursuant to which the authenticity of the message can be "tested" by various devices such as identification codes or other security information in the control of the customer designed to provide certainty that the message is that of the customer identified in the payment order as its sender.

In the funds transfer business, the concept of "authorized" is different from the concept found in agency law. A payment order is treated as the order of the person in whose name it is issued if it is properly tested pursuant to a security procedure and the order passes the test. Risk of loss rules regarding unauthorized payment orders with respect to which verification pursuant to a security procedure is in effect are stated in 4A–202 and 4A–203. The general rule is that a payment order is effective as the order of the customer, whether or not authorized, if the security procedure is commercially reasonable and the receiving bank proves that it accepted the order in good faith after verifying the order in compliance with the security procedure. There are certain exceptions and qualifications to this rule that are explained in the Comments to 4A–203. The general rule is based on the assumption that losses due to unauthorized payment orders can best be avoided by the use of commercially reasonable security procedures, and that the use of such procedures should be encouraged. If a commercially reasonable security procedure is not in effect or if the bank fails to comply with a commercially reasonable procedure, ordinary rules of agency apply with the effect that, if the payment order was not authorized by the customer, the receiving bank acts at its peril in accepting the order.

The Article 4A rules are designed to protect both the customer and the receiving bank. A receiving bank needs to be able to rely on objective criteria to determine whether it can safely act on a payment order. Employees of that bank can be trained to "test" a payment order according to the various steps specified in the security procedure. The bank is responsible for the acts of these employees. The interests of the customer are protected by providing an incentive to a receiving bank to make available to the customer a security procedure that is commercially reasonable. Prudent banking practice may require that security procedures be utilized with respect to virtually all payment orders, except for those in which personal contact between the customer and the bank eliminates the possibility of an unauthorized order. The burden of making available commercially reasonable security procedures is imposed on receiving banks because generally they determine what security procedures can be used and are in the best position to evaluate the efficacy of procedures offered to customers to combat fraud. The burden on the customer is to supervise its employees to assure compliance with the security procedure, to safeguard confidential security information, and to restrict access to transmitting facilities so that the security procedure cannot be breached.

Sections 4A–202 and 4A–203 were among the most contentious provisions in the drafting of Article 4A. Customers strongly believed that they should not be liable for unauthorized funds transfers: the banks control the security procedures and if a fraudulent payment order penetrates the security controls the bank should bear the loss. Bank representatives were just as firm in their belief that they could not transfer trillions of dollars a day all over the world at great speed in a highly automated process if they had to be concerned about whether the customer had actually authorized the payment order: if the payment order "tests," that is, meets their security procedures, they should be able to send the order without fear of liability. Sections 4A–202 and 4A–203 represent a compromise solution which satisfied neither side. Each time the authorization issue was discussed, customer representatives brought up the possibility that a brilliant hacker might crack even the most sophisticated security procedure and pull off the world's biggest bank robbery at the expense of the customer. Bankers said that it was tried every day and just couldn't be done.

PROBLEMS

1. Bank One received a payment order to send $1 million to Account #567891234 in Bank Two for Boniface, a customer of Bank Two. The originator's name on the payment order was SoCorp, a customer of Bank One. The payment order complied with all security procedures agreed to by SoCorp and was accepted by Bank One and, subsequently, by Bank Two. Boniface disappeared after withdrawing the money from its account in Bank Two. When SoCorp learned of the transaction, it denied that it had authorized the payment order and demanded its money back from Bank One, which had deducted the amount of the transfer from SoCorp's account. An investigation showed that SoCorp did not authorize the payment order. As between SoCorp and Bank One, who should bear the loss of the funds that resulted from the fraud under 4A–202 and 4A–203? What additional information do you need before you can decide this case?

2. Under the heading "Cyber Caper," the Wall Street Journal reported that a 28–year–old Russian biochemistry grad student, "Vova," who worked for a trading company in St. Petersburg, broke into Citicorp's computers on Wall Street and, over a period of months, transferred about $12 million from customer's accounts to banks in Finland, Israel, Netherlands, San Francisco and Switzerland, where his confederates attempted to withdraw the funds. They succeeded in getting $400,000 out before the accounts were traced and frozen. Since, according to the Journal article, Citicorp moves about $500 billion a day in funds transfers, Vova seemed almost restrained in his thievery. Customers of Citicorp in Buenos Aires and Jakarta were shocked to learn that unauthorized transfers had been made from their accounts. In order to get into Citicorp's computers, Vova had to penetrate a security system so sophisticated that industry experts said what he did was "almost impossible." William M. Carley and Timothy L. O'Brien, Cyber Caper: How Citicorp System Was Raided and Funds Moved Around World, Wall St. J., Sept. 12, 1995, at A1. Assume that Vova was a brilliant hacker who penetrated the security system without the assistance of anyone associated with Citicorp or its customers whose accounts were debited, as between the customers whose accounts were charged and Citicorp, where would 4A–202 and 4A–203 throw the loss in the Cyber Caper case?

––––––––––

By way of a postscript, when Vova was eventually extradited to this country, he pled guilty to charges of conspiracy to commit bank, wire and computer fraud. He admitted that he had used passwords acquired from "another Russian." Citibank doesn't know how the accomplice obtained the passwords, but there is no evidence that its employees were involved. Citibank has beefed up its security system. Dean Starkman, Russian Hacker Enters Fraud Plea in Citicorp Case, Wall St. J., Jan. 26, 1998, at B9A.

9. INCORRECTLY IDENTIFIED BENEFICIARY

When 4A–207 was conceived, the drafters had in mind the type of fraud transaction involved in the following Problem in which the name identifies one person and the account number identifies a different person. The hypothetical case set out in Comment 2 to 4A–207 is similar to this Problem.

PROBLEM

In the 1990s billions of dollars flowed into stock and bond mutual funds; new funds sprung up daily. These developments caught the attention of Thief who reasoned that these novice funds were unlikely to be as fraud-sensitive as his old prey, commercial banks. Thief developed a new MO for mutual funds and he employed it with success in the following case: He impersonated Investor, who owned shares in a mutual fund (Fund) worth more than $1 million, by sending forged documents to Fund requesting redemption of $1 million of his shares and the wire transfer of these funds to Investor's account number 987654 in Dallas Bank. Thief preceded the redemption by agreeing to pay Coin Dealer $1 million for gold coins (impossible to trace) by wiring the funds to Coin Dealer's account in Dallas Bank. Fund was taken in by the impersonation and sent a payment order to Boston Bank requesting it to transfer $1 million to Investor as beneficiary to be credited to account number 987654 in Dallas Bank. Boston Bank carried out the instructions. When Dallas Bank received the payment order, designating the Investor as the beneficiary and the account number as 987654, it credited the designated account number which, of course, was the account of Coin Dealer, not Investor, who had no account in this bank. When Dallas Bank notified Coin Dealer of the credit, Coin Dealer released the gold coins to Thief who absconded. After Fund learned of the theft, it recredited Investor's account and sued Dallas Bank for return of the money, relying on 4A–207(b)(1), (c) and (d). Dallas Bank relied on a pre-Article 4A case, Bradford Trust Co. of Boston v. Texas American Bank-

Houston, 790 F.2d 407 (5th Cir.1986), which held on similar facts that Fund should take the loss because it was the party in the best position to avoid the loss, it dealt directly with the impostor, and it sent the funds to the wrong account. What result under 4A–207? See Comments 2 and 3 to 4A–207.

Murphy's Law being what it is, virtually the first case arising under 4A–207 was Corfan in which the account number identified no one.

Corfan Banco Asuncion Paraguay v. Ocean Bank

District Court of Appeal of Florida, 1998.
715 So.2d 967.

■ SORONDO, JUDGE.

Corfan Banco Asuncion Paraguay, a foreign banking corporation (Corfan Bank), appeals the lower court's entry of a Final Summary Judgment in favor of Ocean Bank, a Florida bank.

On March 22, 1995, Corfan Bank originated a wire transfer of $72,972.00 via its intermediary Swiss Bank to the account of its customer, Jorge Alberto Dos Santos Silva (Silva), in Ocean Bank. The transfer order bore Silva's name as the recipient and indicated that his account number was 010070210400 (in fact, this was a nonexistent account). Upon receipt of the wire transfer, Ocean Bank noticed a discrepancy in this number and before depositing the money, confirmed with Silva that his correct account number was 010076216406. Ocean Bank did not, however, inform Corfan Bank or Swiss Bank of the error. Once the correct number was confirmed by Silva, Ocean Bank accepted the wire transfer and credited Silva's account.

The next day, Corfan Bank became aware of the account number discrepancy and, without first checking with either Silva or Ocean Bank, sent a second wire transfer of $72,972.00 to Silva's correct account number at Ocean Bank. The second transfer order did not indicate that it was a correction, replacement or amendment of the March 22nd transfer. Because the information of the transfer was correct, it was automatically processed at Ocean Bank and was credited to Silva's account. Several days later, Corfan Bank inquired of Ocean Bank regarding the two transfers, maintaining that only one transfer was intended. By that time, Silva had withdrawn the proceeds of both wire transfers. When Ocean Bank refused to repay $72,972.00 to Corfan Bank, this litigation ensued. Corfan Bank proceeded on two claims, one based on the section 670.207, Florida Statutes (1995), which codifies as Florida law section 4A–207 of the Uniform Commercial Code (UCC), and one based on common law negligence. Ocean Bank answered denying liability under the statute and also contending that the negligence claim was precluded by the preemptive statutory scheme.

The trial court, emphasizing that Florida's adoption of the UCC sections concerning wire transfers did not abrogate the basic tenets of commercial law, found that Ocean Bank had not contravened § 4A–207 by crediting the erroneous March 22nd wire transfer to Silva's account. Finding that Corfan Bank was the party best situated to have avoided this loss, the court held that Corfan Bank must bear that loss and, therefore, the court granted Ocean Bank's motion for summary judgment as to count one (the UCC count). Additionally, the court dismissed count two (the negligence count).

We begin with a review of the exact language of § 4A–207(a):

(a) Subject to subsection (b), if, in a payment order received by the beneficiary's bank, the name, bank account number, *or* other identification of the beneficiary refers to a nonexistent or unidentifiable person or account, no person has rights as a beneficiary of the order and acceptance of the order cannot occur.

Corfan Bank argues that this language is clear and unambiguous, where a name or bank account number, or other identification refers either to a nonexistent or unidentified person *or* a nonexistent account, the order *cannot* be accepted. Ocean Bank responds that such a "highly technical" reading of the statute is "contrary to commercial and practical considerations and common sense." It suggests that we look to the legislative intent and conclude that the "or" in the statute should be given conjunctive rather than disjunctive effect. We respectfully decline Ocean Bank's invitation to look behind the plain language of the statute and conclude that given its clarity it must be read as written.

In Capers v. State, 678 So.2d 330 (Fla. 1996), the Florida Supreme Court stated:

[T]he plain meaning of statutory language is the first consideration of statutory construction. St. Petersburg Bank & Trust Co. v. Hamm, 414 So.2d 1071, 1073 (Fla. 1982). Only when a statute is of doubtful meaning should matters extrinsic to the statute be considered in construing the language employed by the legislature. Florida State Racing Comm'n v. McLaughlin, 102 So.2d 574, 576 (Fla. 1958).

Id. at 332. * * * These cases preclude the analysis urged by Ocean Bank. Although Ocean Bank's position has been noted in the legal literature,[4]

---

4. One respected treatise on the Uniform Commercial Code analyzes the code provision, 4A–207(a), which is identical to the statute in question, as follows:

The requirements of subsection 4A–207(a) are stated in the disjunctive. Thus, apparently, if the payment order name and bank account number provide an identifiable or known person but "other identification of the beneficiary" refers to a nonexistent or unidentifiable person or account, subsection 4A–207(a)

is literally applicable. The express deference in subsection 4A–207(a) to subsection 4A–207(b) does not appear to resolve this conundrum. Subsection 4A–207(b) provides rules only for payment orders in which the beneficiary is identified "by both name and an identifying or bank account number" in the instance in which the name and the number identify different persons.

"unambiguous language is not subject to judicial construction, however wise it may seem to alter the plain language." *Jett*, 626 So.2d at 693. * * *

* * *

The Supreme Court of Florida has fashioned only one exception to this general rule: "[t]his Court will not go behind the plain and ordinary meaning of the words used in the statute unless an unreasonable or ridiculous conclusion would result from failure to do so." Holly v. Auld, 450 So.2d 217, 219 (Fla. 1984). The plain and ordinary meaning of the words of the statute under review do not lead to either an unreasonable or ridiculous result. As discussed more thoroughly below, one of the critical considerations in the drafting of Article 4A was that parties to funds transfers should be able to "predict risk with certainty, to insure risk with certainty, to adjust operational and security procedures, and to price funds transfer services appropriately." See 19A Fla. Stat. Ann. 15 (U.C.C. cmt. 1995). All of these goals are reasonable and assured by the plain statutory language.

In the present case, although the payment order correctly identified the beneficiary, it referred to a nonexistent account number. Under the clear and unambiguous terms of the statute, acceptance of the order could not have occurred. As the Florida Supreme Court stated in *Jett*:

> We trust that if the legislature did not intend the result mandated by the statute's plain language, the legislature itself will amend the statute at the next opportunity.

Jett, 626 So.2d at 693.

As indicated above, the trial court dismissed count two of the complaint which sounded in negligence. The court concluded that the statutory scheme preempts the common law remedy of negligence. * * *

* * *

In addressing this issue we restrict our analysis to the pleadings and facts of this case. In pertinent part, count two reads as follows:

Ocean Bank owed Corfan Bank a duty of care to follow the accepted banking practice of the community, and to return the funds from the first transfer to Corfan Bank upon receipt due to the reference in the first transfer to a non-existent account number.

It does not appear that this anomaly in subsection 4A–207(a) was intended; nonetheless, the subsection 4A–207(a) suggests only one preventive mechanism for avoiding this conundrum: the sender should include no "other identification of the beneficiary" which might "refer ... to a nonexistent or unidentifiable person or account." Then subsection 4A–207(a) would be harmonized with subsection 4A–207(b) as long as the name and account number refer to the same identifiable person or account. If they refer to different identifiable persons or accounts then subsection 4A–207(b) controls. If either the name or account number refers to a nonexistent or unidentifiable person then subsection 4A–207(a) is again applicable.

William D. Hawkland & Richard Moreno, Uniform Commercial Code Series, § 4A-207:01 (1993)(emphasis added).

The duty claimed to have been breached by Ocean Bank in its negligence count is exactly the same duty established and now governed by the statute. Under such circumstances we agree with the trial judge that the statutory scheme preempts the negligence claim in this case and affirm the dismissal of count two.[5] We do not reach the issue of whether the adoption of Article 4A of the UCC preempts negligence claims in all cases.

We reverse the Final Summary Judgment entered by the trial court in favor of Ocean Bank as to count one of the complaint and affirm the dismissal of count two. We remand this case for further proceedings consistent with this opinion.

■ LEVY, J., concurs.

■ NESBITT, JUDGE, dissenting: [Opinion omitted.]

NOTE

In a case like *Corfan* in which the account number identifies no one, 4A–207 doesn't work as intended. Corfan Bank is responsible for the error and should bear the loss, but under the plain meaning of the statute, the court placed the loss on Ocean Bank. Section 4A–207(b) contains a drafting error and should be amended. One solution would be to amend subsection (b) by deleting the words in brackets and adding the underlined words as follows:

> (b) If a payment order received by the beneficiary's bank identifies the beneficiary both by name and by an identifying or bank account number and the name and number [identify different persons] do not refer to the same person, the following rules apply:
>
> > (1) Except as otherwise provided in subsection (c), if the beneficiary's bank does not know that the name and number [refer to different persons] do not refer to the same person, it may rely on the number as the proper identification of the beneficiary of the order. The beneficiary's bank need not determine whether the name and number refer to the same person.
> >
> > (2) If the beneficiary's bank pays the person identified by name or knows that the name and number [identify different persons] do not refer to the same person, no person has rights as

---

5. We note that allowing a negligence claim in this case would "create rights, duties and liabilities inconsistent" with those set forth in § 4A-207. In a negligence cause of action, Ocean Bank would be entitled to defend on a theory of comparative negligence because Corfan Bank provided the erroneous account number which created the problem at issue and then initiated the second transfer without communicating with Ocean Bank. Section 670.207 does not contemplate such a defense. (Oddly enough, allowing Corfan Bank's negligence claim in this case might actually inure to Ocean Bank's benefit). As explained in the comment, one of the primary purposes of the section is to enable the parties to wire funds transfers to predict risk with certainty and to insure against risk. The uniformity and certainty sought by the statute for these transactions could not possibly exist if parties could opt to sue by way of pre-Code remedies where the statute has specifically defined the duties, rights and liabilities of the parties.

beneficiary except the person paid by the beneficiary's bank if that person was entitled to receive payment from the originator of the funds transfer. If no person has rights as beneficiary, acceptance of the order cannot occur.

Since subsection (a) is subject to (b), if subsection (b) were amended as indicated, that subsection would apply to a case like *Corfan* because the name on the payment order referred to Silva and the account number did not refer to anyone. Thus, the name and number did not refer to the same person. Subsection (b)(2) would control.

10.   AUTOMATED CLEARING HOUSE (ACH)

a.   CONSUMER TRANSFERS

A lower cost, somewhat slower means of making electronic payments is through the automated clearing house (ACH) system, used to transfer money to or from consumer bank accounts through the ACH network, which links a large number of financial institutions, by "batching" numerous payments and sending them together. These transfers may be either credit or debit transfers. The difference between the two is discussed in Comment 4 to 4A–104. In a credit transfer the instruction to pay is given by the person making the payment, as is the case in Article 4A transfers. In a debit transfer the instruction to pay is made by the person receiving payment. An example of a credit transfer is one in which an employer pays its employees by direct deposit to their bank accounts. Suppose its employees have accounts in ten banks in the area. In such a case, the employer will prepare a magnetic tape or other electronic record with information concerning the bank accounts of each employee in which a deposit is to be made. This information will go to the employer's bank which electronically forwards it to an ACH facility in the area. The ACH performs its clearing house function by repackaging this information for each bank in which the employees have accounts, which it forwards electronically to these banks. ACH allows the party initiating the transfer to time the dates when the payments will be credited to the employees' accounts by their banks and when the debits will be made to the originator's account in its bank. After the ACH has determined the net balances between the employer's bank and the employees' banks, these banks will settle through the Federal Reserve System. Numerous government payments, like social security and other benefits and pensions are made in this manner.

Equally common is the debit transaction. An example is one in which the debtor authorizes its creditor to draw each month on its bank account to make its monthly mortgage payments. The mortgage lender (mortgagee) will prepare a tape or other electronic device giving information on all mortgagors whose payments are due on a given date and give this tape or other electronic device to its bank. The bank will forward this information electronically to an ACH that will send the relevant information to each bank in which mortgagors have accounts. These banks will debit the mortgagors' accounts on the prescribed date. The mortgagee's bank will credit the mortgagee's account on that date and settlement between the banks will be made through the Federal Reserve System. Insurance premiums, and other recurring payments, are frequently made in this manner.

Since ACH transfer is a cheap, reliable method of moving credit from one bank account to another, it is used in many transactions in addition to those have we have mentioned above. For instance, as we will see in the next section, ACH plays an important part in the growing Internet payments systems.

The operational details of the ACH system are discussed in Donald I. Baker & Roland E. Brandel, The Law of Electronic Fund Transfer Systems, Chapter 3 (1988 & Cum. Supp. 1995); James V. Vergari & Virginia V. Shue, Fundamentals of Computer–High Technology Law 463–472 (1991), and 1 Clark & Clark, The Law of Bank Deposits, Check Collections and Credit Cards & 6.04 (Rev. ed. 1999). There are some 40 ACHs in the nation, most of which are operated by the Fed. According to Melanie L. Fein, Law of Electronic Banking § 5.02[A] (2003 Supp.), ACH networks are used by over 20,000 financial institutions, 500,000 businesses and 60% of all households. The ACH system processed trillions of dollars annually in transfers, including direct deposits of payrolls, pensions and annuities, as well as preauthorized bill payments and corporation-to-corporation payments. The ACH trade association is the National Automated Clearinghouse Association (NACHA), which prescribes operating rules for ACH transfers. 3 White & Summers, Uniform Commercial Code § 22–2 (4th Prac. ed. 1995), discusses the intricacies of what law governs ACH payments and concludes that for all practical purposes the NACHA rules effectively do so. Clark & Clark, supra, concurs.

b. COMMERCIAL TRANSFERS

At the beginning of this Chapter we referred to an article by Fred R. Bleakley, Electronic Payments Now Supplant Checks at More Large Firms, Wall St. J., Apr. 13, 1994, at A1, to show how burdensome it is for banks to manage the vast bulk of checks that must be cleared each day. The point of this article was that major corporations are moving to electronic payments to avoid having to use checks. The usual method employed by these corporations to pay their bills electronically to suppliers and governmental units is by ACH payments. One executive is quoted as saying: "We want computers talking to computers." Since ACH is a value-dated system, cash managers can plan the exact date payments will be credited to their payees' accounts and debited to their own accounts, and this knowledge allows them to utilize their funds more efficiently.

The use of ACH to pay bills is similar in concept to Fedwire and Chips payments in that, for the most part, these business-to-business payments are credit transfers. But there are important differences. Fedwire and Chips are "big dollar" wholesale wire transfers that can often give same-day service. Although many more transfers are made by ACH, the amount of money sent is much less. Credit transfers over ACH between businesses are nominally covered by Article 4A, but 4A–501(b) effectively cedes gover-nance to the NACHA rules.

B.   EMERGING TRENDS IN FUNDS TRANSFERS

1.   STORED VALUE CARDS

The plastic cards that we call credit or debit cards are merely bearers of information, encoded in machine readable form on a magnetic strip on the back of a card. A stored value (or "prepaid" or "value-added") card uses a computer chip or magnetic strip to hold information that allows the cardholder to make purchases. More recent stored value cards ("smart" cards) use computer chips, which reliably retain information and allow encryption to avoid duplication or unauthorized use of the card. Long used in Europe and Asia, "smart" cards are being introduced in the United States. In Hong Kong, they are used in subways, movie theaters, parking meters, and even McDonald's, as well as for security purposes at schools and residential complexes. Stacy Forster, Smart Cards Escape the U.S. Mind, Wall St. J., July 16, 2002, at D2. Because they can store large quantities of information, their potential use is unlimited. "Smart" cards can serve as a health insurance card, containing the patient's medical records, or as electronic "dog tags" for soldiers. China is using these cards to allow their security authorities to store personal information about its citizens on ID cards with embedded microchips. Andrew Batson, China Orders Up To A Billion Smart Cards, Wall St. J., Aug. 12, 2003, at A10.

When used as a means of payment, the cards store a "value" of funds available for the cardholder's use. The balance of funds recorded on the card is debited at the merchant's terminal when the cardholder makes a purchase. Stored value cards therefore serve as substitutes for cash, al-though the information stored on the cards is not itself cash. Use of the card does not transfer funds to the merchant; it only transfers information informing it of its right to be paid by the card sponsor. Stored value cards are extensively treated in Donald I. Baker & Roland E. Brandel, The Law of Electronic Fund Transfer Systems, Chapter 9 (1988, Cum. Supp. 1995), and in 2 Clark & Clark, The Law of Bank Deposits, Collections and Credit Cards & 16.07 (Rev. ed. 1999).

Our interest in stored value cards is in their function as cash substi-tutes. Stored value card systems are of two basic sorts: "online" and "off line" systems. The stored value card systems differ as to whether transac-tions are made with or without communication with a central data facility operated by the system provider. "Online" systems process use of the card by communication from the facility giving authorization for a transaction. A record of the balance of funds available to the cardholder is maintained only at a central data facility. Off line systems involve card use without contact with a central data facility. These systems differ in turn according to where the primary record of the balance of funds on the card is maintained. If the primary record is maintained at a central data facility, the system is considered an off line "accountable" system. If the primary record is maintained on the card itself, the system is an off line "unaccountable" system. See Federal Reserve Board, Proposed Rules, 61 Fed. Reg. 19696 (1996). Almost all stored value card systems currently in use are off line unaccountable systems.

A simple example of card use in an off line unaccountable system is one in which the card is "loaded" with a sum of money, say $500, that the cardholder can use to purchase goods or services from participating merchants, telephone companies, transit systems and the like. The cardholder obtains the card by buying it from a bank teller, retailer, or by using a bank dispenser by inserting money or an ATM or credit card. It is disposable; when used up, it is worthless and may be thrown away. If the cardholder makes a purchase from a merchant, no identification is sought; the card has its own verification and passwords. The merchant deducts the sale price by running the card through a terminal. The balance record contained in the card in turn is reduced by the amount of the sale price and is ascertainable by ATM or POS terminals. (In an off line accountable system, the primary balance record is reduced at the central data storage facility as well.) The merchant aggregates balances stored in its transaction records, usually on a daily basis, and transmits them electronically in a "batched" transmission to the system provider. Upon verifying the validity of the transmission, the provider transfers funds to the merchant equal to the aggregate amount of the transmissions minus a discount fee reflecting the system provider's expenses. At least with respect to the cardholder and participating merchant, the card is a complete substitute for cash.

More sophisticated cards may be "reloadable" by accessing the cardholder's bank account through an ATM machine or the Internet. They may be online through the use of ATM or POS terminals, and, like debit cards, the cardholder's bank account is debited upon use. However, until reloaded, these cards can transfer value only to the extent of the amount stored on the card. College students are familiar with these cards because a growing number of universities have combined them with the student's identification card, allowing the student to make on-campus purchases. Credit card companies have developed technologies that allow consumers to download dollar amounts from their bank accounts onto cards.

The question facing banks and merchants is whether the potential for stored value cards justifies the costs of converting from the present magnetic strip technology to one that will accommodate these cards. If sufficiently high volume can be obtained, banks may profit handsomely from stored value cards by the "float," that is, having cardholder's money until the card is used up, by charging fees from participating merchants and by keeping the few cents left on the card when the cardholder discards it. (In principle, competitive pressure could force card providers to pay interest on unused funds deposited with the provider, thus reducing profit from the "float.") As is true with the introduction of any new operational technology, the chicken-and-egg dilemma arises: banks and merchants would prefer not to convert to stored value cards until there are enough customers to promise ultimate profitability; customers would like not to go to the trouble of obtaining stored value cards until enough providers of goods and services are prepared to accept them.

Stored value cards have had a slow start in this country. Banks made a major promotional effort to popularize them in connection with the 1996 Olympic Games in Atlanta. They signed up merchants with some 1500 retail outlets, mostly fast food outlets and gas stations, and the Atlanta transit system. There results were encouraging but hardly a gold medal performance. Nikhil Deogun, The Smart Money is on "Smart Cards," but Electronic Cash Seems Dumb to Some, Wall St. J., Aug. 5, 1996 at B1. In 1997 VisaUSA, MasterCard International, Citibank and Chase Manhattan distributed 80,000 stored value cards to New Yorkers on Manhattan's Upper West Side; 700 merchants signed up to accept them. In 1998 they ended the program, citing little support from consumers and merchant complaints of slow processing. Brian Tracey, The Color of Money, Wall St. J., Nov. 16, 1998, at R28. Smart cards have been more successful in continental Europe, where governments along with some banks have ensured demand by installing pay telephones, bus-ticket machines and parking meters that accept (sometimes exclusively) smart cards. In America and Britain, where such decisions are more decentralized, guaranteeing demand for smart cards is harder. Keep the Change, The Economist, Nov. 21, 1998, at 73.

In the article, cited above, Stacy Forster concludes that so far stored value cards have been a failure in the U.S. in part because retailers have been reluctant to install the higher-end processing equipment necessary to read them. He refers to the Upper West Side flop and the view of Americans that the cards have to do more than serve as cash-substitutes before they will embrace them. Kathy Chu, Prepaid Cash Cards See Mixed Results, Wall St. J., September 10, 2003, at B4B, chronicles the lack of success of prepaid, reloadable cash cards aimed at teenagers and college students.

2. INTERNET PAYMENTS

The commercialized Internet began in 1995 and has already become a powerful global medium for the sale of goods, the providing of services, particularly financial services, and information of all kinds. The volume of goods sold on the Internet is huge and growing. Online stock transactions are vast. A growing percent of mortgage loans originate online. The examples of the commercial use of the Internet are endless. Not only the largest merchants have Web sites but tiny boutiques do so as well. The electronic catalog function of the Internet is inexpensive and unbounded in territory. Andy Grove, chairman of Intel, predicts that the term "Internet company" will become meaningless: "all companies will be Internet companies." George Anders, Buying Frenzy, Wall St. J., July 12, 1999, at R6.

The use of the Internet for remote shopping of all kinds is well established, but making payments through the Internet is less common. For a remote payments system to develop on a large scale, there must be a means of moving credit through the banking system. Leaving aside the wholesale funds transfer systems of Fedwire and CHIPS, the two means commonly used for this task are the credit card clearing and settlement systems (e.g., the Visa and MasterCard networks) and the automated clearing house (ACH) system that connects nearly all banks. By far the most popular method of paying for consumer obligations incurred in Internet shopping is by credit cards, but in recent years interest has developed in offering individuals the convenience of making payments on the Internet merely by clicking a mouse.

Programs are being developed that allow payments to be made over the Internet. One successful example arose out of the great success of online auction selling. Many of the noncommercial auction sellers on eBay, some of whom may have just cleaned out their attics, cannot be expected to be authorized credit card merchants. This is also true for some small merchants who sell by auction over the Internet. Online-payment services companies have been created to meet the needs of these sellers. The procedure is for online senders and recipients to set up accounts with an online-payment service. A sender's account may be funded from the sender's bank account through ACH or by credit card; the transfer of funds by ACH is much cheaper. The sender can activate a transfer of funds from this account through the service company to another account holder of the company merely by sending an e-mail. After the online auction in which the sender made a purchase, the payment, less a discount for the online-payment service (usually about 2% of the amount of the transaction), is added to the recipient's account. Will Morton, Check It Out (subtitled: The Web is suddenly crowded with online-payments services. Here's how they compare), Wall St. J., Dec. 10, 2001, at R13. If the recipient doesn't have an account with the online-payments service at the time of the sale, the service may notify it that the sender's money has arrived and will be added to the seller's account when one is opened. David Colker, EBay to Acquire Online Payment Service Pay Pal, LA Times, July 9, 2002, at C1. Recipients may withdraw the money from their accounts by debit cards issued by the online-payment service, by credits to a credit card account, or by ACH transfers made to their bank accounts.

Morton points out that even merchants who are authorized to accept credit cards sometimes prefer to use an online-payment service because the costs of Internet payments made through the ACH batching system are lower than the charges made by the credit card networks for the clearing and settlement of credit card payments. In the future, interbank agreements may reduce the need for an intermediary such as an online-payment service entity. For a detailed treatment of Internet person-to-person payments, see Melanie L. Fein, Law of Electronic Banking § 6.05[B] (2003 Supp.), and Clarks' Bank Deposits and Payments Monthly, Vol. 9, No. 9, p. 4, March 2000.

3. ONLINE BANKING AND BILL PAYING

Banks are pressing their customers to do their banking and bill paying online. They have strong incentives to do so: most charge their customers fees for online payment services; online payment users tend to stay with their banks longer and hold higher balances; and a banking transaction completed over the Internet costs the bank only a penny, compared with 27 cents for an ATM and $1.07 for a teller. Some banks give premiums to customers who convert to online bill paying. By the end of 2002, 24.3 million households were expected to bank online. All the customer need do is to go to her bank's Web site, create a user name and password and indicate which account is to be accessed. At this point the customer can do just about anything online that can be done on a telephone: pay bills, transfer money between accounts, apply for credit cards, mortgages or other loans. See Stephanie Miles, What's a Check? (Subtitled: After years of false starts, online banking is finally catching on.), Wall St. J., Oct. 21, 2002, at R5. Customers avoid the monthly chore of writing checks to pay their bills; no search for stamps and licking envelopes; busy customers save time and banks make money.

In theory, customers can use online banking to make payments to anyone having a bank account, and the payments can be scheduled a year in advance. Thus, a customer can schedule at the beginning of the year all recurring payments to be made during the year; can keep her money in interest bearing savings accounts until the time of payment when the money can be transferred into a checking account; and can get a confirmation on the screen for every transaction. A problem is that a transfer can be made electronically only to a payee whose bank and account number are known either to the customer or the payor bank. To meet this problem, banks have signed up large numbers of businesses that are prepared to accept electronic payments to their accounts. Thus, in the usual case of a payment to a business, all the customer has to be sure about is the name and address of the payee, for the bank will know its account number. In cases in which the databank does not contain the payee's account number and the payee has not provided that number to the customer, payment may be made by the customer's bank's sending that person a paper check drawn on the customer's account. This must also be done when the payee is not equipped to receive electronic payments.

An alternative method of online bill paying is to accept the invitation of a growing number of companies that encourage debtors to pay their bills directly at the biller's Web site by authorizing the biller to charge the debtor's bank account or credit card. After giving the biller the information about the debtor's bank account or credit card to be charged the first time a payment is made, subsequently, all the debtor has to do is to click the "pay" button on the biller's Web site and the money is withdrawn from the bank account or charged to the credit card. Presumably, clearing is done through the ACH system if a credit card is not used. The downside of direct billing is that the debtor must visit each Web site in order to pay. Customers can also arrange for automatic deductions to pay periodic bills. Michelle Higgins, Honest the Check Is in the E–Mail, Wall St. J., Sept. 4, 2002, at D1.

There is wide-spread belief that online bill paying will not replace checks until the industry has incorporated electronic bill presentment or delivery as a feature of online bill paying. At present the customer usually receives bills by mail, but systems have been developed in which bills are received online. These systems turn paper bills into electronic bills if the customer arranges for her bills to be sent to a processing facility. See the Higgins article, supra. This enables customers, having been alerted by a message "You have bills," to log onto a Web site and view any bills that had been presented; payment can be made by a click. Rebecca Buckman, Bills, Bills (Click), More Bills ... A Race Is On for Best Paperless–Payment System, Wall St. J., Nov. 19, 1998, at C1. Electronic bill presentment is regarded as likely to lead to much broader acceptance of computer banking.

CHAPTER 5

FRAUD, FORGERY, AND ALTERATION

A. FORGERY

1. ALLOCATION OF LOSS BETWEEN CUSTOMER AND PAYOR BANK

a. INTRODUCTION

Suppose Customer has a checking account in Payor Bank. Thief steals Customer's checkbook, writes a check payable to Payee, and signs Customer's name to the check as drawer. Because Thief was not authorized to sign Customer's name, the signature is ineffective as the signature of Customer unless some provision of Article 3 or Article 4 makes it effective. 3–403(a). Since Customer did not sign the check and did not authorize Thief to sign the check, Customer is not liable on the check. 3–401(a). The check, however, is not a nullity. Although it is not Customer's check, Article 3 treats it as Thief's check even though Thief signed it by using Customer's name. 3–403(a) and 3–401(b). Checks such as the check in this example, i.e., a check bearing a forged drawer's signature, are known as "forged checks." Such checks sometimes are transferred for value and paid by the drawee bank. Rights of a holder with respect to such checks can be acquired by persons who take them.

A more common type of forgery can be illustrated by the following example. Customer writes a check to the order of Payee, signs it as drawer, and mails it to Payee. Thief steals the check from Payee, indorses the check by signing Payee's name on the back of the check, and obtains payment of the check from Payor Bank. The check in this example is not a forged check because Customer's signature was not forged. Rather, the infirmity of the check is that it bears a "forged indorsement." Under 3–403(a) and 3–401 the signature by Thief is ineffective as the indorsement of Payee. Since Payee did not indorse the check, Thief cannot negotiate the check and no one can obtain rights as a holder unless some provision of Article 3 otherwise provides. 3–201(b) and 3–109(b).

What are the rights of Customer and Payor Bank toward each other if Payor Bank pays the forged check in the first example or the check bearing the forged indorsement in the second example? Under 4–401(a) a payor bank "may charge against the account of a customer an item that is properly payable from that account" and, to be properly payable, the check must be "authorized by the customer." Thus, in the case of the forged check, the Payor Bank may not debit Customer's account and is not entitled to reimbursement from Customer. The risk of loss falls on Payor Bank even though it may have had no way of discovering the forgery.

The result is the same in the case of the check bearing the forged indorsement. By the terms of the check Payor Bank was ordered by Customer to pay the check to the order of Payee. Since Payee did not receive payment and did not order payment to anybody else, Payor Bank did not comply with the terms of the check. Since Payor Bank did not pay a holder or other person entitled to receive payment, it has no right to reimbursement from Customer.

The general rule protecting Customer from loss from forgery is changed in some cases by other provisions of Article 3 or Article 4. Two of the most important provisions that may allow Payor Bank to shift the forgery loss to Customer are 3–406(a), discussed in *Thompson Maple Products,* and 4–406, discussed in *Espresso Roma.*

b. NEGLIGENCE OF CUSTOMER CONTRIBUTING TO FORGERY

With respect to payment by a payor bank of a forged check or a check bearing a forged indorsement, if the bank can prove a failure by the customer to exercise ordinary care that substantially contributed to the making of the forged signature, the customer is precluded from asserting the forgery. 3–406(a). "Ordinary care" is defined in 3–103(a)(9). The leading case on the meaning of the words "substantially contributes to * * * the making of a forged signature" in 3–406(a) is *Thompson Maple Products,* the case that follows. Comment 2 to 3–406 discusses the meaning of the quoted words. In the absence of proof of negligence by the bank contributing to the loss, the effect of the preclusion is to give to the bank a right to reimbursement from the customer for the amount paid on the check. Under Former 3–406, discussed in *Thompson Maple Products,* the preclusion against the customer did not occur if the bank was negligent in paying the check. This result is changed by Revised 3–406. Negligence by the bank does not prevent the preclusion from arising but, under subsection (b), the loss from the forgery can be apportioned between the negligent customer and the negligent bank.

Thompson Maple Products, Inc. v. Citizens National Bank

Superior Court of Pennsylvania, 1967.
211 Pa.Super. 42, 234 A.2d 32.

■ HOFFMAN, JUDGE.

* * *

The plaintiff [Thompson Maple Products] is a small, closely-held corporation, principally engaged in the manufacture of bowling pin "blanks" from maple logs. Some knowledge of its operations from 1959 to 1962 is essential to an understanding of this litigation.

The plaintiff purchased logs from timber owners in the vicinity of its mill. Since these timber owners rarely had facilities for hauling logs, such transportation was furnished by a few local truckers, including Emery Albers.

At the mill site, newly delivered logs were "scaled" by mill personnel, to determine their quantity and grade. The employee on duty noted this information, together with the name of the owner of the logs, as furnished by the hauler, on duplicate "scaling slips."

In theory, the copy of the scaling slip was to be given to the hauler, and the original was to be retained by the mill employee until transmitted by him directly to the company's bookkeeper. This ideal procedure, however, was rarely followed. Instead, in a great many instances, the mill employee simply gave both slips to the hauler for delivery to the company office. Office personnel then prepared checks in payment for the logs, naming as payee the owner indicated on the scaling slips. Blank sets of slips were readily accessible on the company premises.

Sometime prior to February, 1959, Emery Albers conceived the scheme which led to the forgeries at issue here. Albers was an independent log hauler who for many years had transported logs to the company mill. For a brief period in 1952, he had been employed by the plaintiff, and he was a trusted friend of the Thompson family. After procuring blank sets of scaling slips, Albers filled them in to show substantial, wholly fictitious deliveries of logs, together with the names of local timber owners as suppliers. He then delivered the slips to the company bookkeeper, who prepared checks payable to the purported owners. Finally, he volunteered to deliver the checks to the owners. The bookkeeper customarily entrusted the checks to him for that purpose.

Albers then forged the payee's signature and either cashed the checks or deposited them to his account at the defendant bank, where he was well known. * * *

In 1963, when the forgeries were uncovered, Albers confessed and was imprisoned. The plaintiff then instituted this suit against the drawee bank, asserting that the bank had breached its contract of deposit by paying the checks over forged endorsements. * * *

The trial court determined that the plaintiff's own negligent activities had materially contributed to the unauthorized endorsements, and it therefore dismissed the substantial part of plaintiff's claim. We affirm the action of the trial court.

Both parties agree that, as between the payor bank and its customer, ordinarily the bank must bear the loss occasioned by the forgery of a payee's endorsement.

* * *

The trial court concluded, however, that the plaintiff-drawer, by virtue of its conduct, could not avail itself of that rule, citing § 3–406 of the Code: "Any person who by his negligence substantially contributes to * * * the making of an unauthorized signature is precluded from asserting the * * * lack of authority against * * * a drawee or other payor who pays the instrument in good faith and in accordance with the reasonable commercial standards of the drawee's or payor's business." * * *

Before this Court, the plaintiff Company argues strenuously that this language is a mere restatement of pre-Code law in Pennsylvania. Under those earlier cases, it is argued, the term "precluded" is equivalent to "estopped," and negligence which will work an estoppel is only such as "directly and proximately affects the conduct of the bank in passing the forgery * * *." See, e.g., Coffin v. Fidelity–Philadelphia Trust Company, 374 Pa. 378, 393, 97 A.2d 857, 39 A.L.R.2d 625 (1953); Land Title Bank and Trust Company v. Cheltenham National Bank, 362 Pa. 30, 66 A.2d 768 (1949). The plaintiff further asserts that those decisions hold that "negligence in the conduct of the drawer's business," such as appears on this record, cannot serve to work an estoppel.

Even if that was the law in this Commonwealth prior to the passage of the Commercial Code, it is not the law today. The language of the new Act is determinative in all cases arising after its passage. This controversy must be decided, therefore, by construction of the statute and application of the negligence doctrine as it appears in § 3–406 of the Code. * * *

Had the legislature intended simply to continue the strict estoppel doctrine of the pre-Code cases, it could have employed the term "precluded," without qualification, as in § 23 of the old Negotiable Instruments Law, 56 P.S. § 28 (repealed). However, it chose to modify that doctrine in § 3–406, by specifying that negligence which *"substantially contributes to * * * the making of an unauthorized signature * * *."* will preclude the drawer from asserting a forgery. [emphasis supplied]. The Code has thus abandoned the language of the older cases (negligence which "directly and proximately affects the conduct of the bank in passing the forgery") and shortened the chain of causation which the defendant bank must establish. "[N]o attempt is made," according to the Official Comment to § 3–406, "to specify what is negligence, and the question is one for the court or jury on the facts of the particular case."

In the instant case, the trial court could readily have concluded that plaintiff's business affairs were conducted in so negligent a fashion as to have "substantially contributed" to the Albers forgeries, within the meaning of § 3–406.

Thus, the record shows that pads of plaintiff's blank logging slips were left in areas near the mill which were readily accessible to any of the haulers. Moreover, on at least two occasions, Albers was given whole pads of these blank logging slips to use as he chose. Mrs. Vinora Curtis, an employee of the plaintiff, testified:

"Q. Did you ever give any of these logging slips to Mr. Albers or any pads of these slips to Mr. Albers?

"A. Yes.

* * *

"Q. What was the reason for giving [a pad of the slips] to him, Mrs. Curtis?

"A. Well, he came up and said he needed it for [scaling] the logs, so I gave it to him."

Mrs. Amy Thompson, who also served as a bookkeeper for the plaintiff, testified:

"Q. As a matter of fact, you gave Mr. Albers the pack of your logging slips, did you not?

"A. Yes, I did once.

"Q. Do you remember what you gave them to him for?

"A. I don't right offhand, but it seems to me he said he was going out to look for some logs or timber or something and he needed them to mark some figures on * * *.

"Q. Well, if he was going to use them for scratch pads, why didn't you give him a scratch pad that you had in the office?

"A. That's what I should have done."

In addition, the plaintiff's printed scaling slips were not consecutively numbered. Unauthorized use of the slips, therefore, could easily go undetected. Thus, Mr. Nelson Thompson testified:

"Q. Mr. Thompson, were your slips you gave these haulers numbered?

"A. No, they were not.

"Q. They are now, aren't they?

"A. Yes.

"Q. Had you used numbered logging slips, this would have prevented anybody getting logging slips out of the ordinary channel of business and using it to defraud you?

"A. Yes."

Moreover, in 1960, when the company became concerned about the possible unauthorized use of its scaling slips, it required its own personnel to initial the slips when a new shipment of logs was scaled. However, this protective measure was largely ignored in practice. Mrs. Amy Thompson testified:

"Q. And later on in the course of your business, if you remember Mr. Thompson said he wanted the logging slips initialed by one of the so-called authorized people?

"A. Yes.

"Q. [D]idn't you really not pay too much attention to them at all?

"A. Well, I know we didn't send them back to be sure they were initialed. We might have noticed it but we didn't send them back to the mill.

"Q. In other words, if they came to you uninitialed, you might have noticed it but didn't do anything about it.

"A. Didn't do anything about it."

The principal default of the plaintiff, however, was its failure to use reasonable diligence in insuring honesty from its log haulers including Emery Albers. For many years, the haulers were permitted to deliver both the original and the duplicate of the scaling slip to the company office, and the company tolerated this practice. These slips supplied the bookkeeper with the payees' names for the checks she was to draw in payment for log deliveries. Only by having the company at all times retain possession of the original slip could the plaintiff have assured that no disbursements were made except for logs received, and that the proper amounts were paid to the proper persons. The practice tolerated by the plaintiff effectively removed the only immediate safeguard in the entire procedure against dishonesty on the part of the haulers.

Finally, of course, the company regularly entrusted the completed checks to the haulers for delivery to the named payees, without any explicit authorization from the latter to do so.

While none of these practices, in isolation, might be sufficient to charge the plaintiff with negligence within the meaning of § 3–406, the company's course of conduct, viewed in its entirety, is surely sufficient to support the trial judge's determination that it substantially contributed to the making of the unauthorized signatures.[6] In his words, that conduct was "no different than had the plaintiff simply given Albers a series of checks signed in blank for his unlimited, unrestricted use."

* * *

Judgment affirmed.

■Watkins, J., dissents.

PROBLEMS

1. In *Thompson Maple Products*, Albers either cashed or deposited the checks with his forged indorsement in the same bank on which they were drawn by the Thompson company. Banks call this an "on us" check, meaning the drawee bank is also the depositary bank. Note that 3–406(b) embraces a form of comparative negligence. If this case had been decided under Revised Article 3, could a case be made that Bank's conduct in *Thompson Maple Products* was not in exercise of ordinary care in paying the checks that were presented to it by Albers over a period of years that were payable to timber producers? Is there any legitimate reason why the

---

6. In this connection, the trial court also noted that the plaintiff at all times prior to the commencement of this litigation failed to keep an accurate inventory account. It could not therefore verify, at any given point in time, that it actually possessed the logs which it had paid for.

payees would transfer the checks to Albers? Wouldn't the payees normally deposit these checks to their accounts?

2. Assume that the facts in *Thompson* were these: the checks made to the timber companies were made to corporate payees, and the indorsements of these companies would ordinarily be printed and "look official." Albers forged the indorsements of these companies by handwritten indorsements that were crudely done. Albers then wrote his own name under each of these indorsements. He deposited these checks in his account in Depositary Bank and withdrew the proceeds of the checks once they cleared. The checks were presented to the drawee, Citizens National Bank, which paid the checks. In subsequent litigation, the drawer, Thompson Maple Products, contended that the drawee bank is precluded from relying upon the drawer's negligence as a defense under 3–406 because of the drawee's failure to verify the indorsements. The drawee bank defended on the ground that a drawee has no duty to examine indorsements on checks that it has received from a depositary bank. Under the facts in this Problem, Albers had no deposit account in drawee bank and the drawee had no reason to be familiar with his signature. Is drawee bank correct in this case? See Guardian Life Ins. Co. of America v. Weisman, 223 F.3d 229 (3d Cir. 2000).

c. FAILURE OF CUSTOMER TO REPORT FORGERY

In cases involving forged checks, the malefactor often forges a series of checks on the same account over a period of time. Forgery with respect to a single check is much more likely to involve a forged indorsement rather than a forgery of the drawer's signature. Typically, repeated forged check cases involve a dishonest employee of the person whose signature is forged. Usually the employee has access to the employer's checkbook and often has duties related to bookkeeping. In the case of repeated forgeries the later forgeries could have been easily prevented if the person whose signature was forged had detected the earlier forgeries. Such detection is relatively easy because in most cases the payor bank, after paying a check, returns the cancelled check to the customer on whose account the check was drawn. The customer should be able to determine whether a check written on the its account is a forgery. On the other hand it may be very difficult for the payor bank to detect forgery. Since it is easy for the customer to detect a forgery, 4–406 imposes a duty on the customer to report forged checks to the bank. Failure of the customer to comply with this duty can, in some cases, result in a shifting of the loss from the bank to the customer. Although 3–406 applies to checks bearing a forged indorsement as well as forged checks, 4–406 does not apply to forged indorsements. Both sections also apply to altered checks which are discussed later in this chapter.

Given the rule that a payor bank bears the loss on a check it pays over a forged drawer's signature, banks had traditionally engaged in the labor intensive activity of sight review of all checks drawn on the bank. Bank employees compared the signature on each check with that on the signature specimen card on file. For a large bank, a typical setting was a big room, crammed with desks, with soft music, free softdrinks and aspirin, and other amenities designed to keep these unfortunate workers from losing their minds. As the volume of checks grew and automation became the norm, banks abandoned sight review except for checks that met certain risk criteria, the principal one being the amount of the check.

Now that forgers utilize desktop printers, sight review has become obsolete for the large volume of corporate and government checks on which signatures are printed. Even on personal checks in which a signature is written in ink, a sight reviewer, who can normally spend only a few seconds on each check, is no match for a skillful forger. Thus, banks came to the conclusion that sight review was not cost effective. Some banks purported to find no greater forgery losses without sight review than with it, and others contended that whatever losses they might suffer on the payment of forged checks of relatively small amounts did not justify the heavy labor costs involved. As we shall see, payor banks have better ways of fighting forgeries than sight review.

The legal problems raised by the abandonment of sight review occupied the courts for years. Julianna J. Zekan, Comparative Negligence Under the Code: Protecting Negligent Banks Against Negligent Customers, 26 U. Mich. J.L. Reform 125, 166–178 (1992). Under 4–406, the customer is obliged to examine its cancelled checks for forgeries and to notify the payor bank if any are found. If it fails to do so in a timely manner, the customer is precluded from raising the forgery *unless the bank fails to exercise ordinary care.* Before the 1990 revision of Articles 3 and 4 became effective, the case law was sharply divided on the issue whether a bank that did not conduct sight review of the checks in question was exercising ordinary care. In Medford Irrigation District v. Western Bank, 66 Or.App. 589, 676 P.2d 329 (Or.Ct.App.1984), the bank's automated system was programmed to pay all checks of $5,000 or less unless there was a hold or stop order on the check; checks for amounts in excess of that sum were selected out by the check sorting machine and individually reviewed. The court held that the bank was precluded from raising the customer's negligence on the ground that in order to exercise ordinary care a bank's system must be reasonably related to the detection of forged signatures. Since in this case the bank had no procedure for detecting forgeries in checks under $5,000 the bank was negligent *as a matter of law.*

The *Medford* view has been rejected in a number of cases. The Illinois Supreme Court held in Wilder Binding Co. v. Oak Park Trust & Savings Bank, 135 Ill.2d 121, 552 N.E.2d 783 (Ill. 1990), that whether a bank exercised ordinary care in paying a check is a question of fact. In Rhode Island Hospital Trust National Bank v. Zapata Corp., 848 F.2d 291 (1st Cir.1988) (Breyer, J.), the court approved the cost-benefit analysis rejected in *Medford.* Judge Breyer opined that there was no evidence that any increased forgery loss from the bank's automated system was unreasonable in light of the costs that the new practices would save. He relied on Learned Hand's view that duty should be defined by calculating the probability of injury times the gravity of harm to determine the burden of precaution that is warranted. United States v. Carroll Towing Co., 159 F.2d 169 (2d Cir.1947).

In the revision of Articles 3 and 4, the Drafting Committee was mindful of the need to make sure that Revised Article 4 would accommodate a system of electronic presentment, discussed in the preceding chapter, if such a system were developed. This tipped the scale in favor of adopting the line of authority rejecting *Medford*. This was implemented in the definition of "ordinary care" in 3–103(a)(9), discussed in Comment 5 to 3–103 and Comment 4 to 4–406. The following case discusses 3–103(a)(9) and is instructive in showing how banks attempt to prove ordinary care under that provision.

Espresso Roma Corporation v. Bank Of America, N.A.

Court of Appeal, First District, California, 2002.
124 Cal.Rptr.2d 549.

■ STEIN, ACTING P.J.

Espresso Roma Corporation, Pacific Espresso Corporation, and David S. Boyd dba Hillside Residence Hall (appellants) appeal from a judgment dismissing their complaint alleging several causes of action against Bank of America, N.A. (Bank), based upon its payment of forged checks drawn on appellants' accounts by one of their former employees. The court entered judgment in favor of the Bank after it granted the Bank's motion for summary judgment on the ground that appellants were precluded by California Uniform Commercial Code section 4406, subdivisions (d) and (e) from asserting any claims against the Bank for unauthorized payment of checks drawn on their accounts. We shall affirm the judgment.

David S. Boyd is the president of Espresso Roma and Pacific Espresso Corporations and also runs Hillside Residence Hall. All three businesses had checking accounts with the Bank.

From late 1996 through April 1999, appellants employed Joseph Montanez, who eventually assumed certain bookkeeping responsibilities, learned how to generate company checks on the computer, and had access to blank checks. Starting in October 1997, Montanez downloaded company computer programs, stole blank checks, and printed company checks on his home computer which he used to pay his personal bills, and for personal purchases. He concealed his actions by removing the forged checks from the bank statements when he sorted the mail.

Boyd did not discover the forgeries, or report them to the Bank until May 1999. After Montanez left the company, a check was returned by a stereo company, bearing a signature that Boyd did not recognize. Boyd then reviewed the records and discovered that, from October 1997 through April 1999, Montanez had forged company checks in an amount totaling more than $330,000.

The Bank's motion for summary judgment was based upon section 4406, which limits a payor bank's liability to its customer for making payment upon checks with alterations or unauthorized signatures.

Pursuant to subdivision (f) of section 4406, the Bank asserted that appellants were absolutely precluded from asserting forgeries processed more than one year before the forgery was reported. By its terms subdivision (f) applies, "[w]ithout regard to care or lack of care of either the customer or the bank," (italics added) and precludes "a customer who does not within one year after the statement or items are made available to the customer ... discover and report the customer's unauthorized signature" from asserting it against the Bank. The Bank also relied upon the conditional preclusion established by subdivisions (d) and (e) of section 4406. Subdivision (c) of section 4406 imposes a duty upon the customer promptly to review monthly statements or checks made available to the customer by the bank, to exercise reasonable care in discovering any unauthorized signature or alteration, and promptly to notify the bank of the discovery of such items. Pursuant to subdivision (d), if the customer fails to comply with these duties, when the same person has forged checks on the account, the customer is precluded from making a claim against the bank for the unauthorized payment unless the customer notified the bank no more than 30 days after the first forged item was included in the monthly statement or canceled checks, and should have been discovered. (§ 4406, subd. (d)(2).) This preclusion is conditional because the customer may avoid its application by establishing that the bank "failed to exercise ordinary care in paying the item and that the failure contributed to [the] loss." (§ 4406, subd. (e) * * *.

In its order granting summary judgment, the court held that appellants were precluded by "sections 4406(d) and 4406(e) from asserting claims against the [B]ank for unauthorized payments of checks drawn on [appellants'] checking accounts." The court specifically ruled that appellants failed to create a triable issue of fact as to whether "the [B]ank's system of processing checks for [appellants' accounts] violated the [B]ank's ... procedures" or varied unreasonably from general banking usage in the area. The court also ruled that the declaration of appellant's expert failed to create a triable issue of fact "as to whether the [B]ank failed to exercise ordinary care," and that the Bank had no duty to sight review the checks.[2]

Appellants argue that the burden never shifted to them to create a triable issue of fact because the Bank failed to meet its "burden of production to make a prima facie showing of the nonexistence of any triable issue of fact," that (1) despite the availability of monthly statements and

---

2. The Bank contends that, even if triable issues of fact existed on the issue of exercise of ordinary care, the absolute preclusion set forth in section 4406, subdivision (f) applied, and was shortened by contract to a period of six months, thereby barring nearly half of appellants' claim without regard to exercise of ordinary care. We need not reach this contention because we shall uphold the summary judgment upon the ground that no triable issue of fact existed with respect to the application of the conditional preclusion set forth in section 4406, subdivisions (d) and (e).

canceled checks, appellants failed to discover and notify the Bank of the forgery within 30 days, and (2) it exercised ordinary care in paying the item. * * * Appellants further contend that, even if the burden did shift to them, the declaration of their own expert created a triable issue of fact on the issue whether the bank exercised ordinary care, precluding summary judgment in the Bank's favor.

1.   APPELLANTS' FAILURE TO DISCOVER AND REPORT THE FORGERIES

Pursuant to section 4406, subdivision (d), the customer is precluded from making a claim against the bank for unauthorized payment unless the customer notified the bank no more than 30 days after the *first* forged item was included in the monthly statement or canceled checks and should have been discovered. (§ 4406, subd. (d)(2); see also Official Comments on U. Com. Code, West's Ann. Cal. U. Com.Code, (2002 ed.) com. 2, § 4406, p. 190.)[3]

According to the complaint, the forged checks were presented for payment between October 1997 and May 1999, but appellants did not discover or report them until on or about May 15, 1999. To establish its prima facie case that the conditional issue preclusion created by section 4406, subdivision (d) applied, the Bank presented the deposition testimony of Boyd, that it made monthly account statements and canceled checks available to appellants shortly after the closing period of each statement. Boyd testified that he received statements on a monthly basis, and they included canceled checks. When Boyd began to suspect unauthorized checks were being written and reviewed the statements and checks in May 1999, he was able to identify, and reported, the forgery. This evidence supports the inference that the first monthly statement that would have reflected the forgery by Montanez would have been in November 1997 * * * Yet, despite having the means to discover the forgeries, more than a year and a half elapsed before appellants discovered and reported any of them, far beyond the 30 days specified in section 4406, subdivision (d). * * *

2.   EVIDENCE THAT THE BANK EXERCISED ORDINARY CARE

Having established a prima facie case that the Bank made monthly statements and checks available, and that appellants failed to notify the Bank within 30 days, the issue preclusion pursuant to section 4406,

---

3. The California Uniform Commercial Code comment 2 explains: "Subsection (d)(2) applies to cases in which the customer fails to report an unauthorized signature or alteration with respect to an item . . . and the bank subsequently pays other items of the customer with respect to which there is an alteration or unauthorized signature of the customer and the same wrongdoer is involved. If the payment of the subsequent items occurred after the customer has had a reasonable time, (not exceeding 30 days) to report *with respect to the first item,* and before the bank received notice of the unauthorized signature or alteration *of the first item,* the customer is precluded from asserting the alteration or unauthorized signature with respect to the subsequent items." (Official Comments on U. Com. Code, 23B West's Ann. Cal. U. Com.Code, *supra,* Com. 2, foll. § 4406 (2002 ed.) p. 190, italics added.)

subdivision (d) applies unless the customer can establish that the bank, "failed to exercise ordinary care in paying the item and that the failure contributed to [the] loss." (§ 4406, subd. (e).) "Ordinary care" is defined by section 3103, subdivision (a)(7) as follows: " 'Ordinary care' in the case of a person engaged in business means observance of reasonable commercial standards, prevailing in the area in which the person is located, with respect to the business in which the person is engaged. In the case of a bank that takes an instrument for processing for collection or payment by automated means, reasonable commercial standards do not require the bank to examine the instrument if the failure to examine does not violate the bank's prescribed procedures and the bank's procedures do not vary unreasonably from general banking usage not disapproved by this [D]ivision or Division 4 (commencing with Section 4104.)"

As explained in *Story Road Flea Market, Inc. v. Wells Fargo Bank* (1996) 42 Cal.App.4th 1733, 1742, 50 Cal.Rptr.2d 524, a case in which the court upheld a motion for summary judgment in the Bank's favor based upon section 4406, subdivisions (d) and (e), ordinary care as used in section 4406 is a " 'professional negligence' standard of care which looks at the procedures utilized in the banking industry rather than what a 'reasonable person' might have done under the circumstances." (*Id.* at p. 1741, 50 Cal.Rptr.2d 524.) " '[R]easonable commercial standards do not require the bank to *examine the instrument* if the failure to examine does not violate the bank's prescribed procedures and the bank's procedures do not vary unreasonably from general banking usage.' " (*Id.* at p. 1742, 50 Cal.Rptr.2d 524, italics added.)

The Bank, in support of its motion for summary judgment, presented a prima facie showing that it exercised ordinary care, through the declaration of its expert, Jack Thomas. In addition to stating his qualifications as an expert in the field, Thomas declared that he was "familiar with the check processing strategies and procedures employed by banks similarly sized to Bank of America, including those within the San Francisco Bay area, which are 'bulk file bookkeeping' banks." He further explained that "Bank of America is a 'bulk file bookkeeping' check processor," meaning that it processes checks automatically and does not visually examine individual checks or verify signatures. Thomas declared that Bank of America processes in excess of one million checks per day in California, and although it uses fraud filters, they are not designed to "catch a crooked employee who forges his employer's checks, which only the employer would know are forged." Thomas declared that the Bank's "practices and procedures are consistent with those of all other large 'bulk file bookkeeping' banks in California." Thomas also "verified with the responsible [B]ank officer that [the Bank] followed its procedures with respect to the checks at issue in this litigation when it processed the checks." He concluded that the Bank "exercised ordinary care in processing [appellants'] checks ... in observance of reasonable commercial standards prevailing in the area in which Bank of America is located, and where [appellants] maintained their accounts."

Appellants argue that this declaration was insufficient to define the reasonable commercial standard "in the area," (§ 3103, subd. (a)(7)) and failed to demonstrate that the Bank's automated check processing did not vary unreasonably from general banking usage, because the expert stated that the Bank's practices conformed to commercial standards for "bulk file bookkeeping" in all of California and considered only the practices of similarly sized banks. Appellant, however, takes the reference to the entire State of California in isolation and out of context, because the expert specifically stated that he was also familiar with the practices of similarly sized banks in the "San Francisco Bay area." Thus, read as a whole, the expert's declaration expressed the opinion that the Bank's practices conformed not only with those of similarly sized banks in the Bay Area, but also with similarly sized banks in the State of California. Nor are we persuaded by appellant's contention that it was necessary to offer expert opinion that the Bank's practices were consistent with those of *all* banks in the area, not just those of similarly sized banks. To the contrary, section 3103, subdivision (a)(7) defines ordinary care as "observance of reasonable commercial standards, prevailing in the area in which the person is located, with respect to the business in which the person is engaged," meaning the standard of reasonableness is set by comparable businesses. (See Com. com. 4, West's Ann.Cal. U. Com.Code, § 4406, p. 191 [ordinary care is established if the bank's "procedure is reasonable and is commonly followed by other comparable banks in the area" and was followed by the bank in processing the checks in issue.] Size is a relevant factor in identifying comparable businesses because, in the banking context, a reasonable commercial standard for processing checks at a small bank with a relatively small volume of checks, and personal familiarity with its customers, would be quite different than what is reasonable for a large bank that processes upwards of a million checks per day. Thomas's declaration therefore established that the reasonable industry standard prevailing in the area for similarly sized banks was to bulk process checks through an automated system that employs fraud filters, but does not include sight review of individual checks for signature verification. The Bank's procedures conformed to this standard, which also was consistent with general bank usage as reflected by the practices of other bulk file bookkeeping banks in California, and it followed those procedures in this case. We conclude that Thomas's declaration was sufficient to establish a prima facie case that the Bank exercised ordinary care, thereby shifting the burden to appellant to create a triable issue of fact. (*Story Road Flea Market, Inc. v. Wells Fargo Bank, supra,* 42 Cal.App.4th 1733, 1738, 1743, 50 Cal.Rptr.2d 524 [expert declaration that bank processed checks, none of which were selected for sight review, in accordance with its own procedures, and consistent with reasonable commercial standards in the area, and general banking practices, shifted burden to plaintiff to create a triable issue of fact].)

Although appellants submitted the declaration of its own expert, John Moulton, in opposition, the trial court correctly concluded that it failed to create a triable issue of fact on the question whether the Bank "failed to exercise ordinary care in paying the item *and* that the failure contributed to [the] loss." (§ 4406, subd. (e), italics added.) Moulton declared that he called upon "large and small banks in Alameda County to inquire of their actual practices." These banks make decisions for payment of items at the branch where the account is kept and have the "means to check signatures for forgeries" present, whether it be by signature card or digital imaging. He also declared that these banks would manually examine checks which resulted in an overdraft, were unsigned, or exceeded a certain amount. He further declared that there were four instances of daily overdrafts occurring on days in which forged checks were processed, and one unsigned check that was processed and paid, all without selecting the checks for manual review.

The fundamental defect in Moulton's declaration is that, instead of defining the applicable reasonable commercial standard of care by looking at comparably sized banks using bulk file bookkeeping, he bases his opinion that the standard of care requires certain checks be selected for sight review, or other special handling, upon the practices of large and small banks. Without a showing that *comparable* banks in the area select individual checks for sight review, the fact that the Bank's system did not select individual checks for sight review, or signature verification, is insufficient to create a material issue of fact because section 3103, subdivision (a)(7) specifies that "reasonable commercial standards *do not require the bank to examine the instrument if the failure to examine does not violate the bank's prescribed procedures and the bank's procedures do not vary unreasonably from general banking usage.*" (Italics added.) Therefore, Moulton's declaration does not create a triable issue of fact with respect to the Bank's showing that its system of bulk processing of checks, which does not include sight review for signature verification, is commercially reasonable, and consistent with the practice of other comparably large banks in the area and in California.

Moreover, assuming arguendo that reasonable commercial standards did require that the Bank have established criteria for selecting some checks for sight review, Moulton's declaration still fails to create a triable issue of fact because it provides no basis to infer that the failure to have such a system *contributed to the loss*. (§ 4406, subd. (e) [the customer must show the Bank "failed to exercise ordinary care in paying the item *and* that the failure contributed to [the] loss" (italics added)].) Moulton does not specify what the criteria should be, in an automated check processing system that selects some checks for sight review, other than reviewing a check that causes an overdraft, or is in excess of some unspecified amount. Although Moulton declares that daily overdrafts occurred on four of the days forged items were processed, Moulton does not declare that it was forged checks which caused the overdrafts. Similarly, although Moulton identifies a check that was paid without a signature, he does not state whether this check is one of the items that appellants contend were paid without authorization, or how such a check would be identified and selected for sight review under the criteria he declares are commercially reasonable. Nor does he declare that any forged check was in an amount that, pursuant to the criteria he suggests, would have resulted in its selection for sight review. Therefore, even if such a system of selection for sight review had been used by the Bank, the declaration provides no basis for inferring that any of the unauthorized checks would have been selected for sight review, resulting in earlier discovery of the forgeries. Therefore, the declaration does not create a triable issue that the failure to have such a system contributed to the loss. (See *Story Road Flea Market, Inc. v. Wells Fargo Bank, supra,* 42 Cal.App.4th 1733, 1744, 50 Cal.Rptr.2d 524 [expert declaration that unauthorized checks were out of sequence failed to create an issue of fact, because under stated criteria for selecting checks for sight review, unauthorized checks would still not have been selected for sight review].) * * *

We conclude that the court properly granted the Bank's motion for summary judgment on the ground that section 4406, subdivisions (d) and (e) precluded appellants from asserting claims against the Bank for unauthorized payments of checks drawn on their checking accounts, and that appellants failed to create a triable issue of fact as to whether they failed to exercise ordinary care in paying the items and that the failure contributed to their loss.

The judgment is affirmed.

NOTES

1. Should a bank be allowed to raise the 4–406(f) one-year bar if it was in bad faith when it paid the check? The subsection and the Comments are silent on the issue. Take this case: Drawer Company (D) employed Margaret Marvic in its accounts payable department. She fraudulently signed the name of D's treasurer, Travis, to a number of checks over a three-year period. These checks were all made payable to Margaret and drawn on D's account in Bank. Margaret's husband, Lazlo Marvic, an officer of Bank made certain that no questions were raised about the validity of the checks upon payment. When D finally began to raise questions about Margaret's honesty, she and Lazlo disappeared. When D demanded recredit of its account in Bank for the amount of the forged checks, Bank raised the one-year bar of 4–406(f). D countered by contending that Bank could not raise this barrier because it paid the checks in bad faith.

The authorities are divided on the bad faith issue. The thrust of 4–406 is to place on the drawer the burden of discovering a forged signature when the bank has returned the periodic bank statement and notifying the bank of the forgery. Under 4–406(f), without respect to the lack of due care of the bank, if the drawer has not reported the forgery within a year, the drawer is precluded from raising the forgery. But under the hypothetical facts given, the drawer has been hindered in performance of its duty to discover forgeries and give the requisite notice by the bad faith intervention of an officer of the bank. This is different from mere lack of care. Falk v. The Northern Trust Co., 763 N.E.2d 380 (Ill. App. 2001), held that the one-year limitation does not apply if the bank is in bad faith. But Halifax

Corp. v. First Union Nat. Bank, 546 S.E.2d 696 (Va. 2001), noting that 4–406(f) says nothing about good faith while 4–406(d) and (e) do mention it, drew the negative implication and held the contrary. In neither case was there a clear case of bad faith. See 1–201(b)(20) "good faith." Unless the statute is amended, more judicial analysis will be required before we can be confident of the trend of the law in this area.

2. If the customer and payor bank enter into the increasingly common agreement that allows the bank to retain the cancelled checks and to send the customer a periodic statement of account, does the customer have enough information to detect forged checks drawn on its account? 4–406(a) and (b). Comment 1 to 4–406. The Federal Reserve Board has approved a plan to allow banks to send periodic statements and disclosure information to customers electronically if the customers consent. Banks can utilize e-mail or their Web site. Jonathan Nicholson, Fed Plan To Let Banks Send E–Mail Statements, Wall St. J., Aug. 19, 1999, at A2.

3. There has been disagreement in the courts on the question of what constitutes reasonable promptness by the customer in discovering an unauthorized signature and in notifying the bank when the wrongdoer is the person designated by the customer to check the monthly statement. Under 1–202(f), the customer would seem to be bound by the information supplied by the bank when that information reaches the customer's employee who is authorized to receive it and act on it. Under the law of agency, if that employee fails to notify the bank of the forgery, the customer should be bound by the employee's conduct regardless of whether the employee's failure to notify is due to negligence or is the deliberate act of the employee to cover up the employee's wrongdoing. The issue should not be whether the customer was negligent in the procedure chosen for reviewing the bank statements, if the employee receiving and acting on the statements was the designated agent of the customer for that purpose. See Warren Seavey, Notice Through An Agent, 65 U. Pa.L. Rev. 1, 7–8 (1916).

PROBLEMS

The agreement between Bank and its corporate customer, Company, is that Bank is authorized to pay checks drawn on Company's account only if they are signed by the chief financial officer, Hardy, and her deputy, Olsen. Signature specimens of these two parties were on file with Bank.

1. Olsen signed his name to the check in dispute but Hardy did not. Bank paid the check. When Company demanded that Bank re-credit its account with the amount of the check, Bank contended that this should not be treated as an unauthorized signature on the part of Company because the signature on the check was not forged. Is Bank correct? See 3–403(b).

2. Olsen fraudulently wrote three checks on Company's account payable to the order of Olsen. Olsen signed his name to each check and forged the name of Hardy.

a. The first check, in the amount of $1,000, was paid by Bank on January 2 by automated equipment without any human examination of the check. The cancelled check was returned to Company on January 4.

b. The second check, in the amount of $2,000, was paid by Bank on February 20 by automated equipment without any human examination of the check. The cancelled check was returned to Company on March 3.

c. The third check, in the amount of $5,000, was paid by Bank on February 28. Before the check was paid, an employee of Bank examined the check but failed to detect the forgery of Hardy's signature. The cancelled check was returned to Company on March 3.

Under the established procedures of Bank, checks presented for payment in amounts less than $2,500 were not examined by anybody before payment. All checks paid by Bank were returned to Company each month along with the monthly statement of account.

The fraud by Olsen was discovered by Company in June. Olsen, who is insolvent, used the proceeds of the three checks to pay gambling debts. Company notified Bank of the forged checks on June 7, immediately after discovery of the fraud. Company demanded that Bank restore to Company account the $8,000 debited to the account as a result of payment of the checks.

With respect to each of the checks, state your opinion whether, under 4–406, Company is entitled to recover from Bank.

NOTE: FRAUD PREVENTION MEASURES

Banks have attempted to reduce fraud losses by adopting fraud prevention measures. These are described in 1 Clark & Clark, ¶ 10.01 (Rev. ed. 2003). Traditional methods involving sight review or random examination are not very effective against professionals who have available desktop computers that can scan and alter documents to produce accurate reproductions, as well as color printers and copiers, unless precautions are taken by the customer or bank.

A common protection against alteration and counterfeiting (producing checks like those of the drawer) is the use of paper stock for checks with security features. Examination of checks will normally warn a potential forger that the check has safety features. Some of these are visible, like the legend "original document" which has a ghostly presence on the back of some checks and is difficult to copy. Others are warnings, such as the admonition that some awful things will happen to the check if photocopied. Still others are not revealed at all, leaving the would-be malefactor to worry about what he might be up against if he transgresses. Of course, security devices in the paper stock are not effective in the common insider case in which the forger has access to the genuine checks of the customer. 1 Clark & Clark, supra, ¶ 10.01[8][2], at 10–14.

Some banks offer a service identified as "positive pay." In its most common form the bank's business customers notify the bank daily of the checks drawn by them. The information provided to the bank typically includes the MICR line, dollar amounts and payee identification. When checks drawn by that customer are presented for payment, the bank compares these checks with the list given by the customer. If the checks don't match, they are returned to the presenting bank. See ABA Subcommittee on Payments, Check Fraud: The Model Positive Pay Services Agreement and Commentary, 54 Bus. Law. 637 (1999). Banks have begun to offer imaging positive pay services, under which the bank posts online for the customer's benefit the entire image of suspect checks, not just their MICR line. When the returned checks reach the depositary bank, it will erase the provisional credit given its depositor. If the depositary bank has already allowed the depositor to withdraw the funds, it has the burden of pursuing this person to get the money back. Since banks under Regulation CC are making funds available for most checks either on the day of deposit or the next day, as we indicated in an earlier chapter, it is likely that the money has been withdrawn in cases in which the forger is the depositor.

After Regulation CC one of the favorite handiworks of skilled forgers has been cashier's checks, the proceeds of which must be available for withdrawal by the depositor the day after deposit. Some banks take thumb prints of persons cashing checks, which can then be compared with FBI files to identify a forger.

Software companies have developed programs that allow banks to scan accounts for possible forgeries without the assistance of customers. The program allows a bank to review the past activity of customers' accounts in order to construct an archive for each account that shows a profile of the customer's usage. Checks presented for payment on these accounts will be reviewed for aberrations from this profile that may point to suspect checks. Fraud detection factors may include whether the check is larger in amount than checks drawn on this account in the past, whether the check number duplicates other checks already paid, whether the check number is out of sequence with other checks the customer is currently drawing, whether the check lacks any check number, and whether the volume of activity in the customer's account exceeds past levels. 1 Clark & Clark, supra, & 10.01[6].

d. VALIDITY OF CONTRACTUAL "CUTDOWN" CLAUSES

Section 4–406 states two time limitations bearing on the customer's duty to discover and report unauthorized signatures or alterations. One appears in 4–406(d)(2) and bears on the repeat forgery issue. It provides that if there is a repeat forgery, the customer is precluded from asserting the forgery against the bank if payment was made before the bank received notice of the forgery "after the customer had been afforded a reasonable period of time, not exceeding 30 days, in which to examine the item or statement of account and notify the bank." The other is the overriding one-year notice preclusion in 4–406(f) that we discussed in Note 1 in the previous section. This is a strong statement of the policy of giving banks an outer time limit beyond which they no longer need to be concerned about forged checks even if the bank's negligence had led to the forgery. But 4–103(a) allows the parties to vary the effect of the terms of Article 4 by agreement, a subject that we will discuss in greater detail in the next chapter. Does this mean that the deposit agreement between the bank and its customer can cutdown this one-year period to six months, or 60 days, or 20 days? If so, the risk of forgery loss on the part of banks may be substantially reduced.

National Title Insurance Corporation Agency v. First Union National Bank

Supreme Court of Virginia, 2002.
559 S.E.2d 668.

■ Opinion By JUSTICE CYNTHIA D. KISNER.

Pursuant to the provisions of Code § 8.4–406(f), a bank's customer is precluded from asserting against the bank an unauthorized signature or alteration on an item if the customer fails to report such fact to the bank within one year after a statement of account showing payment of the item is made available to the customer. The dispositive issue in this appeal is whether a bank and its customer may, by contractual agreement, shorten the one-year period provided in Code § 8.4–406(f). Because we conclude that Code § 8.4–103(a) permits the parties to vary that time period, we will affirm the judgment of the circuit court holding that an agreement reducing the period to 60 days is binding on the parties.

National Title Insurance Corporation Agency (National Title) opened an escrow checking account with First Union National Bank (First Union) in April 1996. At that time, the parties entered into a "DEPOSIT AGREE-MENT AND DISCLOSURES For Non–Personal Accounts" (Deposit Agreement) that defined and governed the relationship between them. The provisions of Paragraph 12 of that Deposit Agreement, which are at issue in this appeal, absolve First Union of any liability for paying an item containing an unauthorized signature, an unauthorized indorsement, or a material alteration if National Title does not report such fact to First Union within 60 days of the mailing of the account statement describing the questioned item. In pertinent part, Paragraph 12 states:

> You should carefully examine the statement and canceled checks when you receive them. If you feel there is an error on the statement, or that some unauthorized person has withdrawn funds from the account, notify us immediately. The statement is considered correct unless you notify us promptly after any error is discovered. Moreover, because you are in the best position to discover an unauthorized signature, an unauthorized [i]ndorsement or a material alteration, you agree that we will not be liable for paying such items if . . . (b) you have not reported an unauthorized signature, an unauthorized [i]ndorsement or material alterations to us within 60 days of the mailing date of the earliest statement describing these items. . . .

Subsequently, First Union paid two checks ostensibly drawn on National Title's account, both of which were counterfeit checks and were not executed by an authorized signatory to the account. The first check, paid in November 1998, was described in an account statement mailed on December 5, 1998, and the second check, paid in December 1998, was described in National Title's account statement mailed on January 5, 1999. National Title did not report either of the unauthorized signatures to First Union within 60 days of the mailing of the respective account statements describing the two checks.

After First Union refused to credit National Title's account in the amounts paid on the two checks bearing unauthorized signatures, National Title filed a motion for judgment seeking to recover its losses from First Union. In its answer, First Union asserted, among other things, that National Title was precluded from making this claim because it had failed to report the unauthorized signatures within the 60–day time period specified in Paragraph 12 of the Deposit Agreement between the parties.

Ruling on the parties' cross-motions for summary judgment, the trial court concluded that First Union and National Title could contractually reduce the one-year period for reporting unauthorized signatures set forth in Code § 8.4–406(f) and that the 60–day period agreed upon by the parties in this case is not "manifestly unreasonable" under the provisions of Code § 8.4–103. The court therefore denied National Title's motion for summary judgment and granted First Union's motion, entering judgment in favor of First Union. National Title now appeals from that final judgment.

Title 8.4 of Virginia's Uniform Commercial Code (UCC) establishes the rights and duties between banks and their customers with regard to deposits and collections. A bank may charge against the account of its customer only those items that are properly payable from that account. *See* Code § 8.4–401(a). Items bearing unauthorized signatures, such as the checks in this case, are not properly payable. *Id.*

However, a customer has certain duties with regard to discovering and reporting an unauthorized signature or alteration on an item. If a bank sends or makes available to its customer a statement of account showing payment of items for the account, "the customer must exercise reasonable promptness in examining the statement or the items to determine whether any payment was not authorized because of an alteration of an item or because a purported signature by or on behalf of the customer was not authorized." Code § 8.4–406(c). A customer must promptly report to the bank any unauthorized payment that the customer "should reasonably have discovered" based on the statement or items provided. *Id.*

If a customer fails to comply with these duties, the customer is precluded from asserting against the bank the unauthorized signature or alteration on the item. Code § 8.4–406(d)(1). However, if a customer establishes that the bank "failed to exercise ordinary care in paying the item and that the failure substantially contributed to loss, the loss is allocated between the customer precluded and the bank asserting the preclusion according to the extent" that the failure of each party contributed to the loss. Code § 8.4–406(e).[2] Finally, if a customer does not discover and report an unauthorized signature or alteration on an item within one year after the statement or items are made available to the customer, the customer is thereafter precluded from asserting against the bank the unauthorized signature or alteration. Code § 8.4–406(f). This preclusion applies irrespective of whether the bank paid the item containing the unauthorized signature or alteration in good faith. *Halifax Corp. v. First Union Nat'l Bank,* 262 Va. 91, 101, 546 S.E.2d 696, 703 (2001).

On appeal, National Title first argues that Code § 8.4–406(f) is a statute of repose, i.e., a rule of substantive law, and that the one-year period set forth in that section is, therefore, not subject to contractual modification by the parties. Next, National Title posits that Paragraph 12 of the Deposit Agreement imports the time bar established in Code § 8.4–406(f) into subsection (c), thereby rendering the preclusion in subsection (f) meaningless. National Title further asserts that Paragraph 12 impermissibly changes the comparative negligence provisions established in Code § 8.4–406(e) and reinstates the concept of contributory negligence into Code § 8.4–406(c). Finally, National Title contends that the 60–day time limit for reporting an unauthorized signature or alteration on an item is "manifestly unreasonable," but that, if Paragraph 12 is enforceable, the 60–day limit should be construed as the parties' definition of "reasonable promptness" in determining comparative negligence, rather than as an absolute bar to National Title's claim against First Union. We do not agree with National Title.

The issue in this appeal is whether a bank may, through a contractual agreement with its customer, shorten the one-year period provided in Code § 8.4–406(f) to a period of 60 days. In *Halifax Corp.,* 262 Va. at 101, 546 S.E.2d at 703, we characterized that one-year period as a statutorily prescribed notice that operates as "a condition precedent to the customer's right to file an action against the bank to recover losses caused by the unauthorized signature or alteration." * * * This condition precedent does not limit a customer's claim against a bank but requires that the customer first perform the duty to discover and report any unauthorized signature or alteration on an item before bringing suit against the bank. However, that characterization of subsection (f) as a condition precedent is not, as National Title suggests, determinative of the question whether a customer and a bank can, by agreement, shorten the one-year period. The provisions of Code § 8.4–103(a) provide the analytical framework for resolving that question.

Code § 8.4–103(a) states that

[t]he effect of the provisions of this title may be varied by agreement but the parties to the agreement cannot disclaim a bank's responsibility for its lack of good faith or failure to exercise ordinary care or limit the measure of damages for the lack or failure. However, the parties

---

2. If a bank does not pay an item in good faith, the preclusion under Code § 8.4– 406(d) as to the customer does not apply. Code § 4.6–406(e).

may determine by agreement the standards by which the bank's responsibility is to be measured if those standards are not manifestly unreasonable.

According to Official Comment 2 regarding § 4–103 of the UCC, "[s]ubsection (a) confers blanket power to vary all provisions of the Article by agreements of the ordinary kind." Thus, this statute allows a bank and its customer to vary by agreement the effect of the provisions of Title 8.4 as long as the agreement does not: (1) "disclaim a bank's responsibility for its lack of good faith," (2) "[disclaim a bank's responsibility for its] failure to exercise ordinary care," or (3) "limit the measure of damages for the lack or failure." Code § 8.4–103(a).

The clause in Paragraph 12 of the Deposit Agreement reducing the one-year period in Code § 8.4–406(f) to a period of 60 days does not run afoul of these limitations on the authority to vary the effect of the provisions of Title 8.4. The Deposit Agreement does not absolve First Union of its duty to exercise ordinary care or good faith, nor does it limit the measure of damages. Instead, Paragraph 12 merely varies the effect of Code § 8.4–406(f) in that the period of time in which National Title must report an unauthorized signature or alteration on an item, without having its claim for losses precluded by the bar in subsection (f), is shortened from one year to 60 days. * * * This reduction in the length of the statutory notice period is consistent with the concept embodied in Code § 8.4–406(f) that a bank can be held potentially liable for paying an item containing an unauthorized signature or alteration only for a limited period of time. Thus, we conclude that a bank and its customer may contractually shorten the one-year period contained in Code § 8.4–406(f) and that First Union and National Title did so in Paragraph 12 of the Deposit Agreement.

Notwithstanding this reduced time period, if National Title complies with its duty to exercise reasonable promptness in examining its account statement and reporting any unauthorized signature or altered item, First Union remains liable for paying an item bearing an unauthorized signature or alteration. Likewise, the comparative negligence provisions contained in Code § 8.4–406(e) remain in effect during the 60–day period after First Union makes available to National Title a statement showing payment of items from National Title's account. Thus, the provisions of Paragraph 12 at issue do not alter the scheme of liability between banks and their customers as set forth in Code § 8.4–406. * * *

Finally, National Title contends that the 60–day period for reporting unauthorized signatures or alterations is "manifestly unreasonable" under Code § 8.4–103(a). As used in subsection (a), this term is the test for determining the validity of an agreement that sets the standards by which a bank's responsibility for its lack of good faith or failure to exercise ordinary care is to be measured. While it is not necessary for us to decide in this case whether the test of manifest unreasonableness also applies to a determination regarding the validity of a reduction in the time period contained in Code § 8.4–406(f), we will utilize that standard in this appeal since it is the one advanced by National Title. In doing so, we conclude that the 60–day time limitation set forth in Paragraph 12 of the Deposit Agreement is not "manifestly unreasonable." Other jurisdictions have likewise upheld the validity of reductions in the one-year period provided in Code § 8.4–406(f) to periods similar to or shorter than 60 days.[4] * * *

A condition precedent such as the one set forth in Code § 8.4–406(f) recognizes that a customer is in a better position than a bank to know whether a signature is authorized or an item has been altered. * * * A reduction in the one-year period allowed in subsection (f) to a period of 60 days encourages diligence by a customer and is " 'in accord with public policy by limiting disputes in a society where millions of bank transactions occur every day.' " *Basse Truck Line, Inc. v. First State Bank,* 949 S.W.2d 17, 22 (Tex.App.1997) (quoting *Parent Teacher Ass'n,* 524 N.Y.S.2d at 340).

For these reasons, we will affirm the judgment of the circuit court.

NOTE

The validity of cut-down clauses has been much litigated. Clark & Clark, ¶ 10.05[1][c] (Rev. ed. 2003). If a 60–day limitation is permissible, what about a 20–day limit? See Stowell v. Cloquet Co-op Credit Union, 557 N.W.2d 567 (Minn. 1997).

2.   RIGHT OF PAYOR BANK TO RECOVER MISTAKEN PAYMENT OF CHECK

a.   FORGED CHECKS

The law of mistake and restitution recognizes the general principle that a person who confers a benefit upon another person because of a mistake is entitled to restitution from the person receiving the benefit. For example, a shopkeeper receives a $10 bill from a customer in payment of goods purchased by the customer for a price of $8. The shopkeeper, who has an obligation to give the customer $2 change, gives the customer $12 because of a mistaken belief that the customer had paid with a $20 bill. The shopkeeper is entitled to get back the $10 paid by mistake. Restatement of Restitution § 19 (1937).

Mistake can also occur when money is paid for a negotiable instrument either by a person who buys the instrument or by a person such as a payor bank who pays the instrument. The law of mistake and restitution applies to negotiable instrument cases, but special rules apply in some cases. The mistake cases fall into various categories and most of the cases involve payment or acceptance of a check or other draft by the drawee. The principal categories involve forged checks, checks bearing a forged indorsement, altered checks, checks on which the drawer has stopped payment, and checks drawn on an account with insufficient funds to cover the check.

---

4. We do not decide today whether a period shorter than 60 days would be "mani-   festly unreasonable."

The seminal case in this area is Price v. Neal, 3 Burr. 1354, 97 Eng. Rep. 871 (K.B. 1762), which involved two forged bills of exchange drawn on Price and indorsed to Neal, a bona fide purchaser for value. Price paid Neal on the first bill and then accepted the second bill which was subsequently purchased by Neal. After Price paid the second bill he learned that the signature of the drawer of the bills had been forged. Price sued Neal to get his money back. Lord Mansfield, in deciding in favor of the defendant, stated:

> It is an action upon the case, for money had and received to the plaintiff's use. In which action, the plaintiff can not recover the money, unless it be against conscience in the defendant, to retain it: and great liberality is always allowed, in this sort of action.

> But it can never be thought unconscientious in the defendant, to retain this money, when he has once received it upon a bill of exchange indorsed to him for a fair and valuable consideration, which he had bona fide paid, without the least priority or suspicion of any forgery.

> Here was no fraud: no wrong. It was incumbent upon the plaintiff, to be satisfied "that the bill drawn upon him was the drawer's hand," before he accepted or paid it: but it was not incumbent upon the defendant, to inquire into it. Here was notice given by the defendant to the plaintiff of a bill drawn upon him: and he sends his servant to pay it and take it up. The other bill he actually accepts; after which acceptance, the defendant innocently and bona fide discounts it. The plaintiff lies by, for a considerable time after he has paid these bills; and then found out "that they were forged:" and the forger comes to be hanged. He made no objection to them, at the time of paying them. Whatever neglect there was, was on his side. The defendant had actual encouragement from the plaintiff himself, for negotiating the second bill, from the plaintiff's having without any scruple or hesitation paid the first: and he paid the whole value, bona fide. It is a misfortune which has happened without the defendant's fault or neglect. If there was no neglect in the plaintiff, yet there is no reason to throw off the loss from one innocent man upon another innocent man: but, in this case, if there was any fault or negligence in any one, it certainly was in the plaintiff, and not in the defendant.

Payment or acceptance by the drawee of a forged check or other draft is addressed in 3–418(a) and (c) and 3–417(a)(3). Under these provisions the rule of Price v. Neal is preserved. Section 4–208(a)(3) is identical in effect to 3–417(a)(3) and applies specifically to warranties made in the bank-collection process to a payor bank with respect to an Article 4 "draft" (4–104(a)(7)), which includes a check.

PROBLEM

Taylor, an employee of Juliet, needed money to meet overdue bills. He broke into a storeroom and stole a pad of company checks. Taylor forged Juliet's name to a check for $307 drawn on Payor Bank which he made payable to him. He used the check to pay for groceries at Best Foods whose policy was to accept third-party checks only if they appeared to be paychecks, and this check clearly did. The name printed at the top of the check was Juliet's d/b/a, "Juliet Company," and Taylor typed on the signature line the company name, followed by a written signature of Juliet. The forgery was skillfully done and even a handwriting expert would have had difficulty in detecting it. Best Foods deposited the check in its account in Depositary Bank which presented the check to Payor Bank for payment. Payor Bank paid the check in ordinary course and Best Foods withdrew the amount from its account in Depositary Bank. Taylor shortly filed in bankruptcy.

(a) When Payor Bank learned of the forgery, it demanded that Depositary Bank reimburse it for the amount of the check. Is it entitled to recover on the basis of the Code provisions set out in the paragraph preceding the Problem?

(b) When Payor Bank learned of the forgery, it demanded that Best Foods, the party that dealt with the forger, reimburse it for the amount of the check. Is it entitled to recover? See the Code provisions set out above and, in addition, 3–416(a)(2) and its Article 4 counterpart, 4–207(a).

(c) Did Depositary Bank breach the warranty stated in 3–417(a)(1)?

─────────────

During the redraft of Article 3 and 4, active consideration was given to rejecting the rule of Price v. Neal, but the doctrine has been retained. Does that doctrine allocate the loss resulting from forged checks in a fair manner in this Problem?

b.   FORGED INDORSEMENT

PROBLEM

Drawer drew a check to the order of Payee. The check was stolen from Payee by Thief who signed Payee's name to the check as a blank indorsement. Thief then delivered the check to Jennifer, who purchased for value, in good faith and without notice that the indorsement was forged. Jennifer indorsed and deposited the check with Depositary Bank which presented the check and received payment from Payor Bank. Depositary Bank credited Jennifer's account and the credit was withdrawn. Payee then notified Drawer of the theft. Drawer notified Payor Bank, but was told that the check had already been paid. Is Payor Bank entitled to recover the amount of the check from either Depositary Bank or Jennifer? 3–417(a)(1), 4–208(a)(1), and Comments 2 and 3 to 3–417. If Depositary Bank has to pay, is Depositary Bank entitled to recover from Jennifer? 3–416(a)(1) and (2), 4–207(a)(1) and (2).

─────────────

How can you reconcile this case with Price v. Neal? That case announced a finality policy for forged checks: it is better to end the transaction on an instrument when it is paid rather than reopen and upset a series of transactions at a later date when forgery is discovered. But the result reached in the Problem above with respect to forged indorsements is inconsistent with a finality policy. Is it justified because a transferee from a forger may achieve some protection against a forged indorsement by requiring identification while a drawee cannot? For a judicial discussion of these issues, see Perini Corp. v. First National Bank of Habersham County, 553 F.2d 398 (5th Cir. 1977).

c. PRE–AUTHORIZED CHECKS

Telemarketing has proved effective in selling goods and services. In the usual transaction the payment mechanism is a credit card; the buyer gives the credit card number to the telemarketer caller and is charged for the sale on its next statement. What if the buyer wants the article being offered but has no credit card or her credit cards are "maxed out"? No problem. If the buyer has a bank account, the telemarketer asks the buyer to read off the information on the MICR line (the payor bank's routing and transit number and the buyer's account number) of a check. If the buyer is willing to provide this information, the telemarketer prints a check drawn on buyer's account in the payor bank payable to itself, stamps on the signature line "customer authorized draft," or words to that effect, and deposits the check for collection in telemarketer's depositary bank. Unless the buyer stops payment, the check will be paid by the payor bank on the basis of the MICR information with no review of the signature.

If the buyer did not authorize the check, the rule of Price v. Neal places the loss of the unauthorized signature on the payor bank rather than the depositary bank. This is a bad result because the depositary bank is in a better position to monitor the behavior of its customer, the telemarketer, than is the payor bank. The 2002 revisions of Article 3 impose the risk of an unauthorized signature on the depositary bank, following the lead of several states that had done so by amendments earlier. "Remotely-created consumer item" is defined in 3–103(a)(16) as meaning a check that "does not bear a handwritten signature purporting to be the signature of the drawer." Under 3–416(a)(6) the telemarketer warrants to the depositary bank that the check is authorized by the person on whom the check is drawn, and 3–417(a)(4) provides that the telemarketer and depositary bank warrant the same to the payor bank. These amendments are described in Comment 8 to 3–416 as implementing "a limited rejection of Price v. Neal."

These amendments to the UCC do nothing to address the concern that the use of "remotely-created" checks by telemarketers is subject to abuse. Congress intervened to provide a degree of consumer protection by enacting the Telemarketing and Consumer Fraud and Abuse Prevention Act in 1994, which requires the Federal Trade Commission to issue rules "prohibiting deceptive telemarketing acts or practices." 15 U.S.C. § 6102(a)(1).

Pursuant to this, the FTC rule provides that it is a deceptive telemarketing practice to submit for payment a draft drawn on a person's deposit account without that person's "express verifiable authorization." Authorization is deemed verifiable if the customer's authorization is obtained either in writing or on tape or if written confirmation of the transaction is sent to the customer prior to submission for payment of the customer's draft. 16 CFR § 310.3(a)(3). The pre-authorized check issue is extensively discussed in 1 Clark & Clark, The Law of Bank Deposits, Collections and Credit Cards & 10.02[2] (Rev. ed. 2003).

The FTC's Telemarketing Sales Rule, establishing the "Do–Not–Call" registry, 16 CFR § 310.4(b)(1)(iii), Mar. 31, 2003, should significantly reduce the volume of telemarketing sales, and, presumably, the abuses associated with telemarketing. Congress ratified the FTC Rule in HR 3161, Public Law No. 108–82, Sept. 25, 2003.

d. OVERDRAFTS

If a payor bank pays a check that is forged or which bears a forged indorsement, it is clear that the bank paid the check by mistake. No bank would knowingly pay such a check because the check is not properly payable and the payor bank is not entitled to charge the account of the drawer. The payment of a check drawn on an account in which there are insufficient funds to cover the check is different. Under 4–401(a) such a check is properly payable and the drawer's account can be charged. Thus, it may not be clear at the time of payment whether the payor bank paid by mistake or intended to grant credit to the drawer. Intentional payment of checks that create overdrafts is very common. There is some authority denying a payor bank any right of restitution in overdraft cases, but most courts follow Restatement of Restitution § 29 (1937), which recognizes a limited right of restitution in such cases. In Article 3, overdraft cases are governed by 3–418(b) which gives to the payor bank a right to recover "to the extent permitted by the law governing mistake and restitution." But 3–418(b) is subject to 3–418(c). No right of restitution may be asserted against a person who took the check in good faith and for value or who in good faith changed position in reliance on payment of the check.

3. CONVERSION ACTIONS REGARDING CHECKS BEARING FORGED INDORSEMENT

a. ACTION BY PAYEE

(1) INTRODUCTION

Section 3–420(a) restates the common law rule: "An instrument is * * * converted if it is taken by transfer, other than a negotiation, from a person not entitled to enforce the instrument or a bank makes or obtains payment with respect to the instrument for a person not entitled to enforce the instrument or receive payment." Thus, a person, including a depositary bank, taking after a forged indorsement is a converter, as is a drawee bank that pays such an instrument. A payee or other holder from whom the instrument has been taken has a choice of suing either the depositary bank (3–420(c)) or the drawee bank for the conversion even though neither knew that the indorsement was forged. Bear in mind in considering the liability of depositary banks that almost as many checks are deposited as are written—more than 50 billion a year. Solve the following Problem on the basis of the text set out below and the statutes cited.

PROBLEM

Electronic Supply Co. (ESC) sells products by mail order and over the Internet as well as at its retail store, which also serves as its headquarters. Most of its sales are paid for by credit cards or cash but some are by checks drawn on banks throughout the nation. Thief, a former employee, broke into the retail store after the close of business and stole cash and unindorsed checks payable to ESC from buyers. He had prepared a stamp, bearing ESC's name, which he used to indorse the stolen checks. Beneath the stamped indorsement, Thief signed the name he used as an account holder at Depositary Bank (DB) and made an ATM deposit of the stolen checks in DB before dawn. The various payor banks on which the checks were drawn paid the checks when presented by DB though banking channels. DB allowed Thief to withdraw the proceeds of the checks before the forgeries were discovered. What are ESC's remedies with respect to (i) the drawers of the checks, (ii) the several payor banks on which the checks were drawn, and (iii) DB? Which remedy would you advise ESC to use? Why?

In a common type of forged indorsement case, the check is stolen by an employee of the payee. The check is an ordinary check mailed to the payee by the drawer in payment of an obligation owed to the payee. The check is received by the payee when the mail delivery is made and the payee becomes a holder of the check at that time. Suppose the check is stolen by an employee of the payee who works as a clerk in the payee's mailroom. The employee forges the payee's name as an indorsement of the check, and obtains payment from the drawee bank. How does the theft of the check and its collection affect the payee's rights with respect to the check and the obligation of the drawer to the payee that the check was intended to pay? Under 3–310(b), the obligation for which the check was received becomes "suspended" at the time the payee receives the check. In the hands of the payee, the check represents a right to receive money, which is a property right of the payee. This property right is provisionally substituted for the right of the payee to enforce the obligation for which the check was received. If the payee receives payment of the check, the obligation for which the check was received is discharged to the extent of the payment. 3–310(b)(1). If the payee presents the check for payment and the check is dishonored, the payee has a cause of action against the drawer of the check either on the check (3–414(b)) or on the obligation for which the check was received. 3–310(b)(3).

What rights does the payee have if the check is stolen from the payee and the thief obtains payment from the drawee? Under 3–310(b)(1) "[p]ayment * * * of the check" results in discharge of the obligation for which a check was taken, but under 3–602(a), the check is not paid unless payment is made to a person entitled to enforce the check. Payment to the thief or a transferee of the thief does not result in payment of the check, and the obligation of the drawer on the check is not discharged. The payee of the check remains the owner of the check and the person entitled to enforce it. 3–301 and 3–309 (lost instruments). The drawee's payment to a person not entitled to enforce the check does not affect the payee's rights in the check. The payee, however, does not have a right to enforce the obligation for which the check was received. That obligation remains suspended under 3–310(b) because neither dishonor nor payment of the check has occurred. Under the last sentence of 3–310(b)(4), the payee of a stolen check who is not in possession of the check, has rights against the drawer only on the check. 3–309, 3–414, and Comment 4 to 3–310. Thus, the payee has the burden of asserting rights with respect to the stolen check, and there are several possible courses of action available to the payee against third parties as well as the drawer.

Although the payee from whom a check has been stolen has no right to obtain a substitute check from the drawer, sometimes the drawer will issue such a check. In the case in which payment with respect to the stolen check has not yet been made by the drawee, the drawee can be informed of the theft and payment to the thief may be avoided. If payment by the drawee has already been made, the drawer can insist that the drawee recredit the drawer's account because payment to the thief did not entitle the drawee to debit the drawer's account. 4–401. If the drawer refuses to issue a replacement check, the payee has a remedy against the drawer on the stolen check, but that remedy may not be convenient. 3–309. Often a forged indorsement case involves thefts of many checks from one payee by the same thief. Actions against the various drawers of the stolen checks may not be feasible. An action against the person who took the checks from the thief is usually a better remedy.

In the hands of the payee, a check is property and, if that property is stolen, the rules of conversion applying to personal property also apply to the check. Thus, the payee of the stolen check has an action in conversion against the thief for the amount of the check. But the law of conversion also allows an action to be brought against "innocent converters," i.e. persons who exercise dominion over stolen property without knowledge that it was stolen. Thus, if a thief sells stolen goods to a good faith purchaser for value, the owner has an action against the BFP as well. A stolen check bearing the forged indorsement of the payee can be turned into money by selling it to a depositary bank or other purchaser for cash, by depositing it to the thief's bank account for bank credit that can subsequently be withdrawn, or by presenting the check for payment to the drawee bank. Each of these takers of the check is a potential defendant. The common law was clear that a conversion action could be brought by the payee against the person who bought the check. The common law cases were divided on the issue of whether the drawee bank was liable in conversion if it paid a stolen check bearing a forged indorsement, but most courts held that a conversion action was available and that view was adopted by Article 3. Article 3 states the rules regarding conversion in 3–420.

(2) DELIVERY OF CHECK TO PAYEE

Pre-revision authorities were divided on whether the payee of a check could sue a depositary bank for conversion when the check had been stolen before it was delivered to the payee. Section 3–420(a)(ii) states the view that a payee cannot bring conversion unless it has received delivery. Comment 1 explains that a payee has no interest in the check until it receives delivery. If a check has not been delivered to the payee, its rights against the drawer have not been affected by the theft; the drawer is still liable to the payee on the underlying obligation.

Article 3 does not define "delivery." It states that delivery may either be made directly to the payee or to an agent or co-payee. 3–420(a)(ii). Comment 1 to 3–420 says that a payee receives delivery when the check comes into the payee's possession. Words like "delivery," "agency," and "possession" are familiar but inexact terms, and Article 9 leaves their meaning to the body of common law that has grown around them. Clearly, delivery of a settlement check to the plaintiff's dishonest attorney is delivery to the plaintiff's agent. Leeds v. Chase Manhattan Bank, 752 A.2d 332 (N.J. Super. 2000). Comment 1 opines on a recurring issue when it observes that a payee has possession when a check is put into its mailbox. The court in Hancock Bank v. Ensenat, 819 So.2d 3 (Miss. App. 2001), relied on this Comment to hold that possession occurs when the check arrives at the payee's home mailing address.

(3) LIABILITY OF DEPOSITARY BANK AS AGENT FOR COLLECTION

When a check is transferred to a depositary bank by its customer, the bank sometimes purchases the check from the customer by giving cash for it or by giving the customer a credit to the customer's account immediately available for withdrawal as of right. More commonly the depositary bank doesn't buy the check. Rather, it takes the check as agent of the customer to obtain payment of the check from the payor bank and pays the proceeds of the check to the customer after the check is paid. This distinction can have some importance in Article 3 because the status of the depositary bank as a holder in due course may depend upon whether it had given value for the check at the time the check was presented for payment. But in Article 4 the depositary bank is normally treated as an agent for collection whether or not the bank gave value to the customer for the check. 4–201(a).

Under Former Article 3, the statute appeared to provide that a depositary bank, as well as subsequent collecting banks, was not liable for conversion if it acted merely as an agent for collection. This was a reversal of the common law rule, and some courts, by using creative statutory construction, refused to follow the literal wording of the statute. In justifying their deliberate misreading of the statute, courts pointed out that to do otherwise produced the ridiculous result that forced the payee to sue the payor bank in conversion and the payor bank to proceed against the depositary bank for breach of its presentment warranty. Two lawsuits instead of one. The issue is well discussed in Denn v. First State Bank, 316 N.W.2d 532 (Minn.1982), in which the court reluctantly read the statute literally but acknowledged that to do so produced a bad result.

Section 3–420(a) and (c) return to the pre-UCC rule that allowed the payee to sue the depositary bank directly in conversion. Not only is judicial economy served because the bank of first deposit is ultimately liable in forged indorsement cases owing to its presentment warranty to the payor bank under 3–417(a)(1), 4–208(a)(1), but also it is usually the most convenient defendant for the payee to sue in the common case of multiple forgeries in which an employee has forged the indorsement of the employer on checks drawn on many different payor banks, some in different states. Comment 3.

(4) UNAUTHORIZED INDORSEMENT

If a check is made payable to two persons, ambiguity sometimes arises whether both must indorse for the instrument to be negotiated or whether either may do so. Section 3–110(d) provides that if an instrument is payable to two or more persons alternatively, either may indorse, but if it is payable to them "not alternatively," all signatures are required. Section 3–403(b) states that the signature of an organization is unauthorized if one of the required signatures is lacking. How can we be sure when an instrument is payable to them alternatively so that one signature may constitute a negotiation?

PROBLEM

In each of the following cases, the check was indorsed only by Michael Bijlani & Assoc. and was deposited in Bank. Under 3–110(d), in which case or cases should Bank have demanded Bay Village Inc.'s signature before taking the check?

Case #1.   The check was payable to "Bay Village Inc. Michael Bijlani & Assoc." See Bijlani v. Nationsbank of Florida, 25 UCC Rep. Serv. 2d 1165, 1995 WL 264180 (Fla. Cir. Ct. 1995).

Case #2.   How would Case #1 be decided if there were a slash (/) or virgule between "Inc." and "Michael"? See Purina Mills, Inc. v. Security Bank & Trust, 215 Mich.App. 549, 547 N.W.2d 336 (Mich.App. 1996); Danco, Inc. v. Commerce Bank/Shore, N.A., 675 A.2d 663 (N.J.Sup.Ct. 1996).

Case #3. How would Case #1 be decided if there were a hyphen between "Inc." and "Michael"? See J.R. Simplot, Inc. v. Knight, 988 P.2d 955 (Wash. 1999).

(5) FORGERY BY ENTRUSTED EMPLOYEE OF PAYEE

As we stated earlier, perhaps the most common cases of forged indorsements are the "inside jobs." An employee entrusted with the responsibility of dealing with checks payable to the employer forges the indorsement of the employer and covers up the forgery in the reconcilement process. Section 3–406(a) provides that if the payor bank can prove that the employer's failure to supervise the employee's activities and to check the financial records that the employee kept substantially contributed to the forgery, it can throw the forgery loss back on the employer. In the drafting of Revised Article 3, the contention was made that it was unfair to impose on the bank the burden of proving the employer's negligence. If the employer chose to entrust responsibility to an employee and the employee betrayed the trust, isn't it fair to put the risk of loss with respect to the employee's misconduct on the employer rather than the bank? The original Code recognized in Comment 4 to former 3–405 that in such cases the loss should fall on the employer as the risk of its business enterprise because it is normally in a better position to prevent forgeries by reasonable care in selecting or supervising employees "or if he is not, is at least in a better position to cover the loss by fidelity insurance." Section 3–405 implements this policy.

The following scenario is a summary of some of the facts, somewhat modified, of Cooper v. Union Bank, 9 Cal.3d 371, 107 Cal.Rptr. 1, 507 P.2d 609 (Cal. 1973). This fact situation is one of the templates the drafters had in mind in writing 3–405 and its analysis offers an informative journey through the statute. See Comment 3, Case #3.

> Stell, a lawyer, was retained by Ruff to represent her in connection with her insolvency and litigation brought against her by several creditors. She informed Stell that her financial difficulties were primarily due to gambling losses she had sustained. A short time later Stell hired Ruff as a secretary and bookkeeper. Ruff's duties included posting the amounts of checks received by Stell to the proper accounts in Stell's accounting records and reconciling the monthly bank statement of deposits and withdrawals with respect to Stell's checking account with Stell's accounting records. Over a period of a year and a half, Ruff stole 29 checks payable to Stell that were received in the mail, and forged Stell's indorsement to these checks. Most of these checks were cashed over the counter at Depositary Bank at which both Stell and Ruff had checking accounts. A few of the checks were deposited to Ruff's account in Depositary Bank. Stell was well known to the tellers at the bank as a customer of the bank and Ruff was well known as Stell's secretary. It was the policy of Depositary Bank to allow checks payable to known customers to be cashed over the counter by the customer or the customer's secretary. The forgeries by Ruff

were so well done that only a handwriting expert could have detected them.

Stell exercised almost no supervision over Ruff, never reviewed the books that she kept, and never checked the bank reconciliation of deposits to Stell's checking account. Stell brought an action in conversion against Depositary Bank with respect to the 29 checks that were transferred by Ruff to that bank.

Under the second sentence of 3–420(a), Depositary Bank is liable to Stell as a converter of the 29 checks that Ruff transferred to it if (1) Depositary Bank did not become the holder of the checks as a result of the transfer, i.e., the transfer was not a negotiation, and (2) Ruff was not a person entitled to enforce the checks when she transferred them to Depositary Bank, i.e., she was not a holder at the time of the transfer. Both of these elements depend upon whether the forgery by Ruff of Stell's signature was effective as Stell's indorsement in spite of the fact that it was a forgery. Section 3–405 addresses this issue.

Section 3–405 applies to this case if a "fraudulent indorsement" (3–405(a)(2)) was made by Ruff, and Ruff was entrusted by Stell, her employer, with "responsibility" (3–405(a)(3)) with respect to the checks that she transferred to Depositary Bank. Under the first sentence of 3–405(b), is the indorsement by Ruff effective as the indorsement of Stell? The first and last paragraphs of Comment 1 to 3–405 address this issue. The Ruff–Stell scenario should be compared with Case #1, Case #3, and Case #4 of Comment 3 to 3–405. If Stell is not entitled to recover from Depositary Bank as a converter of the 29 checks because of the first sentence of 3–405(b), is Stell entitled to any recovery against Depositary Bank based on the last sentence of 3–405(b)? Under that sentence is there any difference in result with respect to the checks cashed over the counter and the checks deposited to Ruff's account?

b. ACTION BY DRAWER

Forged indorsement cases usually involve a theft of the check from the payee, but sometimes the theft of the check occurs before the check is received by the payee. In *Stone & Webster,* which follows, an employee of the drawer of several checks stole the checks from the drawer before the checks could be mailed to the payee. The stolen checks were intended to pay debts of the drawer to the payee. In such a case the payee has no legal claim with respect to the checks because the payee never received them. The theft of the check and payment by the drawee to the thief do not change payee's rights with respect to the debt for which the check was written. The payee never became the owner of the check and the drawer's debt to the payee remains unpaid. 3–310(b) does not apply. The drawer of the stolen check has a continuing obligation to pay the debt for which the check was issued and thus is obliged to issue a replacement check to the payee.

The drawer normally will not suffer any loss with respect to a check bearing a forged indorsement if the drawer is free of negligence contributing to the theft and forgery. 3–406. The payor bank may not charge the drawer's account because a check bearing a forged indorsement is not properly payable according to Comment 1 to 4–401(a). Thus, the drawer is entitled to have the account in the payor bank credited for the amount of the payment. This remedy of the drawer is clear and convenient since in most cases the drawer's account will be in a local bank. Nevertheless, there have been a number of cases in which the drawer, instead of suing the payor bank, sued the depositary bank. Such a suit might be brought in the uncommon case in which the depositary bank is a local bank and the payor bank is out of state, or the drawer may simply be reluctant to sue the payor bank with which the drawer has a favorable business relationship. The issue in these cases is whether the drawer of a check stolen from it has a property right in the check that can be asserted in a conversion action. The authority on the issue was divided under original Article 3. The view expressed in the seminal case of *Stone & Webster* was adopted by 3–420(a)(i).

Stone & Webster Engineering Corp. v. First National Bank & Trust Co.

Supreme Judicial Court of Massachusetts, 1962.
345 Mass. 1, 184 N.E.2d 358.

■ WILKINS, CHIEF JUSTICE.

In this action of contract or tort in four counts for the same cause of action a demurrer to the declaration was sustained, and the plaintiff, described in the writ as having a usual place of business in Boston, appealed. G.L. (Ter.Ed.) c. 231, § 96. The questions argued concern the rights of the drawer against a collecting bank which "cashed" checks for an individual who had forged the payee's indorsement on the checks, which were never delivered to the payee.

In the first count, which is in contract, the plaintiff alleges that between January 1, 1960, and May 15, 1960, it was indebted at various times to Westinghouse Electric Corporation (Westinghouse) for goods and services furnished to it by Westinghouse; that in order to pay the indebtedness the plaintiff drew three checks within that period on its checking account in The First National Bank of Boston (First National) payable to Westinghouse in the total amount of $64,755.44; that before delivery of the checks to Westinghouse an employee of the plaintiff in possession of the checks forged the indorsement of Westinghouse and presented the checks to the defendant; that the defendant "cashed" the checks and delivered the proceeds to the plaintiff's employee who devoted the proceeds to his own use; that the defendant forwarded the checks to First National and received from First National the full amounts thereof; and that First National charged the account of the plaintiff with the full amounts of the checks and has refused to recredit the plaintiff's checking account; wherefore the defendant owes the plaintiff $64,755.44 with interest.

Count 2, also in contract, is on an account annexed for money owed, namely $64,755.44, the proceeds of checks of the plaintiff "cashed" by the defendant on forged indorsements between January 1, 1960, and May 15, 1960.

Counts 3 and 4 in tort are respectively for conversion of the checks and for negligence in "cashing" the checks with forged indorsements.

By order, copies of the three checks were filed in court. The checks are respectively dated at Rowe in this Commonwealth on January 5, March 8, and May 9, 1960. Their respective amounts are $36,982.86, $10,416.58 and $17,355. They are payable to the order of "Westinghouse Electric Corporation, 10 High Street, Boston." The first two checks are indorsed in typewriting, "For Deposit Only: Westinghouse Electric Corporation By: Mr. O. D. Costine, Treasury Representative" followed by an ink signature "O. D. Costine." The Third check is indorsed in typewriting, "Westinghouse Electric Corporation By: [Sgd.] O. D. Costine Treasury Representative." All three checks also bear the indorsement by rubber stamp, "Pay to the order of any bank, banker or trust co. prior indorsements guaranteed * * * [date][1] The First National Bank & Trust Co. Greenfield, Mass."

The demurrer, in so far as it has been argued, is to each count for failure to state a cause of action.

* * *

1.   Count 1, the plaintiff contends, is for money had and received. We shall so regard it. "An action for money had and received lies to recover money which should not in justice be retained by the defendant, and which in equity and good conscience should be paid to the plaintiff." Cobb v. Library Bureau, 268 Mass. 311, 316, 167 N.E. 765, 767; Adams v. First Nat. Bank, 321 Mass. 693, 694, 75 N.E.2d 502; Trafton v. Custeau, 338 Mass. 305, 308, 155 N.E.2d 159.

The defendant has no money in its hands which belongs to the plaintiff. The latter had no right in the proceeds of its own check payable to Westinghouse. Not being a holder or an agent for a holder, it could not have presented the check to the drawee for payment. * * * See Uniform Commercial Code § 3–419, comment 2: "A negotiable instrument is the property of the holder." See also Restatement 2d: Torts, Tent. draft no. 3, 1958, § 241A. The plaintiff contends that "First National paid or credited the proceeds of the checks to the defendant and charged the account of the plaintiff, and consequently, the plaintiff was deprived of a credit, and the defendant received funds or a credit which 'in equity and good conscience' belonged to the plaintiff."

---

1. The respective dates are January 13, March 9, and May 11, 1960. Each check bears the stamped indorsement of the Federal Reserve Bank of Boston and on its face the paid stamp of The First National Bank of Boston.

In our opinion this argument is a non sequitur. The plaintiff as a depositor in First National was merely in a contractual relationship of creditor and debtor. * * * The amounts the defendant received from First National to cover the checks "cashed" were the bank's funds and not the plaintiff's. The Uniform Commercial Code does not purport to change the relationship. * * * Section 3–409(1) provides: "A check or other draft does not of itself operate as an assignment of any funds in the hands of the drawee available for its payment, and the drawee is not liable on the instrument until he accepts it." * * * Whether the plaintiff was rightfully deprived of a credit is a matter between it and the drawee, First National.

If we treat the first count as seeking to base a cause of action for money had and received upon a waiver of the tort of conversion—a matter which it is not clear is argued—the result will be the same. In this aspect the question presented is whether a drawer has a right of action for conversion against a collecting bank which handles its checks in the bank collection process. Unless there be such a right, there is no tort which can be waived.

The plaintiff relies upon the Uniform Commercial Code § 3–419, which provides, "(1) An instrument is converted when * * * (c) it is paid on a forged indorsement." This, however, could not apply to the defendant, which is not a "payor bank," defined in the Code, § 4–105(b), as "a bank by which an item is payable as drawn or accepted." * * *

A conversion provision of the Uniform Commercial Code which might have some bearing on this case is § 3–419(3). This section implicitly recognizes that, subject to defences, including the one stated in it, a collecting bank, defined in the Code, § 4–105(d), may be liable in conversion. In the case at bar the forged indorsements were "wholly inoperative" as the signatures of the payee, Code §§ 3–404(1), 1–201(43), and equally so both as to the restrictive indorsements for deposits, see § 3–205(c), and as to the indorsement in blank, see § 3–204(2). When the forger transferred the checks to the collecting bank, no negotiation under § 3–202(1) occurred, because there was lacking the necessary indorsement of the payee. For the same reason, the collecting bank could not become a "holder" as defined in § 1–201(20), and so could not become a holder in due course under § 3–302(1). Accordingly, we assume that the collecting bank may be liable in conversion to a proper party, subject to defences, including that in § 3–419(3). See A. Blum, Jr.'s, Sons v. Whipple, 194 Mass. 253, 255, 80 N.E. 501, 13 L.R.A.,N.S., 211. But there is no explicit provision in the Code purporting to determine to whom the collecting bank may be liable, and consequently, the drawer's right to enforce such a liability must be found elsewhere. Therefore, we conclude that the case must be decided on our own law, which, on the issue we are discussing, has been left untouched by the Uniform Commercial Code in any specific section. * * *

The authorities are hopelessly divided. We think that the preferable view is that there is no right of action. * * *

We state what appears to us to be the proper analysis. Had the checks been delivered to the payee Westinghouse, the defendant might have been liable for conversion to the payee. The checks, if delivered, in the hands of the payee would have been valuable property which could have been transferred for value or presented for payment; and, had a check been dishonored, the payee would have had a right of recourse against the drawer on the instrument under § 3–413(2). Here the plaintiff drawer of the checks, which were never delivered to the payee * * *, had no valuable rights in them. Since, as we have seen, it did not have the right of a payee or subsequent holder to present them to the drawee for payment, the value of its rights was limited to the physical paper on which they were written, and was not measured by their payable amounts. * * *

The enactment of the Uniform Commercial Code opens the road for the adoption of what seems the preferable view. An action by the drawer against the collecting bank might have some theoretical appeal as avoiding circuity of action. * * * It would have been in the interest of speedy and complete justice had the case been tried with the action by the drawer against the drawee and with an action by the drawee against the collecting bank. * * * So one might ask: If the drawee is liable to the drawer and the collecting bank is liable to the drawee, why not let the drawer sue the collecting bank direct? We believe that the answer lies in the applicable defences set up in the Code.

The drawer can insist that the drawee recredit his account with the amount of any unauthorized payment. Such was our common law. * * * This is, in effect, retained by the Code §§ 4–401(1), 4–406(4). But the drawee has defences based upon the drawer's substantial negligence, if "contributing," or upon his duty to discover and report unauthorized signatures and alterations. §§ 3–406, 4–406. As to unauthorized indorsements, see § 4–406(4). Then, if the drawee has a valid defence which it waives or fails upon request to assert, the drawee may not assert against the collecting bank or other prior party presenting or transferring the check a claim which is based on the forged indorsement. § 4–406(5). * * * If the drawee recredits the drawer's account and is not precluded by § 4–406(5), it may claim against the presenting bank on the relevant warranties in §§ 3–417 and 4–207, and each transferee has rights against his transferor under those sections.

If the drawer's rights are limited to requiring the drawee to recredit his account, the drawee will have the defences noted above and perhaps others; and the collecting bank or banks will have the defences in § 4–207(4) and § 4–406(5), and perhaps others. If the drawer is allowed in the present case to sue the collecting bank, the assertion of the defences, for all practical purposes, would be difficult. The possibilities of such a result would tend to compel resort to litigation in every case involving a forgery of commercial paper. It is a result to be avoided.

[The court sustained demurrers to all plaintiff's counts.]

PROBLEM

Employee stole an unindorsed check from her employer, Payee, forged Payee's indorsement and deposited it in Depositary Bank (DB) for collection. Payor Bank (PB) paid the check upon presentment and debited Drawer's account for the amount of the check. When the forgery was discovered, PB erased the debit to Drawer's account and relied on DB's breach of presentment warranty in demanding the return of the amount that it paid DB in settlement for the check. DB defended on the ground that Drawer's lack of due care substantially contributed to the forgery and that PB should debit Drawer's account under 3–405 or 3–406 rather than proceeding against DB for breach of its warranty. If Drawer's conduct contributed to the forgery, should PB be allowed to shift the loss from the drawer to DB? See 3–417(c), Comment 6 to 3–417, and 4–208(c). DB's liability to PB is only to reimburse it for any loss resulting from the breach of warranty. 3–417(b), 4–208(b). If Drawer may not raise the forgery against PB because of 3–405 or 3–406, has PB been damaged by DB's breach of presentment warranty?

4. IMPOSTORS AND FICTITIOUS PAYEES

We have seen that in forged indorsement cases, as a general rule, the loss falls on the bank of first deposit, the bank that dealt with the forger. But exceptions have been made to this rule in certain situations in which it seems unfair to allocate the loss in this manner. One of these exceptions is the impostor cases, covered by 3–404(a). Another is the fictitious payee cases, governed by 3–404(b). Still another is the payroll-padding cases to which 3–405 and other provisions apply. The drafting stratagem used to identify these cases in Article 3 is largely based on the intent of the issuer of the instrument with respect to the person to whom the instrument is payable. Hence, before looking at the exceptions, we examine the intent issue.

a. INTENT OF ISSUER

In some cases in which a forged indorsement is alleged, it may not be clear whether there is a forged indorsement because it is not clear to whom the instrument is payable. In identifying the person to whom the instrument is payable, the starting point is 3–110.

Suppose Jane Doe writes a check to the order of Richard Roe. Under 3–110(a) the intent of Doe determines to whom the check is payable. There may be many people in the world named Richard Roe, but only the Richard Roe intended by Doe is the payee of the check. If the check gets into the hands of a different Richard Roe, an indorsement by that Richard Roe is ineffective as an indorsement of the payee of the check.

Change the facts. Suppose Doe made a mistake in writing the check. Intending to issue a check to a person that she thinks is Richard Roe, she writes that name as the payee of the check. In fact the name of the person to whom she intended to issue the check is Peter Poe and Poe has never used the name Richard Roe. If Doe delivers the check to Poe, Poe becomes the holder of the check even though the check states that it is payable to Richard Roe. An indorsement by Poe is effective because Poe is the payee of the check. Poe may indorse by signing either the name on the check or Poe's name. 3–110(a) and 3–204(d).

The rules stated in 3–110(a) apply to the issuer of a negotiable instrument in determining to whom the instrument is initially payable and the same rules apply in determining to whom an instrument is subsequently made payable by a holder making a special indorsement. 3–205(a). Thus, if Jane Doe is the payee of the check rather than the drawer and she indorses the check with the indorsement "Pay to Richard Roe," the person to whom the check becomes payable is determined by Doe's intent according to the rules in 3–110.

Section 3–110 is also important with respect to forged checks. Suppose Thief steals Jane Doe's checkbook and forges her name to a check on her bank account. The check is made payable to Richard Roe. Although Thief's act of signing Doe's name to the check is ineffective as the signature of Doe, the signature is effective as Thief's signature. 3–403(a). Under 3–110(a), it is the intention of Thief, the drawer of the check, that determines to whom the check is payable.

An organization such as a corporation must act through human agents in the drawing of checks, and the organization normally identifies officers who are authorized to sign checks in behalf of the organization. Often, the organization requires that its checks be signed by more than one authorized officer. Under 3–110(a) the intent of the authorized officer or officers signing in behalf of the organization determines to whom the check is payable. But in many cases, checks of organizations do not bear any manually-made signature in behalf of the organization. Rather, the check is produced by a check-writing machine and the signature of the drawer is a printed or facsimile signature. The terms of the check, including the name of the payee, are determined by information entered into the computer that controls the check-writing machine. The person providing the information usually is an authorized employee acting in good faith in behalf of the organization, but sometimes the person providing the information is acting fraudulently and might be either an employee authorized to operate the machine or a wholly unauthorized person. In all of these cases the intention of the person supplying the information determines to whom the check is payable. 3–110(b).

People engaged in fraud usually try to mask the fraud. For example, an employee authorized to operate a corporation's check-writing machine wishes to steal money by obtaining payment of checks produced by the machine. Instead of causing the machine to produce checks payable to the employee, the employee causes the machine to produce checks payable to a different payee. The payee named on the check may be an imaginary person, a so-called "fictitious payee," or the check may name as payee a real person who is not intended to have any interest in the check. In either case, the intent of the dishonest employee is to produce a check for the employee's benefit that the employee can turn into cash after indorsing it by signing the name of the payee indicated on the check. In either case, to whom is the check payable? Is the indorsement by the employee an effective indorsement or a forgery? These cases are governed by 3–404(b) which validates the indorsement and allows the check to be negotiated by the employee.

b.   IMPOSTORS

Although 3–110(a) states that the intent of the person writing the check determines to whom the check is payable, in some cases it is not possible to clearly identify the payee that way. These cases involve issuance of checks to impostors. For example, if Rogers by impersonating Jacobs induces Drawer to issue to her an instrument payable to Jacobs, Drawer might well have dual intent: to make the check payable to the person to whom he issued the instrument (Rogers) and to the person he thought Rogers was (Jacobs). In this case the statute resolves the case by providing that if Rogers induced Drawer to issue the instrument to him by impersonating Jacobs, Roger's indorsement of Jacobs' name on the instrument is effective. 3–404(a). Since business organizations must operate through the acts of their agents, cases involving malefactors who impersonate agents are common. Unlike its predecessor, 3–404(a) applies to such impersonations.

PROBLEMS

1.   Pauley fraudulently induced Martini to write a check on Bank One for $5,000 payable to Herman by convincing Martini that Pauley was Herman, a person of high repute. Pauley took the check from Martini, indorsed Herman's name on the back of the check and deposited the check in Pauley's account in Bank Two. The check was presented by Bank Two to Bank One, Martini's bank, which paid the check. Pauley withdrew all the funds in his account in Bank Two and absconded. Martini claims that Bank One cannot debit his account for the amount of the check because Herman's indorsement was forged. Is Martini correct? See 3–404(a).

2.   Pauley induced Martini to write a check on Bank One for $5,000 to the Red Cross of Cook County by leading Martini to believe that Pauley was chair of the local Red Cross chapter. Pauley wrote two indorsements on the check: first, "Cook County Red Cross", and second, "Pauley". Pauley deposited the check in his account in Bank Two, which presented it to Bank One, Martini's bank, which paid the check. Pauley withdrew the funds representing the check from his account and absconded. Martini claims that Bank One cannot debit his account for the amount of the check because Pauley forged the indorsement by writing "Cook County Red Cross" on the back of the check. Is Martini correct. See Comment 1 to 3–404.

The following case compares the former and the present impostor provisions with respect to agency impersonations. How does it help you solve the preceding problems?

Title Insurance Company of Minnesota v. Comerica Bank–California

Court of Appeal, Sixth District, 1994.
27 Cal.App.4th 800, 32 Cal.Rptr.2d 735.

■ MIHARA, ASSOCIATE JUSTICE.

At issue in this appeal is the applicability and scope of the "impostor rule," which makes an indorsed check effective if the drawer was induced to issue the check by an impersonator of the payee. (Com.Code, § 3404, subd. (a); former Com.Code, § 3405, subd. (1)(a).) Plaintiff Title Insurance Company of Minnesota contends the trial court erroneously applied this rule in sustaining the demurrer of the drawee bank, respondent Comerica Bank–California ("Bank"), to plaintiff's complaint for negligence. We agree that the impostor rule is not applicable under the circumstances presented, and accordingly reverse the judgment of dismissal.

ALLEGATIONS OF THE COMPLAINT

* * *

Plaintiff is the assignee of the interests of First National Mortgage Company ("FNMC"), who made two equity loans to Helen Nastor ("Helen"), secured by deeds of trust. Plaintiff issued a policy of land title insurance for each of these loans.

On September 22, 1988, FNMC issued a check payable to Helen in the amount of $58,659.29, the proceeds of the first loan. FNMC gave the check to Helen's son, Rudy Nastor ("Rudy"), for delivery to Helen. That day, someone impersonating Helen indorsed the check and presented it to Bank, where FNMC held an account. Bank paid the impersonator the full amount of the check.

On December 29, 1988, FNMC made a second loan to Helen in the amount of $108,300. Part of the proceeds of this loan were used to pay off the first loan. The remainder was issued to Rudy in the form of a check made payable to him.

When FNMC failed to receive payment on the $108,300 loan, it initiated nonjudicial foreclosure proceedings against Helen's property. On October 17, 1989, Helen's attorney informed FNMC that its deed of trust on the property was invalid because it had been executed by Rudy using a forged power of attorney. Helen thereafter testified by deposition that she had not executed the power of attorney, nor had she indorsed or presented the check to Bank for payment.

FNMC made a claim for payment under the second title insurance policy, and plaintiff paid FNMC $108,300. Plaintiff, acting as subrogee and assignee with respect to FNMC's claim, then sued Bank for negligence, seeking recovery of the $108,000. According to the first amended complaint, Bank had a duty "to establish and practice such procedures and business practices as are or may be reasonably necessary and effective to avoid a breach of any of the duties of care owed by BANK . . . to the depositors and customers of BANK ... including therein a duty to immediately inform customers such as FNMC when impostors and/or forgers attempt to cash a check drawn on such customers' accounts with BANK." Bank breached this duty, plaintiff alleged, by failing to ensure "that only properly endorsed and presented checks of its depositors [were] paid." Had Bank "caught" the impostor trying to cash the check payable to Helen, it would have informed FNMC of the attempt, and FNMC would have discovered the forged power of attorney before it made the second loan.

APPLICABILITY OF THE IMPOSTOR RULE

Bank's demurrer is based entirely on the asserted applicability of the impostor rule, which, according to Bank, interposes an "absolute defense" against plaintiff's allegations of negligence. Bank relies on the current provisions of section 3404, subdivision (a) (hereafter, "section 3404(a)"), which makes an indorsement by any person effective if an impostor had induced the issuance of the instrument to either the impostor or "a person acting in concert with the impostor."[1] In this case, argues Bank, Rudy was acting in concert with the impostor (the impersonator of Helen), who presented the check to Bank for payment.

Plaintiff responds that section 3404(a) is not applicable, because it was not enacted until 1992, after the events alleged in the complaint. Instead, plaintiff maintains, this case is controlled by former section 3405, subdivision (1)(a) (hereafter, "former section 3405(1)(a)"). The expression of the rule in the latter statute is substantially the same as that of the current provisions, but excluded from its reach are false representations of agency. Because Rudy obtained the check from FNMC by falsely representing that he was authorized to act as Helen's agent, plaintiff argues the transaction at issue is outside the scope of the impostor rule.

We agree with plaintiff that former section 3405(1)(a) governs the disposition of this case, since the events at issue took place in 1988, while that statute was still in effect. Former section 3405(1)(a) provided: "An indorsement by any person in the name of a named payee is effective if (a) An impostor by use of the mails or otherwise has induced the maker or drawer to issue the instrument to him or his confederate in the name of the payee...."

This section does not protect Bank from liability under the circumstances presented. As one California court explained prior to the enactment of former section 3405, the impostor rule is applicable only when the issuance of the check has been accomplished through *impersonation* of the payee: "[W]here a check is delivered to an impostor as payee and the drawer believes that the impostor is the person upon whose endorsement it

---

1. Section 3404(a) states: "If an impostor, by use of the mails or otherwise, induces the issuer of an instrument to issue the instrument to the impostor, or to a person acting in concert with the impostor, by impersonating the payee of the instrument or a person authorized to act for the payee, an indorsement of the instrument by any person in the name of the payee is effective as the indorsement of the payee in favor of a person who, in good faith, pays the instrument or takes it for value or for collection."

will be paid, the endorsement by such impostor in the name which he is using to impersonate another is not a forgery.... The soundness of the rule obtains in the fact that the money has actually been paid to the person for whom it was really intended. Because another person might bear the very name assumed by the impostor and might have some contractual relationships with the impostor does not subject to a loss the drawee bank when it has paid the check to the person intended as the payee." (Schweitzer v. Bank of America (1941) 42 Cal. App.2d 536, 540, 109 P.2d 441.) * * *

The reasoning of the *Schweitzer* court directs our analysis in the present case. If FNMC (the drawer) had been induced *by an impostor* of Helen to issue the check either to Rudy or to the impostor, then the indorsement would be considered effective as to FNMC under the impostor rule. The rationale for this result is that Bank has paid the person whom FNMC intended to receive the money. When viewed under principles of negligence or estoppel, the outcome of this scenario would be the same: the risk of loss would be shifted to the drawer of the instrument (FNMC), who was in a better position to detect the fraud. (See Fireman's Fund Ins. Co. v. Security Pacific Nat. Bank (1978) 85 Cal. App.3d 797, 830, 149 Cal. Rptr. 883 [burden of loss on party who deals with the forger]; Intelogic v. Merchants Nat. Bank (Ind.App. 2 Dist.1993) 626 N.E.2d 839, 842 [under UCC, loss resulting from forged indorsement should fall upon party best able to prevent it]; East Gadsden Bank v. First City Nat. Bank of Gadsden (1973) 50 Ala.App. 576, 281 So.2d 431, 433 [intended payee theory distinguished from negligence or estoppel theory].)

This case presents different facts, however. Here, FNMC made the check payable to the true Helen, not to an impostor representing herself as Helen. FNMC intended that Helen herself—not a person it believed to be Helen—indorse the check and receive the proceeds. There is no question that FNMC intended to deal solely with Helen. The rationale underlying the protection of the impostor rule thus does not apply here. * * *

A person's false representation that he or she is an agent of the payee is not sufficient. Uniform Commercial Code Comment 2 to former section 3405 notes: " 'Impostor' refers to impersonation, and does not extend to a false representation that the party is the authorized agent of the payee. The maker or drawer who takes the precaution of making the instrument payable to the principal is entitled to have his indorsement." (See Uniform Com.Code com., 23B to § 3405.) Here, Rudy obtained issuance of the check to Helen not by impersonating her, but by falsely representing that he was authorized to act on her behalf. Although clearly fraudulent, this conduct does not constitute impersonation and thus cannot be considered an inducement to issue the instrument within the meaning of former section 3405(1)(a). * * *

Bank's emphasis on the asserted fact that Rudy was acting in concert with Helen's impostor is of no consequence. To invoke the protection of former section 3405(1)(a) Bank would have to point to facts showing that *by impersonation* the impostor induced FNMC to issue the check either to her or to Rudy, her confederate. The complaint alleges no such facts, however. The only impersonation that took place was in the presentation of the check to Bank. * * *

The result is no different even under section 3404(a), the current version of the rule. The only significant change in this section is its recognition that the impostor may pretend to be either the payee or the payee's agent. As the Uniform Commercial Code Comment to the revised law notes, "Under former Section 3–405(1)(a), if Impostor impersonated Smith and induced the drawer to draw a check to the order of Smith, Impostor could negotiate the check. If Impostor impersonated Smith, the president of Smith Corporation, and the check was payable to the order of Smith Corporation, the section did not apply.... Section 3–404(a) gives Impostor the power to negotiate the check in both cases." (See Uniform Com.Code com., 23B to § 3404.) This comment makes it clear that impersonation is still required to invoke the impostor rule, whether the perpetrator of the deception pretends to be the principal or the agent. Misrepresentation of the perpetrator's agency status does not suffice. * * *

We must conclude, therefore, that the impostor rule is inapplicable under these circumstances. By correctly identifying himself as Rudy but falsely representing himself to be Helen's agent Rudy did not engage in the impersonation required by the impostor rule, as expressed both in former section 3405, which was applicable at the time of the transactions at issue, and in its contemporary form, section 3404(a). The impersonation by Helen's impostor cannot be said to have induced FNMC to issue the check, since it took place only afterward, when the impostor presented the check to Bank.

Bank does not challenge the legal sufficiency of the complaint in any respect other than the asserted bar of the impostor rule. Accordingly, we hold that the trial court incorrectly sustained Bank's demurrer based on the application of the impostor rule. * * *

NOTE

Contrast these two cases: Case #1. Rudy induced Drawer to issue a check to Helen Corporation by falsely representing that he was the treasurer of that organization. Case #2. Rudy induced Drawer to issue a check to Helen Corporation by representing that he was Barnes, who actually was the treasurer of Helen Corporation. How would 3–404(a) apply to these cases? Which of these cases most resembles *Title Insurance Company*?

c. FICTITIOUS PAYEES

The two basic fictitious payee cases are set out in Comment 2 to 3–404. In Case #1 Treasurer, authorized to draw checks in behalf of Corporation, fraudulently draws a corporate check to Supplier Co., a non-existent company. 3–404(b)(ii). In Case #2 the facts are the same except that Supplier Co. is an actual company that does business with Corporation, but Treasurer does not intend Supplier Co. to have any interest in the check. 3–404(b)(i). In both cases the Treasurer indorses the checks in the name of

Supplier Co and deposits them in Depositary Bank in an account controlled by Treasurer. Some cases had distinguished between Case #1 in which the payee is truly fictitious and Case #2 in which the payee is an actual person with which Corporation does business. Section 3–404(b) sweeps away this distinction and treats the indorsements as effective as the indorsement of the payee in both cases in favor of Corporation's Payor Bank and the Depositary Bank, if, in good faith, the Payor Bank paid the check or the Depositary Bank cashed the check over the counter or took it for collection.

The effect of the fictitious payee rule under 3–404(b) is to shift the loss to the Drawer instead of the Depositary Bank. Since the indorsement is effective as the indorsement of the payee, Payor Bank can charge Drawer's account because the check is properly payable under 4–401. The statement in Comment 1 to 4–401 that a check containing a forged indorsement is not properly payable does not apply because there is no forged indorsement. If Payor Bank does not charge Drawer's account and elects to proceed against Depositary Bank on breach of its presentment warranty under 4–208(a)(1), it cannot succeed because at the time of presentment Depositary Bank was a holder under 3–404(b)(1). Section 4–208(c) specifically empowers Depositary Bank to defend a breach of warranty suit by Payor Bank by proving that the indorsement is effective under 3–404(b).

Pre-revision 3–405(1) provided that "[a]n indorsement by any person in the name of a named payee is effective" if the drawer did not intend the payee to have an interest in the instrument. Some courts frustrated the manifest policy of this section by holding that even a slight variation between the indorsement and the name of the "named payee" precluded the section from applying, thereby making the indorsement a forgery, with the loss falling on the innocent depositary bank. Section 3–404(c)(i) addresses this problem by providing that an indorsement is made in the name of the person to whom the instrument is payable if it is made in a name substantially similar to the name of that person. Perhaps of greater importance is the provision in 3–404(c)(ii) that no indorsement at all is needed if the check is deposited in an account in a name substantially similar to the name of the person to whom the instrument is made payable.

The most important novelty in 3–404 is subsection (d) which allows "the person bearing the loss" in a fictitious payee case—usually the drawer—to recover from a person who fails to exercise due care in paying or taking an instrument for collection—usually the depositary bank—if that failure substantially contributes to the loss resulting from the payment of the instrument. See Comment 3 to 3–404. An example of the kind of case this provision is intended to deal with is set out in Comment 4 to 3–405: Malefactor works the fictitious payee scam and possesses a check for a large amount payable to the Ford Motor Company, a supplier of Malefactor's employer; Malefactor opens an account in Ford's name in Depositary Bank, asserting that he is the manager of a new Ford branch; he indorses the check in Ford's name, deposits the check and withdraws the proceeds by a wire transfer to a foreign country. Depositary Bank failed to require Malefactor to produce a corporate resolution or other evidence of authorization to act for the corporation when the account was opened. The premise of 3–404(d) is that in some cases the person taking the check might have detected the fraud and prevented the loss by exercise of ordinary care. If that person did not exercise ordinary care, it is reasonable to impose loss on that person to the extent its failure contributed to the loss. Comment 3. We see an application of this provision in *Gina Chin* in the next section.

5. THE DOUBLE FORGERY

We have seen that in cases of a forged drawer's signature the loss is generally borne by the payor bank and in cases of a forged indorsement the loss usually falls on the depositary bank, subject to the important exceptions discussed in this chapter. But what of the case—the all-time favorite negotiable instruments examination question—in which both the drawer's signature and the payee's indorsement are forged, the so-called double forgery? In the following case, Lehman, an employee of Chin, forged the signature of one of Chin's officers on checks payable to Chin's suppliers; Lehman then forged the indorsement of the payee of these checks and deposited them in his account in First Union. Before revision of Article 3, the courts had reached consensus that such cases should be treated as forged check cases, not as forged indorsement cases. The loss should fall on the drawee bank and not the depositary bank because the indorsement is not forged. In short, there is no double forgery; there is only one, the signature of the drawer. How would this case be decided under 3–404(b)? See Case #5 in Comment 2 to 3–404. How does 3–404(d) change this result? Comment 3 to 3–404. 1 Clark & Clark, The Law of Bank Deposits, Collections and Credit Cards & 12.07[3][b] (Rev. ed. 1999); White & Summers, Uniform Commercial Code §§ 15–6, 16–4e (4th ed. 1995).

Gina Chin & Associates, Inc. v. First Union Bank

Supreme Court of Virginia, 1998.
500 S.E.2d 516.

■ LACY, JUSTICE.

Gina Chin & Associates, Inc. (Chin) filed a motion for judgment against First Union Bank alleging that First Union was negligent when it accepted checks drawn on Chin's accounts bearing both forged signatures of the drawer and forged indorsements of the payees. The trial court sustained First Union's demurrer and entered summary judgment. We awarded Chin an appeal, and we will reverse the judgment of the trial court because we conclude that Chin's motion for judgment pled a cause of action pursuant to §§ 3–404 and –405 of the Uniform Commercial Code.

In reviewing a case decided on a demurrer, we accept as true the facts alleged in the motion for judgment and all reasonable inferences to be drawn therefrom. * * * Chin, a food wholesaler, maintained checking accounts at Signet Bank and Citizens Bank of Washington, D.C. (the drawee banks). During 1994 and 1995, an employee of Chin, Amie Cheryl

Lehman, forged the signature of one of Chin's officers on a number of checks that were payable to Chin's suppliers. Lehman then forged the payees' indorsements and, with the assistance of a First Union teller, deposited the checks in an account which she held at First Union. The drawee banks then paid the checks and debited a total amount of $270,488.72 from Chin's accounts.

First Union asserts that, under the UCC, it is amenable to suit only by the drawee banks based on a breach of warranty of title theory. § 4–207. Chin's sole cause of action, according to First Union, is against the drawee banks for improperly charging Chin's accounts for the amount of the forged checks. See §§ 4–401–406. Under First Union's interpretation of §§ 3–404 and –405, Chin does not have a cause of action against it pursuant to those sections because they only apply to instances involving a forged indorsement of the payee and not to the circumstances where both the payee's indorsement and the signature of the drawer were forged.

While First Union correctly states that the UCC provides a drawer with a cause of action against a drawee bank that charges a drawer's account based on checks containing a forged signature of the drawer, its conclusion that §§ 3–404 and –405 cannot be utilized by a drawer against the depositary bank in a double forgery situation is erroneous.

Sections 3–404 and –405 were part of the 1992 revisions to the UCC. Revised § 3–404(b) provides that where the payee on a check is fictitious or not the person intended to have an interest in the check by the person determining to whom the check is payable, a forged payee's indorsement on the check is nevertheless effective for one who takes the check in good faith.[2] Similarly, where an employee vested with the responsibility for processing, signing, or indorsing the employer's check makes a fraudulent indorsement of such check, revised § 3–405 continues the prior provision's rule that the indorsement is effective if taken or paid in good faith. However, both revised sections provide that if the person taking the check fails to exercise ordinary care, "the person bearing the loss may recover from the person failing to exercise ordinary care to the extent the failure to exercise ordinary care contributed to the loss." §§ 3–404(d)–405(b).

The revisions to §§ 3–404 and –405 changed the previous law by allowing "the person bearing the loss" to seek recovery for a loss caused by the negligence of any person paying the instrument or taking it for value based on comparative negligence principles. The concept of comparative negligence introduced in the revised sections reflects a determination that all participants in the process have a duty to exercise ordinary care in the drawing and handling of instruments and that the failure to exercise that duty will result in liability to the person sustaining the loss. Nothing in the statutory language indicates that, where the signature of the drawer is forged, the drawer cannot qualify as a "person bearing the loss" or that the drawer is otherwise precluded from seeking recovery from a depositary

2. The person whose intent determines to whom an instrument is payable includes a person who forges the drawer's signature. See § 3–110(a).

bank under these sections. In the absence of any specific exclusion, we conclude that the sections are applicable in double forgery situations.

This conclusion is consistent with Comment 2 of the Official Comments to § 3–404, which states that subsection (b) "also applies to forged check cases." Another commentary also concludes that § 3–404 applies to double forgery situations. Remarking that under the previous law, double forgery cases were treated solely as forged drawer's signature cases, allowing the depositary bank to avoid liability, the commentary concludes that the result under the revised section "differs sharply."

> In fictitious payee double forgeries under the Revision, some of the ultimate loss will end up on the shoulders of the company that hired the dishonest bookkeeper and failed to supervise the miscreant. The rest will be shouldered by the depositary bank for [its] negligence....

Barkley Clark & Barbara Clark, The Law of Bank Deposits, Collections and Credit Cards & 12.07[3][b] (Rev. ed. 1995).

Accordingly, we hold that Chin was not precluded from asserting a cause of action against First Union pursuant to §§ 3–404 or –405. In light of this conclusion, we next examine Chin's motion for judgment to determine whether it is sufficient to state a cause of action under these sections.

Chin seeks recovery for a loss sustained as a result of the negligent actions of First Union. Chin alleged that its employee, Lehman, forged both its signature and the indorsement of the payees on a number of checks and, with the cooperation of an employee of First Union, deposited the checks into Lehman's account at First Union. The motion for judgment specifically alleged that the acceptance of the forged checks by First Union for payment "was negligent and was in contravention of established banking customs and standards" and "was due to the negligent failure of First Union Bank to supervise its employee." The pleading further asserts that this negligence caused Chin to suffer a loss of over $270,000.

These allegations are sufficient to state a cause of action against First Union pursuant to §§ 3–404 and –405. Accordingly, the trial court erred in sustaining First Union's demurrer. The judgment of the trial court is reversed and the case is remanded for further proceedings.

NOTE

Since Chin's signature on the checks was forged, under 4–401(a) the drawee banks were not entitled to charge Chin's account, unless 3–406 or 4–406 applies, and these are not in issue in this case. If the drawee banks cannot charge Chin's account, how does Chin qualify as a "person bearing the loss" under 3–404(d)? In the last paragraph of Comment 3 to 3–404, the statement is made that in Case #5, which is a double forgery case in which the indorsement is effective under 3–404(b), the drawee bank has a cause of action under subsection (d).

6. PAYROLL PADDING

We have seen examples of employee fraud that involve forgery of the employer's signature either as an indorsement of checks payable to the employer or as drawer of a check drawn on the employer's bank account. Another common type of employee fraud does not involve forgery of the employer's signature. This type of fraud is sometimes referred to as "payroll padding," and it can be illustrated by the following cases.

Case #1. Corporation pays its employees by check. Treasurer is authorized to sign checks on behalf of Corporation, but a signature by one other officer of Corporation is also necessary. Treasurer signed checks to pay employees on the April payroll. Intending to defraud Corporation, Treasurer included in the checks for that month three checks payable either to fictitious people or real people who sometimes work for Corporation but who did not work in April and therefore were not entitled to any pay. At the request of Treasurer, Vice President also signed the checks. Vice President did not know who was entitled to payment and did not raise any question about the checks. The checks were returned to Treasurer after they were signed. Treasurer took the three fraudulent checks and indorsed each of them by signing the name of the payee. She then deposited each of the checks in a bank in which she had an account. The checks were paid and Treasurer withdrew the proceeds of the checks. Assume Treasurer is judgment proof. If the indorsements by Treasurer are effective as indorsements of the payees of the three checks, Corporation takes the loss. If the indorsements are treated as forged indorsements, the depositary banks that collected the checks will take the loss. 3–417(a)(1), 4–208(a)(1). In this case the intent of Treasurer determines the person to whom each of the three checks is payable. 3–110(a) (last sentence). Under 3–404(b), Treasurer became the holder of each check and her indorsement in the name of the stated payee was effective as the indorsement of the payee of the check. Thus, Corporation takes the loss.

Case #2. Same as Case #1 except that Corporation's checks are produced by a check-writing or facsimile signature machine. Treasurer had access to the computer that operates the machine. She made entries in the computer that caused the machine to issue the three fraudulent checks. She obtained possession of the checks and then proceeded as in Case #1. Under 3–110(b) the intent of Treasurer determines the person to whom each of the three checks is payable. The analysis of Case #2 is identical to that of Case #1.

Case #3. Treasurer signs checks on behalf of Corporation to pay employees, but Clerk prepares the April payroll that tells Treasurer to whom to issue the checks and in what amount. This time the culprit is Clerk. Intending to defraud Corporation, Clerk includes in the payroll the names of three people who work part time for Corporation, but who performed no work during April. Clerk prepared checks of Corporation in accordance with the payroll and gave them to Treasurer for signature. Treasurer signed the checks and returned them to Clerk.

Clerk took the three fraudulent checks, indorsed each in the name of the payee named in the check, and dealt with the checks as Treasurer did in Case #1. This case is more complex. Assume Treasurer knew each of the three employees named in the three fraudulent checks, but she did not know that they did not work in April. Treasurer intended each check to be payable to the payee named in the check and, under 3–110(a), Treasurer's intent controls; hence 3–404(b) doesn't apply. Thus, Clerk's indorsements are forged indorsements and the normal result is that the loss is taken by the depositary bank that collected the check. In Case #1 and Case #2, Corporation took the loss because it was held responsible for the conduct of Treasurer, its faithless employee. In Case #3 the faithless employee is Clerk. Is there any good reason why Corporation should not also be responsible for the conduct of Clerk? In each case the faithless employee had duties with respect to the issuance of checks. The three cases are essentially similar. In Case #3, Treasurer performed the same function as Vice President did in Case #1 and the check writing machine did in Case #2. By preparing the payroll, Clerk as a practical matter determined to whom Corporation's checks were to be made payable. However, the result in Case #3 is not determined solely by 3–110(a) because 3–405 also applies. We previously examined cases covered by 3–405(a)(2)(i). This time the relevant provision is 3–405(a)(2)(ii).

7.   ALLOCATION OF LOSS BY CONTRACT

How far can banks go in protecting themselves from fraud or forgery losses by contracts with their customers? Section 4–103(a) gives broad authority to vary the effect of the statute by agreement, but there are limits beyond which banks cannot go in disclaiming their liability. We will discuss these limits in more detail in Chapter 16. At this point we include a case on a bank's attempt to disclaim liability for paying counterfeit checks containing unauthorized facsimile signatures. We place the case here rather than in Chapter 16 so that you can assess the reasonableness of the bank's broad disclaimer provisions in the context of the material you have just studied on fraud and forgery.

Jefferson Parish School Board v. First Commerce Corporation

Court of Appeal of Louisiana, Fourth Circuit, 1996.
669 So.2d 1298.

■ JONES, JUDGE.

Jefferson Parish School Board appeals a judgment of the trial court granting defendant First National Bank of Commerce's ("First NBC") Motion for Summary Judgment.

Appellant Jefferson Parish School Board maintained a checking account titled "general account," number 7003–42931, with appellee, First

NBC. Appellant desired to utilize a facsimile signature machine, and accordingly, adopted a facsimile signature resolution with First NBC.

In November of 1992, various instruments purporting to be checks made by appellant and drawn on the subject account were presented for payment and paid by First NBC. Upon receiving the monthly bank statement, appellant observed the instruments to be counterfeit. The checks were returned to First NBC each with an individual "Affidavit of Forgery, Alteration, Loss or Threat of Instrument." First NBC maintained that, pursuant to the resolution adopted by appellant, they were entitled to honor the instruments and appellant should bear the loss.

Appellant filed suit in the Civil District Court for the Parish of Orleans in October of 1993 seeking recovery of the amount paid on the checks. First NBC filed a motion for summary judgment alleging that the resolution adopted by appellant precludes such an action. The district court agreed and granted First NBC's Motion for Summary Judgment.

In their only assignment of error, appellant argues that the trial court erred in dismissing their case based on the adoption of the facsimile signature resolution. This assignment of error has no merit. The resolution contains the following provision:

> RESOLVED: That the First National Bank of Commerce, New Orleans, hereinafter referred to as "Bank", as a designated depository of this corporation, be and it is hereby requested, authorized and directed to honor, for the account and to the debit of the corporation, all checks, drafts, or other orders for the payment of money (inclusive of any such as may be payable to any of the officers of this Corporation or other persons hereinafter specified or whose names appear thereon as signor or signors thereof) drawn in the name of this Corporation on the account(s) of this Corporation with the Bank when bearing *or purporting to bear* the facsimile signatures as of any of the following: [facsimile signatures] and the Bank is and shall be entitled to honor and to charge this Corporation for all such checks, drafts, or other orders, *regardless of by whom or by what means the actual or purported facsimile signature or signatures thereon may have been affixed thereto, if such facsimile signature or signatures resemble the facsimile specimens* from time to time duly certified to or filed with the Bank by the Secretary or other officer of the Corporation. (emphasis added).

The resolution further provides:

> *That the said bank may rely on these resolutions until the receipt by the Bank of a certified copy of a resolution by the Board of Directors of this Corporation revoking the same, this Corporation expressly assuming all risks involved in any unauthorized use of such facsimile signature and agreeing that this Corporation shall be responsible for and chargeable with the amount of all checks, drafts, or other orders bearing such facsimile signature or signatures resembling the same, whether or not placed thereon by the authority of this Corporation.* (emphasis added).

The language of the facsimile agreement, a contract between the parties, is clear and unambiguous. The bank is authorized to honor *all checks* "purporting to bear" the facsimile signatures, "regardless of by what means" the actual or purported signature is affixed as long as the "signatures resemble the facsimile specimens." This is the only requirement imposed on the bank by the contract between the parties—to insure that any signatures "resemble" those provided by the Board on the signature card. This comports with the provision of § 4–103(1) in effect at the time of the agreement. The provision provides:

> The effect of the provisions of this chapter may be varied by agreement except that no agreement can disclaim a bank's responsibility for its own lack of good faith or failure to exercise ordinary care or can limit the measure of damages for such lack of failure; *but the parties may agree to determine the standards by which such responsibility is to be measured if those standards are not manifestly unreasonable.* (emphasis added).

Agreements confected pursuant to this statute are not unusual. See Springhill Bank and Trust Co. v. Citizens Bank and Trust Co., 505 So.2d 867 (La.App. 2d Cir.1987), and Perini Corp. v. First National Bank of Habersham County, 553 F.2d 398 (5th Cir.1977). In *Perini*, the court held that there was no cause of action for recovery of funds paid on forged checks where a resolution was adopted authorizing the drawee's payment of checks bearing signatures resembling the machine-endorsed facsimile signature.

The appellant erroneously argues that First NBC cannot prove any negligence on the part of the appellant's employees regarding the safeguarding of their checks on that account and of the facsimile signature plates of the employees used on that account. This argument incorrectly suggests that the appellant should not bear the burden of the loss if the facsimile plates were not used in the forgery. This position is clearly contrary to the resolution adopted by the appellants. As previously stated, the resolution provides that the bank is authorized to honor checks "regardless of by whom or by what means" the actual or purported signature is affixed as long as the "signatures resemble the facsimile specimens."

Additionally, appellants contend that the checks at issue contained errors that a diligent perusal of the documents would have revealed to experienced bank employees. Appellants base this argument on the fact that the checks in question were printed on different paper. This argument also lacks merit. First NBC is obligated to pay on any paper on which the signature of the drawer matches the signature on file. It is very common for customers to order their checks from different sources.

When reviewing trial court judgments on motions for summary judgment, appellate courts must use the same criteria applied by the trial courts. Thus, a summary judgment should be affirmed when "the pleadings, depositions, answers to interrogatories, and admissions on file, together with affidavits, if any, show that there is no genuine issue of material fact, and that the mover is entitled to judgment as a matter of law." * * * The only material fact in this case is the nature of the signatures and there is no dispute that the signatures are nearly identical to the facsimile signatures submitted by the appellants.

Therefore, for the reasons stated above, the judgment of the trial court is affirmed.

PROBLEM

A fundamental principle of banking law, established in Price v. Neal, is that the drawee bank bears the loss in forged check cases. *Jefferson Parish* allowed Bank to contract out of this basic liability by obtaining a resolution from the Board exculpating Bank from liability for paying forged facsimile checks bearing a drawer's signature that resembles the Board's signature specimens. Would a resolution be valid that extends the bank's protection from facsimile machine forgery losses to all cases in which the drawer's signature, whether written by *hand* or by machine, resembles that of the drawer's signature specimens?

NOTE

The School Board was not negligent in this case and its facsimile machine was not used by the counterfeiter; none of its employees had any connection with the counterfeiter. The Board saw itself as an innocent bystander. In this light, why isn't the disclaimer clause "manifestly unreasonable" as applied to this case? Compare Cumis Insurance Society, Inc. v. Girard Bank, 522 F.Supp. 414 (E.D.Pa.1981), in which the court reached a different result in a forged facsimile signature case. See 1 Clark & Clark, The Law of Bank Deposits, Collections and Credit Cards & 10.02[1] (Rev. ed. 1999).

The limits of parties under 4–103(a) to vary their statutory rights and obligations also has been tested with respect to stop payment orders, discussed further in Chapter 16. Section 4–403(a) obligates a bank to stop payment on a check when ordered to do so by its customer or authorized drawer if it has a reasonable opportunity to act. Banks' deposit contracts with customers frequently specify the conditions under which stop payment orders will be honored, and the litigated issue has been whether the specified conditions are "manifestly unreasonable" under 4–103(a). The results have been mixed. Compare Poullier v. Nacua Motors, Inc., 439 N.Y.S.2d 85 (N.Y.Sup.Ct.1981) (bank's stipulation of information needed for stop payment orders to be executed upheld), with FJS Electronics, Inc. v. Fidelity Bank, 431 A.2d 326 (Pa.Super.Ct. 1981) (refusing to give effect to stipulation when inaccuracy in stop payment order insignificant). Some refusals to enforce contractually imposed restrictions are based on the extrastatutory requirement that the bank clearly disclose them to the customer; see, e.g., Staff Service Associates, Inc. v. Midlantic National Bank, 504 A.2d 148 (N.J.Super.Ct. 1985). Is there a problem of nondisclosure in *Jefferson Parish*, where the Parish School Board's resolution authorized honor of instruments containing signatures "purporting to bear" the facsimile signature? Cf. SOS Oil Corp. v. Norstar Bank of Long Island, 563 N.E.2d 258 (N.Y.Ct.App.1990). Or is the *Jefferson Parish* court simply refusing to regulate the substantive allocation of forgery risk between the customer and bank?

B.   ALTERATION

1.   COMPLETE INSTRUMENTS

"Alteration," defined in 3–407(a), refers to a change that purports to modify the obligation of a party to an instrument if the change is unauthorized. Thus, if the payee raises the amount of a check without the consent of the drawer the check has been altered. But if the payee's act is authorized by the drawer before any other person becomes obligated on the check, the check has not been altered; the change is treated as a change made by the drawer.

The definition of alteration is very broad. It includes fraudulent changes as well as changes made in good faith. For example, the holder of a note changes the due date of the note because the holder believes in good faith that the original due date was erroneous. Even if the holder was mistaken, the alteration is not fraudulent. Under the second sentence of 3–407(b), the non-fraudulent alteration is ineffective to modify the obligation of the maker and the note is enforceable according to its original terms. Non-fraudulent alteration is described in the first paragraph of Comment 1 to 3–407.

The concept of alteration can apply to incomplete instruments described in 3–115 as well as complete instruments, but the effect of alteration is not the same in each case. A discussion of alteration of incomplete instruments follows in the next section.

Fraudulent alteration is the principal focus of 3–407 and can be illustrated by the following hypothetical case:

> An authorized employee of Drawer, a large corporation, signed and delivered a typewritten check for $10 payable to the order of Payee. Without Drawer's consent Payee raised the amount of the check to $10,000 by adding a comma and three zeroes after the figure "10" and the word "thousand" after the word "ten." Payee deposited the check in Payee's account with Depositary Bank and the bank obtained $10,000 from Drawee in payment of the check. Drawee then debited Drawer's account in the same amount. Payee withdrew the $10,000 that had been credited to Payee's account in Depositary Bank with respect to the check. When Drawer learned that Drawee had debited $10,000 to Drawer's account with respect to the check, Drawer notified Drawee of the alteration.

Who takes the loss in the hypothetical case? The liability of the drawer with respect to a check is based on the terms of the order to pay made by the person against whom the drawer's liability is asserted. Liability on an altered check can be compared to liability on a forged check. In the absence of fault, the person whose signature as drawer is forged has no liability on the check because the order to pay on which liability is asserted was not made by that person. In the case of the check in the hypothetical case, Drawer can reasonably be held liable with respect to the order to pay $10 because that order was made by Drawer, but, in the absence of fault by Drawer, it is not reasonable to hold Drawer liable with respect to the raised amount because Drawer did not order payment of that amount.

How is this analysis reflected in 3–407? In the hypothetical case, to what extent is Drawee entitled to debit Drawer's account with respect to the check? 3–407(c). If Drawee had dishonored the check, to what extent would Depositary Bank have had a right to recover from Drawer? 3–414(b) and 3–407(c). What is the significance of the first sentence of 3–407(b), which states that "a party whose obligation is affected by the alteration" is discharged? See Comment 1 (second paragraph) to 3–407. If Drawee pays the check but is not entitled to full reimbursement from Drawer, what remedy does it have against Depositary Bank? 3–417(a)(2) and (b). If Depositary Bank is liable to Drawee, what recourse does Depositary Bank have against Payee? 3–416(a)(3) and (b).

Suppose, in the hypothetical case, that the employee who wrote the check in behalf of Drawer left blank spaces in the amount lines on the check, allowing Payee to raise the amount of the check without leaving any easily detectable evidence that the check had been altered. How does this additional fact affect your answers to the questions asked in the preceding paragraph? 3–406. See the following case.

HSBC Bank USA v. F & M Bank Northern Virginia

United States Court of Appeals, Fourth Circuit, 2001.
246 F.3d 335.

■ HAMILTON, SENIOR CIRCUIT JUDGE:

On or about March 31, 1999, Donald Lynch purchased a check (the Check) from Allied Irish Bank (AIB) in Ireland. The Check was made payable to Advance Marketing and Investment Inc. (AMI) in the amount of US$250.00, which was hand written as "Two Hundred + Fifty" on the center line of the Check (with "US Dollars" hand written on the line below), (*i.e.,* the written portion of the Check), and "US$250.00" hand written on the upper right-hand side of the Check (*i.e.,* the numerical portion of the Check). The manner in which AIB made out the Check left just less than one-half inch of open space in the numerical portion and one inch of open space in the written portion.

The drawee/payor on the Check was Marine Midland Bank, now known as HSBC Bank USA (HSBC). Prior to the Check's deposit into AMI's account at F & M Bank Northern Virginia (F & M), the amount of the Check was altered from $250.00 to $250,000.00 by adding three zeros and changing the period to a comma in the numerical portion of the check and adding the letters "Thoud" in the written portion. The alteration was unauthorized, and the Check was endorsed "A.M.I., Inc."

F & M presented the Check for payment to HSBC. In so doing, F & M warranted, pursuant to Virginia Code § 8.4–207.2(a)(2), that the Check "had not been altered." Va.Code Ann. § 8.4–207.2(a)(2) (Cum.Supp.2000). HSBC honored the Check as presented and paid $250,000.00 to F & M, and debited AIB's account for that amount.

HSBC was subsequently advised by AIB of the Check's unauthorized alteration. HSBC then recredited AIB's account for the amount of the unauthorized alteration and brought the present diversity action against F & M in the United States District Court for the Eastern District of Virginia. Among other claims not relevant to the present appeal, F & M alleged a claim for breach of presentment warranty pursuant to Uniform Commercial Code § 4–207(1)(c) and (2)(c).

Using the Virginia Commercial Code as the substantive law governing HSBC's breach of presentment warranty claim, on July 12, 2000, the district court conducted a bench trial on the claim.[1] F & M asserted as an affirmative defense that by leaving the open spaces as it did in the numerical and written portions of the Check, AIB failed to exercise ordinary care in preparing the Check, which failure substantially contributed to the unauthorized alteration of the Check.[2] The only evidence F & M

---

1. The parties agreed that Virginia's Commercial Code governed HSBC's breach of presentment warranty claim. The applicable provision of Virginia's Commercial Code provides as follows:

> (a) If an unaccepted draft is presented to the drawee for payment or acceptance and the drawee pays or accepts the draft, (i) the person obtaining payment or acceptance, at the time of present-ment, and (ii) a previous transferor of the draft, at the time of transfer, warrant to the drawee that pays or accepts the draft in good faith that: ... (2) the draft has not been altered....

Va.Code Ann. § 8.4–207.2(a)(2) (Cum.Supp. 2000).

2. F & M asserted its affirmative defense pursuant to Virginia Commercial Code § 8.4–207.2(c), which provides, in relevant part, as follows:

If a drawee asserts a claim for breach of warranty under subsection (a) based on ... an alteration of the draft, the warrantor may defend by proving that ... the drawer is precluded under [Virginia Commercial Code] § 8.3A 406 ... from asserting against the drawee the ... alteration.

Va.Code Ann. § 8.4–207.2(c). To restate this section using the names of the actual parties in this case, the section provides that F & M, the warrantor, can defend against the warranty claim of HSBC, the drawee, by proving that AIB, the drawer, is precluded under Virginia Commercial Code § 8.3A–406 from asserting the unauthorized alteration of the Check against HSBC. Of relevance in this appeal, AIB is precluded from asserting the unauthorized alteration of the Check against HSBC under Virginia Commercial Code § 8.3A–406(a), if AIB failed to exercise ordinary care in preparing the check and such failure substantially contributed to the unauthorized alteration of the Check. Va.Code Ann. § 8.3A–406(a). Notably, the question of whether AIB failed to exercise ordinary care in preparing the Check is a question to be answered by the trier of fact. Va.Code Ann. § 8.3A–406 cmt. 1 (Cum.Supp.2000).

actually submitted in support of its affirmative defense was the Check itself.

The district court found that HSBC had established all elements of its breach of presentment warranty claim under Virginia Commercial Code § 8.4–207.2(a)(2). The district court also found that AIB had exercised ordinary care in preparing the Check. In this last regard, the district court stated:

> I have examined this check. And, of course, there does have [sic] to be sufficient writing on a check that there is not an open space so someone can fill it in for additional amounts and alter the check.

> But regardless of what you do about writing in zero, zero over 100 and then put a line in, which is, I guess, the standard way to do it—I don't know that if I looked at all the checks in this country that I would know the standard. It is the way I have always done it. There is still some kind of an open space regardless of what you do.

> And so, the test has got to be is that line sufficiently filled so that someone cannot come along and add into that writing in a way that just alters the check so that it will go through unnoticed.

> That certainly wasn't done on this check. This check was substantially written across the line. As a matter of fact, it was written far enough along the line that you could not write the word "thousand" in. It had to be scrawled up in the manner in which it was.

> And I just[,] looking at this check[,] and the way it is made out, I can't find that the preparer was negligent or participated in the alteration of it.

> There was sufficient writing there that any alteration that was made was obvious. And I can't find negligence in that regard.

(J.A. 242).

Subsequently, on July 31, 2000, the district court entered an order stating that for the reasons stated from the bench, judgment should be entered in favor of HSBC in the amount of $249,750.00, plus interest at the rate of 9% from April 13, 1999 to the date of the entry of judgment. The docket sheet reflects that such judgment was entered on July 31, 2000. F & M noted a timely appeal.[3]

On appeal, F & M contends the district court's factual finding that AIB exercised ordinary care in preparing the Check is clearly erroneous. F & M seeks reversal of the judgment in favor of HSBC solely upon this basis. For the reasons stated below, we affirm.

F & M concedes that if the district court's factual finding that AIB exercised ordinary care in preparing the Check is not clearly erroneous, it cannot successfully rely upon its affirmative defense to HSBC's breach of

---

3. On September 13, 2000, a consent order was entered staying the effect of the judgment pending appeal upon F & M Bank's posting a supersedeas bond of $249,000, which it did.

presentment warranty claim and, therefore, the judgment in favor of HSBC should be affirmed. Fed.R.Civ.P. 52(a) (providing that a district court's finding of fact shall not be set aside unless clearly erroneous). We now turn to consider whether the district court's factual finding that AIB exercised ordinary care in preparing the Check is clearly erroneous. * * *

The only evidence submitted by F & M in support of its burden of proving that AIB failed to exercise ordinary care in making out the Check was the Check itself. The district court physically examined the Check, including the just less than one-half inch of open space in the numerical portion of the Check and the one inch of open space in the written portion of the Check. Based upon this physical examination, the district court found that AIB had filled in the open spaces in the numerical and written portions of the check sufficiently such that "any alteration that was made was obvious." Accordingly, the district court found that AIB had exercised ordinary care in making out the Check.

After reviewing a copy of the Check contained in the joint appendix (the sole evidence on this issue presented below), we are not left with a definite and firm conviction that the district court's finding that AIB exercised ordinary care in making out the Check is wrong, mistaken, or implausible. Indeed, we see sound logic in the district court's rationale that if the written portion of the Check contained enough writing such that the Check's alteration could only be accomplished with the "scrawled up," abbreviated form of the word "thousand," *i.e.* "Thoud," ordinary care was exercised in making out the Check. (J.A. 242). In short, we hold that the district court's factual finding that AIB exercised ordinary care in making out the check is not clearly erroneous.

We also note that F & M's reliance upon the following comment to Virginia Commercial Code § 8.3A–406 is misplaced:

> 3. The following cases illustrate the kind of conduct that can be the basis of a preclusion under Section 3–406(a): ... Case #3. A company writes a check for $10. The figure "10" and the word "ten" are typewritten in the appropriate spaces on the check form. A large blank space is left after the figure and the word. The payee of the check, using a typewriter with a type face similar to that used on the check, writes the word "thousand" after the word "ten" and a comma and three zeros after the figure "10." The drawee bank in good faith pays $10,000 when the check is presented for payment and debits the account of the drawer in that amount. The trier of fact *could* find that the drawer failed to exercise ordinary care in writing the check and that the failure substantially contributed to the alteration. In that case the drawer is precluded from asserting the alteration against the drawee if the check was paid in good faith.

Va.Code Ann. § 8.3A–406, cmt. 3 (Cum.Supp.2000) (emphasis added). This illustration is easily distinguishable from the facts of the present case. First, the illustration involves typewritten preparation of a check. The small nature of typewritten characters obviously would take up much less space than the handwriting involved in the present case. Furthermore, the actual number of words and numbers typed on the check that is discussed in the commentary prior to alteration is significantly less than the number of words and numbers AIB hand wrote on the Check prior to its alteration.

Because the district court's finding that AIB exercised ordinary care in making out the Check is not clearly erroneous, we affirm the judgment in favor of HSBC.

NOTE

If the Drawer had left more open space on the check, would it have qualified as an incomplete instrument under 3–115(a)?

2.   INCOMPLETE INSTRUMENTS

Section 3–115(a).   Incomplete Instrument.

(a) "Incomplete instrument" means a signed writing, whether or not issued by the signer, the contents of which show at the time of signing that it is incomplete but that the signer intended it to be completed by the addition of words or numbers.

Assume that A is indebted to B but is not sure of the precise amount of the debt. In payment of the debt A sends to B a check payable to B, leaving the amount of the check blank. A instructs B to complete the check by filling in the amount of the debt. If the amount of the debt is $10 and B fills in the check for that amount, there is no difficulty in enforcing the check against A. The intent of A has been carried out by B's completion of the check. The result is the same as if A had personally completed the check. When the check was received by B, the check was an "incomplete instrument," defined in 3–115(a). Because the amount of the check was not stated, the check was not a negotiable instrument under 3–104 and the last sentence of 3–115(b) applies. If B completes the check by writing in $10 as its amount, the check becomes an instrument under 3–104 and the last sentence of 3–115(b) states that the check can be enforced as completed. There is no alteration.

But if B fills in $10,000 rather than $10, the act of B is not authorized by A. Under 3–115(c) there is an alteration of the incomplete instrument and 3–407 applies. The case is analogous to the hypothetical case in the material in the previous section in which a check payable in the amount of $10 was altered by changing the amount to $10,000. In each case the drawer intended a check in the amount of $10 and in each case the payee raised the intended amount to $10,000.

Suppose B deposited the altered check to B's account in Depositary Bank and the bank obtained $10,000 from Drawee Bank in payment of the check. Drawee Bank then debited A's account in the same amount. B withdrew the $10,000 that had been credited to B's account in Depositary Bank with respect to the check. When A learned that Drawee Bank had debited $10,000 to A's account with respect to the check, A notified Drawee Bank of the alteration. Who takes the loss in this case? To what extent is

Drawee Bank entitled to debit A's account with respect to the check? 3–407(c). If Drawee Bank had dishonored the check, to what extent would Depositary Bank have had a right to recover from A? 3–414(b) and 3–407(c).

Compare the results in this case with the results in the hypothetical case in the previous section. Why are the results different? Is there any relationship between 3–406 and 3–407(c) as it applies to fraudulent completion of incomplete instruments?

C.   RESTRICTIVE INDORSEMENTS

Indorsement of an instrument may serve several purposes, but most commonly an indorsement is made in order to negotiate the instrument. 3–204(a). The form of the indorsement can affect rights with respect to the instrument if it is stolen and collected or transferred to a third party. If a check indorsed in blank by the holder is stolen, the thief may negotiate the check to a transferee who may obtain rights as a holder in due course. If the stolen check was payable to an identified person and the payee made a special indorsement or did not indorse the check at all, the thief cannot negotiate the check and nobody taking through the thief can become a person entitled to enforce the check. Thus, the rights of a person taking a stolen check may depend upon whether an indorsement by the holder was made and whether the indorsement was special or in blank. The rights of the taker, however, can also depend upon whether the holder made a "restrictive indorsement," governed by 3–206.

The purpose of a restrictive indorsement is to restrict payment of the instrument. That restriction can be expressed as part of a special indorsement or an indorsement in blank. For example, an indorsement of a check consisting solely of the signature of the holder under the words "for deposit only" is a blank indorsement because it does not identify a person to whom it makes the check payable, and is a restrictive indorsement because it indicates that the check is to be deposited to an account. This restrictive indorsement is governed by 3–206(c). Comment 3 to 3–206. An indorsement "Pay to John Doe in trust for Jane Doe" is a special indorsement because it identifies John Doe as the person to whom the check is payable, and is a restrictive indorsement because it indicates that the proceeds of the check are to be paid for the benefit of Jane Doe. This restrictive indorsement is governed by 3–206(d). Comment 4 to 3–206.

Some attempts to restrict payment of an instrument by an indorser are nullified by 3–206. An indorsement "Pay to John Doe only" is ineffective to prohibit payment to any other holder. In spite of the indorsement, John Doe may indorse the instrument to another person and that person may become entitled to enforce the instrument. 3–206(a). An indorsement that attempts to prohibit payment unless a stated condition is satisfied is also ineffective to restrict payment. 3–206(b). Invalid restrictions are discussed in Comment 2 to 3–206.

PROBLEM

Banking by mail is a common practice. This problem considers the degree of protection the payee of a check gains by using a restrictive indorsement under 3–206. Peter, the payee of a check for $10,000 drawn on Payor Bank, indorsed and mailed the check to Bank One where he had an account. Before the check arrived at Bank One, Thief stole the check and wrote Thief's name under Peter's indorsement. Thief then deposited the check to Thief's account in Bank Two. Bank Two presented the check to Payor Bank and Payor Bank paid the check. Thief then withdrew the $10,000 that had been credited to Thief's account in Bank Two with respect to the check.

What are Peter's rights against Bank Two and Payor Bank if Peter's indorsement were as follows?

Case #1

For deposit only

Peter

Case #2

Pay to Bank One for Account No. 1234321

Peter

Case #3

Peter

For deposit only

———————

When we are sending checks to our bank for deposit by mail, many of us use the kinds of restrictive indorsements set out in either Case #1 or Case #3. You may be surprised to learn that the court in Spencer v. Sterling Bank, 74 Cal.Rptr.2d 576 (Cal.Ct.App.1998), tells us that what we've been doing accomplishes nothing. The court held that under the plain meaning of 3–206(c)(2) a check indorsed "X, for deposit only" can be deposited in anyone's account in any bank; the depositary bank need not deposit the proceeds in the account of the person indorsing the check, usually the payee of the check, because the blank indorsement does not specify where or for whose benefit such a check is to be deposited. A few cases agree with *Spencer*, but the majority does not. The following case states the majority view. Which view do you believe is a correct interpretation of the statute?

State of Qatar v. First American Bank

United States District Court, E.D. Virginia, 1995.
885 F.Supp. 849.

■ ELLIS, DISTRICT JUDGE.

At issue in this sequel to State of Qatar v. First American Bank of Virginia ("Qatar I")[1] is the meaning and legal significance of the phrase

1. 880 F.Supp. 463 (E.D.Va.1995)

"for deposit only" following an indorsement on the back of a check. More specifically, the question presented is whether a depositary bank complies with the restrictive indorsement "for deposit only" when it deposits a check bearing that restriction into *any* person's account, or whether that restriction requires a depositary bank to deposit the check's proceeds only into the account of the named payee. For the reasons that follow, the Court holds that the unqualified language "for deposit only" following an indorsement on the back of a check requires a depositary bank to place the check's proceeds into the payee's[2] account, and the bank violates that restrictive indorsement when it credits the check to any other account.

The facts underlying this case are more fully set forth in *Qatar I* and are only briefly reiterated here. Plaintiffs are the State of Qatar and certain of its agencies (collectively, "Qatar"). From approximately 1986 to 1992, one of Qatar's employees, Bassam Salous, defrauded his employer by having checks drawn on Qatar's account in purported payment of false or duplicate invoices that he had created. Although all of the unauthorized checks were made payable to individuals and entities other than Salous, he nonetheless successfully deposited the checks into his own personal accounts with Defendant First American Bank of Virginia ("First American") and Central Fidelity Banks, Inc. (collectively, "the depositary banks").

After Qatar discovered this fraudulent scheme in 1992, it brought suit against the depositary banks for conversion. * * *

Only one category of checks remains in dispute. These checks all bear the forged indorsement of the payee named on the face of the check, followed by a stamped "for deposit only" restriction. In *Qatar I*, the Court denied the depositary banks' motion for summary judgment with respect to these checks on the ground that the depositary banks could be held liable for applying the proceeds of the checks in violation of the restrictive indorsements. *Qatar I*, 880 F.Supp. at 469, 470–71. Specifically, the Court stated:

> [W]hile the forged signature presented no barrier to payment given the effect of [U.C.C.] § 3–405, the accompanying restriction ("FOR DEPOSIT ONLY") provided a clear instruction to the depositary banks to deposit the funds only into the account of the last indorser—here, the named payee.

The Court did not hold the depositary banks liable as a matter of law with respect to these checks, but decided to await the banks' presentation of defenses, if any, at trial. At trial, the depositary banks raised no defenses, but instead challenged for the first time the Court's assumption in *Qatar I* that the phrase "for deposit only", without further specification, directs a depositary bank to deposit the funds only into the account of the named

---

2. Throughout this Memorandum Opinion, "payee" is intended to refer to the last purported indorser.

payee. An indorsement in this form, they argued, is far less restrictive, as it merely directs that the check's proceeds be *deposited* in an account, not that they be deposited into a particular account. Thus, the depositary banks urged, they fully complied with the restrictive indorsements on these checks when they deposited the proceeds into Salous' account. Although this issue properly should have been raised at the summary judgment stage, the Court permitted the parties to research the matter and submit post-trial legal memoranda regarding this final, narrow issue. Qatar and First American did so, and the matter is now ripe for disposition.

It is now established that First American may be liable to Qatar for handling a check's proceeds in violation of a restrictive indorsement. *Qatar I*, 880 F.Supp. at 469, 470–71.[8] Under § 3–205(c) of the pre–1993 Uniform Commercial Code ("U.C.C." or "Code"),[9] restrictive indorsements are defined to "include the words 'for collection,' 'for deposit,' 'pay any bank,' or like terms signifying a purpose of deposit or collection." Thus, the U.C.C. makes clear that the phrase "for deposit only" is, in fact, a restrictive indorsement. But the Code does not define "for deposit only" or specify what bank conduct would be inconsistent with that restriction.[10] Nor does Virginia decisional law provide any guidance on this issue. As a result, reference to decisional law from other jurisdictions is appropriate.

Not surprisingly, most courts confronted with this issue have held that the restriction "for deposit only", without additional specification or directive, instructs depositary banks to deposit the funds only into the payee's account. In addition, commentators on commercial law uniformly agree that the function of such a restriction is to ensure that the checks' proceeds be deposited into the payee's account.[11]

---

8. It is important to note for the reader unfamiliar with *Qatar I* that First American is liable in conversion to Qatar, the drawer, for violating restrictive indorsements only because the forged indorsements are "effective" pursuant to former § 3–405(1)(c). Were this not a § 3–405(1)(c) case, the forged indorsements would be ineffective to negotiate the instrument, and any money paid to the depositary banks on the forged checks would be deemed to come from the drawee bank's own funds, not from Qatar's account. See *Qatar I*, 880 F.Supp. at 467–68.

9. Article three of the U.C.C. governs the law of negotiable instruments and was substantially amended effective January 1, 1993. Because all of the relevant events surrounding this case occurred prior to 1993, the former U.C.C. provisions apply here. All U.C.C. citations are to Va.Code, Title 8.3, amended by Va.Code, Title 8.3A (Supp.1994).

10. The amended Code provision on restrictive indorsements provides more guidance on the meaning of "for deposit only."

§ 3–206. Specifically, in describing particular types of restrictive indorsements, § 3–206(c)(ii) refers to indorsements "using the words 'for deposit,' 'for collection,' *or other words indicating a purpose of having the instrument collected by a bank for the indorser or for a particular account*" (emphasis added).

11. See, e.g., 1 William H. Lawrence, Commercial Paper and Payment Systems § 3.6[b][3], at 3–37 (1990) ("A payee who endorses a check 'for deposit only' provides notice to the depository [sic] bank that the check is to be credited to the payee's account.... The only way that a depository [sic] bank can apply value consistently with the endorsement is to credit the payee's account"); 4 William D. Hawkland & Lary Lawrence, U.C.C. Series § 3–206:05 (Art. 3), at 366 (1994) (rejecting proposition that "for deposit only" "would permit the proceeds to be credited to any account"); 2 Frederick M. Hart & William F. Willier, Bender's Uniform Commercial Code Service, Commercial Paper

This construction of "for deposit only" is commercially sensible and is adopted here. The clear purpose of the restriction is to avoid the hazards of indorsing a check in blank. Pursuant to former § 3–204(2), a check indorsed in blank "becomes payable to bearer." It is, essentially, cash. Thus, a payee who indorses her check in blank runs the risk of having the check stolen and freely negotiated before the check reaches its intended destination. To protect against this vulnerability, the payee can add the restriction "for deposit only" to the indorsement, and the depositary bank is required to handle the check in a manner consistent with that restriction. § 3–206(3). And in so adding the restriction, the payee's intent plainly is to direct that the funds be deposited into her own account, not simply that the funds be deposited into some account.[14] See 1 William H. Lawrence, Commercial Paper and Payment Systems § 3.6[b][3] (1990). Any other construction of the phrase "for deposit only" is illogical and without commercial justification or utility. Indeed, it is virtually impossible to imagine a scenario in which a payee cared that her check be deposited, but was indifferent with respect to the particular account to which the funds would be credited.

First American opposes this result, contending that the unqualified restriction "for deposit only" merely requires a depositary bank to deposit the check into an account, irrespective of which one. * * *

* * *

While it is true that the literal command of the bare words "for deposit only" is simply that the check be deposited, such rigid reliance on linguistics in disregard of practical considerations and plain common sense is both unwarranted and imprudent. This is especially so given that the individuals writing and relying upon these restrictive indorsements are not apt to be well versed in the subtleties of negotiable instruments law. As evidenced by numerous authorities, see supra note 12, and common experience, the unqualified phrase "for deposit only" is almost universally taken to mean "for deposit only *into the payee's account*." To disregard this common understanding in support of an illogical construction is to elevate form over substance. First American's argument to the contrary is a little like saying

under the Uniform Commercial Code § 3A.02 (1994) ("When an instrument is indorsed 'For Deposit,' the indorsee, almost always a bank, is obligated to put any money received for the instrument in the indorser's account"); Julian B. McDonnell, Bank Liability for Fraudulent Checks: the Clash of the Utilitarian and Paternalist Creeds under the Uniform Commercial Code, 73 Geo.L.J. 1399, 1415 (1985) ("indorsers must deposit checks restrictively indorsed 'for deposit only' into the account of the indorser, rather than cash the check or deposit it into another's account"); James S. Rogers, Negotiability as a System of Title Recognition, 48 Ohio St.L.J.

197, 223 n. 94 (1987) ("the mechanism of restrictive indorsement 'for deposit only' enables a payee to [indorse a check in blank] without facing any of the risks that would otherwise flow from converting the instrument into bearer form"). See also 1 James J. White & Robert S. Summers, Uniform Commercial Code § 13–10 (3d ed. 1994 Supp.).

14. Of course, the payee can direct that the funds be delivered into someone else's account by including the particular account name or number in the restriction (e.g., "for deposit only into account of X" or "for deposit only into account #123456").

that a store sign reading "shirts and shoes required" does not restrict a trouserless man from entering the store.

Finally, it is worth noting that the new revisions to the negotiable instruments provisions of the U.C.C., see supra note 10, support the result reached here. Although these revisions are inapplicable to this case, the commentary following § 3–206 states that the new subdivision dealing with "for deposit only" and like restrictions "continues previous law." § 3–206 comment 3. Shortly thereafter, the commentary provides an example in which a check bears the words "for deposit only" above the indorsement. In those circumstances, the commentary states, the depositary bank acts inconsistently with the restrictive indorsement where it deposits the check into an account other than that of the payee. Id. Although the restriction in that example precedes the signature, whereas the restrictions on the checks at issue here follow the signature, this distinction is immaterial. The clear meaning of the restriction in both circumstances is that the funds should be placed into the payee's account.[17]

Therefore, First American violated the restrictive indorsements in depositing into Bassam Salous' account checks made payable to others and restrictively indorsed "for deposit only." Pursuant to the holding in *Qatar I*, then, First American is liable to Qatar for conversion in the amount of the total face values of these checks.

PROBLEM

Peter, the payee of a check for $10,000 drawn on Payor Bank, gave the check to Faith, the legal guardian of Ward, her elderly father who had become legally incompetent. Peter told Faith that the check was a contribution to defray Ward's nursing home expenses. Before giving the check to Faith, Peter indorsed the check as follows:

> Pay to Faith as Guardian for Ward
>
> Peter

Faith indorsed the check by signing her name under Peter's indorsement and deposited the check to her personal account in Depositary Bank. Faith also had a fiduciary account as guardian for Ward in the same bank. Pursuant to her instructions, Depositary Bank credited Faith's personal account $10,000 and obtained payment of the check from Payor Bank. Faith subsequently withdrew the $10,000 that had been credited to her

---

17. The facts of this case are unusual in that it was the forger, Bassam Salous, who added the restriction "for deposit only." While *his* intent clearly was not to direct that the funds be placed into the account of the named payee, the general purpose and meaning of the phrase "for deposit only" is unaltered. Cf. Society Nat'l Bank v. Security Fed. Sav. & Loan, 71 Ohio St.3d 321, 643 N.E.2d 1090 (1994). Although it is difficult to speculate regarding why Salous so indorsed the checks, Salous' idiosyncratic subjective intent is immaterial to First American's obligation to abide by the terms of the restrictive indorsement, an obligation which, if fulfilled, would have put an earlier stop to the ongoing fraud.

personal account by writing checks on the account for her personal expenses.

Suit on behalf of Ward has been brought against Faith for breach of trust and against Depositary Bank and Payor Bank. Faith is insolvent and has no funds. What is the liability of Depositary Bank and Payor Bank? 3–206.

CHAPTER 6

THE BANK–CUSTOMER RELATIONSHIP

A. INTRODUCTION

A customer with a deposit account in a bank has a contractual relationship with the bank that is governed by Part 4 of Article 4. If the bank pays a check written on the customer's account, 4–401(a) allows the bank to charge the customer's account only if the check is "properly payable," that is, if the customer has authorized the payment and it violates no agreement between the customer and the bank. Thus, a bank cannot charge a customer's account if the customer's signature is forged, but may charge the account even though the charge creates an overdraft. Of course, the bank does not have to pay an overdraft unless it has agreed to do so. 4–402(a). Agreements by banks to pay overdrafts up to specified limits are common. If a bank fails to pay a check that is properly payable and covered by funds in the customer's account, the bank has wrongfully dishonored the check under 4–402(a) and may be liable in damages under 4–402(b). A customer has the right for any reason or no reason to order a bank to stop payment of checks on the customer's account or to close the account, and if the bank fails to do so it may be liable for the loss caused by its failure. 4–403. However, a bank is not liable for dishonoring a "stale" check, one presented more than six months after its date. 4–404.

The provisions of Article 4 are only one source of rules on the bank-customer relationship. Federal statutes and Federal Reserve regulations are another source. The Truth-in-Savings Act, discussed later, became effective in 1992; it requires disclosure of the terms of consumer deposit accounts. The Expedited Funds Availability Act and Regulation CC expressly override the UCC. Regulation J does so as well. Still another source is provided by 4–103(a) under which the "effect of the provisions" of Article 4 may be varied by bank-customer agreements; it is customary for banks to have some form of deposit agreement with their customers. Section 4–103(a) restates and even enlarges upon the "freedom of contract" principle embodied in 1–302. Comment 1 to 4–103 says: "This section, therefore, permits within wide limits variation of the effect of provisions of the Article by agreement." Since deposit agreements have aspects of contracts of adhesion, a continuing matter of dispute between banks and their customers concerns the extent of the "wide limits" referred to in the Comment. We discuss this issue later in this chapter.

B. STOP-PAYMENT ORDERS

Section 4–403(a) affords a customer an unrestricted right to stop payment on checks drawn on the customer's account or to close the account. Comment 1 to 4–403 is a ringing affirmation of this cherished right of bank customers, and Comment 7 adds that a payment in violation of a stop order is an improper payment even though made by inadvertence or mistake. The broad right given drawers by 4–403(a) to stop payment of checks is unique in payment systems, and it can be very valuable to drawers. Even if the check was given in payment of an obligation of the drawer on a valid contract, a stop payment order by the drawer deprives the payee of the coveted status of being a paid obligee, forcing the payee to proceed against the obligor by legal process for payment of the obligation. When a contract is breaking down, this is a huge tactical advantage for the drawer; facing the expense of enforcing its rights at law, the payee-obligee may give up and let the drawer out of the contract.

Answer these elementary introductory questions about 4–403.

Question #1.   Saxton is the remitter of a cashier's check issued by Bank. She learns that the payee of the check, who now has possession of the check, has possibly defrauded her. She orders Bank to stop payment of the check. Must Bank do so?

Question #2.   Payee learns that his paycheck has been stolen from his wallet. He immediately notifies Bank on which the check was drawn to stop payment of the check. Must Bank do so?

Question #3.   Baker and Able are partners but they don't trust each other. Their agreement with Bank is that both must sign any partnership check. Both signed a check for $10,000 payable to Payton. After the check had been delivered to Payton, Baker had second thoughts and ordered Bank to stop payment on the check. Must Bank do so?

Question #4.   Husband and Wife have a joint account in Bank. Wife disapproved of some checks that Husband had been writing on the account and, without Husband's consent, ordered Bank to close the account even though this would result in the dishonor of several checks Husband had already written. Must Bank do so?

1. PROVING LOSS UNDER 4–403(C)

Subsection 4–403(a) grants a drawer an unlimited right to stop payment on checks and Comment 1 to 4–403 states that this right is a basic service that bank customers are entitled to receive whatever the inconvenience to the bank, but in a seeming contradiction subsection (c) imposes the burden of establishing any loss resulting from a bank's violation of a stop order on the customer. What justification is there for this provision? If the bank is the wrongdoer, shouldn't it bear the burden of proving absence of loss?

Although the meaning of 4–403(c) seems clear, courts have disagreed widely on its import. We use the facts of Hughes v. Marine Midland Bank, 127 Misc.2d 209, 484 N.Y.S.2d 1000 (City Ct. Rochester 1985), as the basis for discussing the divergence of views:

Customer wrote a check payable to a real estate agent for advance rental on a vacation cottage in Florida. When Customer arrived at the cottage she found that it was not as advertised and stopped payment on the check in ample time for her Bank, located in New York, to act on the stop order. When Customer received her cancelled checks at the end of the month, she found to her surprise that Bank had mistakenly paid the check. She immediately demanded that Bank recredit her account for the amount of the check. Bank declined to recredit the account on the ground that Customer had not established her loss by merely showing that Bank had violated the stop order and had refused to recredit her account. The real estate agent was located in Florida, and Bank had no way of knowing about the transaction between Customer and the agent. For all Bank knew, Customer may have owed the money to the agent, thus Bank's payment might have paid a legitimate debt of Customer. Since only Customer knew these facts, Bank argued that she should have the burden of convincing Bank before it returned the money to her.

Minority view. Customer sued Bank for the amount of the check. Her proof of loss was her showing that Bank had paid the check over her valid stop order and had refused to recredit her account. A summary judgment for Customer was entered. The court held that Bank should have recredited Customer's account immediately and sought its remedy under 4–407. Under that provision, if Bank can show that its payment was made either to a holder in due course (4–407(1)) or to a holder of the check who was entitled to payment from Customer (4–407(2)), in order to prevent unjust enrichment, Bank is subrogated to the right of the holder to recover the amount of the check from Customer. If Bank finds that it has paid a holder who was not entitled to payment from Customer (e.g., this would be true if the agent had defrauded Customer), in order to prevent unjust enrichment, Bank is subrogated to Customer's right to get the money back from the holder (4–407(3)).

Majority view. Most courts believe that holdings like *Hughes* do not give adequate weight to the requirement of 4–403(c) that the customer must establish the loss. A statement of this view is found in the following quotation from Siegel v. New England Merchants National Bank, 386 Mass. 672, 437 N.E.2d 218, 222–223 (1982):

> The rule of § 4–403(3), that a depositor must prove his loss, may at first seem at odds with our earlier conclusion that § 4–401(1) provides the depositor with a claim against the bank in the amount of the check, leaving the bank with recourse through subrogation under § 4–407. * * * We believe, however, that § 4–403(3) was intended to operate within the process of credit and subrogation established by §§ 4–401(1)

and 4–407. See § 4–403, comment 8. When a bank pays an item improperly, the depositor loses his ability to exercise any right he had to withhold payment of the check. His "loss," in other words, is equivalent to his rights and defenses against the parties to whose rights the bank is subrogated—the other party to the initial transaction and other holders of the instrument. Section 4–403(3) simply protects the bank against the need to prove events familiar to the depositor, and far removed from the bank, before it can realize its subrogation rights. The depositor, who participated in the initial transaction, knows whether the payee was entitled to eventual payment and whether any defenses arose. Therefore, § 4–403(3) requires that he, rather than the bank, prove these matters. * * *

This view of the three relevant sections of the code suggests a fair allocation of the burden of proof. The bank, which has departed from authorized bookkeeping, must acknowledge a credit to the depositor's account. It must then assert its subrogation rights, and in doing so must identify the status of the parties in whose place it claims. If the bank's subrogation claims are based on the check, this would entail proof that the third party subrogor was a holder, or perhaps a holder in due course. This responsibility falls reasonably upon the bank, because it has received the check from the most recent holder and is in at least as good a position as the depositor to trace its history.

The depositor must then prove any facts that might demonstrate a loss. He must establish defenses good against a holder or holder in due course, as the case may be. See UCC §§ 3–305, 3–306. If the initial transaction is at issue, he must prove either that he did not incur a liability to the other party, or that he has a defense to liability. Thus, the bank, if it asserts rights based on the transaction, need not make out a claim on the part of its subrogor against the depositor. Responsibility in this area rests entirely with the depositor, who participated in the transaction and is aware of its details. Further, the depositor must establish any consequential loss.

A few courts have adopted a variant of the majority rule, assigning shifting burdens of production. See, e.g., Mitchell v. Republic Bank & Trust Co., 239 S.E.2d 867 (N.C.Ct.App.1978); Thomas v. Marine Midland Tinkers National Bank, 381 N.Y.S.2d 797 (N.Y.Sup.Ct. 1976). These courts allocate the burden of proof as to loss to the customer. However, burdens of production of evidence of loss are allocated between the customer and the bank. The customer must present evidence that the bank paid a check against an effective stop-payment order. Thereafter the bank must present evidence that the customer did not suffer a loss when it paid against the order. The variant of the majority rule apparently does not read 4–403(c)'s requirement that customer bears "[t]he burden of establishing the fact and amount of loss" as including both burdens of production and proof.

Section 4–403(c) has long been a bone of contention between customers and banks. In violating a customer's stop-payment order, even if the payment is made to a holder on a valid debt of the customer, the bank has deprived the customer of the tactical advantage of forcing the holder to proceed against the customer for payment. Had the stop order in *Hughes* been honored by the bank, the agent might well have been unwilling to undertake the expense of suing the customer for the amount of the check, and might have given up on the transaction. But there is no basis in 4–403 or 4–407 for compensating a customer for this kind of loss.

A major difference between the majority and minority views is that under the majority view the bank usually keeps the money while the parties litigate; under the minority view the bank must recredit the customer's account upon learning that it has paid over a valid stop-payment order and then must proceed under 4–407 to get its money back from either the holder or the customer. The banks seek to shore up the policy of the majority view by claiming that many stop-payment orders are the result of "buyer's remorse" rather than valid defenses on the part of the customer; moreover, they strongly object to getting tied up in messy contract disputes between obligors and obligees. Customers find unfairness in a system that allows a bank that has wrongfully paid out over a stop-payment order to sit back and force the customer to proceed against it to get its money back.

A number of attempts were made to redraft 4–403(c) during the revision of Article 4, but no solution found consensus. The only substantive change made was the addition of the last sentence in 4–403(c), which clarified an issue on which there was some dispute in the case law. If a customer's checks presented subsequent to the violation of the stop order are dishonored because the check that should not have been paid depleted the customer's account balance, the customer can proceed against the bank under 4–402 to recover damages for wrongful dishonor. Since it costs money to attract customers and banks are reluctant to lose them, anecdotal evidence indicates that banks have worked out informal procedures to satisfy meritorious customer demands for a recredit after the bank violates a stop order. Under one plan, discussed by the Drafting Committee as a possible model for the redraft of Article 4, if the bank believes the customer's representations that it had paid out money the customer did not owe, it required the customer (1) to sign an affidavit stating facts indicating that the payment was made on a debt for which the customer was not liable, and (2) to enter into an agreement that it would cooperate in any litigation the bank might have to bring against the person who received the mistaken payment. Once this was done the bank would recredit the customer's account and initiate proceedings against the person who received payment.

A case applying the majority rule to interesting facts follows. Which has the better of the argument, the majority or the dissent?

Dunnigan v. First Bank

Supreme Court of Connecticut, 1991.
217 Conn. 205, 585 A.2d 659.

■ BORDEN, ASSOCIATE JUSTICE.

In this appeal, we are called upon to define the meaning and scope of § 4–403(3) of the Uniform Commercial Code (Code) as applied to the facts of this case. The defendant bank appeals, after a court trial, from the judgment of the trial court in favor of the plaintiff, the trustee in bankruptcy of Cohn Precious Metals, Inc. (Cohn), a customer of the bank. We transferred the appeal to this court pursuant to Practice Book § 4023, and we now reverse the trial court's judgment.

The plaintiff brought this action against the bank for wrongfully paying a check issued by Cohn over Cohn's valid stop-payment order. The trial court determined that the plaintiff had established a loss within the meaning of § 4–403(3) as a result of the bank's payment of the check, and that the subrogation provisions of General Statutes § 4–407 did not defeat the rights of Cohn. The court accordingly rendered judgment for the amount of the check. This appeal followed.

The bank claims that judgment was improperly rendered for the plaintiff because (1) as a matter of law, Cohn did not suffer a loss within the meaning of § 4–403(3), and (2) the bank was subrogated to the rights of the payee of the check and of the collecting banks, pursuant to § 4–407. We agree with the bank's first claim and therefore need not reach its second claim. Furthermore, it is not necessary to define the relationship between §§ 4–403(3) and 4–407.

The parties stipulated to the following facts. On November 8, 1978, pursuant to purchase order 1142, Lamphere Coin, Inc. (Lamphere), a trader in coins and precious metals, delivered to Cohn certain silver dollars with a unit price of $1.71 and with a total value of $27,492.07. Cohn's bookkeeper incorrectly recorded the unit price of those coins, however, as $17.10, resulting in an erroneous total value of $47,098.93. On November 9, 1978, Cohn paid Lamphere $47,098.93 by wire transfer to Lamphere's bank account, resulting in an overpayment to Lamphere by Cohn of $19,606.86. On November 10, 1978, Lamphere delivered three and one-half bags of silver dollars to Cohn pursuant to Cohn's purchase order 1145. The value of the silver dollars was $21,175. On the same day, Cohn issued two checks drawn on its account at the bank to Lamphere, one in the amount of $12,175 and one in the amount of $9000, totaling $21,175.

Between November 10 and November 15, Cohn discovered its bookkeeper's error and, on November 14, 1978, directed the bank to stop-payment on the two checks totaling $21,175 that had been issued on November 10, 1978. The bank stopped payment on the $9000 check, but on or about November 20, 1978, the bank inadvertently honored the $12,175 check over the valid stop-payment order. Cohn retained the three and one-half bags of silver dollars, but never recovered its overpayment from Lamphere. As of November 20, 1978, the date of the improper payment of the check by the bank, and at all times thereafter Lamphere owed Cohn in excess of $13,000 as a result of these transactions.

The merits of this controversy revolve around the meaning of § 4–403(3), which provides that "[t]he burden of establishing the fact and amount of loss resulting from the payment of an item contrary to a binding stop order is on the customer." The bank argues that where there is good consideration for a particular check, or where the check was given as payment on a binding contract, the bank that paid the check over a valid stop payment order is not liable to its customer, because there was no "loss resulting from [its] payment...." Thus, in the bank's view a customer cannot establish a loss under this provision of the code by relying on the loss of credits due the customer from prior unrelated transactions between the customer and the payee of the check. The plaintiff argues, as the trial court concluded, that whether a customer has incurred a "loss" within the meaning of § 4–403(3) cannot be determined solely by focusing on the transaction underlying the particular check involved, but must be determined by focusing on the entire relationship between the customer and the payee of the check. The plaintiff contends that it is unreasonable to disregard the relative positions of the parties, especially where they have demonstrated a continuing course of business dealings, where there are likely to be such credits. Under such circumstances, the plaintiff claims that focusing on a single transaction is contrary to the intent of the Code. Thus, in the plaintiff's view, Cohn would have had a good "defense" to a claim by Lamphere on the check because of the overpayment, and by paying the check the bank caused Cohn a loss within the meaning of § 4–403(3).

The issue, therefore, is whether, on the facts of this case, the bank customer who sought to establish "the fact and amount of loss resulting from the payment of an item contrary to a binding stop payment order" pursuant to § 4–403(3) was entitled to do so by resorting to credits from prior transactions unrelated to that for which the check was issued, or whether the customer was limited to the facts of the particular transaction for which the check was issued. We conclude that the customer was limited to the facts of the particular transaction for which the check was issued, and that § 4–403(3) does not contemplate taking into account a loss by the customer of credits that arose from prior unrelated transactions. * * *

Under § 4–403(1), a bank customer has the right to order his bank to stop-payment on a check, so long as he does so in a timely and reasonable manner, and, under § 4–403(2), an oral stop-payment order is binding on the bank for a limited period of time. The fact that the bank has paid the check over the customer's valid stop-payment order does not mean, however, that the customer is automatically entitled to repayment of the amount of the check. Under § 4–403(3), the customer must also establish "the fact and amount of loss resulting from" the bank's improper payment.

The case law makes clear that "[t]he loss ... must be more than the mere debiting of his account." * * * Siegel v. New England Merchants National Bank, 386 Mass. 672, 437 N.E.2d 218 (1982) * * *. The commentators agree. See W. Hillman, Basic UCC Skills 1989, Article 3 and Article 4, p. 302; E. Peters, A Negotiable Instruments Primer (1974) p. 79; 1 J. White & R. Summers, Uniform Commercial Code (3d Ed. 1988) § 18–6, pp. 909–10. Otherwise, § 4–403(3) would be superfluous. Furthermore, whether the customer has suffered such a loss is in the first instance a question of fact. * * *

The cases and commentators also agree that where the check in question was supported by good consideration, or where the payee has enforceable rights against the maker based on the transaction underlying the check, the customer has suffered no loss within the meaning of § 4–403(3). Siegel v. New England Merchants National Bank, supra 386 Mass. at 678–79, 437 N.E.2d 218; * * * W. Hillman, supra, 302; E. Peters, supra; J. White & R. Summers, supra. As then Professor Peters explained, it "is implicit in § 4–403(3) that if a check was issued for good consideration . . . failure to observe a stop-payment order does no more than to accelerate the drawer's inevitable liability, and is therefore a defense to the payor bank." E. Peters, supra.

Applying these principles to the facts of this case, we conclude that as a matter of law Cohn suffered no "loss" within the meaning of § 4–403(3). The check was supported by good consideration because it was issued in payment for the silver coins that Lamphere delivered to Cohn. Furthermore, on the basis of that underlying transaction Lamphere had enforceable rights to payment by Cohn for those coins.

The plaintiff argues, however, that, although the particular check was supported by valid consideration and although there were no defenses available to it arising out of that particular transaction, the previous transaction between Cohn and Lamphere had supplied Cohn with a defense to payment of the check based on Cohn's overpayment to Lamphere. We disagree.

First, the language of § 4–403(3) suggests a narrower reading than would be required by the plaintiff's position. Section 4–403(3) places on the bank's customer the "burden of establishing the *fact and amount of loss resulting from the payment* of an item contrary to a binding stop-payment order. . . ." (Emphasis added.) By contrast, § 4–402, which deals with a bank's liability to its customer for a wrongful *dishonor*, as opposed to a wrongful payment, provides as follows: "A payor bank is liable to its customer for *damages proximately caused by the wrongful dishonor* of an item. When the dishonor occurs through mistake liability is limited to actual damages proved. If so proximately caused and proved damages may include damages for an arrest or prosecution of the customer or other consequential damages. Whether any consequential damages are proximately caused by the wrongful dishonor is a question of fact to be determined in each case." (Emphasis added.) Thus, pursuant to § 4–402 the wrongfully dishonoring bank may be liable for all consequential damages proximately caused by its wrongful conduct, including damages resulting from arrest or prosecution of the customer, whereas there is a conspicuous absence from § 4–403(3) of language indicating such a broad scope of liability for wrongful payment.

This difference in the scope of the language used in § 4–403(3), as compared to that used in § 4–402, is consistent with the notion that § 4–403(3) is intended to impose a limited, rather than broad, form of liability on banks. "The trade-off for requiring banks to accept stop orders under § 4–403(1) was the limitation of their liability under §§ 4–403(3) and 4–407." E. Peters, supra.

The case law and commentary support this more restrictive view of the scope of § 4–403(3). In determining whether a customer has established a "loss" under this section of the code, they focus on the check itself and on the transaction underlying it, and not on whether there were other prior, unrelated transactions between the maker and payee of the check. "In order to prove a loss under [§ 4–403(3) of] the Code, a customer must prove he was not liable to the payee *on the check*. White & Summers, Uniform Commercial Code 560 (2d ed. 1980); Brady, Brady on Bank Checks § 20.20 p. 20–45 (5th ed. 1979); 6 Reitman & Weisblatt, Banking Law § 133.B07(2) (Bender's Banking Law Service 1981)." (Emphasis added.) Bryan v. Citizens National Bank In Abilene, 628 S.W.2d 761, 763 (Tex. 1982) * * *. Although Cohn had an offset or counterclaim available to it with respect to Lamphere, it did not have a defense to payment of the check itself. * * *

In this case, the plaintiff seeks more than to establish a loss caused by the bank's failure to honor Cohn's stop-payment order. That "loss" occurred in fact on November 9, 1978, when Cohn overpaid for the coins it had received. Rather, the plaintiff seeks to recoup a loss resulting from a prior transaction separate from and independent of the stopped check. Thus, the plaintiff's position would permit the customer to establish a "loss" based on offsets or counterclaims against the payee based on prior unrelated transactions, no matter how remote from the check in question or from the transaction underlying it. We do not believe that the intent of § 4–403(3) ranges that far. * * *

The judgment is reversed, and the case is remanded with direction to render judgment for the defendant.

In this opinion CALLAHAN and HULL, JJ., concurred.

■ SHEA, ASSOCIATE JUSTICE, WITH WHOM GLASS, ASSOCIATE JUSTICE, JOINS, DISSENTING.

In this case it is undisputed that the drawer, Cohn Precious Metals, Inc. (Cohn), complied fully with General Statutes § 4–403(1) in stopping payment on the checks it had delivered to Lamphere Coin, Inc. (Lamphere), on November 10, 1978, while unaware of the overpayment of $19,606.86 on November 9, 1978. It is also clear that, but for the negligence of the bank in paying the $12,175 check contrary to the stop-payment order, Cohn could have offset its overpayment of the previous day against the value of the coins received from Lamphere on November 10, 1978. Thus, as the trial court concluded, the plaintiff trustee, on behalf of Cohn, sustained his "burden of establishing the fact and amount of loss resulting from payment of an item contrary to a binding stop-payment order" by the defendant bank, as § 4–403(3) requires.[1]

---

1. On the basis of the facts before us, the trial court's award of $12,175 damages may have been excessive. The amount of the overpayment of November 9, 1978, was

The majority opinion does not challenge, as unsupported by the evidence, the trial court's factual finding that Cohn suffered a loss resulting from the bank's negligent payment of the $12,175 check to Lamphere, but rejects this straightforward "but for" causation analysis in favor of a narrower view of the "resulting from payment" provision of § 4–403(3). The majority would restrict a bank's liability for paying a check contrary to a stop order to losses arising from the transaction in which the check was issued, such as a failure of consideration. I disagree, because there is nothing in the text of § 4–403(3) or its history to support such an unjustifiable curtailment of the right of the drawer recognized by § 4–403(3) to stop-payment on a check for any reason, so long as the order is given to the bank in a timely and reasonable manner, as in this case. The right, of course, would be illusory without recourse against the negligent bank. * * *

The majority stresses the difference between the "resulting from" causation language of § 4–403(3) and the more elaborate provision of § 4–402 that expressly makes the bank liable for consequential damages for wrongfully dishonoring a check, including such damages as may result from the arrest or prosecution of the customer. Such a provision in § 4–402 is probably necessary if liability for such damages is to be imposed because of the contract law limitation of damages to those that are reasonably foreseeable at the time of the contract. 3 Restatement (Second), Contracts § 351(1). Such a provision in § 4–403(3) is unnecessary to make a bank liable for the amount of a check it has paid after a stop-payment order, however, because it is obvious that such a loss to the drawer from the bank's oversight is readily foreseeable.

* * * The view of the majority that a drawer should be made to bear a loss that would have been avoided but for the bank's neglect, because it did not arise from the transaction in which the check was issued, places a substantial restriction on the right to stop-payment that § 4–403(1) purports to give.

With respect to § 4–407 and the defendant's claim to be a holder in due course, there is nothing in the record to indicate that the collecting bank ever allowed the payee to draw on the check after it was deposited. Since there is no proof that the collecting bank gave value, the defendant's claim to be subrogated to the status of a holder in due course is without foundation.

Accordingly, I dissent.

$19,606.86. The value of the silver dollars received by Cohn on November 10, 1978 was $21,175. Before the two checks totaling $21,175 were issued for this purchase, Cohn owed Lamphere $1568.14. That debt was discharged by the bank's erroneous payment of the $12,175 check. Thus, Cohn received good consideration of $1568.14 as a result of the bank's payment and its loss is limited to the balance of the amount paid on the $12,175 check, $10,606.86.

2. OPERATIONAL ISSUES

If the customer gives an oral order to stop-payment, 4–403(b) provides that the order lapses after 14 calendar days unless confirmed in writing within that period. Usually the check will be presented and dishonored within the 14–day period after the oral order was given, but if the check is not presented during that period and the customer fails to confirm the order in writing, the bank may have a customer relations problem. Although 4–403(b) allows the bank to treat an unconfirmed oral stop-payment order as having no effect after the 14–day period, if the bank later pays the check, the customer may contend that it had not understood that it had to confirm in writing within a short period of time. Playing back the tape recording of the conversation regarding the stop-payment order to the customer is not likely to placate the customer; the directions to the customer may have been couched in banker's talk that customers (and sympathetic juries) find difficult to understand. On the other hand, if the bank suspects that the customer wants the stop-payment order to continue even though not confirmed and dishonors the subsequently presented check, the bank risks being held for wrongful dishonor. Banks customarily try to prevent misunderstandings in these cases by sending a written confirmation form to the customer as quickly as possible after the oral order is received with an exhortation to the customer to return the form immediately. The matter is discussed in 1 Clark & Clark, The Law of Bank Deposits, Collections and Credit Cards & 3.06[1][b] (Rev. ed. 1999).

PROBLEMS

1. Customers ordered Bank to stop-payment on check number 292 drawn on their account number 315–726 for $1000. The stop order was communicated to Bank in plenty of time to act on it. However, since the correct number of the check in question was 280 and not 292, Bank's computer, which was directed to identify only checks on a customer's account which bore the correct check number, did not identify the check, and it was paid. Bank denied liability for violating the stop order because under 4–403(a) banks must stop-payment on a check only if the check is described by the customer "with reasonable certainty." Bank conceded that its computer could have been directed to stop-payment by (1) check number alone, (2) by check number and amount of check, or (3) by amount of check alone. Did Customers identify the check with reasonable certainty? See Comment 5 to 4–403.

2. Would the decision in Problem 1 be affected by a clause in the bank's stop order form stating: "In order to stop-payment on a check, you must inform the bank of the exact amount of the item, the number of the check, and your account number; otherwise our computer may not catch the stop order. Unless this is done the bank will not be responsible for any loss resulting from its failure to stop-payment"? 1 Clark & Clark, The Law of Bank Deposits, Collections and Credit Cards & 3.06[1][b] and [d] (Rev. ed. 1999). Is this clause valid under 4–103(a) as determining "the standards by which the bank's responsibility is to be measured" or is it invalid as an attempt to disclaim the bank's responsibility for its "failure to exercise ordinary care"? Comment 1 to 4–403.

3. Suppose Bank induces its customer to sign a stop-payment form containing the following clause: "In requesting you to stop-payment of this or any other item, the undersigned agrees to hold you harmless for all expenses and costs incurred by you on account of refusing payment of said item, and further agrees not to hold you liable on account of payment contrary to this request if same occurs through inadvertence, accident or oversight, or if by reason of such payment other items drawn by the undersigned are returned insufficient." Is this clause, or any part of it, enforceable? 4–103(a) and 4–403. See Opinion of Attorney General of Connecticut, 25 U.C.C. Rep. Serv. 238, 1978 WL 23495 (1978).

4. Given that the customer has an absolute right to stop-payment by complying with 4–403, is the drawee bank entitled to impose a charge for processing a stop-payment order? See Opinion of Attorney General of Michigan, 30 U.C.C. Rep. Serv. 1626, 1981 WL 137970 (1981); 33 U.C.C. Rep. Serv. 1445, 1981 WL 138014 (1981). 1 Clark & Clark, supra, & 3.06[1][b]. If a typical charge for a stop order is $20, could a bank legally impose a $200 charge?

NOTE: POSTDATED CHECKS

A luxury that manual processing of checks allowed customers was the postdated check. The customer could hold off an impatient creditor by writing a check for the debt and could control the time of payment by postdating the check. The customer could be confident that the check would not be paid before its date because a bank clerk would examine the check for date before payment by the bank. Under original Article 3 and pre–1990 Article 4, the check was not properly payable until the date of the check, and the bank could not charge the customer's account until that time. But when automated processing of checks became universal in the 1960s, there was no visual examination of the vast majority of checks. Checks were paid or dishonored on the basis of the balance in the account and the machine-readable information on the MICR line. Since there is no space on that line for the date of the check, the usual result is that the check is paid or dishonored without regard to its date. A bank prematurely paying a postdated check that depleted the customer's account balance could be liable for wrongfully dishonoring subsequent checks that would have been paid had the postdated check not been paid. A bank might seek protection against this liability by a clause in the bank-customer agreement allowing payment of any check at the time of presentment regardless of the date of the check. To the extent such a clause was enforceable, it deprived the customer of the ability to rely on postdating.

Section 4–401(c) offers a compromise that enables customers to post-date checks while protecting banks from potential liability for failure to examine each check for its date. Under this provision the bank can pay all checks at the time of presentment unless it has received a notice of postdating from the customer. This allows the bank time to order its computer to identify the described check when it is presented so that its date may be examined before a decision to pay is made. Banks charge a fee for processing notices of postdating just as they charge for stop-payment orders.

C. SECTION 4–303 AND THE "FOUR LEGALS"

1. CLAIMS AFFECTING THE CUSTOMER'S ACCOUNT

In Chapter 13 we considered when a check is paid in order to determine how long a payor bank has to decide whether to dishonor. A related issue concerns the priority of parties who assert rights that affect the customer's bank account as against a check that is presented for payment from that account. Whether a payor bank will pay a check depends on whether the balance in the customer's account is large enough to cover the check. A number of events may occur after a check has been presented for payment that give rise to claims that affect the size of the customer's balance. The priority between these claims, often referred to as the "four legals," and the right of the holder of the check to be paid is governed by 4–303(a). The events enumerated in 4–303(a), are (1) knowledge or notice by the bank of the customer's death, incompetency or bankruptcy; (2) a customer's order received by the bank to stop-payment; (3) legal process (e.g., garnishment) served on the bank by a creditor of the customer; and (4) setoff against the customer's account exercised by the payor bank. The "four legals" are discussed in 1 Clark & Clark, The Law of Bank Deposits, Collections and Credit Cards & 6.03 (Rev. ed. 1999); 2 White & Summers, Uniform Commercial Code § 21–7 (4th Prac. ed. 1995).

We have seen in the previous section that a customer has an absolute right to stop-payment on a check under 4–403(a), and the payor bank must honor a stop order received at a time that gives the bank "a reasonable opportunity" to act on it. Just as a bank's authority to pay a check of a customer may be revoked by the express direction of the customer, as in the case of a stop-payment order, it may also be revoked by operation of law as in the case of the death, adjudication of incompetency or bankruptcy of the customer. The risk to the bank in making unauthorized payment in these cases is similar to that involved in the case of stop-payment orders. Section 4–405(a) deals specifically with the bank's authority in the case of death or incapacity and 4–405(b) gives to the bank additional authority in the case of death. On the latter point see Comments 2 and 3 to 4–405.

The authority of the bank to act in the case of the bankruptcy of the customer is not dealt with by the UCC because the question is governed by federal rather than state law. Under Bankruptcy Code § 541(a) the property of the bankrupt (including bank accounts) passes to the estate in bankruptcy when the bankruptcy case is commenced. Thus, after bankruptcy, payment by the bank of a check drawn on the account would be a payment of funds owned by the bankruptcy estate rather than by the bankrupt customer. Authority to dispose of property of the bankruptcy estate rests with the trustee in bankruptcy, and in the case of a Chapter 7 bankruptcy, this means that the bankrupt has no right to dispose of assets of the estate. But, under Bankruptcy Code § 542(c) a bank, until it has "actual notice [or] actual knowledge" of the bankruptcy of its customer, may continue to pay checks of the customer. The latter provision codifies the result of Bank of Marin v. England, 385 U.S. 99 (1966), which recognized the same right of the bank under the previous statute, the Bankruptcy Act of 1898.

Attaching and judgment creditors of the customer are given the right under conditions set out in state statutes to reach the customer's bank accounts by legal process. The asset reached is the debt the payor bank owes the customer for the amount of the account. The process used is generally described as garnishment, under which a writ is served on the payor bank notifying it to pay over to a judicial officer for the benefit of the creditor the amount in the account up to the unpaid balance of the claim.

If the payor bank itself is a creditor of the customer, the bank may collect its debt extrajudicially by exercise of its traditional right of setoff. The bank may offset debts the customer owes the bank (loans the bank has made to the customer) against the debt the bank owes the customer (the balance of the customer's bank account). No legal process is involved in the bank's exercise of its right of setoff; bookkeeping entries indicating that the money has been withdrawn from the account suffice to effectuate the setoff.

2.   PRIORITY RULES OF SECTION 4–303

The problem that must be solved is at what point a check has reached the stage in the payor bank's payment process that the amount of that check can no longer be considered part of the customer's account balance and subject to the "legals." Section 4–303(a) addresses this issue. Under 4–303(a)(1), when a bank certifies a check, the amount of that check is no longer considered to be in the customer's account for purpose of the legals. The same is true when the check is presented over the counter for immediate payment and the presenter receives cash (4–303(a)(2)) or a cashier's or teller's check (4–303(a)(3)). See Comment 3 to 4–303. If the check has been effectively paid by expiration of the midnight deadline, any subsequent claim under one of the legals comes too late to be prior to the check (4–303(a)(4)).

A special rule is set out in 4–303(a)(5) for checks that will apply to the great bulk of checks that are presented to payor banks through banking channels. This provides that if a check is presented to a payor bank on Day 1, the amount of that check is no longer considered to be included in the customer's account for purposes of the legals after the close of the banking day on Day 2. However, the bank can shorten that period by setting a cutoff hour on Day 2 no earlier than one hour after the opening of business. This means that if a garnishment order is served on the payor bank after that cutoff hour, the balance of the account subject to the garnishment does not include the amount of the check in question, and the bank is protected if it pays the check. By the same token, the balance of the account subject to the payor's bank's right of setoff is similarly reduced after this point. Nor can a customer stop-payment on the check after the cutoff hour. However, if a bankruptcy proceeding has been commenced involving the customer, Bankruptcy Code § 362(a)(7) prevents the bank from exercising its setoff right, even if the bank does not know that the proceeding has been commenced. In this case the bank must obtain the permission of the bankruptcy court to do so.

W & D Acquisition, LLC v. First Union National Bank

Supreme Court of Connecticut, 2003.
262 Conn. 704, 817 A.2d 91.

■ BORDEN, J.

The dispositive issue in this appeal is whether, as a matter of law, a banking institution has until the "midnight deadline" described in General Statutes § 42a–4–104 (a)(10) to comply with garnishment process under General Statutes § 42a–4–303 (a). The plaintiff, W & D Acquisition, LLC, claims that the duration of the "reasonable time" period in which to comply with garnishment process pursuant to § 42a–4–303 (a) is not defined by the midnight deadline, but is to be measured by a "reasonable time," considering the facts of the case. We agree with the plaintiff and, accordingly, we reverse the judgment of the trial court to the contrary.

The plaintiff brought this writ of scire facias alleging that the defendant, First Union National Bank, had failed to secure garnished funds held in the accounts of one of its customers, R.K.E. Associates (R.K.E.), which was a defendant in the underlying action. The defendant moved for summary judgment, arguing that it was not obligated to secure the garnished funds until its midnight deadline,[5] at which time only a nominal sum remained in the accounts subject to garnishment. The trial court ruled that, as a matter of law, a banking institution has until that time to secure garnished funds. Accordingly, the court granted the defendant's motion for summary judgment, except as to the nominal sum that remained in the accounts at the midnight deadline, as to which the court rendered judgment for the plaintiff. This appeal followed.

The parties presented the following undisputed facts on the motion for summary judgment. The plaintiff is a construction materials supplier that brought an action against R.K.E., a building contractor, for breach of a provisional credit contract. In that action, the plaintiff alleged that it had supplied R.K.E. with $45,436.40 worth of construction materials on credit and that R.K.E. had failed to pay any of that balance. After demonstrating

---

5. In this case, the midnight deadline would be midnight of the banking day following service of the garnishment process.

to the trial court that there was probable cause to believe that a judgment would enter in its favor, the plaintiff obtained an ex parte prejudgment garnishment order for up to $70,000 of the goods or estate of R.K.E. to secure the potential judgment. The defendant was one of four named garnishees, all of which were banking institutions where R.K.E. allegedly had deposited funds. At approximately noon on October 27, 1997, the plaintiff served a copy of the writ of garnishment and a copy of the complaint on the defendant at one of the defendant's branch locations in Danbury. At that time, R.K.E. held two accounts with the defendant, which are known here as account 1 and account 2. The balance in account 1 was $34,163.79, and it fluctuated with debits and credits throughout the ensuing hours. The balance in account 2 was $30.54, and it remained at that level throughout the entire relevant time period.

The defendant did not secure the money in either account when the garnishment papers were served. At 3:26 p.m. on that same day, an agent of R.K.E. entered the same Danbury branch location of the defendant and, by means of a counter withdrawal,[7] withdrew $32,318.26 in cash from account 1, leaving a balance of approximately $1845. Additional credits and debits reduced the balance of account 1 to $200.39 at the close of business on October 27, and $30.43 at the close of business on October 28. At midnight on October 28, 1997, the midnight deadline following the garnishment, the balance of account 1 remained at $30.43.

The plaintiff then brought this writ of scire facias to recover funds that it alleged the defendant should have secured in response to the garnishment. The defendant moved for summary judgment on the basis that it was not obligated to secure the garnished funds until the midnight deadline. The trial court granted the motion, and rendered judgment for the plaintiff in the amount of $60.97, the sum that remained in R.K.E.'s accounts at the midnight deadline.

On appeal, the plaintiff claims that the trial court improperly determined that, as a matter of law, a banking institution has until the midnight deadline described in § 42a–4–104 (a)(10) to comply with garnishment process pursuant to § 42a–4–303 (a). Specifically, the plaintiff claims that General Statutes §§ 42a–4–303 (a) and 52–329[9] require a bank to comply

---

7. The term "counter withdrawal" refers to the common practice of withdrawing funds from a bank account in person by filling out, signing and presenting a withdrawal slip to a bank teller. The withdrawal slip used in the transaction at issue in this case was a nonnegotiable encoded document, with fields for the account number, name of the account holder, authorized signature, date and dollar amount.

9. General Statutes § 52–329 provides in relevant part that *"from the time of leaving [a] copy* [of the necessary garnishment process on a garnishee] all the effects of the defendant in the hands of any such garnishee, and any debt due from any such garnishee to the defendant ... shall be secured in the hands of such garnishee to pay such judgment as the plaintiff may recover...." (Emphasis added.) Nonetheless, the parties agree, as do we, that this provision cannot feasibly or fairly be applied literally, because a bank necessarily requires some period of time from the moment the process is left with it to take the practical steps necessary to secure the funds in its depositor's account.

Thus, both sides agree that this provision means that a bank has a reasonable time

with garnishment process within a "reasonable time" period, the precise duration of which will vary from case to case, depending upon the factual circumstances. We agree with the plaintiff. * * *

The statutory provision primarily at issue in this appeal is § 42a-4–303 (a). We first turn to its language. The language of § 42a–4–303 (a) strongly suggests that the relevant time period is a reasonable time depending upon all of the relevant facts and circumstances, rather than a fixed period terminating on the bank's midnight deadline.

Section 42a–4–303 (a) provides that "[a]ny ... legal process served upon ... a payor bank comes too late to terminate, suspend, or modify the bank's right or duty to pay an item or to charge its customer's account for the item if the ... legal process is received or served and *a reasonable time for the bank to act* thereon expires ... after the earliest of the following: (1) [t]he bank accepts ... the item; (2) the bank pays the item in cash...." (Emphasis added.) In other words, under § 42a–4–303 (a), a banking institution is obligated to secure funds within a "reasonable time" after receiving garnishment process, a form of "legal process," to prevent distribution of those funds in response to an "item." The "item[s]" at issue in this case include a withdrawal slip[10] tendered in exchange for $32,318.26 in cash as well as several checks drawn against account 1 in the hours that followed.[11]

Section 42a–4–303 (a) expressly provides that a banking institution must act within a "reasonable time"; it does not expressly provide that a banking institution must act before its midnight deadline. We do not decide the meaning of "reasonable time," as used in § 42a–4–303 (a), in a vacuum. General Statutes § 42a–1–[12] 204 further defines "reasonable time" as used in § 42a–4–303 (a). Section 42a–1–204 (1) specifically provides that the standards that it contains apply to conduct governed by "this title...." "[T]his title" is title 42a of the General Statutes, the Uniform

in which to act. They differ, however, regarding how to measure that reasonable time. The plaintiff contends that the reasonable time must be determined on a case-by-case basis, depending on all of the facts and circumstances. The defendant contends that, as a matter of law, its midnight deadline is the appropriate measurement of what is a reasonable time.

10.   See footnote 7 of this opinion.

11.   * * * [T]he withdrawal slip that R.K.E. handed to the defendant's teller was an "item" within the meaning of § 42a–4–303 (a). General Statutes § 42a–4–104 (a)(9) defines an " 'item' " as, inter alia, "an ... order to pay money handled by a bank for collection or payment...." An " '[o]rder' " is defined in General Statutes § 42a–3–103 (a)(6) as "a written instruction to pay money signed by the person giving the instruc-

tion...." The withdrawal slip at issue in this appeal was a written instruction to pay out $32,318.26 in cash, handled by a bank, namely, the defendant, for payment, and signed by the agent of R.K.E., who gave the bank the instruction to pay. See footnote 7 of this opinion.

12.   General Statutes § 42a–1–204 provides: "(1) Whenever this title requires any action to be taken within a reasonable time, any time which is not manifestly unreasonable may be fixed by agreement.

"(2) What is a reasonable time for taking any action depends on the nature, purpose and circumstances of such action.

"(3) An action is taken 'seasonably' when it is taken at or within the time agreed or if no time is agreed at or within a reasonable time."

Commercial Code. The requirement in § 42a–4–303 (a) that a bank act within a "reasonable time," is a provision of the Uniform Commercial Code. Thus, the standards set forth in § 42a–1–204, which define the phrase "reasonable time," apply to § 42a–4–303 (a). Section 42a–1–204 (2) specifically provides: "What is a reasonable time for taking any action depends on the nature, purpose and circumstances of such action." Thus, textually, § 42a–4–303 (a) strongly indicates, by its open-textured language and by virtue of § 42a–1–204 (2), that its meaning is what is normally meant by the statutory use of the phrase "reasonable time," namely, a fact-specific inquiry depending on all of the circumstances of the case.

The conclusion that the phrase "reasonable time" as used in § 42a–4–303 (a) requires a fact-specific inquiry and is not synonymous with the midnight deadline is also consistent with the official commentary of the Uniform Commercial Code dealing with the very same "reasonable time" provision. Section 42a–4–303 is our state's version of § 4–303 of the Uniform Commercial Code. The official commentary to § 4–303 is a part of the circumstances surrounding the enactment of § 42a–4–303 (a), and, as such, is relevant to the legislature's intent. * * * Official comment 6 to § 4–303 of the Uniform Commercial Code provides in relevant part: "In the case of . . . legal process the effective time for determining whether [it was] received too late to affect the payment of an item and a charge to the customer's account by reason of such payment, is receipt plus a reasonable time for the bank to act on [the service of process]. . . . Usually, a relatively short time is required to communicate to the accounting department advice of one of these events but certainly some time is necessary. . . ." Thus, the official commentary unequivocally states that the time period is variable and depends upon the factual circumstances. It makes no mention of the bright-line rule created by the midnight deadline.

This conclusion is consistent with what we perceive to be the purpose of § 42a–4–303 (a), namely, to balance the interests of the garnishor in securing its potential debtor's funds against the need for the bank to have the necessary time in which to take the steps necessary to effectuate that security. Although, as the defendant suggests, a midnight deadline would give a bank more certainty and, in all likelihood, more time to take those steps, we see nothing in either the language or the purpose of the statute to justify that bright-line rule. * * *

The judgment is reversed and the case is remanded for further proceedings according to law.

PROBLEM

Payee deposited a check for $25,000 in Depositary Bank (DB) for collection. The check was drawn by Drawer on her account in Payor Bank (PB) and was presented through banking channels to PB at 10 a.m. on Day 1. At the time the check was presented, Drawer had $30,000 in collected funds in her account. At noon on Day 2, PB examined the check and noted that paying the check would leave only $5,000 in Drawer's account. This was of concern to PB because Drawer owed PB $20,000 on an overdue loan. At 2 p.m. on Day 2, PB made the bookkeeping entries that were required to setoff its $20,000 claim against Drawer's account. Since this act reduced Drawer's account to $10,000, PB returned the check, marked "not sufficient funds," to the presenting bank at 6 p.m. on Day 2. The close of PB's banking day was 5 p.m., and it had not opted for an earlier cutoff hour. Payee challenged PB's right to setoff against the check 26 hours after it had been presented to PB. Is Payee correct? See 4–303(a)(5) and Comment 4.

D.   "HIGH-TO-LOW" BASIS OF POSTING

Bank receives five checks drawn on Customer's account that are presented on the same day: $1500 mortgage payment, $500 car payment, $100 credit card payment, $65 florist payment, and $60 gift shop payment. But Customer's account contained only $1525 on that date. Bank paid the $1500 check and returned the four others, charging the customer a $25 NSF (not sufficient funds) fee for each returned check. When Customer learned that Bank could have paid the four smaller checks and assessed only a single $25 NSF fee, he complained loudly. Bank explained that it followed the "high-to-low" posting basis, which meant that its policy was to pay the largest check first; moreover, the law clearly gives it the option of choosing this payment basis. Section 4–303(b) states: " * * * items may be accepted, paid, certified, or charged to the indicated account of its customer in any order."

Different banks use different posting rules. According to Rick Brooks, How Banks Make the Most of Bounced Checks, Wall St. J., Feb. 25, 1999, at B1, among the nation's five largest banks, three pay the largest checks first and two pay the smallest checks first. Other banks pay checks on the basis of check number; others say that they will sometimes deviate from their policy to give a customer a break when they see that a number of checks are likely to bounce. Some high-low banks justify their policy by maintaining that their customers tell them they want the largest checks paid first; they would rather owe the florist than have their mortgage check bounce. Before Revised Article 4, banks usually had clauses in their deposit agreements with their customers saying about what 4–303(b) now says. At the time Revised Article 4 was being drafted, the codification of these agreements was not controversial. But, during the enactment process, consumer groups in California and Texas were sufficiently concerned about the potential for abuse in 4–303(b) to persuade their legislatures to append the following to the Official Comments:

> The only restraint on the discretion given to the payor bank under subsection (b) is that the bank act in good faith. For example, the bank could not properly follow an established practice of maximizing the number of returned checks for the sole purpose of increasing the amount of returned check fees charged to the customer.

Over time, enough customers have become sufficiently aggrieved by high-low posting that lawsuits have challenged the practice as merely a device for increasing banks' income from NSF fees. According to the Brooks' article, out of the 173 million checks processed daily, 1.3 million are NSF, and, with fees running up as high as $30 per check, the stakes are high. When pre-trial discovery in some of these suits turned up damaging intra-bank communications proposing that the high-low formula be adopted in order to increase revenue, the fat was in the fire. So far the banks have been winning these cases. See, e.g, Hill v. St. Paul Federal Bank for Savings, 768 N.E.2d 322 (Ill. App. 2002), which held that even if the motive of the bank in adopting the high-low posting order was to maximize profits, the motive was irrelevant because 4–303(b) authorizes high-low posting. Since issue in 2001 by the Comptroller of the Currency of Interpretative Letter #916 that is favorable to high-low posting, litigation appears to have diminished. See Clarks' Bank Deposits and Payments Monthly, Vol. 10, No. 6, Nov. 2001, at p.1, and Vol. 11, No. 8, Jan. 2003, at p.3.

E.   WRONGFUL DISHONOR

Most business lawyers at some time receive a call from an irate client whose check has been bounced by a bank. Sometimes the bank has not been sufficiently contrite about its error, and your client wants to "teach that bank a lesson." What can you do for this client? As we will see, the answer to this in most cases is very little, other than to extract an apology from the chastened bank. Nonetheless, the lawyer would do well to ask the client some detailed questions about the facts surrounding the wrongful dishonor, for, under certain circumstances, 4–402(b) not only offers the wronged customer direct damages but is one of the few provisions in the UCC that offers consequential damages.

Section 4–402(b) is only the latest step in a long series of judicial and legislative efforts to strike a balance between the erring bank and the wronged customer. In nineteenth century rural America, in which everyone knew everyone else's business, wrongful dishonor of checks was treated as slander against the character of a business person ("trader"). 1 Clark & Clark, supra, & 3.05[9][c] (Rev. ed. 1999). Being a "no account" was a serious accusation. The so-called "trader rule" was stated in 2 Morse, Banks and Banking 1007–1008 (6th ed., Voorhees, 1928):

> [T]he better authority seems to be, that, even if * * * actual loss or injury is not shown, yet more than nominal damages shall be given. It can hardly be possible that a customer's check can be wrongfully refused payment without some impeachment of his credit, which must in fact be an actual injury, though he cannot from the nature of the case furnish independent distinct proof thereof. It is as in cases of libel and slander, which description of suit, indeed, it closely resembles, inasmuch as it is a practical slur upon the plaintiff's credit and repute in the business world. Special damage may be shown, if the plaintiff be able; but, if he be not able, the jury may nevertheless give such

[temperate] damages as they conceive to be a reasonable compensation for that indefinite mischief which such an act must be assumed to have inflicted, according to the ordinary course of human events.

This was a plaintiff's lawyer's dream: if a bank wrongfully dishonored the check of a business customer, the customer got to the jury without showing any actual damage, and juries weren't any more fond of banks then than now. The banks fought back in the legislatures. At the behest of the American Bankers Association, a number of states enacted a version of the following: "No bank shall be liable to a depositor because of the nonpayment through mistake or error, and without malice, of a check which should have been paid unless the depositor shall allege and prove actual damage by reason of such nonpayment and in such event the liability shall not exceed the amount of damage so proved." Cal. Civ. Code § 3320 (repealed).

The original version of what is now 4–402(b) read: "A payor bank is liable to its customer for damages proximately caused by the wrongful dishonor of an item. When the dishonor occurs through mistake liability is limited to actual damages proved. If so proximately caused and proved damages may include damages for an arrest or prosecution of the customer or other consequential damages. Whether any consequential damages are proximately caused by the wrongful dishonor is a question of fact to be determined in each case." Comment 1 to Revised 4–402 contains a critique of this language and discusses the changes made in the revision.

Loucks v. Albuquerque National Bank

Supreme Court of New Mexico, 1966.
76 N.M. 735, 418 P.2d 191.

■ LA FEL E. OMAN, JUDGE, Court of Appeals.

The plaintiffs-appellants, Richard A. Loucks and Del Martinez, hereinafter referred to as plaintiffs, Mr. Loucks and Mr. Martinez, respectively, were partners engaged in a business at Albuquerque, New Mexico, under the partnership name of L & M Paint and Body Shop.

By their complaint they sought both compensatory and punitive damages on behalf of the partnership, on behalf of Mr. Loucks, and on behalf of Mr. Martinez against the defendants-appellees, Albuquerque National Bank and W. J. Kopp, hereinafter referred to as defendants, the bank, and Mr. Kopp, respectively.

Prior to March 15, 1962 Mr. Martinez had operated a business at Albuquerque, New Mexico, under the name of Del's Paint and Body Shop. He did his banking with defendant bank and he dealt with Mr. Kopp, a vice-president of the bank.

On February 8, 1962 Mr. Martinez borrowed $500 from the bank, which he deposited with the bank in the account of Del's Paint and Body Shop. He executed an installment note payable to the bank evidencing this indebtedness.

On March 15, 1962 the plaintiffs formed a partnership in the name of L & M Paint and Body Shop. On that date they opened a checking account with the bank in the name of L & M Paint and Body Shop and deposited $620 therein. The signatures of both Mr. Loucks and Mr. Martinez were required to draw money from this account. The balance in the account of Del's Paint and Body Shop as of this time was $2.67. This was drawn from this account by a cashier's check and deposited in the account of L & M Paint & Body Shop on April 18, 1962.

Two payments of $50.00 each were made on Mr. Martinez' note of February 8, 1962, or on notes given as a renewal thereof. These payments were made by checks drawn by plaintiffs on the account of L & M Paint and Body Shop. The checks were payable to the order of the bank and were dated June 29, 1962 and August 28, 1962. A subsequent installment note was executed by Mr. Martinez on October 17, 1962 in the principal amount of $462 payable to the order of the bank. This was given as a replacement or renewal of the prior notes which started with the note of February 8, 1962.

Mr. Martinez became delinquent in his payments on this note of October 17, 1962 and the bank sued him in a Justice of the Peace court to recover the delinquency.

As of March 14, 1963 Mr. Martinez was still indebted to the bank on this note in the amount of $402, and on that date, Mr. Kopp, on behalf of the bank, wrote L & M Paint and Body Shop advising that its account had been charged with $402 representing the balance due "on Del Martinez installment note," and the indebtedness was referred to in the letter as the "indebtedness of Mr. Del Martinez."

The charge of $402 against the account of L & M Paint and Body Shop was actually made on March 15, 1963, which was a Friday.

Although Mr. Martinez at one time testified he telephoned Mr. Kopp on either Friday or the following Monday about this charge, when he was questioned more closely he admitted he discussed the matter with Mr. Kopp by telephone on Friday. Mr. Loucks testified that as he recalled, it was on Monday. Both plaintiffs went to the bank on Monday, March 18, and talked with Mr. Kopp. They both told Mr. Kopp that the indebtedness represented by the note was the personal indebtedness of Mr. Martinez and was not a partnership obligation. Mr. Loucks explained that they had some outstanding checks against the partnership account. Mr. Kopp refused to return the money to the partnership account. There was evidence of some unpleasantness in the conversation. The partnership account, in which there was then a balance of only $3.66, was thereupon closed by the plaintiffs.

The bank refused to honor nine, and possibly ten, checks drawn on the account and dated between the dates of March 8 and 16, inclusive.

The checks dated prior to March 15 total $89.14, and those dated March 15 and 16 total $121.68. These figures do not include the tenth check to which some reference was made, but which was not offered into evidence and the amount of which does not appear in the record.

The case came on for trial before the court and a jury. The court submitted the case to the jury upon the question of whether or not the defendants wrongfully made the charge in the amount of $402 against the account of L & M Paint and Body Shop. The allegations of the complaint concerning punitive damages and compensatory damages, other than the amount of $402 allegedly wrongfully charged by the defendants against the partnership account, were dismissed by the court before the case was submitted to the jury. The jury returned a verdict for the plaintiffs in the amount of $402.

The plaintiffs have appealed and assert error on the part of the trial court in taking from the jury the questions of (1) punitive damages, (2) damages to business reputation and credit, (3) damages for personal injuries allegedly sustained by Mr. Loucks, and (4) in disallowing certain costs claimed by plaintiffs.

* * *

The plaintiffs, as partners, sought recovery on behalf of the partnership of $402 allegedly wrongfully charged against the partnership account. This question was submitted to the jury, was decided in favor of the partnership, and against the defendants, and no appeal has been taken from the judgment entered on the verdict. They also sought recovery on behalf of the partnership of $5,000 for alleged damages to its credit, good reputation, and business standing in the community, $1,800 for its alleged loss of income, and $14,404 as punitive damages.

Each partner also sought recovery of $5,000 for alleged damages to his personal credit, good reputation and business standing. Mr. Martinez sought punitive damages individually in the amount of $10,000, and Mr. Loucks sought punitive damages individually in the amount of $60,000. Mr. Loucks also sought $25,000 by way of damages he allegedly sustained by reason of an ulcer which resulted from the wrongful acts of the defendants.

The parties have argued the case in their respective briefs and in their oral arguments upon the theory that the questions here involved, except for Point IV, which deals with the disallowance by the trial court of some claimed costs, are questions of the damages which can properly be claimed as a result of a wrongful dishonor by a bank of checks drawn by a customer or depositor on the bank, and of the sufficiency of the evidence offered by plaintiffs to support their claims for damages.

Both sides quote UCC § 4–402. * * *

It would appear that the first question to be resolved is that of the person, or persons, to whom a bank must respond in damages for a wrongful dishonor. Here, the account was a partnership account, and if there was in fact a wrongful dishonor of any checks, such were partnership checks.

We have adopted the Uniform Commercial Code in New Mexico. In UCC § 4–402 it is clearly stated that a bank "is liable to its customer." In UCC § 4–104(1)(e), entitled "Definitions and index of definitions" it is stated that:

"(1) In this article unless the context otherwise requires

"(e) 'Customer' means any person having an account with a bank or for whom a bank has agreed to collect items and includes a bank carrying an account with another bank; * * * "

This requires us to determine who is a "person" within the contemplation of this definition. Under part II, article I of the Uniform Commercial Code, entitled "General Definitions and Principles of Interpretation," we find the term "person" defined in § 1–201(30) as follows: " 'Person' includes an individual or an organization * * *."

Subsection (28) of the same section expressly includes a "partnership" as one of the legal or commercial entities embraced by the term "organization."

It would seem that logically the "customer" in this case to whom the bank was required to respond in damages for any wrongful dishonor was the partnership. The Uniform Commercial Code expressly regards a partnership as a legal entity. This is consistent with the ordinary mercantile conception of a partnership. * * *

The Uniform Partnership Act, which has been adopted in New Mexico and appears as chapter 66, article I, N.M.S.A.1953, recognizes that a partnership has a separate legal entity for at least some purposes. * * *

Suits may be brought in New Mexico by or against the partnership as such. * * * A partnership is a distinct legal entity to the extent that it may sue or be sued in the partnership name. National Surety Co. v. George E. Breece Lumber Co., 60 F.2d 847 (10th Cir. 1932).

* * *

The relationship, in connection with which the wrongful conduct of the bank arose, was the relationship between the bank and the partnership. The partnership was the customer, and any damages arising from the dishonor belonged to the partnership and not to the partners individually.

The damages claimed by Mr. Loucks as a result of the ulcer, which allegedly resulted from the wrongful acts of the defendants, are not consequential damages proximately caused by the wrongful dishonor as contemplated by § 4–402. In support of his right to recover for such claimed damages he relies upon the cases of Jones v. Citizens Bank of Clovis, 58 N.M. 48, 265 P.2d 366 and Weaver v. Bank of America Nat. Trust & Sav. Ass'n., 59 Cal.2d 428, 30 Cal. Rptr. 4, 380 P.2d 644. The California and New Mexico courts construed identical statutes in these cases. The New Mexico statute appeared as § 48–10–5, N.M.S.A.1953. This statute was repealed when the Uniform Commercial Code was adopted in 1961.

Assuming we were to hold that the decisions in those cases have not been affected by the repeal of the particular statutory provisions involved and the adoption of the Uniform Commercial Code, we are still compelled by our reasoning to reach the same result, because the plaintiffs in those cases were the depositor in the California case and the administratrix of the estate of the deceased depositor in the New Mexico case. In the present case, Mr. Loucks was not a depositor, as provided in the prior statute, nor a customer, as provided in our present statute. No duty was owed to him personally by reason of the debtor-creditor relationship between the bank and the partnership.

It is fundamental that compensatory damages are not recoverable unless they proximately result from some violation of a legally-recognized right of the person seeking the damages, whether such be a right in contract or tort. * * *

Insofar as the damage questions are concerned, we must still consider the claims for damages to the partnership. As above stated, the claim on behalf of the partnership for the recovery of the $402 was concluded by judgment for plaintiffs in this amount. This leaves (1) the claim of $5,000 for alleged damage to credit, reputation and business standing, (2) the claim of $1,800 for alleged loss of income, and (3) the claim of $14,404 as punitive damages.

The question with which we are first confronted is that of whether or not the customer, whose checks are wrongfully dishonored, may recover damages merely because of the wrongful dishonor. We understand the provisions of UCC § 4–402 to limit the damages to those proximately caused by the wrongful dishonor, and such includes any consequential damages so proximately caused. If the dishonor occurs through mistake, the damages are limited to actual damages proved.

It is pointed out in the comments to this section of the Uniform Commercial Code that:

" * * * *

"This section rejects decisions which have held that where the dishonored item has been drawn by a merchant, trader or fiduciary he is defamed in his business, trade or profession by a reflection on his credit and hence that substantial damages may be awarded on the basis of defamation 'per se' without proof that damage has occurred. * * * " Uniform Commercial Code, § 4–402, Comment 3.

If we can say as a matter of law that the dishonor here occurred through mistake, then the damages would be limited to the "actual damages proved." Even if we are able to agree, as contended by defendants in their answer brief, that the defendants acted under a mistake of fact in " * * * that Mr. Kopp acting on behalf of the bank thought that the money was invested in the partnership and could be traced directly from Mr. Martinez to the L & M Paint and Body Shop," still defendants cannot rely on such mistake after both Mr. Martinez and Mr. Loucks informed them on March 15 and 18 that this was a personal obligation of Mr. Martinez and that the partnership had outstanding checks. At least it then became a question for the jury to decide whether or not defendants had wrongfully dishonored the checks through mistake.

The problem then resolves itself into whether or not the evidence offered and received, together with any evidence properly offered and improperly excluded, was sufficient to establish a question as to whether the partnership credit and reputation were proximately damaged by the wrongful dishonors. There was evidence that ten checks were dishonored, that one parts dealer thereafter refused to accept a partnership check and Mr. Loucks was required to go to the bank, cash the check, and then take the cash to the parts dealer in order to get the parts; that some persons who had previously accepted the partnership checks now refused to accept them; that other places of business denied the partnership credit after the dishonors; and that a salesman, who had sold the partnership a map and for which he was paid by one of the dishonored checks, came to the partnership's place of business, and ripped the map off the wall because he had been given "a bad check for it."

This evidence was sufficient to raise a question of fact to be determined by the jury as to whether or not the partnership's credit had been damaged as a proximate result of the dishonors. This question should have been submitted to the jury.

Damages recoverable for injuries to credit as a result of a wrongful dishonor are more than mere nominal damages and are referred to as " * * * compensatory, general, substantial, moderate, or temperate, damages as would be fair and reasonable compensation for the injury which he [the depositor] must have sustained, but not harsh or inordinate damages. * * * " 5A Michie, Banks and Banking, § 243 at 576.

What are reasonable and temperate damages varies according to the circumstances of each case and the general extent to which it may be presumed the credit of the depositor would be injured. * * * The amount of such damages is to be determined by the sound discretion and dispassionate judgment of the jury. * * *

The next item of damages claimed on behalf of the partnership, which was taken from the jury, was the claim for loss of income in the amount of $1,800 allegedly sustained by the partnership as a result of the illness and disability of Mr. Loucks by reason of his ulcer. We are of the opinion that the trial court properly dismissed this claim for the announced reason that no substantial evidence was offered to support the claim, and for the further reason that the partnership had no legally-enforceable right to recover for personal injuries inflicted upon a partner.

Even if we were to assume that a tortious act had been committed by defendants which proximately resulted in the ulcer and the consequent personal injuries and disabilities of Mr. Loucks, the right to recover for such would be in him. An action for damages resulting from a tort can only be sustained by the person directly injured thereby, and not by one claiming to have suffered collateral or resulting injuries. * * *

As was stated by Mr. Justice Holmes in Robins Dry Dock & Repair Co. v. Flint, 275 U.S. 303, 48 S.Ct. 134, 72 L.Ed. 290:

> " * * * no authority need be cited to show that, as a general rule, at least, a tort to the person or property of one man does not make the tort-feasor liable to another merely because the injured person was under a contract with that other, unknown to the doer of the wrong. * * * The law does not spread its protection so far."

The last question of damages concerns the claim for punitive damages. The trial court dismissed this claim for the reason that he was convinced there was no evidence of willful or wanton conduct on the part of defendants. Punitive or exemplary damages may be awarded only when the conduct of the wrongdoer may be said to be maliciously intentional, fraudulent, oppressive, or committed recklessly or with a wanton disregard of the plaintiffs' rights. * * *

Malice as a basis for punitive damages means the intentional doing of a wrongful act without just cause or excuse. This means that the defendant not only intended to do the act which is ascertained to be wrongful, but that he knew it was wrong when he did it. * * *

Although, as expressed above, we are of the opinion that there was a jury question as to whether defendants acted under a mistake of fact in dishonoring the checks, we do not feel that the unpleasant or intemperate remark or two claimed to have been made by Mr. Kopp, and his conduct, described by Mr. Martinez as having "run us out of the bank more or less," are sufficient upon which an award of punitive damages could properly have been made. Thus, the trial court was correct in taking this claim from the jury. * * *

It follows from what has been said that this cause must be reversed and remanded for a new trial solely upon the questions of whether or not the partnership credit was damaged as a proximate result of the dishonors, and, if so, the amount of such damages.

NOTES

1. *"Liable to its customer."* Since *Loucks*, interesting developments have taken place on the issue of who can recover for damages incurred from a wrongful dishonor of the check of a corporate customer. Obviously a corporation cannot suffer emotional distress or acquire ulcers resulting from the bank's mistake, much less the personal embarrassment and social ostracism stemming from being jailed for writing a check that was wrongfully dishonored. But in a closely held corporation these damages may well be sustained by the individuals who own and operate the business. In an era in which plaintiffs are successfully seeking more adequate awards for their injuries, it comes as no surprise that courts are finding ways of reading the term "customer" more flexibly or finding alternative bases for liability. In Kendall Yacht Corp. v. United California Bank, 50 Cal.App.3d 949, 123 Cal.Rptr. 848 (Cal.Ct.App.1975), Corporation was the depositor and Laurence and Linda Kendall were officers and prospective shareholders who personally guaranteed Corporation's debts to Bank. Corporation never issued stock, and "it was, in effect, nothing but a transparent shell, having no viability as a separate and distinct legal entity." 123 Cal.Rptr. at 853. The court held that the Kendalls were "customers" within the meaning of 4–402. "Thus it was entirely foreseeable that the dishonoring of the Corporation's check would reflect directly on the personal credit and reputation of the Kendalls and that they would suffer the adverse personal consequences which resulted when the Bank reneged on its commitments." 123 Cal.Rptr. at 853. The court allowed recovery by the Kendalls of damages for emotional distress under 4–402.

Parrett v. Platte Valley State Bank & Trust Co., 236 Neb. 139, 459 N.W.2d 371 (1990), goes beyond *Kendall Yacht*. Parrett was the principal shareholder and president of the corporate customer. He personally participated in the business relationship between the corporate customer and the bank and entered into a personal guaranty for the corporation's obligations to the bank. When the bank wrongfully dishonored the corporate customer's check, Parrett was charged with felony theft and went to trial on the charge; at trial the charge was dismissed. Parrett sued for wrongful dishonor under 4–402. The lower court sustained the bank's demurrer on the ground that Parrett was not the customer. The Supreme Court of Nebraska, relying on *Kendall Yacht*, reversed and said:

> As reflected by Parrett's petition, the parties' business relationship, which included Parrett's personal guaranty for P & P Machinery's obligations to the bank, was such that it was foreseeable that dishonoring the corporation's check would reflect directly on Parrett. This is borne out by the fact that a criminal charge based on the dishonored check was brought against Parrett, but was dismissed during Parrett's trial. Since the consequences of the wrongful dishonor fell upon Parrett, it would elevate form over substance to say that he was not the bank's "customer" within the meaning of § 4–402. This is not to say that in every case a corporate officer has a wrongful dishonor action against the depository bank on which the corporation's check has been drawn and later dishonored. However, in view of the facts of this case alleged in Parrett's petition, Parrett has a cause of action against the bank.

459 N.W.2d at 378. Although the majority opinion in *Parrett* purported to rely on *Kendall Yacht*, the dissent pointed out that the key factor in that case was that the corporation was not a separate legal entity; the decision was based on veil-piercing. But in *Parrett* the corporate customer was clearly a separate legal entity and had always been treated as such by the bank.

Another line of decisions has held fast to the view expressed in *Loucks* that only the corporate customer can proceed under 4–402. See, e.g., Farmers Bank v. Sinwellan Corp., 367 A.2d 180 (Del.1976) (president of corporate customer denied right to sue under 4–402 for damages resulting from a criminal action brought against him because of the dishonor). An approach to allowing insiders to recover in cases in which corporate checks have been dishonored, even in jurisdictions taking the *Sinwellan* point of view, is to contend that 4–402 does not displace any cause of action that such an insider may have had against the bank at common law. See 1–103(b) and Comment 5 to 4–402.

2. *Damages.* Section 4–402(b) provides very broadly that a bank is liable for any damages proximately caused by a wrongful dishonor. Comment 1 to 4–402 describes a customer's right to sue as a "statutory cause of action." In most cases no damages can be proved, but if economic loss can be shown consequential damages will be awarded. Skov v. Chase Manhattan Bank, 407 F.2d 1318 (3d Cir.1969). The principal damages issue has been whether aggrieved customers can recover for emotional distress. Certainly a wrongful dishonor can proximately cause emotional distress, and this type of damage is within the limitation in the second sentence of 4–402(b) that the damages must be "actual." Although courts show their concern about the potential for abuse present in allowing damages for emotional distress, a number of courts have awarded customers damages for emotional distress in wrongful dishonor cases. The precedents are collected and discussed in Buckley v. Trenton Saving Fund Society, 111 N.J. 355, 544 A.2d 857 (1988). In that case the court held that the facts did not justify recovery for mental anguish and said:

> To some extent, slight emotional distress arising from the occasional dishonor of a check is one of the regrettable aggravations of living in today's society. See *Restatement,* [(Second) of Torts], § 436A comment b. Accordingly, we are reluctant to allow compensation for the intentional infliction of emotional distress when a bank wrongfully dishonors a check unless the bank's conduct is intentional, as well as reckless or outrageous, and the distress is severe or results in bodily injury. See *Hume,* 178 N.J.Super. 310, 428 A.2d 966; *Restatement,* [(Second) of Torts], § 46. When those conditions are met, a customer should be compensated for the emotional distress that is caused by the wrongful dishonor of a check.

544 A.2d at 864. Other courts are similarly restrictive on allowing damages for emotional distress in wrongful dishonor cases. See, e.g., Maryott v. First National Bank of Eden, 624 N.W.2d 96 (S.D. 2001).

Comment 1 to 4–402 points out in its last sentence that whether punitive damages are appropriate depends, under 1–305(a), on non–UCC state law. The matter is discussed in *Buckley.*

3. *Consequential damages.* Two further questions arise in connection with 4–402(b). First, why is the bank liable for consequential damages under 4–402(b) while a receiving bank that improperly executes or fails to execute a wire transfer is not liable for consequential damages under 4A–305(c)–(d), unless it expressly agrees to assume liability? Both 4–402(b) and 4A–305(c) set default rules; the question is why the default rules are set differently. The precaution-taking abilities of banks and customers, and the array of possible loss from wrongful dishonor of a check and improper execution of a wire transfer, seem to be the same. The costs of contracting around a default rule also do not appear to differ as between 4–402(b) and 4A–305(c). What, then, justifies setting different default rules? There might be a political explanation. Banks might have conceded an expanded potential liability under 4A–402(c)'s "money-back guarantee" and 4A–202 and 4A–203's unauthorized payment order provisions in exchange for limitations on recoverable damages under 4A–402(c). A similar sort of trade-off possibly was infeasible in the case of Article 4.

Second, does 4–402(b) set the default rule correctly with respect to consequential damages? There is room for doubt. Where contracting parties have asymmetric information and the less well informed party is the superior risk bearer, an important purpose of default rules can be to induce the party with the better information to disclose it to the less well informed party. See Ian Ayres & Robert Gertner, Filling Gaps in Incomplete Contracts: An Economic Theory of Default Rules, 99 Yale L. J. 87 (1989). This seems warranted in the context of wrongful dishonor of checks because customers typically are better informed than banks about the impact of wrongful dishonor on them. In order for banks to take the appropriate precautions, they need this information. However, allowing customers to recover consequential damages, including for emotional distress, under some plausible assumptions gives them a disincentive to disclose information to banks. As a result, banks might take inefficient precautions against wrongful dishonor. To see this, assume that customers are of two sorts, "low injury" and "high injury," and that banks cannot identify in advance a customer as being of one sort or another. "Low injury" customers suffer few consequential damages from wrongful dishonor, and no loss from emotional distress; "high injury" customers suffer significant consequential damages, including emotional distress. Banks will charge each customer a rate reflecting its expected liability to a mixed population of low and high injury customers. Thus, each customer pays this blended charge. Low injury customers pay a higher rate, and high injury customers a lower rate, than if banks could identify each customer's risk profile. Here high injury customers are subsidized by low risk customers. Banks in turn take inefficient levels of precaution because they overinvest in preventative measures for low injury customers and underinvest in them for high injury customers. An efficient default rule gives high and low injury customers incentives to reveal information about their respective types to banks.

Section 4–402(b) doesn't induce customers to do so. By allowing recovery of consequential damages, including damages for emotional distress, 4–402(b) gives all customers an enhanced level of protection. High injury customers therefore have no incentive to disclose information about their likely emotional distress resulting from banks' wrongful dishonor. They are protected by 4–402(b) and already benefit from the cross-subsidy provided by low injury customers. Low injury customers, who don't need 4–402(b)'s enhanced protection, also might not have an incentive to disclose their type to banks. For instance, if the population of customers contains a significant number of high injury customers and relatively few low injury customers, the subsidy provided to high injury customers might be slight. Disclosure therefore would produce a modest reduction in rates charged to low injury customers. If so, the costs of contracting around 4–402(b), to reduce the banks potential liability, might exceed the benefits of doing so for low risk customers. On the other hand, if the default rule excluded particular sorts of consequential damages, such as damages for emotional distress, high injury customers would be unprotected. Low injury customers would not need to incur contracting costs because the default rule already protects them. High injury customers would have to contract with banks, thus disclosing information about their type, but they receive a benefit in the form of enhanced protection (for an enhanced charge). Thus, 4–402(b) might be an inferior default rule.

This conclusion obviously is sensitive to the assumptions made. A realistic estimate of the population of customers would not divide it into two simplified sorts of customer: low and high injury. The more accurate assumption is that customers come in a continuum of risk profiles, from businesses suffering no emotional distress from wrongful dishonor, to the thick-skinned customer, to the socially sensitive or financially precarious customer. The extent of other sorts of consequential damage also realistically varies among customers, as does the size of contracting costs for customers of bargaining around a default rule. Section 4–402(b)'s default rule might be superior to other candidates, given the limited information available to lawmakers in designing or applying default rules. For the important effect of such details on the choice of default rule, see Barry E. Adler, The Questionable Ascent of Hadley v. Baxendale, 51 Stan. L. Rev. 1547 (1999); Alan Schwartz, The Default Rule Paradigm and the Limits of Contract Law, 3 S. Cal. Interdisc. L. J. 389 (1993); Lucian Ayre Bebchuk & Steven Shavell, Information and the Scope of Liability for Breach of Contract: The Rule of Hadley v. Baxendale, 7 J. L. Econ. & Org. 284 (1991).

F.   THE BANK-CUSTOMER AGREEMENT

1.   DISCLOSURE: THE TRUTH-IN-SAVINGS ACT

Among the demands that consumer groups have made of deposit-holding institutions, one of the most persistent has been the call for improved disclosure of the terms of deposit accounts so that customers may better understand the agreements they are entering into with banks. The drive for improved disclosure has been at the core of the consumer movement in the second half of the last century. At the earliest stage of this movement, Senator Paul Douglas of Illinois, a former economics professor, noted that financial institutions quoted their finance charges to consumers in several different ways: annual percentage rate, monthly percentage rate, annual dollar amount, and so forth. These practices made it difficult for consumers to do effective credit shopping because they could not be sure which creditor was offering the lowest rates. He proposed what sounded like a modest solution: require all creditors to state their finance charges as an annual percentage rate or "simple annual interest," as he liked to put it. Creditors, seeing the head of the federal camel under the tent, tried to head off the legislation by asserting that the variety and complexity of consumer credit transactions were so great that such a law would be operationally impossible for creditors to comply with. After many years of heated discussions about the subject, Congress passed the Truth-in-Lending Act in 1968, which required disclosure of finance charges in terms of an annual percentage rate. 15 U.S.C. § 1601 et seq. Congress passed on to a reluctant Federal Reserve Board the task of solving by regulations the innumerable operational problems encountered. Regulation Z, 12 C.F.R. Part 226, resulted. There now is a considerable body of legislative, administrative and case law on the subject of the disclosure of consumer finance charges. The Truth-in-Lending Act served as a model for the deposit account disclosure legislation that came along more than two decades later.

Consumers had the same problems in attempting to compare the terms offered by banks and other depository institutions with respect to deposit accounts. These terms are usually contained either in the bank-customer agreement or in a separate brochure and are selectively publicized in advertisements designed to attract more depositors. Consumers complained that although most deposit institutions disclosed the interest rates they were paying on deposit accounts as an annual percentage rate based on the full amount of the principal in the account, others used methods that made it appear that the interest rate offered was higher than it actually was. As was the case with Truth in Lending, negotiations leading to Truth in Savings went on for years in Congress before the Act was finally passed in 1991 as part of the Federal Deposit Insurance Act, 12 U.S.C. § 4301 et seq. Again Congress fobbed off on the Fed the task of making the law workable, and Regulation DD, 12 C.F.R. Part 230, was completed in 1992 for this purpose. The Act and the Regulation are extensively discussed in 2 Clark & Clark, Bank Deposits, Collections and Credit Cards, Chapter 19 (Rev. ed. 1999).

(1) *Initial disclosure.* In brief, the Truth-in-Savings Act (TISA) requires federal and state deposit-holding institutions, e.g., banks, savings and loan associations, and credit unions, to disclose in a uniform manner the terms of their consumer deposit accounts at the time of entering into the deposit relationship with the customer. This initial disclosure must include interest rate information, the amounts of any service charges or other fees that may be imposed in connection with the account, and other salient features of the deposit account like minimum balance requirements, time account features (e.g., the effect of early withdrawal), and transaction limitations (e.g., limitations on the number of withdrawals or deposits). Regulation DD § 230.4. Although TISA applies to credit union accounts, Regulation DD does not; credit unions have parallel regulations. Regulation DD § 230.1(c).

The key items disclosed are the interest rate and the "annual percentage yield" (APY), which is the yield the interest rate produces with compounding. Regulation DD § 230.2(c). It is this figure that should be most useful to consumers in interest rate shopping. The model clause suggested by the Appendix to Regulation DD is:

> The interest rate on your account is _____% with an annual percentage yield of _____%.

(2) *Periodic statement disclosures.* Additional disclosures must be made in the periodic, usually monthly, statements that depository institutions send to their customers. Regulation DD § 230.6. These disclosures must include the "annual percentage yield earned" during the statement period, the dollar amount of the interest earned during that period, the dollar amounts and kinds of fees imposed and the number of days in the statement period or the beginning and ending dates of the period.

(3) *Advertising.* The third level of disclosure regulation relates to advertising. As is true with any law attempting to regulate advertising, Regulation DD § 230.8 is very complex. In an attempt to force the depository institution to be fair in its advertising, Regulation DD calls for so much explanatory language that it will probably result in either less advertising or an information overload in the ads that are published. If the printed ad states a rate of return, it must state the rate as an APY, but if it does so it must include a host of additional disclosures if they relate to the kind of deposit being advertised, e.g., explanations concerning variable rates, the period of time the APY is offered, any minimum balance required to obtain the APY advertised, any minimum opening balance, a statement that the fees charged could reduce the earnings, a number of features of time accounts, and on and on. However, if the advertising is being done on radio, TV or billboards, the disclosure requirements are much reduced.

(4) *Changes in the terms of the deposit account.* Advance notice, usually 30 days, is required for changes "if the change may reduce the annual percentage yield or adversely affect the consumer." Regulation DD § 230.5. Normally the bank-customer agreement will give the bank the right to change unilaterally certain terms of the account so long as some prior notice is given. Among the most common changes made are those in the service charges and fee amounts. Despite the specific reference in the quotation above to changes in annual percentage yield, 2 Clark & Clark, supra, & 19.02[2][t] and & 19.07[1][e][iv], points out that the broad definition of "variable-rate account," Regulation DD § 230.2(v), as "an account in which the interest rate may change after the account is opened," means that most interest rate changes need not be disclosed in a change-in-terms notice unless the bank specifically commits to give advance notice of rate decreases. This result flows from Regulation DD § 230.5(a)(2)(i), which provides that no notice of change need be given for changes in interest rates in variable rate accounts. Since all deposit accounts in which the bank has the power to change rates are arbitrarily considered to be variable rate accounts under the broad definition of the term in Regulation DD § 230.2(v), which bears no relation to the common meaning of the term, the most important information that a customer needs to know, that the bank is lowering its interest rate, need be disclosed to the customer

only if the bank has specifically agreed to make the disclosure. This result seems absurd.

2.   "FREEDOM OF CONTRACT" UNDER SECTION 4–103(1)

The UCC adopts the principle of freedom of contract in 1–302(a), which provides that: "Except as otherwise provided in subsection (b) or elsewhere in [the Uniform Commercial Code], the effect of provisions of [the Uniform Commercial Code] may be varied by agreement." How far can the parties go in contracting away the provisions of the Code? Section 1–302(b) states that: "The obligations of good faith, diligence, reasonableness, and care prescribed by [the Uniform Commercial Code] may not be disclaimed by agreement. The parties, by agreement, may determine the standards by which the performance of those obligations is to be measured if those standards are not manifestly unreasonable." Comment 1 to 1–302 cautions that it is only the "effect" of the provisions of the UCC that may be varied by agreement, but "[t]he meaning of the statute itself must be found in its text, including its definitions, and in appropriate extrinsic aids; it cannot be varied by agreement."

Section 4–103(a) reiterates the freedom-of-contract principle for Article 4: "The effect of the provisions of this Article may be varied by agreement * * *." At bottom, almost all of Article 4's provisions are default rules only. Comment 1 to 4–103 seems to go even further to say that constant technological changes affecting banking warrant giving parties even greater latitude than with respect to 1–302 to make changes by agreement. This seems to suggest that the provisions of Article 4 are even more subject to variation than other parts of the UCC. The Comment asserts that it would be unwise to interpret Article 4 as freezing the law in this dynamic area by mandatory rules. It concludes: "This section, therefore, permits within wide limits variation of the effect of provisions of the Article by agreement." This Comment impliedly recognizes two short-comings of the UCC. First, amending the provisions of the Code is a cumbersome procedure that usually takes a minimum of ten years before the changes are adopted in all states; thus the Code is not good at keeping up with technological change. Second, there is no state administrative agency devoted to keeping the Code up to date by issuance of regulations in the Article 4 area. To an extent, the Federal Reserve Board serves as such an administrative agency. Section 4–103(b) recognizes the Fed's power to make regulations varying the provisions of Article 4, and the Fed has frequently acted to modernize the law of bank collections. But the Fed is not particularly interested in bank-customer relations; its focus is on interbank relations.

Article 4's drafters concluded that private ordering is preferable to statutory regulation as a means of keeping the Code responsive to the needs of modern banking collection operations. Is this a defensible conclusion? The question raises the familiar problem of the comparative benefits and costs of setting contract terms by regulation or contract. The problem is a basic one of institutional design. Certainly there must be some limits on the degree to which terms in a deposit agreement can vary Article 4's provisions. It is difficult, however, to specify exactly those limits. True, deposit agreements have all the earmarks of contracts of adhesion: contracts drafted by the bank and offered to the prospective customer on a take-it-or-leave-it basis. If a customer does not like particular terms in the agreement, its only choice is to go to another bank. The recent trend in bank consolidations means that fewer competing banks are available and therefore possibly less variation in the terms of deposit agreements being offered. But it can't be concluded that the terms in deposit agreements, even if adhesion contracts, are adverse to the interests of customers. Adhesion contracts can be transaction cost saving devices and therefore consistent with either monopoly power or convergence of contract terms produced by competitive market competition.

The prominent terms of deposit agreements, such as conditions placed on stop-payment orders, authorized signatures, and waiver provisions, implicate issues of fairness and efficiency. They affect the incentives of customers and banks, and alter the costs of banking services for classes of customers. The central issue of statutory drafting is whether fairness and efficiency is better pursued by the terms being set by private ordering or substantive regulation. Given the fast pace of technological change in banking services and their price impact on all depositors, the political and judicial barriers to updating statutes, and the demanding informational requirements for effective substantive regulation in the area, Article 4's drafters presumably favored private ordering announced by 4–103(a). It is perhaps significant that the Federal Reserve Board to date has taken the same view with respect to many of the terms governing electronic payments systems; see Chapter 14 supra.

The only limitations stated in 4–103(a) are that "[t]he parties to the agreement cannot disclaim a bank's responsibility for its lack of good faith or failure to exercise ordinary care or limit the measure of damages for the lack or failure. However, the parties may determine by agreement the standards by which the bank's responsibility is to be measured if those standards are not manifestly unreasonable." Hostility to 4–103(a)'s freedom-of-contract principle is well expressed by Grant Gilmore, who described agreements which alter Article 4's default rules as "carrying a good joke too far." Grant Gilmore, The Uniform Commercial Code: A Reply to Professor Beutel, 61 Yale L. J. 364, 375 (1952). How should a court apply 4–103(a) to the following Problems? The issues raised by these Problems are discussed in detail in 1 Clark & Clark, The Law of Bank Deposits, Collections and Credit Cards § 3.01[3] (Rev. ed. 1999), and White & Summers, Uniform Commercial Code § 18–2 (5th ed. 2000).

PROBLEMS

1. Husband (H) and Wife (W) have a joint checking account in Bank. Their deposit agreement with Bank provides, among other matters: (1) that either party may write checks on the account, may stop-payment of any check drawn on the account, or may close the account, and (2) that Bank may pay an overdraft drawn by either party, the account may be debited for the overdraft, and either party is liable for the amount of the overdraft without respect to whether that party signed the check or benefited from the overdraft. H wrote a check which Bank paid that overdrew the account. W did not know of the overdraft and she did not benefit in any way from the proceeds of the overdraft. H is insolvent and Bank seeks to hold W liable for the amount of the overdraft. May it do so? 4–401(b).

2. Corporate depositor (D) opens a demand deposit account in Bank from which D intends to pay its bills. The deposit agreement that D entered into with Bank contains the following clause: "You [D] may authorize the use of a facsimile signature device by a corporate resolution communicated to Bank. If you have authorized the use of a facsimile signature device, Bank may honor any check that bears or appears to bear your facsimile signature even if it was made by an unauthorized person or with a counterfeit facsimile device." Use of a facsimile device was duly authorized. Burglar breaks into D's premises and uses the facsimile machine to write a check to himself which Bank pays on presentment. May Bank debit D's account? Is the quoted clause enforceable in the face of 3–403(a), which provides that an unauthorized signature is ineffective, and 4–401(a), which provides that a bank may charge a customer's account only for checks that are properly payable? Comment 1 to 4–401 states "[a]n item containing a forged drawer's signature * * * is not properly payable." 1 Clark & Clark, supra, & 3.01[3][c][iii], cites cases on both sides of the question, and, like White & Summers, supra, § 18–2 a., favors upholding the exculpatory clause. The quoted clause is based on one that appears in a model deposit account set out in 1 Clark & Clark, supra, & 3.13[1].

3. Corporate depositor (D) opens a demand deposit account in Bank from which D intends to pay its bills. The deposit agreement that D entered into with Bank contains the following clause: "Unless you [D] shall notify Bank within fifteen calendar days of the delivery or mailing to you of any statement of account and cancelled checks of any objection to any check or item on the account, all objections for any cause or reason whatsoever, whether known or unknown, shall be absolutely barred and waived." A forged check was returned by Bank to D on June 1; D's reconciliation process did not turn up the forgery until July 15, at which time D gave Bank prompt notice of the forgery. Bank claimed that because D had failed to give the notice within the 15–day period prescribed in the agreement, D had no right to challenge its payment of the check. D noted that under 4–406(f), it had a year in which to object. Is Bank protected by the quoted clause? National Title Insurance Corporation Agency v. First Union National Bank, reprinted in Chapter 15, upheld a 60–day contract cutdown clause; Stowell v. Cloquet Co–Op Credit Union, 557 N.W.2d 567 (Minn. 1997), upheld a 20–day contract cutdown clause. 1 Clark & Clark, supra, & 3.01[3][c][ii], cites some cases tending to uphold similar clauses. White & Summers, Uniform Commercial Code § 18–2 (4th ed. 1995), questions whether a clause with a 15–day cutoff date should be upheld. Herzog, Engstrom & Koplovitz P.C. v. Union National Bank, 640 N.Y.S.2d 703 (N.Y.App.Div.1996), refused to enforce a 14–day cutoff period.

3. SERVICE CHARGES AND FEES

a. INTRODUCTION

Most banks impose charges on depositors for services performed by the bank in processing stop-payment orders, overdrafts, and checks deposited in the customer's account that have been returned because they were not paid by the bank on which they were drawn (NSF items), and many other services. Until the early '80s, regulations prohibited commercial banks from paying competitive interest rates on deposits; they lured customers by giving them gifts. But they also provided many free services: no per-check charges or the like. After deregulation, banks started paying market interest rates on deposits, but in order to cover their increased costs, banks began to impose charges for various services performed. The process was called "unbundling." Bankers believe that customers have never gotten used to service charges; they still view banks as quasi-public utilities that should be giving them toasters rather than charging them service fees. The story is told in Karen Hube & Matt Murray, New Charges Make Banking More Confusing, Wall St. J., Nov. 11, 1997, at C1. Bear in mind that since 1992, TISA has required that banks make an initial disclosure of the types and amounts of these fees, Regulation DD § 230.4(b)(4); that periodic statements must disclose the types and amounts of fees imposed during the statement period, Regulation DD § 230.6(a)(3); and that a 30–day advance notice must be given of any new fees or any increase in the amounts of fees, Regulation DD § 230.5(a).

The emergence of class actions to vindicate consumer rights allowed consumers to challenge banks on the validity of the terms of that classic example of a contract of adhesion, the bank-customer deposit agreement. The rules of the game were well known: if the class was certified and the plaintiff could get by a demurrer, the case could go to the jury. The plaintiffs had won the case because at this point the bank would usually settle. It would be difficult to find a juror who does not believe that bank service charges are excessive. An early example of the ensuing blizzard of class action litigation against banks is the following oft-cited case.

Perdue v. Crocker National Bank

Supreme Court of California, 1985.
38 Cal.3d 913, 216 Cal.Rptr. 345, 702 P.2d 503.

■ BROUSSARD, JUSTICE.

Plaintiff filed this class action to challenge the validity of charges imposed by defendant Crocker National Bank for the processing of checks drawn on accounts without sufficient funds. (The parties refer to such checks as NSF checks and to the handling charge as an NSF charge.) He appeals from a judgment of the trial court entered after that court sustained defendant's general demurrer without leave to amend.

On July 3, 1978, plaintiff filed suit on behalf of all persons with checking accounts at defendant bank and a subclass of customers who have paid NSF charges to the bank. The complaint first alleges a contract under which the bank furnishes checking service in return for a maintenance charge. It then asserts that "It is the practice of defendants to impose and collect a unilaterally set charge for processing checks presented against plaintiffs' accounts when such accounts do not contain sufficient funds to cover the amount of the check." "Defendants have at various times unilaterally increased the NSF charge to an amount the defendants deemed appropriate, without reference to any criteria, and defendants imposed and collected the said increased amount without any explanation or justification by defendants to plaintiffs." At the time of filing of the suit, the charge was $6 for each NSF check, whether the check was honored or returned unpaid, even though "the actual cost incurred by the defendants in processing an NSF check is approximately $0.30."

The bank requires each depositor to sign a signature card which it uses "to determine and verify the authenticity of endorsements on checks". In extremely small (6 point) type, the signature card states that the under-signed depositors "agree with Crocker National Bank and with each other that ... this account and all deposits therein shall be ... subject to all applicable laws, to the Bank's present and future rules, regulations, prac-tices and charges, and to its right of setoff for the obligations of any of us." The card does not identify the amount of the charge for NSF checks, and the bank does not furnish the depositor with a copy of the applicable bank rules and regulations.

On the basis of these allegations, plaintiff asserts * * * causes of action: (1) for a judicial declaration that the bank's signature card is not a contract authorizing NSF charges; [and] (2) for a judicial declaration that such charges are oppressive and unconscionable * * *.

I. PLAINTIFF'S FIRST CAUSE OF ACTION: WHETHER THE SIGNATURE CARD IS A CONTRACT AUTHORIZING NSF CHARGES.

* * *

We conclude that plaintiff here is not entitled to a judicial declaration that the bank's signature card is not a contract authorizing NSF charges. To the contrary, we hold as a matter of law that the card is a contract authorizing the bank to impose such charges, subject to the bank's duty of good faith and fair dealing in setting or varying such charges. Plaintiff may, upon remand of this case, amend his complaint to seek a judicial declara-tion determining whether the charges actually set by the bank are conso-nant with that duty. * * *

II. PLAINTIFF'S SECOND CAUSE OF ACTION: WHETHER THE BANK'S NSF CHARGES ARE OPPRESSIVE, UNREASONABLE, OR UNCONSCIONABLE.

Plaintiff's second cause of action alleges that the signature card is drafted by defendant bank which enjoys a superior bargaining position by reason of its greater economic power, knowledge, experience and resources. Depositors have no alternative but to acquiesce in the relationship as offered by defendant or to accept a similar arrangement with another bank. The complaint alleges that the card is vague and uncertain, that it is unclear whether it is intended as an identification card or a contract, that it imposes no obligation upon the bank, and permits the bank to alter or terminate the relationship at any time,[8] then asserts that "The disparity between the actual cost to defendants and the amount charged by defendants for processing an NSF check unreasonably and oppressively imposes excessive and unfair liability upon plaintiffs." Plaintiff seeks a declaratory judgment to determine the rights and duties of the parties.

Plaintiff's allegations point to the conclusion that the signature card, if it is a contract, is one of adhesion. The term contract of adhesion "signifies a standardized contract, which, imposed and drafted by the party of superior bargaining strength, relegates to the subscribing party only the opportunity to adhere to the contract or reject it." (Neal v. State Farm Ins. Co. (1961) 188 Cal. App.2d 690, 694, 10 Cal. Rptr. 781 * * * The signature card, drafted by the bank and offered to the customer without negotiation, is a classic example of a contract of adhesion; the bank concedes as much.

In Graham v. Scissor–Tail, Inc., 28 Cal.3d 807, 171 Cal. Rptr. 604, 623 P.2d 165, we observed that "To describe a contract as adhesive in character is not to indicate its legal effect.... [A] contract of adhesion is fully enforceable according to its terms [citations] unless certain other factors are present which, under established legal rules—legislative or judicial—operate to render it otherwise." (Pp. 819–820, 171 Cal. Rptr. 604, 623 P.2d 165, fn. omitted.) "Generally speaking," we explained, "there are two judicially imposed limitations on the enforcement of adhesion contracts or provisions thereof. The first is that such a contract or provision which does not fall within the reasonable expectations of the weaker or 'adhering' party will not be enforced against him. [Citations.] The second—a principle of equity applicable to all contracts generally—is that a contract or provision, even if consistent with the reasonable expectations of the parties, will be denied enforcement if, considered in its context, it is unduly oppressive or 'unconscionable.' " (P. 820, 171 Cal. Rptr. 604, 623 P.2d 165, fns. omitted.)

In 1979, the Legislature enacted Civil Code section 1670.5, which codified the established doctrine that a court can refuse to enforce an unconscionable provision in a contract. Section 1670.5 reads as follows: "(a) If the court as a matter of law finds the contract or any clause of the contract to have been unconscionable at the time it was made the court may refuse to enforce the contract, or it may enforce the remainder of the contract without the unconscionable clause, or it may so limit the application of any unconscionable clause as to avoid any unconscionable result. [&] (b) When it is claimed or appears to the court that the contract or any clause thereof may be unconscionable the parties shall be afforded a

---

8. The depositor also has the right to terminate the relationship at any time, but lacks the right asserted by the bank to alter the relationship without terminating it.

reasonable opportunity to present evidence as to its commercial setting, purpose, and effect to aid the court in making the determination."

In construing this section, we cannot go so far as plaintiff, who contends that even a conclusory allegation of unconscionability requires an evidentiary hearing. We do view the section, however, as legislative recognition that a claim of unconscionability often cannot be determined merely by examining the face of the contract, but will require inquiry into its setting, purpose, and effect.

Plaintiff bases his claim of unconscionability on the alleged 2,000 percent differential between the NSF charge of $6 and the alleged cost to the bank of $0.30.[11] The parties have cited numerous cases on whether the price of an item can be so excessive as to be unconscionable. The cited cases are from other jurisdictions, often from trial courts or intermediate appellate courts, and none is truly authoritative on the issue. Taken together, however, they provide a useful guide to analysis of the claim that a price is so excessive as to be unconscionable.

To begin with, it is clear that the price term, like any other term in a contract, may be unconscionable. * * * Allegations that the price exceeds cost or fair value, standing alone, do not state a cause of action. * * * Instead, plaintiff's case will turn upon further allegations and proof setting forth the circumstances of the transaction.

The courts look to the basis and justification for the price (cf. A & M Produce Co. v. FMC Corp., supra, 135 Cal. App.3d 473, 487, 186 Cal. Rptr. 114), including "the price actually being paid by ... other similarly situated consumers in a similar transaction." (Bennett v. Behring Corp., supra, 466 F.Supp. 689, 697, italics omitted.) The cases, however, do not support defendant's contention that a price equal to the market price cannot be held unconscionable. While it is unlikely that a court would find a price set by a freely competitive market to be unconscionable (see Bradford v. Plains Cotton Cooperative Assn. (10th Cir.1976) 539 F.2d 1249, 1255 [cotton futures]), the market price set by an oligopoly should not be immune from scrutiny. Thus, courts consider not only the market price, but also the cost of the goods or services to the seller (Frostifresh Corporation v. Reynoso (N.Y.Dist.Ct.1966) 52 Misc.2d 26, 274 N.Y.S.2d 757; Toker v. Westerman (1970) 113 N.J. Super. 452, 274 A.2d 78), the inconvenience imposed on the seller (see Merrel v. Research & Data, Inc., supra, 589 P.2d 120, 123), and the true value of the product or service (American Home Improvements, Inc. v. MacIver (1964) 105 N.H. 435, 201 A.2d 886, 889).

In addition to the price justification, decisions examine what Justice Weiner in *A & M Produce* called the "procedural aspects" of unconsciona-

---

11. The bank's briefs claim the alleged $0.30 cost is too low and plaintiff's briefs admit that a higher figure, but still $1 or less, might be more accurate. We do not, however, find in plaintiff's briefs a sufficiently clear concession to enable us to depart from the general principle that, in reviewing a judg- ment after the sustaining of a general demurrer without leave to amend, we must assume the truth of all material factual allegations in the complaint. (Alcorn v. Anbro Engineering, Inc., supra, 2 Cal. 3d 493, 496, 86 Cal. Rptr. 88, 468 P.2d 216.)

bility. (See *A & M Produce Co.*, supra, 135 Cal. App.3d at p. 489, 186 Cal. Rptr. 114.) Cases may turn on the absence of meaningful choice (Patterson v. Walker–Thomas Furniture Co., supra, 277 A.2d 111, 113 and cases there cited), the lack of sophistication of the buyer (compare Geldermann & Co., Inc. v. Lane Processing, Inc. (8th Cir.1975) 527 F.2d 571, 576 [relief denied to sophisticated investor] with Frostifresh Corporation v. Reynoso, supra, 274 N.Y.S.2d 757 [relief granted to unsophisticated buyers]) and the presence of deceptive practices by the seller (ibid.; Vom Lehn v. Astor Art Galleries, Ltd., supra, 380 N.Y.S.2d 532).

Applying this analysis to our review of the complaint at hand, we cannot endorse defendant's argument that the $6 charge is so obviously reasonable that no inquiry into its basis or justification is necessary. In 1978 $6 for processing NSF checks may not seem exorbitant,[13] but price alone is not a reliable guide. Small charges applied to a large volume of transactions may yield a sizeable sum. The complaint asserts that the cost of processing NSF checks is only $0.30 per check, which means that a $6 charge would produce a 2,000 percent profit; even at the higher cost estimate of $1 a check mentioned in plaintiff's petition for hearing, the profit is 600 percent.[14] Such profit percentages may not be automatically unconscionable, but they indicate the need for further inquiry.

Other aspects of the transaction confirm plaintiff's right to a factual hearing. Defendant presents the depositor with a document which serves at least in part as a handwriting exemplar, and whose contractual character is not obvious. The contractual language appears in print so small that many could not read it. State law may impose obligations on the bank (e.g., the duty to honor a check when the account has sufficient funds (Allen v. Bank of America, supra, 58 Cal. App.2d 124, 127, 136 P.2d 345)), but so far as the signature card drafted by the bank is concerned, the bank has all the rights and the depositor all the duties. The signature card provides that the depositor will be bound by the bank's rules, regulations, practices and charges, but the bank does not furnish the depositor with a copy of the relevant documents. The bank reserves the power to change its practices and fees at any time, subject only to the notice requirements of state law.

In short, the bank structured a totally one-sided transaction. The absence of equality of bargaining power, open negotiation, full disclosure, and a contract which fairly sets out the rights and duties of each party

13. Defendant cites Merrel v. Research & Data, Inc., supra, 589 P.2d 120, which held a $5 fee imposed by merchants for NSF checks was a "modest" amount (p. 123) and not unconscionable. NSF checks pose a substantial inconvenience to a seller, who has been deceived into an involuntary extension of credit to a customer whose credit standing may not be very good. A bank, however, is not deceived. It checks the balance of the account, and may reject any overdraft. A fee reasonable to compensate the merchant for the cost, inconvenience, and risk of an NSF check may be excessive if exacted by a bank.

14. The complaint does not state the market price for the service of processing NSF checks, although one might infer it is similar to defendant's price since plaintiff alleges that if he did not contract with defendant, he would be "forced to accept a similar arrangement with other banks." The complaint does not set a figure for the "fair" or "true" value or worth of the service.

demonstrates that the transaction lacks those checks and balances which would inhibit the charging of unconscionable fees. In such a setting, plaintiff's charge that the bank's NSF fee is exorbitant, yielding a profit far in excess of cost, cannot be dismissed on demurrer. Under Civil Code section 1670.5, the parties should be afforded a reasonable opportunity to present evidence as to the commercial setting, purpose, and effect of the signature card and the NSF charge in order to determine whether that charge is unconscionable.

* * *

NOTE

Perdue was trouble for California banks. Now every deposit account fee charged was open to challenge on whether it was unconscionable. Anecdotal evidence suggests that virtually every bank in California was subjected to class actions on their service fees. Most of the cases were settled, after presumably enriching counsel on both sides of the suits. The Comptroller of the Currency found this situation intolerable.

b.   FEDERAL PREEMPTION

In a reaction to *Perdue* and the numerous class actions against banks that it spawned, the Comptroller of the Currency intervened decisively to preempt the area of deposit-related charges. The effect has been to make national banks virtually immune to attacks on the validity of the deposit service charges.

The following provision concerning deposit account service charges for national banks is found in 12 C.F.R. § 7.4002.

(a) Authority to impose charges and fees. A national bank may charge its customers non-interest charges and fees, including deposit account service charges.

(b) Considerations. (1) All charges and fees should be arrived at by each bank on a competitive basis and not on the basis of any agreement, arrangement, undertaking, understanding, or discussion with other banks or their officers. (2) The establishment of non-interest charges and fees, their amounts, and the method of calculating them are business decisions to be made by each bank, in its discretion, according to sound banking judgment and safe and sound banking principles. A national bank establishes non-interest charges and fees in accordance with safe and sound banking principles if the bank employs a decision-making process through which it considers the following factors, among others:

(1) The cost incurred by the bank in providing the service;

(2) The deterrence of misuse by customers of banking services;

(3) The enhancement of the competitive position of the bank in accordance with the bank's business plan and marketing strategy; and

(4) The maintenance of the safety and soundness of the institution.

(c) *Interest.* Charges and fees that are "interest" within the meaning of 12 U.S.C. 85 are governed by § 7.4001 and not by this section.

(d) *State law.* The OCC applies preemption principles derived from the United States Constitution, as interpreted through judicial precedent, when determining whether State laws apply that purport to limit or prohibit charges and fees described in this section. * * *

PROBLEM

The practice of banks in State A is to impose an additional charge for the use of their ATM machines by non-customers. Two cities in State A passed ordinances prohibiting this practice. National banks in these cities sought to have these ordinances permanently enjoined on the authority of § 7.4002. What result? See Bank of America v. City and County of San Francisco, 309 F.3d 551 (9th Cir. 2002).

4. ARBITRATION CLAUSES

a. FEDERAL ARBITRATION ACT

A major struggle between customers and banks today is the enforceability of clauses in which the customer is asked to give up its rights with respect to jury trial and class actions by agreeing to arbitration to resolve all disputes. In Green Tree Financial Corp. v. Randolph, 531 U.S. 79 (2000), the Supreme Court strongly supported arbitration clauses. In that case Green Tree financed Randolph's purchase of a mobile home. The contract provided that all disputes arising from or relating to the contract would be resolved by binding arbitration. In enlarged type the contract said: "The parties voluntarily and knowingly waive any right they have to a jury trial either pursuant to arbitration under this clause or pursuant to a court action by assignee (as provided herein)." 531 U.S. at 83, fn 1. Randolph sued Green Tree, alleging that it violated the Truth in Lending Act by failing to disclose as a finance charge the cost of required insurance. The Court upheld Green Tree's motion to compel arbitration.

The Court said: "[W]e are mindful of the Federal Arbitration Act's purpose 'to reverse the longstanding judicial hostility to arbitration agreements ... and to place arbitration agreements upon the same footing as other contracts.' In the light of that purpose, we have recognized that federal statutory claims can be appropriately resolved through arbitration, and we have enforced agreements to arbitrate that involved such claims. * * * We have likewise rejected generalized attacks on arbitration that rest on 'suspicion of arbitration as a method of weakening the protection afforded in the substantive law to would-be complainants.' * * * In determining whether statutory claims may be arbitrated, we first ask whether the parties agreed to submit their claims to arbitration, and then ask whether Congress has evinced an intention to preclude a waiver of judicial remedies for the statutory rights at issue." 531 U.S. at 89–90.

Courts agree that disputes may be arbitrated "so long as the prospective litigant effectively may vindicate [his or her] statutory cause of action in the arbitral forum." 531 U.S. 90. The effect of an arbitration clause is usually to bar the claimant from participating in a class action. In cases in which class actions would ordinarily be contemplated, the issue arises whether an arbitration proceeding effectively vindicates a plaintiff's cause of action. Johnson v. West Suburban Bank, 225 F.3d 366 (3d Cir. 2000), considered that issue when the plaintiff argued that the legislative history of Truth in Lending legislation showed that Congress approved of class actions in the enforcement of claims under the Act. "Rather than simply provided restitution, [plaintiff] asserts, such litigation is meant to serve public policy goals through plaintiffs who act as private attorneys general, for the class action device is necessary to ensure meaningful deterrence to creditors who might violate the acts." 225 F.3d at 369. The court rejected this contention: "In sum, though pursuing individual claims may well be less attractive than pursuing a class action the courts, we do not agree that compelling arbitration of the claim of a prospective class action plaintiff irreconcilably conflicts with TILA's goal of encouraging private actions to deter violations of the Act." 225 F.3d at 374–375. There remains the opposite question: whether an arbitration agreement between the bank and its customer can prohibit class arbitration. In Green Tree Financial Corp. v. Bazzle, 539 U.S. 444, 123 S.Ct. 2402 (2003), the Court implicitly gave an affirmative answer, finding the matter to be one of contract interpretation to be decided by the arbitrator. A 2003 agreement between a credit card issuer and a cardholder addresses the issue: "If either party elects to resolve a Claim by arbitration, that Claim shall be arbitrated on an individual basis. *There shall be no right or authority for any Claims to be arbitrated on a class action basis or on bases involving Claims brought in a purported representative capacity on behalf of the general public, other Cardmembers or other persons similarly situated*." (Emphasis in original.)

b. UNCONSCIONABILITY

An emerging basis for attacking arbitration clauses in contracts, such as bank-customer deposit agreements, is the claim that these contracts are contracts of adhesion and in this context the arbitration clauses are unconscionable. The Federal Arbitration Act, 9 U.S.C. § 2, states:

A written provision in * * * a contract evidencing a transaction involving commerce to settle by arbitration a controversy thereafter arising out of such contract or transaction * * * shall be valid, irrevocable, and enforceable, save on such grounds as exist at law or equity for the revocation of any contract.

Generally applicable contract defenses such as fraud, duress or undue influence may be raised to invalidate an arbitration clause under the italicized language of section 2 above. The accepted view is that this language also includes unconscionability. See Doctor's Associates, Inc. v. Casarotto, 517 U.S. 681, 682 (1996); "[G]enerally applicable contract defenses, such as fraud, duress or unconscionability, may be applied to invalidate arbitration agreements without contravening § 2." Proof of unconscionability focuses on the existence of both procedural and substantive unconscionability. Procedural unconscionability examines the manner in which the contract was negotiated and the circumstances of the parties: inequality of bargaining power, lack of disclosure, such as a clause hidden in boiler-plate contract, coercion on part of stronger party. Substantive unconscionability centers on whether the terms of the agreement are so one-sided as to shock the conscience.

A majority of cases have refused to find arbitration clauses unconscionable. The authorities taking this view are marshaled in Hutcherson v. Sears Roebuck & Company, 342 Ill.App.3d 109 (Ill. App. 2003). In that case the court held that there was no procedural unconscionability because there was a clearly stated, conspicuous arbitration clause that gave the debtor the right to opt out if it did not agree to arbitration. Substantive unconscionability was absent because the court found no unfairness in the agreement and, moreover, federal policy strongly favors enforcement of arbitration provisions, even at the cost of the debtor's waiving her right to a class action. There is more than a whiff of federal preemption in the opinion.

Other courts have refused to enforce arbitration agreements on unconscionability grounds, citing the inequality of bargaining power and the take-it-or-leave-it basis on which arbitration clauses are offered as proof of procedural unconscionability. The wholly one-sided terms of arbitration agreements are relied on as showing substantive unconscionability. Ingle v. Circuit City Stores, Inc., 328 F.3d 1165 (9th Cir. 2003), forcefully presents this view.

Emboldened by passage of the Federal Arbitration Act and aggrieved by high class action recoveries, banks and other financial institutions have stampeded toward inclusion of arbitration clauses in their agreements with customers. This is easily done with respect to new customers but banks have faced difficulties in adding such clauses to their agreements with existing customers. Banks customarily reserve the right to change their deposit agreements by notifying customers of the intended change and providing that if the customer continues to use the account the change will apply to all past and future transactions. When a bank acting under such a clause sent a proposed change incorporating an arbitration clause as a "bill stuffer" in the same envelope that contained the customer's periodic statement, the court in Badie v. Bank of America, 79 Cal.Rptr.2d 273 (Cal. Ct. App. 1998), held that the amendment did not bind the customer because under the circumstances customers would not have reasonably anticipated that a mere bill stuffer amending an agreement that was almost wholly devoted to such mundane subjects as various fee schedules was intended to deprive them of their constitutional right to jury trial. Most other courts have disagreed with Badie. See, e.g., Hutcherson, supra.

CHAPTER 7

LETTERS OF CREDIT

A. INTRODUCTION

Letters of credit are ubiquitous and important financial instruments. They have a wide variety of uses, such as paying for goods, guaranteeing commercial paper and municipal and corporate bonds, and backing up the performance of nonfinancial contracts. Simply put, a letter of credit is an undertaking in a writing or other record by one person to pay or deliver an item of value to a named person on that person's satisfaction of documentary conditions, if any, stipulated in the record. 5–102(a)(10). In its most basic form the instrument involves three parties: the issuer, the applicant (or "customer") and the beneficiary. The issuer is the party making the record undertaking, the applicant is the party requesting the issuer to make the record undertaking (almost always for a fee), and the beneficiary is the party who is to receive payment or deliver an item of value. The letter of credit provides that the issuer will pay the beneficiary a stipulated amount upon the beneficiary's satisfaction of stipulated documentary conditions by a specified date. It may even provide that the issuer will deliver an item of value to the beneficiary, such as stock certificates. The legal relationship between the beneficiary and applicant may vary, as can their identity. The beneficiary and applicant may be, respectively, a seller and buyer in a sales contract, a contractor and owner in a construction contract, a creditor and debtor, or a donee and donor. Although the relationship between parties and the transactions can change, the elementary form of the letter of credit is the same: an issuer's record undertaking, made at the request of an applicant, to give specified value to a beneficiary upon its satisfaction of documentary conditions, if any, stated in the record.

A letter of credit may involve additional parties. The issuer can engage a party, called the adviser, to notify the beneficiary of the existence and terms of the credit. 5–102(a)(1), 5–107(c). Another party, called the confirmer, may be engaged by the issuer to pay the beneficiary upon the beneficiary's presentation of documents required by the confirmation. 5–102(a)(4). A confirmed letter of credit is a separate instrument from the issuer's letter of credit. 5–107(a). Often the same party may undertake both to advise and confirm the issuer's letter of credit. Letters of credit issued in international transactions frequently involve advisers and confirmers. This is because applicants and beneficiaries often are strangers to each other. An advisor local to the beneficiary can vouch reliably for the genuineness and accuracy of the terms of a foreign letter of credit. A local confirmer provides a convenient and reliable source of payment as well as other advantages such as avoidance of foreign currency exchange controls. Where an advice and confirmed letter of credit is warranted, a prudent beneficiary will require them as part of the terms of transaction that calls for the issuance of a letter of credit.

Letter of credit contracts are traditionally called commercial or mercantile "specialties." They are contracts subject to special rules, not the ordinary rules that apply to other contracts. Some commentators and courts describe the letter of credit as a "unique" or "idiosyncratic" instrument. For instance, the issuer's obligation to the beneficiary is not the product of the beneficiary's acceptance of an offer by the issuer. The issuer's obligation also is enforceable without consideration, although typically consideration will support its obligation. See 5–105. Essential to letter of credit law is the rule that the issuer's payment obligation to the beneficiary is conditioned only on the documentary terms described in the credit. Only these terms govern the issuer's obligation to the beneficiary. Terms or facts bearing on the relationship or contracts between the beneficiary and the applicant, or between the applicant and issuer, have no effect on the issuer's obligation to the beneficiary. In this sense the issuer's obligation to the beneficiary is "primary": it is independent of facts or terms bearing on relationships between other parties. The issuer's undertaking to the beneficiary alone controls its payment obligation to the beneficiary. Thus, a letter of credit isn't a guarantee because the issuer's obligation isn't conditional on the default of the principal obligor; the issuer's liability isn't "secondary." In contrast, the guarantor's liability is secondary. See Restatement (Third) of Suretyship and Guaranty § 34 (1995). The letter of credit contract also doesn't give the issuer or applicant rights of a third party beneficiary: neither can use the rights of others to affect the issuer's payment obligation to the beneficiary. Legally, the insulation of the issuer's payment obligation from other transactions makes the letter of credit a distinctive financial instrument. See Comment 1 to 5–102.

In a typical transaction involving a letter of credit, three separate contracts are involved: (1) the contract between the beneficiary and the applicant that calls for the establishment of the credit or gives rise to it; (2) the contract between the issuer and beneficiary requiring payment against presentation of the documents; and (3) the contract of reimbursement between the issuer and the applicant. It is standard to refer to contract (1) as the underlying contract, contract (2) as the letter of credit contract, and contract (3) as the reimbursement contract. The distinctiveness of letter of a credit as a financial instrument derives from the independence of the letter of credit contract from the other two sorts of contract. Thus, issuer's obligations to the beneficiary under the letter of credit are "primary" and therefore unaffected by the underlying or reimbursement contracts.

There are two types of letters of credit: commercial and standby letters of credit. They are distinguished by their intended financial purposes and the sorts of documentary conditions specified credits. A commercial letter of credit serves as a mechanism for payment owed on the underlying contract. For instance, a contract for the sale of goods might require the buyer-applicant to establish a letter of credit naming the seller as the beneficiary. The terms of the credit require the issuer to pay a specified amount equal to the contract price to the beneficiary upon the beneficiary's presentation to it of documents described in the credit. The described documents can be of any sort. They typically include a draft drawn by the seller on the buyer, a commercial invoice, a bill of lading or other document of title, and certificates of origin or inspection certificates. Where the underlying contract involves a sale of assets other than goods, such as real estate or securities, different documentation will be required. The seller is paid the contract price by the issuer if the seller-beneficiary presents documents to it that comply with the terms of the credit. Because the issuer undertakes to pay the seller-beneficiary, the commercial credit adds the issuer's obligation to that of the buyer. Thus, the seller won't receive the contract price only if both the buyer and issuer are unable or unwilling to pay it. Because issuers frequently are banks with low risks of insolvency and a great concern for their reputations as reputable financial intermediaries, a commercial credit reduces the seller-beneficiary's risk of nonpayment significantly. The use of commercial credits in sales transactions is discussed in Clayton P. Gillette and Steven D. Walt, Sales Law: Domestic and International 406–454 (2d ed. 2002).

A standby letter of credit has a different purpose and specifies different documentary conditions. Standby letters of credit function to guarantee performance of an underlying contract or transaction. They do not serve as a risk-reducing device for payment of the contract price. Typically a standby credit provides that the issuer will pay the beneficiary if the beneficiary presents specified documentary evidence of default by the applicant or some other party in an underlying contract or transactions. Unlike the commercial letter, the issuer of a standby credit does not usually expect the beneficiary to draw on the credit. ("Direct pay" credits are variant standby credits in which the credit serves as a payment mechanism for discharging financial obligations, and the issuer expects to pay upon the beneficiary's presentation of a draft or documentary demand.) Required documents generally include a draft and noncommercial documents, typically a certificate of default of specified content. Thus, presentation of documentary evidence of default allows the beneficiary to obtain payment from the issuer. In this way the issuer's obligation backs up the applicant or another's obligation under the underlying contract or transactions. The standby credit thereby shifts the risk of the applicant's insolvency, nonpayment or nonperformance from the beneficiary to the issuer. Standby credits that back up financial obligations owed in an underlying transaction are called "financial" standby credits. "Performance" standby credits back up nonmonetary obligations owed in the underlying transaction. As a standby credit, the issuer's obligation to the beneficiary in each case depends only on the beneficiary's presentation of documentary evidence of default in an underlying transaction, not on nondocumentary facts bearing on default.

Standby credits serve a guarantee function in a variety of underlying transactions. Issuers of commercial paper can market the paper at a higher price by backing it up with letters of credit. The credits can be drawn upon by the holders of the paper if the paper isn't paid at maturity. Purchasers of limited partnerships on credit can guarantee their partnership interests by having issued a credit that undertakes to pay the beneficiary-sellers upon certification of the purchasers' default on its payment obligations. In securitization transactions standby credits serve to enhance the credit rating of securities issued by the securitization vehicle: the credit guarantees the payment of interest and principal on securities the vehicle issued. Finally, a standby credit might serve as an alternative to withholding progress payments under a construction contract. Rather than withhold progress payments, the owner can have the contractor-applicant establish a standby credit in the owner's favor. The credit can allow the owner-beneficiary to draw stipulated amounts if the owner presents documentary evidence to the issuer of the contractor's default. The same sort of scheme can allow the buyer-beneficiary in a sales of goods contract to prepay for the goods and draw on credit upon documentary presentation of the seller-applicant's default under the sales contract. Its wide range of uses and the comparatively low fees charged by issuers of standby credits apparently make the standby credit an attractive financial instrument. In 2001 U.S. FDIC-insured depository banks issued approximately 296.2 billion dollars in standby credits. During the same period they issued about 23.3 billion dollars in commercial credits. See FDIC Statistics on Banking C–12 (Table RC–6) (2001). A form standby letter of credit and reimbursement agreement appear at the end of this Chapter.

B. SOURCES OF LETTER OF CREDIT LAW

Most letter of credit law consists of domestic law and institutional rules, and much of it is uniform across jurisdictions. Letter of credit law has five sources: (1) In the United States Article 5 of the UCC and extra-Code common law; (2) Publication Number 500 of the Uniform Customs and Practice for Documentary Credits of the International Chamber of Commerce ("UCP 500" or "UCP"); (3) the Uniform Law for Demand Guarantees of the International Chamber of Commerce; (4) the International Standby Practices of the International Chamber of Commerce ("ISP 98"); and (5) the United Nations Convention on Independent Guarantees and Standby Letters of Credit ("U.N. Convention"). To date, six countries have ratified the U.N. Convention; the United States has not done so. Thus, domestic law such as Article 5 and the International Chamber of Commerce's institutional rules remain the most important rules governing credits. Treatises describing the sources of letter of credit law include John F. Dolan, The Law of Letters of Credit: Commercial and Standby Credits (rev. ed. 2003); 3 James J. White & Robert S. Summers, Uniform Commercial Code, Chapter 26 (4th prac. ed. 1995) (herein White & Summers; prac. ed.); and Brooke Wunnicke et al., Standby and Commercial Letters of Credit (3d ed. 2003). A brief summary appears in Boris Kozolchyk, Commercial and Standby Letters of Credit, in 3 United States Law of Trade and

Investment, Chapter 24 (B. Kozolchyk & J.F. Molloy eds. 2001). This Chapter focuses almost exclusively on Article 5 and the UCP.

Article 5 of the UCC governs both commercial and standby letters of credit. Since the International Chamber of Commerce has no legislative authority, its institutional rules apply only if the credit incorporates them. Credits frequently incorporate UCP 500 in particular as a source for principles governing letter of credit transactions. To be applicable, both UCP 500 and ISP 98 require that the incorporation be express. UCP 500 art. 1; ISP 98 art. 1.01(b). Almost all international credits and many domestic commercial credits issued in New York, for instance, are made subject to the UCP. Over half of the standby credits currently issued by Citibank and J.P. Morgan Chase are reported to be governed by the ISP 98. A few courts have held that the UCP can apply to a credit by virtue of trade usage even when the credit does not refer to the UCP. Article 5 governs credits issued by banks or other persons, but excludes credit undertakings issued by consumers. UCP 500 applies to both commercial and standby credits issued only by banks. The ISP 98 applies to standby credits issued by any person. See UCP 500 art. 2; ISP 98 art. 1.04. Both UCP 500 and ISP 98 allow parties to opt-in to the respective rules by incorporation in the credit when the credit would not otherwise be covered. UCP 500 art. 1; ISP 98 art. 1.01(b); cf. U.N. Convention art. 1(2).

Incorporation of institutional rules in most cases displaces conflicting default rules under Article 5. Section 5–116(c) is clear that if a credit is made subject to the UCP or other "rules of custom or practice," the UCP or other rules of custom or practice displace Article 5 only if there is a conflict and the conflict involves a default rule of Article 5. See Comment 3 to 5–116. If Article 5's conflicting rule is mandatory, its rule continues to apply. Article 5's rules, default or mandatory, also continue to apply when they have no counterpart under UCP 500, such as rules concerning fraud or standards of documentary compliance. In these cases there is no conflict between rules. For the most part, Article 5's very few mandatory rules are consistent with the UCP 500's rules, the current version of the UCP. The exceptions bearing on comparatively nuanced rules concerning the expiration of a credit, and the assignment of credit proceeds are isolated. Cf. 5–106(c), UCP 500 art. 42; 5–114(c), UCP 500 art. 49. Thus, although future versions of the UCP might contain rules in conflict with Article 5, at present there are few conflicts. Article 5 therefore effectively allows parties to select between its rules and the UCP.

Article 5, along with most other domestic letter of credit law, allows parties virtually unrestricted freedom of choice over the terms of the credit. Almost all of Article 5's rules are default rules: they apply unless the parties agree to vary them. As just noted, very few of Article 5's rules are mandatory. Section 5–103(c)'s lists the following mandatory rules: the exclusion of consumer-issuers and noncredit undertakings from Article 5, restrictions on the stipulated expiration date for a credit, regulation of the issuer's withholding of consent to the assignment of credit proceeds, obligations of good faith, and subrogation rights. See 5–102(a)(8), (10), 5–

106(d), 5–114(d), 1–302(b), 5–117(d). All of Article 5's other rules are default rules. In fact, even Article 5's mandatory rules are in effect default rules too. This is because Article 5 allows parties to select law governing the letter of credit, without restriction. Section 5–116(a) provides that the law of the jurisdiction chosen by the "affected parties" controls the liability of the issuer, nominated person or adviser, and the law selected "need not bear any relation to the transaction." Parties therefore can select applicable law that does not contain Article 5's mandatory rules. Thus, Article 5's mandatory rules apply only if affected parties fail to select the law of a jurisdiction that does not contain the same rules. See Comment 2 to 5–103 (second paragraph).

C. FORMAL REQUIREMENTS

Under 5–106(a), a letter of credit is enforceable when issued. The credit in turn is issued when the issuer sends or transmits the credit to the beneficiary. Because a credit is "sent" when it is mailed or delivered for transmission by the usual means, 1–201(36)(A), the credit becomes enforceable upon dispatch. Article 5 does not explicitly provide when a confirmed credit becomes enforceable. However, Comment 1 to 5–107 instructs us to treat the terms "confirmation" and "letter of credit" interchangeably throughout Article 5. Thus, the same rules concerning issuance and dispatch apply to confirmed letters of credit. Under 5–106(a), UCP 500 art. 6(c), and ISP 98 art. 1.06(a), a letter of credit is irrevocable unless it states otherwise. Irrevocability means that the issuer cannot cancel or amend the credit without the beneficiary's consent. 5–106(b). This default rule makes sense for the vast majority of beneficiaries, who might want to rely on the credit in advance of drawing on it. Section 5–106(c) provides that if there is no stated expiration date in a credit, it expires one year after issuance, and 5–106(d) provides that if the credit purports to be perpetual, it expires five years after issuance. The latter is a mandatory rule.

To be a letter of credit, a financial instrument must take a certain form. Section 5–104 sets out the formal requirements a credit must satisfy. However, to be a letter of credit in the first place, the financial instrument must contain a particular sort of undertaking. Since the essential feature of a letter of credit is that the credit is independent of the underlying contract, the instrument must reflect this fact. Form must reflect function. Thus, an instrument is a letter of credit only if it conditions the issuer's obligation on satisfaction of documentary conditions. Section 5–102(a)(10) defines a letter of credit as a "definite undertaking ... to honor a documentary presentation by payment...." This definition describes a mandatory rule ((5–103(c)), and an agreement to treat an instrument that is not a letter of credit under 5–102(a)(1) therefore is ineffective. In the following case, Notes and Problems, we inquire after the conditions in a written undertaking that undermine the writing's character as a letter of credit. The Problems following the case also investigate 5–104's formal requirements.

Wichita Eagle and Beacon Publishing Company, Inc. v. Pacific National Bank of San Francisco

United States Court of Appeal, Ninth Circuit, 1974.
493 F.2d 1285.

■ BEFORE CHAMBERS and BROWNING, CIRCUIT JUDGES, and KING, DISTRICT JUDGE.

■ PER CURIAM:

The facts are summarized in the district court's opinion, 343 F.Supp. 332 (N.D.Cal.1971).

* * *

[Summary by Eds. Lessors leased a site on which Lessee (Circular Ramp Garages), under the terms of the lease, undertook to build a parking garage. In order to assure Lessors that Lessee would perform, Lessee obtained from Bank (Pacific National Bank) a writing addressed to Lessors in which Bank established its "Letter of Credit No. 17084" in favor of Lessors for payment of $250,000 "available by drafts drawn at sight on the Pacific National Bank providing that all of the following conditions are met at the time said draft is received by the undersigned." The conditions were (1) that Lessee has failed to perform the terms of the lease; (2) that Lessors have given Bank an affidavit stating that it has given notice to Lessee and its contractor specifying how Lessee has failed to perform its lease; and (3) that either Lessee or its contractor has failed to cure defaults under the lease during a period of thirty days after receiving Lessor's notice. Lessee failed to obtain the financing necessary to build the parking garage and defaulted on the lease. Lessors' assignee (Plaintiff) presented to Bank a draft for $250,000 drawn upon Letter of Credit No. 17084, together with the required documents. When Bank refused payment, Plaintiff brought suit against Bank. The district court concluded that "Although the question is not free from doubt, the Instrument denominated 'Letter of Credit No. 17084' should be treated as a letter of credit and be subject to the law respecting letters of credit to the extent applicable and appropriate." 343 F.Supp. at 339.]

We do not agree with the district court that the instrument sued upon is a letter of credit, though it is so labeled. Rather, the instrument is an ordinary guaranty contract, obliging the defendant bank to pay whatever the lessee Circular Ramp Garages, Inc., owed on the underlying lease, up to the face amount of the guaranty. Since the underlying lease clearly contemplated the payment of $250,000 in case of default, and since this provision appears to be a valid liquidated damages clause, the judgment below must be modified to award the plaintiff $250,000 plus interest.

We do not base our holding that the instrument is not a letter of credit on the fact that payment was triggered by default rather than performance or on the fact that the instrument was written in a lease context, for we recognize that the commercial use of letters of credit has expanded far beyond the international sales context in which it originally developed.
* * *

The instrument involved here strays too far from the basic purpose of letters of credit, namely, providing a means of assuring payment cheaply by eliminating the need for the issuer to police the underlying contract. * * * The instrument neither evidences an intent that payment be made merely on presentation on a draft nor specifies the documents required for termination or payment. To the contrary, it requires the actual existence in fact of most of the conditions specified: * * * for payment, that the lessee have failed to perform the terms of the lease and have failed to correct that default, in addition to an affidavit of notice.

True, in the text of the instrument itself the instruments is referred to as a "letter of credit," and we should, as the district court notes, "giv[e] effect wherever possible to the intent of the contracting parties." 343 F.Supp. at 338. But the relevant intent is manifested by the terms of the agreement, not by its label. * * * And where, as here, the substantive provisions require the issuer to deal not simply in documents alone, but in facts relating to the performance of a separate contract (the lease, in this case), all distinction between a letter of credit and an ordinary guaranty contract would be obliterated by regarding the instrument as a letter of credit.

It would hamper rather than advance the extension of the letter of credit concept to new situations if an instrument such as this were held to be a letter of credit. The loose terms of this instrument invited the very evil that letters of credit are meant to avoid—protracted, expensive litigation. If the letter of credit concept is to have value in new situations, the instrument must be tightly drawn to strictly and clearly limit the responsibility of the issuer.

* * *

NOTES

1. The conceptual issue presented in *Wichita Eagle* concerns the character of the instrument issued by the Bank: is it a guarantee or a standby letter of credit? The issue is important as a matter of bank regulation. Banks in the United States generally are not permitted to issue guarantees. They are permitted, however, to issue letters of credit, subject to regulation. As noted above, in function guarantees and standby letters of credit are indistinguishable, both involving the enhancement of an obligor's promise by adding the promise of a creditworthy third party. In fact, European banking terminology sometimes refers to standby credit as "bank guarantees." Conceptually they are distinguishable by the nature of the issuer's obligation and the conditions under which its obligation attaches. As to the issuer's obligation, it is primary: the issuer cannot invoke defenses against the beneficiary available to the applicant to resist honoring the credit. A guarantor's obligation is secondary: it can invoke defenses available to the obligor to resist payment to the obligee. Because banks generally can only issue letters of credit, the conceptual distinction between credits and guarantees is crucial.

The Office of the Comptroller of the Currency regulates the issuance of letters of credit by focusing on documentary conditions. By the Comptroller's interpretive ruling, national banks may issue letters of credit, including standby letters of credit, only if the obligation to honor "depends upon the presentation of specified documents and not upon nondocumentary conditions or resolution of questions of fact or law at issue between the account party and the beneficiary." 12 C.F.R. 7.1016(a) (1998). State chartered banks usually are subject to a similar sort of regulation.

An important question is the effect of a bank issuing a guarantee in violation of bank regulations. Issuing banks or applicants sometimes adopt the odd litigation posture of urging the illegal issuance of a guarantee as a defense to enforcement of the guarantee. This is the "ultra vires" defense to honor. See Republic National Bank v. Northwest National Bank, 578 S.W.2d 109 (Tex.1978); *Witchita Eagle*. Although a few courts have accepted the ultra vires defense, the majority of case law has rejected it. See, e.g., Federal Dep. Ins. Corp. v. Freudenfeld, 492 F.Supp. 763 (E.D.Wis.1980); First American National Bank v. Alcorn, Inc., 361 So.2d 481 (Miss.1978); Dolan, Letters of Credit & 12.03[2]. In *Witchita Eagle*, for instance, the court enforced the instrument as a guarantee. The rejection of the ultra vires defense makes a good deal of sense. The issuer or applicant almost always is in a better position than the beneficiary to avoid violating applicable bank regulations or detecting their violation. Bank regulating agencies also are better positioned than beneficiaries to monitor issuers and applicants. Accordingly, not allowing the defense to enforcement increases the cost to issuers of violating the regulation against the issuance of guarantees. It serves as a partial substitute for closer monitoring of a bank's investment activities by bank regulating agencies.

2. *Wichita* Eagle was decided under the version of Article 5 in effect before its revision in 1995. How would this case be decided under current version of Article 5? See 5–102(a)(10) ("letter of credit") and Comment 6 to 5–102. How could the document in *Wichita Eagle* be rewritten to remove all doubt about its status as a letter of credit? Does 5–108(g) allow the court in this case to find that the writing is a valid letter of credit by disregarding the two nondocumentary conditions? Comment 9 to 5–108. See Dolan, Letters of Credit & 2.05; 3 White & Summers, Prac. ed. § 26–2. If the undertaking is a letter of credit, the disregard of nondocumentary conditions does not mean that the issuer can ignore them. As a matter of the reimbursement agreement between the applicant and the issuer, their honor might be required. Section 5–108(g)'s injunction only means that the issuer's obligations to the beneficiary under the letter of credit do not depend on the satisfaction of nondocumentary conditions. See Comment 9 to 5–108.

3. The cardinal principle of letter of credit law, the "independence principle," is codified in 5–103(d). Section 5–104 recognizes that the day of an exclusively paper-based system of letter of credit transactions has long since passed. Comment 3 notes: "Many banking transactions, including the issuance of many letters of credit, are now conducted mostly by electronic means. * * * By declining to specify any particular medium in which the letter of credit must be established or communicated, Section 5–104 leaves room for future developments." See the definitions of "document" (5–102(a)(6)) and "record" (5–102(a)(14)).

4. The documents to be presented to the issuer of the letter of credit to obtain payment are usually accompanied by a draft drawn by the beneficiary (5–102(a)(3)) on the issuing bank (5–102(a)(9)) payable "at sight" (that is on presentment) to the order of the beneficiary. A sight draft is merely a demand for payment that may be negotiable in form, thus conferring upon the beneficiary the power to transfer the draft to a third person who may take the rights of a holder in due course. Comment 11 to 5–102.

PROBLEMS

1. Paysaver Credit Union executed the following writing at the request of Wells and Titan Tool, which owed Transparent Products $33,000 on open account:

Transparent Products Corporation

Bensenville, IL 60101

RE: Thomas Wells

Gentlemen:

We hereby establish our letter of credit at the request of Thomas Wells of 1315 South 3rd Avenue, Maywood up to the aggregate amount of fifty-thousand dollars ($50,000).

Titan wanted to buy more plastics from Transparent and obtained Paysaver's issuance of the writing directed to Transparent to bolster Titan's creditworthiness. Wells is an employee of Titan who was not indebted to Transparent. It was Wells' $50,000 certificate of deposit with Paysaver that apparently persuaded Paysaver to issue this writing. Transparent ultimately declined to extend more credit to Titan and, when the latter filed in bankruptcy, Transparent demanded payment under Paysaver's "letter of credit" to defray the remaining $33,000 debt. Is the quoted writing sufficiently "definite" to be a letter of credit under 5–102(a)(10)? See Comment 6 to Rev. 5–102. If it is not, is the instrument effective as a guaranty? A guarantor undertakes to pay the debt of another and can raise the principal debtor's defenses; the issuer of a letter of credit is primarily liable and cannot set up defenses of the applicant. The facts are based on Transparent Products Corp. v. Paysaver Credit Union, 864 F.2d 60 (7th Cir.1988). Comment 1 to 5–104 states: " * * * a letter of credit will typically specify the amount available, the expiration date, the place where presentation should be made, and the documents that must be presented to entitle a person to honor."

2. (a) What would be the result in Problem 1 if the body of the writing had said: "We hereby establish our letter of credit at the request of

Thomas Wells of 1315 South 3rd Avenue, Maywood up to the aggregate amount of fifty-thousand dollars ($50,000) on which Transparent Products Corporation may draw at any time within the next year by presentation of a draft payable at sight for any amount up to the credit limit"? See 5–102(a)(6) ("document"), (10) ("letter of credit") and (12) ("presentation").

(b) What would be the result in Problem 1 if the body of the writing had said: "This is a guarantee, not a letter of credit. At the request of Thomas Wells of 1315 South 3rd Avenue, Maywood, we hereby undertake to pay Transparent Products Corporation up to the aggregate amount of fifty-thousand dollars ($50,000) at any time within the next year upon the following three conditions: (1) Transparent presents a written demand for payment; (2) Transparent not make the presentation before 1 p.m. eastern standard time; and (3) Transparent recites to our representative that the writing represented is a written demand for payment"?

D. ISSUER'S DUTY TO HONOR OR DISHONOR

1. THE STRICT COMPLIANCE STANDARD

A letter of credit is a highly efficient instrument in which banks or others issue suitably definite undertakings to honor complying documentary presentations and the beneficiaries present the prescribed documents and are paid. Indirect evidence of the credit's efficiency is the comparatively low fees issuers charge compared to fees charged for other comparable financial instruments. Central to the credit's cost advantage is the issuer's duty to honor complying documentary presentations. Under 5–108(a), the standard of documentary compliance is strict: "... [A]n issuer shall honor a presentation that, as determined by the standard practice referred to in subsection (e), appears on its face strictly to comply with the terms and conditions of the letter of credit." The domestic law of most legal systems apparently also adopts the strict compliance standard. See Boris Kozolchyk, Commercial Letters of Credit in the Americas 72, 259 (1966). Neither the UCP nor ISP 98 expressly adopts a standard of documentary compliance. See UCP 500 art. 13(a); ISP 98 art. 4.01. Accordingly, in credits governed by the UCP or ISP 98 that otherwise do not address the standard of compliance, domestic law standards continue to apply. The strict compliance standard therefore likely will control under applicable law in these cases.

The importance of a documentary discrepancy is irrelevant under the standard. As a Law Lord put it in Equitable Trust Co. of New York v. Dawson Partners Ltd., [1927] 27 Lloyd's List. L. R. 49, 52 (Summer L.), a leading letter of credit case, "[t]here is no room for documents which are almost the same, or which will do just as well." Of course, facts about the underlying transaction also are irrelevant to the issuer's duty to the beneficiary. If the documents presented correspond to the terms of the credit, the issuer must pay. Otherwise, not. As we will discuss below, an issuer who honors a noncomplying documentary presentation risks not being reimbursed by the applicant.

The strict compliance standard resists an informative and precise statement. Strict compliance does not require literal, letter-for-letter correspondence between the contents of prescribed documents and the credit's terms. Comment 1 to 5–108 states that the standard does not mean "slavish conformity to the terms of the credit." On the other hand, both the strict compliance standard and Comment 1 reject a substantial compliance standard, which judges compliance by an undefined measure of the degree to which documents comply with the credit's terms. Thus, the standard seems to treat documents as complying if they less than literally comply, but more than substantially comply, with the credit's terms. Courts and commentators have had trouble identifying the permissible range of less than perfect compliance. Even courts that do not insist on absolute compliance sometimes disagree on what is strict but less than literal compliance. A rough working notion of compliance under 5–108(a) finds that documents strictly comply when the issuer, using standard practices of issuers, determines that they correspond on their face with the credit's terms. Put another way, the notion is that the documents comply if a reasonable issuer, examining only the documents and the credit, and charged with knowledge of the practices of issuers, would decide that a documentary discrepancy is substantial. For a brief history of applications of the standard, see Peter Ellinger, The Doctrine of Strict Compliance: Its Development and Current Construction, Lex Mercatoria: Essays on International Commercial Law in Honour of Francis Reynolds 187–198 (2000). The strict compliance standard and related issues are extensively discussed in 2 Barkley Clark & Barbara Clark, The Law of Bank Deposits, Collections and Credit Cards 14.05 (rev. ed. 1999); Dolan, Letters of Credit Ch. 6; and 3 White & Summers, Prac. ed. § 26–6.

In this section we examine perhaps the most litigated issue in the letter of credit law: the duty of the issuer to both the beneficiary and applicant to honor or dishonor a presentation. At issue in most of the litigation is the application of the strict compliance standard in the face of documentary discrepancies. Strict compliance tests documentary presentations by the standard practice of financial institutions that regularly issue credits. Using slightly different terms, 5–108(a) and (e), UCP 500 art. 13(a) and ISP 98 art. 4.01(b) refer to such practice. The following case, involving a credit subject to UCP 500, is a good example of the courts' struggle to define the relevant practice of financial institutions that regularly issue credits.

Voest-Alpine Trading USA Corp. v. Bank of China

United States District Court, S.D. Texas, 2000.
167 F.Supp.2d 940.

■ GILMORE, DISTRICT JUDGE.

On February 16–17 and 21–23, 2000, a bench trial was held in the above-styled case. Having considered the evidence in this case and the applicable law, the Court enters the following findings of fact and conclusions of law.

On June 23, 1995, Plaintiff Voest–Alpine Trading USA Corporation ("Voest–Alpine") entered into a contract with Jiangyin Foreign Trade Corporation ("JFTC") to sell JFTC 1,000 metric tons of styrene monomer at a total price of $1.2 million. To finance the transaction, JFTC applied for a letter of credit through Defendant Bank of China. The letter of credit provided for payment to Voest–Alpine once the goods had been shipped to Zhangjiagang, China and Voest–Alpine had presented the requisite paperwork to the Bank of China as described in the letter of credit. The letter of credit was issued by the Bank of China on July 6, 1995 and assigned the number LC9521033/95. In addition to numerous other typographical errors, Voest–Alpine's name was listed as "Voest–Alpine USA Trading Corp." instead of "Voest–Alpine Trading USA Corp" with the "Trading USA" portion inverted. The destination port was also misspelled in one place as "Zhangjiagng," missing the third "a". The letter of credit did indicate, however, that the transaction would be subject to the 1993 Uniform Customs and Practice, International Chamber of Commerce Publication Number 500 ("UCP 500").

By the time the product was ready to ship, the market price of styrene monomer had dropped significantly from the original contract price between Voest–Alpine and JFTC. Although JFTC asked for a price concession in light of the decrease in market price, Voest–Alpine declined and, through its agents, shipped the styrene monomer on July 18, 1995. All required inspection and documentation was completed. On August 1, 1995, Voest–Alpine presented the documents specified in the letter of credit to Texas Commerce Bank, the presenting bank. Texas Commerce Bank found discrepancies between the presentation documents and the letter of credit which it related to Voest–Alpine. Because Voest–Alpine did not believe that any of the noted discrepancies would warrant refusal to pay, it instructed Texas Commerce Bank to forward the presentation documents to the Bank of China.

Texas Commerce Bank sent the documents via DHL courier to the Bank of China on August 3, 1995. According to the letter of credit, Voest–Alpine, the beneficiary, was required to present the documents within fifteen days of the shipping date, by August 2, 1995.[1] As the documents were presented on August 1, 1995, they were presented timely under the letter of credit. Bank of China received the documents on August 9, 1995.

On August 11, 1995, the Bank of China sent a telex to Texas Commerce Bank, informing them of seven alleged discrepancies between the letter of credit and the documents Voest–Alpine presented, six of which are

---

1. Originally, the Bank of China cited late presentation as one of its reasons for refusing to honor the letter of credit, but has since conceded that Voest–Alpine presented the documents in a timely fashion.

the subject of this action. The Bank of China claimed that 1) the beneficiary's name differed from the name listed in the letter of credit, as noted by the presenting bank; 2) Voest–Alpine had submitted bills of lading marked "duplicate" and "triplicate" instead of "original"; 3) the invoice, packing list and the certificate of origin were not marked "original"; 4) the date of the survey report was later than that of the bill of lading; 5) the letter of credit number in the beneficiary's certified copy of the fax was incorrect, as noted by the presenting bank; and 6) the destination was not listed correctly in the certificate of origin and the beneficiary's certificate, as noted by the presenting bank. The telex further stated. "We are contacting the applicant of the relative discrepancy [sic]. Holding documents at your risks and disposal."

On August 15, Texas Commerce Bank faxed the Bank of China, stating that the discrepancies were not an adequate basis to refuse to pay the letter of credit and requested that the bank honor the letter of credit and pay Voest-Alpine accordingly. The telex identified Voest–Alpine as the beneficiary in the transaction. Voest–Alpine also contacted JFTC directly in an effort to secure a waiver of the discrepancies but was unsuccessful.

On August 19, 1995, the Bank of China sent another telex to Texas Commerce Bank further explaining what it believed to be discrepancies between the letter of credit and the documentation presented by Voest–Alpine according to the UCP 500. In relevant part, the telex provided:

> You cannot say [the discrepancies] are of no consequence. The fact is that our bank must examine all documents stipulated in the credit with reasonable care, to ascertain whether or not they appear, on their face, to be incompliance [sic] with the terms and conditions of the credit. According to Article 13 of UCP 500. An irrevocable credit constitutes a definite undertaking of the issuing bank, providing that the stipulated documents are complied with the terms and conditions of the credit according to Article UCP 500. Now the discrepant documents may have us refuse to take up the documents according to article 14(B) of UCP 500.

The Bank of China returned the documents to Voest–Alpine and did not honor the letter of credit.

II.

The commercial letter of credit is a payment device often used in international trade which permits a buyer in a transaction to substitute its financial integrity with that of a stable credit source, usually a bank. Alaska Textile Co., Inc. v. Chase Manhattan Bank, N.A., 982 F.2d 813, 815 (2d Cir.1992).

"[A letter of credit] transaction usually comprises three separate contracts: '[f]irst, the issuing bank enters into a contract with its customer to issue the letter of credit. Second, there is a contract between the issuing bank and the party receiving the letter of credit. Third, the customer who procured the letter of credit signs a contract with the person receiving it,

usually involving the sale of goods or the provision of some service.' "
Resolution Trust Corporation v. Kimball, 963 F.2d 820, 820 (5th Cir.
1992)(quoting East Girard Sav. Ass'n v. Citizens National Bank, Etc., 593
F.2d 598, 601 (5th Cir.1979)). The underlying principle of the letter of
credit transaction is the independence of the three contracts. Philadelphia
Gear Corp. v. Central Bank, 717 F.2d 230, 235 (5th Cir.1983). The issuing
bank does not verify that all the terms of the underlying contract have
been fulfilled and must pay on a draft properly presented by a beneficiary,
without reference to the rights or obligations of the parties to the contract.
Tex. Bus. & Comm.Code Ann § 5.108(a), (f)(1) (Vernon's 2000). The
issuing bank need only make a facial examination of the presenting
documents to determine whether the beneficiary has complied with the
terms of the letter of credit, however, the bank bears the risk of any
misinterpretation of the beneficiary's demand for payment. Tex. Bus. &
Comm.Code Ann. § § 5.108(i)(4) (Vernon's 2000).

Prior to the amendments to the Texas Business and Commercial Code
in 1999, a beneficiary was not required to make its presentation documents
strictly comply with the letter of credit, but to present documents that on
their face "appear[ed] to comply" with the letter of credit in order to
receive payment. Tex. Bus. & Comm.Code Ann. § 5.109(b)(Vernon's 1998);
see also Vest v. Pilot Point Nat'l Bank, 996 S.W.2d 9, 12 (Tex.Civ.App.
1999)(finding that the language in section 5.109 did not mandate strict
compliance). The current statutory law requires an issuer to honor a
presentation that, as determined by standard practice of financial institutions that regularly issue letters of credit, "appears on its face strictly to
comply with the terms and conditions of the letter of credit." Tex. Bus. &
Comm.Code Ann. § 5.108(a), (e) (Vernon's 2000). Determination of what
constitutes standard practice of financial institutions is a "matter of
interpretation for the court." Tex. Bus. & Comm.Code Ann. § 5.108(e)
(Vernon's 2000).

The Uniform Customs and Practices for Documentary Credits, first
issued in 1930 by the International Chamber of Commerce and revised
approximately once every ten years since, is a compilation of international-
ly accepted commercial practices which may be incorporated into the
private law of a contract between parties. Banco General Runinahui, S.A. v.
Citibank Int'l, 97 F.3d 480, 482 (11th Cir.1996)(citing Alaska Textile, 982
F.2d at 816). In this case, the parties expressly adopted the UCP 500 as the
governing authority in the letter of credit. Where parties explicitly refer to
the UCP 500 in their contracts, the UCP has been interpreted to apply to
the transaction. Vest, 996 S.W.2d at 15. Accordingly, the Court will look to
the UCP for guidance in analyzing whether the actions of the Bank of
China were in conformity with "standard practice" of financial institutions.

* * *

III.

Voest–Alpine claims that the six remaining discrepancies cited by the
Bank of China are mere technicalities and typographical errors that do not

warrant the rejection of the documents. Voest–Alpine argues for a "functional standard" of compliance, contending that if the whole of the documents obviously relate to the transaction covered by the credit, the issuing bank must honor the letter of credit. The Bank of China argues that the discrepancies were significant and that if the documents contain discrepancies on their face, it is justified in rejecting them and is not required to look beyond the papers themselves.

Section 13(a) of the UCP 500 provides:

> Banks must examine all documents stipulated in the Credit with reasonable care, to ascertain whether or not they appear, on their face, to be in compliance with the terms and conditions of the Credit. Compliance of the stipulated documents on their face with the terms and conditions of the Credit shall be determined by international standard banking practice as reflected in these Articles. Documents which appear on their face to be inconsistent with one another will be considered as not appearing on their face to be in compliance with the terms and conditions of the Credit.

INTERNATIONAL CHAMBER OF COMMERCE, ICC UNIFORM CUSTOMS AND PRACTICE FOR DOCUMENTARY CREDITS, ICC PUBLICATION NO. 500 19 (1993).

The UCP 500 does not provide guidance on what inconsistencies would justify a conclusion on the part of a bank that the documents are not in compliance with the terms and conditions of the letter of credit or what discrepancies are not a reasonable basis for such a conclusion. The UCP 500 does not mandate that the documents be a mirror image of the requirements or use the term "strict compliance."

The Court notes the wide range of interpretations on what standard banks should employ in examining letter of credit document presentations for compliance. Even where courts claim to uphold strict compliance, the standard is hardly uniform. The first and most restrictive approach is to require that the presentation documents be a mirror image of the requirements. See Banco General Runinahui, S.A. v. Citibank Int'l, 97 F.3d 480, 483 (11th Cir.1996) ("This Court has recognized and applied the 'strict compliance' standard to requests for payment under commercial letters of credit ... '[T]he fact that a defect is a mere technicality' does not matter.'") (quoting Kerr–McGee Chem. Corp. v. FDIC, 872 F.2d 971, 973 (11th Cir.1989)); Alaska Textile Co. v. Chase Manhattan Bank, 982 F.2d 813, 816 (2d Cir.1992)(noting that documents that are nearly the same as those required by the letter of credit are unacceptable for presentation in a letter of credit transaction).

Second, there are also cases claiming to follow the strict compliance standard but support rejection only where the discrepancies are such that would create risks for the issuer if the bank were to accept the presentation documents. See Flagship Cruises Ltd. v. New England Merchants Nat'l Bank of Boston, 569 F.2d 699, 705 (1st Cir.1978) ("We do not see these rulings as retreats from rigorous insistence on compliance with letter of credit requirements. They merely recognize that variance between documents specified and documents submitted is not fatal if there is no possibility that the documents could mislead the paying bank to its detriment"); Crist v. J. Henry Schroder Bank & Trust Co., 693 F.Supp. 1429, 1433 (S.D.N.Y.1988)(where a party who has succeeded by operation of law to the rights of the beneficiary of a letter of credit, refusal was improper, even though the terms of the credit provided for payment only to the beneficiary); Bank of Cochin, Ltd. v. Manufacturers Hanover Trust Co., 612 F.Supp. 1533, 1541 (S.D.N.Y.1985)(even under the strict compliance standard, a variance is permitted between the documents specified in a letter of credit and the documents *947 presented thereunder where "there is no possibility that the documents could mislead the paying bank to its detriment"); Vest, 996 S.W.2d at 14 (noting that strict compliance does not demand "oppressive perfectionism").

A third standard, without much support in case law, is to analyze the documents for risk to the applicant. See INT'L CHAMBER OF COMMERCE, COMM'N ON BANKING TECHNIQUE AND PRACTICE, PUBLICATION NO. 511, UCP 500 & 400 COMPARED 39 (Charles del Busto ed.1994) (discussion of a standard that would permit "deviations that do not cause ostensible harm" to the applicant); see also Breathless Assoc. v. First Savings & Loan Assoc., 654 F.Supp. 832, 836 (N.D.Tex.1986) (noting, under the strict compliance standard, "[a] discrepancy ... should not warrant dishonor unless it reflects an increased likelihood of defective performance or fraud on the part of the beneficiary").

The mirror image approach is problematic because it absolves the bank reviewing the documents of any responsibility to use common sense to determine if the documents, on their face, are related to the transaction or even to review an entire document in the context of the others presented to the bank. On the other hand, the second and third approaches employ a determination-of-harm standard that is too unwieldy. Such an analysis would improperly require the bank to evaluate risks that it might suffer or that might be suffered by the applicant and could undermine the independence of the three contracts that underlie the letter of credit payment scheme by forcing the bank to look beyond the face of the presentation documents.

The Court finds that a moderate, more appropriate standard lies within the UCP 500 itself and the opinions issued by the International Chamber of Commerce ("ICC") Banking Commission. One of the Banking Commission opinions defined the term "consistency" between the letter of credit and the documents presented to the issuing bank as used in Article 13(a) of the UCP to mean that "the whole of the documents must obviously relate to the same transaction, that is to say, that each should bear a relation (link) with the others on its face ..." INT'L CHAMBER OF COMMERCE, BANKING COMM'N, PUBLICATION NO. 371, DECISIONS (1975–1979) OF THE ICC BANKING COMMISSION R. 12 (1980). The Banking Commission rejected the notion that "all of the documents should be exactly consistent in their wording." Id. (emphasis in original).

A common sense, case-by-case approach would permit minor deviations of a typographical nature because such a letter-for-letter correspondence between the letter of credit and the presentation documents is virtually impossible. See INT'L CHAMBER OF COMMERCE, COMM'N ON BANKING TECHNIQUE AND PRACTICE, PUBLICATION NO. 511, UCP 500 & 400 COMPARED 39 (Charles del Busto ed.1994)(noting the difficulty in attaining mirror-image compliance). While the end result of such an analysis may bear a strong resemblance to the relaxed strict compliance standard, the actual calculus used by the issuing bank is not the risk it or the applicant faces but rather, whether the documents bear a rational link to one another. In this way, the issuing bank is required to examine a particular document in light of all documents presented and use common sense but is not required to evaluate risks or go beyond the face of the documents. The Court finds that in this case the Bank of China's listed discrepancies should be analyzed under this standard by determining whether the whole of the documents obviously relate to the transaction on their face.

First, the Bank of China claimed that the beneficiary's name in the presentation documents, Voest–Alpine Trading USA, differed from the letter of credit, which listed the beneficiary as Voest–Alpine USA Trading. While it is true that the letter of credit inverted Voest–Alpine's geographic locator, all the documents Voest–Alpine presented that obviously related to this transaction placed the geographic locator behind "Trading", not in front of it. Furthermore, the addresses corresponded to that listed in the letter of credit and Texas Commerce Bank's cover letter to the Bank of China identified Voest–Alpine Trading USA as the beneficiary in the transaction with JFTC. The letter of credit with the inverted name bore obvious links to the documents presented by Voest–Alpine Trading USA. This is in contrast to a misspelling or outright omission. See Beyene v. Irving Trust Co., 762 F.2d 4 (2d Cir.1985)(listing beneficiary as "Soran" rather than "Sofan" was sufficient basis for refusal); Bank of Cochin, Ltd. v. Manufacturers Hanover Trust Co., 612 F.Supp. 1533 (S.D.N.Y.1985) (omitting "Ltd." from corporate name justified rejection). In contrast with these cases, the inversion of the geographic locator here does not signify a different corporate entity. The expert testimony of Professor Byrne supports the finding that this is not a discrepancy that warrants rejection of the presentation documents because the UCP 500 does not impose a standard of exact replication.

Second, the Bank of China pointed out that the set of originals of the bill of lading should have all been stamped "original" rather than "original," "duplicate" and "triplicate." It should be noted that neither the letter of credit nor any provision in the UCP 500 requires such stamping. In fact, the ICC Banking Commission expressly ruled that "duplicate" and "triplicate" bills of lading did not need to be marked "original" and that failure to label them as originals did not justify refusal of the documents. INT'L CHAMBER OF COMMERCE, BANKING COMM'N, PUBLICATION NO. 565, OPINIONS OF THE ICC BANKING COMM'N 1995–1996 38 (Gary Collyer ed.1997). While it is true that this clarification by the ICC came after the transaction at issue in this case, it is clear from the face of the documents that these documents are three originals rather than one original and two copies. The documents have signatures in blue ink vary slightly, bear original stamps oriented differently on each page and clearly state on their face that the preparer made three original bills. Further, one possible definition of duplicate is "[t]o make or execute again" and one definition of triplicate is "[o]ne of a set of three identical things." WEBSTER'S II NEW RIVERSIDE UNIVERSITY DICTIONARY 410, 1237 (1994). While the "duplicate" and "triplicate" stamps may have been confusing, stamps do not make obviously original documents into copies.

Third, the Bank of China claimed that the failure to stamp the packing list documents as "original" was a discrepancy. Again, these documents are clearly originals on their face as they have three slightly differing signatures in blue ink. There was no requirement in the letter of credit or the UCP 500 that original documents be marked as such. The ICC's policy statement on the issue provides that, "banks treat as original any document that appears to be hand signed by the issuer of the document." (Int'l Chamber of Commerce, Comm'n on Banking Technique and Practice, The determination of an "Original" document in the context of UCP 500 sub-Article 20(b) July 12, 1999). <http://www.iccwbo.org/home/statements rules/statements /1999/the_ determination_of_an_original_document.asp>. The failure to mark obvious originals is not a discrepancy.

Fourth, the Bank of China argues that the date of the survey report is after the bill of lading and is therefore discrepant. A careful examination of the survey *949 report reveals that the survey took place "immediately before/after loading" and that the sample of cargo "to be loaded" was taken. The plain language of the report reveals that the report may have been issued after the bill of lading but the survey itself was conducted before the ship departed. The date does not pose a discrepancy.

Fifth, the Bank of China claims that the letter of credit number listed in the beneficiary's certified copy of fax is wrong. The letter of credit number was listed as "LC95231033/95" on the copy of fax instead of "LC9521033/95" as in the letter of credit itself, adding an extra "3" after "LC952." However, adding the letter of credit number to this document was gratuitous and in the numerous other places in the documents that the letter of credit was referenced by number, it was incorrect only in one place. Moreover, the seven other pieces of information contained in the document were correct. The document checker could have easily looked to any other document to verify the letter of credit number, or looked to the balance of the information within the document and found that the document as a whole bears an obvious relationship to the transaction. Madame Gao, the document checker who reviewed Voest–Alpine's presentation documents for the Bank of China, testified that she did not look beyond the face of this particular document in assessing the discrepancy. The cover letter from Texas Commerce Bank, for example, had the correct number.

Finally, the Bank of China claims that the wrong destination is listed in the certificate of origin and the beneficiary's certificate. The certificate of origin spelled Zhangjiagang as "Zhangjiagng" missing an "a" as it is misspelled once in the letter of credit, making it consistent. The beneficiary's certificate, however, spelled it "Zhanjiagng," missing a "g" in addition to the "a", a third spelling that did not appear in the letter of credit. Madame Gao first considered the discrepancy a "misspelling" rather than an indication of the wrong port, according to her notes. There is no port in China called "Zhangjiagng" or "Zhanjiagng." "Gng" is a combination of letters not found in Romanized Chinese, whereas "gang" means "port" in Chinese. The other information contained in the document was correct, such as the letter of credit number and the contract number, and even contained the distinctive phrase "by courie lukdt within 3 days after shipment", presumably meaning by courier within three days after shipment, as in the letter of credit. The document as a whole bears an obvious relationship with the transaction. The misspelling of the destination is not a basis for dishonor of the letter of credit where the rest of the document has demonstrated linkage to the transaction on its face.

Based on the foregoing, the Court finds in favor of the plaintiff, Voest–Alpine.

NOTES

1.   Section 5–108(a)'s strict compliance standard applies unless the credit provides otherwise. UCP 500 does not explicitly address the standard of compliance or otherwise displace 5–108(a). Noting that the credit in *Voest-Alpine* incorporated the UCP 500, the *Voest-Alpine* court looked to the UCP for guidance in determining whether the Bank of China's actions were in conformity with "standard practice" of financial institutions. The court therefore relies on the practice of financial institutions to test whether Voest–Alpine's documentary presentation complied with the credit. Why then does the court go on to find that "a moderate, more appropriate standard lies within the UCP 500 itself and the opinions issued by the [ICC] Banking Commission"? The suggestion apparently is that the standard implied in both sources is not one of strict compliance. Does the court's test require that documentary discrepancies be measured only by international issuer practice, not strict compliance? Or is it enough that international issuer practice determines when a documentary presentation strictly complies with the credit's terms? Section 5–108(a)'s standard measures strict compliance by the applicable issuer practice referred to in 5–108(e).

2.   Section 5–108(a)'s strict compliance standard is a default rule. As with most aspects of the letter of credit, it can be varied by the reimbursement agreement between the applicant and the issuer when their interests and capabilities favor doing so. See 5–103(c); Comment 2 to 5–103; Comment 1 to 5–108. Reimbursement agreements sometimes are altered accordingly. For example, see ¶ 8 of the Letter of Credit Agreement form reprinted at the end of this Chapter. Another example is ISP 98 art. 4.09(c), which requires exact compliance in the documentary presentation when the credit calls for "exact" or "identical" wording in documents. Even when the parties do not opt out of the default rule, 1–102(3) allows the reimbursement agreement to set standards of documentary compliance. Thus, whether a strict compliance standard is preferable to an alternative compliance standard depends on the preferences and capacities of typical parties to a letter of credit. Which rule is likely to minimize the costs of effecting payment under a credit for the typical applicant? The following observations bear on the pricing of a letter of credit.

> Consider the letter of credit department in a large bank. When the presented documents arrive, they are routed to an examining clerk. He pulls the related letter of credit from the bank's files and lays it next to the presented documents. He compares these documents against the letter's requirements and decides whether compliance has occurred. This happens daily for many sets of documents. Some are presented against a commercial letter, others against a standby. Yet the routine stays the same. It must move along steadily.
>
> Each time, the examiner has only the letter's words and the face of the presented documents to go by. Much may be going on outside these papers. For example, a presented certificate may swear customer's default even though such default is being honestly disputed. Or a bill of lading may show goods loaded on a ship that later sank in a storm. Or perhaps some practice in customer's or beneficiary's industry shades the meaning of a presented document and none of the papers before the examiner explain such practice. The document examiner is ill-equipped to deal with outside events like these. He has no lawyer by his side. He will probably have little or no command of any industry practice not within banking spheres. Nor can he afford the expense, risk, and delay of any elaborate reasoning as he checks the presented papers against the letter's requirements. For the letter of credit to work quickly as a cheap and sure device, then, the examiner must disregard outside influences like these as he routinely asks, "From what appears on their face, do the presented documents meet all the letter's requirements?"

Albert J. Givray, Letters of Credit, 44 Bus.Law 1567, 1589 (1989).

3. Section 5–108(e) states that "[a]n issuer shall observe standard practice of financial institutions that regularly issue letters of credit. Determination of the issuer's observance of the standard practice is a matter of interpretation for the court." Under both 5–108(a) and UCP 500 art. 13(a), the degree of documentary compliance is determined by the "standard practice" of issuers. However, although close in meaning, the two provisions are not identical. They differ in the "practice" referred to: 5–108(e)'s "standard practice" is that of financial institutions that regularly issue credits; UCP 500 art. 13(a)'s "practice" is that of international banking practice. Given the number of non-bank issuers of domestic credits in the United States, the difference might be potentially important. Comment 8 to 5–108 discusses the intended meaning of "standard practice."

The ICC has attempted to describe some of the specific "best practices" for examining documents among international banks. See ICC Document No. 645, International Standard Banking Practice (ISBP) (2003). For example, ISBP para. 69 finds acceptable a description of the quantity of goods in the invoice that varies by +-5% from the quantity required by the credit. ISBP para. 32 requires that each document be presented in at least one original, unless the credit allows otherwise. ISBP para. 28 considers misspellings or typographical errors in a document nondiscrepant as long as they do not alter the meaning of the word or sentence in which they occur.

Section 5–108(e) allocates to the court the determination of the issuer's observance of standard practice. Comment 1 explains, ". . . it is hoped that there will be more consistency in the outcomes and speedier resolution of disputes if the responsibility for determining the nature and scope of standard practice is granted to the court, not to a jury." Does this unconstitutionally deprive the parties of a jury trial? See Margaret L. Moses, The Uniform Commercial Code Meets the Seventh Amendment: The Demise of Jury Trials Under Article 5, 72 Ind. L. J. 681 (1997). Compare also §§ 1–205(2), 2–202, 2–302 and 4A–202(c) which use a similar approach. Section 5–108(e)'s treatment of the issue of standard practice as a question of law is controversial. Three states have adopted nonuniform amendments to the subsection eliminating the offending portion of subsection (e). See N.Y. U.C.C. § 5–108(e) (McKinney 2003); Pa. Stat. Ann. 13 § 51–8(e) (2003); Wyo. Stat. Ann. § 34.1–5–108(e) (2003).

4. Do 5–108(a) and (e) advance the cause of certainty in letter of credit law? Accepting Comment 1's statement that strict compliance does not mean "slavish conformity," how should American Coleman Co. v. Intrawest Bank, 887 F.2d 1382 (10th Cir. 1989) be decided under 5–108? In that case the triggering event for the bank's obligation to pay was presentation to the bank of a sight draft accompanied by a written statement by the beneficiary that the "Note and Security Agreement dated November 21, 1984" were in default. Even though there was no such note, the beneficiary's statement contained the required representation. Out of an abundance of caution and because of its unease about representing that the customers were in default on a nonexistent note, the beneficiary added the fatal words "and the Promissory Note dated November 16, 1984," which described the true note on which the customers were actually in default. The court held that under former Article 5 the documentary presentation was not in compliance owing to the additional language. In one of the cases expressly approved in Comment 1 to 5–108, New Braunfels National Bank v. Odiorne, 780 S.W.2d 313 (Tex. Ct. App. 1989), the correct letter of credit number was 86–122–S but the request for payment listed it as 86–122–5. The court held that the bank's dishonor was wrongful and observed that strict compliance meant "something less than absolute, perfect compliance." Did the *American Coleman* court demand absolute, perfect compliance? Or did it find that, judged by prevailing banking standards of documentary examination, the reference to the November 16 note was significantly at odds with the statements required by the letter of credit? In other words, did the *American Coleman* court in effect find that, although literal compliance is not required, the documentary discrepancy at issue was not on the order of a typographical error?

5. Does the strict compliance standard enhance the reliability of letters of credit as payment mechanisms? Or does it encourage an issuing bank to find a minor defect in the documents in cases in which the bank doesn't want to pay, such as cases in which the applicant has gone into bankruptcy and reimbursement of the bank's claim against the applicant may be difficult? Observers consistently have found a high frequency of noncomplying documentary presentations, typically exceeding 50%. In an informal survey of selected banks issuing commercial credits, the issuers reported that 73% of the documentary presentations contained discrepancies. See Ronald J. Mann, The Role of Letters of Credit in Payment Transactions, 98 Mich. L. Rev. 2494 (2000). Concerned about the number of discrepant presentations, the ICC has tried to create uniformity in international banking practices for handling documentary discrepancies by publishing a set of "best practices." See Document No. 645, ISBP.

In assessing the wisdom of the strict compliance standard, recognize three points. First, in most commercial credits the beneficiary doesn't care if the documents presented contain discrepancies, because the issuer will honor the presentation anyway. Where the market price of goods contracted for in the underlying transaction is stable or rising, the applicant-buyer will want the goods and therefore will have the issuer waive its right to insist on conforming documents. Alternatively, under these markets conditions the issuer may waive the discrepancy at its own risk. Thus, most of the time obtaining conforming documents isn't cost-justified for beneficiary-sellers. See John F. Dolan, Why High Discrepancy Rates Do Not Discourage L/C Use, 2003 Ann. Survey Let. Credit L. & Prac. 36. The few beneficiaries who are concerned about the prospect of a falling market can opt-out of strict compliance by insisting that the reimbursement agreement provide a more forgiving standard of compliance.

Second, there is a powerful market mechanism controlling strategic rejections of discrepant documents by issuers. Issuers operate in a market in which reputation matters. Because issuance fees are comparatively low, an issuer's profit from operating a credit department depends on it generating a high volume of credits. The issuer therefore must both obtain repeat business and attract potential applicants and beneficiaries. The number of issuers is relatively small, and information about their handling of credits often can be obtained from other issuers. An issuer may seize on a discrepancy to avoid honor because it fears not being reimbursed or is undercollaterized or wants to avoid involvement in the applicant's bankruptcy or simply wants to placate its applicant. But doing so risks a loss of credit business since potential beneficiaries will insist that credits be issued by issuers that are reliable sources of payment. The presenting beneficiary also is unlikely to do business with the issuer again. Thus, prospect of a loss in reputation often suffices to prevent issuers from strategic rejections even under a strict compliance standard.

Third, less stringent standards of compliance require judicial intervention, and courts are poorly positioned to intervene effectively. For instance, the court in *Voest-Alpine* considers and rejects a standard that finds documentary discrepancies when the deviation in the document risks harming the applicant in the underlying transaction. Application of this standard encourages parties to litigate the issuer's decision to honor or dishonor a documentary presentation. Courts (and issuers) are unfamiliar with the facts necessary to make this determination of harm at the time the issuer must decide to honor the presentation. They know nothing about industry practices bearing on the underlying transaction. Standards less stringent than strict compliance therefore undermine the credit's efficient payment function. Professor White reaches the same conclusion and states, without remorse, that "the issuer may examine the documents microscopically and may assert small discrepancies to excuse its duty to pay." 3 White & Summers, Prac. ed. § 26–5, at 140–41.

6. Under 5–108(a), an issuing bank must honor a conforming presentation. Must it dishonor a nonconforming presentation? Suppose in the case of questionable documentation like that in *American Coleman*, the bank called the applicant and asked its consent to the bank's payment of the credit. If the applicant gave its consent, (1) may the bank safely pay the credit? (2) May it safely decline to pay the credit? 5–108(a) and Comment 7 to 5–108. (3) Does the issuer have a duty to seek a waiver from the applicant in the case of a nonconforming presentation? Comment 2 to 5–108; see Bombay Industries, Inc. v. Bank of NY, 649 N.Y.S.2d 784 (N.Y.App.Div.1996).

7. Matter of Coral Petroleum, Inc., 878 F.2d 830 (5th Cir.1989), presented the issue of whether impossibility excuses strict compliance with a letter of credit. Seller sold Buyer 31,000 barrels of West Texas Intermediate crude oil for $880,400 and required Buyer to obtain a standby letter of credit in a form acceptable to Seller for the price. Bank issued the letter of credit under Buyer's instructions that the credit would be payable upon receipt of certain documents including (1) a statement by Seller that West Texas Intermediate oil had been delivered to Buyer and (2) a copy of the shipper's transfer order showing transfer to Buyer of 31,000 barrels of "WTNM SO or SR." Buyer's instructions were mistaken. West Texas Intermediate crude is a sweet oil (meaning not containing certain undesirable elements found in sour oil), but "WTNM SO or SR" refers to sour oil. Thus, the letter of credit required two documents that were contradictory: a shipper's order showing transfer of sour oil to Buyer and a statement that sweet oil had been delivered to Buyer. After Buyer filed in bankruptcy under Chapter 11, Seller demanded payment under the letter of credit. Bank refused to pay because Seller's demand was accompanied by a shipper's order showing transfer of sweet oil to Buyer. Seller had inspected the letter of credit before accepting it and did not ask that the erroneous description be corrected. Seller argued that the terms of the credit were impossible to perform. Seller could not deliver sweet oil to Buyer and procure a shipper's transfer order showing that sour oil had been delivered. Seller also argued that the letter of credit was ambiguous and the ambiguity should be construed against Bank. The court held that the letter of credit was not ambiguous. The fact that it was impossible for Seller to comply did not excuse compliance by Seller. Bank is not required to know the meaning of technical trade terms used in the letter of credit. See also In re Sanders–Langsam Tobacco Co., Inc., 224 B.R. 1 (Bankr.E.D.N.Y.1998). Moreover, Seller was negligent in accepting a letter of credit with requirements that could not be met. Accord: First State Bank v. Diamond Plastics Corp., 891 P.2d 1262 (Okla.1995).

In Albert J. Givray, Letters of Credit, 44 Bus. Law. 1567, 1587 (1989), it is suggested that issuers add a conspicuous legend stating "Please examine this letter of credit at once. If you feel unable to meet any of its requirements, either singly or together, please contact customer immediately to see if the letter of credit can be amended. Otherwise, you risk losing payment under this letter of credit for failure to comply strictly with its terms as written." Would the suggested legend be likely to help parties in Seller's position in *Coral Petroleum*? If Seller discovered the inconsistency after Buyer had filed a bankruptcy petition and Buyer were willing to have the credit amended to remove the inconsistency, the automatic stay could prevent it from doing so. See Bankruptcy Code § 362(a)(3). If the discovery and amendment were made prior to Buyer's bankruptcy filing, preference law could be implicated.

2. NOTICE OF DISCREPANCIES: WAIVER AND PRECLUSION

An issuer can respond to a documentary presentation in either of two ways: by honoring or dishonoring it. Both Article 5 and the UCP describe the steps that an issuer must take when documents are presented under a credit and the consequence of failing to take them. The two sets of rules prescribe the same steps. If the documents appear to comply with the credit's terms, both 5–108(a) and UCP 500 art. 13(b) require the issuer to honor the presentation. If the documents are discrepant and the discrepancy allows the issuer to refuse honor, the issuer has a choice: it can waive its right to insist on a complying presentation and honor the discrepant presentation or it can dishonor the presentation. (An issuer who waives the discrepancy does so at its own risk, unless the customer has agreed to the waiver.) Under both 5–108(b) and UCP 500 art. 13(b), 14(c) and (d), the issuer must honor or dishonor a presentation within a reasonable time after the documentary presentation, but not beyond seven business days after receipt of the documents, unless the credit provides otherwise. Comment 2 to 5–108 notes that this seven-day period is not a safe harbor: the issuer must act within a reasonable period, but no later than the end of the seven-day period. The failure to decide to honor or dishonor within the prescribed "reasonable period" constitutes dishonor by the issuer. See Comment 2 to 5–108.

Waiver is an intentional relinquishment of a known legal right and applies to Article 5 via 1–103(a), as a supplementing principle of extra-UCC common law. A waiver can be oral, unless the reimbursement agreement requires otherwise. Paragraph 11 of the Letter of Credit Agreement form at the end of the Chapter requires that waivers be in writing. UCP 500 art. 14(c) explicitly allows the issuer to waive its rights against the applicant. The UCP is silent as to the issuer's waiver against the beneficiary. A few courts have divided over whether common law doctrines such as waiver apply to credits subject to the UCP. Compare Banco General Runinahui, S.A. v. Citibank Int'l, 97 F.3d 480 (11th Cir. 1996) with Alaska Textile Co., Inc. v. Chase Manhatten Bank, N.A., 982 F.2d 813 (2d Cir. 1992).

In deciding whether to waive a documentary discrepancy, prudent issuers usually approach their applicants to obtain their consent. This is because the applicant's consent modifies the reimbursement agreement to allow for the issuer's reimbursement if it honors the presentation. Sometimes issuer's waive discrepancies at their own risk, without the consent of their applicants. In all cases, waiver is a right of the issuer that it can exercise within its discretion. The issuer has no obligation to waive a discrepancy, even if the applicant consents to the waiver. See Suntex Industrial Corp., Ltd. v. The CIT Group/BBC, Inc., 2001 U.S. Dist. Lexis 17656 (D. Del. 2001). It need not even approach the applicant to elicit the applicant's consent. See Note 6 above. ISP 98 arts. 5.05 and 5.06(a) are to the same effect. Comment 7 to 5–108 construes waiver narrowly, so that waiver of one or more presentations does not waive subsequent discrepant presentations.

The issuer's second alternative is to dishonor a discrepant documentary presentation. Article 5 follows the UCP's approach both to the sufficiency of notice that must be given to the presenter and the effect of the failure to give timely notice and sufficient notice of dishonor. Section 5–108(b) requires that, in the case of dishonor, the issuer must communicate both the fact and grounds of dishonor to the presenter. See Comment 2 to 5–108 (second paragraph); cf. UCP 500 art. 14(d)(i), (ii). Thus, 5–108(b) contemplates two possibilities: either the issuer fails to make a timely decision to honor or dishonor, or the issuer's timely decision fails to give timely notice of the grounds for dishonor. In both cases 5–108(c) precludes the issuer from relying as a ground for dishonor on discrepancies it has delayed communicating to the presenter within 5–108(b)'s prescribed time limit. (Strictly, the UCP 500's preclusion rule only applies to the failure to give timely notice of the grounds for dishonor; see UCP 500 art. 14(e). It does not apply to the failure to make a timely decision to honor the presentation; see UCP 500 art. 13(b).)

Section 5–108(b)'s preclusion rule is not a rule concerning waiver or estoppel. Courts tend to mix waiver and estoppel together, and sometimes treat both as preclusion. See, e.g., *American Coleman*, 887 F.2d at 1387 ("waiver-estoppel rule"); *Banco General Runinahui, S.A.*, 97 F.3d at 485 n.11 (preclusion as "strict estoppel"). The notions are distinct. Preclusion isn't waiver because it doesn't require the issuer to intentionally relinquish its right to a complying presentation. Section 5–108(b)'s preclusion rule applies when the issuer simply fails to give timely notice of the grounds for dishonor within the prescribed period. Preclusion also isn't estoppel, because estoppel requires detrimental reliance and 5–108(b)'s rule does not require reliance. It therefore requires no showing that the presenter has been harmed by the issuer's failure to give timely notice of the fact, or grounds, of dishonor. For the same reasons, UCP 500 art. 14(e)'s preclusion rule isn't a waiver or estoppel rule. See Toyota Tsusho Corp. v. Comerica Bank, 929 F.Supp. 1065 (E.D.Mich. 1996). Unlike waiver and estoppel, Article 5 and the UCP 500s' preclusion rules avoid the proof costs associated with litigating over relinquishment of a right to a complying presentation (waiver) or detrimental reliance on a failure to give timely notice of a discrepancy (estoppel).

Both 5–108(b) and UCP 500 art. 14(d)'s prescribed time periods set an outer limit of seven business days, but requires the decision to honor or dishonor be within a "reasonable time" within the seven-day period. The issue what is a "reasonable time" to decide or give notice of discrepancies has been troubled courts construing the UCP. Courts under former Article 5 treated the three-day period prescribed by former 5–112(1) as a safe harbor: notice of dishonor given by the end of the period is effective, even if the decision to dishonor has been made at the beginning of the period. 3 White & Summers, Prac. Ed. § 26–9(c). Because the seven-day period under 5–108(b) is not a safe-harbor, only an outer limit, courts applying the subsection face the same issues concerning the time for giving notice of discrepancies as courts face in applying UCP 500. ISP 98 art. 5.01(a)(i) resolves some of the uncertainty, when applicable, by deeming notice given within three business days "not unreasonable." The following UCP case discusses these matters. Although application of an earlier version of the UCP's preclusion rule is at issue in the case (UCP 400 art. 16(c)), the interpretation of a "reasonable time" in the rule remains relevant under UCP 500's art. 14(d)'s time period.

Esso Petroleum Canada v. Security Pacific Bank

United States District Court, D. Oregon, 1989.
710 F.Supp. 275.

■ FRYE, DISTRICT JUDGE:

The matters before the court are the motion for summary judgment (#45) of defendant, The Oregon Bank (the Bank), on all claims brought by plaintiff, Esso Petroleum Canada (Esso), and Esso's motion for partial summary judgment on its first and third claims for relief (#).

Esso alleges that the Bank wrongfully dishonored its irrevocable standby letter of credit by failing to specify the discrepancies which caused the Bank to reject the documents submitted by Esso or to notify Esso of the discrepancies in a timely fashion.

UNDISPUTED FACTS

Esso is a division of Imperial Oil Limited, a company organized and existing under the laws of Canada, with its principal place of business in Toronto, Canada. The Bank, presently known as Security Pacific Bank, is a banking corporation organized and existing under the laws of the State of Oregon.

Prior to October 22, 1987, Esso entered into a contract with Valley Oil Co., Inc. (Valley Oil) to sell to Valley Oil amounts of aviation gasoline for a total purchase price of $1,196,580. As a condition of sale, Esso required Valley Oil to obtain a standby letter of credit naming Esso as the beneficiary. As a condition to issuing the standby letter of credit, the Bank required Valley Oil to obtain a backup letter of credit from Western Pioneer, Inc., dba Delta Western (Delta), Valley Oil's customer. On October 21, 1987, Delta transferred by wire $1,288,140 to the Bank for deposit to Valley Oil's account.

On October 22, 1987, the Bank executed and delivered to Esso an irrevocable standby letter of credit, a copy of which is attached as Exhibit "A." On November 1, 1987, Esso delivered the aviation fuel to Delta.

The letter of credit issued by the Bank to Esso on October 22, 1987 provides that it is subject to the Uniform Customs and Practice for Documentary Credits (1983 Revision) International Chamber of Commerce (Publication 400) (the UCP). Article 48 of the UCP provides that letters of credit expiring on a day on which the issuing bank is not open for business do not expire until the end of the following day on which the bank is open for business. Therefore, since November 15, 1987 fell on a Sunday, the letter of credit did not expire until Monday, November 16, 1987.

At approximately 1:00 p.m. on Friday, November 13, 1987, Esso presented its draft for $1,218,116.90, drawn on the Bank under the letter of credit, and documents fulfilling the terms and conditions of the letter of credit. Esso demanded immediate payment.

At 5:15 p.m. on Friday, November 13, 1987, the Bank informed Esso that it would not honor Esso's draft and demand for payment due to certain discrepancies. In a Memorandum for Credit Files dated November 16, 1987, Fred Hammack, commercial loan officer for the Bank, states that although Fulvio Santin, supervisor for foreign crude oil supply and scheduling for Esso, demanded a list of these discrepancies on November 13, 1987, the Bank did not inform Esso of them at that time. This memorandum reads as follows:

On 11/13/87 at approximately 5:15 pm, I informed Mr. Santin that the Bank had uncovered discrepancies in the documents and would give to him by 9:00 am on 11/16/87 a written response stating what these discrepancies were.

Mr. Santin asked me if I could tell him what those discrepancies were. I told Mr. Santin and the other representatives that the discrepancies involved the supporting documents but that I could not give him specifics since it was the obligation of the International Banking Department who is responsible for the review process to give the written response. I further stated that this response per Bank policy must be signed by the Head of the International Banking Department. He would be back in his office by 7:30 on 11/16/87 and would be available to sign the letter in order to meet the 9:00 am delivery time. The Head of the International Banking Department was not in the office today.

In a deposition dated August 30, 1988, Hammack states that on behalf of the Bank he informed Esso's representatives on November 13, 1987 that they would have to wait for a written response by the Bank to discover the discrepancies in the documents they had submitted to the Bank on that date. The relevant portion of this deposition states:

Q What was their response?

A They wanted to know what the discrepancies were.

Q What was your response?

A I said, I did not know.

Q What did they say?

A They implored me again about the discrepancies, and if they could talk, I believe, to someone upstairs.

Q What was your response?

A My response was they had to wait for the written response by the bank.

Q Did that satisfy them?

A I think the conversation ended, I don't think it satisfied them.

The Bank sent Esso a list of the discrepancies in a letter dated Monday, November 16, 1987. This letter stated that Esso's draft under the letter of credit:

remains unpaid due to the following discrepancies:

—Invoice does not show beneficiary as stated in Letter of Credit.

—Merchandise description on invoice not per Letter of Credit.

—Applicant name and address on invoice not per Letter of Credit.

—Documentary requirement number 2 as stated in the Letter of Credit not presented.

On November 16, 1987, Esso attempted to correct these discrepancies and again presented its draft for $1,218,116.90 drawn on the Bank under the letter of credit demanding immediate payment. The Bank again refused to honor Esso's draft on the grounds of uncorrected discrepancies.

On January 20, 1988, various creditors of Valley Oil filed a petition in the United States Bankruptcy Court for the District of Oregon, naming Valley Oil as the debtor.

On February 10, 1988, Esso filed this action against the Bank seeking money damages in the amount of $1,218,116.90 plus interest, $935,000 in punitive damages, and costs incurred in this action.

The second amended complaint states several claims for relief in contract, equity and tort. The contract and equity claims are as follows:

(1) that the Bank wrongfully dishonored its irrevocable standby letter of credit;

(2) that the Bank failed to specify the discrepancies which caused it to reject the draft and documents submitted by Esso;

(3) that the Bank failed to notify Esso of the discrepancies in a timely fashion;

(4) that the Bank wrongfully set off amounts owed to it by Valley Oil against funds from the special deposit made by Delta;

(5) that the Bank's conduct in this matter amounted to a waiver of its opportunity to claim that the alleged discrepancies were not in accordance with the letter of credit; and

(6) that the Bank's conduct estops it from asserting the alleged discrepancies as a defense in this action.

Esso also seeks punitive damages on the grounds that the Bank tortiously breached its obligation to deal in good faith by wrongfully, deliberately, or recklessly disregarding Esso's rights under the letter of credit.

* * *

DISCUSSION

I. Dishonor of Letter of Credit—(Claims for Relief 1, 2, 3, 5, 6 and 7).

Esso alleges that the Bank wrongfully dishonored the Bank's irrevocable standby letter of credit when Esso properly presented Esso's draft drawn on the Bank under the letter of credit for payment. Esso contends that Article 16(e) of the UCP precludes a bank from dishonoring the letter of credit once the Bank failed to timely notify Esso of the specific discrepancies on November 13, 1987.

The Bank responds that it properly dishonored the letter of credit on both November 13, 1987 and on November 16, 1987 because the documents presented by Esso on those dates contained numerous discrepancies. In addition, the Bank contends that the letter of credit is subject to the Oregon Commercial Code, arguing that the Bank gave Esso sufficient and timely notice of the discrepancies under O.R.S. 75.1120, which grants banks three days to determine whether to dishonor letters of credit.

Both parties concede that they are bound by the UCP. Article 16 of the UCP provides, in pertinent part, that:

c. The issuing bank shall have a reasonable time in which to examine the documents and to determine ... whether to take up or to refuse the documents.

d. If the issuing bank decides to refuse the documents, it must give notice to that effect without delay by telecommunication or, if that is not possible, by other expeditious means, to the bank from which it received the documents (the remitting bank), or to the beneficiary, if it received the documents directly from him. such notice must state the discrepancies in respect of which the issuing bank refuses the documents and must also state whether it is holding the documents at the disposal of, or is returning them to the presentor (remitting bank or the beneficiary, as the case may be). The issuing bank shall then be entitled to claim from the remitting bank refund of any reimbursement which may have been made to that bank.

e. If the issuing bank fails to act in accordance with the provisions of paragraphs (c) and (d) of this article and/or fails to hold the documents at the disposal of, or to return them to, the presentor, the issuing bank shall be precluded from claiming that the documents are not in accordance with the terms and conditions of the credit.

UCP Article 16(c)–(e) (emphasis added).

The issue is not whether the Bank had cause to reject the documents presented by Esso, but whether, once the Bank made its decision to reject those documents, it properly notified Esso of its decision by specifying the alleged discrepancies in accordance with Article 16(d).

In Bank of Cochin v. Manufacturers Hanover Trust Co., 808 F.2d 209 (2d Cir.1986), the Second Circuit held that an issuing bank was estopped under the UCP from asserting the confirming bank's noncompliance with the terms of a letter of credit where the issuing bank delayed twelve to thirteen days in notifying the confirming bank of specific defects in the presented documents and of its intent to return those documents. The court stated that " '[w]ithout delay' is defined neither in Article 8 nor in any case law dealing with international letters of credit. However, the phrase is akin to 'immediate (at once), instant, instantaneous, instantly, prompt.' W. Burton, Legal Thesaurus 1053 (1980). All of these synonyms connote a sense of urgent action within the shortest interval of time possible." Id. at 213.

In Datapoint Corp. v. M & I Bank, 665 F.Supp. 722 (W.D.Wis.1987), the United States District Court held that a bank was precluded from claiming that a draft varied from the terms of the letter of credit where it failed to notify the beneficiary of the dishonor by telecommunication or other expeditious means. The court found that "[u]nder the provisions of the Uniform Customs and Practice, incorporated by the Letter of Credit, once defendant decided to refuse the Original Draft, it was obligated to notify plaintiff to that effect without delay by telecommunication or, if that was impossible, by other expeditious means." Id. at 727.

In the present action, Esso presented its draft for $1,218,116.90, drawn on the Bank under the letter of credit, at 1:00 p.m. on November 13, 1987. The Bank notified Esso of its decision to dishonor the letter of credit by 5:15 p.m. that afternoon. Under Article 16(d) of the UCP, the Bank was required to state the discrepancies in respect of which it refused the documents at the time it notified Esso of its refusal to honor the letter of credit. Since the Bank's notice did not state these discrepancies at that time, under UCP Article 16(e), the Bank is now precluded from claiming that the documents were not in accordance with the terms and conditions of credit. Esso is, therefore, entitled to collect funds from the Bank under the terms of the letter of credit.

Esso's motion for partial summary judgment on its first and third claims for relief is granted. Since the court has granted Esso summary judgment under its claim of wrongful dishonor of the letter of credit, it need not address Esso's equitable claim for money had and received.

* * *

NOTE

How would this case be decided under 5–108? See Comments 2 and 4 to 5–108. In Rhode Island Hospital Trust Nat. Bank v. Eastern General Contractors, Inc., 674 A.2d 1227 (R.I.1996), a UCP case, the beneficiary made presentation on Thursday, September 26, 1985. On Friday, September 27, the bank did not open for business owing to Hurricane Gloria. Monday, September 30 was the expiry date. On Tuesday, October 1, the bank notified the beneficiary of certain discrepancies and stated that it would hold the documents for beneficiary's disposal. The court concluded that the trial court erred in directing a verdict for the bank. Expert testimony was to the effect that the bank did not act within a reasonable time; if the date of receipt of the presentation to the issuing bank is close to the expiry date of the credit, common banking procedure is to act expeditiously, presumably so that any discrepancy can be cured before expiration of the credit.

PROBLEMS

1. Over the period of a year, Beneficiary presented three drafts for payment to Issuer. Each presentation contained the same discrepancy. The first two times Issuer paid the draft without objection after receiving permission of the Applicant to pay despite the nonconformity. The third time Applicant refused to consent to payment and Issuer dishonored the draft on the ground that the presentation was nonconforming. Has Issuer wrongfully dishonored? Comment 7 to 5–108. 3 White & Summers, Prac. ed. § 26–9(a).

2. Bank issued a letter of credit subject to the UCP 500 and with an expiration date of January 9. The credit undertook to pay Beneficiary $100,000 (U.S.) upon Beneficiary's presentation of three documents: a commercial invoice, a bill of lading and a certificate of inspection. The terms of the credit required the documents to cover "100 pounds of widgets," and invoice and certificate of inspection to state that the widgets were "quality 100%." On January 1, Beneficiary presented all three documents to Bank. The commercial invoice described the goods as "105 pounds of widgets of 95% quality." The bill of lading described the goods as "105 pounds of widgit ... all received on board for shipment." The certificate of origin described them as "105 pounds of WGS," "WGS" being an abbreviation for widgets commonly used in the widget trade.

Bank notified Beneficiary on January 2 to the effect that it "finds discrepancies in the invoice presented by you going to the quantity and quality of widgets described." On January 5 it notified Beneficiary that it "rejects the bill of lading based on the failure of the description of the goods in the bill ('105 pounds of widgit') to conform to the terms of the credit." Bank gave notice to Beneficiary on January 6 that it "rejects the certificate of inspection because the description of goods ('WGS') fail to conform to the terms of the credit." Each notice was accompanied by Bank's statement that it was returning the documents to Beneficiary, and Bank did so. This did Beneficiary no good because Beneficiary was unable make another presentation by January 9, the date on which the credit expired. Bank refused to pay Beneficiary $100,000.

(1) Did Beneficiary's documentary presentation comply with the terms of the credit? Consult ISBP paras. 28 and 69 reproduced below. (2) If not, is Bank entitled to dishonor Beneficiary's noncomplying documentary presentation? See UCP 500 arts. 14(d)(i), (ii), (e).

ICC, International Standard Banking Practices (ISBP) (2003)

28.   Misspellings or typing errors that do not affect the meaning of a word or the sentence in which it occurs, do not make a document discrepant.... However, a description as "model 123" instead of "model 321" would not be regarded as a typing error and would constitute a discrepancy.

69.   The quantity of the goods required in the credit may vary within a tolerance of +/–5%. This does not apply if the a credit stipulates that the quantity must not be exceeded or reduced, or if a credit stipulates the quantity in terms of a stated number of packing units or individual items."

3.   ISSUER'S RIGHT TO REIMBURSEMENT AND OTHER REMEDIES

a.   REIMBURSEMENT

Section 5–108(i) arms the issuer with a statutory right of reimbursement against the applicant. Credits usually also provide for reimbursement, as in the opening paragraph of the Letter of Credit Agreement at the end of this Chapter.

The credit risk that an issuer takes with respect to payment of a letter of credit depends on whether the transaction involves a commercial or a standby letter of credit. Commercial letters of credit are payment mechanisms and are meant to be paid in every case, usually upon presentation of the seller-beneficiary's bill of lading covering the goods sold to the buyer-applicant. When the issuer has paid, it receives possession of the bill of lading which the applicant must obtain from the issuer in order to receive the goods from the carrier that issued the bill of lading. 5–108(i)(2). The issuer can secure its claim for reimbursement by holding the bill of lading until the applicant either pays or arranges for credit.

A standby letter of credit functions as a guaranty and is usually meant to be paid only in case of the applicant's failure to perform the underlying contract. When the issuer pays a standby letter of credit, it receives no bill of lading or similar document that can be used to induce the applicant to pay. Functionally, a letter of credit is a conditional loan made to the applicant by the issuer, and issuing banks treat it as such. Since it is a loan that will usually not have to be funded unless the applicant is in financial difficulty, as when the applicant is in bankruptcy, the statutory reimbursement right under 5–108(i) is invariably supplemented with an express reimbursement agreement between the issuer and applicant containing the usual terms of commercial loans with respect to security, interest rates, set-off, and the like. See ¶¶ 4,5 and 9 of the Letter of Credit Agreement form reprinted at the end of this Chapter.

As we have said before, if obligees are able to obtain standby letters of credit from their obligors, they are in a position far superior to that of secured parties under Article 9. Upon default by their obligor, they can go to the issuing bank and obtain prompt payment of the obligation. They do not need to engage in the expensive and time-consuming exercise of collecting the debt by repossessing and foreclosing on collateral, with all the attendant problems that we raised in the preceding chapters of this book, problems that are exacerbated by the obligor's bankruptcy. If no rational obligee would take a security interest in preference to a standby letter of credit, does this mean the death of security interests? Not at all; it merely changes the identity of the secured party from the obligee to the bank issuing the letter of credit. Unless the applicant is a customer who could borrow money on unsecured credit, banks will usually not issue standby letters of credit without receiving a security interest in the applicant's property. Efficiencies flowing from this tripartite arrangement have contributed to the great popularity of standby letters of credit. The creditworthiness of the obligor is determined by the bank, a professional credit grantor, rather than by the obligee who may be a seller of goods, a centerfielder, or others who are not in the business of credit granting. In this respect, the efficiency of the standby letter of credit resembles that present in the consumer bank credit card transaction. Retail stores, hotels, restaurants and others who sell goods and services can rely on a credit card issued by a bank that will guarantee payment on transactions made pursuant to the card; they don't need to maintain credit departments making costly credit evaluations of their customers. Banks will make the determination of the consumer's creditworthiness in deciding whether to issue the credit card.

b.   STANDARD OF COMPLIANCE

Under 5–108(i), an issuer is entitled to reimbursement from the applicant only if it "has honored a presentation as permitted or required by this article." Under 5–108(a) an issuer must dishonor a presentation that does not strictly comply with the terms of the letter of credit. Comment 1 to 5–108 says that "[t]he standard of strict compliance governs the issuer's

obligation to the beneficiary and to the applicant." The view adopted by
Article 5 that an issuing bank that pays on a presentation that does not
strictly comply with the terms of the letter of credit cannot receive
reimbursement from the applicant was rejected by some cases under the
old law which applied a "bifurcated" standard of compliance. This approach applied a strict compliance standard for the issuer's liability to the
beneficiary for wrongful dishonor but a substantial compliance standard for
the issuer's liability to the applicant for wrongful honor. The bifurcation
view was thought to be justified by an appreciation of the difficulty an
issuing bank experiences in a case in which the applicant is demanding that
the bank dishonor while the beneficiary is threatening suit if the bank does
not pay.

In rejecting the bifurcated approach, Article 5 takes the realistic
position that institutions issuing letters of credit, usually commercial
banks, are sophisticated parties which are eminently capable of looking out
for themselves. Section 5–108(a) recognizes that an issuing bank can safely
pay on a noncomplying presentation if the applicant will waive the discrepancy and consent to the payment. But what if the bank is uncertain about
whether there is a discrepancy in the presentation and the applicant will
not waive the potential discrepancy? Section 5–103(c) allows the parties to
contract around 5–108(a)'s standard of compliance as it applies to the
issuer's right to reimbursement. Prudent issuers will safeguard themselves
against liability for wrongful payment by including exculpatory clauses in
the reimbursement agreement designed to allow them to obtain reimbursement, even when they honor a credit in which a discrepant presentation
has been made. See ¶ 8 of the Letter of Credit Agreement form reprinted at
the end of this Chapter. Provisions imposing a standard of only substantial
compliance on issuing banks with respect to their duty to dishonor are
clearly enforceable. Comment 2 to 5–103. However, under the last sentence
of 5–103(c), terms "generally excusing liability or generally limiting remedies for failure to perform obligations" are unenforceable.

c.   SUBROGATION, RESTITUTION AND BREACH OF WARRANTY

As we have seen, the prudent issuer of a standby letter of credit makes
sure that if it has to pay the credit the applicant will be able to reimburse
it. This is usually done by requiring that the applicant give security for its
reimbursement obligation. However, if the security proves worthless and
the applicant is insolvent, the issuer is unable to obtain reimbursement
from the applicant. In these cases the issuer will explore alternative
remedies. If the applicant has given the beneficiary security, the issuer may
seek to be subrogated to the beneficiary's rights to the security. If the
issuer can claim to have paid because of fraud or mistake, it may demand
restitution from the beneficiary. Or the issuer may claim that the beneficiary has breached its presentation warranties to the issuer. In the materials
below we will examine the availability of these remedies.

Whether an issuer, having paid the beneficiary of a letter of credit, is
entitled to the equitable remedy of subrogation has been much litigated.

For reasons discussed in *Ochoco Lumber Company* below, a majority of courts have denied issuers the right to subrogation. Section 5–117(a) recognizes subrogation for issuers: "An issuer that honors a beneficiary's presentation is subrogated to the rights of the beneficiary to the same extent as if the issuer were a secondary obligor of the underlying obligation owed to the beneficiary and of the applicant to the same extent as if the issuer were the secondary obligor of the underlying obligation owed to the applicant." The subsection does not itself give an issuer a right of subrogation. It instead gives the issuer whatever rights a secondary obligor would have in the same circumstances ("as if the issuer were a secondary obligor . . ."). Thus, 5–117(a) removes a doctrinal barrier based on the issuer's "primary obligation" to granting issuers rights of subrogation. *Ochoco Lumber Company,* below, rehearses and adopts Judge Becker's dissenting opinion in Tudor Development Group, Inc. v. United States Fidelity & Guaranty Company, 968 F.2d 357 (3d Cir. 1992). Professor White, the Reporter of Revised Article 5, states in 3 White & Summers, Prac. ed. § 26–15, at 212–14 that Judge Becker's dissenting opinion in *Tudor* is the correct analysis of the problem, and Comment 1 to 5–117 indorses the Becker position. *Ochoco Lumber Company* shares this understanding of 5–117(a).

Ochoco Lumber Company v. Fibrex & Shipping Company, Inc.

Court of Appeals of Oregon, 2000.
994 P.2d 793.

■ KISTLER, J.

The trial court ruled that neither the applicant nor the issuer on a standby letter of credit can be subrogated to the beneficiary's claims. The court accordingly granted defendants' motion to dismiss plaintiff's equitable subrogation claims, denied plaintiff leave to replead, and entered judgment on those claims. We reverse and remand.

In 1993, defendant Fibrex & Shipping Co., Inc., entered into an agreement to purchase timber in Montana. To fund the purchase, Fibrex borrowed $3,900,000 from West One Idaho Bank.[1] West One imposed two conditions on the loan. First, it required that Fibrex's sole shareholder, Akira Saheki, and his wife, Saeko Saheki, personally guarantee the loan. Second, "[a]s security for repayment of [Fibrex's] note," West One required a standby letter of credit "in an amount no less than the amount of the principal balance of th[e] note."

Fibrex obtained the letter of credit by entering into an agreement with plaintiff Ochoco Lumber Company. Fibrex agreed to sell and Ochoco agreed to buy up to six and one-half million board feet of harvested ponderosa pine logs. As part of their agreement, Ochoco provided for an irrevocable standby letter of credit for $3,900,000, which First Interstate Bank issued

---

1. West One Idaho Bank has since been acquired by U.S. Bank.

for the benefit of West One. The letter of credit both served as security for Ochoco's performance under its agreement with Fibrex and also "was used by Fibrex to fulfill its obligations under [its loan from West One]."[2]

In 1994 and 1995, Fibrex failed to fulfill its obligations under its agreement with Ochoco. In May 1995, Ochoco and Fibrex renegotiated their agreement. In August 1995, Fibrex, Ochoco, and the persons who owned the timber entered into an amended timber purchase agreement. In September 1996, Fibrex's loan from West One came due. Fibrex failed to pay the loan, and West One drew over two million dollars on First Interstate's letter of credit. Ochoco reimbursed First Interstate Bank in full.[3] Ochoco then demanded repayment from Fibrex. After Fibrex refused to repay Ochoco, Ochoco notified West One that it was subrogated to West One's rights against both Fibrex and the Sahekis, the guarantors of Fibrex's loan.

When West One refused to acknowledge Ochoco's equitable subrogation rights, Ochoco brought an action alleging, among other things, four claims for relief that were based on equitable subrogation. Ochoco sought a declaration that it is subrogated to West One's rights, it sued Fibrex on the note that Fibrex had given West One, and it sued the Sahekis on their guarantee. Ochoco also sought injunctive relief against Fibrex and the Sahekis.[4] Defendants moved to dismiss Ochoco's claims for relief that were based on equitable subrogation. Relying on *Tudor Dev. Group, Inc. v. U.S. Fid. & Guar. Co.*, 968 F.2d 357 (3d Cir.1992), and *Shokai v. U.S. National Bank of Oregon*, 126 F.3d 1135 (9th Cir.1997), defendants argued that equitable subrogation is not available to the parties on a standby letter of credit. The trial court agreed. It dismissed Ochoco's subrogation claims without leave to replead and entered judgment on those claims pursuant to ORCP 67 B.

On appeal, defendants advance two arguments. They argue initially that equitable subrogation is available only to persons who are secondarily liable for a debt. They reason that the issuer's contractual obligation to pay on a standby letter of[5] credit means that the issuer is primarily, not

---

2. Fibrex agreed to use the funds it received from Ochoco's log purchases to reduce the balance on its loan with West One and thus reduce Ochoco's exposure on the letter of credit.

3. The complaint does not allege specifically that Ochoco reimbursed First Interstate. Ochoco acknowledged this oversight at the Rule 21 hearing and stated that it would replead to include that allegation. The trial court, however, dismissed Ochoco's subrogation claims without leave to replead, thereby preventing Ochoco from alleging that it had reimbursed First Interstate pursuant to its obligations under the letter of credit. Fibrex neither objected to Ochoco's request to replead at the Rule 21 hearing nor disputes

Ochoco's contention on appeal that it reimbursed First Interstate in full. We accordingly assume that Ochoco has paid First Interstate the amount it paid West One.

4. Ochoco alleged other claims for relief, but only its first, second, and third claims for relief and the first count of its thirteenth claim for relief are based on equitable subrogation and are at issue here.

5. A letter of credit "is an engagement by an issuer, usually a bank, made at the request of the [applicant] for a fee, to honor a beneficiary's drafts or other demands for payment upon satisfaction of the conditions set forth in the letter of credit." *Tudor Dev. Group, Inc.*, 968 F.2d at 360; *accord* Peter R.

secondarily, liable. They argue alternatively that, in any event, the particular facts of this transaction make subrogation inappropriate. Ochoco responds that a standby letter of credit is no different from a surety bond or a guarantee in that the issuer's obligation to pay on a standby letter of credit does not arise until there is a default. It follows, Ochoco reasons, that equitable subrogation should be equally available to the parties to a standby letter of credit; the transactions are in substance no different.

We begin with the statutes that govern letters of credit. When First Interstate issued the letter of credit in this case, the Oregon statutes did not address whether equitable subrogation was available on a standby letter of credit. Nothing should be inferred from that omission, however. ORS 75.1020(3) (1991) specifically recognized that "ORS 75.1010 to 75.1170 deal with some but not all the rules and concepts of letters of credit as such rules or concepts have developed * * * or may hereafter develop." It added: "The fact that ORS 75.1010 to 75.1170 state a rule does not by itself require, imply or negate application of the same or a converse rule to a situation not provided for * * * by ORS 75.1010 to 75.1170." ORS 75.1020(3) (1991). The statute thus explicitly left to judicial development those rules that were not codified in ORS chapter 75.

In 1997, the legislature authorized issuers of and applicants for letters of credit to seek equitable subrogation but made the new statute applicable to letters of credit issued on or after January 1, 1998.[6] Or. Laws 1997, ch. 150, §§ 20, 27 & 29. The Ninth Circuit has concluded that because Oregon's 1997 law applies prospectively, the Oregon legislature must have believed that prior law did not allow subrogation. *See Shokai,* 126 F.3d at 1136. Defendants find the Ninth Circuit's reasoning "instructive" and urge us to follow it. We decline to do so.

The 1997 Legislature amended many of the provisions in ORS chapter 75 governing letters of credit. *See* Or. Laws 1997, ch. 150, §§ 3–20. The fact

Jarvis, *Standby Letters of Credit—Issuers' Subrogation and Assignment Rights,* 9 UCC LJ 356, 356–60 (1977). There are two major types of letters of credit transactions. A commercial letter of credit is typically used when the seller is unfamiliar or uncertain about the buyer's credit history. *Id.* The beneficiary of a commercial letter of credit (usually the seller) may draw upon the letter by showing that it has performed and is entitled to the funds. *Id.* A standby letter of credit, on the other hand, typically requires the production of documents showing that the applicant has defaulted on its obligation to the beneficiary, which triggers the beneficiary's right to draw on the letter. *Id.*

6. Oregon Laws 1997, chapter 150, section 20, provides:

"(1) An issuer that honors a beneficiary's presentation is subrogated to the rights of

the beneficiary to the same extent as if the issuer were a secondary obligor of the underlying obligation owed to the beneficiary and of the applicant to the same extent as if the issuer were the secondary obligor of the underlying obligation owed to the applicant.

"(2) An applicant that reimburses an issuer is subrogated to the rights of the issuer against any beneficiary, presenter or nominated person to the same extent as if the applicant were the secondary obligor of the obligations owed to the issuer and has the rights of subrogation of the issuer to the rights of the beneficiary stated in subsection (1) of this section."

By its terms, this law applies only to letters of credit issued on or after January 1, 1998. Or. Laws 1997, ch. 150, §§ 27 & 29.

that the legislature provided that all those amendments would apply prospectively hardly reflects a judgment on the existing state of the law with respect to each or any of them. *See* Or. Laws 1997, ch. 150, § 27. The inference the Ninth Circuit drew is, at best, a weak one and is at odds with the long-standing principle that one legislature's view on an earlier state of the law is entitled to little or no weight. *Cf. DeFazio v. WPPSS*, 296 Or. 550, 561, 679 P.2d 1316 (1984) ("[t]he views legislators have of existing law may shed light on a new enactment, but it is of no weight in interpreting a law enacted by their predecessors"). Even if, however, the inference that defendants urge were textually permissible, it is not required and the legislative history points in the opposite direction. The Oregon Bankers' Association, which sponsored the 1997 legislation, told the legislature that the courts had not agreed on the availability of equitable subrogation, giving rise to confusion in the law. Testimony, Senate Committee on Business, Law and Government, SB 246, January 22, 1997, Ex H (statement of Frank E. Brawner). Although the legislature sought to clarify the law for letters of credit issued after the effective date of the act, the text, context, and the legislative history of the 1997 act do not suggest that the legislature made any judgment about the parties' right to equitable subrogation for letters of credit issued before the act's effective date. We are accordingly left to resolve that issue under common-law principles.

The court has explained that subrogation is " 'the substitution of another person in place of the creditor to whose rights he succeeds in relation to the debt, and gives to the substitute all of the rights, priorities, remedies, liens and securities of the party for whom he is substituted.' " *Maine Bonding v. Centennial Ins. Co.*, 298 Or. 514, 521, 693 P.2d 1296 (1985) (quoting *United States F. & G. Co. v. Bramwell*, 108 Or. 261, 277, 217 P. 332 (1923)). The purpose of subrogation is to prevent unjust enrichment. *See Barnes v. Eastern & Western Lbr. Co.*, 205 Or. 553, 596, 287 P.2d 929 (1955). Simply stated, subrogation is an equitable device used " 'to compel ultimate discharge of a debt by [the person] who in equity and good conscience ought to pay it * * *.' " *Maine Bonding*, 298 Or. at 521, 693 P.2d 1296 (quoting *United States F. & G. Co.*, 108 Or. at 277, 217 P. 332).

As a general rule, the courts have required that the party seeking subrogation must have paid a debt for which it was secondarily liable. *Wasco Co. v. New England E. Ins. Co.*, 88 Or. 465, 469–71, 172 P. 126 (1918); *accord Tudor Dev. Group, Inc.*, 968 F.2d at 361. The party must not have acted as a volunteer but must have paid to protect its own interests. *Id.* Finally, equitable subrogation "will not be enforced where it will work injustice to those having equal equities." *Id.* The Oregon courts have not specifically addressed how these requirements apply to standby letters of credit.[7] A handful of courts and commentators have done so, although their

---

7. In *Marshall-Wells Co. v. Tenney*, 118 Or. 373, 244 P. 84 (1926), the court used the terms letter of credit and guarantee interchangeably, but its reasoning reveals that it was considering the parties' rights under a guarantee, not a letter of credit. *See* Jarvis, 9 UCC LJ at 375.

decisions have not been uniform. *See Tudor Dev. Group, Inc.*, 968 F.2d at 361–62 (collecting cases).

The majority and minority views are perhaps best illustrated by the two opinions in *Tudor Dev. Group, Inc.* The majority in *Tudor* focused on whether the issuer is primarily or secondarily liable for the debt. 968 F.2d at 362. It reasoned, as a majority of courts have, that the issuer is primarily liable because a letter of credit imposes an independent obligation on the issuer to pay. *Id.* The majority reasoned that the issuer is "satisfying its own absolute and primary obligation to make payment rather than satisfying an obligation of its customer." *Id.* The majority recognized that the issuer's obligation on a standby letter of credit is secondary in the sense that it does not arise until the applicant has defaulted, but it still declined to view an issuer as comparable to a guarantor.

The dissent in *Tudor* responded that the majority's reasoning proved too much. A surety also has a contractual obligation to pay, but that fact neither means that the surety is primarily liable nor prevents it from seeking equitable subrogation. In the dissent's view, the fact that there is a contractual obligation to pay provides no basis for saying that the issuer of a standby letter of credit is not secondarily liable. Rather, like a surety or guarantor, the issuer of a standby letter of credit only has an obligation to pay if and when there is a default. In this case, for example, the note between West One and Fibrex required Fibrex to obtain a letter of credit as "security for repayment of [Fibrex's] note."

The relevant question, in the dissent's view, was whether allowing equitable subrogation would defeat the independence principle that distinguishes letters of credit from guarantees and suretyships. Guarantors generally may assert defenses available to the party whose obligation is guaranteed. *Tudor Dev. Group, Inc.*, 968 F.2d at 366. Under the independence principle, however, the issuer of a standby letter of credit may not assert those defenses. Rather, it must pay if the documents presented by the beneficiary satisfy the conditions set out in the letter of credit. *Id.*

In the dissent's view, once the issuer has honored the letter of credit, the purpose of the independence principle—ensuring prompt payment on the letter of credit according to its terms—has been satisfied. *Id.* at 368. The dissent reasoned that denying equitable subrogation after the issuer had paid the letter of credit would not advance the purposes of the one principle that distinguishes letters of credit from guarantees. *Id.* Rather, in the dissent's view, denying subrogation after payment amounts to "[i]nsistence on * * * pointless formalism." *Id.* Although the dissent's view has only gained minority support among the courts, it has been generally supported by the commentators. *See* James J. White & Robert S. Summers, *Uniform Commercial Code* § 26–15 (4th ed. 1995); Peter R. Jarvis, *Standby Letters of Credit, Issuers' Subrogation and Assignment Rights*, 10 UCC LJ 38 (1977); *cf.* Task Force on the Study of U.C.C. Article 5, *An Examination of U.C.C. Article 5 (Letters of Credit)* 21 (Sept. 29, 1989), *reprinted in* 45 Bus.L. 1527 (1990).

Faced with these two positions, we conclude that the minority view is more persuasive. It recognizes that First Interstate was a *de facto* surety for Fibrex's obligations and is thus consistent with the long-standing principle in Oregon law that equity looks to the substance of the transaction rather than its form. *General Electric Co. v. Wahle,* 207 Or. 302, 317, 296 P.2d 635 (1956); *Decker v. Berean Baptist Church,* 51 Or.App. 191, 199, 624 P.2d 1094 (1981).[8] It is also consistent with the general practice on standby letters of credit—that the issuer's obligation to pay on the letter of credit only arises if there is a default. *See* Jarvis, 9 UCC LJ at 368–71 (comparing standby letters of credit and guarantees). More importantly, it is consistent with our legislature's recognition that having paid the beneficiary, the issuer (and the applicant if it has reimbursed the issuer) should be able to step into the beneficiary's shoes and assert its rights. Accordingly, we hold that equitable subrogation is available to both the issuer and the applicant on a standby letter of credit. * * *

Reversed and remanded.

NOTE

The most common case in which the subrogation issue is litigated concerns the applicability of Bankruptcy Code § 509(a), which states: "Except as provided in subsection (b) or (c) of this section, an entity that is *liable with the debtor* on, or that has secured, a claim of a creditor against the debtor, and that pays such claim, is subrogated to the rights of such creditor to the extent of such payment" (emphasis added). In CCF, Inc. v. First National Bank & Trust, 69 F.3d 468 (10th Cir.1995), the court held that the independence principle under which an issuer is not "liable with the debtor" precluded subrogating an issuer to the beneficiary's right to setoff against funds of the applicant that the beneficiary had collected on behalf of the applicant. Accord Hamada v. Far East National Bank, 291 F.3d 645 (9th Cir. 2002). Although 5–117 was not yet law in the jurisdiction in question, the court was aware of it and said: "Although the revised Article Five provides an issuer with the remedy of subrogation, the UCC does not determine the availability of subrogation in a bankruptcy proceeding. Rather, § 509 of the Bankruptcy Code governs an entity's eligibility for subrogation in a bankruptcy proceeding. Thus, the effect of the Rev. § 5–117 on § 509 subrogation is presently undecided, and suitable for resolution by a future court." 69 F.3d at 476 n.7.

---

8. Defendants argue that the court's reasoning in *Newell v. Taylor,* 212 Or. 522, 532–33, 321 P.2d 294 (1958), supports a contrary position, but the court's reasoning in that case cannot be divorced from the statutory rights established by the workers' compensation laws. As the court explained, the Workers' Compensation Commission had a statutory obligation to pay the injured worker, regardless of whether the injury was due to a third party's negligence. *Id.* at 532, 321 P.2d 294. This case is far closer to the court's later. decision in *Jenks Hatchery v. Elliott,* 252 Or. 25, 30–31, 448 P.2d 370 (1968), where the court held, under common-law principles, that an accommodation maker that had paid on a note could sue on it.

Courts remain uncertain about whether § 509 provides the exclusive source of subrogation in bankruptcy or whether equitable subrogation instead continues to be available. The issue is one of bankruptcy law and is unaffected by nonbankruptcy law such as 5–117(a). In concluding that the issuer lacked subrogation rights in bankruptcy, the *Hamada* court analyzed the issuer's rights under both § 509 and state law of equitable subrogation. In re AGF Direct Gas Sales & Servicing, Inc., 47 UCC Rep. Serv.2d 445, 2002 WL 826817 (D.N.H. 2002), offered the same analysis, adding in passing that it is not "apparent" that a ruling to the effect that § 509 preempted state law of equitable subrogation would constitute legal error. Id. at 449. The court's analysis didn't rely on this observation.

NOTE: RESTITUTION AND BREACH OF WARRANTY

Issuers who have honored a draft drawn under a letter of credit but have been unable to obtain reimbursement from the applicant may attempt to get their money back from the beneficiary under doctrines of restitution or breach of warranty. The applicable common law of restitution may allow one who has paid out under mistake or who has honored a forged or fraudulent presentation to recover the payment. Former Article 5 was silent on the subject. Section 5–108(i)(4) provides that an issuer who has honored a presentation is "except as otherwise provided in Sections 5–110 and 5–117, precluded from restitution of money paid or other value given by mistake to the extent the mistake concerns discrepancies in the documents or tender which are apparent on the face of the presentation * * *." Section 5–110 states: "(a) If its presentation is honored, the beneficiary warrants: (1) to the issuer, any other person to whom presentation is made, and the applicant that there is no fraud or forgery of the kind described in § 5–109(a); and (2) to the applicant that the drawing does not violate any agreement between the applicant and beneficiary or any other agreement intended by them to be augmented by the letter of credit."

Under 5–110, after its presentation has been honored, the beneficiary makes two warranties. One warranty, created by 5–110(a)(1), is to the applicant, issuer and persons who received the presentation. The beneficiary warrants that there is no forgery or material fraud. As is made clear below, forgery involves a document presented whereas material fraud need not. Material fraud may involve fraud in the nondocumentary aspects of the underlying transaction. A party protected by 5–110(a)(1)'s warranty might prefer to recover under it even when the party can recover on some other basis, such as in tort. This is because forgery or documentary fraud typically presents fewer problems of proof than other bases of recovery.

A second warranty, created by 5–110(a)(2), runs only to the applicant. The beneficiary warrants that the drawing did not violate either an agreement between the applicant and beneficiary or any other agreement underlying the credit. Section 5–110(a)(2)'s warranty is more complicated than 5–110(a)(2)'s warranty, and leaves some uncertainty. It applies to any agreement that is part of the transaction underlying the letter of credit.

Thus, even if the applicant isn't a party to the underlying agreement, the beneficiary breaches its 5–110(a)(2) warranty to the applicant if its draw "violates" the agreement. For instance, the warranty applies when an applicant has a credit issued at the request of a party to underlying agreement other than beneficiary. Usually, of course, the applicant has no need for 5–110(a)(2)'s warranty when it is a party to the agreement with the beneficiary. It can rely on warranties created by the underlying agreement. See Comment 2 to 5–110.

An uncertainty remains with respect to the "violations" referred to in 5–110(a)(2). Does a draw following any breach of the underlying agreement constitute a "violation" or must the breach rise to the level of seriousness on par with forgery or material fraud? Comment 2 (last sentence) to 5–110 suggests the former: the beneficiary warrants that it has performed all acts under the underlying agreement necessary for it to demand honor. If so, a beneficiary's draw upon presentation of documents indicating "due performance" of the underlying contract breaches the beneficiary's 5–114(a)(2) warranty to the applicant when the beneficiary has breached the underlying contract. Professor White agrees; 3 White & Summers, Prac. Ed. at 164. The position has a lot going for it. After the issuer has honored a presentation and paid, none of the concerns about disturbing the credit's payment function apply. Finality of payment by the issuer isn't jeopardized by the beneficiary's warranty against "violations," because the warranty runs only to the applicant against the beneficiary. In any case, finality of payment isn't a first principle of letter of credit law. Its principle, if any, is "pay first, litigate later." Both of 5–110's warranties arise only if honor has occurred. Thus, there seems to be no good reason to restrict 5–110(a)(2)'s warranty to breaches ("violations") of the underlying agreement on the order of forgery or material fraud. For an argument reaching the opposite conclusion, see Richard F. Dole, Jr., Warranties by Beneficiaries of Letters of Credit Under Revised Article 5 of the UCC: The Truth and Nothing But the Truth, 39 Houston L. Rev. 375, 394–97 (2002).

The UCP contains no warranties. Professor White, the Reporter for Revised Article 5, notes that of the "hotly debated issues" in Article 5's drafting, 5–110(a)'s warranty provision was the only one that "went against" the UCP. See James J. White, The Influence of International Practice on the Revision of Article 5 of the UCC, 16 Nw. J. Int'l L. & Bus. 189, 207 (1995). This does not mean that the UCP conflicts with 5–110(a)'s warranties. It merely means that the ICC's representatives preferred that warranty provisions not apply to a credit also subject to the UCP. They were disappointed. Given 5–110(a), its warranties apply to credits subject to the UCP, unless Article 5 is otherwise inapplicable or the credit excludes 5–110(a)'s application.

PROBLEMS

In the following Problems assume the following facts: Applicant, a movie producer with limited assets, engaged Beneficiary to appear in a new film, entitled "Legal Nights." In order to induce Beneficiary to agree to perform, Applicant caused Bank to issue a standby letter of credit to her payable on presentation to Bank of the letter of credit, a draft drawn on Bank payable 15 days after the date of presentation, and an affidavit that Beneficiary had satisfactorily completed the film and had not been paid by Applicant. Upon presentation by Beneficiary, Bank honored the draft but was unable to obtain reimbursement from Applicant. Bank proceeded against Beneficiary invoking the remedies of restitution and breach of warranty. What result in the following two cases under Article 5? The issues in these Problems are discussed in 3 White & Summers, Prac. ed. § 26–8 (warranties), § 26–9(e) (restitution).

1. The documents presented by Beneficiary included a draft drawn on Bank "at sight," meaning at the time of presentation. Bank did not notice that the draft did not comply with the documents specified by the letter of credit and paid the draft according to its terms. Had the draft complied with the terms of the credit, Bank might not have paid it at all because during the 15–day period Applicant filed in bankruptcy and Bank's right of reimbursement became virtually worthless.

2. The documents presented by Beneficiary complied with the requirements of the credit, including the affidavit of completion. After honoring the draft, Bank learned that Beneficiary had not completed the film and had breached her contract with Applicant.

4. DAMAGES FOR WRONGFUL DISHONOR

As we have seen, it is fundamental that the letter of credit undertaking between an issuer and a beneficiary is independent of the underlying contract between the beneficiary and the applicant. 5–103(d). Does it follow that if the issuer wrongfully dishonors a draft presented under a letter of credit, the beneficiary can recover the full amount of the draw from the issuer, leaving the applicant to litigate with the beneficiary in a separate action over any amount the beneficiary has received in excess of its rights on the underlying contract? Yes. Under 5–111(a), the beneficiary or any other presenter can recover from the issuer the face amount of the draw under the credit if the issuer wrongfully dishonors the draw. The presenter also can recover incidental damages, but not consequential damages. Section 5–111(a) doesn't require the presenter to mitigate its damages in these circumstances. Because the issuer will have paid the presenter according to the credit's terms, as required by 5–111(a) (the dishonor was wrongful), the issuer's reimbursement agreement requires the applicant to reimburse it. The applicant in turn is left to recover from the beneficiary or other presenter in a separate action.

Section 5–111(b) governs the remedies of an applicant against the issuer. Under 5–111(b), the applicant can recover damages from the issuer who wrongfully dishonors a draft or other presentation under the credit. As under 5–111(a), incidental damages are recoverable but not consequential damages. Unlike 5–111(a)'s recovery, the applicant is required to mitigate its damages under 5–111(b). Article 5 does not provide a remedy in cases of improper honor by the issuer. Instead, recoverable damages are left to the courts. See Comment 2 to 5–111.

Section 5–111(e) requires courts to award reasonable attorney's fees and other litigation expenses to the prevailing party for any action in which a remedy is obtained under Article 5. The subsection overrules the "American rule" under which each party bears its own litigation costs. Section 5–111(e)'s mandatory award is not limited to remedies available under 5–111. The operative language of 5–111(e) is "under Article 5." Thus, a party prevailing on a breach of warranty claim against a beneficiary under 5–110, for instance, must be awarded reasonable attorney's fees and other litigation expenses. Would an injunction issued to prevent a materially fraudulent draw, discussed below, be a "remedy . . . obtained under Article 5"? Unsurprisingly, both 5–111(e) and the exclusion of consequential damages have proven controversial. Connecticut and Louisiana have adopted nonuniform amendments to 5–111 allowing recovery of consequential damages, and several states have enacted nonuniform versions of 5–111(e). New Jersey and Texas, for instance, simply allow the award of attorney's fees and litigation expenses. New York's enactment of Article 5, significantly, omits 5–111(e) entirely. See 2B U.L.A. § 5–111 (2003). How would you apply 5–111 to the following Problems?

PROBLEMS

1. Seller in New York agreed to sell goods to Buyer in Los Angeles by rail shipment with payment to be made pursuant to a commercial letter of credit. Buyer obtained issuance of a letter of credit by Issuer, Buyer's bank. The credit was payable to Seller on presentation to Issuer of a bill of lading, invoice, inspection and insurance certificates, sight draft drawn on Issuer, and the letter of credit. Issuer sent the letter of credit to Seller in New York (this is usually done through an "adviser" bank; 5–102(a)(1)). Seller shipped the goods and obtained an order bill of lading from the carrier. Seller then assembled the required documents and sent them through banking channels to Issuer for payment. Buyer decided that it had made a bad bargain and urged Issuer to dishonor the credit. Buyer threatened that if Issuer honored the letter of credit, Buyer would take its business elsewhere. Issuer reluctantly dishonored. When the goods arrived in Los Angeles, Seller ordered the carrier to store them in a warehouse. Several months later, Seller sold the goods for only a fraction of their invoice price. Seller sued Issuer for wrongful dishonor and sought the face amount of the draft drawn pursuant to the letter of credit in damages. Issuer contended that Seller should have mitigated damages, and that the goods should have been sold for a much higher price; moreover, at the very least, Seller must offset the amount actually recovered from the resale against its claim on the letter of credit.

(a) What result under 5–111(a)? See Comment 1 to 5–111. (b) What incentive does an Issuer have not to dishonor wrongfully? Comment 6 to 5–111. The explanation of the phrase "expenses of litigation" in that comment should be enough to chill the blood of any banker. (c) When might Seller have an incentive to seek recovery under law other than Article 5? See 5–111(e).

2.   Applicant planned to develop a recreational community. County approval of Applicant's subdivision was conditional on Applicant's agreement to provide a standby letter of credit payable to the County as beneficiary to ensure that Applicant would complete roads and related improvements in accordance with subdivision design specifications. The required letter of credit was obtained from Issuer. Applicant never commenced construction of the roads or other improvements. Issuer wrongfully dishonored the letter of credit upon presentation. The County sued Issuer for the face amount of the credit plus interest from the date of the demand for payment. Issuer defended on the ground that the County would receive a windfall since it had not expended or committed itself to expend any funds to complete the improvements. The facts are based on Colorado National Bank v. Board of County Commissioners, 634 P.2d 32 (Colo.1981). What result under 5–111(a)? Dolan, Letters of Credit & 9.02[5][b][ii] and 3 White & Summers, Prac. ed. § 26–14(b), at 207 & 207 n.15., discuss the existing law.

3.   Sport manufactured running shoes for various retail chains. It made the shoes to the specifications of retailers who sold the shoes under their own brand names. Sport was thinly capitalized and the business was highly competitive. Sport had contracts for large deliveries to Retailer A on March 1, Retailer B on June 1, and Retailer C on September 1. Sport required A to obtain a standby letter of credit for the invoice price of the goods on which Sport could draw if A failed to pay for the goods within 15 days of delivery. When the shoes arrived, A contended that they were defective and ordered Issuer not to honor the letter of credit. Sport made timely presentation to Issuer of the required documents and Issuer wrongfully dishonored. Sport immediately implored Issuer to pay, explaining that without the proceeds of this large sale it would be unable to fulfill its obligations to B and C and would lose the profits that it anticipated making on these contracts. When Issuer continued to refuse payment, Sport sued Issuer for wrongful dishonor and claimed damages measured by the face amount of the credit plus the amount of lost profits on its contracts with B and C. What result under 5–111(a)? Do you believe that this is a desirable result? See Comment 4 to 5–111.

E.   FORGERY AND FRAUD

The influential pre-Code case, Sztejn v. J. Henry Schroder Banking Corp., 177 Misc. 719, 31 N.Y.S.2d 631 (N.Y.Sup.Ct.1941), was a concession to the reality that the independence principle, however important, must have limits. The facts of *Sztejn* are summarized in the following case. In brief, the contract of sale between the applicant and beneficiary was for the beneficiary to ship bristles to the applicant, and the bill of lading presented to the issuing bank described the goods as bristles, but the applicant had discovered that the beneficiary had actually shipped what the court described as rubbish. The applicant sought to enjoin the issuer from honoring the draft on the ground of fraud. On the pleadings, assuming the applicant was correct about the fraud, the court held for the applicant. Although the documents were in compliance on their face, they were not genuine and therefore the issuer did not have to honor.

This case seemed to undermine the independence principle in that it allowed the court to look outside the documents presented to determine whether the issuer must honor. Would this mean that honor could be enjoined if the applicant could make a showing that the goods shipped by the beneficiary were defective in a degree amounting to a breach of warranty of quality? Or if the applicant could show that it had been induced to enter into the underlying sale transaction by misrepresentations by the beneficiary about the goods? Former 5–114, set out in the case below, was an attempt to codify and delimit *Sztejn*. It allowed the applicant to obtain an injunction against honor even though the documents appear on their face to be in compliance so long as a required document "is forged or fraudulent or there is fraud in the transaction." The breadth of the "fraud in the transaction" test seemed to place the independence principle in peril. The following case is the leading case on how this language has been construed by the courts. After *Intraworld*, we will examine the Revised Article 5 treatment of the subject in 5–109. For an extensive discussion of fraud in the transaction, see Dolan, Letters of Credit & 7.04.

Intraworld Industries, Inc. v. Girard Trust Bank

Supreme Court of Pennsylvania, 1975.
461 Pa. 343, 336 A.2d 316.

■ ROBERTS, JUSTICE.

This appeal requires us to review the trial court's denial of a preliminary injunction to restrain honor of a draft under an international letter of credit. A precise statement of the facts, which are complex, is necessary for a proper understanding.

On February 11, 1972, a lease was executed by Intraworld Industries, Inc., a corporation headquartered in Wilkes–Barre, Pennsylvania, and Paulette Cymbalista, a citizen of Switzerland and resident of Italy. Cymbalista agreed to lease to Intraworld the Hotel Carlton, a luxury hotel located in St. Moritz, Switzerland, for a term of 15 years at an annual rental of 800,000 Swiss francs, payable in semi-annual installments.[2] The lease provided that Intraworld was required to prepay the rent for the initial 18–month period. Intraworld was also obligated to procure, within the first 100

---

2. The lease contained a formula for the adjustment of the annual rental with respect to changes in the value of the Swiss franc. At the time of the execution of the lease, the annual rental was approximately equivalent to $200,000.

days of the term, a performance bond in the amount of $500,000 "to insure to lessor the payment of the rent."[3]

Intraworld entered into possession of the hotel on May 1, 1972. Shortly thereafter, Intraworld assigned its interest in the lease to its subsidiary, Vacanze In Paradiso Hotels, S.A., a Swiss corporation.[4]

At a later time, Intraworld and Cymbalista executed an addendum to the lease (to which the parties have referred by its German title "Nachtrag"). The Nachtrag cancelled Intraworld's obligation to procure a performance bond and substituted a duty to provide letters of credit issued by "the Girard Trust Company of Philadelphia" in order to guarantee rental payments one year in advance. Two letters of credit were specifically required, each in the amount of $100,000, maturing in November, 1973, and May, 1974, to secure the rent due at those times. After each rental payment, Intraworld was to provide a new letter of credit "in order that the lessor remains secured one years [sic] rent in advance." The Nachtrag also provided:

> "In the event the lessee should not fulfill its obligation to pay, so that the letter of credit must be used, . . . then the lessor can terminate the lease immediately without further notice. In this case, the lessor retains the rent paid or guaranteed for the following year as a stipulated penalty for non-performance of the contract from the lessee, in doing so the lessor retains the right to make a claim for additional damages not covered by the stipulated penalty."

On September 1, 1972, Intraworld and the Girard Trust Bank, Philadelphia, entered into an agreement to provide the letters of credit required by the Nachtrag. Girard agreed to

> "issue a letter of credit . . . in the amount of $100,000 under which the Lessor may draw a sight draft on [Girard] for payment of the sum due under said lease (a) on November 10, 1973 and (b) May 10, 1974. Under the terms of such letter of credit, payments will be made if the Lessor presents a draft as provided in such letter of credit. Each such letter of credit will expire . . . on the twentieth day after the payment under said lease is due."[6]

In accordance with the agreement, Girard issued two irrevocable letters of credit on September 5, 1972. Each authorized Cymbalista to draw a draft on Girard in the amount of $100,000.00 if Intraworld failed to pay the rent when due.[7]

---

3. The record does not establish whether Intraworld performed its obligation to procure a performance bond.

The lease also provided: "This agreement shall be governed by the Swiss law. The competent forum shall be in Saint Moritz Court."

4. For convenience we will refer to the lessee as Intraworld.

6. The agreement also provided: "This agreement shall be construed in accordance with the law of the State of Pennsylvania and the Acts of Congress of the United States affecting transactions under the provisions hereof."

7. "IRREVOCABLE   LETTER   OF CREDIT

NO. 35798

In the summer of 1973, the relationship between Cymbalista and Intraworld began to go awry. Norbert Cymbalista, Paulette's husband, visited the hotel in August and, after discussions with the manager, became very concerned over the hotel's financial condition. He discovered that there were unpaid bills in excess of $100,000, that all telephone and Telex communications had been cut off for nonpayment of bills, and that the filing of mechanics liens against the hotel was imminent. After a trans-Atlantic telephone call, the Cymbalistas travelled to the United States within several days of Norbert's discoveries to attempt to resolve the hotel's difficulties with Intraworld. However, as Norbert testified,

> "I tried to reach [the president of Intraworld] innumerable times by telephone and each time his secretary answered that he would call me back and he never did. I stayed a whole month in the United States trying continually to reach him and it was never possible."

On August 20, 1973, apparently while the Cymbalistas were in the United States, their Swiss counsel sent a letter to Intraworld reciting the unpaid bills, erosion of the Carlton's reputation, and internal corporate difficulties (apparently of Intraworld's Swiss subsidiary). It concluded:

> "Based upon [Swiss law] and in reference to the provisions of the Lease Contract, we herewith extend to you a final time limit up to September 15, 1973 in order to:
>
> (a) to pay all due debts,

Date: September 5, 1972

"Amount: $100,000.00

"Beneficiary: Paulette Cymbalista
                  c/o Carlton Hotel
                  St. Moritz, Switzer-
                  land

"For account of: Intraworld Indus-
                  tries, Inc.
                  116 South Main
                  Street
                  Wilkes Barre, PA
                  18701

"Madam:

"You are hereby authorized to draw on us at sight the sum of One Hundred Thousand and 00/100 Dollars United States Currency ($100,000.00) due on November 10, 1973 under a lease, a copy of which is attached to both Beneficiary's copy and Bank's copy of this letter of credit as Exhibit 1, available by your draft for said amount, accompanied by:

"1. Simple receipt for amount drawn.

"2. A signed statement of the drawer of the draft to the effect that the drawer is the lessor under said lease and that the lessee thereunder has not paid the installment of rent due under said lease on November 10, 1973 within 10 days after said installment was due and payable.

"This credit expires on November 30, 1973.

"Drafts under this credit must contain the clause 'drawn under Credit No. 35798 of Girard Trust Bank, dated September 5, 1972.'

"Girard Trust Bank hereby agrees with the drawers, endorsers and bona fide owners of the bills drawn strictly in compliance with the terms of this credit that the same will be duly honored upon presentation.

"Except so far as otherwise expressly stated, this credit is subject to the uniform customs and practices for documentary credits (1962 revision), International Chamber of Commerce Brochure No. 222."

Credit No. 35799 was identical to 35798, except that it applied to the rent due on May 10, 1974, and expired on May 30, 1974.

(b) to supply the necessary means to safeguard proper management of the business,

(c) to complete the Board of Directors according to the law.

Within this time limit you must prove to the Hotel Owners that the aforementioned measures have been effectuated. Should you [fail to?] comply with this demand within the time-limit, the Lease Contract will be regarded as void."

Intraworld's Swiss counsel replied to the August 20 letter (but this reply is not in the record). Finding this reply unsatisfactory, Cymbalista's Swiss counsel answered on September 18, 1973:

"As [Intraworld] did not comply with our demand within this time-limit, we regard the leasing contract as terminated effective from 15 September 1973.... From now on, the proprietor will have direct and sole control over the hotel real estate respective to the hotel management."

Further correspondence was exchanged by Swiss counsel, including, apparently, a demand on November 3 for the rent due in November. On November 7, 1973, Intraworld's Swiss counsel wrote to Cymbalista's counsel:

"You state on behalf of the lessor that [Intraworld] has the obligation to pay ... rent by November 1. My client [Intraworld], who is presently in close contact with their American Bank [Girard], however, have [sic] informed me that the payment of the rent can be made up to November 10 ... My client informed me further that accordingly these payments shall be legally undertaken by the 'Girard Trust Bank' ... [M]y client cannot agree with your position according to which the lease contract can be considered as terminated either because of [Swiss law] or because of the terms of the lease agreement...."

That letter was followed on November 9, 1973, by another from Intraworld's counsel to Cymbalista's counsel in which he stated:

"If the transfer of the rent from the United States should not be made in timely fashion, your client [Cymbalista] is at liberty to obtain payment by way of the guarantee contracts [i.e., letters of credit]. In any event, there exist the two guarantee contracts, valid until November 30, 1973 and May 30, 1974, respectively, in order to preserve the rights of your client."

The rent due on November 10, 1973, was not paid by Intraworld. Accordingly, on November 21, 1973, Cymbalista's American counsel presented to Girard a draft drawn on Girard for $100,000 under Credit No. 35798. The draft was accompanied, all parties agree, by documentation that conformed to the terms of the credit. In his letter to Girard, Cymbalista's counsel stated:

"Your attention is directed to correspondence dated November 7 and November 9, 1973, copies of which are attached, in which Swiss counsel representing the Lessee invites the Lessor to draw upon the

Letters of Credit; our client, as Lessor, takes the position that the lease ... has terminated for various reasons, including the failure timely to pay the amount due pursuant to the 'Nachtrag'...."

Girard informed Intraworld on November 21 that it intended to honor the draft. Intraworld immediately filed an action in equity in the Court of Common Pleas of Philadelphia seeking injunctive relief prohibiting Girard from honoring the draft. Cymbalista filed a petition to intervene, which was granted by the trial court.

The November action was terminated on December 6, 1973, by agreement of all parties. Pursuant to the agreement, Girard placed $100,000 in escrow with a Swiss bank, with entitlement to that fund to be determined by the courts of Switzerland.

The situation remained unchanged for about six months. The rent due on May 10, 1974, was not paid. On May 21, 1974, Cymbalista's American counsel presented to Girard a draft for $100,000 under Credit No. 35799, accompanied by conforming documentation. Girard immediately advised Intraworld that it intended to honor the draft.

On May 24, Intraworld filed this equity action in the Court of Common Pleas of Philadelphia. It sought preliminary and permanent injunctions restraining Girard from honoring Cymbalista's draft under the letter of credit. The court issued a preliminary restraining order and set a date for a hearing. Cymbalista again petitioned for leave to intervene, which the court granted on May 29.

After the filing of additional pleadings, including preliminary objections and an amended complaint, a hearing was held and testimony taken on May 30 and 31, 1974. On July 11, the trial court issued a memorandum and decree in which it denied a preliminary injunction. Intraworld has appealed to this Court. We affirm.

* * *

Girard's obligations to Cymbalista are "subject to" the Uniform Customs and Practice. However, the UCP "is by definition a recording of practice rather than a statement of legal rules," and therefore does not purport to offer rules which govern the issuance of an injunction against honor of a draft. Harfield, Practice Commentary, N.Y.U.C.C., § 5–114 (McKinney's Consol.Laws, c. 38, 1964).

All parties have briefed and argued the case on the assumption that the Pennsylvania Uniform Commercial Code controls, and with this assumption we agree. * * *

* * *

The great utility of letters of credit flows from the independence of the issuer-bank's engagement from the underlying contract between beneficiary and customer. Long-standing case law has established that, unless otherwise agreed, the issuer deals only in documents. If the documents presented conform to the requirements of the credit, the issuer may and must honor demands for payment, regardless of whether the goods conform to the underlying contract between beneficiary and customer. Absent its agreement to the contrary, the issuer is, under the general rule, not required or even permitted to go behind the documents to determine if the beneficiary has performed in conformity with the underlying contract. * * *

This principle of the issuer's right and obligation to honor upon presentation of conforming documents has been codified in § 5–114:

"(1) An issuer must honor a draft or demand for payment which complies with the terms of the relevant credit regardless of whether the goods or documents conform to the underlying contract for sale or other contract between the customer and the beneficiary....

"(2) Unless otherwise agreed when documents appear on their face to comply with the terms of a credit but a required document ... is forged or fraudulent or there is fraud in the transaction

. . .

"(b) in all other cases as against its customer, an issuer acting in good faith may honor the draft or demand for payment despite notification from the customer of fraud, forgery or other defect not apparent on the face of the documents but a court of appropriate jurisdiction may enjoin such honor."

Intraworld seeks to enjoin honor under § 5–114(2)(b) on the basis that there is "fraud ... not apparent on the face of the documents." It points to what it believes are two respects in which Cymbalista's demand for payment and supporting documentation are false and fraudulent, although conceding that the documents on their face conform to the credit. First, it contends that Cymbalista's statement (as required by the credit) that "lessee ... has not paid the installment of rent due under said lease on May 10, 1974," is false and fraudulent because, after Cymbalista purported to terminate the lease in September, 1973, Intraworld was not obligated to pay rent and because the statement failed to disclose the termination of the lease. Second, it argues that the demand is fraudulent because Cymbalista is not seeking rent at all (as, Intraworld contends, she represents in the documents) but rather the "stipulated penalty" pursuant to the Nachtrag.

In light of the basic rule of the independence of the issuer's engagement and the importance of this rule to the effectuation of the purposes of the letter of credit, we think that the circumstances which will justify an injunction against honor must be narrowly limited to situations of fraud in which the wrongdoing of the beneficiary has so vitiated the entire transaction that the legitimate purposes of the independence of the issuer's obligation would no longer be served. A court of equity has the limited duty of

"guaranteeing that [the beneficiary] not be allowed to take unconscientious advantage of the situation and run off with plaintiff's money on a pro forma declaration which has absolutely no basis in fact."

Dynamics Corp. of America v. Citizens and Southern National Bank, 356 F.Supp. 991, 999 (N.D.Ga.1973) (emphasis supplied).

The leading case on the question of what conduct will justify an injunction against honor is Sztejn v. J. Henry Schroder Banking Corp., 177 Misc. 719, 31 N.Y.S.2d 631 (Sup.Ct.1941). In that case as here, the customer sought an injunction against the issuer of a letter of credit restraining honor of a draft drawn by the beneficiary. The customer had contracted to purchase a quantity of bristles from the beneficiary and arranged to have the issuer issue a letter of credit in favor of the beneficiary. The credit required that the draft be accompanied by an invoice and bill of lading.

The beneficiary placed fifty cases of merchandise on a steamship and obtained a bill of lading describing the material as bristles. The beneficiary then drew a draft and presented it, along with the required documents, through a collecting bank. The customer's complaint alleged that the material shipped was not bristles as described in the documents, but rather "cowhair, other worthless material and rubbish [shipped] with intent to simulate genuine merchandise and defraud the plaintiff...."

The collecting bank moved to dismiss the complaint for failure to state a cause of action. The court, assuming the pleaded facts to be true, denied the motion. The court recognized that the issuer's obligation was independent from the underlying contract between customer and beneficiary. That independence is predicated, however, on the genuineness of the documents. The court noted:

> "This is not a controversy between the buyer and seller concerning a mere breach of warranty regarding the quality of the merchandise; on the present motion, it must be assumed that the seller has intentionally failed to ship any goods ordered by the buyer."

177 Misc. at 721, 31 N.Y.S.2d at 634. When the beneficiary has intentionally shipped no goods at all, the court held, the documentation was not genuine and therefore the predicate of the independence of the issuer's engagement was removed.

We conclude that, if the documents presented by Cymbalista are genuine in the sense of having some basis in fact, an injunction must be refused. An injunction is proper only if Cymbalista, comparable to the beneficiary in *Sztejn,* has no bona fide claim to payment under the lease. Dynamics Corp. of America v. Citizens and Southern National Bank, 356 F.Supp. 991, 999 (N.D.Ga.1973). Of course, neither the trial court nor this Court may attempt to determine Cymbalista's actual entitlement to payment under the lease. Such is not the proper standard for the grant or denial of an injunction against honor. Moreover, questions of rights and obligations under the lease are required by the lease to be determined under Swiss law in the courts of Switzerland. See Dynamics Corp. of America v. Citizens and Southern National Bank, supra.

On this record, we are unable to conclude that Intraworld established that Cymbalista has no bona fide claim to payment or that the documents presented to Girard have absolutely no basis in fact. Intraworld's argument rests on the basic premise that the lease was terminated in September, 1973. From this premise Intraworld asserts the falsity of Cymbalista's representations that she is the lessor and that the rent was due and unpaid. However, Intraworld did not attempt to prove to the trial court that, under Swiss law, Cymbalista's attempted termination was effective. In fact, Intraworld's Swiss counsel informed Cymbalista's counsel on November 7, 1973, that Intraworld "cannot agree with your position according to which the lease contract can be considered as terminated...." Counsel added that Cymbalista was "at liberty to obtain payment by way of" the letters of credit. Thus, Intraworld failed to prove that, under Swiss law, Cymbalista had no bona fide claim to rent under the lease despite Intraworld's repudiation of termination.

Intraworld's argument that Cymbalista fraudulently concealed the purported termination from Girard is unpersuasive. When presenting the draft and documents to Girard in November, 1973, Cymbalista's American counsel candidly admitted that "our client, as Lessor, takes the position that the lease has terminated ... for various reasons...." In addition, Girard was a party to the first equity action and its counsel joined the agreement which terminated that action. Cymbalista could reasonably have assumed in May, 1974, that Girard was fully aware of the positions of both Intraworld and Cymbalista.

Intraworld's further contention that Cymbalista's demand was fraudulent in that she was not seeking "rent" at all but the "stipulated penalty" pursuant to the Nachtrag is more substantial but, under scrutiny, also fails. It argues that payment under the credit was permitted only for "rent," and that Cymbalista (as she concedes) was in fact seeking the "stipulated penalty," which is not "rent." Intraworld concludes that Cymbalista was fraudulently attempting to draw under the credit for satisfaction of an obligation not secured by the credit. There are two flaws in this argument.

First, we are not persuaded that the credit was issued for payment of "rent," narrowly defined, only. The letter of credit (see note 7 supra) authorized Cymbalista to draw "the sum ... due ... under [the] lease," without specifying that the "sum due" contemplated was only "rent." The letter required that a draft must be accompanied by Cymbalista's statement that "the lessee ... has not paid the installment of rent due under said lease." This is not equivalent to a limitation on availability of the credit only for nonpayment of rent; in fact, such nonpayment of rent is precisely the condition which triggers Cymbalista's entitlement to the "stipulated penalty." In short, Intraworld has failed to persuade us that the letter of credit was not available to Cymbalista for satisfaction of the "stipulated penalty."

Second and more important, the Nachtrag does not, in our view, create the sharp distinction between "rent" and "stipulated penalty" that Intraworld hypothesizes. It provides that "[i]n the event the lessee should not fulfill its obligation to pay, so that the letter of credit must be used," then the lessor was entitled to terminate the lease and "retain the *rent* paid or *guaranteed* [by the letters of credit] for the following year as a stipulated penalty for non-performance of the contract...."(Emphasis supplied.) Because Intraworld did fail to pay the rent due on November 10, 1973, and May 10, 1974, Cymbalista could reasonably and in good faith have concluded that she had the right to draw on the credit for the "rent ... guaranteed for the following year."

Whether Intraworld was in fact obligated to pay the rent nonpayment of which triggered Cymbalista's right to retain the "rent guaranteed" by the credit or whether Cymbalista is not entitled to the "stipulated penalty" for some other reason are questions to be decided under Swiss law in the courts of Switzerland. We hold only that Intraworld failed to establish that Cymbalista lacked a bona fide claim to the "rent ... guaranteed ... as a stipulated penalty" or that her demand under the credit lacked some basis in fact. Therefore, her documented demand was not shown to be fraudulent because she was seeking satisfaction of the "stipulated penalty."

In summary, we are unable to conclude on this record that Intraworld succeeded in proving that Cymbalista had no bona fide claim for payment under the lease and that her documented demand had absolutely no basis in fact. Accordingly, it is clear that there is an apparently reasonable ground for refusing an injunction.

In addition, Intraworld alleged in its complaint and contends in this Court that Girard's decision to honor Cymbalista's draft was not formed in good faith. Intraworld asserts that Girard's bad faith constituted an additional ground justifying an injunction. It is clear that an issuer of a letter of credit must act in good faith, see §§ 5–114(2)(b), 5–109(1). However, we are not persuaded that issuer bad faith is a circumstance justifying an injunction against honor; in most if not all instances of issuer bad faith, it would seem that a customer would have an adequate remedy at law in a claim against the issuer or a defense against the issuer's claim for reimbursement. In any event, in this case Intraworld has failed to prove the existence of bad faith on the part of Girard. It has proved no more than that Girard failed to resolve the dispute over the rights and obligations of the parties to the lease in Intraworld's favor. This Girard was not obligated to do. Its obligations included a careful scrutiny of the documents, but once it determined that the documents conformed to the requirements of the credit, it bore no responsibility for the performance of the lease obligations or the genuineness of the documents. § 5–109(1)(a) & (2). It would, we think, place an issuer in an intolerable position if the law compelled it to serve at its peril as an arbitrator of contract disputes between customer and beneficiary.

* * *

NOTES

1. Applicants seeking to enjoin honor by issuers have more than the tough *Intraworld* standards to contend with. They must also comply with the law of the jurisdiction on granting injunctions. 5–109(b)(3). This normally requires a showing of irreparable harm. An equitable suit for an injunction is not appropriate if there is an adequate remedy at law. Since the remedy would usually be an action by the applicant against the beneficiary for a money judgment, an injunction would be inappropriate if the beneficiary were solvent and subject to service of process. Moreover, the applicant must show that it is more likely than not to succeed on the merits of the fraud or forgery issue. 5–109(b)(4).

2. Professor White concedes that the Drafting Committee was unable to agree on a definition of fraud. 3 White & Summers, Prac. ed. § 26–10, at 185. Section 5–109(a) adopts the standard of "material fraud" and its Comment 1 embraces the *Intraworld* test: "Material fraud by the beneficiary occurs only when the beneficiary has no colorable right to expect honor and where there is no basis in fact to support such a right to honor." Does the addition of the adjective "material" make the inquiry as to fraud any more manageable? Without a working notion of fraud, 5–109(a)'s requirement that the fraud be material is unhelpful. The U.N. Convention on Independent Guarantees tries, without using the term, to make the fraud inquiry more manageable. It does not obligate an issuer to pay when it is "manifest and clear" that payment is not due on the basis asserted in the demand or documents presented. See U.N. Convention art. 19(1).

The *Sztejn* court distinguished between what it called "active fraud" and a "mere" breach of warranty without precisely characterizing the distinction. See *Sztejn*, 31 N.Y.S.2d at 634–635. To see the difficulty, consider a sales contract calling for Seller to deliver new widgets and a letter of credit requiring documents describing the goods delivered as "new widgets." Is there fraud in Seller's performance of the sales contract in the following four circumstances? (1) Seller intentionally delivers an automobile, not new widgets. (2) Seller intentionally delivers new widgets with very minor scratches. (3) The same as (2) except the market price for widgets has increased so that scratched widgets sell for more than new widgets were previously sold. (4) Seller intentionally delivers seriously malfunctioning new widgets. Notice that Seller has breached an express warranty in all four circumstances. Circumstance (4) arguably is an easy case: deliberately delivering seriously defective goods is egregious behavior characteristic of fraud. The extent of breach differs in the other three circumstances, and a standard is needed to find fraud nonarbitrarily in one or more of them. Article 5 apparently decided not to provide one.

Section 5–109(a) also abandons the "fraud in the transaction" formulation which had led scholars and courts to differ on whether the transaction meant was only the credit transaction or whether it extended to the underlying transaction as well. A critique of the differing positions on this issue appears in 3 White & Summers, Prac. ed. § 26–10, at 179–80. With the addition of "or honor of the presentation would facilitate a material fraud by the beneficiary on the issuer or applicant," 5–109(a) expressly applies to fraud in the underlying transaction. Prevailing authority finds that Article 5's fraud exception continues to apply to credits governed by the UCP. See Mid–America Tire, Inc. v. PTZ Trading Ltd., 768 N.E.2d 619 (Ohio 2002).

3. Section 5–109(a)'s fraud provision is not limited to forgery or fraud by the beneficiary. By its terms, 5–109(a) applies when "a required document is forged or materially fraudulent." Thus, if 5–109(b)'s conditions for injunctive relief are satisfied, an applicant can enjoin an issuer from honoring a draw by the beneficiary even if the beneficiary has not perpetrated the forgery or fraud.

In some cases applicants have attempted to forestall payment under a letter of credit by seeking to enjoin the beneficiary from making presentation to the issuer. An occasional opinion has applied a lesser standard for granting an injunction in such a case than in the usual case of an injunction against the issuer. Dolan, Letters of Credit & 7.04[4][f]. Section 5–109(b) makes clear that the same standards must apply to limit injunctions in both cases by the addition of the language: "or grant similar relief against the issuer or other persons." Comment 5 to 5–109.

4. Article 5 distinguishes between two classes of presenters: presenters whose conforming documentary presentations the issuer must honor even if there is fraud in the transaction and presenters whose conforming presentations the issuer in good faith is permitted to honor or dishonor when there is fraud. See 5–109(a)(1), (b). The former class of presenters are protected against dishonor: fraud does not allow the issuer to dishonor their conforming presentations. Under 5–109(b)(4), the issuer also cannot be enjoined from honoring the draw. Protected presenters are all transferees of documents under the letter of credit. See 5–109(a)(1)(i)–(iv). (Recognizing developments in letter of credit practice, 5–109(a)(1)(iv) protects an assignee under a deferred obligation credit, a relatively recent type of credit first issued in Southeast Asia.) For instance, a negotiating bank, holder of a draft, or good faith purchaser of documents can be protected purchasers. To be protected, the presenter must take the documents or draft in good faith and without notice of the fraud. See 5–109(a)(1). All other presenters are not protected, and the issuer therefore in good faith can dishonor conforming presentations by them. Because a beneficiary under the credit does not purchase the draft or documents, it is a not transferee and therefore not a protected presenter.

Section 5–109(a)(2) deals with the rights of the issuer against unprotected presenters. It allows the issuer to honor ("may honor") presentations by them, even when the presentation involves forgery or material fraud, as long as the issuer does so in good faith. Is an issuer acting in good faith if it honors after the applicant has given it notice of the fraud or forgery? A common tactic used by applicants is to send a barrage of evidence to the issuer in advance of honor documenting the alleged fraud. The purpose is to present a risk to the issuer that a judge or jury ex post will find the issuer to have honored the draw in bad faith. Prudent practice sometimes leads issuers to resort to interpleader in these and other circumstances. See Dolan, Letters of Credit 7.04[4][g]. White & Summers, Prac. ed. § 26–10 at, 183 disapproves of the practice.

Notice how 5–109 allocates the risk of the beneficiary's fraud. In the case of a protected presenter, the applicant bears this risk. This is because the issuer honoring the draw is entitled to be reimbursed by the applicant either by contract or by statute, or both. 5–108(i)(1). The applicant therefore must recover from the beneficiary. Because the issuer can dishonor an unprotected presenter's conforming presentation, the presenter bears the risk of the beneficiary's fraud when dishonor occurs. It must recover from the beneficiary (or its transferor, who ultimately must recover from the beneficiary). Thus, the unprotected presenter bears the risk of the beneficiary's fraud. Article 5's implicit judgment is that protected presenters are in an inferior position to the applicant or issuer to detect the beneficiary's fraud. Allocating fraud risk to either the applicant or unprotected presenters but never to protected presenters is thought to be the cost-minimizing solution. Is the judgment sound? In support, it is usually observed that the applicant has dealt with the beneficiary whereas a presenter may have purchased a draft or documents from a remote transferor and never have dealt directly with the applicant. See United Bank Ltd. v. Cambridge Sporting Goods, 360 N.E.2d 943, 949 n. 6 (N.Y.1976). The applicant's costs in taking appropriate precautions therefore are thought generally to be lower than those facing the ultimate transferee's precaution costs. The observation has no force when the presenter purchases directly from the beneficiary. Consider also that often issuers or confirmers are local banks who know the beneficiary or can easily acquire information about it. Article 5's allocation of fraud risk is justifiable only if most documentary drafts are discounted in markets to strangers to the underlying contract. Neither the Comments to 5–109 nor its drafting history discuss this assumed empirical generalization.

5. "Good faith" is defined in 5–102(a)(7) as "honesty in fact." This is a subjective standard. Section 1–201(20) contains the operative standard of good faith in the Articles of the UCC: " 'Good faith,' except as otherwise provided in Article 5, means honesty in fact and the observance of commercially reasonable standards." The generally applicable definition includes both subjective and objective elements. Why is the "commercially reasonable standards" language not included in the Article 5 definition of good faith? See Comment 3 to 5–102. Professor White reports that in Article 5's drafting representatives of a banking industry trade group argued that "Europeans and other nonAmericans were frightened by the threat of a runaway good faith doctrine, particularly by American courts' applying good faith in unforeseen cases." James J. White, The Influence of International Practice on the Revision of Article 5 of the UCC, 16 Nw. J. Int'l L. & Bus. 189, 207 (1995).

Comment 3 finds 5–102(a)(7)'s subjective standard of good faith appropriate because it "creates greater certainty" in the issuer's obligations. The finding goes against the usual assessment of the effects of subjective standards. Standards such as "honesty in fact" make potentially relevant large bodies of evidence, encourage prelitigation coaching of witnesses, and potentially extend the course of judicial proceedings going to the issue of good faith. Objective standards of good faith, by contrast, typically involve more limited evidence, less prelitigation jockeying, and more truncated proceedings. The usual assessment is that subjective standards produce indeterminacy and high costs in the application of otherwise clear rules. See, e.g., Richard A. Epstein, Simple Rules for a Complex World (1995); Robert D. Cooter & Edward L. Rubin, A Theory of Loss Allocation for Consumer Payments, 66 Tex. L. Rev. 63 (1987). Comment 3's different assessment depends on a confidence that the requisite showing of "honesty in fact" is so easy (and a showing of "dishonesty in fact" so hard) as to discourage investment in litigation of the issue.

PROBLEM

At Buyer's request Bank One issued a letter of credit in Beneficiary's favor. At Beneficiary's-Seller's insistence, Buyer also asked Bank One to have a bank known to Beneficiary, Bank Two, confirm the credit, and Bank One did so. Bank Two accordingly notified Beneficiary of its confirmation. Later, Buyer learns that Beneficiary has intentionally breached the underlying sales contract by shipping nothing but will present documents to Bank Two for payment under Bank Two's credit. The documents will evidence shipment in accordance with the sales contract, as required under the credit. (a) At Buyer's urging, can Bank One obtain an injunction to prevent Bank Two from honoring Beneficiary's presentation? See 5–107(a), 5–109(b). (b) Can Buyer obtain an injunction against Bank Two in these circumstances? See 5–109(b); 5–107(a); Comment 1 to 5–107 (third paragraph); International Trade Relationship & Export v. Citibank, N.A., 41 UCC Rep. Serv.2d 626, 2000 WL 343899 (S.D.N.Y. 2000).

F.   TRANSFER, ASSIGNMENT AND SECURITY INTERESTS

1.   TRANSFER AND ASSIGNMENT

There are two ways to transfer rights in a letter of credit: by "transferring" the credit and by assigning the proceeds of the credit. The two notions are different. Section 5–112(a) defines "transfer" to mean the transfer of the beneficiary's right to draw on the letter of credit. Transferring the credit changes the party who must present documents to the issuer for honor. See also UCP 500 art. 48(a). Section 5–114 defines "proceeds of a letter of credit" to mean cash, checks or other items of value paid by the issuer upon honor of the letter of credit. Thus, assignment of the proceeds merely changes the party entitled to receive them. Assignment doesn't change the party who must present the documents for honor.

Letter of credit law treats transfer of the credit very differently from assignment of the credit's proceeds. Under 5–112(a) transfer convey to a third party the beneficiary's right to draw on the credit by signing and presenting its own draft and other documents. See UCP 500 art. 48(i). Further, in the words of Comment 2 to 5–112, "[i]t contemplates not merely payment to but also performance by the transferee." That is, the beneficiary's duties are delegated to the transferee, and it may submit documents showing that it rather than the beneficiary performed the underlying contract. The applicant loses control over the identity of the person who will perform. In short, it is analogous to a novation. Comment 2 to 5–112.

Transfer of the right to draw is a radical change in the original deal in which an applicant obtained an issuer's undertaking to pay a beneficiary, who is usually a party to whom the applicant is or will be indebted for performance. In the commercial letter of credit setting, the applicant is usually a buyer and the beneficiary a seller. Since after the transfer, the issuer's undertaking is to pay another person who may perform the beneficiary's contract, how are the applicant's rights protected in transfer cases? A letter of credit can be transferred only if the credit provides that it is transferable. 5–112(a); see also UCP 500 art. 48(b). Section 5–112(a) sets the default rule against transfer to reflect the preferences of most applicants. If the applicant doesn't want to give the beneficiary the right to transfer, it must be sure that the credit it procures from the issuer does not permit transfer. In this case the issuing bank must dishonor any presentation of invoices of third persons; the applicant bargained for performance by its beneficiary and only its invoices will do. But if the credit is transferable on its face, Comment 2 to 5–112 states: "The issuance of a transferable letter of credit with the concurrence of the applicant is ipso facto an agreement by the issuer and applicant to permit a beneficiary to transfer its drawing right and permit a nominated person to recognize and carry out that transfer without further notice to them." Issuing banks may counter this by a requirement in the letter of credit that the beneficiary obtain the bank's permission before transfer so that the bank can anticipate who will make the presentation. 5–112(b)(2).

Transferable credits often are used by intermediate sellers to finance sales to their buyers. In the simplest form of such transactions the intermediate seller has its buyer have issued a transferable credit in the amount of the contract price naming the seller as the beneficiary. Typically the credit requires the seller to present its invoice and draft. The seller in turn asks the issuer to transfer part of the credit to the supplier of the goods it is selling to its buyer. This is called a "partial transfer" of the credit because the issuer is being asked to allow the transferee to draw less than the full amount payable under the credit. The issuer notifies the supplier of the terms of the transfer, agreeing to pay the amount of the supplier's invoice and draft upon the supplier's presentation of conforming documents. If the documents comply with the notice of transfer, the issuer pays the supplier the face amount of the supplier's draft. It also pays over to the intermediate seller the difference between the amount it paid to the supplier and the amount of the credit—the seller's profit from the sale to its buyer. The issuer substitutes the intermediate seller's invoice, draft and other documents it has received from the seller for the supplier's documents. This is done in order to avoid disclosing to the buyer the supplier's identity and its lower invoice price. See UCP 500 art. 48(i). The issuer then delivers the substituted documents to the buyer. Transferable credits usually involve more parties such as advisers of the credit, who may themselves undertake to allow transfer.

The notion of assignment is straightforward. It simply means assignment by the beneficiary of the proceeds that it is entitled to receive upon honor of the credit by the issuer. Proceeds are always assignable. Assignment of proceeds does not include the beneficiary's drawing rights. 5–114(a). The right to draw on the credit remains in the beneficiary, and the assignee's rights are contingent upon whether the beneficiary's presentation for honor complies with the terms and conditions of the credit. See Comment 2 to 5–112 and 5–114(b). Further, the issuer and the beneficiary can amend the credit without the assignee's consent. The beneficiary may assign its rights to part or all of the proceeds, and it may do so after the credit is established but before presentation. Presumably the beneficiary may also assign the proceeds even after presentation if the issuer wrongfully dishonors. In re XYZ Options, Inc., 154 F.3d 1276 (11th Cir.1998), so held, interpreting former Article 5. Comment 1 to 5–114 appears to support this sensible holding by its statement that assignments of proceeds are valid if made after the credit is established "but before the proceeds are realized." Section 5–114(a)'s default rule allowing assignment presumably reflects the preferences of most beneficiaries under credits.

Section 5–114(c) provides that an issuing bank can ignore an assignment of proceeds "until it consents to the assignment." Professor White, Reporter for the 1995 Revision to Article 5, describes this as a "significant concession" to issuing banks. 3 White & Summers, Prac. ed. § 26–12, at 200. Comment 3 to 5–114 states that the requirement of the issuer's consent conforms to "recognized national and international letter of credit practices." Common practice is for the beneficiary to sign a form giving the issuer notice of the assignment and instructing the issuer to pay the assignee directly upon presentation. Noting that it is always advisable for assignees to obtain the consent of the issuer, the Comment says: "When notice of an assignment has been received, issuers normally have required signatures on a consent form. This practice is reflected in the revision. By unconditionally consenting to such an assignment, the issuer or nominated person becomes bound * * * to pay the assignee the assigned letter of credit proceeds that the issuer or nominated person would otherwise pay to the beneficiary or another assignee."

Thus does banking practice become law. Some amelioration is found in 5–114(d), which provides that though an issuer is not obliged to consent, "consent may not be unreasonably withheld if the assignee possesses and exhibits the letter of credit and presentation of the letter of credit is a condition to honor." The assignee's exhibition to the issuer of a letter of credit presumably gives the issuer sufficient evidence of the assignment to make unreasonable its refusal to consent. Presumably the issuer may consent in advance to assignments by a provision in the letter of credit. Dolan, Letters of Credit, Ch. 10 contains an extensive discussion of transfer and assignment of letters of credit. The subject is also treated in Barkley

Clark, The Law of Secured Transactions Under the Uniform Commercial Code, Ch. 7 (rev. ed. 2003), and 3 White & Summers, Prac. Ed. § 26–12.

PROBLEMS

Beneficiary transferred a letter of credit payable on presentation of the draft without further documents, designated as transferable, to its supplier, Transferee. On a false pretext, Beneficiary retained the letter of credit and, later, fraudulently assigned the proceeds to Assignee who took delivery of the letter of credit for value without knowledge of the previous transfer.

1. Transferee made timely presentation of its draft to Issuer, together with the papers documenting the transfer from Beneficiary. The draft was honored. Later, Assignee presented the letter of credit, papers showing the assignment, and a draft drawn by Beneficiary. Issuer dishonored because the credit had already been paid to Transferee. Is Issuer liable to Assignee? See 5–114(e) and Comment 2 to 5–114.

2. Assignee presented the letter of credit, papers showing the assignment, and a draft drawn by Beneficiary. Issuer, who knew nothing of the previous transfer to Transferee, honored the draft. Later, Transferee presented its own draft. Issuer informed Transferee that it had not known of the transfer and had previously honored beneficiary's draft. Is Issuer liable to Transferee?

3. How should the parties guard by contract and conduct against the risks inherent in a system like that in Revised Article 5 in which Transferee has the right to draw on a letter of credit that is in the possession of Assignee? See 5–112(b)(2) and Comment 1 to 5–112.

2. SECURITY INTERESTS

The most common reason for a beneficiary to assign the proceeds of a letter of credit is to secure the beneficiary's obligation to a creditor. Security interests in the proceeds of a credit fall within Article 9. Section 5–114(f) provides that "[t]he mode of creating and perfecting a security interest in or granting an assignment of a beneficiary's rights to proceeds is governed by Article 9 or other law." Article 9 governs only the right to proceeds of the credit. It does not control rights in the letter of credit itself. Article 9 calls the right to proceeds of the credit "a letter-of-credit right." Comment 5(e) to 5–102. Under 9–102(a)(51) a letter-of-credit right is "a right to payment or performance under the letter of credit ... The term does not include the right of the beneficiary to demand payment or performance under a letter of credit." Thus, the term does not include the right to draw on the credit. The transfer of rights to draw is controlled by Article 5. 5–114(e).

To obtain a property right in a letter-of-credit right, the creditor's security interest must attach to it. Attachment allows enforcement of the right against the debtor. It occurs when three conditions are satisfied. § 9–203(b). Two of the conditions are easily met in letter of credit contexts involving a loan or other value provided to the beneficiary: that the creditor give value to the debtor-beneficiary, and that the debtor-beneficiary have a right to the letter of credit proceeds. The third condition is disjunctive: the debtor must either authenticate a security agreement describing the letter-of-credit right or the secured creditor obtain "control" of the right pursuant to the debtor's security agreement or the secured creditor obtain a security interest in collateral for which the letter-of-credit right is a "supporting obligation." 9–203(b)(3).

Thus, under the third condition, a security interest can attach to the letter-of-credit right in either of two different ways. Attachment occurs if the right is described in a security agreement authenticated by the debtor or the creditor obtains control of the letter-of-credit right pursuant to the debtor's security agreement. Alternatively, the security interest attaches to the letter-of-credit right if it attaches to collateral for which the letter-of-credit right is a "supporting obligation." The next section discusses the letter-of-credit right as a "supporting obligation." Section 9–409(a) treats as ineffective restrictions on the creation of security interests in letter of credit proceeds. This allows a security interest to attach when the restriction otherwise would prevent attachment. Comment 2 to 9–409.

Perfection of a security interest allows enforcement of a security interest against third parties. It requires attachment plus the secured creditor to take steps, usually acts of public notice, prescribed by Article 9. 9–308(a), 9–310. Under 9–312(b)(2) a security interest in a letter-of-credit right as original collateral may be perfected only by "control." Thus, control is a particularly effective (but sometimes costly) means of attachment because a security interest that attaches by control also is perfected. Control, according to 9–107, occurs when the issuer "has consented to an assignment of proceeds of the letter of credit under Section 5–114(c)." Section 5–114(c) in turn provides that an issuer need not recognize an assignment of credit proceeds until it consents to the assignment. Where the assignee possesses and exhibits the credit to the issuer, the issuer cannot withhold its consent unreasonably. Article 5 gives no further guidance on obtaining the issuer's consent, and Comment 2 to 9–107 states that the details of the consenting issuer's duty to pay the assignee are left to the parties' agreement.

Article 9's use of the concept of control is borrowed from Article 8. First used in Article 8 to govern the rights of purchasers and secured parties in investment property, Article 9 adapts and applies the concept to security interests in deposit accounts, electronic chattel paper, letter-of-credit rights, and investment property. It replaces the old system of requiring possession of the credit by the assignee in order to perfect a security interest in the credit proceeds. The requirement of possession was cumbersome, contrary to industry practice and in the case of partial assignments of the credit sometimes impossible to satisfy. See Barkley Clark, The Law of Secured Transactions Under the Uniform Commercial Code 7.14[1] (rev. ed. 2003). Control doesn't require possession of the credit.

In the two cases below determine whether the secured parties have control over the described letter-of-credit proceeds.

Case #1.   Beneficiary assigned 1/3 of the credit proceeds to A1, its secured creditor, and delivered possession of the letter of credit to A1. Subsequently Beneficiary assigned 1/3 of the letter-of-credit proceeds to each A2 and A3. Beneficiary notified the issuer of all three assignments.

Case #2.   Foreign Buyer had issued a letter of credit for $1,000,000 from Foreign Issuer payable to US Seller. Issuer sent the letter of credit to its US correspondent bank to serve as an advising and confirming bank, which delivered Issuer's letter of credit to Seller. Seller granted a security interest to SP Bank in the credit proceeds to secure a loan of $500,000, and a second security interest to US Distributor to secure an existing $250,000 obligation. Advising Bank's invariable practice when notified of assignments of letter-of-credit rights was to demand and retain possession of the credit and note on it the terms of the assignment. It followed the practice in this case. When Seller filed a bankruptcy petition, its trustee sought to avoid the security interests of SP Bank and Distributor in the proceeds of the letter of credit. Seller's trustee can avoid their security interests if the interests are unperfected.

Revised Article 9 leaves unaddressed the rights and priority of a secured creditor when it becomes the transferee of a letter of credit. A transferee acquires all of the beneficiary's rights under the letter of credit, and therefore transferring the credit is a good way to secure the beneficiary's obligations. Section 9–109(c)(4) makes Article 9 inapplicable to the rights of a transferee beneficiary given priority under 5–114(e). And Section 5–114(e) in turn gives the transferee priority over the assignee's right to credit proceeds as well as over claims of competing secured creditors in the proceeds. See Comment 3 to 9–329. Thus, Article 9 leaves undisturbed 5–114(e)'s grant of paramount rights in the letter of credit proceeds to the transferee beneficiary, even when the transferee is a secured creditor. Article 9 therefore does not govern at least two situations: (1) the rights of a beneficiary-debtor against the transferee beneficiary-secured creditor; and (2) the priority of the transferee beneficiary-secured creditor against competing secured creditors. In situation (1), a distinction between an outright transfer and the grant of a security interest has to be made. In situation (2), a conflict between Article 9's priority rules and 5–114(e)'s priority rule is possible. Section 9–329's "control priority" rule gives priority to the security party first obtaining control of the letter of credit right. Section 5–114(e), however, gives priority to the transferee beneficiary over competing claimants to the letter of credit proceeds. Suppose Secured Creditor 1 obtains control over credit proceeds of a transferable letter of credit. Later, Secured Creditor 2 becomes a transferee beneficiary under the same letter. It never obtains control over the credit proceeds. Section 9–329(1) awards priority to Secured Creditor 1. Section 5–114(e) awards it to Secured Creditor 2. Comment 4 to 9–329 recognizes the two unaddressed situations and simply counsels courts to give "appropriate consideration to the policies and provisions of Article 5 and letter-of-credit practice as well as Article 9."

3.   LETTERS OF CREDIT AS SUPPORTING OBLIGATIONS

Article 9 has special rules that apply to letter-of-credit rights when the letter of credit is a "supporting obligation" under 9–102(a)(77). This term "means a letter-of-credit right or secondary obligation that supports the payment or performance of an account, chattel paper, a document, a general intangible, an instrument, or investment property." Collateral described in (a)(77) is the "supported obligation," and the letter-of-credit right is the "supporting obligation." When a letter-of-credit right "supports" the sort of collateral described in 9–102(a)(77), it serves to enhance the value of the supported collateral. Given the frequent use of standby credits as credit enhancement devices, our guess is that in the great majority of cases letter-of-credit rights will be supporting obligations. If a sports franchise assures a basketball player that if its promissory note for the athlete's salary is not paid, the athlete can rely on a standby letter of credit, the letter of credit is a supporting obligation. The same is true when a dealer assigns its accounts to a financer and backs the accounts by a letter of credit. The examples are endless.

Article 9's special rules for attachment, perfection and priority of a security interest in a letter-of-credit right treat the right as an incident of the collateral it supports. Comment 5f. to 9–102. Accordingly, the secured creditor's rights in the credit proceeds derive from its rights in the collateral supported by the credit proceeds. Thus, under 9–203(f) a security interest automatically attaches to the letter-of-credit right when it attaches to the supported collateral. So, for example, there is no need for an authenticated security agreement describing the supported obligation to describe or contain any reference to the letter-of-credit right supporting it. Under 9–308(d) perfection in the supported collateral is perfection in the letter-of-credit right. And under 9–322(c), with one significant exception, priority in the supported collateral is priority in the letter-of-credit right.

Article 9's control concept must be understood taking into account its special rules for supporting obligations. Two points are important. First, the role of control is significantly qualified for letter-of-credit rights when they are supporting obligations. If a letter-of-credit right is not a supporting obligation, 9–312(b)(2) provides that perfection may be achieved only by control. But the requirement doesn't apply to supporting obligations. In this case perfection of the security interest in the supported collateral automatically perfects a security interest in the supported obligation. Some commercial and most standby transactions letter-of-credit rights are supporting obligations. Thus, in many cases attachment and perfection in these rights is automatic. Control isn't necessary and will be a more expensive alternative.

Second, and by far more important, are Article 9's special priority rule for supporting obligations. Section 9–322(b)(2) describes Article 9's basic priority rule for supporting obligations. Under it the time for filing and perfection as to the supported obligation is also the time of filing and perfection as to the supported obligation. This priority rule treats priority in the supporting obligation as derivative: the priority of the supporting obligation is the priority of the supported collateral. However, 9–322(b)(2)'s basic rule is subject to an important exception contained in 9–322(c). Section 9–322(c)(1) provides in relevant part that the rule that a security interest in the supporting obligation takes the priority of a security interest in the supported collateral, subject to 9–329(1). Section 9–329(1) in turn provides that if there are conflicting security interests in the same letter-of-credit right, the security interest of the secured party having control has priority over a security interest of a secured party that does not have control. Hence, for example, if a bank files first against accounts, it is perfected with respect to a supporting letter-of-credit right. However, it will not be prior as to that right if a financer who filed second against the same accounts but perfected its security interest in the supporting letter of credit right by control. Thus, to be sure of their priority, secured parties claiming security interests in letter-of-credit rights that are supporting obligations must obtain control. Control remains the central tenet of the law of secured transactions in letter-of-credit rights.

G.   LETTERS OF CREDIT IN BANKRUPTCY

If a standby letter of credit is to be useful as the functional equivalent of a guaranty, it must pass muster in bankruptcy. So far it has. Discharge of the applicant in bankruptcy does not effect the liability of the issuer on a letter of credit. BC 524(e). The initial question is whether the automatic stay of BC 362(a) restrains the beneficiary from drawing on the issuer after the applicant's bankruptcy. If it does, the utility of letters of credit is greatly impaired because the beneficiary would be forced to go through the expensive and time-consuming procedure to lift the stay under BC 362(d). As we have shown, the usual letter of credit transaction involves three undertakings: the letter of credit between the issuer and the beneficiary; the underlying contract between the applicant and the beneficiary; and the reimbursement contract between the applicant and the issuer. There is no question that the automatic stay precludes any action by the beneficiary against the applicant on the underlying contract as well as any action by the issuer against the applicant on the reimbursement agreement.

That BC 362(a) does not stay the beneficiary's draw against the issuer was decided in In re Page, 18 B.R. 713 (D.D.C.1982), and has been widely accepted. Accord In re War Eagle Construction Co., Inc., 283 B.R. 193 (S.D.Va. 2002). The applicant in *Page* granted security interests in its assets to issuer to secure its obligation to reimburse the issuer if the issuer had to pay the letter of credit. Later the applicant filed in bankruptcy and the beneficiary presented the letter of credit for honor. The bankruptcy court held that unless payment of the letter of credit were stayed, the issuer, after payment, would be able to realize on its security interest in debtor's property, thereby reducing the assets available to the other creditors. The district court reversed on the ground that before the applicant had filed in bankruptcy the issuer already had a perfected security interest in the applicant's assets to secure its contingent claim for reimbursement. In its payment of the letter of credit, the issuer merely liquidated its claim against the applicant for reimbursement, and applicant's other creditors are no worse off because the property of the applicant's bankruptcy estate has not been depleted. The letter of credit was not, of course, property of the applicant's estate. The court demonstrated its respect for the importance of the independence principle of letter of credit law: "Moreover, enjoining the payment of the letter of credit, even temporarily, would frustrate the commercial purposes of letters of credit to the detriment of financial institutions as well as their customers. * * * If payment on a letter of credit could be routinely delayed by the filing of a Chapter 11 petition the intended substitution of a bank for its less credit-worthy customer would be defeated." 18 B.R. at 717.

The more difficult problems concerning letters of credit in bankruptcy have arisen in the area of voidable preferences law as illustrated in the following case.

Matter of Compton Corp.

United States Court of Appeals, Fifth Circuit, 1987.
831 F.2d 586.

■ JERRE S. WILLIAMS, CIRCUIT JUDGE:

This is a bankruptcy preference case in which a bankruptcy trustee seeks to recover a transfer made via a letter of credit for the benefit of one of the debtor's unsecured creditors on the eve of bankruptcy. The bankruptcy court and the district court found there to be no voidable preference. We reverse.

I.   FACTUAL BACKGROUND

In March 1982, Blue Quail Energy, Inc., delivered a shipment of oil to debtor Compton Corporation. Payment of $585,443.85 for this shipment of oil was due on or about April 20, 1982. Compton failed to make timely payment. Compton induced Abilene National Bank (now MBank–Abilene) to issue an irrevocable standby letter of credit in Blue Quail's favor on May 6, 1982. Under the terms of the letter of credit, payment of up to $585,443.85 was due Blue Quail if Compton failed to pay Blue Quail this amount by June 22, 1982. Compton paid MBank $1,463.61 to issue the letter of credit. MBank also received a promissory note payable on demand for $585,443.85. MBank did not need a security agreement to cover the letter of credit transaction because a prior 1980 security agreement between the bank and Compton had a future advances provision. This 1980 security agreement had been perfected as to a variety of Compton's assets through the filing of several financing statements. The most recent financing statement had been filed a year before, May 7, 1981. The letter of credit on its face noted that it was for an antecedent debt due Blue Quail.

On May 7, 1982, the day after MBank issued the letter of credit in Blue Quail's favor, several of Compton's creditors filed an involuntary bankruptcy petition against Compton. On June 22, 1982, MBank paid Blue Quail $569,932.03 on the letter of credit after Compton failed to pay Blue Quail.

In the ensuing bankruptcy proceeding, MBank's aggregate secured claims against Compton, including the letter of credit payment to Blue Quail, were paid in full from the liquidation of Compton's assets which served as the bank's collateral. Walter Kellogg, bankruptcy trustee for Compton, did not contest the validity of MBank's secured claim against Compton's assets for the amount drawn under the letter of credit by Blue Quail. Instead, on June 14, 1983, trustee Kellogg filed a complaint in the bankruptcy court against Blue Quail asserting that Blue Quail had received a preferential transfer under § 547 through the letter of credit transaction. The trustee sought to recover $585,443.85 from Blue Quail pursuant to § 550.

Blue Quail answered and filed a third party complaint against MBank. On June 16, 1986, Blue Quail filed a motion for summary judgment asserting that the trustee could not recover any preference from Blue Quail because Blue Quail had been paid from MBank's funds under the letter of credit and therefore had not received any of Compton's property. On August 27, 1986, the bankruptcy court granted Blue Quail's motion, agreeing that the payment under the letter of credit did not constitute a transfer of debtor Compton's property but rather was a transfer of the bank's property. The bankruptcy court entered judgment on the motion on September 10, 1986. Trustee Kellogg appealed this decision to the district court. On December 11, 1986, the district court affirmed the bankruptcy court ruling, holding that the trustee did not establish two necessary elements of a voidable transfer under § 547. The district court agreed with Blue Quail and the bankruptcy court that the trustee could not establish that the funds transferred to Blue Quail were ever property of Compton. Furthermore, the district court held that the transfer of the increased security interest to MBank was a transfer of the debtor's property for the sole benefit of the bank and in no way benefitted Blue Quail. The district court therefore found no voidable preference as to Blue Quail. The trustee is appealing the decision to this Court.

II. THE LETTER OF CREDIT

It is well established that a letter of credit and the proceeds therefrom are not property of the debtor's estate under § 541. * * * When the issuer honors a proper draft under a letter of credit, it does so from its own assets and not from the assets of its customer who caused the letter of credit to be issued. * * * As a result, a bankruptcy trustee is not entitled to enjoin a post petition payment of funds under a letter of credit from the issuer to the beneficiary, because such a payment is not a transfer of debtor's property (a threshold requirement under § 547(b)). A case apparently holding otherwise, In re Twist Cap., Inc., 1 B.R. 284 (Bankr.Fla.1979), has been roundly criticized and otherwise ignored by courts and commentators alike.

Recognizing these characteristics of a letter of credit in a bankruptcy case is necessary in order to maintain the independence principle, the cornerstone of letter of credit law. Under the independence principle, an issuer's obligation to the letter of credit's beneficiary is independent from any obligation between the beneficiary and the issuer's customer. All a beneficiary has to do to receive payment under a letter of credit is to show that it has performed all the duties required by the letter of credit. Any disputes between the beneficiary and the customer do not affect the issuer's obligation to the beneficiary to pay under the letter of credit.

Letters of credit are most commonly arranged by a party who benefits from the provision of goods or services. The party will request a bank to issue a letter of credit which names the provider of the goods or services as the beneficiary. Under a standby letter of credit, the bank becomes primarily liable to the beneficiary upon the default of the bank's customer to pay for the goods or services. The bank charges a fee to issue a letter of credit and to undertake this liability. The shifting of liability to the bank rather than to the services or goods provider is the main purpose of the letter of credit. After all, the bank is in a much better position to assess the risk of its customer's insolvency than is the service or goods provider. It should be noted, however, that it is the risk of the debtor's insolvency and not the risk of a preference attack that a bank assumes under a letter of credit transaction. Overall, the independence principle is necessary to insure "the certainty of payments for services or goods rendered regardless of any intervening misfortune which may befall the other contracting party." In re North Shore, 30 B.R. at 378.

The trustee in this case accepts this analysis and does not ask us to upset it. The trustee is not attempting to set aside the post petition payments by MBank to Blue Quail under the letter of credit as a preference; nor does the trustee claim the letter of credit itself constitutes debtor's property. The trustee is instead challenging the earlier transfer in which Compton granted MBank an increased security interest in its assets to obtain the letter of credit for the benefit of Blue Quail. Collateral which has been pledged by a debtor as security for a letter of credit is property of the debtor's estate. In re W.L. Mead, 42 B.R. at 59. The trustee claims that the direct transfer to MBank of the increased security interest on May 6, 1982, also constituted an indirect transfer to Blue Quail which occurred one day prior to the filing of the involuntary bankruptcy petition and is voidable as a preference under § 547. This assertion of a preferential transfer is evaluated in Parts III and IV of this opinion.

It is important to note that the irrevocable standby letter of credit in the case at bar was not arranged in connection with Blue Quail's initial decision to sell oil to Compton on credit. Compton arranged for the letter of credit after Blue Quail had shipped the oil and after Compton had defaulted in payment. The letter of credit in this case did not serve its usual function of backing up a contemporaneous credit decision, but instead served as a back up payment guarantee on an extension of credit already in jeopardy. The letter of credit was issued to pay off an antecedent unsecured debt. This fact was clearly noted on the face of the letter of credit. Blue Quail, the beneficiary of the letter of credit, did not give new value for the issuance of the letter of credit by MBank on May 6, 1982, or for the resulting increased security interest held by MBank. MBank, however, did give new value for the increased security interest it obtained in Compton's collateral: the bank issued the letter of credit.

When a debtor pledges its assets to secure a letter of credit, a transfer of debtor's property has occurred under the provisions of § 547. By subjecting its assets to MBank's reimbursement claim in the event MBank had to pay on the letter of credit, Compton made a transfer of its property. The broad definition of "transfer" under § 101 is clearly designed to cover such a transfer. Overall, the letter of credit itself and the payments thereunder may not be property of debtor, but the collateral pledged as a security interest for the letter of credit is.

Furthermore, in a secured letter of credit transaction, the transfer of debtor's property takes place at the time the letter of credit is issued (when the security interest is granted) and received by the beneficiary, not at the time the issuer pays on the letter of credit. * * *

The transfer to MBank of the increased security interest was a direct transfer which occurred on May 6, 1982, when the bank issued the letter of credit. Under § 547(e)(2)(A), however, such a transfer is deemed to have taken place for purposes of § 547 at the time such transfer "takes effect" between the transferor and transferee if such transfer is perfected within 10 days. The phrase "takes effect" is undefined in the Bankruptcy Code, but under Uniform Commercial Code Article 9 law, a transfer of a security interest "takes effect" when the security interest attaches. Because of the future advances clause in MBank's 1980 security agreement with Compton, the attachment of the MBank's security interest relates back to May 9, 1980, the date the security agreement went into effect. The bottom line is that the direct transfer of the increased security interest to MBank is artificially deemed to have occurred at least by May 7, 1981, the date MBank filed its final financing statement, for purposes of a preference attack against the bank.[4] This date is well before the 90 day window of § 547(b)(4)(A). This would protect the bank from a preference attack by the trustee even if the bank had not given new value at the time it received the increased security interest.* MBank is therefore protected from a

---

4. UCC § 9–312(7) specifies that for purposes of priority among competing secured parties, the security interest for a future advance has the same priority as the security interest for the first advance. Conflicting security interests rank according to priority in time of filing or perfection. UCC § 9–312(5).

* [Editors' Note: The "relation back" theory of the Court is not supported by the Bankruptcy Code. The Court is correct in stating that the phrase "at the time such transfer takes effect" in § 547(e)(2)(A) refers to the time the security interest "attaches" under the UCC. The time of attachment is governed by UCC § 9–203. In this case at-

preference attack by the trustee for the increased security interest transfer under either of two theories: under § 547(c)(1) because it gave new value and under the operation of the relation back provision of § 547(e)(2)(A). The bank is also protected from any claims of reimbursement by Blue Quail because the bank received no voidable preference.

The relation back provision of § 547(e)(2)(A), however, applies only to the direct transfer of the increased security interest to MBank. The indirect transfer to Blue Quail that allegedly resulted from the direct transfer to MBank occurred on May 6, 1982, the date of issuance of the letter of credit. The relation back principle of § 547(e)(2)(A) does not apply to this indirect transfer to Blue Quail. Blue Quail was not a party to the security agreement between MBank and Compton. So it will not be able to utilize the relation back provision if it is deemed to have received an indirect transfer resulting from the direct transfer of the increased security interest to MBank. Blue Quail, therefore, cannot assert either of the two defenses to a preference attack which MBank can claim. Blue Quail did not give new value under § 547(c)(1), and it received a transfer within 90 days of the filing of Compton's bankruptcy petition.

III. DIRECT/INDIRECT TRANSFER DOCTRINE

The federal courts have long recognized that "[t]o constitute a preference, it is not necessary that the transfer be made directly to the creditor." National Bank of Newport v. National Herkimer County Bank, 225 U.S. 178, 184 (1912). "If the bankrupt has made a transfer of his property, the *effect* of which is to enable one of his creditors to obtain a greater percentage of his debt than another creditor of the same class, circuity of arrangement will not avail to save it." Id. (Emphasis added). To combat such circuity, the courts have broken down certain transfers into two transfers, one direct and one indirect. The direct transfer to the third party may be valid and not subject to a preference attack. The indirect transfer, arising from the same action by the debtor, however, may constitute a voidable preference as to the creditor who indirectly benefitted from the direct transfer to the third party.

tachment occurred when three events occurred: (1) value was given by MBank; (2) the debtor had rights in the collateral; and (3) the debtor signed a security agreement providing for the security interest. The second and third events occurred before May 6, but MBank did not give value with respect to the transfer challenged by the trustee in bankruptcy until the letter of credit was issued on May 6. Thus, under § 547(e)(2)(A), the transfer could not have occurred before May 6. Under UCC § 9–303, the security interest that attached on May 6 was perfected at the time it attached because the filing of a financing statement—the applicable step required for perfection—had already occurred before May 6. Because May 6 is the day of both attachment and perfection, the result under § 547(e)(2)(A) is that the transfer from the debtor to MBank occurred on May 6. It is irrelevant under § 547 that UCC § 9–312(5) and (7) date the priority of MBank with respect to the May 6 transaction from the time MBank filed its financing statement. § 547(e)(2)(A) refers to the time of attachment and perfection, not to the date of priority. There is no avoidable preference in this case, however. The Court correctly holds that the giving of value by MBank and the transfer by the debtor to MBank were a contemporaneous exchange under § 547(c)(1).]

This is the situation presented in the case before us. The term "transfer" as used in the various bankruptcy statutes through the years has always been broad enough to cover such indirect transfers and to catch various circuitous arrangements. Katz v. First National Bank of Glen Head, 568 F.2d 964, 969 n. 4, (2d Cir.), cert. denied, 434 U.S. 1069 (1978). The new Bankruptcy Code implicitly adopts this doctrine through its broad definition of "transfer."[6] Examining the case law that has developed since the *National Bank of Newport* case yields an understanding of what types of transfers the direct/indirect doctrine is meant to cover.

In Palmer v. Radio Corporation of America, 453 F.2d 1133 (5th Cir.1971), a third party purchased from the debtor a television station for $40,000 cash and the assumption of certain liabilities of the debtor, including unsecured claims by creditor RCA. This Court found the direct transfer from the debtor to the third party purchaser constituted an indirect preferential transfer to creditor RCA. We found that the assumption by the third party purchaser of the debt owed by the debtor to RCA and the subsequent payments made thereunder constituted a voidable transfer as to RCA. The court noted that such indirect transfers as this had long been held to constitute voidable preferences under bankruptcy laws. 453 F.2d at 1136.

* * *

In Virginia National Bank v. Woodson, 329 F.2d 836 (4th Cir.1964), the debtor had several overdrawn accounts with his bank. The debtor talked his sister into paying off $8,000 of the overdrafts in exchange for an $8,000 promissory note and an assignment of some collateral as security. The debtor's sister made the $8,000 payment directly to the bank. The $8,000 technically was never part of the debtor's estate. The court, however, held that the payment of the $8,000 by the sister to the bank was a preference as to the bank to the extent of the value of the collateral held by the sister. The court noted that the measure of the value of a voidable preference is diminution of the debtor's estate and not the value of the transfer to the creditor.

In the *Woodson* case the sister was secured only to the extent the pledged collateral had value; the remainder of her loan to her brother was unsecured. Swapping one unsecured creditor for another unsecured creditor does not create any kind of preference. The court held that a preference in such a transaction arises only when a secured creditor is swapped for an unsecured creditor. Only then is the pool of assets available for distribution to the general unsecured creditors depleted because the secured creditor has priority over the unsecured creditors. Furthermore, the court held that

---

6. "Transfer" means every mode, direct or *indirect,* absolute or conditional, voluntary or involuntary, of disposing of or parting with property or with an interest in property, including retention of title as a security interest and foreclosure of the debtor's equity of redemption. § 101(50) (emphasis added). See also the Notes of the Committee on the Judiciary under 11 U.S.C. 101 ("The definition of transfer is as broad as possible.")

the bank and not the sister had received the voidable preference and had to pay back to the trustee an amount equal to the value of the collateral.

* * *

IV. THE DIRECT/INDIRECT DOCTRINE IN THE CONTEXT OF A LETTER OF CREDIT TRANSACTION

The case at bar differs from the cases discussed in Part III supra only by the presence of the letter of credit as the mechanism for paying off the unsecured creditor. Blue Quail's attempt to otherwise distinguish the case from the direct/indirect transfer cases does not withstand scrutiny.

In the letter of credit cases discussed in Part II supra, the letters of credit were issued contemporaneously with the initial extension of credit by the beneficiaries of the letters. In those cases the letters of credit effectively served as security devices for the benefit of the creditor beneficiaries and took the place of formal security interests. The courts in those cases properly found there had been no voidable transfers, direct or indirect, in the letter of credit transactions involved. New value was given contemporaneously with the issuance of the letters of credit in the form of the extensions of credit by the beneficiaries of the letters. As a result, the § 547(c)(1) preference exception was applicable.

The case at bar differs from these other letter of credit cases by one very important fact: the letter of credit in this case was issued to secure an antecedent unsecured debt due the beneficiary of the letter of credit. The unsecured creditor beneficiary gave no new value upon the issuance of the letter of credit. When the issuer paid off the letter of credit and foreclosed on the collateral securing the letter of credit, a preferential transfer had occurred. An unsecured creditor was paid in full and a secured creditor was substituted in its place.

The district court upheld the bankruptcy court in maintaining the validity of the letter of credit issued to cover the antecedent debt. The district court held that MBank, the issuer of the letter of credit, could pay off the letter of credit and foreclose on the collateral securing it. We are in full agreement. But we also look to the impact of the transaction as it affects the situation of Blue Quail in the bankrupt estate. We hold that the bankruptcy trustee can recover from Blue Quail, the beneficiary of the letter of credit, because Blue Quail received an indirect preference. This result preserves the sanctity of letter of credit and carries out the purposes of the Bankruptcy Code by avoiding a preferential transfer. MBank, the issuer of the letter of credit, being just the intermediary through which the preferential transfer was accomplished, completely falls out of the picture and is not involved in this particular legal proceeding.

MBank did not receive any preferential transfer—it gave new value for the security interest. Furthermore, because the direct and indirect transfers are separate and independent, the trustee does not even need to challenge the direct transfer of the increased security interest to MBank, or seek any relief at all from MBank, in order to attack the indirect transfer and recover under § 550 from the indirect transferee Blue Quail.

We hold that a creditor cannot secure payment of an unsecured antecedent debt through a letter of credit transaction when it could not do so through any other type of transaction. The purpose of the letter of credit transaction in this case was to secure payment of an unsecured antecedent debt for the benefit of an unsecured creditor. This is the only proper way to look at such letters of credit in the bankruptcy context. The promised transfer of pledged collateral induced the bank to issue the letter of credit in favor of the creditor. The increased security interest held by the bank clearly benefitted the creditor because the bank would not have issued the letter of credit without this security. A secured creditor was substituted for an unsecured creditor to the detriment of the other unsecured creditors.

* * *

The precise holding in this case needs to be emphasized. We do not hold that payment under a letter of credit, or even a letter of credit itself, constitute preferential transfers under § 547(b) or property of a debtor under § 541. The holding of this case fully allows the letter of credit to function. We preserve its sanctity and the underlying independence doctrine. We do not, however, allow an unsecured creditor to avoid a preference attack by utilizing a letter of credit to secure payment of an antecedent debt. Otherwise the unsecured creditor would receive an indirect preferential transfer from the granting of the security for the letter of credit to the extent of the value of that security. Our holding does not affect the strength of or the proper use of letters of credit. When a letter of credit is issued contemporaneously with a new extension of credit, the creditor beneficiary will not be subject to a preferential attack under the direct/indirect doctrine elaborated in this case because the creditor will have given new value in exchange for the indirect benefit of the secured letter of credit. Only when a creditor receives a secured letter of credit to cover an unsecured antecedent debt will it be subject to a preferential attack under § 547(b).

* * *

NOTES

1. The trustee in *Compton* elected to recover from Blue Quail, the beneficiary of Compton's grant of a security interest to Mbank. In dicta the court suggested that the trustee could not recover from Mbank because it did not receive a preference. See Douglas G. Baird, Elements of Bankruptcy 191 (Rev. ed. 1993). This conflicts with Levit v. Ingersoll Rand Financial Corp., 874 F.2d 1186 (7th Cir.1989), as well as four other circuits. These courts have held that a transfer voidable as a preference under BC 547(b) can be recovered from a transferee who was not preferred as the "initial transferee of such transfer" under BC 550(a)(1). Because the creation of a security interest is a transfer under the Bankruptcy Code and Mbank is the "initial transferee," they would allow recovery from Mbank under BC 550(a)(1) in the circumstances described in *Compton*. (Further, BC 550(b)'s good faith defense to recovery does not apply to initial transferees to protect Mbank.) The 1994 Bankruptcy Reform Act altered BC 550 in response to *Levit*, adding BC 550(c) to limit recovery from an insider transferee of an indirect preference. However, Congress left BC 550(a)(1) untouched. Congress' action arguably signals approval of *Levit*'s literal reading of the subsection, to the effect that, as Baird puts it, "if a transfer is preferential as to anyone, the trustee may recover from the initial transferee." Id.

2.   In *Compton* we see that a debtor who already owes a debt makes a voidable preference to the creditor if it causes a bank to issue a letter of credit to the creditor to secure the debt within 90 days of bankruptcy. If the debtor had paid the creditor or had granted the creditor a security interest in the debtor's property during the 90–day period, there would clearly be a preference. The debtor cannot alter this result by use of a letter of credit. But letters of credit are not normally used to secure antecedent debts. The usual case is one in which the letter of credit is issued to the creditor at the inception of the credit transaction between the beneficiary and applicant. An example is one in which the beneficiary sells goods to the debtor-applicant on credit and takes a standby letter of credit to protect itself against the debtor-applicant's failure to pay. Here the seller-beneficiary gives new value at the time it receives the letter of credit. Is it possible for a preference problem to arise in such a case?

Take two cases:

Case #1.   Beneficiary sold goods to Applicant on 60–day credit for $100,000 and demanded a letter of credit to secure it against Applicant's default. Applicant induced Bank to issue the letter of credit by granting Bank a security interest in its property worth in excess of $100,000 to secure its agreement to reimburse Bank. Applicant was unable to pay for the goods at the end of the credit period but induced Beneficiary not to draw on the letter of credit for a month. At the end of the month Applicant, though thoroughly insolvent, paid $100,000 to Beneficiary in satisfaction of the debt. Within 90 days of the payment, Applicant filed in bankruptcy and its trustee sought to recover the payment as a voidable preference. There should be no preference in this case under BC 547(b)(5), and it shouldn't matter if payment to Beneficiary came from Bank or Applicant. The transfer of assets from Applicant's estate occurred when the security interest was granted to Bank, and Bank gave new value for that transfer by undertaking to pay Beneficiary. If Bank pays Beneficiary, Bank has a valid secured claim in Applicant's bankruptcy for $100,000. If Applicant pays, Bank's claim to the security is released and, although Applicant's unsecured creditors have lost $100,000 in the cash payment Applicant made to Beneficiary, they have gained the same amount in the release of Bank's claim against Applicant's property. The transfer of assets that depleted

Applicant's estate to the detriment of its creditors took place before the beginning of the 90–day period.

Case #2. Difficulties arise when we change only one fact in the case above. Assume that Applicant either granted no security interest in its property to Bank or, more realistically, granted a security interest in property that eventually turned out to be worth much less than $100,000. Let's assume for purposes of discussion that the collateral became worthless. If Bank pays Beneficiary on the letter of credit, there is no preference because Bank's payment does not transfer property of Applicant's estate. Before payment Applicant owed $100,000 to Beneficiary on an unsecured claim; after payment Applicant owes the same amount to Bank on an unsecured claim. The problem arises if Applicant, rather than Bank, pays the Beneficiary. Here $100,000 in cash has been taken from Applicant's estate for the benefit of Beneficiary during the 90–day period. We look at preferences from the point of view of the debtor's unsecured creditors. Are they worse off after the transfer than before? True, Applicant has been relieved of Bank's unsecured contingent claim for reimbursement, but that does not put money into the Applicant's estate for the benefit of its creditors. In re Powerine Oil Co., 59 F.3d 969 (9th Cir.1995), held that payment by the Applicant in such a case is preferential, even though payment by the Bank in the same case would not be. Noting that the result of this case makes Beneficiary better off if its debtor, the Applicant, defaults, the court observed that "law can be stranger than fiction in the Preference Zone." 59 F.3d at 971. The Bankruptcy Appellate Panel had held that the payment was not a preference because it did not enable the Beneficiary to obtain more than it would in a Chapter 7 bankruptcy. If Applicant hadn't paid it, Bank would have had to. Could you contend that Bank rather than Beneficiary is the recipient of the preference in *Powerine*?

FORM. LETTER OF CREDIT APPLICATION AND AGREEMENT

When an applicant requests a standby letter of credit, banks require completion of the following form which states the agreement between the applicant and issuing bank and the terms under which the bank must honor upon presentation of the letter of credit.

CITY NATIONAL BANK

INTERNATIONAL OPERATIONS CENTER

606 South Olive Street, Suite 300   Date:
CABLE ADDRESS "CINABANK LSA"   Los Angeles, California 90014
                                                    TELEX 825717

IRREVOCABLE STANDBY LETTER OF CREDIT APPLICATION AND LETTER OF CREDIT AGREEMENT

TO: CITY NATIONAL BANK (CNB)

☐ Cable

We (Applicant) request you to establish by   ☐ Overnight courier service   an irrevocable standby Letter of Credit on

☐ Same day messenger service

the following terms and conditions:

ADVISING BANK (name and address)	APPLICANT (name and address)
BENEFICIARY (name and address)	**AMOUNT** indicate currency—i.e., U.S. $—and specify amount in figures and words
EXCEPT SO FAR AS OTHERWISE EXPRESSLY STATED THIS CREDIT WILL BE SUBJECT TO INTERNATIONAL STANDBY PRACTICES 1998 (ISP98), INTERNATIONAL CHAMBER OF COMMERCE PUBLICATION AS IN FORCE AS OF THE DATE OF ISSUANCE OF THE LETTER OF CREDIT	EXPIRY DATE AT CNB's ISSUING OFFICE

available by Draft(s) at sight on CNB and accompanied by the following:

APPLICANT'S AGREEMENT TO PAY CNB

Applicant agrees immediately upon CNB's demand or if no demand is made then on _____, to repay to CNB the total amount of each disbursement by CNB under this Letter of Credit, together with interest thereon at the rate of __ percent per year in excess of the Prime Rate. The "Prime Rate" shall mean the floating loan rate of CNB announced from time to time as its "Prime Rate". Any change in the interest rate resulting from a change in the Prime Rate shall be effective on the effective date of change in the Prime Rate. Interest shall be calculated on a basis of a 360-day year and actual days elapsed. We further authorize you to charge, without further notice, our account, (or an account of any of us) for all such amounts when and as such are due and payable.

THE OPENING OF THIS CREDIT IS SUBJECT TO THE TERMS AND CONDITIONS AS SET FORTH IN THE LETTER OF CREDIT AGREEMENT APPEARING ON THE REVERSE HEREOF TO WHICH WE AGREE. WE FURTHER AGREE THAT THE CREDIT AS ISSUED SHALL INCLUDE SUCH REVISIONS OF THE LANGUAGE SET FORTH ABOVE AS YOU DEEM NECESSARY.

(APPLICANT)

FOR BANK USE ONLY:
APPROVAL OF CREDIT:

   Lending Officer

   Sr. Loan Officer (when applicable)

   Branch

ACCOUNT TO BE DEBITED:
(   ) Branch G/L No. 11305000
(   ) Customer Acct. No.

FIRM NAME

AUTHORIZED SIGNATURE

SOCIAL SECURITY/TAXPAYER I.D. NO.

LETTER OF CREDIT AGREEMENT

In consideration of your opening, at our request, a letter of Credit (herein called "the Credit"), the terms and conditions of which appear on the reverse side hereof we hereby agree as follows:

1. As to drafts under or purporting to be under the Credit, which are payable in lawful United States funds, we agree to pay you on demand at your issuing office in lawful United States funds, the amount of such draft(s) on the presentment to you thereof or, at your request in advance.

2. As to drafts under or purporting to be under the Credit, which are payable in foreign currency, we agree to pay you at your office on demand, the equivalent of each such draft in lawful United States funds at your then prevailing rate of exchange effective for sales of that other currency for cable transfer to the country of which it is the currency.

3. We also agree to pay to you any attorneys' fees incurred in the enforcement of this Letter of Credit Agreement, your service charge in accordance with your Schedule of Fees and Charges now existing or as hereafter adopted, and all other charges and expenses paid or incurred by you in connection therewith.

4. We agree to reimburse you for any losses and charges incurred by you or made against you in connection with this Agreement and related to the reevaluation or fluctuations in the exchange rate of any currency whether United States or any other.

5. We hereby convey and transfer to you a security interest in all goods, documents and instruments which shall come into your control or into your possession or that of any of your correspondents as the result of opening or in connection with any transactions under the Credit, which goods, documents and instruments are and shall be granted to you as security (a) for all payments made or to be made by you or your correspondents under the Credit; (b) for any interest, commission or other customary charges in relation to the Credit and (c) for any other obligations or liabilities (absolute or contingent) of us to you, which now exist or are hereafter created. Upon any default by us in any of the undertakings set forth in this Letter of Credit Agreement, you are authorized to sell, under the provisions of the Commercial Code of the State of California, any or all goods, documents and instruments; in the event of any deficiency, we will pay the same to you immediately or in the event of any surplus, you shall pay the same to us or to the persons entitled thereto. In the event such described property should suffer any decline in value we will upon demand, deliver to you additional collateral to your satisfaction.

6. We agree that your rights and duties under the Credit are, except as otherwise provided herein, governed by the International Standby Practices 1998 (ISP98), International Chamber of Commerce Publication as in force on the date of issuance of the Credit.

7. We agree that in the event of any amendments or modifications of the terms of the Credit, this Agreement shall be binding upon us with regard to the Credit so amended. You may (at your option) issue the requested Credit through a correspondent of your choice.

8. The users of the Letter of Credit shall be deemed our agents and we assume all risks of their acts of omissions. Neither you nor your correspondents shall be responsible for/or: the validity, sufficiency, or genuineness of documents, even if such documents should in fact prove to be in any or all respects invalid, insufficient, fraudulent or forged; the solvency or responsibility of any party issuing any documents; delay in arrival or failure to arrive of any documents; delay in giving or failure to give notice of arrival or any other notice; failure of any draft to bear adequate reference to the Credit; failure of documents to accompany any draft at negotiation, or failure of any person to note the amount of any draft on the reverse of the Credit, to surrender or take up the Credit or to send documents apart from drafts as required by the terms of the Credit, each of which provisions, if contained in the Credit itself, it is agreed may be waived by you; errors, or omissions, or interruptions or delays in transmission or delivery of any message by mail, cable, telegraph, wireless or otherwise; nor shall you be responsible for any error, neglect, or default of any of your correspondents; and none of the above shall affect, impair, or prevent the vesting of any of your rights or powers hereunder. In furtherance and extension and not in limitation of the specific provisions hereinbefore set forth, we agree that any action taken by you or your correspondent of you under or in connection with the Credit or relative drafts or documents, if taken in good faith, shall be binding on us and shall not put you or your correspondent under any resulting liability to us.

9. We agree at any time and from time to time, on demand, to deliver, convey, transfer, or assign to you, as security for any and all of our obligations and liabilities hereunder, and also for any and all other obligations and liabilities, absolute or contingent, due or to become due, which are or may at any time hereafter be owing to you, additional security of a value and character satisfactory to you, or to make such cash payment as you may require. We agree that all property belonging to us, or in which we may have an interest, conveyed, transferred, assigned, or paid to you, or coming into your possession or into the possession of anyone for you in any manner whatsoever, whether expressly as security, or for safekeeping or otherwise including any items received for collection or transmission and the proceeds thereof, whether or not such property is in whole or in part released to us on trust of bailee receipt, is security for each and all such obligations and liabilities. We agree that upon our failure at all times to keep a margin of security with you satisfactory to you, or upon the making by us of any assignments for the benefit of creditors, or upon the filing of any voluntary or involuntary petition in bankruptcy by or against us, or upon any application for the appointment of a receiver of any of our property, or upon any act of bankruptcy or state of insolvency of us, or if you in good faith deem yourself insecure at any time, or upon the death of any of us, all of such obligations and liabilities shall become and be immediately due and payable without demand or notice notwithstanding any credit or time allowed to us, or any instrument evidencing any such obligation or otherwise; and each of us, and all of us, as to property in which we may have any interest, expressly authorize you in any such event, or upon our failure to pay any of such obligations or liabilities when it or they shall become or be made due, to sell all such property, in accordance with the Commercial Code of the State of California and to apply the

net proceeds of such sale or sales, together with any balance of deposits and any sum credited by or due from you to us, in general accounts or otherwise, to the payment of all of our obligations or liabilities to you however arising.

10. Your rights specified in this Agreement are in addition to any created by statute or rule of law. You are expressly given the right to execute and file and record endorsements, assignments, financing statements, and other instruments in the name of any of us with respect to documents, property and interests relative to the Credit or any property of any of us in which you have a security interest which may at any time come into your possession under the Credit or by virtue of this Agreement. We agree to pay all expenses, filing fees and other charges incurred by you relative to the perfection or enforcement of your rights and security interests hereunder.

11. You shall not be deemed to have waived any of your rights hereunder, unless you or your authorized agent shall have signed such waiver, in writing. No such waiver unless expressly stated therein shall be effective as to any transaction which occurs subsequent to the date of such waiver, nor as to any continuance of a breach after such waiver.

12. We understand that any credit issued pursuant to this Agreement is the direct obligation of you established in favor of our designated beneficiaries. Once established, such credit is irrevocable and is not subject to recall or stop payment, and any claim or demand by us to stop payment thereunder is void and of no effect.

13. The word "property" as used in this Agreement includes goods, merchandise, securities, funds, choses in action, and any and all other forms of property, whether real, personal or mixed and any right or interest therein.

14. This Agreement incorporates the provisions on the reverse hereof. Time is of the essence. Acceptance by you of partial or delinquent payments or your failure to exercise any right, power or remedy shall not waive any obligation of us or modify this Agreement. You, your successors and assigns have all rights, powers and remedies herein and as provided by law, and may exercise the same and effect any set-off and proceed against any security for the obligations of us at any time notwithstanding any cessation of our liability or running of any statute of limitations, which we hereby waive to the fullest extent permitted by law. Notice to you must be given at the office of City National Bank to which this Credit and Agreement is addressed.

15. We hereby agree to pay all reasonable fees and costs incurred by you and arising out of any act or action you may take to enforce any provision of this Agreement or to enforce collection of any sums, payments or obligations owing from us to you.

16. If this Agreement is signed by one individual the terms, "we", "our", "us", shall be read throughout as "I", "my", "me", as the case may be. If this Agreement is signed by two or more parties, it shall be the joint and several Agreement of such parties.

APPENDIX

PROMISSORY NOTES

 **CITY NATIONAL BANK**

REVOLVING NOTE
(INTEREST TIED TO PRIME)

On *, *, the undersigned, * ("Borrower"), promises to pay to the order of **City National Bank**, a national banking association ("CNB"), at its office in this city, in lawful money of the United States of America and in immediately available funds, the principal sum of *** Dollars (\$*)**, or so much thereof as may be advanced and be outstanding, with interest thereon to be computed on each advance from the date of its disbursement at a rate computed on the basis of a 360–day year, actual days elapsed, equal to the Prime Rate of CNB, as it exists from time to time, plus * percent (*%) per year. "Prime Rate" shall mean the rate most recently announced by CNB at its principal office in Beverly Hills, California, as its "Prime Rate." Any change in the Prime Rate shall become effective on the same business day on which the Prime Rate shall change, without prior notice to Borrower.

All or any portion of the principal of this Note may be borrowed, repaid and reborrowed from time to time prior to maturity, provided at the time of any borrowing no Event of Default (as herein defined) exists, and provided further that the total borrowings outstanding at any one time shall not exceed the principal amount stated above. Each borrowing and repayment hereunder shall be noted in the books and records of CNB. The excess of borrowings over repayments shall evidence the principal balance due hereon from time to time and at any time. Borrowings hereunder shall be conclusively presumed to have been made to or for the benefit of Borrower when made as noted in such books and records.

Interest accrued on this Note shall be payable on the * day of each *, commencing *, *.

The occurrence of any of the following with respect to any Borrower or any guarantor of this Note or any general partner of such Borrower or guarantor, shall constitute an "Event of Default" hereunder:

1. The failure to make any payment of principal or interest when due under this Note;

2. The filing of a petition by or against any of such parties under any provisions of the Bankruptcy Code;

3. The appointment of a receiver or an assignee for the benefit of creditors;

4. The commencement of dissolution or liquidation proceedings or the disqualification of any such parties which is a corporation, partnership, joint venture or any other type of entity;

5. The death or incapacity of any of such parties who is an individual;

6. The revocation of any guaranty of this Note, or any guaranty becomes unenforceable as to any future advances under this Note;

7. Any financial statement provided by any of such parties to CNB is false or misleading;

8. Any material default in the payment or performance of any obligation, or any default under any provisions of any contract or instrument pursuant to which any of such parties has incurred any obligation for borrowed money, any purchase obligation or any other liability of any kind to any person or entity, including CNB;

9. Any sale or transfer of all or a substantial or material part of the assets of any of such parties other than in the ordinary course of business; or

10. Any violation, breach or default under any letter agreement, guaranty, security agreement, deed of trust or any other contract or instrument executed in connection with this Note or securing this Note.

Upon the occurrence of any Event of Default, CNB, at its option, may declare all sums of principal and interest outstanding hereunder to be immediately due and payable without presentment, demand, protest or notice of dishonor all of which are expressly waived by each Borrower, and CNB shall have no obligation to make any further advances hereunder. Each Borrower agrees to pay all costs and expenses, including reasonable attorneys' fees, expended or incurred by CNB (or allocable to CNB's in-house counsel) in connection with the enforcement of this Note or the collection of any sums due hereunder and irrespective of whether suit is filed. Any principal or interest not paid when due hereunder shall thereafter bear additional interest from its due date at a rate of five percent (5.0%) per year higher than the interest rate as determined and computed above, and continuing thereafter until paid.

Should more than one person or entity execute this Note as a Borrower, the obligations of each Borrower shall be joint and several.

This Note and all matters relating thereto, shall be governed by the laws of the State of California.

REVOLVING NOTE (With Accounts Receivable Borrowing Base)

On *, *, a * ("Borrower"), promises to pay to the order of City National Bank, a national banking association ("CNB"), at its office in this city, in United States Dollars and in immediately available funds, the principal sum of * Dollars ($*) ("Revolving Credit Commitment"), or so much thereof as may be advanced and be outstanding, with interest thereon to be computed on each advance from the date of its disbursement at a rate computed on a basis of a 360–day year, actual days elapsed, equal to the "Prime Rate" of CNB, as it exists from time to time, plus * percent (*%) per year. "Prime Rate" shall mean the rate most recently announced by CNB at its principal office in Beverly Hills, California, as its "Prime Rate." Any change in the Prime Rate shall become effective on the same business day on which the Prime Rate shall change, without prior notice to Borrower.

As provided herein, the principal of this Note may be borrowed, repaid and reborrowed from time to time prior to maturity, provided at the time of any borrowing no Event of Default (as hereinafter defined) exists, and provided further that the total borrowings outstanding at any one time shall not exceed the lesser of (i) the Revolving Credit Commitment or (ii) * percent (*%) of the total Eligible Accounts Receivable owing to Borrower from time to time. Each borrowing and repayment hereunder shall be noted in the books and records of CNB. The excess of borrowings over repayments shall evidence the principal balance due hereon from time to time and at any time. Borrowings hereunder shall be presumed to have been made to or for the benefit of Borrower when made as noted in such books and records.

Interest accruing on this Note shall be payable on the * day of each month, commencing *, *.

Eligible Accounts Receivable shall mean those accounts receivable owed to Borrower:

A. Upon which Borrower's right to receive payment is absolute and not contingent upon the fulfillment of any condition whatsoever;

B. Against which is asserted no defense, counterclaim, discount or setoff, whether well-founded or otherwise;

C. That is a true and correct statement of a bona fide indebtedness incurred in the amount of the account receivable for goods sold or leased and delivered to, or for services rendered to and accepted by, the account debtor;

D. That is owned by Borrower free and clear of all liens, encumbrances, charges, interests and rights of others, except security interests granted to CNB;

E. That does not arise from a sale or lease to or for services rendered to any employee, stockholder, director, *[S]ubsidiary or affiliate of Borrower or any entity in which any employee, stockholder, director, *[S]ubsidiary or affiliate of Borrower has any interest;

F. That is not the obligation of an account debtor that is the federal government unless perfected under the Assignment of Claims Act;

G. That is not the obligation of an account debtor located in a foreign country;

H. That is due and payable not more than thirty (30) days from the date of the billing therefor unless otherwise agreed to in writing by CNB;

I.   As to which not more than ninety (90) days have elapsed since the original invoice date;

J.   As to which the account debtor has not:

(i) died, suspended business, made a general assignment for the benefit of creditors, become the subject of a petition under the *Bankruptcy Code* or consented to or applied for the appointment of a receiver, trustee, custodian or liquidator for itself or any of its property;

(ii) become more than sixty (60) days past due, under the original terms of sale, with respect to 20% or more of the amounts owed by such account debtor to Borrower;

(iii) had its check in payment of an account receivable returned unpaid; or

(iv) become or appear to have become unable, in the opinion of CNB, to pay the account receivable in accordance with its terms; and

K.   That does not, when added to all other accounts receivable that are obligations of the account debtor to Borrower, at any time result in a total sum that exceeds twenty percent (20%) of the total balance then due on all accounts receivable.

The occurrence of any of the following with respect to any Borrower or guarantor of this Note or any general partner of such Borrower or guarantor, shall constitute an "Event of Default" hereunder:

1.   Failure to make any payment of principal or interest when due under this Note;

2.   Filing of a petition by or against any of such parties under any provision of the *Bankruptcy Code*;

3.   Appointment of a receiver or an assignee for the benefit of creditors;

4.   Commencement of dissolution or liquidation proceedings or the disqualification (under any applicable law or regulation) of any of such parties which is a corporation, partnership, joint venture or any other type of entity;

5.   Death or incapacity of any of such parties which is an individual;

6.   Revocation of any guaranty of this Note, or any guaranty of this Note becomes unenforceable as to any future advances under this Note;

7.   Any financial statement provided by any of such parties to CNB is false or materially misleading;

8.   Any material default in the payment or performance of any obligation, or any default under any provision of any contract or instrument pursuant to which any of such parties has incurred any

obligation for borrowed money, any purchase obligation or any other liability of any kind to any person or entity, including CNB;

9. Any sale or transfer of all or a substantial part of the assets of any of such parties other than in the ordinary course of business;

10. Any violation, breach or default under this Note, any letter agreement, guaranty, security agreement, deed of trust, subordination agreement or any other contract or instrument executed in connection with this Note or securing this Note;

11. Failure of Borrower, after twenty (20) days' written notice from CNB to Borrower, to reduce the principal balance hereunder to * percent (*%) of the total Eligible Accounts Receivable owing to Borrower;

12. Any obligee of *[S]ubordinated [D]ebt* shall fail to comply with the subordination provisions of the documents or instruments, including, without limitation, any subordination agreement, evidencing or relating to such *[S]ubordinated [D]ebt*;

13. Failure of Borrower to furnish CNB, within the times specified, the following statements:

    13.1. Within *[forty-five (45)/sixty (60)]* days after the end of each quarterly accounting period of each fiscal year, a financial statement consisting of not less than a balance sheet, *[and income statement, reconciliation of net worth and statement of cash flows,]* with notes thereto, prepared in accordance with generally accepted accounting principles consistently applied, which financial statement may be internally prepared;

    13.2. Within *[ninety (90)/one hundred twenty (120)]* days after the close of each fiscal year, a copy of the annual *[audit report/review report/compilation report]* for such year for Borrower and the Subsidiaries including therein a balance sheet, income statement, reconciliation of net worth and statement of cash flows, with notes thereto, the balance sheet, income statement and statement of cash flows to be *[audited/reviewed/ compiled]* by a certified public accountant acceptable to CNB, and *[certified by such accountants to have been]* prepared in accordance with generally accepted accounting principles consistently applied and accompanied by Borrower's certification as to whether any event has occurred which constitutes an Event of Default, and if so, stating the facts with respect thereto;

    13.3. *[Monthly/quarterly]* reports of agings of Borrower's accounts payable and accounts receivable, together with a current list of names and addresses of all account debtors, as soon as available, but in no event later than thirty (30) days after the end of each *[month/fiscal quarter]*;

13.4.   The Federal Income Tax Return for Borrower and each guarantor of this Note, *[and each general partner of Borrower or guarantor,]* within ten (10) days after its filing of each Return, respectively; and

13.5.   Such additional information, reports and/or statements as CNB may, from time to time, reasonably request.

14.   Failure of Borrower to furnish current financial statements of each guarantor of this Note *[and each general partner of Borrower or such guarantor]* on CNB's form or in such other form acceptable to CNB, certified by such guarantor *[or general partner]* to be true and correct, delivered within ninety (90) days after Borrower's fiscal year end of each year;

15.   Failure of Borrower to maintain the following:

15.1.   Tangible Net Worth *[plus Subordinated Debt]* of not less than $* at all times;

15.2.   A ratio of Total Senior Liabilities to Tangible Net Worth *[plus Subordinated Debt]* of not more than * to 1 at all times;

15.3.   A ratio of Current Assets to Current Liabilities of not less than * to 1 at all times;

15.4.   A ratio of Quick Assets to Current Liabilities of not less than * to 1 at all times; and

15.5.   Working Capital of not less than $* at all times.

For purposes of this Note, the following terms have the following meanings:

"**Current Assets**" shall be determined on a consolidated basis for Borrower and the Subsidiaries in accordance with generally accepted accounting principles, consistently applied, excluding, however, from the determination of Current Assets, loans to shareholders, management or employees, amounts due from Subsidiaries or affiliates, deferred costs, and other intangible assets.

"**Current Liabilities**" shall be determined on a consolidated basis for Borrower and the Subsidiaries in accordance with generally accepted accounting principles, consistently applied, and shall include without limitation (a) all payments on Subordinated Debt required to be made within one (1) year after the date on which the determination is made; and (b) all indebtedness payable to stockholders, affiliates, Subsidiaries or officers regardless of maturity, unless such indebtedness shall have been subordinated to CNB, on terms satisfactory to CNB.

"**Quick Assets**" shall mean the sum of cash, plus cash equivalents, plus accounts receivable, plus securities classified as short-term marketable securities according to generally accepted accounting principles, consistently applied, as such items appear on Borrower's consolidated balance sheet, determined in accordance with generally accepted accounting principles consistently applied.

"**Subordinated Debt**" shall mean indebtedness of Borrower or any Subsidiary the repayment of principal and interest of which is subordinated to CNB, on terms satisfactory to CNB.

"**Subsidiary**" shall mean any corporation, the majority of whose voting shares are at any time owned, directly or indirectly by Borrower and/or by one or more Subsidiaries.

"**Tangible Net Worth**" shall mean the total of all assets appearing on a balance sheet prepared in accordance with generally accepted accounting principles consistently applied for Borrower and the Subsidiaries on a consolidated basis, minus (a) all intangible assets, including, without limitation, unamortized debt discount, affiliate, employee and officer receivables or advances, goodwill, research and development costs, patents, trademarks, the excess of purchase price over underlying values of acquired companies, any covenants not to compete, deferred charges, copyrights, franchises and appraisal surplus; minus (b) all obligations which are required by generally accepted accounting principles consistently applied to be reflected as a liability on the consolidated balance sheet of Borrower and the Subsidiaries; minus, (c) the amount, if any, at which shares of stock of a non-wholly owned Subsidiary appear on the asset side of Borrower's consolidated balance sheet, as determined in accordance with generally accepted accounting principles consistently applied; minus (d) minority interests; and minus (e) deferred income and reserves not otherwise reflected as a liability on the consolidated balance sheet of Borrower and the Subsidiaries.

"**Total Senior Liabilities**" shall mean, as of any date of determination, the amount of all obligations that should be reflected as a liability on a consolidated balance sheet of Borrower and the Subsidiaries prepared in accordance with generally accepted accounting principles, consistently applied, less Subordinated Debt.

"**Working Capital**" shall mean Current Assets minus Current Liabilities.

Upon the occurrence of any Event of Default, CNB, at its option, may declare all sums of principal and interest outstanding hereunder to be immediately due and payable without presentment, demand, protest or notice of dishonor all of which are expressly waived by Borrower, and CNB shall have no obligation to make any further advances hereunder. Borrower agrees to pay all costs and expenses, including reasonable attorneys' fees (which counsel may be CNB employees), expended or incurred by CNB (or allocable to CNB's in-house counsel) in connection with the enforcement of this Note or the collection of any sums due hereunder and irrespective of whether suit is filed. Any principal or interest not paid when due hereunder shall thereafter bear additional interest from its due date at a rate of five percent (5.0%) per year higher than the interest rate as determined and computed above, and continuing thereafter until paid.

Should more than one person or entity execute this Note as Borrower, the liability and obligations of each Borrower shall be joint and several.

This Note and all matters relating thereto, shall be governed by the laws of the State of California.

INDEX

433

†

1-58778-740-7

90000

9 781587 787409